THE WILEY BICENTENNIAL—KNOWLEDGE FOR GENERATIONS

*E*ach generation has its unique needs and aspirations. When Charles Wiley first opened his small printing shop in lower Manhattan in 1807, it was a generation of boundless potential searching for an identity. And we were there, helping to define a new American literary tradition. Over half a century later, in the midst of the Second Industrial Revolution, it was a generation focused on building the future. Once again, we were there, supplying the critical scientific, technical, and engineering knowledge that helped frame the world. Throughout the 20th Century, and into the new millennium, nations began to reach out beyond their own borders and a new international community was born. Wiley was there, expanding its operations around the world to enable a global exchange of ideas, opinions, and know-how.

For 200 years, Wiley has been an integral part of each generation's journey, enabling the flow of information and understanding necessary to meet their needs and fulfill their aspirations. Today, bold new technologies are changing the way we live and learn. Wiley will be there, providing you the must-have knowledge you need to imagine new worlds, new possibilities, and new opportunities.

Generations come and go, but you can always count on Wiley to provide you the knowledge you need, when and where you need it!

WILLIAM J. PESCE
PRESIDENT AND CHIEF EXECUTIVE OFFICER

PETER BOOTH WILEY
CHAIRMAN OF THE BOARD

Hazard Mitigation and Preparedness: Building Resilient Communities

Anna J. Schwab, Katherine Eschelbach, and David J. Brower

BICENTENNIAL
1807
WILEY
2007
BICENTENNIAL

Credits

PUBLISHER
Anne Smith

PROJECT EDITOR
Laura Town

MARKETING MANAGER
Jennifer Slomack

EDITORIAL ASSISTANT
Tiara Kelly

PRODUCTION MANAGER
Kelly Tavares

PRODUCTION ASSISTANT
Courtney Leshko

CREATIVE DIRECTOR
Harry Nolan

COVER DESIGNER
Hope Miller

COVER PHOTO
Tobias Schwarz/Reuters/Landov LLC

This book was set in Times New Roman, printed and bound by R. R. Donnelley.

The cover was printed by Phoenix Color.

To order books or for customer service please, call 1-800-CALL WILEY (225-5945).

ISBN-13 978-0-471-79019-8

ISBN-10 0-471-79019-2

Printed in the United States of America

10 9 8 7 6 5 4 3

PREFACE

As we embarked on the venture of writing *Hazard Mitigation and Preparedness: Building Resilient Communities* for use in beginning courses in Emergency Planning, Hurricane Katrina was unfolding before our very eyes and the eyes of all America. The storm struck the Gulf Coast in August 2005, impacting the states of Alabama, Mississippi, and Louisiana, after having ripped through Cuba, Florida, and Georgia. Katrina continued to produce heavy rains and flooding as it dissipated through the Mississippi Basin and Tennessee Valley. New Orleans, the "Big Easy," was particularly hard hit, as the force of the hurricane caused levees, which had protected the city from flooding, to breach in several places, engulfing the city with water that reached up to 20 feet in some locations.

The sheer magnitude of the catastrophe was overwhelming, as daily, hourly, and minute-by-minute newscasts displayed graphic images of human suffering on a scale not experienced in our country since the end of the Civil War. With each media sound bite, we became increasingly aware of the number of communities ravaged by the storm's wind, rain, and storm surge; Most tragic of all, was the number of people displaced and homeless, packed into shelters like subhuman beasts under conditions so appalling it horrified viewers and shocked our collective consciousness. Many of those who would not or could not evacuate the region before the hurricane struck drowned in the rising floodwaters. Others died from hunger, dehydration, exposure, or from injuries, infection, diabetes, heart disease, and other medical conditions that went untreated.

With many notable exceptions in the form of countless brave and sacrificing first responders who saved hundreds of victims from certain death, the government response to the disaster—federal, state, and local—was abysmal. Many agencies and government officials at all levels have been lambasted for their response, or lack thereof, to the Katrina disaster; Some have been chastised for being utterly incompetent and out of touch at best. At worst, they have been portrayed as unfeeling, uncaring bigots and snobs, completely removed from and incapable of recognizing the immediacy and dire nature of the situation. Issues of race, ethnicity, class, and income disparity are deeply entwined in the disaster that was Katrina, a disaster that, uncomfortably and unnervingly, brought to the foreground the plight of the impoverished during times of crisis.

As additional information about the Hurricane and its aftermath was disseminated over the days and weeks that followed, we realized that we must address Hurricane Katrina in this book. We grappled with how best to deal with the uncertainties of unreliable data and unconfirmed statistics, knowing that, though new information gathered and reported would continue to shed light on the immense scale and far-reaching consequences of this national disaster, we would never gain a complete picture of all that occurred before, during, and after. We arrived at the conclusion that the best way we could discuss the implications of the disaster amidst so much uncertainty, while at the same time helping our students learn from what occurred, was by presenting one issue at a time in small, bite-sized pieces.

Pathways Books

College classrooms bring together learners from many backgrounds with a variety of aspirations. Although the students are in the same course, they are not necessarily on the same path. This diversity, coupled with the reality that these learners often have jobs, families, and other commitments, requires a flexibility that our nation's higher education system is addressing. Distance learning, shorter course terms, new disciplines, evening courses, and certification programs are some of the approaches that colleges employ to reach as many students as possible and help them clarify and achieve their goals.

Wiley Pathways books, a new line of texts from John Wiley & Sons, Inc., are designed to help you address this diversity and the need for flexibility. These books focus on the fundamentals, identify core competencies and skills, and promote independent learning. The focus on the fundamentals helps students grasp the subject, bringing them all to the same basic understanding. These books use clear, everyday language, presented in an uncluttered format, making the reading experience more pleasurable. The core competencies and skills help students succeed in the classroom and beyond, whether in another course or in a professional setting. A variety of built-in learning resources promote independent learning and help instructors and students gauge students' understanding of the content. These resources enable students to think critically about their new knowledge, and apply their skills in any situation.

Our goal with *Wiley Pathways* books—with its brief, inviting format, clear language, and core competencies and skills focus—is to celebrate the many students in your courses, respect their needs, and help you guide them on their way.

Organization of Hazard Mitigation and Preparedness

CASE Learning System. To meet the needs of working college students, *Hazard Mitigation and Preparedness* uses a four-step process: The CASE Learning System. Based on Bloom's Taxonomy of Learning, CASE presents key hazard mitigation and preparedness topics in easy-to-follow chapters. The text then prompts analysis, synthesis, and evaluation with a variety of learning aids and assessment tools. Students move efficiently from reviewing what they have learned, to acquiring new information and skills, to applying their new knowledge and skills to real-life scenarios. Each phase of the CASE system is signaled in-text by an icon:

▲ Content
▲ Analysis
▲ Synthesis
▲ Evaluation

Using the CASE Learning System, students not only achieve academic mastery of emergency planning topics, but they master real-world emergency planning skills. The CASE Learning System also helps students become independent learners, giving them a distinct advantage whether they are starting out or seeking to advance in their careers.

Organization, Depth and Breadth of the Text

▲ **Modular format.** Research on college students shows that they access information from textbooks in a non-linear way. Instructors also often wish to reorder textbook content to suit the needs of a particular class. Therefore, although *Hazard Mitigation and Preparedness* proceeds logically from the basics to increasingly more challenging material, chapters are further organized into sections (4 to 6 per chapter) that are self-contained for maximum teaching and learning flexibility.

▲ **Numeric system of headings.** *Hazard Mitigation and Preparedness* uses a numeric system for headings (for example, 2.3.4 identifies the fourth sub-section of Section 3 of Chapter 2). With this system, students and teachers can quickly and easily pinpoint topics in the table of contents and the text, keeping class time and study sessions focused.

Special Feature: Hurricane Katrina Mini-Case Studies

Because Hurricane Katrina and its aftermath taught us so much about hazard mitigation and preparedness, every chapter save one of this book contains a Hurricane Katrina Scenario: a vignette of the event that illustrates one particular aspect of the disaster and reflects the broader concepts discussed in that chapter. For instance, in Chapter 1, "Hazards vs. Disasters," we use the Hurricane Katrina disaster to highlight the differences between a natural hazard (a phenomenon of nature) and a disaster (a natural hazard that occurs where people and structures are located). In Chapter 4, "Manmade Hazards," we describe some of the hazardous materials that entered Gulf Coast floodwaters from damaged petro-chemical facilities and other types of manmade hazards that arose during Katrina. Our intent in including these "mini case-studies" about Katrina in this book is to show that natural hazards themselves cannot be managed, but characteristics of the built environment can, and should be managed to reduce the impact of hazards on our communities

Chapter Overviews

The major thrust of this book is that we have choices when planning and building our communities in ways that increase resiliency, reduce risk, and minimize damage and losses from both natural and manmade hazards, largely through mitigation and preparedness action taken at the local level. Material is presented in what we consider a logical sequence, although each chapter is designed to stand on its own as it focuses on one particular topic related to mitigation and preparedness. Here is a summary of the highlights of each chapter.

Chapter 1, Hazards vs. Disasters, provides a broad overview of building resilience at the community level, and defines both hazard mitigation and preparedness as part of the emergency management cycle.

Chapter 2, Meteorological and Hydrological Hazards, Chapter 3, Geological Hazards, and Chapter 4, Manmade Hazards, present the major categories of hazards. Each also includes a discussion of terrorism and technological hazards. Because students are not necessarily expected to have a background in meteorology, geology, or technological hazards management, Chapters 2, 3, and 4 are very basic, focusing on the key characteristics of each type of hazard that are pertinent to the emergency manager.

The next few chapters introduce the reader to the institutional framework within which emergency managers must carry out their hazard mitigation and preparedness functions. Chapter 5, Hazards Management Framework, highlights the patchwork nature of our system of governance with regard to managing development in hazardous areas, and the sometimes divergent roles that the various levels of government can play.

Chapter 6, The Role of the Federal Government, presents information about the practice and politics of mitigation policy at the federal level.

Chapter 7, Mitigating Hazards at the State Level, speaks to the role of the states in mitigating hazards, including some state policies that may inadvertently encourage growth and development in hazard areas.

Chapter 8, Local Government Powers, presents an overview of local government powers to manage hazard areas within their jurisdiction.

Chapter 9, Community Resilience and the Private Sector, focuses on how the private sector can contribute to strong local economies through wise land use and business protection planning.

The next few chapters provide more in-depth information about how mitigation and preparedness are carried out, beginning with a discussion of risk assessment, a process of identifying hazards and assessing vulnerability, in Chapter 10, Risk Assessment.

Risk assessment is an essential component of emergency management, because the level of risk helps us choose what preparedness activities we must undertake in the short term to be ready for potential hazards as described in Chapter 11, Preparedness Activities.

The most appropriate mitigation tools and techniques to reduce vulnerability are discussed in Chapter 12, Hazard Mitigation Tools and Techniques.

Chapter 13, Hazard Mitigation Planning, takes the reader through the process of hazard mitigation planning, where risk assessment helps inform the development of goals, policies, and strategies for creating resilient communities.

We conclude the book with Chapter 14, Building a Culture of Prevention, which highlights the role of personal responsibility, and describes how the principles of sustainable development can be applied to the creation of resilient communities for a safer tomorrow.

Pre-reading Learning Aids

Each chapter of *Hazard Mitigation and Preparedness* features the following learning and study aids to activate students' prior knowledge of the topics and orient them to the material.

▲ **Pre-test.** This pre-reading assessment tool in multiple-choice format not only introduces chapter material, but it also helps students anticipate the chapter's learning outcomes. By focusing students' attention on what they do not know, the self-test provides students with a benchmark against which they can measure their own progress. The pre-test is available online at www.wiley.com/college/schwab.

▲ **What You'll Learn in This Chapter and After Studying This Chapter.** These bulleted lists tell students what they will be learning in the chapter and why it is significant for their careers. They also explain why the chapter is important and how it relates to other chapters in the text. "What You'll Learn…" lists focus on the subject matter that will be taught (e.g. what emergency planning is). "After Studying This Chapter…" lists emphasize capabilities and skills students will learn (e.g. how to write an emergency plan).

▲ **Goals and Outcomes.** These lists identify specific student capabilities that will result from reading the chapter. They set students up to synthesize and evaluate the chapter material, and relate it to the real world.

Within-text Learning Aids

The following learning aids are designed to encourage analysis and synthesis of the material, and to support the learning process and ensure success during the evaluation phase:

▲ **Introduction.** This section orients the student by introducing the chapter and explaining its practical value and relevance to the book as a whole. Short summaries of chapter sections preview the topics to follow.

▲ **"For Example" Boxes.** Found within each section, these boxes tie section content to real-world organizations, scenarios, and applications.

▲ **Figures and Tables.** Line art and photos have been carefully chosen to be truly instructional rather than filler. Tables distill and present information in a way that is easy to identify, access, and understand, enhancing the focus of the text on essential ideas.

▲ **Self-Check.** Related to the "What You'll Learn" bullets and found at the end of each section, this battery of short answer questions emphasizes student understanding of concepts and mastery of section content. Though the questions may either be discussed in class or studied by students outside of class, students should not go on before they can answer all questions correctly. Each Self-Check question set includes a link to a section of the pre-test for further review and practice.

▲ **Summary.** Each chapter concludes with a summary paragraph that reviews the major concepts in the chapter and links back to the "What You'll Learn" list.

▲ **Key Terms and Glossary.** To help students develop a professional vocabulary, key terms are bolded in the introduction, summary and when they first appear in the chapter. A complete list of key terms with brief definitions appears at the end of each chapter and again in a glossary at the end of the book. Knowledge of key terms is assessed by all assessment tools (see below).

Evaluation and Assessment Tools

The evaluation phase of the CASE Learning System consists of a variety of within-chapter and end-of-chapter assessment tools that test how well students have learned the material. These tools also encourage students to extend their learning into different scenarios and higher levels of understanding and thinking. The following assessment tools appear in every chapter of *Hazard Mitigation and Preparedness Building Resilient Communities*.

▲ **Summary Questions** help students summarize the chapter's main points by asking a series of multiple choice and true/false questions that emphasize student understanding of concepts and mastery of chapter content. Students should be able to answer all of the Summary Questions correctly before moving on.

▲ **Review Questions** in short answer format review the major points in each chapter, prompting analysis while reinforcing and confirming student understanding of concepts, and encouraging mastery of chapter content. They are somewhat more difficult than the Self-Check and Summary Questions, and students should be able to answer most of them correctly before moving on.

▲ **Applying This Chapter Questions** drive home key ideas by asking students to synthesize and apply chapter concepts to new, real-life situations and scenarios.

▲ **You Try It Questions** are designed to extend students' thinking, and so are ideal for discussion or writing assignments.

Using an open-ended format and sometimes based on Web sources, they encourage students to draw conclusions using chapter material applied to real-world situations, which fosters both mastery and independent learning.

▲ **Post-Test** should be taken after students have completed the chapter. It includes all of the questions in the pre-test, so that students can see how their learning has progressed and improved.

Instructor and Student Package

Hazard Mitigation and Preparedness: Building Resilient Communities is available with the following teaching and learning supplements. All supplements are available online at the text's Book Companion Website, located at www.wiley.com/college/schwab.

▲ **Instructor's Resource Guide.** Provides the following aids and supplements for teaching:

  ▲ *Diagnostic Evaluation of Grammar, Mechanics, and Spelling.* A useful tool that instructors may administer to the class at the beginning of the course to determine each student's basic writing skills. The Evaluation is accompanied by an Answer Key and a Marking Key. Instructors are encouraged to use the Marking key when grading students' Evaluations, and to duplicate and distribute it to students with their graded evaluations.

  ▲ *Sample syllabus.* A convenient template that instructors may use for creating their own course syllabi.

  ▲ *Teaching suggestions.* For each chapter, these include a chapter summary, learning objectives, definitions of key terms, lecture notes, answers to select text question sets, and at least 3 suggestions for classroom activities, such as ideas for speakers to invite, videos to show, and other projects.

▲ **Test Bank.** One quiz per chapter, as well as a mid-term and a final. Each includes true/false, multiple choice, and open-ended questions. Answers and page references are provided for the true/false and multiple choice questions, and page references for the open-ended questions. Available in Microsoft Word and computerized formats.

▲ **PowerPoints.** Key information is summarized in 10 to 15 PowerPoints per chapter. Instructors may use these in class or choose to share them with students for class presentations or to provide additional study support.

ACKNOWLEDGMENTS

Taken together, the content, pedagogy, and assessment elements of *Hazard Mitigation and Preparedness: Building Resilient Communities* offer the career-oriented student the most important aspects of emergency management as well as ways to develop the skills and capabilities that current and future employers seek in the individuals they hire and promote. Instructors will appreciate its practical focus, conciseness, and real-world emphasis. We would like to thank the following reviewers for their feedback and suggestions during the text's development. Their advice on how to shape the text into a solid learning tool that meets both their needs and those of their busy students is deeply appreciated.

Bernice Carr, Jacksonville State University
Roger Hovis, University of Richmond
Robert Jaffin, American Public University System
Frank Scott, Fairleigh Dickinson University

We would like to express their heartfelt gratitude to Shannon Brownfield of the Department of City and Regional Planning at the University of North Carolina at Chapel Hill for her unfailing cheerfulness, goodwill, and unparalled competence in helping us assemble this manuscript, particularly in the last harrowing days to meet the publisher's deadline. We would also like to thank our reviewers, whose insightful comments contributed greatly to our revisions of each chapter, and in particular, Dr. Gavin Smith, who, in his position as Director of the Office of Response and Renewal in the Office of the Governor of the State of Mississippi, was highly qualified to review our Katrina Scenarios. We would also like to thank the editors and staff at Wiley for their continued strong support and encouragement throughout this project.

Katherine Eschelbach would like to thank Connie Moy for her suggestions on where to find information about NOAA's response following Hurricane Katrina and for her creative ideas on business preparedness. She also thanks her husband, John Eschelbach, for his exemplary photography skills and, as always, his loving support.

In addition to her parents and immediate family, including husband DeWayne Tate and sons Will, T.J., Karlton and Patrick, Anna Schwab must express a deep indebtedness to her niece, Krystle Lyght-Tate for her many hours of underpaid and overworked child-minding of her younger cousins as their mother was otherwise occupied with the writing of this book. She would also like to thank Kate for coming to her rescue, shouldering ever more of the burden as the deadline neared. And as always, Anna Schwab would like to thank her long-time colleague and mentor, David Brower, for the opportunities to be involved in interesting and challenging projects that he continues to provide.

BRIEF CONTENTS

CONTENTS

1

HAZARDS VS. DISASTERS
Defining Resilient Communities

Starting Point

Go to www.wiley.com/college/schwab to assess your knowledge of what defines a resilient community.
Determine where to concentrate your effort.

What You'll Learn in This Chapter

▲ Types of natural and man-made hazards
▲ How hazards differ from disasters
▲ Types of costs associated with disasters
▲ Characteristics of a resilient community
▲ Phases of the comprehensive emergency management cycle
▲ Differences between preparedness and mitigation

After Studying This Chapter, You'll Be Able To

▲ Illustrate how natural hazards relate to the Earth's dynamic equilibrium
▲ Distinguish between hazards and disasters
▲ Analyze why there are more and bigger disasters
▲ Discuss the potential costs of a disaster scenario
▲ Apply the phases of comprehensive emergency management
▲ Demonstrate where mitigation and preparedness fit into the emergency management cycle

Goals and Outcomes

▲ Assess the value of mitigation and preparedness
▲ Estimate the different types of costs associated with natural hazards, man-made hazards, and disasters
▲ Evaluate the tools and techniques used to address the costs associated with hazards
▲ Appraise the basic features of a resilient community
▲ Collaborate with others to determine mitigation strategies
▲ Evaluate decision strategies used in community mitigation and preparedness efforts

INTRODUCTION

Imagine you are an emergency manager in a small coastal town along the Atlantic Ocean. The National Hurricane Center in Florida has just predicted that a hurricane will make landfall a few miles south of your town in less than 72 hours. What steps should you take in the time remaining to prepare for this storm? What actions should you have taken weeks, months, and even years ago to make sure your community is safe from hurricanes like the one that is headed your way now? Throughout this book, we will help you find the answers to some of these questions. Chapter 1 gives a brief overview of the hazards that face our communities, both natural and man-made, and how a hazard differs from a disaster. Also covered in this chapter are the many costs—economic, social, environmental, and human—associated with hazards that affect the built environment. The chapter concludes with an examination of ways that emergency managers, planners, residents, and community leaders can use mitigation and preparedness strategies to make a community more resilient to the impacts of hazards.

1.1 Hazards: Part of the Natural Environment

Disasters are not natural. Of course, there are many natural hazards in the world, and there are many man-made hazards as well. But not every hazard becomes a disaster. This section of Chapter 1 introduces the concept of natural hazards and describes how they are naturally occurring phenomena that play a vital role in the Earth's dynamic equilibrium. This section also introduces man-made hazards as a potential threat to our communities. Section 1.2 of this chapter discusses what must happen for a disaster to result from a natural or man-made hazard event.

1.1.1 Natural Hazards Are Inevitable and Unstoppable

Natural hazards are part of the world around us, and their occurrence is inevitable. Floods, hurricanes, tornadoes, winter storms, earthquakes, tsunamis, volcanoes, landslides, sinkholes, and other extreme events are natural phenomena we cannot control.

Some natural events can change the ecological environment. Consider these impacts caused by natural hazards:

- ▲ Wildfires burn forests and grasslands.
- ▲ Coastal storms erode beaches, flatten dunes, and create or fill inlets.
- ▲ Flooding inundates wetlands and marshes.
- ▲ Volcanic eruptions cover the landscape with molten rock and lava.

Despite the destruction caused by natural hazards, these occurrences are part of the natural system. Hazards have been happening for billions of years on Earth and will continue for eons more. The natural environment is amazingly recuperative and resilient. After a hazard event, ecosystems can regenerate, and habitats are restored in time for the next generation of plant and animal life to begin anew.

1.1.2 The Earth's Dynamic Equilibrium

Many of the events we call "hazards" are in fact beneficial for the natural environment and help maintain the delicate balance of nature, the Earth's **dynamic equilibrium.** Under normal, undisturbed conditions, natural systems maintain a balanced state over long periods of time through a series of adjustments. Change in one part of the system will be balanced by change in another part so that the entire system regains equilibrium.[1]

Consider the benefits that result when natural systems absorb the impact of some hazard events and readjust through dynamic equilibrium:

▲ Wildfires burn off old growth in forests and allow new species of trees to grow.
▲ Coastal storms change the morphology (shape) of beaches and islands, bringing more sand to some areas and removing sand from others up the coast.
▲ Flooding brings nutrients and sediment to wetlands and marshes, creating a rich habitat for a variety of plant and animal species.
▲ Volcanic lava and ash form fertile soils when they weather and break down,[2] stimulating new plant growth.

These examples illustrate ways in which the environment is well equipped to deal with hazards as part of the natural processes on Earth.

1.1.3 Types of Natural Hazards

Natural hazards can be classified by the types of geophysical processes involved in their occurrence. The four types of natural hazards are:

▲ Meteorological (hurricanes, tropical storms, typhoons, tornadoes, snow and ice storms, thunderstorms, etc.).
▲ Geological (earthquakes, volcanoes, tsunamis, landslides, subsidence, etc.).
▲ Hydrological (floods, droughts, wildfire, etc.).
▲ Extraterrestrial (meteorites impacting the Earth's surface)[3].

Physical parameters of natural hazards include intensity and severity, measures that indicate the relative strength of a particular hazard within a class. Hurricanes, for instance, are often categorized using the Saffir-Simpson Scale, which ranks hurricanes from 1 to 5 according to maximum wind speed, storm surge potential, and barometric pressure. See Chapter 2 for a more detailed discussion of the physical elements of hurricanes and other meteorological and hydrological hazards. Earthquakes are usually described in terms of magnitude using the Richter scale, a unit of measurement that describes the energy release of an earthquake through shock wave amplitude, or the Modified Mercalli scale. See Chapter 3 for a discussion of earthquakes and other geological hazards. Professional meteorologists, hydrologists, seismologists, and other scientists interested in studying and predicting natural hazard events use these systems of hazard measurement. These scales also provide planners, emergency managers, engineers, and decision-makers at all levels with a common terminology to describe, anticipate, plan for, and deal with natural hazards in terms of policy and management.

We will not discuss extraterrestrial hazards further in this book, although the threat of meteorites piercing the Earth's atmosphere and impacting the surface of the planet is considered a natural hazard. Even though catastrophic meteorite impacts have been the grist for Hollywood's mill for years, the scientific community increasingly takes the threat of meteorite impacts seriously. Geologists have documented previous impacts that have left large craters in the Earth's surface. Paleontologists have postulated that one of these catastrophic impacts caused the extinction of the dinosaurs along with vast numbers of species of plant and animal life.[4]

1.1.4 Are Natural Hazards Becoming More Frequent?

There is speculation that natural hazards are becoming more common. Many theories have been posed to explain this increase in hazard occurrence, although scientists and policy makers are not always in full accord on certain points. Some of the reasons that natural hazards may be on the rise include the following:

▲ Climate changes such as El Niño cause fluctuations in weather patterns.

▲ Some hazards occur in natural cycles of frequency. (For example, research shows that hurricanes have a cycle of 30 to 40 years; after experiencing a lull since the 1950s, we are now entering a phase in which hurricanes occur in greater numbers.)

▲ Global warming may cause changes in average worldwide temperatures, creating disturbances in the atmosphere and oceans.

▲ Deforestation and desertification in parts of the world lead to imbalances in global hydrological cycles.

▲ Sea level rise due to melting polar ice caps may increase flooding in low-lying coastal areas.

Natural hazards may also appear to be increasing in frequency because of heightened media exposure. Referred to as the "CNN syndrome," intense media coverage of hazard events can increase awareness of hazard losses worldwide as the capability for reporting and documentation of news expands.[5] In past generations,

---

FOR EXAMPLE

Hazards, Hazards Everywhere

Some natural hazards occur only in certain regions of the United States. Volcanoes are not found in New England, but in Hawaii active volcanoes produce lava, ash, and steam at regular intervals. Other types of hazards are more widely distributed and can be found almost anywhere. Flooding can occur wherever water sources overflow their normal channels. In fact, flash floods can happen even in areas that experience drought most of the year, such as Las Vegas, Nevada. Still other types of hazards occur quite frequently in one part of the country but are also possible in other areas that experience them less often. For example, the risk of earthquakes in California is well documented, but less well known is the large earthquake that struck Charleston, South Carolina, in 1886. The risk of an earthquake occurring there in the near future is quite significant.

---

when communication systems were not instantaneous as they are today, fewer people knew about natural hazards that took place outside their own communities.

1.1.5 Man-Made Hazards

In general terms, there are two major classifications of **man-made hazards**: technological hazards and terrorism. Technological hazards are usually caused by accident—either through incompetence, poor planning, faulty equipment, bad weather, or some other mishap; no one intended the hazard to occur. Terrorism, on the other hand, implies an intentional act; that is, some individual or group means to cause harm in order to further a political agenda; a social, economic or religious mission; or because they are delusional or misguided in some way. See Chapter 4 for further discussion of man-made hazards and their effects.

Intentional man-made hazards (such as a bombing) almost always have humans as their ultimate targets. Unintentional or accidental hazards (such as an oil spill or a train derailment) are more like natural hazards because they do not occur as a result of a malicious plot or an organized activity that is designed to cause damage or injury. Either way, it is very difficult to predict where or when man-made hazards will occur, and our ability to completely prevent either terrorism or technological hazards is limited.

Although the root of the problem for most man-made disasters is different from that for natural processes, there are many factors in common in terms of the impact the two types of events might have on a community. There are also many common ways to prevent damage and to prepare for both natural and human-made hazards. Therefore, during the rest of this chapter, and throughout much of the remainder of this book, we will treat natural and man-made hazards in a similar way.

SELF-CHECK

- Define **natural hazards** and **dynamic equilibrium**.
- Discuss the beneficial functions of three natural hazards.
- Describe the differences between technological hazards and terrorism.

1.2 Hazards and Disasters: Not the Same

Natural hazards occur as part of the balance of nature, and natural environments and ecosystems can usually recover and restore themselves after a hazard event. A disaster is something different. A **disaster** results when a natural hazard takes place where humans are located. To some degree, this distinction is also true for man-made hazards, particularly those caused by accident.

1.2.1 The Official Definition of *Disaster*

The Robert T. Stafford Disaster Relief and Emergency Assistance Act is the primary legislation authorizing the federal government to provide disaster assistance to states, local governments, Native American tribes, and individuals and families. The Stafford Act defines a disaster as

> *Any natural catastrophe (including hurricane, tornado, storm, high water, wind driven water, tidal wave, tsunami, earthquake, volcanic eruption, landslide, mudslide, snowstorm or drought), or, regardless of cause, any fire, flood or explosion, in any part of the United States, which in the determination of the President causes damage of sufficient severity and magnitude to warrant major disaster assistance under this Act to sup- plement the efforts and available resources of States, local governments, and disaster relief organizations, in alleviating the damage, loss, hardship, or suffering caused thereby.*

As this definition indicates, a disaster, whatever its cause, is a "catastrophe" of such magnitude and severity that the capacities of states and local governments are overwhelmed. The threshold for determining what constitutes a disaster depends upon the resources and capabilities of states and local communities, as supplemented by relief organizations such as the American Red Cross. The patch- work of policies and regulations that makes up our system of governance has direct bearing on these resources and capabilities. Chapter 5 elaborates on the hazards management framework that exists in our federalist system of government, and Chapters 6, 7, and 8 give more detailed information about how the federal, state, and local governments carry out their responsibilities for disaster management. It is important to note that the federal government is responsible for providing assistance only after other resources have been depleted. How strictly this policy is actually carried out is discussed in later chapters as well. The "politics of extreme natural events"[6] can significantly affect the way in which disaster declarations are made and how disaster funds are disbursed from the national treasury.

1.2.2 The Intersection of the Human Environment and a Natural Hazard

The human environment—made up of homes, offices, farms, schools, roads, sewage treatment plants and other types of buildings and infrastructure—is not nearly as resilient as the natural one. The occurrence of a natural hazard can debilitate an entire community for many years following the event, and some communities never recover fully from a particularly severe disaster.

The formula for a natural disaster is

$$\text{Natural hazard} + \text{Human environment} = \text{Disaster}$$

In other words, it is only when people are injured and property is damaged by a hazard that we experience a disaster.

Figure 1-1 illustrates what happens when the human environment collides with a natural hazard. At the intersection we have a disaster.

Figure 1-1

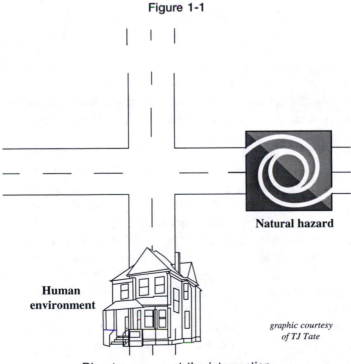

Natural hazard

Human environment

graphic courtesy of TJ Tate

Disaster occurs at the intersection.

FOR EXAMPLE

A Hurricane at Sea Is Not a Disaster

A hurricane is a natural hazard, but if it happens far out to sea, it cannot harm anyone. In the middle of the ocean there are no buildings to be damaged and no people to be injured or killed. Even when a hurricane reaches land, if it makes landfall in an unpopulated area, then no disaster occurs.

1.2.3 Why Are There More and Bigger Natural Disasters?

We mentioned earlier in the chapter that hazard events are possibly occurring more frequently around the world today. Scientists have proposed various theories as to why this may be true. But whether or not *natural hazards* are increasing in frequency, it is very clear that *disasters* are occurring more and more often. It is also certain that disasters are becoming more *costly*. Why is this so?

We are experiencing more disasters than ever before in our nation's history because more infrastructure and more people are in harm's way than ever before. The rate of disasters in this country is rising at an alarming rate, because more people have chosen to live in areas exposed to coastal storms, repeated flooding, seismic activity, and other types of natural hazards, often with little or no attention to the need to protect themselves and their property. As a result, the risk of disasters occurring in the wake of natural hazards has grown exponentially over the past few decades.

Why is this happening? Part of the answer is that the population of the United States is growing very quickly. As cities and towns expand to accommodate more people, they sprawl out into areas that are potentially hazardous. For instance, the cities of Los Angeles and San Francisco are growing by leaps and bounds, despite the well-known risk of earthquakes in California. Other communities are building new shopping centers and subdivisions in the floodplain, even though these areas are flooded on a regular basis. Still others are building on steep slopes where the potential for landslides is high, and others insist on encroaching on the urban-wildland interface despite the likelihood of wildfires. Perhaps the most dramatic increase in population growth and development is occurring on our nation's shorelines. The coastal environment is extremely hazardous due to hurricanes, nor'easters, flooding, storm surge, wind, erosion, inlet migration, and other coastal hazards, yet the shoreline continues to be the most desirable real estate in the country. As long as development and population growth keep expanding into hazardous areas, we can expect more and bigger disasters in the future.

HURRICANE KATRINA: AN IMPRESSIVE NATURAL HAZARD AND A CATASTROPHIC HUMAN DISASTER

Hurricane Katrina is an example of both an extreme natural hazard and a horrifying disaster (see Figure 1-2). This storm was not only extraordinarily powerful, but it also caused a catastrophic amount of damage and a tragic number of human deaths. As a natural hazard, Katrina had a life span in hurricane form of almost four days. During that time, Katrina made landfall twice, first as a Category 1 Hurricane in Florida and then again as a Category 3 Hurricane in Louisiana. It was one of the largest, most intense hurricanes on record in the Atlantic when it reached Category 5 status over the Gulf of Mexico. The storm produced high winds, storm surge, flooding, and tornadoes in parts of Cuba, Florida, Georgia, Alabama, Mississippi, and Louisiana and continued to produce heavy rains and flooding as it dissipated through the Mississippi Basin and Tennessee Valley.

If there had been no people or property in the path of Hurricane Katrina to experience her wrath, or if the hurricane had taken place on open ocean waters, the hurricane would have been counted as one of the strongest storms on record. But the implications of the storm would have been of

Figure 1-2

Satellite image of Hurricane Katrina over the central Gulf of Mexico on August 28, 2005, near the time of peak intensity.

interest merely to professional meteorologists and amateur storm watchers. Unfortunately, the history of Hurricane Katrina tells a very different tale. Thousands of people and structures were within direct reach of Katrina's intense rain bands and swirling winds, resulting in one of the deadliest, as well as the single costliest, hurricane to hit the United States. Katrina struck an area that is particularly vulnerable to storm surge and flooding, resulting in widespread destruction of homes, businesses, schools, farms, infrastructure, and entire ecosystems. The economic ramifications are deep and long-lasting, and the storm will continue to impact the oil and gas industry, fisheries and shellfishery, transportation networks along the Mississippi River system, and the tourism and hospitality industries for years to come. Insured losses caused by Katrina are estimated by the American Insurance Services Group (AISG) to be around $75 billion, about twice the adjusted costs of the next costliest hurricane in US history, Hurricane Andrew.[7] The total number of fatalities directly or indirectly related to Katrina may never be known. At the time of this writing, approximately 1,090 deaths were reported in Louisiana, 228 in Mississippi, 14 in Florida, 2 in Alabama and 2 in Georgia, for a total of 1,336 human lives lost, including hundreds of children and elderly people.[8] Of those that survived, many are displaced in temporary shelters (such as hotels, mobile homes or travel trailers) scattered throughout the country. Some survivors may never return to their homes or communities.

The full impacts of the Hurricane Katrina disaster are still being compiled and are beyond the scope of this book or any single text written at this time. It is indeed a sad and compelling chapter in our nation's modern history. There are short scenarios regarding Hurricane Katrina in each chapter that illustrate some of the mitigation and preparedness concepts discussed in that chapter. These examples hopefully will bring to life some of the obstacles as well as some of the opportunities that confront practitioners in the emergency management field today. If we can learn from studying how this particular disaster happened in the wealthiest and most powerful country on Earth, perhaps we can prevent such a tragedy from occurring again.

SELF-CHECK

- Recite the federal government's definition of **disaster**.
- Explain why disasters are increasing in frequency.
- Discuss how the conditions of a disaster differ from those of a natural hazard.

1.3 The Many Costs of Disasters

There are many different types of costs associated with a disaster. Some costs are obvious, such as the expense of repairing damaged structures. Other costs are less direct and cannot be fully calculated until years after the disaster has passed. Still other costs are not financial in nature, and no monetary value can be placed on them.

1.3.1 Direct Financial Costs

Disasters are very expensive, whether they are caused by a natural hazard or by a human agent. When people are in danger, they must be rescued quickly and safely, then sheltered and fed. When community security is compromised, law enforcement must beef up patrols to protect people and property from looting and vandalism (see Figure 1-3). When power goes out, electricity and telephone lines must be repaired. When buildings and infrastructure are damaged, they must be rebuilt.

It costs millions, sometimes billions of dollars to remove debris, repair infrastructure, rebuild homes, and reestablish commerce and industry when a community has been hit by a disaster. Local governments are often burdened with much of the cost to reconstruct schools, utilities, fire stations, roads, bridges, and other local facilities that are damaged during a disaster. If the local and state governments cannot afford to pay for it all, the federal government covers much of the cost of recovery and reconstruction following a large disaster, as well the costs of short-term assistance to people who lose their homes and jobs. Federal disaster assistance programs are discussed in more detail in Chapter 6.

Who pays for these costs? Taxpayers finance all the activities of local, state, and federal governments before, during, and after a disaster. Property owners who have purchased insurance coverage (homeowners, flood, earthquake, etc.) often receive reimbursement for some of the costs of repairing their homes and businesses following a disaster. But when thousands of people make insurance claims all at once after a large-scale disaster, premiums for everyone, not just for those directly affected, can go up. Churches and other charities and volunteer organizations also contribute generously for disaster recovery, but the funds that they provide to disaster victims could have been directed elsewhere, such as helping the homeless, donating to arts and education, protecting animals, or otherwise serving the original mission of the organization. In other words, *we all pay for disasters*, even if we don't live in the area directly affected.

1.3.2 Long-Term Economic Costs

In addition to the direct financial costs of repair and reconstruction, other costs are often associated with disasters. Long-term economic costs can keep a community from recovering fully after a disaster occurs, even if the direct financial costs of repair and reconstruction are met.

Figure 1-3

East Grand Forks, MN, April 8, 1997: Law enforcement officers patrol the
Sherlock Park area of East Grand Forks.

Following a large-scale disaster that affects a major portion of a community, local businesses may close permanently, either because their capital assets (warehouses, manufacturing plants, equipment, inventory, offices, etc.) are damaged beyond repair and cannot be replaced, or because the company has lost employees displaced by the disaster. Often, employees must move out of the area, either because they have lost their own homes or because they no longer have a place to work. Disruptions in the flow of goods and services can also impact local businesses, as well as industries located out of the disaster region, for a long time. Long-term economic losses are particularly hard for small business owners and farmers, who may not have adequate savings or insurance to cover expenses and who cannot recoup their losses quickly enough to stay financially solvent.

The loss of jobs that occurs when major employers close because of a disaster can have a ripple effect throughout the community (see Figure 1-4). If the job loss is severe enough, the entire economic structure of the locality can be changed permanently. Many smaller communities are dependent upon just one or two industries for their economic base, and when these are destroyed, there is no source of employment for residents. Towns and villages that serve primarily as tourist destinations, for example, can be devastated when a natural hazard obliterates the accommodations and attractions that bring visitors to the area. In turn, the local government loses its main sources of revenue from property, occupancy, and sales taxes, and no longer has means of providing services needed to support the community.

Problems arising from changes to the economic structure and employment base are compounded when municipal services are interrupted and cannot be restored quickly and efficiently. The longer utilities, schools, transportation systems, communications, and other local facilities are off-line, the more difficult it becomes for residents and businesses to return to work and commerce.

A lack of housing is often one of the most serious limitations to the full recovery of a community over the long term. When housing stocks are depleted because of an earthquake, hurricane, or other major disaster, the cost of available housing goes up, further adding to the economic burden of community residents. Building costs typically rise dramatically following a disaster owing to a scarcity of materials, rising prices of material and labor, and a corresponding increase in demand. These high prices further limit the housing choices of new and returning residents.

Figure 1-4

The owner of this small business in New Hope, Pennsylvania spent weeks cleaning up after flooding on the Delaware River. He suffered $100,000 in inventory losses and spent $200,000 in cleaning fees. This business may or may not remain viable after this disaster.

1.3.3 Environmental Costs

Economic losses are not the only costs associated with hazard events. The natural environment can suffer severe damage during a disaster. Environmental damage can be the result of a man-made hazard that affects habitats and ecosystems directly, such as a chemical accident or an oil spill. The environment can also be damaged when a natural hazard causes a secondary hazard to occur, such as an earthquake that causes a gas line to rupture or a tornado that uproots a hazardous waste facility.

Flooding very often causes severe environmental damage when hazardous materials are released into the floodwaters. As floodwaters recede, contaminants may be carried along to surface waters (rivers, lakes, and streams) or seep into the groundwater and eventually may make their way into drinking water supplies. For example, propane, gas, chemicals, solvents, pesticides, and other harmful agents can be released if tanks, barrels, and storage containers are breached during a flooding event. Junkyards, livestock pens, meat and poultry processing plants, sewage treatment facilities, and other sources of contamination can also increase the environmental costs of a flooding disaster. For example, during Hurricane Floyd in 1999, many hog farms in eastern North Carolina were flooded when rivers and streams overflowed their banks following days of heavy rainfall. Tons of raw animal waste spilled over containment lagoons and entered the waterways of the region. Water quality declined precipitously, endangering the health of people, livestock, wildlife, and aquatic animals and fish for a considerable length of time after the event.

Often, with proper cleanup and handling procedures, the damage to ecosystems and habitats can be minimized, but in other cases, wildlife and vegetation are severely impacted for many years following a disaster.

1.3.4 Societal Costs

One of the most insidious effects of a disaster is the impact it can have on society. When a disaster destroys whole neighborhoods and large sections of the community, the social fabric of the community may be ripped to shreds. Consider these possible consequences of a catastrophic event:

▲ Social networks that were in place to support residents are disjointed.

▲ A vibrant neighborhood may suddenly become a ghost town.

▲ Residents are often displaced and forced to live in unfamiliar locations far from family and friends.

▲ Children are suddenly without teachers, friends, and classmates, and the routines of school and home life are disrupted.

▲ Places of worship may lose their congregations, and community centers that once provided assistance to residents may be dismantled.

▲ Incidents of domestic violence and substance abuse often increase following a traumatic event.

> **FOR EXAMPLE**
>
> **Many Katrina Victims Are Poor African Americans**
>
> The impact of Hurricane Katrina in New Orleans and elsewhere on the Gulf Coast in 2005 highlighted some of the many problems associated with poverty, race, and class in areas affected by a natural disaster of that scale. The hardest-hit regions in the Gulf states were already drowning in extreme poverty: Mississippi is the poorest state in the nation, with Louisiana just behind it. Before the storm, New Orleans had a poverty rate of 23%, ranking 7th out of 290 large US cities. In 2000, the city of New Orleans was more than 67% black. Although the national average for elders with disabilities is 39.6%, New Orleans hovers near 57%. Nearly one in four New Orleans citizens did not have access to a car. These pre-Katrina statistics have direct bearing on the conditions in the city following the hurricane, when hundreds of people were stranded without adequate resources to evacuate or to cope with the conditions created by flooding, loss of power, breakdowns in security, and other disaster impacts.[9]

▲ As parents and families frantically try to find food, shelter, clothing, diapers, and other necessities of life, tensions can rise, and stress can cause changes in behavior and reduce coping skills.

▲ Residents who were only marginally able to provide for themselves before the disaster are often disproportionately affected. These individuals with special needs include lower-income, non–English speaking, minority, elderly, disabled, homeless, or otherwise disadvantaged people, and those in single parent households.

All of these impacts put together can cause some communities to lose their sense of place. What was once a source of pride and identity is now lost, and the characteristics that held the society together may never be regained. The social costs of a disaster should never be underestimated, because these costs may never be fully compensated for.

1.3.5 Human Lives Lost

The death of one human being as a result of a natural or man-made hazard is one death too many. Tragically, over a thousand lives were lost during Hurricane Katrina in 2005. Buildings, infrastructure, personal possessions, and other material goods can be restored given enough time and money, but a human life can never be replaced. Our first priority for creating resilient communities must be to reduce the likelihood that people may be killed or injured during a disaster. The loss of any life is an unacceptable cost of disaster and should always be the focus of our mitigation and preparedness efforts.

Table 1-1: Top Ten Natural Disasters in the United States (Ranked by Relief Costs of FEMA)

Event	Year	FEMA Funding
Hurricane Katrina (AL, LA, MS)	2005	$7.2 billion*
Northridge Earthquake (CA)	1994	$6.961 billion
Hurricane Georges (AL, FL, LA, MS, PR, VI)	1998	$2.251 billion
Hurricane Ivan (AL, FL, GA, LA, MS, NC, NJ, NY, PA, TN, WVA)	2004	$1.947 billion**
Hurricane Andrew (FL, LA)	1992	$1.813 billion
Hurricane Charley (FL, SC)	2004	$1.559 billion**
Hurricane Frances (FL, GA, NC, NY, OH, PA, SC)	2004	$1.425 billion**
Hurricane Jeanne (DE, FL, PR, VI, VA)	2004	$1.407 billion**
Tropical Storm Allison (FL, LA, MS, PA, TX)	2001	$1.387 billion
Hurricane Hugo (NC, SC, PR, VI)	1989	$1.307 billion

Source: www.fema.gov/hazard/topten.shtm Last Modified: Wednesday, 05-Apr-2006 12:35:00 EDT

Amount obligated from the President's Disaster Relief Fund for FEMA's assistance programs, hazard mitigation grants, federal mission assignments, contractual services and administrative costs as of March 31, 2006. Figures do not include funding provided by other participating federal agencies, such as the disaster loan programs of the Small Business Administration and the Agriculture Department's Farm Service Agency. **Note: Funding amounts are stated in nominal dollars, unadjusted for inflation.*

***Amount obligated from the President's Disaster Relief Fund for FEMA's assistance programs, hazard mitigation grants, federal mission assignments, contractual services and administrative costs as of May 31, 2005. Figures do not include funding provided by other participating federal agencies, such as the disaster loan programs of the Small Business Administration and the Agriculture Department's Farm Service Agency. **Note:** Funding amounts are stated in nominal dollars, unadjusted for inflation.*

1.3.6 Top Ten Natural Disasters in the United States

The United States has a long history of expensive disasters. Table 1-1 lists the top ten natural disasters in the United States as compiled by the Federal Emergency Management Agency (FEMA). These figures represent only the costs paid or obligated by FEMA for disaster assistance and do not include the amounts paid by other federal agencies, state and local governments, charities and relief organizations, or insurance payouts. Nor do these figures account for the social, environmental, or long-term indirect costs due to these hazards. Also note that fatalities are not listed in this chart.

SELF-CHECK

- List the five categories of costs associated with disaster.
- Discuss how the environment can suffer from a disaster.
- Cite five examples of social costs.

1.4 Mitigation and Preparedness for Resilient Communities

We cannot stop natural hazards from happening, nor can we prevent many man-made hazards, but we *can* take action to reduce the impacts of these hazards so that the damage is less extensive and so that recovery can take place quickly. Actions taken to lower disaster risk can also help reduce losses and their associated costs.

1.4.1 Taking Action to Prevent Disasters

Resilient communities are towns, cities, counties, and states that take action prior to a hazard event so that a disaster does not result. Resilient communities do this in two stages:

1. Preparedness
2. Mitigation

A **disaster resilient community** is a community or region developed or redeveloped to minimize the human, environmental, and property losses, and the social and economic disruption caused by disasters. A resilient community understands natural systems and realizes that appropriate siting, design, and construction of the built environment are essential to advances in disaster prevention.[10]

1.4.2 The Emergency Management System

Comprehensive emergency management is a widely used approach at the local, state, and federal levels to deal with the inevitability of natural hazards and the possibility of man-made hazards and their potential to cause disasters in a community. The four phases of a Comprehensive emergency management system are: **Preparedness, Response, Recovery,** and **Mitigation.** Table 1-2 outlines each of these phases.

Table 1-2: Phases of Comprehensive Emergency Management

Preparedness	• Activities to improve the ability to respond quickly in the immediate aftermath of an incident. • Includes development of response procedures, design and installation of warning systems, evacuation planning, exercises to test emergency operations, and training of emergency personnel.
Response	• Activities during or immediately following a disaster to meet the urgent needs of disaster victims. • Involves mobilizing and positioning emergency equipment and personnel; includes time-sensitive operations such as search and rescue, evacuation, emergency medical care, food and shelter programs, and bringing damaged services and systems back online.
Recovery	• Actions that begin after the disaster, when urgent needs have been met. Recovery actions are designed to put the community back together. • Includes repairs to roads, bridges, and other public facilities, restoration of power, water, and other municipal services, and other activities to help restore normal operations to a community.
Mitigation	• Activities that prevent a disaster, reduce the chance of a disaster happening, or lessen the damaging effects of unavoidable disasters and emergencies. • Includes engineering solutions such as dams and levees; land-use planning to prevent development in hazardous areas; protecting structures through sound building practices and retrofitting; acquiring and relocating damaged structures; preserving the natural environment to serve as a buffer against hazard impacts; and educating the public about hazards and ways to reduce risk.

Figure 1-5

Emergency Management Cycle

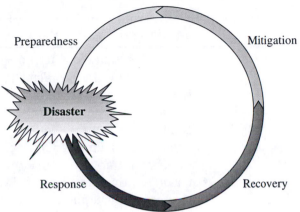

Emergency Management Cycle.

The four phases of comprehensive emergency management are often illustrated in a circular pattern, signifying its cyclical nature (see Figure 1-5). We prepare for disasters before they occur. When a disaster happens, a community must first respond to that particular event and soon thereafter begin recovery. But even while the community is still recovering from one disaster, it must begin the process of mitigating the impacts of the next disaster.

Also known as the **disaster life cycle**, this system describes the process through which emergency managers prepare for emergencies and disasters, respond to them when they occur, help people and institutions recover from them, mitigate their effects, reduce the risk of loss, and prevent secondary disasters such as fires from occurring.[11]

We are always preparing for and mitigating the impacts of disasters (see Table 1-3). These two phases indicate the future orientation of emergency management and are the building blocks for resilient communities. Ironically, the period of recovery following a hazard event often provides a unique opportunity to rebuild in a way that incorporates mitigation concepts into the redevelopment of a damaged community. In fact, the availability of government funding to carry out mitigation plans and projects has historically been highest during the recovery phase of the disaster life cycle. New emphasis is being placed on predisaster mitigation activity, but the postdisaster environment continues to be one of significant increases in fiscal and technical capability.

1.4.3 Preparedness

Preparedness ensures that if a disaster occurs, people are ready to get through it safely and respond to it effectively. Preparedness can be characterized as a state of readiness to respond to any emergency or disaster. It involves anticipating

Table 1-3: Preparedness Activities Are Any Actions Taken Prior to the Emergency That Facilitate the Implementation of a Coordinated Response

Preparedness Activities	Description
Planning	All 56 U.S. states and territories prepare Emergency Operations Plans (EOPs). The EOP establishes a chain of command, designates responsible parties, provides for continuity of government functions, establishes an Emergency Operations Center (EOC), and provides a road map for decision making during emergencies. Evacuation and emergency sheltering are also an important planning function of the preparedness phase.
Training	Emergency managers, first responders, and public officials take classes in emergency planning, disaster management, hazardous materials response, fire service management, and so on.
Exercises & Drills	From "tabletop" discussions of a specific problem to full scale exercises that involve detailed disaster scenarios that unfold over several days, exercise events bring together every agency and volunteer organization that would respond in a real disaster.
Emergency Awareness and Education	Educational messages include teaching children how to make a 911 call, reminding parents to keep emergency supplies on hand, showing homeowners how to make their homes more hazard proof, distributing disaster-specific messages to areas at risk, and so forth.
Warning	Warning activities include development of warning systems, emergency alert systems, and coordination of sirens and other emergency notification methods. Regular testing of warning and notification devices is also involved.

FOR EXAMPLE

Turn Around Don't Drown

People are at risk even in shallow flooding. According to the National Weather Service (NWS), almost half of all flood fatalities occur in vehicles. The next highest percentage of flood-related deaths is due to walking into or near flood waters. Local storms can quickly fill underpasses and cover bridges, and even two feet of water can float most vehicles, including large ones. If the water is moving, vehicles can be swept away. Driving at night during a local flood can be especially hazardous. To increase awareness of the dangers of shallow flooding, the NWS has initiated the "Turn Around Don't Drown" program to help communities educate residents about the dangers of walking or driving in floodwaters (see Figure 1-6).

Figure 1-6

The Federal Highway Administration has approved the Flooding Ahead Don't Drown sign as an official Incident Road Sign.

what might happen during different sorts of hazard events and developing plans to deal with those possibilities. Preparedness also involves carrying out exercises, evaluating plans for shortfalls, and training and education. Although emergency managers must remain flexible and able to adapt their plans to meet immediate needs as the situation warrants, a plan or established protocol for dealing with disasters and emergencies of all sorts is crucial to a successful response. See Chapter 11 for a more detailed discussion of preparedness.

1.4.4 Mitigation

Mitigation is defined as "any sustained action to reduce or eliminate long-term risk to people and property from hazards and their effects".[12] This definition highlights the long-term benefits that effective mitigation can have. This definition also emphasizes that mitigation is an ongoing effort that communities must make on a continuous basis. Mitigation involves planning, strategizing, and implementing action ideas in advance of a hazard event. The ultimate purpose of mitigation plans, strategies, and actions is to avoid placing people and property in harm's way and to make structures safer and stronger when avoidance is impossible or impractical.

1.4.5 The Difference between Preparedness and Mitigation

Preparedness involves the functional, logistical, and operational elements of emergency management. Although preparedness activities are carried out in advance of a hazard event, they are directed to the response and, to a lesser degree, the recovery phases of the emergency management cycle. During preparedness, we gather our supplies and make our plans for what to do when the disaster hits.

Preparedness can be visualized as the phase in which we pose a series of "what if" questions, and seek to find the answers before they become reality. For instance, an emergency manager may consider various worst-case scenarios, such as:

▲ What if the power goes out? Do we have generators and a supply of fuel? What about telecommunications, water, and sewer service?

▲ What if the roads are blocked? How will we deliver needed supplies and medical services to impacted populations?

▲ What if our food supplies are cut off? Do we have access to water, ice, Meals-Ready-to-Eat? Where are these supplies stored, and how quickly can they become available?

▲ What if there are multiple injuries? Who are our medical contacts? Will they need transportation, supplies, a power source, blood?

▲ What if residents have to leave their homes quickly? Is an evacuation plan in place? Does it account for fluctuations in populations, such as the tourist season in a resort community? What about people who are not independently mobile? Those who are ill, old, young, illiterate?

▲ Are community buildings ready to serve as shelters? Are their locations clearly identified and accessible? Who opens the shelters? Are pets provided for as well?

▲ Are first responders ready to carry out search and rescue missions? Have they been trained to serve in disaster conditions? How will they communicate with one another?

These are the types of issues that the preparedness phase attempts to address before emergency conditions render the situation impossible.

Mitigation, in contrast, is the ongoing effort to lessen the impacts of disasters on people and property through predisaster activities. Mitigation can take place months, years, and even decades before a hazard event and continues after a disaster occurs with an eye to the future. Mitigation differs from the other phases of emergency management in that it looks for long-term solutions to reduce hazards. Mitigation involves a different thought process and a different skill set, one that is oriented toward long-range policy and decision-making processes.

One of the primary differences between mitigation and preparedness is the visibility of the respective results. The benefits of mitigation often are not realized for some time, and success is measured by what does *not* occur. Avoidance and prevention are the outcomes of mitigation done well, outcomes that can be difficult to quantify. In the past, some emergency managers have been hesitant to embrace mitigation activities with enthusiasm equal to that for preparedness, perhaps thinking, "I won't lose my job for failing to mitigate, but I might lose my job if I botch a response." The emphasis therefore has been on highly visible, results-oriented action in preparation for the immediacy of an emergency situation rather than the slower, process-oriented strategy of mitigation.

Unfortunately, mitigation is often neglected until after a disaster actually occurs. In the case of natural disasters, history is filled with examples of communities that rebuild in the same places, in the same manner as previously, only to suffer the same perils when the hazard event recurs. Mitigation seeks to break the cycle of unnecessary destruction and reconstruction by adapting human settlement patterns and construction techniques to reflect the threat posed by potential hazards.[13]

SELF-CHECK

- Define **disaster resilient communities, comprehensive emergency management, preparedness, response, recovery,** and **mitigation.**
- List the four stages of comprehensive emergency management cycle.
- Discuss the differences between preparedness and mitigation.

1.5 Mitigation Strategies

Because it is so important, we will restate the definition of mitigation here:

Mitigation is any sustained action to reduce or eliminate long-term risk to people and property from hazards and their effects.

1.5.1 A Mitigation Toolbox

There are a wide variety of tools and techniques that a community can use to reduce the impacts of hazards on people and property. These range from keeping people and property out of harm's way through incentives and acquisition to imposing regulatory standards on all construction in hazard areas.

▲ *Building standards* specify how buildings are constructed. In addition to traditional building codes, building standards can include flood-proofing requirements, such as elevating structures above expected flood heights; seismic design standards; and wind-bracing and anchoring requirements for new construction and similar requirements for retrofitting existing buildings.

▲ *Development Regulations,* which may include zoning and subdivision ordinances, regulate the location, type, and intensity of new development. Development regulations can include flood-zone regulations; setbacks from faults, steep slopes, and coastal erosion areas; and overlay zoning districts that apply additional development standards for sensitive lands such as wetlands, dunes, and hillsides.

▲ *Capital improvement programs* can be an effective way to implement mitigation throughout a community. Local public policies supporting hazard mitigation should be incorporated into these programs. Locating schools, fire stations, and other public buildings, streets, storm sewers, and other utilities outside of high hazard areas provides direct mitigation benefits. When siting public facilities in hazardous locations cannot be avoided, communities can incorporate hazard reduction measures into the design or require retrofits. Public facility siting is a key determinant of the location of new privately financed growth in a community. As such, facilities, particularly roads and utilities, should not be placed where they have the potential to encourage growth in high hazard areas.

▲ *Land and property acquisition* means purchasing properties in hazard-prone areas with public funds and restricting development to uses that are less vulnerable to disaster-related damages. This can be accomplished through acquisition of undeveloped lands, acquisition of development rights, transfer of development rights to lower-risk areas, relocation of buildings, and acquisition of damaged buildings.

▲ *Taxation and fiscal policies* can be used to distribute the public costs of private development onto owners of such properties. Employing impact fees to cover the public costs of development in areas of high hazards or providing tax breaks for reducing land use intensities in hazardous areas are two options.

▲ **Public awareness** through information dissemination on natural hazards and providing educational materials to the construction industry, homeowners, tenants, and businesses is also important. Included in this category are hazard disclosure requirements for the real estate industry and public information campaigns to increase awareness in all sectors of the community.[14]

Each of these types of strategies seeks to reduce the vulnerability of the built environment to the impacts of hazards (see Figure 1-7). Many communities use a combination of strategies to meet their mitigation needs. See Chapter 12 for a more detailed discussion of hazard mitigation tools and techniques.

1.5.2 Strategies to Mitigate Man-Made Hazards

Many of the strategies used to reduce the effects of natural hazards are also effective for mitigating the impacts of man-made hazards. For instance, construction

Figure 1-7

Baldwin County, Alabama: This house has been elevated above the expected flood height. Elevation is one way to mitigate flooding for a home situated in a river's floodplain.

techniques that strengthen buildings to withstand hurricane-force winds may also provide some protection against the force of an explosive device. Following the terrorist attacks of September 11, 2001, greater attention has been paid to prevention and mitigation of terrorism and other intentional hazards, but because these types of incidents are difficult to predict and analyze, this field is still under development. There is some possibility that increased intelligence, surveillance, and security operations can minimize the threats posed by these hazards, but much remains to be done to solidify our approach to dealing with terrorist events while also protecting our civil liberties.

We have had more experience in this country with mitigating other technological hazards. For instance, following the Three Mile Island nuclear accident, the U.S. Nuclear Regulatory Commission implemented several improvements for operations, including increased oversight, more frequent inspections, more comprehensive training and exercises for personnel, and upgrades in equipment at all nuclear reactors in the United States. These improvements significantly decreased the risk of a similar nuclear accident in this country.

1.5.3 Risk Assessment and Mapping

Before a community can implement any of its mitigation strategies, it must have a clear picture of the types of hazards that pose a threat to it and how those hazards may impact people and property. Hazard identification is the necessary first step to reducing vulnerability; it involves a process of culling information about the community's hazard history, profiling various hazard events, and making predictions about the possibility of future hazards. The community must also determine what assets and populations are vulnerable to the hazards that have been identified, including analysis of land use patterns, growth potential, and development trends to evaluate what may be at risk in the *future*. Maps are an important component of a community **risk assessment**, as they can be used to illustrate where hazards intersect with the built environment in a graphic and visual way. The analysis and maps produced during a risk assessment can help a community make important decisions about how to protect local assets and vulnerable populations against likely hazards. See Chapter 10 for a more in-depth discussion about community risk assessment.

Many communities in the United States have an official Flood Insurance Rate Map, or FIRM, that shows the location of flood-prone areas throughout the jurisdiction. These maps indicate the likelihood that a particular home, street or business could be flooded during the next 100-year flood (a flood that has a 1% chance of occurring during a given year). These maps also contain visual information about the frequencies of other flooding events. These maps are used as the basis for developing ordinances that regulate the types of structures that are allowed in the community's floodplain and specify how structures must be protected to mitigate the impacts of various levels of flooding.

1.5.4 Managing Community Growth and Development

One of the most effective approaches to mitigation involves managing community growth and development through land use regulations and planning and controlling the quality of structures that are built through building standards and code requirements. Local governments can place hazardous locations such as floodplains, seismic risk areas, landslide-prone sites, wildfire areas, and other places vulnerable to natural hazards off-limits through zoning and subdivision ordinances. Local governments can also install infrastructure such as roads, utility lines, water and sewage treatment facilities, and other public services to avoid hazardous areas. By making hazardous areas less attractive for development by withholding capital improvements, communities can discourage building on inappropriate sites.

The choices we make regarding where and how we build determine our level of vulnerability to many natural and man-made hazards. Mitigation should not be seen as an impediment to growth and development of a community. On the contrary, incorporating hazard mitigation into decisions related to a community's growth can result in a safer, more resilient community and one that is more attractive to new families and businesses.

1.5.5 Protecting the Environment

Damage to natural ecosystems and resources during and after a hurricane, earthquake, or other major hazard is inevitable. Given time, the natural environment will recuperate and adjust. However, communities, public agencies, and individuals can help reduce the vulnerability of natural ecosystems and resources by preventing releases of hazardous waste through proper handling, storage, and contingency planning. Sound planning and siting of development and infrastructure consistent with realistic disaster scenarios is also an important environmental protection. Preserving and restoring floodplains and wetlands allow these areas to serve as storm and erosion buffers and as temporary storage for floodwaters. Protection of beaches, dunes, floodplains and native vegetation, and appropriate construction regulations that take into consideration natural processes, may help to minimize damage to critical habitats and bolster protection of the built environment.[15]

1.5.6 Tying It All Together with Mitigation Planning

Hazard mitigation planning is the process of determining how to reduce or eliminate the loss of life and property damage that can happen as a result of hazards. An **all-hazards approach** to mitigation planning involves consideration of all hazards with the potential for causing harm, including natural hazards (earthquakes, snowstorms, flooding, hurricanes and the like) as well as man-made hazards such as technological accidents and terrorism. The end product of the process is a **hazard mitigation plan,** a document that presents policies and strategies that will reduce vulnerability to hazards when those policies and strategies are put into

---

FOR EXAMPLE

Eastern Band of Cherokee Indians Is First Native American Tribe in the Southeast to Plan to Reduce Damages from Future Disasters

The Eastern Band of Cherokee Indians (EBCI) in North Carolina was the first American Indian tribe in the eight southeastern states to receive approval of their hazard mitigation plan from FEMA. The EBCI reservation, incorporated under the laws of North Carolina in 1889, is located in the southern Appalachian Mountains of western North Carolina. The Multi-Hazard Mitigation Plan submitted by the Cherokee Tribal Council (the legislative branch of the EBCI) addresses ways to mitigate the ravages of natural and man-made disasters. The plan was developed to help the Cherokee Tribal Council make decisions on how best to minimize damage resulting from natural hazards, including floods, landslides and erosion, wildfires, high winds, earthquakes, droughts and extreme heat, severe winter weather, and selective man-made hazards on the EBCI Reservation.

The plan also calls for reducing the vulnerability of existing infrastructure, providing the basis for grant funding and loans to homeowners and small businesses for the purpose of implementing mitigation measures, capitalizing on federal funding that may become available before or after a disaster strikes, and ensuring the tribe maintains eligibility for the full range of future federal disaster relief. The tribe has also emphasized preparedness for disasters by developing and Emergency Operations Plan that addresses responsibilities for response and recovery activities following an emergency event.[16]

---

action. These policies and action strategies should be based on a sound and thorough assessment of the hazards present in the community and an analysis of what is at risk from those hazards. The planning process helps pull together these important analyses and uses them as background support for changes that will contribute to the resiliency and overall sustainability of the community. See Chapter 13 for further discussion of the hazard mitigation planning process.

SELF-CHECK

- List six categories of mitigation strategies.
- Describe how risk assessment and mapping help inform the mitigation strategy process.
- Discuss the benefits of preparing a hazard mitigation plan.

1.6 The Value of Mitigation and Preparedness

Mitigation, also known as prevention, encourages long-term reduction of hazard vulnerability. (see Table 1-4). The goal of mitigation is to save lives and reduce property damage. Mitigation can accomplish this through cost-effective and environmentally sound actions. This, in turn, can reduce the enormous cost of disasters to property owners, businesses, and all levels of government. In addition, mitigation can protect critical community facilities, reduce exposure to liability, and minimize community disruption. Preparedness saves lives and property and facilitates response operations through predisaster plans and training. Through mitigation and preparedness, individuals and communities can recover more

Table 1-4: Benefits of Mitigation and Preparedness

Mitigation and Preparedness Benefit	Details
Reduces loss of life and damage to property	Communities can save lives and reduce property damage from hazards through mitigation actions, such as moving families and their homes out of harm's way. Mitigation and preparedness also reduce the risk to emergency workers who must rescue people and pets during a disaster.
Reduces vulnerability to future hazards	By having mitigation and preparedness plans in place, a community is able to take steps to permanently reduce the risk of future losses.
Saves money	A community will experience cost savings by not having to provide emergency services, rescue operations, or recovery efforts. Communities also avoid costly repairs or replacement of buildings and infrastructure.
Speeds response and recovery	By considering mitigation and preparation in advance, a community can identify postdisaster opportunities before a disaster occurs. A strategy that is thought out prior to a disaster allows the community to react quickly when the time comes.
Demonstrates commitment to community health and safety	A mitigation and preparedness strategy demonstrates the community's commitment to safeguarding its citizens and protecting its economic, social, and environmental well-being.

rapidly from disasters, lessening the financial burden of disasters on families, the Treasury, state, local, and tribal governments.[17]

1.6.1 Mitigation Contributes to Sustainable Communities

As mitigation serves to protect the environment and reduce disaster-related costs, it can contribute to the community's long-term sustainability, supporting economic vitality, environmental health, and quality of life for the community as a whole. Sustainability is attained when decisions made by the present generation do not reduce the options of future generations. **Sustainable development** is development that "meets the needs of the present without compromising the ability of future generations to meet their own needs."[18] Resilience to disasters is an essential characteristic of a sustainable community. [19]

Sustainability is a concept that can help communities of all sizes and in all locations make decisions that will lead to a better quality of life for all of their members. The principles of sustainability also apply to communities that find they must recover and rebuild in the aftermath of a disaster. The goal of sustainable development and redevelopment is to create and maintain safe, lasting communities through the protection of life, property, the natural environment, and the economy. Resilience, created thorough hazard mitigation and preparedness activities, is a very important part of any effort to become more sustainable.

The guiding principles of sustainable development are intended to provide a sense of direction to decision makers for ensuring the quality of development and redevelopment without necessarily limiting the quantity of development. Sustainability recognizes that the economy and the environment are not in conflict, but are intricately intertwined. These principles are not an impediment to growth; instead, sustainable development fosters quality growth. See Chapter 14 for further discussion of the role of mitigation and preparedness in building community sustainability.

1.6.2 Mitigation Pays

A fundamental premise of mitigation is that current dollars invested in mitigation will significantly reduce the demand for future dollars by reducing the amount needed for emergency response, recovery, repair, and reconstruction following a disaster. By protecting its investment in infrastructure and capital assets, a community will enjoy cost savings over the long term. Mitigation, therefore, is a fiscally responsible activity for a community to pursue (see Figure 1-8). The benefits of mitigation and preparedness accrue equally to business, industry, and other members of the private sector. By reducing risk to hazard losses, companies can protect their employees, their income stream, and company assets, and they are better equipped to maintain fiscal solvency and economic viability even after a disaster. See Chapter 9 for a discussion of private sector mitigation and preparedness activities.

Figure 1-8

Heeding warnings of El Niño rains, the San Diego Zoo Wild Animal Park invested heavily in preventive measures to protect zoo assets and inhabitants, including silt damming, re-grassing, and drainage improvements.

1.6.3 Mitigation Calls for Environmental Integrity

Mitigation calls for conservation of natural and ecologically sensitive areas (such as floodplains, wetlands, and dunes), which allows the environment to absorb some of the impact of hazard events. This open space preservation technique also serves to protect the habitats of many species, enhances water quality, and provides recreational and aesthetic opportunities for the community. In this way, mitigation programs can contribute to a community's environmental integrity.

1.6.4 Window of Opportunity

Although any time is the right time to engage in mitigation activities, the aftermath of a disaster presents a unique window of opportunity for a community to figure out what went wrong and to develop and implement strategies to prevent the same kind of damage from occurring in the future.

During the recovery and reconstruction that take place following a disaster, streets, water systems, schools, and other public facilities can be constructed in safer locations away from hazardous areas in the community. If there are no safer alternatives for locating structures and facilities that were damaged or destroyed, then new homes, businesses, and other buildings can be built according to building

FOR EXAMPLE

Reduce, Reuse, Recycle After a Disaster

Following Hurricane Floyd, many residential structures in the Charlotte-Mecklenburg metropolitan area in North Carolina were severely flooded. The City-County participated in the Hazard Mitigation Grant Program (HMGP) buyout of many of the damaged homes. But the community went beyond mere acquisition and demolition to mitigate flood hazards and extended its program to include the use of two creative alternatives to immediate demolition: stripping of salvageable materials and public safety training. Partnering with Habitat for Humanity of Charlotte, the community identified opportunities to remove and reuse undamaged interior materials such as hardwood floors, ceiling fans, light fixtures, interior doors, kitchen appliances, counter tops, cabinets, sinks, door moldings, mantelpieces, basins, and vanities. Several homes also had furnaces and hot water heaters located in the attic, protecting them from past floodwaters. Volunteers from Habitat Charlotte carried out the work of removing the items and taking them off-site for storage and distribution through Habitat's ReStore.

By salvaging and recycling materials from acquisition/demolition projects, communities can reduce the amount of debris in their landfills, minimize demolition and landfill costs, and even offer opportunities for job training and welfare-to-work programs. Mecklenburg County Soil & Water Conservation District led an effort to rescue plants that would have otherwise been leveled during demolition. Ornamental plants including azalea bushes and other flowering shrubs were saved and replanted at a local nature preserve, a senior citizens' center, and several nearby schools.

Before the demolition was carried out, Charlotte-Mecklenburg made many of the damaged structures available to local public safety personnel for training purposes. The abandoned homes were used by firefighters, law enforcement (including K-9 training for drug searches and S.W.A.T. team training), rescue workers, and other public safety officers.[20]

techniques that make them stronger and more capable of withstanding hazard impacts. A resilient community builds back better, smarter, and stronger after a disaster, so that the next hazard is less likely result in another disaster.

In addition to incorporating principles of resilience into the rebuilding process, the postdisaster period of recovery is also a time of opportunity to rebuild in a more sustainable way. Communities may wish to encourage local residents and business owners to include "green" building techniques in terms of energy efficiency and alternative energy sources (for example, installing solar panels as damaged roofs are repaired) and to use recycled building materials.

The community may also use this chance to provide affordable housing, create walkable neighborhoods, implement water use reduction measures, and protect the environment.

1.6.5 There's More to Be Done

Mitigation and preparedness help communities become more resilient to the impacts of hazards. Although the practice of mitigation and preparedness for man-made hazards is still evolving, we have a comprehensive set of tools for reducing the risk of loss from natural hazards. This does not mean that our job is done. Disaster costs continue to escalate, and we must increase our efforts to keep property out of vulnerable locations thorough implementation of long-lasting and forward-thinking mitigation strategies such as acquisition of at-risk structures, land use regulations to keep development out of hazard areas, and building codes to strengthen homes and businesses against hazard impacts. We have much to do in terms of preparedness as well. The loss of life during Hurricane Katrina highlights the need for vast improvements in our ability to evacuate, shelter, and administer emergency aid to disaster victims. These areas of improvement should serve as a catalyst for further research and study into the most effective means of preventing disasters so that community resiliency becomes reality.

SELF-CHECK

- Define **sustainable development**.
- Discuss the role of community growth in a resilient community's mitigation plan.
- List four benefits of preparedness and mitigation.

SUMMARY

Every community faces the potential for exposure to hazards, both natural and man-made. Only when people are injured and property is damaged by a hazard does a disaster occur. Due to patterns of population growth and development in the United States, disasters now occur more frequently than ever before. Because we all pay for these disasters, directly or indirectly, it is in our best interests to prepare for disasters with responsible emergency management plans. Mitigation and preparedness strategies are critical ways of making a community more resilient against the impacts of hazards.

KEY TERMS

All-hazards approach	Consideration of all the hazards with the potential for causing harm in a community, including natural hazards and man-made hazards, such as technological accidents and terrorism.
Comprehensive emergency management	Approach used to deal with natural hazards and human-caused hazards and their potential to cause disasters in a community.
Disaster	The result when a natural hazard takes place where humans have situated themselves.
Disaster life cycle	The cycle of the four phases of the comprehensive emergency management system as it interacts with a disaster event.
Disaster resilient community	A community or region developed or redeveloped to minimize the human, environmental, and property losses and the social and economic disruption caused by disasters. A resilient community understands natural systems and realizes that appropriate siting, design, and construction of the built environment are essential to advances in disaster prevention.
Dynamic equilibrium	The Earth's natural systems maintain a balanced state over long periods of time through a series of adjustments.
Hazard Mitigation Plan	A document that presents policies and strategies to reduce vulnerability to hazards when those policies and strategies are put into action. These policies and action strategies are based on a sound and thorough risk and vulnerability assessment.
Man-made hazards	Intentional or accidental occurrences caused by human activity; examples include oil spills and acts of terrorism such as bombings.
Mitigation	Any sustained action to reduce or eliminate long-term risk to people and property from hazards and their effects.
Natural hazards	Inevitable and uncontrollable occurrences such as floods, hurricanes, winter storms, and earthquakes.
Preparedness	A state of readiness to respond to any emergency or disaster.

Recovery	Phase in the emergency management cycle that involves actions that begin after a disaster, after emergency needs have been met; examples include road and bridge repairs and restoration of power.
Response	Phase in the emergency management cycle that involves activities to meet the urgent needs of victims during or immediately following a disaster; examples include evacuation as well as search and rescue.
Risk Assessment	The process or methodology used to evaluate risk. Risk assessment typically includes five preliminary steps: (1) identify hazards; (2) profile hazard events; (3) inventory assets and populations; (4) estimate losses; (5) determine future development and population trends. A sixth step, (6) determine acceptable level of risk, is often included in a risk assessment to decide whether further action is warranted.
Sustainable development	Development that meets the needs of the present without compromising the ability of future generations to meet their own needs.

ASSESS YOUR UNDERSTANDING

Go to www.wiley.com/college/schwab to evaluate your knowledge of how to define resilient communities.

Measure your learning by comparing pre-test and post-test results.

Summary Questions

1. Natural hazards are not the same as disasters. True or False?
2. Which of the following is an example of a natural hazard?
   (a) warehouse fire
   (b) sewage overflow
   (c) winter storm
   (d) soil spill
3. The frequency of hazards is increasing. True or False?
4. Disasters are a beneficial part of the balance of nature. True or False?
5. A disaster occurs only when human life and property suffer from damage. True or False?
6. Disasters occur most often in unpopulated areas. True or False?
7. Examples of technological hazards include
   (a) bridge collapse.
   (b) flood.
   (c) bombing.
   (d) tornado.
8. Costs associated with disasters include
   (a) infrastructure repair.
   (b) rise in domestic violence.
   (c) job loss.
   (d) all of the above.
9. Loss of power is a possible environmental cost associated with a flood. True or False?
10. A resilient community is a community that prevents hazards from happening. True or False?
11. Preparedness involves anticipating what might happen during different types of hazard events. True or False?
12. Which of the following is an example of preparedness measures?
    (a) rebuilding water-supply systems
    (b) conserving floodplains
    (c) training those involved in emergency situations
    (d) road repairs

13. The period following a disaster is a valuable time for implementing mitigation measures. True or False?
14. Mitigation is a way to save communities money. True or False?

Review Questions

1. Natural hazards may differ from one geographic area to the next. Discuss a natural hazard for California that is unlikely to affect New Jersey, and vice versa.
2. Hazards help maintain the Earth's dynamic equilibrium. Explain the role of a nor'easter on the coast of Long Island.
3. Give three possible explanations for why it appears that natural hazards are becoming more frequent.
4. How does a natural hazard differ from a disaster?
5. Disasters are increasing in frequency. Explain why.
6. Man-made hazards are another consideration for community planning. Name two types of man-made hazards.
7. How are natural hazards and man-made hazards alike? How are they different?
8. We all pay for the cost of disasters. Explain three ways we do so.
9. Some costs associated with disasters are not financial. Discuss how this is possible.
10. What two stages of the emergency management cycle do resilient communities use to ensure that a disaster does not occur?
11. Citing examples, explain the difference between preparedness and mitigation.
12. A comprehensive emergency management system follows four stages. Name the stages.
13. Mitigation should be considered a wise investment for a community. Explain why.
14. How does mitigation affect a community's decision regarding growth?

Applying This Chapter

1. Natural hazards are uncontrollable events. List three examples of hazards particular to where you live.
2. Compare the disaster potential of Missoula, Montana, versus Miami, Florida.
3. Discuss the direct and indirect costs of an oil spill in a coastal Oregon tourist town.
4. As a resident of a rural farming region of the Midwest, you've suffered through three tornadoes this year. You've faced the obvious costs of

damaged crops, buildings, and equipment; outline some of the social costs your small community will face.

5. Which members of your community should be considered for extra protection during a disaster? How will you identify this vulnerable population?

6. Compare how a town in northern Minnesota would prepare for hazards versus a town in Arizona. Which measures are consistent?

7. As the chief emergency manager in your town, you must present a proposal to the local governing board about a new federal program that requires local governments to engage in hazard mitigation activities. How will you describe what a resilient community is? What will you include in your presentation about the benefits of mitigation? How will you convince the board to authorize spending local resources to reduce the impacts of hazards?

YOU TRY IT

Find Your Local Hazard

What natural hazards take place in your community on a regular basis? Are there hazards that haven't happened in a long time, yet residents can still remember "the big one" that occurred years ago? You can visit the NWS website to find warnings, watches, and advisories for all sorts of natural hazards for all states and territories in the United States. The website is updated about every two minutes around the clock. Go to www.weather.gov to find what the forecast is for your state.

Disasters at Home

Think about your own community or neighborhood. If a major disaster occurred where you live, what buildings and facilities could be damaged or destroyed? Who are the major employers in your city or town? What would happen if these industries and companies suddenly shut down? Could people you know find jobs nearby, or would they be forced to transfer to other areas?

Tracking a Hurricane

As an official with your local government, you have a responsibility to ensure the safety of those who live in your town. You haven't experienced a serious hurricane in decades, but one changed its track last year and narrowly missed affecting your area. Assume that hurricane season is approaching, and outline a public announcement that will update residents about what your town has done to prepare for this year's season. The federal (NOAA) hurricane tracking website (www.nhc.noaa.gov) is an excellent resource.

Judging Resiliency

Assume you are an emergency manager in a flood-prone community. What factors will you look at to determine how resilient your community is to this hazard? How can you determine whether your community will experience a natural hazard event, so that damage is minimal and people are safe, or whether your community will suffer a disaster?

2

METEOROLOGICAL AND HYDROLOGICAL HAZARDS

Hurricanes, Floods, Tornadoes, Severe Winter Weather, and Wildfire

Starting Point

Go to www.wiley.com/college/schwab to assess your knowledge of meteorological and hydrological hazards.
Determine where to concentrate your effort.

What You'll Learn in This Chapter

▲ The difference between meteorological and hydrological hazards
▲ Characteristics of hurricanes
▲ Types of flooding
▲ The role of Flood Insurance Rate Maps (FIRM)
▲ The ratings systems used to measure hurricanes and tornadoes
▲ The types of severe winter hazards common in the United States
▲ The impacts that major meteorological and hydrological hazards can have on a community

After Studying This Chapter, You'll Be Able To

▲ Compare and contrast meteorological and hydrological hazards
▲ Assess the features of a hurricane that are most damaging to property and human life
▲ Discuss the relationship between floodplains and floods
▲ Distinguish between intensities of hurricanes, tornadoes, windchill
▲ Compare several severe winter weather hazards

Goals and Outcomes

▲ Select the appropriate tools to measure meteorological and hydrological hazards
▲ Evaluate the science behind the natural hazards that affect a community
▲ Select the appropriate tools and techniques to recognize patterns in meteorological and hydrological hazards
▲ Collaborate with others to examine patterns of human activity, such as development, taking into account the potential of natural hazards
▲ Evaluate knowledge of past occurrences of weather-based natural hazards to your local area and apply it to emergency plans
▲ Evaluate the use of ratings scales and weather patterns used by managers responsible for community safety

INTRODUCTION

This chapter examines several weather-related hazards and how they can affect a community. We classify these hazards as either *meteorological,* meaning they are due to processes in the Earth's atmosphere, or *hydrological,* which result from the Earth's water systems. This chapter focuses on four major meteorological and hydrological hazards: hurricanes, floods, tornadoes, and severe winter weather. This chapter also includes a discussion of wildfire. Wildfire is not necessarily caused by weather patterns; however, certain weather conditions must be present for wildfire to occur. We discuss some of the major characteristics of these five hazards, what to expect during the course of a hazard event, how the hazards are ranked in terms of severity, and some of the impacts they can have on our communities.

2.1 Weather-Related Natural Hazards

Between the years 1980 and 2004, there were 62 disasters in the United States that reached over 1 billion dollars each in damages as a result of weather-related natural hazards. In 2005, a single weather-related event by the name of Hurricane Katrina exceeded all of the previous disasters in this category in terms of property damage and lives lost. It is clear that hazards present serious problems for communities throughout the country. There are two types of weather-related natural hazards that will be discussed in this chapter:

▲ **Meteorological hazard:** A weather event that occurs because of processes in the Earth's atmosphere.
▲ **Hydrological hazard:** A weather event that occurs as part of the Earth's water systems.

The most prevalent **meteorological** and **hydrological** hazards that occur in the United States include:

▲ Hurricanes
▲ Storm surge
▲ High winds
▲ Torrential rain
▲ Tornadoes
▲ Waterspouts
▲ Floods
▲ Nor'easters
▲ Severe winter weather
▲ Freezing rain
▲ Snowstorms

- ▲ Blizzards
- ▲ Windchill
- ▲ Extreme cold
- ▲ Drought
- ▲ Heat wave
- ▲ Hailstorms
- ▲ Lightning storms
- ▲ Severe thunderstorms
- ▲ Fog

The following sections of this chapter focus on four major hydrological and meteorological hazards: hurricanes, floods, tornadoes, and severe winter weather, along with wildfires. Whereas the previously listed hazards certainly pose serious threats to some communities in certain regions, we discuss these five hazards because they occur most frequently throughout the country, with the highest probability of causing significant damage to property and the highest risk to human life.

The ultimate goal of learning about weather-related hazards is to be able to lessen their impacts on our communities through mitigation and preparedness activities.

FOR EXAMPLE

Choosing a Way of Life

Awareness of the high probability of hurricanes and other coastal storms on the Atlantic and Gulf Coasts is vital to reducing the impacts of wind, rain, and storm surge on properties located along the shoreline. In some coastal communities, regulations and/or personal choice have led residents to adopt various measures to protect their property. In towns such as Gulf Shores, Alabama, structures are built on stilts to reduce the risk of flooding caused by hurricanes. Although these beach houses appear to be perched on top of toothpicks, the stilts are effective in elevating the first-floor of the structure above expected flood heights, offering a degree of protection during storms. Many homeowners also install permanent storm shutters on the exterior of the building or have plywood ready to install over windows and doors when coastal storms are predicted. These prepared residents have learned from first-hand experience or from the experience of others that slab-on-grade building practices do not represent a wise investment in flood-prone areas, or that merely taping windows is not an effective way of preventing damage from hurricane-force winds. These examples indicate the wide range of choices available to property owners living in vulnerable locations such as the coast; property owners can make beneficial choices if they are knowledgeable about natural hazards and their potential impacts on people and property.

SELF-CHECK

- Define **meteorological hazard** and **hydrological hazard**.
- List examples of meteorological and hydrological hazards.
- Explain why a basic knowledge of weather-related hazards is necessary for carrying out hazard mitigation and preparedness activities.

2.2 Hurricanes

A **hurricane** is a revolving mass of wind that circulates around a calm center called the **eye,** which can be 20 to 30 miles wide. The eye is surrounded by **rain bands** that extend in spirals outward from the center of the storm. Hurricanes are extremely powerful forces that can last for more than two weeks over water and can extend across 400 miles. Because hurricanes are large, moving storm systems, they can affect entire states or regions. Not only is coastal development affected, but areas far inland can also suffer direct impacts from hurricanes, including high winds and torrential rain.

2.2.1 Hurricane Formation

Hurricanes originate in tropical ocean waters poleward of about 5° latitude. Thus hurricanes are also referred to as **tropical cyclones.** Hurricanes are "heat engines," meaning they are fueled by the release of latent heat from the condensation of warm water (see Figure 2-1). These conditions exist in tropical areas and supply the energy necessary for a hurricane to form. The prime season for ideal hurricane conditions lasts from June 1 through November 30. This means the hurricane season comprises six months out of every calendar year; much of this period coincides with peak tourist season in many hurricane-prone coastal areas.

Hurricanes begin as tropical depressions. If the proper conditions are maintained, a depression can develop into a tropical storm and then intensify to full-blown hurricane status. Hurricane formation requires the following conditions:

▲ A low pressure disturbance.
▲ Sufficiently warm sea surface temperature.
▲ Rotational force from the spinning of the Earth.
▲ Absence of wind shear in the lowest 50,000 feet of the atmosphere.

2.2.2 Hurricane Characteristics

A hurricane is a *multi-force* natural hazard made up of several distinguishing characteristics, each of which alone can be very destructive. The combination of

Figure 2-1

Formation of the eyewall of a hurricane.

features is often what makes a hurricane so devastating to people and property. The major elements of a hurricane that cause the most damage to property and pose the greatest threat to human life include:

▲ **Storm surge:** Storm surges are large waves of ocean water that sweep across coastlines where a storm makes landfall. The more intense the storm, the greater the height of the water. The higher the storm surge the greater the damage to the coastline. Storm surges inundate coastal areas, wash out dunes, cause backwater flooding in rivers, and can flood streets and buildings in coastal communities.

▲ **Storm tide:** If a storm surge occurs at the same time as high tide, the water height will be even greater. Storm tide is the combination of the storm surge and the normal tide. For example, a 15-foot storm surge along with the normal 2-foot high tide creates a storm tide of 17 feet.

▲ **Inland flooding:** In recent years, most deaths related to hurricane activity have been the result of inland flooding. As hurricanes move across land bringing torrential rains and backwater flooding from the ocean, rivers and streams overflow.

▲ **Water force:** During hurricanes and other coastal storms, coastal areas will experience flooding with velocity or "wave action," defined as areas subject to receiving waves on top of the rising water from coastal flooding. The velocity and the force of the water make flooding even more destructive. The velocity and wave action knock over buildings, move debris, erode dunes, scour the shoreline, and displace and redeposit sand.

▲ **Wind velocity:** The higher the wind speed the greater the damage. Hurricane-force winds can travel hundreds of miles inland, creating substantial damage to buildings, vegetation, and infrastructure. Hurricane-force winds can also create missiles out of loose debris such as roof shingles, tree branches, lawn furniture, even boats and cars. Flying debris often causes more damage than the force of the wind alone.

▲ **Coastal erosion:** Coastal erosion is the wearing away of coastal land. It is commonly used to describe the horizontal retreat of the shoreline along the ocean. Although erosion occurs as a natural coastal process, hurricanes can greatly accelerate the normal rate of erosion along the coastline, even to the point that houses and other structures that were considered safe from ocean waves become suddenly subject to direct wave action or even fall into the sea.

When a hurricane makes landfall and traverses across the land either up the coast or inland, the types of damage that occur vary according to the dominant feature exhibited by that particular storm. Hurricane Fran, for instance, was considered primarily a "wind hurricane." When this hurricane affected the state of North Carolina in 1996, the majority of reported damages included roofs ripped off of homes; trees falling on structures, vehicles and roadways; and damage caused by flying debris. In contrast, when Hurricane Floyd hit North Carolina three years later, most of the damage was caused by severe flooding. The entire eastern third of the state experienced unprecedented high water levels, as rainfall far inland caused rivers and streams to overflow their banks, flooding homes, businesses, hog farms, sewer plants, junkyards, and other features of the built environment throughout the coastal plain.

2.2.3 Measuring a Hurricane: The Saffir-Simpson Scale

Hurricane severity is measured using the Saffir-Simpson Scale, ranging from 1 (minimal) to 5 (catastrophic). The scale categorizes hurricanes based upon maximum sustained winds, minimum barometric pressure, and storm surge potential (see Table 2-1). These three factors are combined to estimate the potential flooding and damage to property given a hurricane's estimated intensity.

Category 3, 4, and 5 hurricanes are the most potentially dangerous and can be categorized as **major hurricanes.** These intense hurricanes cause over 70% of the damage in the United States, even though they account for only 20% of all tropical cyclone landfalls. However, it is important to remember that hurricanes

Table 2-1: Saffir-Simpson Scale

Saffir-Simpson Category	Maximum Sustained Wind Speed			Minimum Surface Pressure	Storm Surge	
	mph	meter/sec	knots	(millibars)	feet	meters
1	74–96	33–42	64–83	Greater than 980	3–5	1.0–1.7
2	97–111	43–49	84–96	979–965	6–8	1.8–2.6
3	112–131	50–58	97–113	964–945	9–12	2.7–3.8
4	132–155	59–69	114–135	944–920	13–18	3.9–5.6
5	156+	70+	136+	Less than 920	19+	5.7+

of all intensities, including category 1 and 2 hurricanes, have the potential to cause massive property damage and pose a risk to human life. Table 2-2 gives examples of the types of damage that can occur with each of the hurricane categories on the Saffir-Simpson Scale.

2.2.4 Landfall

Hurricanes have the greatest potential to inflict damage as they cross the coastline from the ocean, at a point called **landfall**. Because hurricanes derive their strength from warm ocean waters, they generally deteriorate once they make landfall. The forward speed of a hurricane can vary from just a few miles per hour to up to 40 miles per hour. This forward motion, combined with a counterclockwise surface flow, makes the right front quadrant of a hurricane the location of the most potentially damaging winds. Slow-moving hurricanes can actually cause more damage than faster hurricanes because they spend more time in one location, dumping more rain, causing more storm surge, and subjecting the area to prolonged high winds. The worst-case scenario is a hurricane that stalls along the coast, pounding the area for hours or even days.

The site of hurricane landfall is notoriously unpredictable. Although the skill of tropical storm forecasting has greatly improved with advances in technology, hurricane prediction is not an exact science. The track that a hurricane can take once it makes landfall is also somewhat unpredictable. Inland areas far west of the Atlantic coast and north of the Gulf Coast have been devastated by the remnants of tropical storms and hurricanes as they travel with the force of forward momentum. The erratic nature of hurricanes is illustrated on the map in Figure 2-2 from the National Hurricane Center, which shows North Atlantic tropical storm and hurricane tracks from 1851 to 2004. Notice that so many hurricanes occurred in this time period that the entire Southeastern United States appears black.

Table 2-2: Hurricane Category Damage Examples

Category	Level	Description	Example
1	MINIMAL	Damage primarily to shrubbery, trees, foliage, and unanchored homes. No real damage to other structures. Some damage to poorly constructed signs. Low-lying coastal roads inundated, minor pier damage, some small craft in exposed anchorage torn from moorings.	Hurricane Jerry (1989)
2	MODERATE	Considerable damage to shrubbery and tree foliage; some trees blown down. Major damage to exposed mobile homes. Extensive damage to poorly constructed signs. Some damage to roofing materials of buildings; some window and door damage. No major damage to buildings. Coastal roads and low-lying inland escape routes cut off by rising water 2 to 4 hours before arrival of hurricane's center. Considerable damage to piers. Marinas flooded. Small craft in unprotected anchorages torn from moorings. Evacuation of some shoreline residences and low-lying areas required.	Hurricane Bob (1991)
3	EXTENSIVE	Foliage torn from trees; large trees blown down. Most poorly constructed signs blown down. Some damage to roofing materials of buildings; some window and door damage. Some structural damage to small buildings. Mobile homes destroyed. Serious flooding at coast and many smaller structures near coast destroyed; larger structures near coast damaged by battering waves and floating debris. Low-lying inland escape routes cut off by rising water 3 to 5 hours before hurricane's center arrives. Flat terrain 5 feet or less above sea level flooded inland 8 miles or more. Evacuation	Hurricane Ivan (2004)

(continued)

Table 2-2: *(continued)*

Category	Level	Description	Example
		of low-lying residences within several blocks of shoreline may be required.	
4	EXTREME	Shrubs, trees, and all signs blown down. Extensive damage to roofing materials, windows, and doors. Complete failures of roofs on many small residences. Complete destruction of mobile homes. Major damage to lower floors of structures near shore due to flooding and battering by waves and floating debris. Low-lying inland escape routes cut off by rising water 3 to 5 hours before hurricane's center arrives. Flat terrain 10 feet or less above sea level flooded inland as far as 6 miles. Major erosion of beaches. Massive evacuation of all residences within 500 yards of shore and of single-story residences within 2 miles of shore may be required.	Hurricane Katrina (2005)
5	CATASTROPHIC	Shrubs, trees, and all signs blown down. Very severe and extensive damage to windows and doors; extensive shattering of glass in windows and doors. Complete failure of roofs on many residences and industrial buildings; considerable damage to other roofs. Some complete building failures. Small buildings overturned or blown away. Complete destruction of mobile homes. Major damage to lower floors of all structures less than 15 feet above sea level within 500 yards of shore. Low-lying inland escape routes cut off by rising water 3 to 5 hours before hurricane's center arrives. Massive evacuation of residential areas on low ground within 5 to 10 miles of shore may be required.	Hurricane Camille (1969)

Figure 2-2

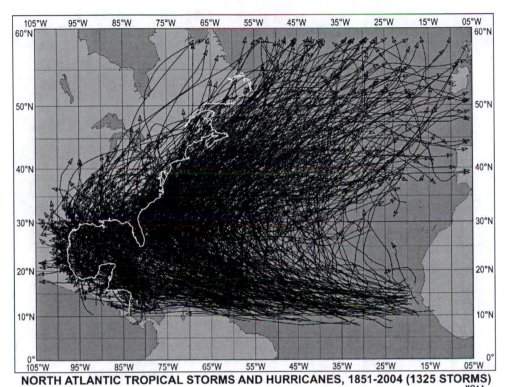

NORTH ATLANTIC TROPICAL STORMS AND HURRICANES, 1851-2004 (1325 STORMS)
NOAA

North Atlantic Tropical Storms and Hurricanes, 1851-2004.

2.2.5 Patterns of Hurricane Activity

Historically, Atlantic hurricane activity has experienced a great deal of variability. Increasingly accurate record keeping of hurricane statistics over the past century and a half has indicated that hurricanes appear to fluctuate in number and intensity over a period of about 30 to 40 years. Some decadal periods have above-normal activity, while others have below-normal activity. These fluctuations result from differences in the number of hurricanes and major hurricanes forming in the tropical Atlantic and Caribbean Sea each year. Hurricane seasons during 1995-2004 averaged 13.6 tropical storms, 7.8 hurricanes, and 3.8 major hurricanes. The National Oceanic and Atmospheric Administration (NOAA) has classified all but two of these ten seasons as above normal, and six of these years as hyperactive. The 2005 season qualified as the seventh hyperactive season in the past eleven years (see Figure 2-3). In marked contrast to this period of extraordinary activity, the hurricane seasons of the preceding period from 1970 to 1994 averaged just 9 tropical storms, 5 hurricanes, and 1.5 major hurricanes.

Figure 2-3

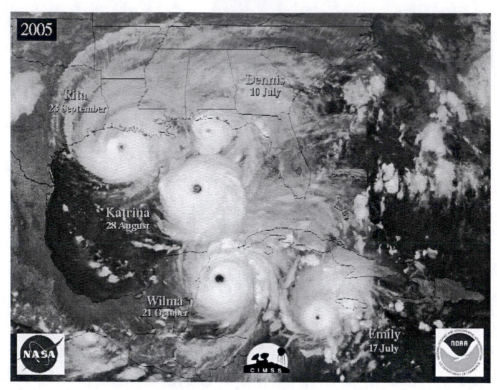

Montage of Atlantic Basin storms from the 2005 hurricane season.

FOR EXAMPLE

2004: Picking on Florida

During the hurricane season of 2004, three hurricanes with a Saffir-Simpson Scale rating of 3 or above hit the state of Florida. Hurricanes Jeanne, Ivan, and Charley combined caused over $35.9 billion in damage and at least 119 deaths. Although Hurricane Frances did not make landfall as a major hurricane, it was the fourth significant hurricane for Florida in 2004. Frances also affected the states of Georgia, South Carolina, North Carolina, and New York, and caused at least 48 deaths and $9 billion in damages.

NOAA classified 12 of the 25 seasons in this period (almost one-half of the total) as below normal, with only 3 as above normal (1980, 1988, 1989) and none as being hyperactive.

2.2.6 Explaining the Increase

We can see from the statistics cited previously that hurricane landfalls in recent years have been striking the Atlantic and Gulf Coasts of the United States with increasing frequency. This is due to the active phase of the multi-decadal cycle, which involves a number of atmospheric factors that contribute to ideal hurricane conditions, including

▲ An increase in sea surface temperatures in the tropical Atlantic.
▲ A favorable African easterly jet stream.
▲ Weaker easterly trade winds.
▲ Higher pressure in the upper atmosphere.
▲ Reduced vertical wind shear.

The combination of these conditions has resulted in a large number of tropical storms and hurricanes. There is speculation in some circles that global warming has contributed to several of the conditions causing the recent pattern of increased hurricane activity. There is further speculation that human activity, particularly the emission of carbon dioxide and other greenhouse gases into the atmosphere caused by burning fossil fuels, is a catalyst for the violent and turbulent weather patterns around the globe.

2.2.7 Patterns of Human Activity

As stated in the previous section, hurricane frequency tends to fluctuate in cycles of a few decades. Not too coincidently, the last period of below-average hurricane activity (1970 to 1994) coincided with a period of intense development and growth along the coastlines of the Atlantic Ocean and the Gulf of Mexico. Although many of the beaches and barrier islands of the Gulf and Atlantic had some development before this time, for the most part structures along the coast were relatively small-scale, single-family cottages, and populations in coastal communities were relatively low. Some areas were completely inaccessible by land, resulting in large stretches of undeveloped properties.

When investors, developers, and vacationers "discovered" the pristine coastlines of states along the Atlantic and Gulf, an unprecedented boom in coastal construction began. The 1980s in particular saw a rapid expansion of high-rise (and high-dollar) properties in the most vulnerable and fragile areas of the coast. The comparative lull in hurricane activity served to bolster the image of the coast as a safe and sound investment opportunity, and relatively few damaging storms proved these investment strategies wrong. When the cycle of calm ended and the current cycle of intense storm activity began, the development patterns in many communities were firmly established. Local communities and states had discovered that coastal development was extremely profitable, not just for the private investor and vacation homeowner, but for the government, as property tax revenues from expensive real estate contributed significantly to the local and state economies. There was little incentive to curb rapid expansion and growth at that time, which set up the scenarios we are experiencing today: massive development, huge population numbers, expensive investment, and tremendous economic benefit coupled with more frequent and damaging hurricane activity. We can see from this discussion that the rapid increase in property damage and loss of life that we have experienced in the last few years is due to the combination of intense hurricane activity intersecting with intense human activity in the narrow strip of land along the coast.

2.2.8 2005: A Record-Breaking Season

The hurricane season of 2005 was the most active Atlantic hurricane season on record to date. There were a total of 26 named tropical storms, 13 of which became hurricanes and 7 of which were major hurricanes. This breaks records for tropical storms set in 1933 and for hurricanes set in 1969. One of these tropical storms, Vince, was the first known tropical cyclone to make landfall as far east as Spain. In addition to these record-breaking statistics, the 2005 season includes the first time since 1951 that 3 hurricanes (Katrina, Rita, and Wilma) reached Category 5 status during their lifespan. A fourth storm, Hurricane Emily, also reached Category 5 strength, although briefly. Hurricane Katrina is both the deadliest and costliest hurricane on record for the United States, making landfall in Florida as a Category 1 hurricane and, most devastatingly, as a Category 4 hurricane in Louisiana on August 29, 2005.

2.2.9 What's In a Name?

To help identify tropical storms and track them across the ocean, the World Meteorological Organization uses six lists of names in rotation. The first tropical storm of the season is named beginning with the letter "A," and following storms' names begin with successive letters of the alphabet, alternating between male and female names. When the alphabet is depleted, subsequent storms are named using letters of the Greek alphabet as occured in 2005, when the last tropical storm of the season was named *Epsilon*. If a hurricane is particularly deadly or costly, its name is retired and a new name is selected to enter the six-year cycle. In 2004, the names Charley, Frances, Ivan, and Jeanne were retired. After the hurricane season of 2005, the names Dennis, Katrina, Rita, Stan, and Wilma went into retirement.

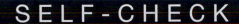

SELF-CHECK

- Define **hurricane, eye, rain band, storm surge,** and **landfall.**
- Describe a hurricane.
- List the four conditions required for the formation of a hurricane.
- Cite four features of a hurricane that cause the most damage to property and risk to human life.
- Name the scale used to measure hurricane activity.
- List five reasons scientists give for the current increase in hurricane activity in the United States.

HURRICANE KATRINA: NATURE AT ITS MOST INTENSE

Hurricane Katrina led a very dynamic life, which included many different characteristics at different points on the storm's path. This scenario will take you through the various stages of Katrina to demonstrate the start-to-finish life cycle of a hurricane.[1]

Katrina was originally designated as a tropical depression on August 23, 2005, over the southeastern Bahamas. The cyclone became Tropical Storm Katrina on August 24, the 11th tropical storm of the 2005 Atlantic hurricane season. The storm next moved northwest, then proceeded westward toward southern Florida on August 25 while developing a stronger inner core. Katrina continued to strengthen and reached hurricane status around 9 P.M. on August 25, less than two hours before it made landfall in Florida as a Category 1 hurricane near the border between Broward and Miami-Dade counties.

The eye became more defined during Katrina's six-hour course over inland Florida, dumping the heaviest rains south and east of its eye in Miami-Dade County. Katrina weakened to a tropical storm and emerged into the Gulf of Mexico at 5 A.M. on August 26, but quickly regained hurricane status an hour later while sending large rain bands through the Florida Keys and Dry Tortugas. While over the Gulf of Mexico, Katrina intensified rapidly, first with an increase in maximum sustained winds and then the formation of a new, outer eyewall. The size of the hurricane nearly doubled in size on August 27, with tropical storm-force winds extending 140 nautical miles from the center.

As Katrina continued westward on August 27, it strengthened from a low-end Category 3 to a Category 5 hurricane in less than twelve hours and reached peak intensity about 170 nautical miles southeast of the mouth of the Mississippi River by the afternoon of August 28. Late that day, hurricane force winds reached out 90 nautical miles from the center, and tropical storm-force winds reached about 200 nautical miles, making it a very large and intense hurricane.

The hurricane weakened rapidly before landfall due to erosion of the inner eyewall and drier ambient air as it approached the coast. Katrina remained very large, however, and made landfall as a strong Category 3 hurricane near Buras, Louisiana, at 11:10 A.M. on August 29 and again near the mouth of the Pearl River on the Louisiana/Mississippi border. As Katrina moved inland over Mississippi on the 29th, it became a Category 1 hurricane by 6 P.M. and weakened to a tropical storm by the end of the day northwest of Meridian, Mississippi. The tropical storm continued to move north and east over the Tennessee Valley and became a tropical depression on August 30. The remnants of what had been Hurricane Katrina were eventually absorbed into a frontal zone the next day over the Great Lakes.

The central pressure of Katrina (902 mb on August 28) was the sixth lowest pressure ever measured in the Atlantic Basin. Katrina produced massive storm surges, the largest of which were estimated to be 30 feet in Hancock County, Mississippi. The storm surge was particularly severe in Mississippi due to the shallow bathymetry and the limited elevation rise onshore, as well as the physical funneling effect toward the coastal counties of Mississippi created by the "boot" of Louisiana. Storm surges of equal or greater heights most likely occurred along other sections of the Gulf Coast of Mississippi but are difficult to document because of widespread tide gauge failures caused by the intensity of the wave action. The storm surge was as high as 10 feet as far east as Mobile, Alabama, causing flooding several miles inland. Approximately 80% of New Orleans flooded up to 20 feet, and rivers in Mississippi flooded anywhere from 8 to 12 miles inland. Katrina caused record rainfall totals throughout the region of impact, including 14.04 inches in Miami-Dade County, Florida; 8-10 inches across southeastern Louisiana and southwestern Mississippi; and 11.63 inches in Slidell, Louisiana. In addition, Katrina produced a total of 33 tornadoes throughout Florida, Georgia, Alabama, and Mississippi.

2.3 Flooding

Flooding is the leading cause of weather-related deaths in the United States. It is the most common natural hazard in the country because of the widespread geographical distribution of river valleys and coastal areas, and the long-standing attraction of human settlements to these areas. Flooding is generally the result of the excessive precipitation that can occur during a hurricane, thunderstorm, or other torrential rainfall. Flooding can also be caused by a dam break or levee failure.

2.3.1 Floodplains, River Basins, and Watersheds

Before we discuss the characteristics of flood hazards in the United States, we will introduce some of the features associated with rivers and how rivers function as part of the natural ecosystem. Quite frequently, floodwaters rise at a very fast rate because the quantity of water deposited during a particular rain event exceeds the capacity of the river channel to hold such a large volume of water at one time. Sometimes with little warning, floodwaters overflow the riverbanks, moving to low-lying areas first. The flat lower-elevation areas that typically lie to either side of a river or stream that experience this inundation make up the waterway's natural **floodplain.**

▲ The **floodway** is the central portion of the floodplain, the area with the greatest water velocities and highest depths.

▲ The **flood fringe** comprises the outer areas on both sides of the floodway and is usually the area of shallower depths and lesser velocities. The flood fringe is also the area that stores water during a flood.

▲ A **river basin** is the land that water flows across or under on its way to a river. As a bathtub catches all the water that falls within its sides, a river basin sends all the water falling on the surrounding land into a central river and out to an **estuary** or the sea. River basins may also be referred to as **catchments,** because they essentially catch, or collect, all of the water from surrounding higher elevations.

A river basin drains all the land around a major river. Basins can be divided into **watersheds,** or areas of land around a smaller river, stream, or lake. The landscape is made up of many interconnected basins or watersheds. Large river basins such as the Mississippi are made up of hundreds of smaller river basins and watersheds. Within each watershed, all water runs to the lowest point—a stream, river, lake, or ocean. On its way, water travels over the surface and across farm fields, forestland, suburban lawns, and city streets as **runoff,** or it seeps into the soil and travels as **groundwater.**[2]

2.3.2 Types of Flooding

Floods generally fall into two categories:

▲ **Flash floods** are the product of heavy localized precipitation in a short time period over a given location.

▲ **General floods** are caused by precipitation over a longer time period and over a given river basin.

2.3.3 Flash Flooding

Flash floods occur within a few minutes or hours of heavy amounts of rainfall, a dam or levee failure, or a sudden release of water held by an ice jam. Flash flood waters move at very fast speeds and can roll boulders, tear out trees, destroy buildings, and obliterate bridges. Walls of water can reach heights of 10 to 20 feet and generally are accompanied by a deadly cargo of debris. During a flash flood cars can easily be swept away in just two feet of moving water. Heavy rains that produce flash floods can also trigger mudslides, a secondary hazard.

Most flash flooding is caused by slow-moving thunderstorms, repeated thunderstorms in a local area, or by heavy rains from hurricanes and tropical storms. Although flash flooding often occurs along mountain streams where the terrain is steep, it is also common in urban areas where much of the ground is covered by impervious surfaces. **Impervious surfaces** are hard, paved areas such as roof tops and parking lots, where rainwater cannot soak through to the ground. Instead, the water flows over the surface as runoff until it reaches a drain or low-lying area. Manmade features such as roads and buildings generate greater amounts of runoff than land with natural groundcover like grass, trees, and other vegetation. Flooding can also occur when drainage channels in urban areas are unable to contain the runoff that is generated by relatively small but intense rainfall events.

FOR EXAMPLE

Tragedy on the Big Thompson

On July 31, 1976, the Big Thompson River near Denver, Colorado overflowed during an extremely heavy thunderstorm. The canyon through which the Big Thompson flows has very high, steep walls in some places, leaving little opportunity for the soils to absorb any precipitation. Usually, the winds above the mountains surrounding Big Thompson Canyon are strong enough to blow rainstorms away quickly, but this storm was an exception. Without the action of the wind, the storm dropped 8 inches of rain in just one hour in a concentrated location and dumped a total of 12 inches during its two-hour span. As a result, a wall of water 19 feet high roared down the Big Thompson Canyon where people were camping, fishing, and exploring the canyon that afternoon. Tragically, the only egress from the Canyon floor was up its steep sides, trapping the visitors as the wave of water rushed down the channel. Over $40 million dollars of property was damaged or destroyed and 140 people perished.[3]

2.3.4 General Flooding

While flash floods occur within hours of a rain event, periodic general flooding is a longer-term event and that can last for several days (see Figure 2-4). The primary types of general flooding are riverine flooding, coastal flooding, and urban flooding.

▲ **Riverine flooding** is a function of precipitation levels and water runoff volumes within the watershed of a stream or river. Periodic flooding of lands adjacent to freshwater rivers and streams is a natural and inevitable occurrence. When stream flow exceeds the capacity of the floodway or normal watercourse, some of the above-normal stream flow spills over onto adjacent lands within the floodplain.

▲ **Coastal flooding** is typically the result of storm surge, wind-driven waves, and heavy rainfall. These conditions are produced by hurricanes during the summer and fall, and nor'easters and other large coastal storms during the winter and spring. Storm surges may overrun barrier islands and push seawater up coastal rivers and inlets, blocking the downstream flow of inland runoff. Thousands of acres inland may be inundated by both saltwater and freshwater. Escape routes, particularly those from barrier islands, may be cut off quickly, stranding residents in flooded areas and hampering rescue efforts.

▲ **Urban flooding** occurs where there has been development within stream floodplains. In many areas of the country, intense development in the floodplain is a result of the use of waterways for transportation purposes when shipment by water was the major form of moving goods and raw materials. Sites adjacent to rivers and coastal inlets provided convenient places to load and receive commodities. The price of this accessibility has been increased flooding of the communities that grew up in the surrounding area. Urbanization increases the magnitude and frequency of floods by increasing impermeable surfaces, increasing the speed of drainage collection, reducing the carrying capacity of the land, and, occasionally, overwhelming sewer systems.

2.3.5 Flood Mapping

Unlike some other meteorological hazards, areas prone to flooding can be mapped with relative precision, depending upon the extent and accuracy of data gathered about the waterway itself and the surrounding floodplain. Factors that are used to map flood-risk areas include:

▲ Proximity to the river.
▲ Amount of vegetative cover.
▲ Soil moisture conditions.
▲ Local historic rainfall records.
▲ Topographic features of the area.

Figure 2-4

Asheville, NC, September 17, 2004: Flooding outside Biltmore Estate after Hurricane Frances.

An assessment of flooding potential requires spatial data (geographic information) of these factors at a relatively small scale. We need the information at this level of detail because flood hazards vary greatly by location and type.

Flood Insurance Rate Maps (FIRMs)

Much of the flood mapping in the United States is carried out under the National Flood Insurance Program (NFIP) administered by the Federal Emergency Management Agency (FEMA). The NFIP offers federally backed flood insurance to residents in communities that choose to participate in the program by regulating development in the floodplain according to standards established by the NFIP (for a more detailed discussion of the NFIP see Chapter 6).

The NFIP provides **Flood Insurance Rate Maps** (FIRMs) to participating communities to help define the local flood risk areas. Terminology used on a FIRM includes the:

▲ **Floodway**: the stream channel and the portion of the adjacent floodplain that must remain open to permit passage of the base flood without raising the water surface elevation by more than one foot.

▲ **100-year floodplain:** applies to an area that has a 1% chance, on average, of flooding in any given year. However, a 100-year flood could occur two years in a row, or once every 10 years. The 100-year flood floodplain is also referred to as the **base flood**: a national standard that represents a compromise between minor floods and the greatest flood likely to occur in a given area. The base flood provides a useful benchmark.

▲ **Base flood elevation (BFE):** the elevation of the water surface resulting from a flood that has a 1% chance of occurring in any given year. The BFE is the height of the base flood, usually in feet, in relation to the National Geodetic Vertical Datum of 1929, the North American Vertical Datum of 1988, or other specified datum.

▲ **Special flood hazard area (SFHA):** the shaded area on a FIRM that identifies an area that has a 1% chance of being flooded in any given year (100-year flood floodplain).

▲ The **500-year flood floodplain:** the area with a 0.2% chance of flooding in any given year.

▲ **Coastal high hazard areas:** coastal areas that are subject to a velocity hazard (wave action).

FIRMs also show different floodplains with different zone designations. These are primarily for insurance rating purposes, but the zone differentiation can be very helpful for other floodplain planning purposes as well. For example:

▲ Zone A: The 100-year or base floodplain. There are 6 types of A zones.

▲ Zones V and VE: The coastal area subject to velocity hazard (wave action).

▲ Zone B: Area of moderate flood hazard, usually the area between the limits of the 100- and 500-year floods.

▲ Zones C X: Areas of minimal flooding hazard.

▲ Zone D: Area of undetermined but possible flood hazard.

2.3.6 Low-Level Flood Risks[4]

Most cities, towns, villages, and counties in the United States have one or more clearly recognizable flood-prone areas, usually along a river, stream, or other large body of water, that are designated as the SFHAs on the community's FIRM. These flood-prone areas are properly the subject of community, state, and federal initiatives to minimize flooding and its impacts. These initiatives include maps, floodplain management criteria, ordinances, and community assistance programs. However, thousands of communities also have shallow, localized flooding problems outside of the SFHA resulting from ponding, poor drainage, inadequate storm sewers, clogged culverts or catch basins, sheet flow, obstructed drainage ways, sewer backup, or overbank flooding from small streams. These kinds of flood events can occur anywhere in a community and can result from even minor storms.

Localized flooding refers to flooding outside the scope of criteria that apply to the SFHA as depicted on a community's FIRM. This includes areas within and outside the B, C, and X zones. Such floods are often referred to as the following:

▲ Stormwater flooding
▲ Nuisance flooding
▲ Flooding on small streams
▲ Carpet wetters
▲ Poor drainage
▲ Ponding

If these localized floods occur infrequently, the problems are minor. However, in some areas localized flooding can be chronic, so that over the years the cumulative damage and recurring disruption from localized flooding can be more than that caused by flooding on major rivers and streams. The costs of insuring buildings that are subject to the repeated damage add up as well, and many property owners outside the SFHA do not purchase flood insurance. Even a few inches of water in the basement or ground floor of a building can cause expensive damage. Carpeting, wallboard, insulation, mattresses, and upholstered furniture must be thrown out and replaced. Flooring, studs, and other wooden parts of the building must be thoroughly cleaned and dried. Business records, photographs, and other papers are often destroyed. Flood waters can block streets, disrupt traffic patterns, and hinder access to homes and businesses. This can affect the entire community, not just those whose property is flooded. Localized flooding also poses safety hazards, as people are at risk even in shallow flooding. It is not unusual for children especially to drown after slipping in shallow water or to be swept into a ditch or storm drain. Even adults can be knocked down by just a few inches of moving water, and cars can be moved with the flow of shallow flooding in roads.

SELF-CHECK

- Define **floodplain, SFHA (special flood hazard area),** and **base flood.**
- List the three types of general flooding.
- Cite five factors used to map flood-risk areas.
- **Discuss FIRMs and SFHAs.**

2.4 Tornadoes

A **tornado** is a violently rotating column of air extending from the base of a thunderstorm (see Figure 2-5). Tornadoes can also form during hurricanes. These dangerous wind events are sometimes called "funnel storms" or "funnel clouds" because of the shape of the rotating column of air, which is typically wider at the top than at the base. Contrary to popular belief, the tornado funnel does not always touch the ground; a debris cloud beneath a thunderstorm may confirm the presence of a tornado despite the absence of a visible funnel. **Waterspouts,** which are weak tornadoes that form over warm ocean waters, can occasionally move inland to become tornadoes.

2.4.1 Tornado Formation

Tornadoes are spawned by a thunderstorm and produced when cool air overrides a layer of warm air, forcing the warm air to rise rapidly. Tornadoes are usually

Figure 2-5

Tornado.

preceded by very heavy rain and, possibly, hail. If hail falls from a thunderstorm, it is an indication that the storm has large amounts of energy and may be severe. In general, the larger the hailstones, the more potential for damaging thunderstorm winds and/or tornadoes.

As powerful as they are, tornadoes account for only a tiny fraction of the energy in a thunderstorm. What makes them dangerous is that their energy is concentrated in a small area, perhaps only a hundred yards across. The damage from a tornado is due to the resulting high **wind velocity,** or speed of the wind as it revolves.

2.4.2 The Fujita-Pearson Tornado Scale

The intensity, path length, and width of tornadoes are rated according to a scale developed in 1971 by T. Theodore Fujita and Allen D. Pearson. The standard Fujita-Pearson Scale is presented below. Under this scaling system, tornadoes classified as F0-F1 are considered weak tornadoes; those classified as F2-F3 are considered strong, while those classified as F4-F5 are considered violent. See *www.ncdc.noaa.gov/oa/satellite/satelliteseye/educational/fujita.html.*

The size of a tornado is not necessarily an indication of its intensity. Large tornadoes can be weak, while small tornadoes can be violent. Tornado intensity may also change during the lifespan of the event. A small tornado may have been larger, and is at the "shrinking" stage of its life cycle.

Evidence from past tornadoes suggests that tornadic wind speeds can be as high as 300 miles per hour in the most violent events. Wind speeds that high can cause automobiles to become airborne, rip homes to shreds, and turn broken glass and other debris into lethal missiles. The most serious threat to humans and other living creatures from tornadoes is from flying debris and from being tossed about in the wind (see Figure 2-6).

The Enhanced Fujita Scale

The original Fujita Scale does not recognize differences in construction, is difficult to apply without any damage indicators, is subject to bias, is based only on the worst damage from an event, and overestimates wind speeds greater than F3[5]. Based on these observations, a team of meteorologists and wind engineers collaborated to develop the updated **Enhanced Fujita Scale,** with an implementation date nationwide of February 1, 2007 (see Table 2-3). The Enhanced Fujita Scale can be used to determine an "EF Number" based on 28 separate damage indicators (see Table 2-4). The damage indicators represent typical types of construction, ranging from single-family residences to multi-story hotels. Depending upon the type of indicator, specific Degrees of Damage can be identified. The Degrees of Damage include associated upper and lower three-second wind gust estimates that would typically cause that type of destruction to happen. These upper and lower wind speeds are then rated according to the Enhanced Fujita Scale to determine the applicable EF Number.

Table 2-3: Fujita-Pearson Scale for Rating Tornado Intensity

F-Scale	Intensity	Wind Speed	Type of Damage Done
F0	Gale Tornado	40–72 mph	Some damage to chimneys; breaks branches off trees; pushes over shallow-rooted trees; damages sign boards.
F1	Moderate Tornado	73–112 mph	Peels surface off roofs; mobile homes pushed off foundations or overturned; moving autos pushed off roads.
F2	Significant Tornado	113–157 mph	Considerable damage. Roofs torn off frame houses; mobile homes demolished; boxcars pushed over; large trees snapped or uprooted; light object missiles generated.
F3	Severe Tornado	158–206 mph	Roof and some walls torn off well-constructed houses; trains overturned; most trees in forests uprooted.
F4	Devastating Tornado	207–260 mph	Well-constructed houses leveled; structures with weak foundations blown off some distance; cars thrown and large missiles generated.
F5	Incredible Tornado	261–318 mph	Strong frame houses lifted off foundations and carried considerable distances to disintegrate; automobile-sized missiles fly through the air in excess of 100 meters; trees debarked; steel re-enforced concrete structures badly damaged.

2.4.3 Tornado Activity in the United States

In an average year, 800-1,000 tornadoes occur across the United States, resulting in 80 deaths and over 1,500 injuries. These figures are based on tornado events that are sited and reported. In less populated areas, tornado frequency may be much higher, but the events remain unobserved. Tornadoes can occur in any state, but are more frequent in the Midwest, Southeast, and Southwest. Although tornadoes may occur at any time of the year, in the southern states,

Figure 2-6

Tornado in a highly populated area of Dallas, Texas.

Table 2-4: The Enhanced Fujita Scale

Fujita Scale		Enhanced Fujita Scale	
F Number	3 Second Gust (mph)	EF Number	3 Second Gust (mph)
0	45–78	0	65–85
1	79–117	1	86–110
2	118–161	2	111–135
3	162–209	3	136–165
4	210–261	4	166–200
5	262–317	5	Over 200

peak tornado season lasts from March until May, while the northern states experience more frequent tornado activity during the summer. Waterspouts are more common in the late fall and winter in the southern states and along the Gulf Coast.

FOR EXAMPLE

Tornado Outbreaks

The worst tornado outbreak in the United States was in early April 1974. There was a total of 148 tornadoes during a 16-hour period that touched down in 13 states. For more on the outbreak, including maps, statistics and eye witness accounts, see the NOAA website www.publicaffairs.noaa.gov/storms.

2.5 Severe Winter Weather

In contrast to tropical storms such as hurricanes, severe winter storms are **extra-tropical cyclones.** These storms form outside the tropics, are characterized by fronts, and have their strongest winds within the upper atmosphere. Unlike tropical cyclones that have a center warmer than the surrounding air, the center of extra-tropical storms is colder. Fueled by strong temperature gradients and an active upper-level jet stream, severe winter storms produce an array of hazardous weather conditions, including

▲ Freezing rain.
▲ Windchill.
▲ Extreme cold.
▲ Snowstorms.

Blizzards, which can involve a combination of all of these hazards, pack a major snowstorm into one cold, windy, low-visibility event. The following sections give a brief description of each of these severe winter weather hazards.

2.5.1 Blizzards

A **blizzard** is a snowstorm characterized by low temperatures (usually below 20°F) that is accompanied by winds that are at least 35 miles per hour or greater. In addition, there must also be sufficient falling and/or blowing snow in the air. This airborne snowfall contributes significantly to the danger posed by a blizzard, as visibility can be reduced to 1/4 mile or less for three hours or longer. A **severe blizzard** is considered to have temperatures at or below 10°F, winds exceeding 45 miles per hour, and visibility reduced to near zero.

Blizzard conditions often develop on the northwest side of an intense storm system. The difference between the lower pressure in the storm and the higher pressure to the west creates a tight pressure gradient, which in turn results in very strong winds. These winds combine with snow and blowing snow to produce extreme conditions. Storm systems powerful enough to cause blizzards

Table 2-5: Notable Blizzard Events in the United States

Name of Storm	Date	Details
The "Knickerbocker" Storm	January 1922	This blizzard took place in Washington, D.C. and caused the roof of the Knickerbocker Theater to collapse, killing almost 100 people.
The New York City Storm	February 1969	There was so much snow in the city that even the snow plows were buried in snow, forcing the city to employ 10,000 workers to clear the streets with shovels.
The Buffalo Storm	February 1977	Areas surrounding western New York state and Ontario, Canada were hit by a blizzard that killed 28, shut down Buffalo, and stranded thousands of people in their cars on the highway.
The Blizzard of the Century	March 1993	This storm took place across a wide area of the eastern United States, from Alabama to Massachusetts. Snowfall rates of between 1 and 2 inches per hour took place in many areas.
The Blizzard of 1996	January 1996	This January blizzard took place in the northeastern United States and was the cause of over 100 deaths.

usually form when the jet stream dips far to the south, allowing cold air from the north to clash with warm air from the south. With the colder and drier polar air comes an atmospheric temperature cold enough for the development of snow, sleet, or freezing rain. A few of the notable blizzard events in the United States are listed in Table 2-5.

2.5.2 Snowstorms

Snow is frozen precipitation in the form of a six-sided ice crystal, commonly known as the snowflake. **Snowstorm** is the phrase used to describe any storm with heavy snow.

Snow requires temperatures to be below freezing in all or most of the atmosphere, from the surface up to cloud level. Snow can fall when surface temperatures are above freezing and form a relatively shallow layer on the ground. Under these conditions, the snow will not have enough time to melt before reaching the ground; the snow will be quite wet and contain large flakes, the result of wet snow crystals sticking to one another to form larger flakes. Generally, 10 inches of snow will melt into one inch of water. Sometimes the snow-liquid ratio may be much higher—on the order of 20:1 or 30:1. This commonly happens when snow falls into a very cold air mass, with temperatures of 20°F or less at ground-level.

High-impact snowstorms in the Northeastern United States are ranked according to the **Northeast Snowfall Impact Scale (NESIS)**, developed by Paul Kocin of The Weather Channel and Louis Uccellini of the National Weather Service.[6] The NESIS consists of five categories of storms in descending order of severity: Extreme, Crippling, Major, Significant, and Notable. The scale rates storms that have large areas of 10-inch snowfall accumulations or greater. A score is assigned to each area affected by the snowstorm as a function of the amount of snow, the area impacted, and the number of people in the path of the storm. Because the score includes population data, the index gives an indication of a storm's societal impacts.

NESIS categories, their corresponding NESIS values, and a descriptive adjective are displayed in Table 2-6.[7]

2.5.3 Freezing Rain

Freezing rain or freezing drizzle is rain or drizzle that occurs when surface temperatures are below freezing. The moisture falls in liquid form but freezes upon impact, resulting in a coating of ice or glaze on all exposed surfaces. **Sleet** is precipitation that falls as frozen water or becomes frozen before it hits the ground.

Freezing rain is caused when there is a warm mass of air in the middle altitudes between the ground and the cloud deck and a mass of freezing air near

Table 2-6: NESIS Categories

Category	NESIS Value	Description
1	1–2.499	Notable
2	2.5–3.99	Significant
3	4–5.99	Major
4	6–9.99	Crippling
5	10.0+	Extreme

the surface. When the precipitation falls from the cloud, it will generally be snow. As it encounters the warm air it will melt to form rain. The melted snowflakes then fall through the shallow freezing layer without refreezing into sleet. As the precipitation reaches ground level, it enters air at below-freezing temperatures, and quickly turns to ice. As a result, when the liquid droplets encounter exposed objects at the surface they freeze upon contact.

Some ice events (up to and including ice storms) are the result of **cold air damming** (CAD). CAD is a shallow, surface-based layer of relatively cold, stably-stratified air entrenched against the eastern slopes of the Appalachian Mountains. With warmer air above, falling precipitation in the form of snow melts, then becomes either super-cooled (liquid below the melting point of water) or re-freezes. In the former case, super-cooled droplets can freeze on impact (freezing rain), while in the latter case, the re-frozen water particles form ice pellets, or sleet (see Figure 2-7).

2.5.4 Windchill and Extreme Cold

A **cold wave** is an unusual fall in temperature to the freezing point or below, exceeding 16 degrees in twenty-four hours or 20 degrees in thirty-six hours. What constitutes extreme cold varies across different regions of the United States. In areas unaccustomed to winter weather, near freezing temperatures are considered extreme cold. In contrast, the more northern and mountainous states require much lower temperatures for conditions to be considered extreme cold.

▲ **Windchill factor** describes what happens to the human body when there is a combination of cold and wind. As wind increases, heat is carried

Figure 2-7

Tree limbs covered in ice.

away from the body at a faster rate, driving down both skin temperature (which can cause frostbite) and eventually the internal body temperature (which can cause death).

▲ **Windchill temperature** is a measure of the combined cooling effect of wind and ambient air temperature. Windchill temperature is a unit of measurement used to describe the windchill factor.

Figure 2-8 is a windchill chart that shows the amount of time it takes for humans to develop frostbite given different windchill temperatures.

2.5.5 Impacts of Severe Winter Weather

The dangers posed by severe winter weather are generally three-fold:

▲ The cold and wet conditions can be extremely hazardous to the health of people and animals that are exposed for prolonged periods of time.

▲ Driving conditions become hazardous as roads, bridges, and overpasses become slick or impassable due to accumulation of snow and ice.

Figure 2-8

Wind Chill Chart

Wind (mph)	Calm	40	35	30	25	20	15	10	5	0	-5	-10	-15	-20	-25	-30	-35	-40	-45
5		36	31	25	19	13	7	1	-5	-11	-16	-22	-28	-34	-40	-46	-52	-57	-63
10		34	27	21	15	9	3	-4	-10	-16	-22	-28	-35	-41	-47	-53	-59	-66	-72
15		32	25	19	13	6	0	-7	-13	-19	-26	-32	-39	-45	-51	-58	-64	-71	-77
20		30	24	17	11	4	-2	-9	-15	-22	-29	-35	-42	-48	-55	-61	-68	-74	-81
25		29	23	16	9	3	-4	-11	-17	-24	-31	-37	-44	-51	-58	-64	-71	-78	-84
30		28	22	15	8	1	-5	-12	-19	-26	-33	-39	-46	-53	-60	-67	-73	-80	-87
35		28	21	14	7	0	-7	-14	-21	-27	-34	-41	-48	-55	-62	-69	-76	-82	-89
40		27	20	13	6	-1	-8	-15	-22	-29	-36	-43	-50	-57	-64	-71	-78	-84	-91
45		26	19	12	5	-2	-9	-16	-23	-30	-37	-44	-51	-58	-65	-72	-79	-86	-93
50		26	19	12	4	-3	-10	-17	-24	-31	-38	-45	-52	-60	-67	-74	-81	-88	-95
55		25	18	11	4	-3	-11	-18	-25	-32	-39	-46	-54	-61	-68	-75	-82	-89	-97
60		25	17	10	3	-4	-11	-19	-26	-33	-40	-48	-55	-62	-69	-76	-84	-91	-98

Frostbite Times　■ 30 minutes　■ 10 minutes　■ 5 minutes

$$\text{Wind Chill (°F)} = 35.74 + 0.6215T - 35.75(V^{0.16}) + 0.4275T(V^{0.16})$$

Where, T= Air Temperature (°F)　V= Wind Speed (mph)　　*Effective 11/01/01*

Windchill Chart.

▲ Power outages can occur when power lines are coated with ice or are knocked down by falling tree limbs.

Winter weather claims nearly 100 lives nationwide annually; the majority of these fatalities can be directly attributable to the impacts of winter storms. About 70% of all winter-related deaths occur in motor vehicle accidents caused by hazardous driving conditions, while nearly 25% are due to prolonged exposure to snow and cold. A significant percentage of winter weather-related deaths are due to heart attacks caused by overexertion while shoveling snow. Deaths have also occurred as a result of poisonous fumes released by generators, propane heaters, gas stoves, and charcoal grills when power outages force people to improvise alternate sources of heat for their homes. Without adequate ventilation in enclosed spaces, these devices can prove deadly within a matter of hours.

Dangers to human health from exposure to extremely cold conditions include frostbite and hypothermia.

▲ **Frostbite** is a severe reaction to cold exposure that can permanently damage body extremities. A loss of feeling and a white or pale appearance of fingers, toes, nose, and ear lobes are symptoms of frostbite.

▲ **Hypothermia** is a condition brought on when internal human body temperature drops below 95°F. Symptoms of hypothermia include uncontrollable shivering, slow speech, memory lapses, frequent stumbling, drowsiness, and exhaustion.

FOR EXAMPLE

Ice Kingdom

Heavy accumulations of ice can bring down trees, electrical wires, telephone poles and lines, and communication towers, disrupting communications and power for days. The massive ice storm of January 1998 covered the St. Lawrence River Valley with a veneer of solid ice. Although the destructive storm hit a region accustomed to severe winter weather, it left more than 4 million people without electricity, including a large number of the area's farmers. Because many of these rural farms were not equipped with generators, livestock suffered. Many lessons were learned from this event about rural emergency preparedness, planning, and action. Today, many more farms and rural homeowners have generators stored in preparation for the next winter event.

SELF-CHECK

- Define **extra-tropical cyclone, blizzard, severe blizzard, snowstorm, windchill factor,** and **hypothermia.**
- List four conditions created by severe winter storms.
- Discuss the difference between a snowstorm and a blizzard.
- Name three dangers that severe winter weather pose.

2.6 Wildfires

A **wildfire** is an uncontrolled burning of grasslands, brush, or woodlands. The potential for wildfire depends upon

▲ Surface fuel characteristics.

▲ Recent climate conditions.

▲ Current meteorological conditions.

▲ Fire behavior.

Hot summers with average or below-average rainfalls and extensive dry vegetative groundcover increase susceptibility to fire in the fall, a particularly dangerous time of year for wildfire.

Wildfires have taken place as a natural process for many thousands of years, playing an important role in the ecological integrity of our natural environment.

FOR EXAMPLE

Wildfire in North Carolina

Fayetteville, North Carolina experienced a devastating fire on May 29, 1831. The fire was considered to be more destructive than the Great Fire of Chicago in 1871. Fayetteville lost 600 homes, 125 businesses, several churches, and the North Carolina State House.[8] In recent years, North Carolina has experienced two significant wildfires. On June 3, 1998, lightning sparked a forest fire just east of Shaw Highway in Pender County that burned 695 acres on the western edge of Holly Shelter Game Land. The event lasted 45 hours. A wildfire was started in the Linville Gorge area on October 28, 2000, and eventually burned hundreds of acres in McDowell County. Extremely dry conditions had persisted across the area, as rain had not been measured for 50 days. The event lasted 60 hours.

Human settlement has significantly influenced changes in the spatial and temporal pattern of wildfire occurrence as well as the risks associated with them for human life and property.

Fire regimes of the eastern United States can be categorized into five basic time periods, as described in Table 2-7.[9]

Natural wildfires still take place on a regular basis. They can be caused by human carelessness, arson, or from lightning strikes on the tops of mountains. Other natural disturbances such as tornadoes and hurricanes can influence the structure and fuel distribution of forests, leading to a change in wildfire intensity and risk. Occurrence and frequency of wildfire also relies greatly upon the type of forest surrounding the community. Figure 2-9 shows a drought index.

The current scale of wildfire risk conditions is measured with the **Keetch-Byram Drought Index (KBDI)**. The KBDI estimates the potential risk for wildfire conditions based on daily temperatures, daily precipitation, and annual precipitation levels on an index of 0 (no drought) to 800 (extreme drought). It is a useful tool for fire fighters, planners, and citizens in understanding the risk of wildfire.

SELF-CHECK

- Define **wildfire** and the **Keetch-Byram Drought Index (KBDI)**.
- List four conditions that can contribute to the start of a wildfire.
- Discuss the different fire regime time periods of the eastern United States.

Table 2-7: Fire Regime Time Periods

Time Period	Fire Description
14,000 to 500 years ago	American Indians used fire for swidden agriculture, hunting visibility, reduction of wildfire fuel, and maintenance of trails.
500 to 100 years ago	European settlers used fire to maintain large amounts of permanent agricultural fields at a much greater scale than before.
Late 1800s into early 1900s	Forests were extensively logged, exacerbating conditions for common occurrence of wildfires.
1900 to 1950s	Response to wildfires was widespread fire suppression.
1950 to Today	Active management; natural role of fire is incorporated through prescribed burning.

Figure 2-9

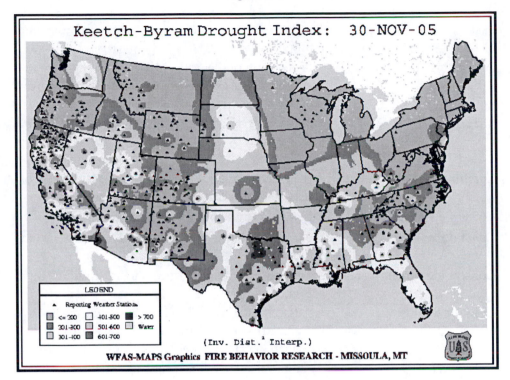

Example of drought index distributed across the U.S. during a very fire-prone winter season in 2005.

SUMMARY

This chapter covers some of the United State's most prevalent—and destructive—meteorological and hydrological hazards. The combination of intense hurricane activity and intense human activity along the coast has resulted in greater loss of life and property than ever before. Similarly, where humans choose to live often leaves them more vulnerable to riverine, urban, and coastal flooding. This chapter also covers the dangerous effects of tornadoes, wildfire, and severe winter weather hazards. Ultimately, a greater knowledge of all of these weather-related hazards will enable us to lessen their impacts on our lives and communities.

KEY TERMS

100-year flood floodplain   The area that has a 1% chance, on average, of flooding in any given year as shown on a community's FIRM.

500-year flood floodplain	An area with a 0.2% chance of flooding in any given year.
Base Flood	The 100-year flood floodplain as shown on a community's FIRM.
Base flood elevation (BFE)	The elevation of the water surface resulting from a flood that has a 1% chance of occurring in any given year as shown on a community's FIRM.
Blizzard	Snowstorm characterized by low temperatures and accompanied by winds that are at least 35 miles per hour.
Catchment	A river basin, or the area surrounding a river that collects water from higher surrounding elevations.
Coastal erosion	The wearing away of the shoreline along the ocean.
Coastal flooding	Flood event that is the result of storm surge, wind-driven waves, and heavy rainfall.
Coastal high hazard area	Areas that are subject to a velocity hazard (wave action).
Cold air damming (CAD)	A surface-based layer of cold air entrenched against the eastern slopes of the Ap-palachian Mountains; results in freezing rain or sleet.
Cold wave	An unusual fall in temperature, to or below the freezing point, exceeding 16 degrees in twenty-four hours or 20 degrees in thirty-six hours.
Enhanced Fujita Scale	An updated tornado index based on the Fujita scale that incorporates 28 damage indicators and degrees of damage estimates to more clearly classify tornado intensity during a tornado event.
Estuary	A semi-enclosed area where fresh water from a river meets salty water from the sea.
Extra-tropical cyclones	Storms that form outside the tropics; severe winter storms.
Eye	Calm center of a hurricane.
Flood Insurance Rate Map (FIRM)	Map of a community that shows both the SFHAs and the risk premium zones applicable to the community. FIRMs are prepared by FEMA.
Flash flood	A flood event occurring with little or no warning where water levels rise at an extremely fast rate.
Flood fringe	The area on both sides of the floodway with lower depths and velocities. The flood fringe stores water during a flood.

Floodplain	Low-lying flat areas that typically lie to either side of a river or stream.
Floodway	The central portion of the floodplain with the greatest water velocities and highest depths.
Freezing rain	Moisture falling in liquid form but freezing upon impact when surface temperatures are below freezing.
Frostbite	A severe reaction to cold exposure that can permanently damage its victims.
General flood	Flood event caused by precipitation over an extended period and over a given river basin.
Groundwater	The water found in cracks and pores in sand, gravel, and rocks below the earth's surface.
Hurricane	An intense tropic cyclone, formed in the atmosphere over warm ocean waters, in which wind speeds reach 74 miles per hour or more and blow in a large spiral around a relatively calm center or "eye."
Hydrological hazard	Weather event that occurs as part of the Earth's water systems.
Hypothermia	A condition brought on when the body temperature drops below 95°F.
Impervious surface	Hard, paved areas where water cannot soak through to the ground.
Inland flooding	Rivers and streams overflow as a hurricane moves across land.
Keetch-Byram Drought Index (KBDI)	The current scale of fire conditions that estimates the potential risk for wildfire based on daily temperatures, daily precipitation, and annual precipitation levels on an index of 0 (no drought) to 800 (extreme drought).
Landfall	The point where a hurricane crosses the coastline from the ocean.
Major hurricane	Category 3, 4, and 5 hurricanes; most potentially dangerous.
Meteorological hazard	Weather event that occurs because of processes in the Earth's atmosphere.
Northeast Snowfall Impact Scale (NESIS)	A scale that has recently been developed to characterize and rank high-impact snowstorms in the Northeast United States.
Rain band	A spiraling arm of rain radiating out from the eye of a hurricane.

River basin	The area surrounding a river that collects water from higher surrounding elevations; the drainage area of a river.
Riverine flooding	Flood event that is a function of precipitation levels and runoff volumes within the watershed of a stream or river.
Runoff	Water that is unable to soak through impervious surfaces such as rooftops or pavement.
Severe blizzard	Snowstorm with temperatures near or below 10°F, winds exceeding 45 miles per hour, and visibility reduced by snow to near zero.
Sleet	Ice pellets.
Snowstorm	Any storm with heavy snow.
Special Flood Hazard Area (SFHA)	An area within a floodplain having a 1% or greater chance of flood occurrence in any given year (100-year floodplain); represented on Flood Insurance Rate Maps by darkly shaded areas with zone designations that include the letter A or V.
Storm surge	Rise in the water surface above normal water level on the open coast due to the action of wind stress and atmospheric pressure on the water surface.
Storm tide	The combination of a hurricane's surge and the normal tide.
Tornado	A violently rotating column of air extending from the base of a thunderstorm.
Tropical cyclones	Storms that form in the tropics; hurricanes.
Urban flooding	Flood event that occurs where there has been development within stream floodplains.
Water force	The wave action of water during a hurricane that makes flooding particularly destructive.
Watershed	All the land drained by a river, stream, or lake; many watersheds make up a river basin.
Waterspout	Weak tornadoes that form over warm ocean waters.
Wildfire	An uncontrolled burning of grasslands, brush, or woodlands.
Wind velocity	The speed of wind.
Windchill factor	As wind increases, heat is carried away from the body at a faster rate.
Windchill temperature	Unit of measurement to describe windchill factor.

ASSESS YOUR UNDERSTANDING

Go to www.wiley.com/college/schwab to evaluate your knowledge of meteorological and hydrological hazards.
Measure your learning by comparing pre-test and post-test results.

Summary Questions

1. Weather-related natural hazards can be classified as either meteorological or hydrological. True or False?
2. Which of the following is not a prevalent hazard in the United States?
   (a) drought
   (b) storm surge
   (c) waterspout
   (d) tsunami
3. A hurricane begins as a
   (a) waterspout.
   (b) tropical storm.
   (c) tropical depression.
   (d) tornado.
4. A hurricane's severity is measure on a scale of 1 to 6. True or False?
5. Hurricane velocity increases after landfall. True or False?
6. The current trend in hurricane landfalls is
   (a) steady.
   (b) decreasing.
   (c) increasing.
   (d) difficult to determine.
7. The World Meteorological Organization relies on Greek names to identify tropical storms and hurricanes. True or False?
8. A catchment is the same as a
   (a) river basin.
   (b) streambed.
   (c) flood hazard zone.
   (d) floodplain.
9. Flash flooding is common in urban areas. True or False?
10. Flood maps are created using
    (a) soil moisture conditions.
    (b) topographic features.

(c) proximity to a river.

(d) all of the above.

11. Which of the following is the most damaging effect of a tornado?

   (a) lightning

   (b) hail

   (c) wind velocity

   (d) heavy rain

12. A small tornado will cause less damage than a large tornado. True or False?

13. Severe winter storms are tropical cyclones. True or False?

14. Blizzard conditions are characterized by extreme cold and wind. True or False?

15. Windchill factor is

   (a) a unit of measurement to describe wind speed.

   (b) the wind temperature during a cold wave.

   (c) the air temperature during a winter storm.

   (d) how a combination of cold and wind affects the human body.

16. Frostbite and hypothermia exhibit similar symptoms. True or False?

Review Questions

1. Hurricanes can affect more than just coastal areas. Explain how.

2. When is hurricane season in the Untied States?

3. Hurricanes typically involve more than one destructive feature. List the six characteristic threats of a hurricane.

4. According to the Saffir-Simpson Scale, what are the hurricane categories and the corresponding levels used to describe them?

5. Hurricane landfalls have increased in the United States in recent years. Explain why.

6. Which hurricane was the deadliest and costliest in United States history? In what year did it occur?

7. When a river overflows, floodwater first moves into the surrounding low-lying, flat areas. What is the name of this area?

8. Flash floods can occur in mountains or urban areas. Explain the role of impervious surfaces in a flash flood.

9. Coastal areas often face the threat of flooding. Name three different ways that coastal communities can be flooded during a storm.

10. Define a tornado. How is a tornado different from a hurricane, and how are they related?

11. Name the scale used to rate tornadoes and give the range for classification.

12. Which natural hazard is often a combination of the following conditions: snowstorm, extreme cold, windchill, freezing rain? And is there an area of the United States that is particularly prone to this hazard?

13. Severe winter weather can be very dangerous. How does windchill affect human safety during winter weather?

14. What are the three dangers that officials must be concerned about during a winter storm?

Applying This Chapter

1. Using the list of the most prevalent meteorological and hydrological hazards in the United States, pick the 10 hazards that most apply to where you live and put them in order of most likely to least likely do occur

2. Working from the list of 10 hazards for your community, predict the likely effect each event would have on your community.

3. Imagine that a hurricane with maximum sustained winds of 125 miles per hour were to strike your area (whether or not you live in a hurricane-prone region). Examine your neighborhood to see how it would be affected.

4. Assume you are an official of a town on a barrier beach island on the Gulf Coast. A large hotel and resort has brought much-needed tourism to the area, but it has also brought a boom in real estate development. Using the example of a real community that was hit hard by a hurricane, draft an introduction to a presentation you'll give about why development should be carefully regulated.

5. Assume that you are an insurance agent in an area that has not experienced serious flood damage in more than 25 years. How could you begin to convince your clients of their need to buy flood insurance for their homes? What kind of information could you provide to them?

6. If a tornado with winds of about 115 miles per hour were to hit your community, what level of tornado would it be, and what kind of damage would be likely? Which buildings would be especially vulnerable?

7. Compare the potential effects of a blizzard to those of an F2 tornado. Which elements are different? Which are the same?

8. With wind speeds of 40 miles per hour and a temperature of 0°F, calculate the windchill and explain what that means for someone who has left his or her broken-down car in a storm to walk an undetermined distance for help.

YOU TRY IT

Find Your Ecological Address

Even if you don't live on the waterfront, the land around your house drains into a river, estuary, or lake somewhere nearby. What river basin are you located in? Into what river or stream does your land eventually drain? Does the water running off your property enter a storm drain, a ditch, or an open field? How fast does runoff enter local streams? How much of the area is paved or covered with hard surfaces such as roads or rooftops?

Flooded with Information

Evaluate your risk of experiencing a flood where you live. Which type of flooding would you be most vulnerable to? You can get more information about floods and estimate your flood risk and your insurance premium from the FEMA National Flood Insurance Program Flood Smart website: www.floodsmart.gov/floodsmart/pages/statistics.jsp.

Risk Assessment

Select one threatened area or population of your community and come up with ideas for how to prepare for a potential natural hazard. For example, consider aging mobile homes that you feel could not withstand a serious wind event. How would you provide information about these hazards to members of your community, even if you couldn't identify which areas are most at risk?

Snow Disaster

Imagine that you'll be spending a winter in Buffalo, New York, an area that can be crippled by intense lake-effect snows. Where will you be when disaster strikes? At work, at school, or in the car? A severe storm event may confine you to your home or force you to evacuate. What would you do if basic services—water, gas, electricity, or telephones—were cut off? Using the following NOAA website, www.nws.noaa.gov/om/brochures/wntrstm.htm, prepare a disaster plan for you and/or your family.

3

GEOLOGICAL HAZARDS
Earthquakes, Volcanoes, Landslides, Coastal Erosion, and Land Subsidence

Starting Point

Go to www.wiley.com/college/schwab to assess your knowledge of geological hazards.
Determine where you need to concentrate your effort.

What You'll Learn in This Chapter

- ▲ Types of geological hazards
- ▲ How earthquakes happen
- ▲ Scales used to rate earthquakes
- ▲ Types of volcanoes and volcanic eruptions
- ▲ Causes of landslides and debris flows
- ▲ The definition of setback rules
- ▲ The consequences of excessive groundwater removal

After Studying This Chapter, You'll Be Able To

- ▲ Differentiate the three layers of the Earth's crust
- ▲ Examine the relationship between geologic hazards and community planning
- ▲ Distinguish between earthquakes based on intensity and effects
- ▲ Examine areas of the United States to find those that are vulnerable to volcanoes
- ▲ Examine the relationship between dynamic equilibrium and coastal erosion
- ▲ Analyze the driving forces behind land subsidence

Goals and Outcomes

- ▲ Prepare reports using the terminology that applies to geologic hazards
- ▲ Select tools and techniques to compare geologic events according to magnitude and intensity
- ▲ Evaluate how certain geologic events are connected
- ▲ Compare the potential impacts of major geological hazards on a community
- ▲ Support and work with others on effective ways to inform communities about geologic hazards
- ▲ Predict the risk of geological hazards for an area using knowledge of past occurrences
- ▲ Evaluate decisions made about real communities based on geologic research

INTRODUCTION

All geological hazards share one thing in common: the build-up of pressure over time. In this chapter, we will describe five geological hazards that have serious consequences for humans. Earthquakes, which can have far-ranging and catastrophic effects, are examined in detail. The chapter also covers volcanoes and landslides and the potential impacts these hazards can have on communities. The implications of coastal erosion are discussed in relation to patterns of building and human activity. The chapter concludes with a section on land subsidence, or the settling of the Earth's surface.

3.1 Geological Hazards

The Earth is composed of the core, mantle, and crust.

- ▲ The **crust** is the paper-thin layer on the surface, extending to about 5 kilometers (3.1 miles) below the oceans and about 30 kilometers (18.64 miles) on average beneath the continents.
- ▲ The **mantle** is the middle layer, estimated to be 2900 kilometers (1802 miles) thick.
- ▲ The **core** is the innermost region of the Earth, over 3500 kilometers (2175 miles) thick.

Much of the action associated with the geological hazards we will be discussing in this chapter occurs in the mantle, but it greatly affects the crust, where

FOR EXAMPLE

Evidence of What's Inside

Earth is about 6370 kilometers (3959 miles) deep from surface to the center, but we have been able to drill wells only a few kilometers deep. So how can we tell what is inside the Earth? Several kinds of evidence have been used, including

- ▲ Study of once-deeply buried rocks that have been uncovered by erosion.
- ▲ Study of interior material that emerges as lava and gases from volcanoes.
- ▲ Analysis of earthquake waves that pass through Earth.
- ▲ Study of the curious configuration of Earth's continents and ocean basins.
- ▲ Study of Earth's movements through space.
- ▲ Study of meteorites.

Collectively, this research has provided evidence of Earth's structure and composition.[1]

we live. Quite literally, the "pressure is on" for the crust of Earth, which is also the most brittle of the Earth's three layers.

This chapter describes five geological hazards that occur at the mercy of these shifting layers over time: earthquakes, volcanoes, landslides, coastal erosion, and subsidence. These natural hazards have very serious consequences for human settlements, posing threats to both people and property. It is important to gain at least a basic understanding of the science behind these hazards in order to take steps to protect our communities from their impacts.

SELF-CHECK

- Define **crust, mantle,** and **core.**
- List the five geologic hazards that are related to the Earth's shifting layers.
- List several pieces of evidence about the composition and structure of Earth's interior.

3.2 Earthquakes

The Greek word *seismos* means to quake; **seismology** is the study of earthquakes.[2] Earthquakes are geologic events that involve movement or shaking of the Earth's crust and upper mantle, otherwise known as the **lithosphere.** The upper part of the mantle is cooler and more rigid than the deep mantle below it; thus it behaves similarly to the overlying crust. The two layers together are broken into the moving plates that contain the continents and oceans. It is the movement of these thin **tectonic plates** that is so influential in an earthquake.

3.2.1 Stress Release

Earthquakes are usually caused by the release of stresses accumulated as a result of the rupture of lithosphere rocks along opposing boundaries, or **fault planes,** in the crust. These fault planes are typically found along borders of the Earth's tectonic plates. The plate borders generally follow the outlines of the continents, with the North American plate following the continental border with the Pacific Ocean in the west, but following the mid-Atlantic trench in the east.

3.2.2 Tectonic Plate Movement: A Constant Wrestling Match

Tectonic plates move only, on average, a few inches a year. However, when the seven large plates (which encompass entire continents and giant portions of oceans) move in opposing directions, a few inches can be highly significant.

The areas of greatest tectonic instability occur at the perimeters of the slowly moving plates because these locations are subject to the greatest strains from plates traveling in opposite directions and at different speeds. Deformation along plate boundaries causes strain in the rock and the consequent buildup of stored energy.

Tectonic plate activity is similar to a constant arm wrestling match underneath our feet, with each side exerting tremendous force against the other. Eventually the built-up stress exceeds the rocks' strength and a rupture occurs. When the rock on both sides of the fault snaps, it releases the stored energy by producing **seismic waves.** These waves are what cause the ground to shake in an earthquake.

3.2.3 Earthquake Motion

The variables that characterize earthquakes are ground motion, surface faulting, ground failure, and seismic activity. **Ground motion** is the vibration or shaking of the ground during an earthquake. When a fault ruptures, seismic waves radiate, causing the ground to vibrate. The severity of the vibration increases with the amount of energy released and decreases with the distance from the causative fault, or **epicenter.** Accordingly, damage is generally most severe at or near the epicenter, although this is not always the case.

▲ **Surface faulting** is the differential movement of two sides of a fracture— the location where the ground breaks apart. The length, width, and displacement of the ground characterize surface faults.

▲ **Liquefaction** is the phenomenon that occurs when ground shaking causes loose soils to lose strength and act like viscous fluid. Liquefaction causes two types of ground failure: lateral spread and loss of bearing strength.

▲ **Lateral spreads** develop on gentle slopes and entail the sidelong movement of large masses of soil as an underlying layer liquefies.

▲ **Loss of bearing strength** results when the soil supporting structures liquefies. This can cause structures to tip and topple.[3]

3.2.4 Rating Earthquakes: Scales of Magnitude, Intensity, and Acceleration

Seismologists use several different standardized scales to measure the severity of earthquakes. These include the Richter magnitude, the Modified Mercalli Intensity, and Peak Ground Acceleration (PGA), among others.

Measuring Magnitude with the Richter Scale

The **Richter Scale** is an open-ended logarithmic scale that describes the energy release of an earthquake through a measure of shock wave amplitude. The instrument that records the amplitude of the seismic waves is called a **seismograph.** The corresponding earthquake magnitude is expressed in whole numbers and decimal fractions. Each unit increase in magnitude on the Richter scale (for example, increasing the magnitude rating from 4 to 5) corresponds to a 10-fold increase in wave amplitude, or a 32-fold increase in energy.

The Richter scale does not have an upper limit. Some earthquakes can have magnitudes of 8.0 or higher. The Sumatra-Andaman Earthquake that caused the December 26, 2005 tsunami in the Indian Ocean had a magnitude of 9.15 on the Richter scale, making it among the highest magnitude ratings to ever be recorded by a seismograph. At the other extreme, an earthquake with a magnitude of less than 2.0 is called a **microearthquake.** Quakes can be detected when they are relatively light in strength; however, the seismograph may need to be closer to the center of the earthquake for measurement purposes.

Measuring Intensity with the Modified Mercalli Intensity Scale

The measurement of earthquake magnitude does not specifically address the various levels of damage that could result from an earthquake event. Damage potential is measured by **intensity.** Earthquake intensity is most commonly measured using the Modified Mercalli Intensity (MMI) Scale, a twelve-level scale based on direct and indirect measurements of seismic effects. The scale levels are typically described using roman numerals, ranging from:

- ▲ *I* imperceptible events (can only be detected by seismographic instruments).
- ▲ *IV* moderate events (can be felt by people who are awake at the time).
- ▲ *XII* catastrophic events (total destruction occurs).

A detailed description of the MMI Scale of earthquake intensity and its correspondence to the Richter scale is shown in the following table. The MMI Scale incorporates the types of damages that can be expected with various earthquake intensities (see Table 3-1).

Measuring Acceleration with the Peak Ground Acceleration

Peak Ground Acceleration (PGA) is a measure of the strength of ground movements. The PGA measurement expresses an earthquake's severity by comparing its acceleration to the normal acceleration due to gravity. For example, an object dropped from a height on the Earth's surface will fall (ignoring wind resistance) toward the Earth faster and faster, until it reaches terminal velocity. This principle is known as **acceleration** and represents the rate at which speed is increasing. The acceleration due to gravity is often called "g," a term popularly associated with roller coasters, rockets, and stock car racing. The acceleration due to gravity at the Earth's surface is 9.8 meters (980 centimeters) per second squared. Thus, for every second an object falls toward the surface of the Earth, its velocity increases by 9.8 meters per second. A 100%g earthquake is very severe.

Consider this analogy: a driver presses the gas pedal of a car forcefully, causing groceries in the trunk to smash against the back of the car. The quicker the

Table 3-1: Modified Mercalli Scale of Earthquake Intensity

Scale	Intensity	Description of Effects	Maximum Acceleration (mm/sec)	Approximate Corresponding Richter Scale
I	Instrumental	Detected only on seismographs	< 10	N/A
II	Feeble	Some people feel it	< 25	< 4.2
III	Slight	Felt by people resting; like a truck rumbling by	< 50	N/A
IV	Moderate	Felt by people walking	< 100	N/A
V	Slightly Strong	Sleepers awake; church bells ring	< 250	< 4.8
VI	Strong	Trees sway; suspended objects swing, objects fall off shelves	< 500	< 5.4
VII	Very Strong	Mild alarm; walls crack; plaster falls	< 1000	< 6.1
VIII	Destructive	Moving cars uncontrollable; masonry fractures, poorly constructed buildings damaged	< 2500	N/A
IX	Ruinous	Some houses collapse; ground cracks; pipes break open	< 5000	< 6.9
X	Disastrous	Ground cracks profusely; many buildings destroyed; liquefaction and landslides widespread	< 7500	< 7.3
XI	Very Disastrous	Most buildings and bridges collapse; roads, railways, pipes, and cables destroyed; general triggering of other hazards	< 9800	< 8.1
XII	Catastrophic	Total destruction; trees fall; ground rises and falls in waves	> 9800	> 8.1

driver presses on the gas, the more eggs are likely to be damaged. This effect is caused by the fast acceleration that forces the contents of the trunk of the car to shift rapidly and violently, not slowly and smoothly. A slower acceleration allows the groceries to remain stationary within the confines of the trunk. The groceries-in-the trunk scenario approximates the behavior of an earthquake. If ground acceleration is rapid, more structures and objects experience damage than if the shaking is relatively slow, even if the ground moves the same distance.[4]

3.2.5 Earthquake Impacts on People and Property

Direct impacts from earthquakes include damage to structures and infrastructure, such as buildings, pipelines, roadways, and bridges. Impacts to a community from an earthquake event can include injury and deaths of citizens and public safety officials; loss of vital services including electricity, gas, and communications systems; lost revenue and economic damage; and increased demand on public safety, health and emergency facilities, and critical services. Secondary impacts are common following earthquakes and include fires, loss of water supply and water pressure, hazardous material releases, gas and other flammable material explosions, and related incidents. Earthquakes can also trigger tsunamis and landslides.

Most injuries and deaths, as well as the majority of property damage from an earthquake are caused by ground shaking. Hard, brittle structures such as buildings and roadways tend to break and crack when they are forced to move due to the underlying ground movement. In contrast, resilient or flexible objects are less likely to suffer breakage. Structures can fail due to both horizontal and vertical shaking. Tall buildings tend to sway or vibrate, depending upon their construction materials and height as well as their distance from the epicenter. The top floors of buildings that are located close to one another may even collide during the swaying motion triggered by a large earthquake. **Pancaking** occurs when high-rise buildings collapse in on themselves because the poured concrete flooring separates from the corner fastenings, causing the floors to drop vertically down.

3.2.6 Earthquake Experience in the United States

Earthquake risk in the United States is significant in many regions of the country. The area of greatest seismic activity is along the Pacific Coast in California and Alaska, but as many as 40 states can be characterized as having at least a moderate earthquake risk. In the past 20 years, scientists have learned that strong earthquakes in the central Mississippi Valley are not freak events but have occurred repeatedly in the geologic past. The New Madrid seismic zone is an area of major earthquake activity that experiences frequent minor shocks. Although earthquakes in the central and eastern United States are less frequent than in the western part of the country, these areas represent considerable seismic risk.

FOR EXAMPLE

The Mississippi Valley Earthquakes

In the winter of 1811–12, the central Mississippi Valley was struck by three of the most powerful earthquakes in U.S. history. Survivors reported that the earthquakes caused cracks to open in the Earth's surface, the ground to roll in visible waves, and large areas of land to sink or rise. The crew of the *New Orleans* (the first steamboat on the Mississippi, which was on her maiden voyage) reported mooring to an island only to awake in the morning and find that the island had disappeared below the waters of the Mississippi River. Damage was reported as far away as Charleston, South Carolina, and Washington, D.C.

Notable Earthquakes

The United States has experienced some very disastrous and catastrophic earthquakes in its history. Of the top ten largest earthquakes to occur in the U.S., seven have taken place in Alaska with magnitudes of 7.9 or higher. The earthquake with the second highest magnitude in the world took place in Prince William Sound, Alaska in 1964, with a magnitude of 9.2. This event took 125 human lives and generated a tsunami wave that reached an estimated height of 200 feet. Other significant earthquakes include

▲ The *San Francisco Earthquake of 1906* occurred on April 18, 1906, at 5:12 in the morning. The epicenter was near San Francisco, and the quake lasted approximately 45–60 seconds. The quake is believed to have been between VII and IX on the MMI scale. The quake could be felt from Southern Oregon to south of Los Angeles, and as far east as central Nevada. Reports of deaths vary from 500 to 700 people, although these figures may be underestimated. Significant damage occurred to the city as a direct result of the quake, but the event is remembered more for the devastating fires that broke out city-wide following the ground shaking. Gas lines snapped, and wood and coal burning stoves overturned. Water mains broke, hampering the work of city fire-fighters. Firebreaks were created throughout the city by blowing up buildings and entire neighborhoods to stop the spread of the flames.

▲ The *Loma Prieta, California Earthquake* occurred on October 18, 1989, at 5:04 P.M., the height of rush hour, measuring 6.7 on the Richter scale, and lasting for 15 seconds. As a result of the quake 63 deaths occurred, with over 3700 people injured. Property damage reached nearly $6 billion, making this the most costly disaster up until that time in the United States. Over 1800 homes were destroyed, 2600 businesses were damaged, and

3000 people were made homeless. The two-tiered Bay Bridge and Nimitz Freeway both collapsed, crushing cars underneath and killing and trapping hundreds of motorists. Fire damage to infrastructure and buildings was extensive, gaping cracks were created in most of the main roads, and landslides were triggered in surrounding areas. Fans waiting to see the World Series baseball game in Candlestick Park rushed onto the field as the whole stadium swayed; the event was televised live nationwide until the broadcast was abruptly disconnected.

▲ The *Northridge Earthquake* occurred on Monday January 17, 1994, at approximately 4:30 A.M.; it measured 6.7 on the Richter scale and lasted 15 seconds. The epicenter was located 20 miles northwest of Los Angeles beneath the San Fernando Valley. Between 57 and 72 deaths and more than 9000 injuries were reported. The death and injury toll would have undoubtedly been much higher had the event not occurred on the Martin Luther King, Jr. holiday, when many commuters were at home. Nearly $44 billion in property damage occurred, with 25,000 dwellings made uninhabitable and thousands more severely or moderately damaged. The damage was so widespread that 9 hospitals were closed, 9 parking garages collapsed, 11 major roads into Los Angeles were closed, 2 bridges on the Interstate 10 Santa Monica Freeway collapsed, and countless other bridges and overpasses were damaged, paralyzing the city for weeks, and severely delaying rescue and recovery efforts.

3.2.7 Lessons Learned

What can we learn from these past earthquake experiences? The 1906 San Francisco Earthquake, which caused millions of dollars in damage, was considered merely ill fortune at the time. San Francisco's citizens thought little of the possibility of future quakes. The city was rebuilt following the disaster in almost identical fashion. Yet, that earthquake provided a wealth of information to scientists and, eventually, to planners and builders, about the nature of earthquake damage and the geological processes involved in causing that damage. In fact, the 1906 Earthquake is considered by some scholars as the most significant quake of all time, primarily because of the scientific knowledge gained rather than the quake's sheer size. Damage reports from the 1906 event gave an early indication of the significance of the fault, although its large horizontal displacement and the great rupture length it displayed were not fully appreciated at the time. Although the theory of plate tectonics was not developed for another half century, reports from the 1906 quake laid a sound foundation for later studies in seismology.

Subsequent earthquakes have provided even more opportunities to learn additional information about how earthquakes happen, and, more significantly for the purposes of mitigation, what types of construction design, techniques, and materials are best suited to withstand earthquake impacts. Damage reports indicate that in many of these events, structures and infrastructure (roads, overpasses, bridges, gas and pipe lines, etc.) that were constructed or retrofitted (strengthened) to handle earthquake impacts fared much better on average than older or less substantially constructed buildings and facilities. Engineers and architects have also learned that building design in earthquake-prone areas should incorporate safeguards against both horizontal and vertical shaking. Structural supports should be carefully designed to avoid potential disasters like upper floors collapsing onto the floors below or onto open space, such as parking decks, that are located on the lower levels. Much research has been conducted on transportation infrastructure (roads, bridges, overpasses, and interchanges) to discover the types of damages that have occurred to the transportation network during past quakes (see Figure 3-1). Bridge performance is particularly critical, because the failure of support columns can cause entire spans of highway to collapse. In California, bridges and overpasses built prior to 1971 are particularly vulnerable; following the 1971 San Fernando Earthquake, standards for earthquake design and construction were toughened considerably.

Studies of past earthquake disasters have also shown that many injuries and deaths occur because of breaking glass, falling objects, and insecure furnishings.

Figure 3-1

Damage to Interstate 5 from the Northridge Earthquake.

Fairly simple and relatively inexpensive retrofitting activities can be implemented to combat these dangers, such as bolting furniture to the wall, anchoring book-cases, and securing appliances like televisions and computers so they remain stable during earthquake shaking.

We have also learned that areas prone to earthquakes can be delineated on maps. Within these areas, seismologists can create various zones of potential earthquake severity based on the underlying geological characteristics of the Earth. This ability to locate earthquake risk potential is critical to hazard mitigation and preparedness efforts. Seismic risk zone information is essential for steering future development away from areas that are most at risk from ground shaking and for targeting at-risk structures for retrofitting.

SELF-CHECK

- Define **seismology, lithosphere, tectonic plate, fault plane, seismic wave, ground motion, epicenter, surface faulting, liquefaction, lateral spread, loss of bearing strength, seismograph, microearthquake, intensity, acceleration,** and **pancaking.**
- Name the three scales used to measure the severity of an earthquake; explain the unit measurement of each scale.
- Describe the effects of a level VI earthquake.
- Discuss ways of reducing human deaths and property damage caused by earthquakes.
- Identify the geographic areas of the United States that are potentially impacted by earthquakes.

3.3 Volcanoes

A **volcano** is a vent in the surface of the Earth through which magma and associated gases and ash erupt. The structure that is produced by the ejected material, usually conical in form, is referred to as a volcano as well. The word *volcano* is derived from the Latin word *Vulcan*, Roman god of the forge.[5]

3.3.1 Reaching the Boiling Point

A volcanic eruption occurs when superheated rock under the Earth's surface rises to areas of lower pressure at the surface. During this movement, the rock undergoes a phase change from solid rock to liquid **magma** (molten rock). Volcanic action can be compared to the action that occurs when water boils and turns to steam, resulting in volume expansion. If the water is boiled while in a closed glass beaker, the container does not have room to hold the additional volume, and the glass will explode to release the pressure. A volcanic eruption works under the same principle, but on a far grander scale. The enormous amount of pressure and heat building up under the surface causes conversion of the rock to magma, and the magma expands. The result is an eruption through the most accessible escape route at the Earth's surface. Magma that reaches the Earth's surface is called **lava.** Lava temperatures can reach 1250 degrees Celsius (over 2000 degrees Fahrenheit).

3.3.2 Types of Volcanic Eruptions

There are six types of volcanic eruptions: Icelandic, Hawaiian, Strombolian, Vulcanian, Vesuvian, and Pilian (see Table 3-2).

Mount St. Helens in Washington State was an example of a Pilian eruption. When Mount St. Helens erupted on May 18, 1980, it erupted with such force that the top 1000 feet of the volcano disappeared within minutes. The blast sent thousands of tons of ash into the upper atmosphere, while simultaneously sending waves of lava, poisonous gas, and mudflow debris laterally out the side and down the slopes of the mountain. Within hours, thousands of acres surrounding the volcano had been destroyed. More than 200 square miles of forestland were transformed into a grey, lifeless landscape. All living creatures within miles were killed, including one geologist who had been stationed nearby to monitor

Table 3-2: Types of Volcanic Eruptions

Type of Volcanic Eruption	Description
Icelandic	Gas escapes easily and lava has low viscosity.
Hawaiian	Gas escapes easily, but lava has slightly more viscosity; builds tall peaks.
Strombolian	Smaller, more continuous eruptions; its central lava pool is easily triggered due to the pressure that builds quickly under its crust.
Vulcanian	Switch between high viscosity lava and large amounts of ash blown out the top of the volcano.
Vesuvian	Even more violent high viscosity lava blasts that are due to trapped gases. These gases can blow ash and rock great distances, either vertically or horizontally.
Pilian	The gas pressure and viscosity of the magma is so high that these volcanoes blow lava and ash laterally, or out of its side (rather than up), to relieve the pressure blockages of the throat of the volcano.

the volcano's activity, and one resident who refused to evacuate the area despite official warnings. In all, 57 people died, including loggers, campers, reporters, and scientists, some as far as 13 miles from the mountain itself.

Some volcanoes erupt violently, while others flow more peacefully. The variation in volcanic force is due to:

▲ Variance in chemical and mineral content of the rock/magma.

▲ Variance in the viscosity, temperature, and water and gas content of the rock/magma.

▲ Variance in geographic positions in relation to tectonic plate edges.

3.3.3 Volcanic Hot Spots

Areas that are prone to frequent volcanic activity are known as **hot spots,** such as the one in the Island of Hawaii. In these areas, volcanoes form when magma rises from a stationary heat source—the hotspot—beneath the Earth's lithosphere. The magma migrates up through fractures in the overriding Pacific plate and extrudes onto the ocean floor, gradually building a mountain of successive lava flows. Over time the mass accumulates until it emerges above sea level, thereby becoming an island volcano.

The Hawaiian Islands are arranged in a chain, and the key to understanding why lies in the relation between the Hawaiian hot spot and the movement of the Pacific plate. The hot spot is a stationary heat source over which the Pacific plate slowly moves toward the northwest. Imagine a conveyor with hamburger patties slowly moving over a stationary gas flame, cooking the burgers one after another. The currently active volcanoes in the hot spot on the Island of Hawaii are Mauna Loa, Kilauea, and Loihi.[6]

3.3.4 The Volcano-Earthquake Connection

A few volcanic eruptions are considered by scientists to be related to earthquakes occurring in the area. It is not understood what the exact triggering mechanism might be, but the subsequent volcanic activity is most likely a response to a pressure change in the magma. This could be a consequence of a change in pressure on the crust in the area of the earthquake or the severe ground shaking caused by the quake.

FOR EXAMPLE

A Quake and a Volcano

The eruption of Kilauea in Hawaii in November, 1975, was directly related to an earthquake. A 7.2 magnitude earthquake, along with many aftershocks, occurred just southeast of the Kilauea volcano's caldera and within its south flank. The volcano erupted for over 16 hours.

3.3.5 Types of Volcanic Structures

There are several varieties of volcanic structure, including:

▲ **Cinder cones,** the simplest type of volcano, have a single vent and are built of cinders. As the lava erupts violently into the air, it breaks into small fragments that solidify and fall as **cinders** around the vent. Over time, these small fragments build up to form a circular cone. Most cinder cones grow to no more than a thousand feet or so above their surroundings and have a bowl-shaped **crater** at the summit.

▲ **Shield volcanoes,** on the other hand, can have many eruptions from the fractures, or rift zones, along the flanks of their cones. Rather than erupting violently, the lava flows out in all directions from the vents. These volcanoes are built almost entirely of fluid lava flows that cool as thin sheets and create a gently sloping cone. Some of the largest volcanoes in the world are shield volcanoes. The largest shield volcano (and the largest active volcano in the world) is Mauna Loa. This volcano on the Big Island of Hawaii sits over 13,000 feet above sea level, but the entire volcano, starting from the sea floor, spans over 28,000 feet.

▲ **Lava domes** are formed by lava piles that are too thick, or viscous, to flow far away from the vent. A dome volcano grows by layering the lava upward and outward, largely by expansion from within. Some domes form short, steep-sided lava flows known as **coulees.** Others form spines over the volcanic vent. Domes commonly occur within the craters or on the flanks of large composite volcanoes.

▲ **Composite volcanoes,** also called **stratovolcanoes,** are large volcanoes that are also mountains. Some of the most breathtaking mountains in the world are composite volcanoes, including Mount Fuji in Japan and Mount St. Helens in Washington. Most have a central crater at the summit, but lava can erupt through fissures on the flanks of the cone or flow from breaks in the crater. These volcanoes build up over time by the fortification of the cone when the cooled lava fills the fissures and when cinders and ash are added to the slopes.

3.3.6 Impacts of Volcanic Activity on People and Property

Volcanoes can pose a serious threat to both people and property. One of the most common risks associated with volcanic activity involves **lava flows.** Although lava rarely travels quickly enough to be life-threatening, it does create havoc to the natural and built environment. For example, the flow of lava from volcanoes in southern Hawaii has destroyed numerous homes and buried highways in its path. Because of its excessive heat, lava quickly burns any consumable material it covers, including trees, houses, roads, crops, and anything else in its way. Lava flows may be slow-moving, but they are unstoppable forces. A few communities in Iceland have tried to stop the advance of lava flows using cold seawater in an attempt to change it from a molten to solid condition. The success of this technique is not widely recognized.

Volcanic ash also can be extremely hazardous to plant and animal life. Volcanic ash can form thick deposits on the ground, causing extensive environmental damage. The ash can contain bits of volcanic glass and can be very abrasive. Violent eruptions can bury whole communities, cause houses to collapse, clog engines in airplanes and vehicles, and cause breathing problems. The ash plume from an erupting volcano can be dispersed a long distance by high-altitude winds, bringing similar problems to areas far removed from the eruption site.

Pyroclastic flows pose another danger to humans and are experienced in the vicinity of explosive volcanoes. A **pyroclastic flow**, also called a **nuee ardente** (French for "glowing cloud"), is an incinerating mixture of gas and volcanic debris, with a temperature from 700 to 1000 degrees Celsius (1300–1800 degrees Fahrenheit). Pyroclastic flows remain close to the ground, but they can travel downhill from the volcano summit very quickly, up to 150 kilometers (90 miles) per hour, incinerating anything in their path as they roar down the slope. One of the most famous pyroclastic flows occurred when Mount Vesuvius erupted in A.D. 79, engulfing the ancient city of Pompeii, Italy. The forests on the sides of Mount St. Helens were flattened by a nuee ardente when that volcano erupted in 1980.

Volcanic mudflows also pose a significant threat to human settlements. A mixture of water and volcanic debris, a mudflow can quickly travel downslope, burying all objects in its path. Mudflows created heavy damage during the eruption of Mount St. Helens, as they traveled along stream valleys carrying trees, structures, and soils into the Columbia River below. The U.S. Army Corps of Engineers had to dredge debris from the river to make it passable to navigation following the event.

Poisonous gases from volcanic activity also pose a danger to humans and animals. Although volcanic gas is primarily made up of water vapor, other elements that may be present include carbon dioxide, sulfur dioxide, carbon monoxide, hydrogen sulfide, sulfuric acid, hydrochloric acid, and hydrofluoric acid. These toxic gases can impact urban areas and agricultural crops in the vicinity, something that occurs on the island of Hawaii fairly frequently. **Vog,** or volcanic fog, occurs a short distance downwind from the eruption site, while **laze** (lava haze) is produced when lava enters the sea and the reaction produces hydrochloric acid fumes.

3.4 Landslides/Debris Flows

Landslides occur when masses of rock, earth, or debris move down a slope. The major driving force behind landslides is gravity, assisted by water. Landslides vary in size, from relatively small, isolated events to quite large, widespread ground movement, and can vary in speed from a slow, gradual creep to a rapid rush of earth and debris raging downhill. Activated by geological hazards, rainstorms, wildfires, and by human modification of the land, landslides pose serious threats to any man-made structures and facilities that lie in their path. Landslides can seriously impact fisheries, tourism, timber harvesting, agriculture, mining, energy production, and transportation, as well as community life.

While some landslides move slowly and cause damage gradually, others move so rapidly that they can destroy property and take lives suddenly and unexpectedly. This type of landslide is called a **debris flow,** which can also manifest itself as a mudslide, mudflow, or debris avalanche. These types of fast-moving landslides generally occur during intense rainfall on water-saturated soil.

Debris flows usually start on steep hillsides as **soil slumps** or slides that liquefy and accelerate to speeds as great as 35 miles per hour or more. They continue flowing downhill and into channels, depositing sand, mud, boulders, and organic material onto more gently sloping ground. Consistency ranges from watery mud to thick, rocky mud (like wet cement), which is dense enough to carry boulders, trees, and cars. Debris flows from many different sources can combine in channels, where their destructive power may be greatly increased.

Areas that are generally prone to landslide hazards include existing old landslides, the bases of steep slopes, the bases of drainage channels, and developed hillsides where leach-field septic systems are used. Areas that are typically considered safe from landslides include areas that have not moved in the past; relatively flat-lying areas away from sudden changes in slope; and areas at the top or along ridges, set back from the tops of slopes.

According to the United States Geological Survey (USGS), landslides are major geologic hazards that occur in all 50 states, cause $1 to $2 billion in damages

Figure 3-2

The Thistle Landslide.

per year and result in an average of more than 25 fatalities annually. Several examples include the Canyonville, Oregon, landslide of 1974 that killed 9; the 1980 Mount St. Helens debris flow, which is the world's largest landslide; and a landslide in Mameyes, Puerto Rico, in 1985 that killed 129 people caused by Tropical Storm Isabel.

While torrential rainfalls such as those that occur during hurricanes or tropical storms commonly act as triggers for landslides, other natural hazards can also cause landslides. The Mount St. Helens debris flow was an instantaneous result of the volcanic eruption that took place there. A landslide in San Fernando, California, started as a result of a 7.5 magnitude earthquake in 1971. A string of wildfires that burned over 4000 acres of vegetative cover in Big Sur, California, exacerbated a landslide on California Highway 1 in 1972 after a series of torrential rainstorms.

The Thistle landslide was the single most costly landslide event in U.S. history, with damages exceeding $400 million (see Figure 3-2). Land began shifting in Thistle, Utah, in 1983 because of groundwater buildup from heavy rains during the previous fall and the melting of deep snowpack from the winter. Within a few weeks, the landslide dammed the Spanish Fork River, destroying U.S. Highway 6 and the main line of the Denver and Rio Grande

Sleeping Bear Dunes Landslide

In February 1995, a 1600-foot stretch of popular beach at Sleeping Bear Dunes National Lakeshore suddenly slid into the waters of northeastern Lake Michigan. USGS and National Park Service scientists believe that repeated coastal landslides at Sleeping Bear Point may be related to increases in fluid pressure in the spaces between the grains of sand (pore pressure) that make up the bluff at the point. The increased amount of water would weaken the slope, making it susceptible to landslides.

Western Railroad. The landslide dam caused flood waters to rise, leading to inundation of the surrounding area. The town of Thistle was completely obliterated.

SELF-CHECK

- Define **landslide, debris flow,** and **soil slump.**
- Identify the two forces that drive a landslide.
- List three types of land areas that are typically prone to landslides.
- Discuss the areas of the United States that are at risk of landslide events.

3.5 Coastal Erosion

Coastal erosion is the wearing away of the land surface by detachment and movement of soil and rock fragments. Erosion can occur during a flood or storm event or over a period of years through the action of wind, water, or other geologic processes. Sea level rise can also contribute to the progression of coastal erosion over time.

Wind, waves, and long shore currents are the driving forces behind coastal erosion. The removal and deposition of sand permanently changes the structure and shape of the beach. Sand is transported throughout the sea/shore system, and can be transported to land-side dunes, other beaches, off-shore banks, and

Figure 3-3

The rate of coastal erosion is about 100 times that of sea level rise. Rising water causes beaches to recede and makes structures near them much more vulnerable to storm damage.

deep ocean bottoms. Rates of coastal erosion can also be affected by human activity, sea-level rise, seasonal fluctuations, and climate change.

The beach system is in a state of **dynamic equilibrium.** Constant movement transfers sand from one location to another, but the total amount of sand within the system does not fluctuate. Winter storms along the coast may remove significant amounts of sand, creating steep, narrow beaches, while during the summer, milder waves return the sand, widening beaches and creating gentle slopes. Sand movement will not be consistent year after year in the same location, however, because of the many factors that influence sand movement within the beach system.

Coastal erosion is a highly localized event that can take place on one end of an island and not at the other (see Figure 3-3). Although much erosion takes place gradually over time, a hurricane or other sudden storm event can drastically increase the amount of coastal erosion that takes place in a short period of time. **Episodic erosion** is induced by a single storm event. This type of erosion can make structures located along the shore suddenly become unstable and prone to collapse, as scouring occurs around foundation supports and undermines the building.

FOR EXAMPLE

Erosion Setbacks in North Carolina

North Carolina first evaluated long-term average erosion rates for the state's 300-mile ocean coastline in 1979, and the state updates the erosion rates about every five years. It's an exacting process that takes nearly a year to complete. The process begins by obtaining new aerial photographs of the ocean shoreline. The photos show the shoreline, defined as the high-water line, or the edge of the wet sand visible, on the photographs. The shoreline is marked and then its position is added to an existing database. A computer program determines the average long-term erosion rate by comparing the current shoreline position to the earliest available position and dividing the distance between them by the number of years that have passed between the dates the photographs were taken.

For most single-family homes, regardless of size, setbacks are determined by multiplying the average annual erosion by 30. The minimum setback is 60 feet. For buildings larger than 5000 square feet, the setback is determined by multiplying the erosion rate by 60, with a minimum setback being 120 feet. All buildings must be behind the frontal dune and landward of the crest of the primary dune, where those exist.

The average erosion rate on the Atlantic coast is roughly 2 to 3 feet per year, but the states bordering the Gulf of Mexico, especially in the deltas of Louisiana, have the nation's highest average annual erosion rate at 6 feet per year. Erosion on the rocky cliffs of the Pacific coast averages 1 foot per year, although large episodic erosion occurs occasionally. The Great Lakes annual erosion rate is highly variable, ranging from 0 to more than 10 feet per year depending on a number of hydrologic and weather-related factors such as fluctuating lake levels and wave action.

Many coastal states have **setback rules** that are based on the erosion rate along the shoreline. The erosion setback is a line, measured landward from some specified point (e.g., the first line of stable, natural vegetation), behind which construction must take place. Setbacks are designed to increase the life of a building by avoiding the wear and tear, or sudden collapse, that can happen close to the oceanfront.

SELF-CHECK

- Define **coastal erosion, dynamic equilibrium, episodic erosion,** and **setback rules.**
- Name six forces behind coastal erosion.
- Discuss the effects of episodic erosion on a beachfront community.

LAND CHANGE IN COASTAL LOUISIANA

The coastal zone of Louisiana contains some of the most environmentally significant lands in the United States. Approximately 40% of the nation's total acreage of marshland and 25% of our wetlands are located in this area.[7] The complex ecological system of marshes, wetlands, and barrier islands serves as a protective buffer against the effects of large coastal storms, effectively decreasing the vulnerability of development located further inland. It is estimated that for every 2½ miles of wetland in Louisiana, storm surge height is reduced by 1 foot.[8] The region is exceedingly dynamic, as the areas of marsh, wetlands, and barrier islands are constantly shifting due to the influences exerted by natural fluxes of sea level, subsidence activities both on and off-shore, and variable quantities of sediment deposit from the Mississippi River.

Many factors over the past century have debilitated the natural barriers of the coastal ecosystem of Louisiana, threatening not just their protective features, but their very existence. One of the most debilitating man-made influences involves the vast system of levees installed by the U.S. Army Corps of Engineers along the Mississippi River. Although originally constructed to decrease flooding of the Mississippi and its tributaries, the levees have had unanticipated negative impacts, primarily by preventing natural sediment runoff from reaching the river channel. This in turn reduces the amount of sediment available to the Mississippi delta, which depends upon the sediment for renourishment. The sediment that does make it to the delta is insufficient in quantity and is washed off the continental shelf, where it cannot contribute to the creation of new marshlands. Thousands of oil and gas wells, combined with their network of pipelines and channels that cut through the marsh, allow movement of salt water through these areas, causing further erosion. Sea level rise only further exacerbates the problems of coastal erosion, salt water invasion, and marsh subsidence in this region. It is estimated that more than 1 million acres of the Louisiana coastal wetlands have been lost since 1930, which accounts for 90% of all coastal land loss in the lower 48 states combined.[9] Furthermore, the loss is continuing at an accelerated rate. In the next 50 years, it is estimated that another 1/3 of a million acres could be lost.

The combined effects of Hurricanes Katrina and Rita converted approximately 118 square miles of marsh to open water in southeastern Louisiana in less than two months time. Some of the impacted marshes may recover, but the majority of the losses are expected to be permanent. The most substantial marsh losses took place in St. Bernard and Plaquemines parishes, with Breton Sound alone accounting for 40.9 square miles of marsh loss. The Pontchartrain, Pearl River, Barataria, and Terrebonne basins contributed an additional 60 square miles of inundation, but the most significant concentrated losses were located between State Highway 300 to the north, Delacroix Ridge to the east, and the Mississippi River levee to the west.[10]

3.6 Subsidence and Collapse

The basic cause of land subsidence and collapse is a loss of support below ground. **Land subsidence** is a gradual settling of the Earth's surface owing to subsurface movement of earth materials. It usually occurs over a period of weeks or months, and can happen slowly enough to be barely perceptible. **Collapse** occurs more quickly, when the land surface opens up and surface materials fall into cavities below. Collapse can take place over just a few hours. **Sinkholes** are an especially dramatic example of the collapse process. Subsidence and collapse are serious geological hazards, posing threats to property and human life.

3.6.1 Causes of Land Subsidence

Subsidence is a problem throughout the world. In the United States, more than 17,000 square miles in 45 states, an area roughly the size of New Hampshire and Vermont combined, have been directly affected by subsidence.

Land subsidence is most often caused by human activities, mainly by the removal of **groundwater** (subsurface water), although natural processes can also induce subsidence. Causal factors of land subsidence include:

▲ Drainage of organic soils.
▲ Dissolving of subsurface limestone rock.
▲ First-time wetting of formerly dry, low-density soils.
▲ Natural compaction of soils.
▲ Underground mining.
▲ Withdrawal of groundwater and petroleum.

FOR EXAMPLE

Sacramento River Delta, California

The Sacramento River delta is a mass of channels, wetlands, and islands. In the delta, streams that drain the Sierra Nevada Mountains meet saltwater moved by tides up the Sacramento River from San Francisco Bay. The organic soils of the delta were drained for agriculture many years ago. The land surface has since subsided an average of about 8 centimeters (3 inches) per year. Many parts of the delta now are below river level and are protected from flooding by dike systems. Humans, structures, and wildlife are jeopardized by flooding during high river stages that overtop or breach the dikes. Also, the dikes could be damaged by an earthquake in this seismic risk zone.

Removal of Ground Water

More than 80% of the identified subsidence in the United States is a consequence of groundwater exploitation. The increasing development of land and water resources means that existing land subsidence problems will likely worsen in the near future, and new problems will undoubtedly arise.

When large amounts of groundwater are withdrawn from certain types of rocks, such as fine-grained sediments, the rock compacts because the water is partly responsible for holding the ground up. When the water is withdrawn, the rock falls in on itself. Land subsidence can be difficult to notice, because it can extend over large geographic areas and can take place gradually over a period of time. Eventually, however, land sinks to such a degree that houses become off-kilter, roads collapse, and flooding worsens because the elevation of the land has been lowered.

Groundwater is used to irrigate crops, to provide drinking water to municipalities, and for use in manufacturing and various industries. But the withdrawal of groundwater has depleted critical groundwater resources and created costly regional-scale subsidence in many areas of the country. In the Santa Clara Valley in northern California, early agricultural groundwater use contributed to subsidence that has permanently increased flood risks in the greater San Jose area. In nearby San Joaquin Valley, one of the single largest human alterations of the Earth's surface topography has resulted from excessive pumping of groundwater to sustain an exceptionally productive agricultural business. Early oil and gas production and a long history of pumping groundwater in the Houston-Galveston area in Texas have also created severe and costly coastal flooding hazards and affected the Galveston Bay estuary—a critical environmental resource. In Las Vegas Valley, Nevada, groundwater depletion and associated subsidence have accompanied the conversion of a desert oasis into a thirsty and fast-growing metropolis. Water-intensive agricultural practices in south-central Arizona have caused widespread subsidence and fissuring of the Earth's surface. In each of these areas, not only have the water resources been dangerously reduced, the action of pumping water out of the ground has created hazardous subsidence conditions.

3.6.2 Mine Collapse

Mining of coal, minerals, and other ores is an important economic mainstay in many communities in particular regions of the United States. However, the process of removing these materials can cause subsidence of the surface above the mines. When mining is carried out near the surface of the ground, the supporting structure for overlying rocks is removed. If too much of the supporting material is removed, the surface will collapse into the mine below, creating dangerous **collapse pits.** The danger of subsidence from abandoned coalmines is particularly acute in Pennsylvania, West Virginia, and Kentucky.

The dangers of mine subsidence can be reduced by filling in the void that is created when the ores are removed. Leftover mining materials (mine waste) can be dumped into the mining holes to support the overlying roof. When this is impractical, sand or cement can be pumped in through access holes.

3.6.3 Sinkholes

Sinkholes are common where rock below the land surface is made up of limestone, carbonate rock, salt beds, or rocks that naturally can be dissolved by groundwater circulating through them. As the rock dissolves, spaces and caverns develop underground, creating what is known as Karst topography (named after an area in Yugoslavia where this occurs regularly). Sinkholes can be dramatic episodes of collapse, because the land usually remains intact up to the point when spaces under the Earth's surface become too large to support the upper layer of earth. At this stage, a sudden collapse of the land surface can occur. These collapses can be small, just a few feet wide, or they can be huge, swallowing up an entire house. The most damage from sinkholes in the United States tends to occur in Florida, Texas, Alabama, Missouri, Kentucky, Tennessee, and Pennsylvania. Sinkholes are different from soil slumps, which are composed of loose, partly to completely saturated sand or silt, or poorly compacted man-made fill composed of sand, silt, or clay. Soil slumps are common on embankments built on soft, saturated foundation materials, in hillside cut-and-fill areas, and on river and coastal floodplains.[11]

New sinkholes may result from groundwater pumping and from construction and development practices. Sinkholes can also form when natural water drainage patterns are changed and new water diversion systems are developed. Some sinkholes form when the land surface is changed, such as when industrial and runoff storage ponds are created. The substantial weight of the new material can trigger an underground collapse of supporting material, thus causing a sinkhole

It is very difficult to predict when a sinkhole might happen. It is critical that homeowners and local officials pay attention to developments on the surface that hint at what lies below, and be particularly aware when limestone is present. Land subsidence and cracks on the surface indicate that the underlying material may have large voids, especially when the cracks occur in a circular pattern. Cracks in walls and foundations of buildings can also indicate that the ground below is becoming frail.

SELF-CHECK

- Define **land subsidence, collapse, sinkhole, groundwater,** and **collapse pit.**
- Cite six reasons for land subsidence.
- Discuss the difference between a **collapse pit** and a **sinkhole.**

SUMMARY

The inevitable shifting of the Earth's layers over time results in equally inevitable geological hazards. This chapter covers earthquakes and their potentially devastating effects on human life and property, particularly in areas along fault lines. Volcanic action can cause significant property damage and risk to human, plant, and animal life during eruptions. The chapter also discusses the risk of landslides, coastal erosion, and land subsidence, each of which presents its own dangers and potential for death and destruction. The information on these hazards can be used by emergency managers and those in land use management to better protect communities from their potential impacts.

KEY TERMS

Acceleration	The rate at which speed of ground movement is increasing.
Cinders	Lava that erupts into the air and breaks into small fragments that solidify.
Cinder cones	The simplest type of volcano; they have a single vent and are built of cinders.
Coastal erosion	The wearing away of the land surface by detachment and movement of soil and rock fragments.
Collapse	When the land surface opens up and surface materials fall into cavities below.
Collapse pit	Hole created when too much supporting material is removed during mining; the surface will collapse into the mine below.
Composite volcanoes	Large volcanoes that are also mountains; also called stratovolcanoes.
Core	The innermost region of the Earth.
Coulees	Short, steep-sided lava flows.
Crater	Bowl-shaped hole at the summit of a volcano.
Crust	The thin layer on the surface of the Earth.
Debris flow	Fast-moving landslides that generally occur during intense rainfall on water-saturated soil.
Dynamic equilibrium	In coastal erosion, when sand is moved from one location to another but it does not leave the system.

Earthquake	Geologic hazard caused by the release of stresses accumulated as a result of the rupture of lithosphere rocks along opposing boundaries in the Earth's crust.
Epicenter	Causative fault of an earthquake; damage is generally most severe at or near the epicenter.
Episodic erosion	Erosion induced by a single storm event.
Fault planes	Ruptures in the Earth's crust that are typically found along borders of the tectonic plates.
Ground motion	The vibration or shaking of the ground during an earthquake.
Groundwater	Subsurface water.
Hot spot	Area prone to volcanic activity.
Intensity	How the damage potential of an earthquake is measured.
Land subsidence	A gradual settling of the Earth's surface.
Landslide	When masses of rock, earth, or debris move down a slope.
Lateral spread	Type of ground failure in an earthquake that develops on gentle slopes and entails the sidelong movement of large masses of soil as an underlying layer liquefies.
Lava	Magma that reaches the Earth's surface.
Lava dome	Type of volcano that grows by layering lava upward and outward, largely by expansion from within.
Lava flows	Moving lava; because of its excessive heat, lava quickly burns any consumable material it covers.
Laze	Lava haze produced when lava enters the sea and chemical reactions produces hydrochloric acid fumes.
Liquefaction	When ground shaking causes loose soils to lose strength and act like viscous fluid.
Lithosphere	The Earth's crust and upper mantle.
Loss of bearing strength	Type of ground failure in an earthquake that results when the soil-supporting structures liquify.
Magma	Molten rock.

Mantle	Middle layer of the Earth.
Microearthquake	An earthquake with a magnitude of less than 2.0.
Nuee ardente	French for "glowing cloud"; an incinerating mixture of gas and volcanic debris; also called pyroclastic flow.
Pancaking	When high-rise buildings collapse in on themselves.
Pyroclastic flow	An incinerating mixture of gas and volcanic debris; also called nuee ardente.
Richter Scale	An open-ended logarithmic scale that describes the energy release of an earthquake through a measure of shock wave amplitude.
Seismic waves	When the rock on both sides of a fault snaps, it releases this stored energy; waves are what cause the ground to shake in an earthquake.
Seismograph	The instrument that records the amplitude of the seismic waves.
Seismology	The study of earthquakes.
Setback rules	Regulations based on the erosion rate along the shoreline. The setback is a line behind which construction must take place.
Shield volcanoes	Type of volcano that can have many eruptions from the fractures, or rift zones, along the flanks of their cones.
Sinkholes	Spaces and caverns that develop underground as the rock below the land surface is dissolved by groundwater circulating through them.
Soil slumps	Loose, partly to completely saturated sand or silt, or poorly compacted man-made fill composed of sand, silt, or clay.
Stratovolcanoes	Large volcanoes that are also mountains; also called composite volcanoes.
Surface faulting	The differential movement of two sides of a fracture; the location where the ground breaks apart.
Tectonic plates	Moving layers of the Earth's surface that contain the continents and oceans.
Vog	Volcanic fog; occurs a short distance downwind from volcanic eruption site.

Volcanic ash	Produced by volcanic eruption; can form thick deposits on the ground, causing extensive environmental damage.
Volcanic mudflows	A mixture of water and volcanic debris.
Volcano	A vent in the surface of the Earth through which magma and associated gases and ash erupt.

ASSESS YOUR UNDERSTANDING

Go to www.wiley.com/college/schwab to evaluate your knowledge of geological hazards.
Measure your learning by comparing pretest and post-test results.

Summary Questions

1. The mantle is the outer layer of the Earth. True or False?
2. Which of the following is the most brittle layer of the Earth?
   (a) mantle
   (b) lithosphere
   (c) crust
   (d) core
3. Liquefaction causes soils to lose strength and act like fluid. True or False?
4. The Richter Scale measures:
   (a) shock wave amplitude.
   (b) surface faulting.
   (c) intensity.
   (d) ground movement.
5. A microearthquake has a magnitude of less than 4.5. True or False?
6. The MMI (Modified Mercalli Intensity) Scale is used to judge earthquake damage potential by measuring:
   (a) speed.
   (b) velocity.
   (c) ground movement.
   (d) intensity.
7. The Richter scale measures earthquakes using values from 1 to 8. True or False?
8. The number of states that have at least moderate earthquake risk is:
   (a) 25.
   (b) 50.
   (c) 40.
   (d) 35.
9. A Vulcanian volcanic eruption is characterized by:
   (a) low-viscosity lava.
   (b) large amounts of ash blown off the top.
   (c) lava and ash blown out of the side.
   (d) small, continuous eruptions.

10. Lava that reaches the Earth's surface is called magma. True or False?

11. An area that is prone to volcanic activity is called a hot spot. True or False?

12. A stratovolcano is a:
    (a) composite volcano.
    (b) coulee.
    (c) microearthquake.
    (d) shield volcano.

13. Vog is a byproduct of a volcanic mudflow. True or False?

14. A debris flow can be dense enough to carry trees and cars. True or False?

15. Landslides can be caused by volcanic eruptions and earthquakes. True or False?

16. Landslide-prone areas include:
    (a) bases of drainage channels.
    (b) areas at the top of ridges.
    (c) areas along the edge of ridges.
    (d) areas that have not moved before.

17. Episodic erosion takes places over a period of many months or even years. True or False?

18. Coastal erosion becomes a hazard as an increasing number of homes and structures are built in vulnerable areas. True or False?

19. The average rate of erosion on the Atlantic coast is:
    (a) 10 feet per year.
    (b) 1 foot per year.
    (c) 2 to 3 feet per year.
    (d) 4 to 5 feet per year.

20. Land subsidence occurs when the land opens up and surface materials fall into cavities. True or False?

21. Most of the land subsidence in the United States is a result of:
    (a) mine collapse.
    (b) sinkholes.
    (c) groundwater removal.
    (d) earthquakes.

Review Questions

1. The Earth is composed of three layers. Name the layers.

2. Which factor is common among the five geologic hazards covered in this chapter?

3. In which layer of the Earth does an earthquake form?

4. Explain the role of seismic waves in an earthquake.

5. Name the four variables that characterize an earthquake.

6. California is typically thought of as a particularly earthquake-prone area. Name two other areas that share the threat.

7. What is the name of the geologic event that occurs when solid rock turns to molten rock?

8. Explain what, if any, connection there may be between volcanoes and earthquakes.

9. Lava flows and volcanic ash are obvious dangers to human life and property. Name three other threats from a volcanic eruption.

10. Explain what makes a debris flow different from a typical landslide.

11. Describe how natural hazards other than hurricanes and tropical storms can affect landslides.

12. Which natural process is coastal erosion a part of?

13. Coastal erosion is the wearing away of land surface, most notably by wind, waves, and long shore currents. Name three other causes of coastal erosion.

14. There are many factors involved in coastal erosion. Explain the role of episodic erosion.

15. Removal of groundwater is the most significant cause of subsidence in the United States. What are three other actions that contribute to subsidence?

16. Explain how withdrawal of groundwater causes regional-scale subsidence in many areas of the United States.

Applying This Chapter

1. Using the geologic hazards covered in this chapter, pick those that apply to where you live and put them in order of most likely to least likely to occur.

2. Imagine you live in an area that experiences an earthquake that measures 6.1 on the Richter scale. Using the MMI Scale, what would be its intensity and what effects would you be likely to experience?

3. Consider the building you're in and predict its ability to withstand an earthquake that measures 5.4 on the Richter scale.

4. As an emergency manager in a town 100 miles from Washington State's Mount St. Helens, what kind of information would you provide to members of your community about the risk of volcanoes and other geologic hazards?

5. Landslides occur in all 50 states. Consider the potential for a landslide in your area. Has one occurred in the past? Where would you predict any high-risk areas to be?

6. A series of historic homes along the shore of New York's Long Island have lost many feet of property in the past decade because of the effects of coastal erosion. What information should be presented to potential home buyers in neighboring areas that have not yet experienced such severe erosion? What should they know about regulations for building new structures?

7. Though agriculture has been responsible for a good deal of the groundwater removal and resulting subsidence, the country's growing population and its need for water (landscaping, drinking water, fire suppression, industry, manufacturing, recreation, etc.) is becoming a major factor. Describe an area of the country that is experiencing such a potentially hazardous boom in development. What are the community's water needs?

YOU TRY IT

Know Your Geology

As an emergency manager in your town, what resources would you use to create a map of your town's geologic high-risk areas? How would you describe the different areas of risk to a homeowner or business owner in your community?

Lava Lookout

You're planning a temporary move to Hawaii. You need to find a home to rent, but you're not sure about how volcanoes really affect Hawaiians. Choose what you think is the least hazardous area to live in and support your decision. Use information from the USGS to make your decision. The USGS Hawaiian Volcano Observatory keeps track of current activity of the Kilauea volcano on the Big Island of Hawaii. You can access this information at hvo.wr.usgs.gov/kilauea/update/main.html.

I Feel the Earth Move

Earthquakes are a major concern in many aras of the United States. What is your community's level of risk from a quake? Use the USGS's earthquake website, earthquake.usgs.gov, to determine when the last earthquake took place in your state. Consider how earthquake preparedness factors into your own emergency plan. Using the website, determine what you should do during an earthquake. For example, should you head for a doorway? Rooftop? Basement? Also, how are the contents of your home likely to withstand seismic activity?

4

MAN-MADE HAZARDS
Terrorism, Technological Hazards, and Civil Unrest

Starting Point

Go to www.wiley.com/college/schwab to assess your knowledge of man-made hazards.
Determine where you need to concentrate your effort.

What You'll Learn in This Chapter

▲ How man-made hazards differ from natural hazards
▲ Types of terrorist acts and tactics
▲ Ways that civil unrest can cause disorder and disruption
▲ Common hazardous materials
▲ Ways in which hazardous materials can affect humans
▲ The emotional consequences of man-made hazards
▲ Notable man-made events in U.S. history

After Studying This Chapter, You'll Be Able To

▲ Analyze the relationship between man-made hazards and the all-hazards approach
▲ Identify the criteria for an act of terrorism
▲ Examine how civil unrest fits into an emergency management plan
▲ Illustrate how hazardous materials can be released into a community
▲ Practice the process of mitigating hazards before they become disasters

Goals and Outcomes

▲ Assess the procedures and tools used to evaluate the risks of man-made hazards
▲ Distinguish among man-made hazards in a given situation
▲ Evaluate a community's preparedness for a hazard event by using an all-hazards approach
▲ Support and collaborate with others to determine the man-made hazards and natural hazards in your community
▲ Assess the public's perception of risk from terrorism and technological hazards
▲ Evaluate the use of mitigation plans for real-world communities

INTRODUCTION

A resilient community must deal not only with recurrent natural hazards, but must also take action to protect itself from man-made hazards, those that are accidental as well as hazards that are intentional in nature. This chapter discusses the difference between natural and man-made hazards, and provides a short list of some of the notable man-made events that have occurred in the United States. The chapter then briefly explores the issue of terrorism, a significant intentional threat to our country. Next, the chapter discusses the role of civil unrest and outlines various technological accidents, such as hazardous materials releases, nuclear reactor incidents, and oil spills. The chapter concludes with a description of some of the psychological effects these types of hazards may produce as well as ways to make our communities less vulnerable to the impacts of man-made hazards.

4.1 The American Experience

When compared with the number of natural hazards such as hurricanes, wildfires, floods, earthquakes, tornadoes, ice storms, landslides, and other feats of nature that have impacted our communities in the past, the United States has experienced relatively few man-made hazards. We have one of the safest transportation systems in the world, a highly regulated nuclear power industry, and stringent laws that restrict the use of chemicals, toxins, corrosives, and other hazardous materials. Yet accidents still happen. Trains can derail, spilling chemicals over the landscape. Nuclear power plants can experience meltdowns, spreading radioactive material into surrounding communities. Shipping tankers can sink, leaking oil and petrochemicals into the sea. We call these and other accidental man-made hazards **technological hazards.** This chapter discusses some of the different types of technological hazards and how they can impact our communities.

This chapter also discusses intentional man-made hazards. This category of man-made hazard includes **terrorism,** the unlawful use of force and violence against persons or property to intimidate or coerce a government and/or the civilian population to advance ideological objectives. This category also includes incidents of **civil unrest** such as riots and looting; these events are often disastrous because they quickly get out of control, not because they were intentionally started to create havoc.

We have a vast array of security measures and safety precautions in place in this country to combat terrorism, yet many people feel that the question of a terrorist attack on American soil is not "if" but "when," and further, "where." Since the events of September 11, 2001, the emergency management community has become increasingly sensitive to the need for diligence in preparing for the next biochemical attack or bombing event. We will continue to direct resources, time, and energy toward reducing the dangers of intentional hazards to increase our homeland's security. In order to do so, we must be knowledgeable about the various threats to which we are potentially exposed.

There are many resources available that provide in-depth information regarding a wide variety of man-made hazards. In fact, much of this chapter is based on information distributed by the Department of Homeland Security (DHS), the Federal Emergency Management Agency (FEMA), the U.S. Occupational Health and Safety Administration (OSHA), and the U.S. Environmental Protection Agency (EPA). You can visit the websites of these and other federal and state agencies to learn more about man-made hazards that could be present in your community.

4.1.1 Distinguishing Between Man-Made and Natural Hazards

The fundamental difference between man-made and natural hazards is that the former are caused by humans. Because man-made hazards are caused by humans, terrorist attacks and technological accidents are by nature unpredictable. This unpredictability can present an array of management challenges that do not arise when dealing with natural hazards.

Natural Hazards: We Know Where They Are

The types, frequencies, and locations of many types of natural hazards are identifiable and even in some cases predictable. Natural hazards are governed by the laws of physics and nature. For instance, we can forecast the possible paths of future hurricanes based on past hurricane tracks. Likewise, we can also map areas of the country where earthquakes are more likely to happen based on known fault zones.

Humans Are Much Less Predictable

On the other hand, malevolence, incompetence, carelessness, and other behaviors are functions of the human mind and, while they can be assumed to exist, they cannot be forecast with any accuracy. Therefore, there is the potential for most, if not all, types of man-made hazards to occur anywhere. This is particularly true of terrorism, because terrorists have the ability to choose among targets and tactics, designing their attacks to maximize the chances of achieving their objective.

Like terrorist attacks, accidents, system failures, and other mishaps that lead to technological accidents are also largely unforeseeable. Their occurrence is not quite random, but nearly so. This makes it very difficult to identify how and where these hazards may take place. Acts of civil unrest are also unforeseeable. We may be able to generalize about the social and economic

---

FOR EXAMPLE

Bank Robbers or Terrorists?

A gang of bank robbers who kill the bank manager, blow up the vault, and escape with the contents would not be considered terrorists. But if the robbers did the same thing with the intent to cause a crisis in public confidence in the banking system and destabilization of the economy, then the gang could be considered terrorists. In this case, the motive and long-term consequences are factors that distinguish between the robbers who are seeking personal gain and robbers who are seeking to make a political statement and cause widespread and lingering impacts through their actions.

---

conditions that may lead to riot or disorderly conduct, but we cannot predict with certainty when or where events involving violence and disruption will happen.

4.1.2 The All-Hazards Approach

Despite the feelings of urgency we may have when we consider the threat of terrorism, and to a lesser degree the dangers of technological accidents and civil unrest, we must be careful to keep in mind the natural hazards that we know with certainty will occur in this country. We know that hurricanes will continue to ravage our coasts. We know that tornadoes will cause great damage in the Midwest. We know that communities will be flooded time after time. We know that California and a few other states are ripe for an earthquake. We know without a doubt that these hazards will take place in these areas. In our efforts to reduce the dangers posed by man-made hazards, we must not lose sight of the fact that natural hazards are a certainty. We must take care that resources devoted to homeland security are not diverted from our efforts to reduce the impacts of natural hazards through mitigation and preparedness. Our prioritization process must consider all types of hazards when we develop our risk reduction polices and strategies. This approach to dealing with both natural and man-made hazards simultaneously is known as the **all-hazards approach.** The all-hazards approach is fully endorsed by FEMA, which encourages all communities to adopt mitigation and emergency operations plans.

The following quotation illustrates the importance of continuing the all-hazards approach to hazard mitigation.

The events of 9/11 created a watershed for the profession of emergency management. In the post-9/11 world, the preoccupation with the threat of terrorism has changed political and administrative priorities. Budget allocations for traditional emergency management programs have been subsumed in the larger allocations for homeland security, often with little assurance of the continuity of traditional programs . . . The all-hazards approach must be continued. The risks posed by earthquakes in California and by hurricanes along the Gulf Coast are potentially far greater than those posed by terrorists. The risks posed by influenza and other diseases (witness the SARS epidemic) are far greater than those posed by terrorists with anthrax, sarin, or other biological and chemical agents.[1]

It is clear that natural hazards of all types are more likely to occur in the average American community than a terrorist attack, an event of civil unrest, or a technological accident. That having been said, however, the impacts of a man-made hazard, although unlikely, could be quite far-reaching and could cause lingering consequences for quite some time. As a case in point, by some estimates, the attacks of September 11, 2001, will continue to affect the commercial airline industry for years to come.

Each community must rank the importance of natural and man-made hazards based on its own unique characteristics. In some communities, susceptibility to a terrorist attack or technological accident is quite low. These communities will focus mainly on the natural hazards that are common in their region. Other communities, however, will find that their vulnerability to a man-made hazard is much higher, perhaps because they provide an attractive target for a terrorist, or because there are multiple locations or occasions where a technological accident could occur. Either way, each community will need to assess for itself what priority it should place on dealing with man-made and natural hazards, by assessing the probability of each type of hazard occurring in the community and factoring in the consequences that could occur if that hazard became reality.

4.1.3 Important Man-Made Events in the United States

Now that we are clear about the priority we should place on the efforts to combat terrorism and technological accidents, let's learn a little about these hazards. Table 4-1 lists a few of the more dramatic events that have occurred in our nation's history. Measured in sheer numbers, the monetary impact and numbers of deaths and injuries come nowhere close to the amount of damage that has been caused by natural hazards over the years. However, these types of hazards have an emotional component to them that is sometimes lacking when we dissect the aftermath of a natural disaster. As an interesting exercise, try to gauge your feelings when you read the short facts listed here. Are you affected in ways that might differ from your reaction if these were events caused by nature and not by fellow humans?

Table 4-1: Selected Man-Made Hazard Events in the United States

Event	Location	Type of Hazard	Description and Impacts
Anthrax Attacks October 2001	Washington, D.C. New York City Boca Raton, FL	Terrorism of Unknown Origin	Letters containing anthrax mailed to news media offices and 2 U.S. Senators; 5 deaths, 22 infected with long-term illness; shutdown government mail service; dozens of buildings decontaminated at estimated cost of more than $1 billion. Case remains unsolved (as of September 2005).
Terrorist Attacks September 11, 2001	Dept. of Defense Headquarters (Pentagon) Washington, D.C. World Trade Center, New York City Rural Somerset County near Shanksville, PA	International Terrorism	Series of suicide attacks using hijacked airliners; 2986 deaths, thousands injured; 25 buildings in Manhattan destroyed; 1.5 million tons of debris in New York City; portion of Pentagon damaged; costs of clean-up, rebuilding, and economic losses in billions of dollars; stock markets worldwide fell; airline industry severely impacted; massive insurance claims against airlines and others; impetus for large-scale "War on Terror."
HazMat Train Derailment July 2001	Baltimore, MD	Technological Accident	Train carrying hazardous chemicals derailed and caught fire in downtown tunnel; caused shutdown of city; traffic snarled; 5-block area evacuated; inner harbor closed to boat traffic; internet service disrupted nationwide due to burned fiber optic cables; no deaths.
Olympic Bombing July 27, 1996	Olympic Centennial Park, Atlanta, GA	Domestic Terrorism	Politically motivated bomb attack; 1 direct death, 1 fatal heart attack, 111 injured; perpetrator Eric Rudolph

(continued)

Table 4-1: (*continued*)

Event	Location	Type of Hazard	Description and Impacts
			captured, also charged with other bombings, and sentenced to life imprisonment.
Oklahoma City Bombing April 19, 1995	Murrah Federal Building, Oklahoma City, Oklahoma	Domestic Terrorism	Bomb made of fertilizer and other readily available materials detonated in rental truck; 168 deaths, more than 500 injured; perpetrators Timothy McVeigh and Terry Nichols captured, tried, and sentenced.
World Trade Center Bombing February 26, 1993	New York City	International Terrorism	Van with bomb driven into basement parking garage and remotely detonated; 6 deaths, more than 1000 injured; $300 million property damage.
L.A. Riots (also known as Rodney King Riots) April 29, 1992	Los Angeles, California	Civil Unrest	6 days of rioting sparked when mostly white jury acquitted 4 police officers accused in videotaped beating of African American motorist Rodney King. Thousands of residents joined in what is described as a race riot, involving mass law breaking, looting, arson, murder. 50-60 deaths; more than 2000 injured; 10,000 arrests; $800 million - $1 billion in property damage.
Exxon Valdez Oil Spill 1989	Prince William Sound, Alaska	Technological Accident	Exxon oil tanker ran aground attributed to negligence of Ship's captain; 40,000 tons of crude oil spilled into ocean and spread along hundreds of miles of coastline; caused severe environmental damage and deaths of marine and coastal wildlife and plants; effects of spill

(*continued*)

Table 4–1: (continued)

Event	Location	Type of Hazard	Description and Impacts
			still evident today; Court ordered Exxon to pay $1 billion in damages used for clean-up and restoration; disaster led to passage of federal Oil Pollution Act; Captain fined & sentenced to community service.
Three-Mile Island Nuclear Accident March 28, 1979	Near Middletown, Pennsylvania	Nuclear Power Plant Accident	Equipment malfunction, design problems, and worker errors led to partial meltdown of reactor core; small off-site release of radioactivity; no deaths; brought about sweeping changes in response training, engineering, radiation protection; caused U.S. Nuclear Regulatory Agency to tighten regulatory oversight. Today reactor is permanently shutdown and de-fueled.
White supremacist attack on 16th Street Baptist Church 1963	Birmingham, Alabama	Domestic Terrorism/Civil Unrest	4 teenaged African American girls killed in bomb attack of church; 23 injured; riots and fires followed in city; 1 suspect acquitted of murder in 1963, re-tried in 1977, found guilty, and sentenced to life in prison; 2 more suspects tried in 2000, 1 convicted.
Great Fire of Chicago October 1871	Chicago	Accidental Fire	Small barn fire turned into raging conflagration; 300 dead; 18,000 buildings destroyed; 1/3 of population made homeless; city rebuilt in 2 years.

SELF-CHECK

- Define **technological hazards, terrorism, civil unrest,** and **all-hazards approach.**
- Explain the difference between man-made and natural hazards.
- Give an example of three types of man-made hazards using the list of past U.S. events.

4.2 Terrorism

The term *terrorism* refers to intentional, criminal, malicious acts. It involves the use of force or violence against persons or property in violation of criminal laws for the purposes of intimidation, coercion, or ransom. Terrorists often use threats to create fear among the public, to try to convince citizens that their government is powerless to prevent terrorism, and to get immediate publicity for their causes.

4.2.1 Defining Terrorism

There is no single, universally accepted definition of *terrorism*, and the term is interpreted in many ways. However, certain criteria are common to most definitions of terrorism:

- ▲ **Violence:** Terrorism generally involves violence and/or the threat of violence.
- ▲ **Target:** Terrorism usually entails the deliberate and specific selection of civilians as direct targets.
- ▲ **Objectives:** Terrorism usually is an attempt to provoke fear and intimidation in the main target audience, to attract wide publicity, and cause public shock and outrage.
- ▲ **Motives:** Terrorist activities may be intended to achieve political or religious goals; terrorists who act as mercenaries may also be motivated by personal gain. Historical grievances, retaliation for past actions, and specific demands such as ransom or policy change may also be motivating factors.
- ▲ **Perpetrators:** War crimes and crimes against humanity are not usually included in the definition of terrorism because these are acts carried out by or on behalf of a government. Overt government oppression of its own civilians (e.g., the Holocaust) is not usually considered terrorism. However, state-sponsored terrorism does involve government support of terrorism carried out in another country.
- ▲ **Legitimacy:** Most definitions of terrorism require that the act be unlawful.

In the United States, the official definition of terrorism as stated in the U.S. Code of Federal Regulations is "…the unlawful use of force and violence against persons or property to intimidate or coerce a government, the civilian population, or any segment thereof, in furtherance of political or social objectives."[2]

4.2.2 Types of Terrorism

The Federal Bureau of Investigation (FBI) characterizes terrorism as either domestic or international, depending upon the origin, base, and objectives of the terrorist actor or group.

- ▲ **Domestic terrorism** involves groups or individuals whose terrorist activities are directed at elements of our government or population without foreign direction.
- ▲ **International terrorism** involves groups or individuals whose terrorist activities are foreign-based and/or directed by countries or groups outside the United States or whose activities cross international boundaries.

The 1995 bombing of the Murrah Federal Building in Oklahoma City was an act of domestic terrorism, while the attacks of September 11, 2001, were international in nature.

Within these broad categories, there are many different forms of terrorist activity. In the United States, most terrorist incidents have involved small extremist groups who use terrorism to carry out a specific agenda. There is often overlap between the various motives and methods of these different types of terrorism, and some sorts of terrorism cannot be easily classified into any one group. The following list includes some of the different types of terrorism.

- ▲ **Nationalist:** A type of terrorism that involves actors trying to form an independent state in opposition to an occupying or imperial force. Examples: Lebanese, Palestinian, and Northern Ireland terrorist activities.
- ▲ **Religious:** The use of violence to further what the actors see as a divinely commanded purpose or objective. Examples: Christian, Jewish, Hindu, Islamic, and other world religion terrorist groups, often fanatical in nature.
- ▲ **Left-wing:** Terrorism growing from social movements on the left. Example: Symbionese Liberation Army of the 1970s.
- ▲ **Right-wing:** The use of terrorist tactics to eliminate threats to what is seen as traditional values or politically right-wing power structures. Examples: Neo-Nazi, white supremacist, anti-communist groups.
- ▲ **State:** Can include terrorist activities carried out, subsidized, or sanctioned by a national government or its proxy.
- ▲ **Racist:** Terrorism related to issues of race or ethnicity; may be carried out by racist, xenophobic, or fascist groups. Examples: Ku Klux Klan, Neo-Nazis, white supremacist groups.

▲ **Narco-Terrorism:** Attempts by narcotics traffickers to influence/intimidate government policies, law enforcement, or the justice system.

▲ **Anarchist:** Terrorism intended to carry out the goals of anarchist groups or the elimination of all forms of government.

▲ **Political:** Terrorism used to influence socio-political events, issues, or policies.

▲ **Eco-Terrorism:** Acts of sabotage, vandalism, property damage, or intimidation in the name of environmental interests; often target large corporations seen as exploiting or otherwise damaging natural resources. Examples: EarthFirst!, Animal Liberation Front, Earth Liberation Front.

4.2.3 Terrorism Tactics and Weapons

Terrorist attacks are conducted through a variety of means. The level of organization, technological expertise, and financial backing of the terrorist group often determines the type of technique used. The nature of the political, social, or religious issue that motivates the attack, as well as the points of weakness in the terrorist's target also factor into the type of tactic employed. In the United States, the most frequent terrorist technique has been the use of bombs. Other possibilities include attacks on transportation facilities, communication or utilities networks, or incidents using chemical or biological contaminants.

The following tactics and weapons are among those that may be used to carry out acts of terrorism:

▲ Conventional bomb
▲ Improvised explosive device
▲ Biological agent
▲ Chemical agent
▲ Nuclear bomb
▲ Radiological agent
▲ Arson/incendiary attack
▲ Armed attack
▲ Cyber-terrorism
▲ Agri-terrorism
▲ Hijacking
▲ Car bomb
▲ Suicide bomb
▲ Kidnapping
▲ Assassination
▲ Sabotage

FOR EXAMPLE

Terrorism in the United States

Before the September 11, 2001, attacks in New York and at the Pentagon, most terrorist incidents in the United States were bombing attacks, involving detonated and un-detonated explosive devices, tear gas, and pipe and firebombs. The anthrax events of 2001 were one of the first known widespread incidents of terrorism that did not involve explosives.

4.2.4 Biological and Chemical Weapons

▲ **Biological agents** are infectious organisms or toxins that are used to produce illness or death in people, livestock, and crops.

▲ **Chemical agents** are poisonous gases, liquids, or solids that have toxic effects on people, plants, or animals. Some chemical agents are odorless and tasteless, making them difficult to detect.

Biological agents can be dispersed as aerosols or airborne particles, and can be used by terrorists to contaminate food or water supplies. Depending on the type of agent used, contamination can be spread via wind and/or water. Light to moderate winds will disburse biological agents, but high winds can break up aerosol clouds. Infection can also be spread through human or animal contact. Sunlight can destroy many, but not all, forms of bacteria and viruses.

Severity of injuries from chemical agents depends on the type and amount used, as well as the duration of exposure. Air temperature can affect the evaporation of chemical aerosols, and ground temperature can affect evaporation of liquids. Rainfall can dilute and disperse chemical agents but can also spread contamination. Wind can disperse vapors but can also cause the target area to be dynamic.

The effects of biological and chemical agents can be either instantaneous or delayed up to several hours or several days. Some biological agents can pose a threat for years depending upon conditions. Biological and chemical weapons have been used primarily to terrorize unprotected civilian populations in other countries, but have not been used on a large scale within the United States.

4.2.5 Impacts of Terrorism

The effects of terrorism can vary significantly from injuries and loss of life to property damage and disruptions in services such as electricity, water supply, food supply, public transportation, and communications. Terrorists often seek visible targets where they can avoid detection before or after an attack, such as international airports, large cities, major international events, resorts, and high-profile landmarks.

When terrorism strikes, communities can receive assistance from state and federal agencies operating within the existing Integrated Emergency Management System (IEMS). FEMA is the lead federal agency for supporting state and local responses to the consequences of terrorist attacks.

FEMA's role in managing terrorism includes both antiterrorism and counterterrorism activities.

▲ **Antiterrorism** refers to defensive measures used to reduce the vulnerability of people and property to terrorist acts.

▲ **Counterterrorism** includes offensive measures taken to prevent, deter, and respond to terrorism.

Within the emergency management arena, antiterrorism is a hazard mitigation activity and counterterrorism falls within the scope of preparedness, response, and recovery. The **Emergency Management Assistance Compact (EMAC)** is a congressionally ratified organization that provides form and structure to interstate mutual aid. Through EMAC, a disaster-impacted state can request and receive assistance from other member states quickly and efficiently, resolving two key issues upfront: liability and reimbursement.[3]

SELF-CHECK

- Define **domestic terrorism, international terrorism, chemical agents, biological agents, antiterrorism,** and **counterterrorism.**
- Name the six criteria common to most acts of terrorism.
- List some of the different types of terrorism.
- Compare biological agents and chemical agents.

4.3 Civil Unrest

Civil unrest is a phrase used to describe a variety of events that can cause disorder and disruption to the normal functions of a community. Incidents of civil unrest often involve violence, looting, vandalism, sabotage, destruction of property, threats, and other forms of anti-social behavior. Civil unrest can occur as an unexpected result of a planned event (for example, a parade or rally), when actions of event participants do not follow the normal planned or authorized course. It can also occur when witnesses to the event react with violence or other disorderly conduct. Civil unrest can also occur as a spontaneous reaction to an external catalyst.

FOR EXAMPLE

Protesting the World Trade Organization

On November 30, 1999, a crowd of 40,000 took to the streets of Seattle, Washington to protest meetings of the World Trade Organization. Many of the protestors intended to conduct non-violent methods of protest, but splinter groups engaged in property destruction and vandalism. Protestors chained themselves together, as police fired tear gas, rubber bullets, and pepper spray into the crowd. The mayor of Seattle imposed a curfew and created a 50-block "No-Protest Zone." The protests caused $2-3 million dollars in property damage, city merchants lost approximately $9-18 million in sales, and further losses in the tourism and travel industries were reported for months following the incident.

4.3.1 Race Riots

A **race riot** is an outbreak of violent civil unrest in which issues of race are a key factor. Such riots often involve tensions between racial or ethnic groups and law enforcement agents who are seen as unfairly targeting these minorities. Socio-economic conditions are an underlying cause of many race riots. Racial profiling, police brutality, institutional racism, racially determined policies and politics, and issues of racial and ethnic identity are often common factors among race riots. Urban renewal (such as the construction or removal of publicly subsidized housing, slum or ghetto improvements, and the elimination of blight) has also been cited as a contributing cause of race riots in the United States.

Race riots in the United States have included attacks on Irish Catholics and other early immigrants in the nineteenth century, massacres of black people in the period following Reconstruction, and uprisings in African-American communities such as the 1968 riots following the assassination of Martin Luther King, Jr.

4.3.2 Looting

Looting is the plundering, stealing, or otherwise taking of valuables or other goods triggered by a change in authority or the absence of authority. Lapses in authority can be the result of war, natural disaster, riot, terrorist attack, or other disruption to normal conditions of law and order.

Looting often occurs as a result of mob mentality—when large crowds participate in an unlawful activity, the barriers of personal responsibility and accountability can break down. Some participants justify their own looting as a way to prevent goods from being wasted or stolen by others. In the case of natural disasters, looters may be residents of the disaster site whose belongings have been damaged or destroyed. Disaster victims are often prompted by survival instinct to loot necessities such as food, water, clothing, and medical supplies.

FOR EXAMPLE

Looting in the Wake of Hurricane Katrina

Following Hurricane Katrina in 2005, the media reported many incidents of looting in the devastated city of New Orleans. Many of the looters were victims of the disaster who took food, diapers, bottled water, shovels, chain saws, and other necessities for survival from grocery and hardware stores. Doctors were seen retrieving medical supplies under armed police escort from flooded pharmacies, while police were forced to siphon gas out of abandoned vehicles in order to operate squad cars. Other residents were filmed taking electronics, alcohol, clothing, and similar luxury items from abandoned shops. Civilian and military authorities, who were also responsible for emergency rescue operations of people in danger, were overwhelmed by the breakdown in security and unable to maintain order in many areas of the city.

Often, extraordinary measures are employed to quell looting during a crisis. Looters may be summarily shot by police, army personnel, or property owners. Extraordinary measures and a show of force are often authorized to discourage further looting and prevent conditions from escalating into full-fledge riots.

SELF-CHECK

- Define **race riot** and **looting**.
- Cite two examples of civil unrest from U.S. history.
- Discuss what happens to turn an assembly of people into an event of civil unrest.

4.4 Technological Hazards

From industrial chemicals and nuclear materials to household detergents and air fresheners, hazardous materials are part of the modern world. These materials are used to make our water safe to drink, generate energy, provide fuel for transportation cars, increase farm production, simplify household chores, aid in medical care and research, and act as key components in many of the products we use every day. As many as 500,000 products pose physical or health hazards and can be defined as *hazardous chemicals*. Each year, more than 1000 new synthetic chemicals are introduced in the United States.[4] Technological hazard incidents occur when hazardous materials are used, transported, or disposed of improperly, and the hazardous substances are released into the community.

4.4.1 What Makes Hazardous Materials Hazardous?

Hazardous materials are substances that, because of their chemical or toxic nature, pose a potential risk to life or health. Many of the properties of chemicals that make them valuable to us, such as their ability to kill dangerous organisms in water and pests on crops, pose a hazard to humans and to the environment if the chemicals are mishandled. Hazardous materials come in the form of explosives, flammable and combustible substances, poisons, and radioactive materials, and can affect urban, suburban, and rural areas.

Hazardous materials in various forms can cause death; serious injury; long-lasting health effects; and damage to buildings, homes, and other property. Many products containing hazardous chemicals are used and stored in homes routinely. These products are also shipped daily on the nation's highways, railroads, waterways, and through pipelines.

Definitions of Hazardous Materials

There are many definitions and descriptive names that are used for the term *hazardous material*, each of which depends on the nature of the problem being addressed. Unfortunately, there is no one list or definition that covers all terms. The United States agencies involved, as well as state and local governments, have different purposes for regulating hazardous materials that, under certain circumstances, pose a risk to the public or the environment. The list that follows includes some of the definitions used by federal agencies.

▲ **Hazardous Materials:** The United States Department of Transportation (DOT) uses the term *hazardous materials* to cover eight separate hazard classes, some of which have subcategories called classifications, and a ninth class covering Other Regulated Materials (ORM). DOT includes in its regulations hazardous substances and hazardous wastes as ORM-E (Other Regulated Materials-Environmental), both of which are regulated by the EPA, if their inherent properties would not otherwise be covered.

▲ **Hazardous Substances:** EPA uses the term hazardous substance for the chemicals that, if released into the environment above a certain amount, must be reported, and, depending on the threat to the environment, federal involvement in handling the incident can be authorized.[5]

▲ **Extremely Hazardous Substances:** EPA uses the term extremely hazardous substance for the chemicals that must be reported to the appropriate authorities if released above the threshold reporting quantity. Each substance has a threshold reporting quantity.[6]

▲ **Toxic Chemicals:** EPA uses the term toxic chemical for chemicals whose total emissions or releases must be reported annually by owners and operators of certain facilities that manufacture, process, or otherwise use a listed toxic chemical.[7]

▲ **Hazardous Wastes:** EPA uses the term hazardous wastes for chemicals that are regulated under the Resource, Conservation and Recovery Act[8]. Hazardous wastes in transportation are regulated by DOT. [9]

▲ **Hazardous Chemicals:** OSHA uses the term hazardous chemical to denote any chemical that would be a risk to employees if exposed in the work place. Hazardous chemicals cover a broader group of chemicals than the other chemical lists.

▲ **Hazardous Substances:** OSHA uses the term hazardous substance in regulation that covers emergency response.[10] Hazardous substances, as used by OSHA, cover every chemical regulated by both DOT and EPA.

Symptoms of Toxic Poisoning

Some of the symptoms that people may exhibit after being exposed to certain hazardous materials include:

▲ Difficulty breathing
▲ Irritation of the eyes, skin, throat
▲ Irritation in the respiratory tract
▲ Changes in skin color
▲ Headaches or blurred vision
▲ Dizziness
▲ Clumsiness or lack of coordination
▲ Cramps or diarrhea
▲ Nausea or vomiting

4.4.2 Sources of Hazardous Materials

Many businesses and facilities throughout the United States use and store hazardous materials. Chemical manufacturers and refineries are among the industries that are well recognized as hazardous materials sites; however, many other locations of hazardous materials are also present in our communities. For example, the food processing industry may have large quantities of hazardous materials such as ammonia in the refrigeration systems of their plants, warehouses, distribution centers, and cargo carriers. Local drinking water systems, sewage treatment plants, and public swimming pools also store toxic chemicals that are used to kill dangerous bacteria in the water.

Many retail commercial sites also use, store, and sell chemicals and toxic substances. Hazardous materials can be found in hardware stores, agriculture supply centers, garden shops, and in pest control businesses. Many small operations, including service stations, dry cleaners, and garages, also routinely use hazardous materials in their daily operations. Hospitals, clinics, and research universities store and use a range of radioactive, combustible, and flammable materials. In all, varying quantities of hazardous materials are manufactured, used, or stored at an estimated 4.5 million facilities in the United States. In addition, there are approximately 30,000 hazardous materials waste sites in the country.

The presence of hazardous chemicals does not necessarily mean that a community is at risk for a hazardous materials incident. These chemicals can be, and usually are, handled safely. Many of these substances pose little risk to the community because, even if spilled, they will not migrate beyond the facility; they may, however, pose risks to workers at the facility. Some chemicals are hazardous only after prolonged exposure. Most of these chemicals are dangerous after prolonged exposure above certain concentrations. For some chemicals, government agencies such as the EPA set standards detailing how much of the chemical can be released safely to the air or water per hour or day.

OSHA has set permissible exposure levels for workers for many chemicals. OSHA requires that **Material Safety Data Sheets** (MSDS)[11] be available to employees for potentially harmful substances handled in the workplace under "Employee right to know" rules. OSHA's Hazard Communication Standard (HCS) specifies certain information that must be included on MSDSs. MSDSs provide useful information regarding acceptable levels of toxin exposure, including data regarding the properties of a particular substance, the chemical's risks, safety, and impact on the environment. An important component of workplace safety, the MSDS is intended to provide workers and emergency personnel with procedures for handling or working with that substance in a safe manner and includes information such as physical data (melting point, boiling point, flash point, etc.), toxicity, health effects, first aid, reactivity, storage, disposal, protective equipment, and spill handling procedures.

MSDS information may also include instructions for the safe use of the material; however, the MSDS for a substance is not primarily intended for use by the general consumer, focusing instead on the hazards of working with the material in an occupational fashion. For example, an MSDS for a cleaning solution is not highly pertinent to someone who uses a can of the cleaner once a year, but is extremely important to someone who does this in a confined space for 40 hours a week.[12]

FOR EXAMPLE

We're Not Flushing Away Our Problems

In an average city of 100,000 residents, 23.5 tons of toilet bowl cleaner, 13.5 tons of liquid household cleaners, and 3.5 tons of motor oil are discharged into city drains *each month*. Many of these substances eventually enter our water supply system.[13]

- Define **hazardous material**.
- Explain how a hazardous material becomes a technological hazard.
- List five symptoms of toxic poisoning.
- Name the federal agency that sets safety regulations for workers exposed to chemicals.
- Discuss the various sources of hazardous materials in a typical community.

4.5 Community Impacts from Technological Hazards

Technological hazards can occur at any time without warning. Even if hazardous materials are handled and used safely, they may be of concern if stored improperly or during an emergency such as a fire. Hazardous materials can enter a community during any stage of the materials' life cycle, including production, storage, transportation, use, and disposal.

4.5.1 Transportation Accidents

Communities and residences located near facilities that handle hazardous materials are considered at higher risk of experiencing a hazardous materials incident. However, hazardous materials are transported regularly over our highways and by rail, and if the materials are released during a traffic or train accident they can spread quickly to any community. Oil tankers and other large supply ships frequently travel along our coastlines and through our rivers and the Great Lakes, and an accidental spill can easily spread petrochemicals and other hazardous substances along the shoreline for many miles from the original leak. Human error is the cause of most transportation incidents involving the release of hazardous materials.

4.5.2 Leaks During Storage and Disposal

There are a number of federal and state regulations that must be met for the safe and proper storage of hazardous chemicals and materials. Chemical storage buildings must be designed to contain liquid spills, leaks, vapors, and explosions to minimize risk to workers in the facility or to the environment. Chemical storage buildings in particular must be designed to prevent the leaking of liquids into the environment. Chemical storage buildings are often constructed with steel grates and sumps in the floor of the building to collect and contain spilled hazardous chemicals. The building might also have partitions to segregate different substances.

Despite the rules and regulations imposed by the EPA, DOT, OSHA, and numerous state agencies, leaks, spills, and other accidental releases from storage facilities have occurred. There is the potential for leaks and spills to go undetected for weeks, months, and even years, especially when storage containers are buried underground. Undetected leaks can cause the substances to leach further into the soil or enter groundwater, endangering to nearby residents.

Hazardous waste disposal sites are heavily regulated by local, state, and federal authorities. Most disposal sites are located in areas removed from human habitation, although problems arise when community growth and development sprawl into areas where hazardous materials have been deposited. Most disposal sites must be lined with materials that are suitable to contain the hazardous wastes deposited there in order to prevent leaching into the surrounding environment. However, many communities have experienced problems with leaking, abandoned, or improperly maintained and monitored sites.

4.5.3 Nuclear Accidents

Nuclear power plants use the heat generated from nuclear fission in a contained environment to convert water to steam, which powers generators to produce electricity. Nuclear power plants operate in most states in the country and produce about 20% of the nation's power. Nearly 3 million Americans live within 10 miles of an operating nuclear power plant.

Although the construction and operation of these facilities are closely monitored and regulated by the U.S. Nuclear Regulatory Commission (NRC), accidents are possible. An accident could result in dangerous levels of radiation that could affect the health and safety of the public living near the nuclear power plant.

Local and state governments, federal agencies, and the electric utilities have emergency response plans prepared in the event of a nuclear power plant incident. The plans define two "emergency planning zones." One zone covers an area within a 10-mile radius of the plant, where people could be harmed by direct radiation exposure. The second zone covers a broader area, usually up to a 50-mile radius from the plant, where radioactive materials could contaminate water supplies, food crops, and livestock.

The most significant danger from an accident at a nuclear power plant is exposure to radiation. This exposure could be caused by the release of radioactive material from the plant into the environment, characterized by a plume (cloud-like formation) of radioactive gases and particles. Wind speed, wind direction, precipitation, and the amount of radiation released from the plant are all factors in determining the area that could be affected. The major hazards to people in the vicinity of the plume are radiation exposure to the body from the cloud and particles deposited on the ground, inhalation of radioactive materials, and ingestion of radioactive materials.[14]

FOR EXAMPLE

Three Mile Island Nuclear Reactor Accident

The accident at the Three Mile Island Unit 2 (TMI-2) nuclear power plant near Middletown, Pennsylvania, on March 28, 1979, was the most serious in U.S. commercial nuclear power plant operating history, even though it led to no deaths or injuries to plant workers or members of the nearby community. But it brought about sweeping changes involving emergency response planning, reactor operator training, human factors engineering, radiation protection, and many other areas of nuclear power plant operations. It also caused the U.S. NRC to tighten and heighten its regulatory oversight.

The Three Mile Island Nuclear Generating Station sits on an artificial island in the Susquehanna River in Dauphin County, Pennsylvania. The accident, which consisted of a partial core meltdown, was caused by a combination of personnel error, design deficiencies, and component failures. The accident unfolded over the course of five tense days, as a number of agencies at the federal, state, and local level attempted to diagnose the problem (the full details of the accident were not discovered until much later) and decide whether or not the on-going accident required a full evacuation of the population. In the end, the reactor was brought under control. No identifiable injuries due to radiation exposure occurred, but the accident had serious economic and public relations consequences, and the cleanup process was slow and costly. It also furthered a major decline in the public popularity of nuclear power, exemplifying for many the worst fears of nuclear technology, and, until the Chernobyl accident seven years later, was considered the world's worst civilian nuclear accident.[15]

FOR EXAMPLE

Flooded Hog Lagoons

When Hurricane Floyd struck eastern North Carolina in September 1999, as many as 50 hog waste lagoons, many of them several acres in size, were inundated by floodwaters. Five lagoons breached, and waterborne animal waste produced nutrient pollution and raised the potential for exposure to pathogens and the risk of disease.

HURRICANE KATRINA RELEASES HAZARDOUS CONTAMINANTS INTO THE ENVIRONMENT

Many structures related to the energy industry are located in the coastal areas of the Gulf of Mexico. This includes multiple offshore oil and gas exploration sites, 42,000 oil and gas wells, 1806 miles of navigation channels, 4200 miles of pipelines, and several of the United State's largest oil refineries.[16] When Hurricane Katrina struck this region in 2005, many of these oil refining and exploration activities were forced to a standstill. Katrina was responsible for flooded refineries, broken pipelines, and 13 severely damaged or destroyed oil rigs along the coastlines of Louisiana, Mississippi, and Alabama.[17] One of these offshore rigs actually washed up near the beach on Dauphin Island, Alabama, and several others were completely dislodged.[18]

According to the National Oceanic and Atmospheric Administration (NOAA) Office of Response and Restoration, the destruction of the oil refining infrastructure led to the release of an estimated 7 to 8 million gallons of oil into Gulf waters.[19] Over 40% of the nation's fish and shellfish are harvested in this area, and a large number of migrating birds and endangered species depend upon the habitats that were affected by the oil spills. This event is not only an ecological disaster of immense proportions, but is also an economic disaster for the fishing industry, recreation and tourism businesses, and local communities (see Figure 4-1). The impacts of these toxic substances may also pose a serious threat to the health of human populations in the area.

Efforts to assess the levels of environmental contamination due to Katrina's destruction of petrochemical facilities in the Gulf region have been undertaken jointly by the NOAA, the EPA, the United States Geological Survey (USGS), the United States Food and Drug Administration (USFDA), state governments and others. One such study led by the NOAA Center for Coastal Monitoring and Assessment National Status and Trends Program produced preliminary results of human health risks following Hurricane Katrina.[20] Field samples were taken one month after the hurricane at 20 different sites. Each of these sites has records on file that assess contaminants over the last 20 years for various chemicals that concentrate in the tissues of oysters (under the NOAA Mussel Watch Project). This study found 120 contaminants in the oysters and sediments measured. Trace elements (metals) in general had higher concentrations when compared to the 20-year record for each site, and some of these metals were at record high levels, including chromium, copper, iron, manganese, nickel, and selenium, substances known or suspected to have toxic effects on organisms.

Efforts to clean up the debris, oil spills, and other man-made contaminants released by Hurricane Katrina will continue for many years to come. As researchers gather more data on the environmental impacts of the storm, additional sources of contamination and pollution will undoubtedly be

Figure 4-1

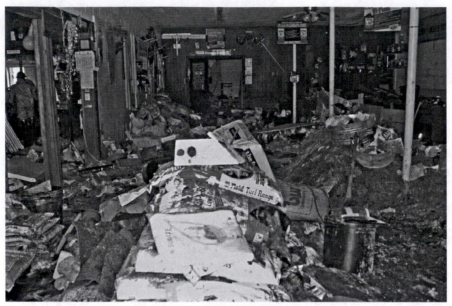

Toxic wastes, such as these exposed in the aftermath of Hurricane Katrina, pose a threat to the environment and to human health.

discovered. Contamination sources that may come to light after further study include hydrocarbon releases in the Mississippi, contents of storm surge waters, seepage from sunken vessels, and leaking hazardous materials containers. These unknown sources will undoubtedly contribute to the problems that have arisen due to the toxins and pathogens contained in the flood waters of New Orleans that have been pumped out of the city and released into the surrounding environment.

4.5.4 Releases During Natural Hazard Events

Natural hazard events, including hurricanes, tornadoes, floods, and earthquakes, have often triggered technological hazards. Natural hazard events can rupture pipelines, spark fires, dislodge tanks and storage containers, and cause safety measures to malfunction.

The occurrence of a technological hazard during a natural hazard event is often called a **secondary hazard,** because it occurs as a result of the primary natural event. Sometimes, the release of hazardous materials during a flood or other natural hazard causes more damage to the environment and surrounding community than the original event itself.

4.5.5 Dangers Lurking at Home

Despite the dangers of chemical leaks and accidents during transportation, storage, and disposal, most victims of chemical accidents are injured at home. These incidents usually result from a lack of awareness or carelessness in using flammable or combustible materials. Local poison control centers are set up nationwide to deal with accidental ingestion or spills of many types of hazardous materials; many of the calls received by these centers involve small children who have gained access to improperly stored hazardous materials such as cleaning solutions, antifreeze, and other substances that can be fatal if swallowed or touched.

Hazardous materials can also be released during routine household chores. Residents may not realize that flushing cleaning solutions and other household substances down the toilet or washing them down the sink allows these dangerous elements to enter our environment directly. The simple act of hosing down a driveway can wash oil, gasoline, and other harmful substances into the local stormwater and drainage systems, where it flows into our rivers and streams and eventually enters our drinking water supplies.

SELF-CHECK

- Define **secondary hazard**.
- List three ways that hazardous incidents can occur during transportation.
- Explain two ways that groundwater can be affected by hazardous materials.
- Cite the hazardous risk associated with nuclear power.
- Give an example of how a natural hazard could trigger a technological hazard.

4.6 Public Perception of Man-Made Hazards

One of the main differences in dealing with man-made disasters as opposed to natural disasters is that the majority of people have not had a personal experience with a man-made event. Although we are keenly aware of the increase in terrorist activities directed against the United States and have some knowledge of the number of industrial hazards located near population centers, the public's perception of the actual degree of risk that we face from terrorism and technological accidents varies widely.

There are many factors that affect how members of the public view the possibility and consequences of man-made hazards in their community.

4.6.1 Media Coverage

The media plays a vital role in shaping our attitude about and perception of terrorism as well as other man-made hazards. We live in an age of near-instant communication. We can mark some of the most dramatic events in our minds because we have seen them on television—sometimes during live coverage. The images that the media chooses to show the public, as well as the news coverage that accompanies those images, directly affect the way we think about man-made hazards that have occurred. Often, the most startling and graphic images are those that sell the most news, and in a for-profit news industry, we may be subjected to the most graphic images of all. This is not to say that these are not newsworthy images, but we must remember that the public's knowledge is often limited to media that is currently available.

4.6.2 Individual Experience

A second element that factors into the public perception of risk involves an individual's experience with various hazard events. Since the time of the Civil War, relatively few people in the United States have actually lived through a man-made hazard event, either intentional or accidental. This is in huge contrast with natural hazard events, where untold thousands of people have at one time or another personally experienced a flood, earthquake, severe winter storm, tornado, hurricane, or other type of natural hazard. Natural disasters in this country cause fewer deaths or serious injuries than in other parts of the world (although Hurricane Katrina in 2005 was a tragic exception to this national

---

FOR EXAMPLE

Watching the Twin Towers on Live Television

The 24-hour news cycle portrays vivid images around the clock, often in real-time as events are unfolding. Repetitive images of hijacked planes impacting the Twin Towers in New York City on September 11, 2001, provided Americans an opportunity to witness one of the most shocking events in our nation's history as that history was being made. These images will be forever seared into our collective consciousness. The terrorist attacks of 9/11 were all the more shocking because they came "like a bolt from the blue."[21] Even after the World Trade Center bombing of 1993, "most Americans did not know of the gathering wave of extreme religious hatred that was fast morphing into a killer event."[22]

average). But property damage from natural hazards is extremely common, and the costs of disasters from natural hazards have risen dramatically over the past few decades. In contrast, there are many fewer property owners who have been affected by a man-made hazard. Interestingly, this reality does not factor into the perception of risk that many people associate with man-made hazards.[23]

4.6.3 A Range of Strong Responses

Because the United States has a relatively short history of man-made hazards, discussions on this subject may be characterized by elements of uncertainty and even fear. Planners and emergency managers who work with the public must realize that there could be strong personal responses as people try to grapple with the idea of the possibility of a terrorist attack or technological hazard. New issues may arise that do not come up when dealing with natural hazards, such as concerns over security, access to information, and civil liberties.[24]

To gain public support for efforts to mitigate and prepare for man-made hazards, emergency managers and planners must be prepared to educate officials, citizens, and the private sector about the hazards that may affect the community and about the prevention and mitigation activities that can help address them. A realistic, comprehensive picture of hazard possibilities is essential, without overstating or inflating the risk, nor underestimating or devaluing the possibilities.

4.6.4 Mitigating and Preparing for Man-Made Hazards

We are not powerless in the face of the many man-made hazards that face our communities. We may not be able to prevent all acts of terrorism or technological accidents from happening, but we can make sure that the possibility of an attack or accident is reduced, and we can take steps to reduce losses by protecting people and the built environment. In this way, our approach to man-made hazards is similar to our approach to dealing with natural hazards. A resilient community is one that realizes that many of these events cannot be stopped, but that action can be taken today to prevent a disaster in the future.

The process of mitigating hazards before they become disasters is similar for both natural and man-made events. Whether we are dealing with natural disasters, threats of terrorism, or hazardous materials incidents, we use a four-step process:

Step 1: Identify and organize resources.
Step 2: Conduct a risk or threat assessment and estimate potential losses.
Step 3: Identify mitigation actions that will reduce the effects of the hazards and create a strategy to place them in priority order.
Step 4: Implement the actions, evaluate the results, and keep the plan up to date.

This step-by-step process is known as mitigation planning, and we will discuss it at length in later chapters.

SELF-CHECK

- Describe the role of the media today in the public's perception of man-made disasters.
- Compare the fear factor of a hurricane versus that of a terrorist attack.
- Identify the four steps of a mitigation planning process.

SUMMARY

Although this country has experienced relatively few man-made hazards, we must be prepared to cope with both accidental and intentional man-made threats. This chapter explains the ways in which natural hazards and man-made hazards differ, but also how emergency managers can approach both effectively. Antiterrorism and counterterrorism activities are at work to reduce the impact of terrorism on our country. The chapter discusses the part that acts of civil unrest such as riots, demonstrations, and looting play in an emergency management system. Hazardous materials are an integral part of life today, but our goal is to keep them from entering our communities in a hazardous event. Finally, the chapter examines the public's changing perception of man-made hazards and what can be done to address fears and concerns.

KEY TERMS

All-hazards approach	A method for dealing with both natural and man-made hazards.
Antiterrorism	Defensive measures used to reduce the vulnerability of people and property to terrorist acts.
Biological agent	Infectious organisms or toxins that are used to produce illness or death in people.
Chemical agent	Poisonous gases, liquids, or solids that have toxic effects on people, plants, or animals.
Civil unrest	Unexpected or planned events that can cause disorder and disruption to a community.

Counterterrorism	Offensive measures taken to prevent, deter, and respond to terrorism.
Domestic terrorism	Groups or individuals whose activities are directed at elements of U.S. government or without foreign direction.
Emergency Management Assistance Compact (EMAC)	A congressionally ratified organization that provides form and structure to interstate mutual aid.
Hazardous material	Chemical or toxic substances that pose a potential threat or risk to life or health.
International terrorism	Acts carried out by groups or individuals whose activities are foreign-based and/or directed by countries or groups outside the United States, or whose activities cross international boundaries.
Looting	Plundering or stealing of valuables or other goods triggered by a change in authority or the absence of authority.
Material Safety Data Sheet (MSDS)	Provides useful information regarding acceptable levels of toxin exposure, including data regarding the properties of a particular substance, the chemical's risks, safety, and impact on the environment; OSHA requires that MSDS be available to employees for potentially harmful substances handled in the workplace.
Race riot	Outbreak of violent civil unrest in which race issues are a key factor.
Secondary hazard	A technological hazard that occurs during, often as a result of, a primary natural event.
Technological hazard	Incident that occurs when hazardous materials are used, transported, or disposed of improperly and the materials are released into a community.
Terrorism	The unlawful use of force and violence against persons or property to intimidate or coerce a government, the civilian population, or any segment thereof, in furtherance of political or social objectives.

ASSESS YOUR UNDERSTANDING

Go to www.wiley.com/college/schwab to evaluate your knowledge of man-made hazards.

Measure your learning by comparing pre-test and post-test results.

Summary Questions

1. The United States has experienced more natural hazards than man-made hazards. True or False?

2. Which of the following would be an intentional man-made hazard?

   (a) oil spill

   (b) train derailment

   (c) anthrax attack

   (d) fire

3. The all-hazards approach is a way for federal agencies to deal with both man-made and natural hazards. True or False?

4. The Olympic bombing in Atlanta, Georgia, in 1996 was an act of international terrorism. True or False?

5. The riots in Los Angeles in 1992 would be classified as:

   (a) an accident.

   (b) domestic terrorism.

   (c) a demonstration.

   (d) civil unrest.

6. Acts of terrorism combine violence, motives, and a target. True or False?

7. A terrorist act targeting Exxon would most likely be which type of terrorism?

   (a) political

   (b) anarchist

   (c) left-wing

   (d) eco-terrorist

8. Contamination from biological agents can be spread by wind and water. True or False?

9. Antiterrorism involves offensive measures to prevent terrorism. True or False?

10. Civil unrest can take place in which of the following forms?

    (a) looting

    (b) rally

    (c) assembly

    (d) all of the above

11. Dizziness and changes in skin color are possible symptoms of hazardous material exposure. True or False?

12. Which of the following is a technological hazard?
    (a) dry cleaner
    (b) overturned petroleum tanker truck
    (c) train crash
    (d) chlorinated swimming pool

13. The EPA provides standards for chemical use. True or False?

14. The probable cause for most transportation-related technological hazards is
    (a) weather.
    (b) computer failure.
    (c) human error.
    (d) leaks.

15. A technological hazard that is triggered as a result of a natural hazard is a
    (a) secondary hazard.
    (b) train derailment.
    (c) primary hazard.
    (d) disaster.

16. Emergency response plans in the event of a nuclear incident define two different emergency planning zones. True or False?

17. A plume is
    (a) a measurement of radioactivity.
    (b) nuclear energy produced by a nuclear power plant.
    (c) an emergency zone surrounding a nuclear power plant.
    (d) a cloud-like formation of radioactive gases and particles.

18. More U.S. residents have experienced a man-made hazard than a natural hazard. True or False?

19. Man-made hazards are likely to produce a more emotional response than natural hazards. True or False?

Review Questions

1. List three examples of accidental man-made hazards.

2. What are the tools that can be used to predict natural hazards that can't be used to predict man-made hazards?

3. Which agencies can be used as resources for information about man-made hazards?

4. What makes terrorism particularly unpredictable?

5. Why is FEMA encouraging communities to adopt the all-hazards approach?

6. What are some of the criteria that are used to define an act of terrorism?

7. Recall the United States' official definition of terrorism.

8. Is it possible for an international terrorist attack to happen in the United States? Explain.

9. Give three examples of tactics used by terrorists.

10. Describe some of the underlying causes of civil unrest, including race riots and looting.

11. Explain how medical facilities such as hospitals and research labs have contact with hazardous materials.

12. Identify five ways that hazardous materials can enter a community.

13. How do hazardous materials affect a home environment?

14. How has the 24-hour news cycle affected the public's perception of man-made hazards?

Applying This Chapter

1. Man-made hazards are not as predictable as some natural hazards. We can, however, judge some of the risk by the hazards of the past. What, if any, man-made hazards have occurred in your area?

2. How would the all-hazards approach be used differently in New York City vs. tornado-prone Indiana?

3. The media has covered certain measures that some larger cities have taken against terrorism (backpack searches on New York City subways, street closures in Washington, DC). List any potential for terrorist activity in your area and any measures that have been taken to protect against the threat.

4. Imagine that a major public meeting has been scheduled about the proposed construction of a hazardous landfill in your community. You expect the meeting to be particularly emotional. What actions should the meeting's organizers take to ensure a peaceful gathering?

5. Consider the household cleaners and other chemicals in your home. Give three examples of ways that an everyday product could have a hazardous effect on your home or your health.

6. In what ways has your life been affected by man-made hazards? Consider both the direct and indirect impacts.

7. What are some of the factors that influence the public's perception of the level of risk we face from man-made hazards? How can this public perception affect how emergency managers and other professionals carry out mitigation and preparedness activities?

YOU TRY IT

Risk Assessment

As the emergency manager in a mid-sized community, how would you go about determining your community's level of risk from man-made hazards as compared to the risk from natural hazards? What local elements would you assess to make your determination?

Transportation and Technological Hazards

Predict the risk of a technological hazards in your community based on any hazardous materials that are regularly transported through or around the area.

Man-Made Precautions

Defend your city's decision to shut down a chemical plant that has experienced two low-grade hazardous accidents in the past seven years. Who is at risk and from what?

Secondary Hazards Hit Home

Assess the likelihood that a natural hazard could trigger a secondary hazard in your community. Base your assessment on geographic, historic, and other data.

5

HAZARDS MANAGEMENT FRAMEWORK
A Patchwork of Policies, Programs, and Players

Starting Point

Go to www.wiley.com/college/schwab to assess your knowledge of the hazards management framework.
Determine where you need to concentrate your effort.

What You'll Learn in This Chapter

▲ Why land use is an important part of managing hazards
▲ The hierarchy of different government levels involved in hazards management
▲ Ways in which the federal, state, and local governments are involved in hazard areas
▲ Types of regional management
▲ The meaning of property ownership
▲ What land controls mean for landowners
▲ Constitutional limits on public land use controls

After Studying This Chapter, You'll Be Able To

▲ Analyze how a land use management approach to hazard mitigation builds resilient communities
▲ Compare the roles of various stakeholders in building resilient communities
▲ Distinguish between federal, state, and local responsibilities
▲ Examine how regional governments are suited to managing ecosystems
▲ Categorize the rights and duties of private property owners
▲ Apply the Fifth Amendment takings rule to land use regulations
▲ Analyze cases in which government controls overstep private property rights

Goals and Outcomes

▲ Master the terminology, understand the policies, and recognize the tools of hazards management
▲ Plan management jurisdictions based on geographic locations and potential hazards
▲ Select the ways in which the U.S. system of government creates both opportunities and challenges for hazard mitigation
▲ Select ways to collaborate with others in evaluating mitigation issues
▲ Predict how property ownership rights will conflict with emergency management
▲ Evaluate land use decisions made by various levels of government

INTRODUCTION

This chapter introduces the reader to the institutional framework within which all mitigation and preparedness activities take place. The chapter first describes how land use and development are related to hazards, and the effectiveness of land use management for reducing damages from certain types of hazards (i.e., those that can be geographically defined). The chapter then introduces the various levels of government that operate in our federal system and the relationships between them. The chapter also discusses the laws that govern hazards management at the federal, state, and local levels, as well as some of the legal and policy issues surrounding hazards management. The chapter concludes with an overview of the types of land use controls that are available to local governments to reduce vulnerability to hazards, as well as some of the constitutional controls and limitations on government intervention.

5.1 Hazard Mitigation through Land Use Management

The objective of this chapter is to highlight how the "patchwork" system of governance in our country impacts mitigation and preparedness efforts. Much of this chapter focuses on land use and development, and the actors, policies, and laws that control how land is used in our country.

We focus so heavily on land use management because a significant number of the hazards that impact communities most dramatically can be geographically defined through the use of maps and other visual data. The hazards for which mapping is possible allow planners and emergency managers to create and display the spatial relationships between hazard locations and vulnerable structures and populations. This is significant for disaster management purposes because one of the most effective mitigation and preparedness strategies concentrates on keeping people and property out of hazardous areas. For the types of hazards that can be delineated with relative precision—earthquakes and flooding, for example—land management is key to reducing the impacts of those hazards on local communities.

5.1.1 Land Use Mitigation Measures

Table 5-1 lists the types of hazards for which land use management is effective for mitigation purposes and gives samples of the types of mitigation strategies that are available to address the potential effects of these hazards. These mitigation actions are discussed in more detail in Chapters 8 and 12. At this point, we merely introduce the concept of employing land use controls as a viable method of reducing the impacts of geographically-definable hazards. This will provide background information for the emphasis of this chapter, namely, the "patchwork" context within which emergency managers carry out these and other types of strategies.

Table 5-1: Hazards for Which Land Use Control Is Effective

Hazard	*Land Use Method*
Hurricane	Limit development in storm surge areas.
	Set structures back from eroding shorelines.
	Elevate structures to reduce flood damage.
	Enforce strict building codes to withstand high winds.
Flood	Limit development in floodplains.
	Relocate buildings out of floodplains.
	Elevate structures to reduce flood damage.
	Inspect private dams to prevent dambreaks.
Earthquake	Limit development in seismic risk areas.
	Set structures back from fault lines.
	Enforce strict building codes to withstand shaking.
Wildfire	Limit development in urban-wildland interface.
	Require fire-resistant landscaping.
	Enforce building codes for fire-resistant materials.
	Design multiple escape routes from neighborhoods.
	Enforce usage of firebreaks in forests and on ranges.
Landslide	Limit development on steep slopes.
	Require slope stabilization for construction.
	Limit grading of hillsides.
	Require sufficient drainage, retaining walls, etc.

FOR EXAMPLE

Regulating Floodplains Through National Flood Insurance Program

Floodplain regulations are an integral part of the National Flood Insurance Program (NFIP), a federal program that allows residents in participating communities to purchase flood insurance for their homes and businesses. A participating community is one that regulates land uses in designated floodplains by enacting ordinances that require buildings to be elevated above flood levels and prohibits building altogether in the most dangerous flood areas as shown on local flood maps.

Land use controls are not effective for reducing the impacts of all types of hazards, including tornadoes and other high wind events, ice, hail, snowstorms, lightning, frost, and most types of terrorism and technological accidents. Most of these are hazards that cannot be located with enough accuracy to restrict development in places where they occur or which cover too broad an area for a land use approach to be practical. While the impacts of these hazards cannot be mitigated by restricting development, other strategies can be effective for making structures safer, such as adding "safe rooms" to buildings in tornado-prone regions of the country or burying utility lines in regions where snow and ice are common.

SELF-CHECK

- Explain how land use relates to natural hazards.
- List the types of hazards for which land use management is effective.
- Discuss why land use control is less effective for hazards such as hail, frost, and terrorism.

5.2 A Patchwork System of Governance

There is no consistent, over-arching program or policy that dictates how land use is managed and regulated in our system of governance. To provide a context for the discussion about the patchwork nature of hazards management, we begin with a brief overview in modern civics as a way of introducing the various levels of government and the relationships between them.

5.2.1 Civics 101

A hierarchy of levels makes up the federalist system of government in the United States. The relationship among the various levels, however, is not a simple top-down distribution of power. The Tenth Amendment to the U.S. Constitution divides power between the national and state governments: "The powers not delegated to the United States by the Constitution, nor prohibited by it to the States, are reserved to the States respectively, or to the people."

The phrase "**states' rights**" refers to the powers that are reserved for the fifty states by the Constitution.

▲ The national government holds supremacy over all other types of powers, such as matters of interstate commerce, national defense, and foreign affairs.

> ⌐ FOR EXAMPLE ¬
>
> ### Statewide Building Code
>
> In North Carolina, a statewide mandatory building code regulates all construction throughout the state. Local governments in North Carolina have not been granted the power to write their own local construction rules. Therefore, all communities in the state enforce and issue building permits under the same uniform code.

▲ Each state government has its own constitution that lays out how that particular state will govern itself within the limits set by the U.S. Constitution.

▲ Local governments are entities of the state.

All towns, cities, counties, parishes, villages, and other forms of local government are created by the government of the state where they are located and are completely dependent upon the state for their authority. If the state has not delegated specific power to a local government to carry out a particular activity, the local government is not authorized to do so.

At the federal, state, and local levels, governmental functions are separated into three distinct branches: legislative, executive, and judicial. Each branch has its own authority and carries out a unique set of duties. Articles 1, 2, and 3 of the U.S. Constitution delegate the powers to each of the three branches at the federal level; each state constitution makes similar distinctions for that state's governing structure.

Because of the hierarchy of government levels in our federalist system and the separation of powers within each level, intergovernmental relations are a significant factor in determining the manner in which public policy is formulated and public programs are carried out in the United States.[1] The lack of centralization and high degree of pluralism in our country has been referred to as a "patchwork" system of governance.[2]

The hodgepodge nature of this system is particularly evident in the programs and policies that govern hazardous areas at the federal, state, and local levels, and in turn affects how private landowners are permitted to use their property. A fragmented patchwork system infers that there is no overarching, consistent policy for governing land use and development in hazard-prone areas, with the result that programs and policies administered by various agencies can often be redundant or can even work at cross-purposes.

5.2.2 Conflicting Public Policy Goals

Our society has conflicting public policy goals with regard to the management of hazardous lands, which must be managed within the patchwork system of governance. On one hand, our society desires and promotes the economically beneficial use of private property, despite the presence of natural hazards. For instance, property located along the oceanfront may have significant value as residential or investment real estate, despite recurrent hurricanes, erosion, flooding, and other coastal hazards. Land along a riverbank may have important commercial access to resources or navigation, despite the risk of frequent flooding. Moreover, much of the land in the United States has already been developed in economically beneficial ways, and there is a reluctance to restrict or prohibit land uses in these developed areas, even if such regulation may prevent property damage from future hazards.[3]

On the other hand, while public policy calls for allowing land to be put to its best use, we also have a strong tradition of protecting public safety through government intervention. Unwise land use decisions can threaten individual property owners and their neighbors, when, for example, structures are built in floodplains or seismic risk zones. Property that is damaged repeatedly is also a drain on public resources, including government expenditures for emergency rescue and response, temporary housing, infrastructure repair, and disaster assistance payments. These tensions between private property rights, protection of public health and safety, and limits on government spending are caused by and contribute to the patchwork system within which emergency managers carry out their duties and responsibilities with respect to reducing hazard risks and preventing disasters.

In the next section of this chapter, we discuss how the patchwork system of governance plays out at the federal, state, regional, and local levels. We then discuss in more detail how private land ownership fits into the overall framework of hazards management.

SELF-CHECK

- Define **states' rights,** national government, state government, and local government.
- Name the three branches of U.S. government.
- Explain why the U.S. government has been described as a "patchwork" system.

5.3 The Role of Government

Under the American system of governance, the states act as sovereign units, except for certain enumerated powers, including interstate commerce, security of the homeland, and foreign affairs, which are delegated by the Constitution to the national government. The sovereignty of the states is particularly evident in terms of land use controls and regulation of growth and development. Although local governments can only act as subunits of the state government, local communities are also a major player in managing land uses within their jurisdiction. In this section, we review how each level of government—federal, state, and local, as well as regional systems of governance—are involved in hazards management.

5.3.1 Federal Government Involvement in Hazards Management

The bulk of the federal government's domestic activities are accomplished through intergovernmental programs, particularly through government appropriations. The federal government is also involved in hazards management as an owner of significant land holdings. Direct federal intervention in land use regulation takes place only in very limited circumstances. We discuss the federal role in hazards management through the use of appropriations and land ownership in this section. Chapter 6 expands on this discussion, and includes an overview of direct federal control in environmentally sensitive areas as well as an overview of some of the capital improvement programs and taxation policies that facilitate development in hazardous areas.

Federal Appropriations

Involvement of the national government in the affairs of state and local government frequently occurs through appropriations of various kinds, many of which are directed toward public health and safety and homeland security programs. The federal government distributes billions of dollars each year to state and local governments in the form of grants and other types of aid. Some grants are given directly to local governments; other federal funds are administered by the state and then funneled to local communities. Federal grants and other aid packages are often used to secure the cooperation of state and local governments through

---

FOR EXAMPLE

Disaster Mitigation Act of 2000 Planning Criteria

Under the Disaster Mitigation Act (DMA) of 2000, Congress requires state and local governments to create and adopt a hazard mitigation plan in order to receive disaster-related funds from a variety of federal programs. DMA regulations establish criteria that must be met for a state or local mitigation plan to be approved by the Federal Emergency Management Agency (FEMA), the agency responsible for administering the Disaster Mitigation Act. Although the federal government cannot mandate the creation of mitigation plans by the states, the requirement that such a plan be adopted as a condition of funding eligibility is a very enticing "carrot".

the imposition of rules and criteria that apply to the use of the funds. The "strings" that are attached to appropriations from Washington, D.C. are a round-about but effective way that the federal government holds a degree of leverage over activities that would otherwise be entirely within the domain of the state and local governments.

The federal government also appropriates vast amounts of funding to state and local governments for post-disaster assistance. Many of the largest grants and aid packages are directed toward post-storm rebuilding, as indicated by federal funding in Louisiana, Mississippi, Florida, and other states for damage caused by Katrina, Wilma, Rita, and other recent storms.[4] Yet some critics claim that the nature of the congressional appropriations process for disaster assistance is one of the chief roadblocks to reducing future hazard losses:

> "It is easier for the appropriators to spend tens of billions of dollars to clean up after Katrina than to spend tens of millions of dollars to prevent the damage. . . . Reducing risks by, say elevating structures or toughening building codes can be expensive. And any federal support for such efforts would have to survive the ordinary budget process. By contrast, hurricane relief funds are provided through emergency supplemental appropriations, which are not constrained by normal budget ceilings. . . . It is a very perverse budget logic."[5]

Most federal grants and other forms of aid are distributed on a cost-share basis, with the federal government providing the bulk of funds and state and local governments providing matching funds. For major development projects, such as those carried out by the U.S. Army Corps of Engineers, the current cost-share formula is typically 65% federal, 35% local. Some critics believe that this system allows state and local governments to shirk their share of the responsibility for the long-term, cumulative impacts that such infrastructure projects may have in the community, including the increased development and growth in hazard locations that may result. Cost-shares that include a greater local contribution may provide more local ownership in a project and thereby a greater level of accountability on the part of local communities.[6]

Federal Real Property

The federal government has vast holdings in many parts of the United States: 28.8% of all land in America (as of September 30, 2004) is owned by the federal government. States with the largest percentage of federal land ownership are located primarily in the west. In Nevada, for example, 84.5% of land is owned by the federal government; in Alaska, 69.1%; and in Oregon, 53.5% is in federal possession.[7]

The Department of the Interior controls the majority of acreage owned by the federal government (68%) and has invested the most in land acquisition costs. The Department of Agriculture controls 28%; twenty-four agencies control the remaining 4%. Of the more than 655.6 million acres of land the federal government owns and leases within the United States, 30% is used for forest and wildlife, 22% is used for grazing, 16% is dedicated to parks and historic Sites, 2% is used for military purposes, while the remaining uses combined represent 32% of total acreage controlled by the federal government.

The federal government also owns and leases thousands of buildings throughout the United States. Close to one-fifth of all the owned and leased federal buildings are used for housing (the second highest category behind office). Other predominant uses include post office, service, storage, research and development, and institutional/school.

The predominate use of infrastructure ranked according to acquisition cost include: power development and distribution, flood control and navigation, utility systems, roads and bridges, and other uses. Of these costs, 16.57% is directed to flood control and navigation, most of which is appropriated to the U.S. Army Corps of Engineers (hereafter referred to as the "Corps").

These statistics are significant, because they indicate the degree of control that the federal government has over land as well as buildings throughout the United States. Areas that are used as timber and grazing lands are usually undeveloped, and relatively few structures (either private or government owned) are exposed to hazard impacts on these lands. Other federal lands, such as military bases owned and operated by the Department of Defense, are intensely used, and many are located in high hazard areas such as the coastal zone.

These statistics also indicate the vast amount of infrastructure that the federal government owns and controls throughout the country. Flood control and navigation structures, for instance, include Corps projects such as levees, dams, seawalls, and beach nourishment activities. These projects have been blamed for some of the boom in coastal development that has occurred over the past few decades. However, the Corps has little, if any, programmatic authority when deploying funds appropriated to it by Congress. The Corps has no independent authority to set construction priorities and little ability to consider the broader effects of the projects that Congress assigns to it, many of which are earmarked in appropriations bills.[8] Furthermore, federal agencies such as the Corps, Department of Transportation, Department of Energy, and other builders of infrastructure are not growth management agencies: "local land use decisions are largely the purview of state and local officials and there is precious little the federal government can do—or wants to do—to keep people away from hazardous areas."[9]

Although impacts of federal property use relating to environmental quality (air and water pollution, habitat destruction, etc.) are routinely disclosed in environmental impact statements as required by the National Environmental Policy Act (NEPA), there is no corresponding requirement that impacts of federal activities on hazard vulnerability be disclosed (NEPA is described in Chapter 6).

5.3.2 Hazards Management at the State Level

By virtue of the Tenth Amendment to the United States Constitution, state governments possess inherent power—the **police power**—to enact reasonable legislation to protect the health, safety, and general welfare of the public. With no overriding public policy regarding how to mitigate natural and man-made hazards, the states have derived their own diverse methods of protecting public health and safety from the impacts of hazards. Some states have taken a direct approach, while others are more hands-off and have delegated responsibility to the local governments. Still others require action on the part of the local governments, but allow implementation decisions to be made at the community level. This inconsistency reflects the fact that the states vary widely in their hazard experiences as well as their political, fiscal, and technical ability to deal with those hazards. State hazards management issues are discussed in greater detail in Chapter 7.

State Regulatory Tools for Hazard Areas

The states have used a variety of regulatory tools to control and manage development in hazard lands. Many states assume administration of certain areas such as environmentally sensitive areas, wetlands, water resource areas, and dunes. Some states impose setback regulations along the shore or in seismic risk zones in an attempt to eliminate buildings in the most hazardous oceanfront and earthquake-prone areas. A few states have enacted legislation that limits the state or local governments from providing public infrastructure such as roads or water and sewer lines into hazardous or environmentally sensitive areas. Many states have enacted mandatory building codes that apply throughout the state, or require local governments to adopt building codes that meet minimum standards. Some states also mandate that local governments prepare local land use plans and specify issues that must be addressed in the plans. Some of these mandated plans must consider natural hazards as a required element, but such a mandate is by no means universal, even among states that experience frequent hazards such as floods and hurricanes.

State Provision of Infrastructure

Along with the federal government, and often in partnership with federal agencies, the states provide a significant portion of the infrastructure built within the state. Much private investment, including investment in private property located in highly hazardous areas such as the coastal zone, is made financially feasible only through state and federal dollars that fund construction and maintenance of roads, bridges, water and sewer lines, communication systems, and other facilities that support and encourage development and growth. State and federal funds are also used to repair public facilities after a storm causes severe damage. While this infrastructure is necessary to encourage and maintain economic growth, often relatively little consideration is made for the increased vulnerability that results from development located in hazardous locations.

In North Carolina, for example, the state has purchased 600 acres of farmland on the outskirts of the small town of Southport with the intention of building one of the largest seaports on the East Coast. The new port is critical to the nation's continued economic growth, as international trade is spawning an enormous increase in shipping traffic. The North Carolina Ports Authority projects an economic boon from the planned Class 1 port, estimating that the facility will create 48,000 jobs in the state and generate $47 million in annual tax revenues. Southport is located in Brunswick County, the southernmost county of North Carolina, directly in the path of past and predicted future hurricanes.[10]

5.3.3 Hazards Management at the Local Level

Through their police power, state governments are authorized to protect public health and safety. The states, in turn, delegate some of these powers to local governments. The local government must have the proper delegation from the state in order to act. This principle is known as **Dillon's Rule.**

The derivative authority granted to local governments under Dillon's Rule varies widely from state to state; however, most local governments are given a fair amount of autonomy to enforce their police power, particularly with regard to emergency management functions. Typically, localities are authorized (and in a few states are required) to adopt at least basic land use management tools (including comprehensive plans, zoning and subdivision ordinances, capital improvement programs, and other types of regulatory actions), some of which may be used to address hazards.

Home Rule

In **Home Rule States**, general police power is delegated by the state legislature to local governments to enact laws and to adopt and enforce regulations that are necessary for it to govern. In these states, the local governments have predominant power over local matters within their jurisdiction. In states that do not follow the Home Rule principle, local governments are only allowed to exercise powers that have been expressly granted to them in the state constitution or by other state laws.

Extraterritorial Jurisdiction

The authority of local governments to regulate behavior and land use is limited to the area within the boundaries of that local government. However, most states establish **extraterritorial jurisdiction** as a way to give municipalities control over development just outside the town or city limits and over areas that eventually could be annexed. The extraterritorial jurisdiction usually extends one mile beyond city limits. In some states, with approval of the county governing board, a city may extend its extraterritorial land use planning jurisdiction to three miles. Extraterritorial jurisdiction is often an effective way for a municipality to broaden the geographic extent of land use controls that help reduce hazard vulnerability. This is particularly effective to mitigate hazard risks that are widely distributed and cross political boundaries, such as flooding. Often, however, residents in outlying areas are resistant to extraterritorial jurisdiction, as they do not receive municipal services or vote for local officials but must abide by municipal zoning and development rules.

Conflicting and Complementary Interests at the Local Level

With power derived from the state, local governments have authority to manage many features of growth and development within their jurisdiction. However, this authority alone does not necessarily ease the decision-making process involved. Regulation of private property can be contentious, and a full range of conflicting issues may arise when local authorities attempt to restrict land use to mitigate the impacts of hazards. Yet, when viewed in the context of the overall wellbeing and sustainability of the community as a whole, these interests may actually be complementary, rather than at odds.

On the one hand, local governments must govern land use for the public good. Protecting public health and safety is a paramount duty of local government. Regulations targeted at reducing damage to property and protecting residents are essential to carry out this duty. On the other hand, local governments are also responsible for providing a full range of services to their citizens, including education, public safety, emergency medical services, health and social services, homeless shelters, public transit, parks and recreation, libraries, recycling and refuse disposal, and other critical needs of the community.

State and federal governments provide some funding for these services, but much of the financial burden falls on the local government. A major source of revenue for local governments lies in their land—property taxes represent a significant portion of most local budgets. In general, developed property is more valuable, and therefore, more lucrative in terms of local taxes, as it can be taxed at a higher rate. In many communities, there is a strong incentive to allow growth and development to occur in order to increase the local tax base. In their eagerness to attract new growth to the area, local jurisdictions may overlook the hazards that pose a risk to the built environment, and may allow or even encourage development in vulnerable locations. Furthermore, many communities, particularly those located in highly desirable areas such as the coast, are already intensely developed, adding to the tensions and conflicting interests at the local level. Avoiding hazard land uses is much more difficult when investments have been made and construction has taken place.

While these local concerns are significant factors in the creation of policies and regulations that concern land uses in hazardous areas, many communities have come to realize that the interests of protecting public health and safety and promoting sound growth and development are not mutually exclusive. Chapter 14 discusses the connection between hazard resiliency and sustainability.

SELF-CHECK

- Explain the role of federal appropriations in emergency management.
- List three types of federal involvement in hazard areas.
- Discuss two state regulatory tools for hazard areas.
- Name five services and facilities that are the responsibility of local government.

5.4 Regional Governments

Although the fragmentation that characterizes our patchwork system of government allows for a degree of flexibility and diversity among and between government levels, many issues and concerns that warrant government attention do not lend themselves to traditional methods of planning and management. In particular, hazards do not follow political boundaries and jurisdictional limits, striking in locations without regard for the regulations and administrative mechanisms that have been established to deal with them.

A regional approach to governance addresses some of the problems that arise when hazard impacts transcend political boundaries and when multiple jurisdictions are responsible for hazards management. Regional agencies are often based on ecosystem boundaries, such as a river basin or watershed. Other regional governments consist of multi-jurisdictional collaborations, such as councils of government that operate within a state, or multi-state compacts and alliances. Regionalism is not widely used in the United States as a way of setting policy or enacting regulations, and it has had limited success for land use planning purposes. However, a few regional entities have been established, although none for the explicit purpose of hazard mitigation.

There are many different approaches to implementing regional or ecosystem management. In some areas, management has been undertaken by a regulatory agency. This may take the form of a free-standing body spanning state borders, or it may operate within a state government, either as a separate entity or as a division of an existing state department or agency. Such regulatory agencies are usually created by the legislatures of the state(s) and may be given both regulatory and enforcement powers.

Other regional management bodies are more administrative in nature, and may perform coordinating functions or act as advisory boards to state and/or local governments. Many states have legislation that enables localities to voluntarily form councils or federations to study regional resources and problems, and to promote cooperative arrangements and coordinated action among their member governments.[11]

> ### FOR EXAMPLE
>
> #### South Florida Has a Vision
>
> The Strategic Regional Policy Plan for South Florida, adopted in 1995, contains specific and extensive guidance on natural hazard reduction. The plan presents an overall vision for South Florida that emphasizes achieving a livable, sustainable, and competitive regional community.

The success of regional organizations in tackling concrete problems such as development in hazard areas has been spotty at best. Some observers have argued that fragmentation among levels of government within a federal system is a fact of life that cannot be changed. The function of regional entities in governing land use in areas prone to natural hazards is likely to remain limited to broad-brush planning, intergovernmental coordination, and capacity-building functions of providing information, education, and technical assistance to local governments.[12] Special purpose regional organizations have been more successful when they have been granted authority to directly implement or compel implementation of their plans and policies.

SELF-CHECK

- Explain the importance of regional governments when it comes to hazard mitigation.
- Discuss ways in which a regional agency's jurisdiction can be determined.
- Give an example of a successful regional agency.

EVACUATING OVER ONE MILLION PEOPLE IN THE PATH OF HURRICANE KATRINA

The evacuation of areas affected by Hurricane Katrina is a story with two endings (see Figure 5-1). For those residents who had the opportunity to flee from the oncoming storm, a framework was in place for efficient, supervised evacuation procedures that were successfully coordinated between local, county, and state officials. However, for those without a personal mode of transportation, those with medical conditions preventing them from moving, and those who lacked sufficient monetary resources to leave, the pre-hurricane evacuation process was an utter failure.

Figure 5-1

Residents from west of New Orleans, east through Biloxi and Gulfport in Mississippi, and east through Mobile, Alabama and Pensacola, Florida were first warned to batten down, and then urged to begin a mass evacuation. More than 300,000 escaped New Orleans, spreading out northwards.

The evacuation of those who were willing and able to evacuate was a resounding success, and is testimony to a well conceived pre-disaster plan that was carried out by multiple levels of government in a coordinated and efficient manner. It demonstrated the ability of the states of Louisiana, Mississippi, and Alabama, along with county and local levels of government, to work together to ensure a safe and timely flow of traffic out of the mandatory evacuation areas. Despite the patchwork nature of the interagency relationships, the multiple jurisdictions involved were prepared for the Katrina evacuation due to recent revisions of their evacuation plans after Hurricanes Ivan and Dennis.[13] In 2004, Hurricane Ivan caused massive traffic jams, especially out of New Orleans, because populations in the southern-most parishes were attempting to evacuate at the same time as the residents of New Orleans and Jefferson Parish. The revised Louisiana state plan initiated the evacuation of the southern-most parishes first, and then incrementally initiated the evacuation of New Orleans and Jefferson Parish.[14] This staging procedure, along with implementation of a pre-conceived contraflow plan (the direction of one-way outbound traffic in all lanes of highway), greatly improved the efficiency of the evacuation before Katrina, resulting in the successful evacuation of over 1 million people in less than a 40-hour period.

Although the Louisiana state plan provided guidance for the overall procedure of the evacuation, plans developed and implemented at the local level also played a key role in carrying out critical elements of the evacuation process. The New Orleans Comprehensive Emergency Management Plan states that "the Mayor of New Orleans is responsible for giving the order for a mandatory evacuation and supervising the actual evacuation of his population. The Mayor's Office of Emergency Preparedness must [c]oordinate with the State . . . on elements of evacuation".[15] These efforts are the joint responsibility of both local and state levels of government because the local jurisdictions have access to information about locally-specific conditions essential for making the mandatory evacuation call, whereas the state is responsible for managing traffic flow and opening shelters. Coordination is also required among states, including states from which populations are evacuating as well as states that are receiving evacuees, which in the case of Katrina involved Texas, Florida, and states beyond.

Although the traffic aspects of the Katrina evacuation were conducted cooperatively at both the state and local levels, the evacuation of those who were not able to leave their homes resulted in a very different scenario. Under standard emergency management procedure, evacuation of endangered populations is preferable to sheltering in place in the face of extraordinarily large storms. This prevents residents from being subjected to the most dangerous elements of the storm, and also avoids the challenges of slow and difficult relief operations involving transportation of personnel and emergency supplies into hurricane-ravaged areas. However, the mandatory evacuation order for New Orleans was issued too late to ensure adequate evacuation time, coming just 19 hours before landfall was projected (on Sunday, August 28 at 11 A.M.). Officials of Jefferson Parish made no mandatory evacuation order at all. In comparison, evacuation from Plaquemines Parish was mandated much earlier (on Saturday, August 27 at 9 A.M.), resulting in the evacuation of 97 to 98% of the population.

Both the Governor of Louisiana, Kathleen Babineaux Blanco, and the Mayor of New Orleans, C. Ray Nagin, emphasized the extreme dangers of remaining in the city as Katrina approached the region, yet their actions did not reinforce their warnings. An estimated 70,000 people remained in New Orleans during the height of Katrina. Of these, a significant number had the means to evacuate yet chose to remain, and must therefore share some of the blame. No amount of government coordination or advance planning can physically force citizens to leave against their will. However, an earlier mandatory evacuation order would have underscored the severity of the situation and would have allowed more time for the ill, the elderly, and those who did not own their own vehicles to find alternative means to evacuate. The New Orleans plan does make provisions for this segment of the population, stating, "Transportation will be provided to those persons requiring public transportation from the area."[16] The city had advance knowledge that approximately 100,000 people in the city would be unable to evacuate due to health reasons or their dependency on public transportation. However, these provisions were not implemented in the days and hours before Katrina struck. Instead, city officials sent personnel from police and fire departments through the city, instructing people to report to bus checkpoints to take them to the Superdome, the shelter of last resort. As a result, thousands of sick, elderly, and impoverished citizens, along with hundreds of children, were forced into a horrific situation with no means of escape.[17]

5.5 Private Land Ownership

Although the government holds title to a portion of the land in the United States, the majority of real property in our country is privately owned, by individuals and by corporations. Property ownership under our legal system encompasses a broad set of rights and duties, some of which offer benefits while others involve restrictions on property use.

5.5.1 Private Property Rights and Privileges

Owners have the right to control their property, which allows them to take advantage of the land's natural resources (timber, water, minerals, oil, etc.). The right of control also allows owners to physically alter the land through grading, filling, construction, and other means of development. Owners also have the right of disposition, whereby the owner may convey all or a portion of the rights in the property to others by sale, gift, donation, or upon death through the laws of inheritance or the terms of a will. This includes the right to hold land for investment purposes and to sell the property in the marketplace in order to realize a profit.

5.5.2 Limitations on Private Property Uses

The rights and privileges of property ownership are not absolute. Owners are subject to certain restrictions and limits as to the use of their property and must carry out certain duties. One such limitation on the use of private property arises from the **law of nuisance**, an ancient legal doctrine that pertains to modern property law. Under the nuisance duty, an owner must refrain from undertaking any activity which interferes with the rights of adjoining property owners or which inflicts injury on the general public. For example, landowners have a duty to secure structures so that they do not become flying missiles during a hurricane or other high wind event. The law of nuisance can also imply a duty to refrain from using property in such a way that increases flooding, endangering neighboring lots.

Land owners are also limited in the use of their property by the police power, which authorizes the government to enact laws and regulations for public health and safety, even when such regulations are contrary to the owner's aspirations. The police power extends to many types of regulations that can restrict development or which impose development standards. For instance, a landowner is obligated to follow the state and local building codes when building a structure on private property. Such codes might include provisions for making the structure more resilient to high winds or require it to be elevated above the flood level. Landowners must also follow local zoning, subdivision, and other land use regulations when using their property.

Landowners are further subject to the government's power of **eminent domain**, whereby private property may be taken (condemned) for public use upon payment of just compensation. In addition, landowners are under the duty to pay all property taxes. Unpaid property taxes constitute a lien, or claim, against the real estate, and the government may force a sale of the property to satisfy the lien. Landowners must also pay all other taxes associated with the property, including inheritance taxes, taxes on capital gains, and taxes on rental income, and must follow other provisions of local, state, and federal tax laws.

5.5.3 Dividing Property Rights

Each of the rights and duties inherent in property ownership can be viewed as separate from one another and can, under certain circumstances, be divided among multiple owners. The right to develop the land, for instance, can be transferred to another owner, while the underlying rights to the property remain unchanged. The right to exploit the natural resources can also be conveyed, while the land itself does not change hands, as when, for example, timber cutting or coal mining rights are sold or leased, but the seller retains control of the other uses of the parcel. Property owners can also assign particular rights of use through the granting of easements, or can impose deed restrictions that carry with the title when the land is transferred to another owner. Rights in property can also be divided in time, which occurs when land or buildings are leased to a tenant for a period of months or years. The landlord retains ownership rights to the property, but the tenant or lessee has the right to occupy the space under the terms of the lease agreement.

5.5.4 Understanding Property Ownership

No matter how the various uses are segregated, either temporally or physically, the combination of ownership privileges and duties makes up the entire bundle of property rights. These concepts associated with property ownership recur throughout this book, when, for example, we discuss public acquisition of property as a

FOR EXAMPLE

Restrictions on Property Use in the Floodplain

Many court cases have upheld regulations that restrict owners from using property located in the floodplain. *Turnpike Realty Co. v. Town of Dedham* is a typical case. The court upheld a floodplain ordinance that allowed only passive uses and prohibited any building or structure, even though these restrictions allegedly reduced the value of the property from $431,000 to $53,000. The court noted that floodplain regulation protects individuals who might choose to build in floodplains despite the flood danger, protects other landowners from floodplain development, and protects the entire community from individual choices of land use which require subsequent public expenditures for infrastructure repair and disaster relief.[18]

form of hazard mitigation. In that instance, the government purchases the entire bundle of property rights from the owner of land that has been subjected to repetitive flooding or other recurrent hazards; under most public acquisition programs, deed restrictions prevent the land from being used for development purposes in perpetuity (see Chapters 8 and 12 for discussion of various types of acquisition strategies). The rights and duties of property ownership also provide a context for discussion in Chapter 9, when we describe the decision-making process of private landowners who invest, develop, and sell land in hazard locations such as the coastal zone. An understanding of property ownership also provides the background for further discussion of the police power and the types of land use regulations that governments impose on private landowners as a way of reducing hazard vulnerability in the community.

SELF-CHECK

- Define **law of nuisance**, **police power**, and **eminent domain**.
- List two rights of land ownership.
- List four duties or limits of land ownership.

5.6 Land Use Controls

Public controls on private property are not a recent innovation. Land use laws existed in various forms in England long before the United States existed, and even extend back into the ancient Roman past. The earliest code of Roman law, the Twelve Tables (451–540 B.C.), required setbacks for structures from parcel boundaries and regulated the distances between trees and lot lines. From the time the concept of private ownership arose in our legal tradition, property has literally been subject to the "law of the land".

What the law of the land entails for the average landowner has been variously interpreted over the years, vacillating between times of expansion and retrenchment depending upon the societal and economic conditions of the day. Early on, judge-made law, such as the law of nuisance, was sufficient to handle land use conflicts, but as our society became more complex and populous, and as increasing demands were placed on limited natural resources, there arose the need for more extensive public land use controls. These land use controls are adopted by state and local governments under the police power.

5.6.1 Exercise of the Police Power through Zoning

Before zoning became widespread, the police power was used by local governments for relatively simple controls, such as fire safety and limitations on nuisance-like uses in locations where they would be incompatible with surrounding uses (such as prohibiting a brickyard in a residential neighborhood). Comprehensive zoning greatly expanded the tools available to local governments to control land uses within their jurisdiction.

Once zoning came into judicial favor, it allowed governments to protect certain uses in certain districts, or zones. At its core, zoning continues the basic nuisance protections of former land use controls, but allows much more specific restrictions and enables the government to predetermine the uses that will be permitted in particular locations, *before* development occurs. In its early stages, zoning focused on protecting single-family housing from encroaching commercial, industrial, and multi-family uses. Zoning today is much more complex and has evolved well beyond the mere protection of single-family homes from apartments and marketplaces. Companion land use controls, including subdivision ordinances, environmental regulations, growth management, and similar measures have continued to expand the repertoire of the police power. Many of these land use controls can be used to increase the resiliency of our communities.

5.6.2 Limits on the Police Power

By the late nineteenth and early twentieth centuries, the courts were accepting land use controls as a legitimate means to protect public health and safety. Yet even early on, it was clear that the police power was not unlimited. Modern courts stress that land use controls such as zoning cannot be exercised arbitrarily or capriciously, cannot be unreasonable, must be applied uniformly upon all landowners in similar circumstances, and above all, cannot confiscate private property without payment of just compensation. **Just compensation** is defined as fair market value.

Courts continue to wrangle with the issue of how far the police power can go in restricting private property owners, and land use cases are often hotly debated and closely followed by government regulators and property owners alike. One of the most contentious and murky of land use issues involves the Fifth Amendment to the Constitution, otherwise known as the "Takings Law." **Takings** requires that the owner of private property that is physically occupied by the government or regulated past a certain point must receive just compensation. There have been attempts over the years to more clearly define the limits on land use controls, but this is still a field in flux, and there is no clear predictor or litmus test to determine how a particular land use case may be resolved.

5.6.3 Constitutional Limitations on Government Intervention: the Fifth Amendment

At the heart of the takings issue is the dilemma of how we as a society should best balance the rights of the private property owner with public objectives of safety, health, and general welfare of the people as a whole. The final clause of the Fifth Amendment to the United States Constitution (referred to as the "Takings Clause"), states: "...nor shall private property be taken for public use without just compensation." Most states have a comparable provision in their own constitutions.

Physical Invasions

It is clear that the Fifth Amendment requires the government to pay just compensation when private property is taken—that is, physically taken—for public use. The amount of space that is occupied or the way in which the property is used is irrelevant—a physical occupation of land by the government is a taking under the Fifth Amendment, and the property owner must be compensated.

FOR EXAMPLE

Takings Big and Small

In the Supreme Court Case *Pumpelly v. Green Bay Co.* (1871), the Court ordered the government to pay the landowner compensation for the permanent flooding of his property that occurred when a dam was built upstream. In *Loretto v. Teleprompter Manhattan CATV Corp.* (1982), the Supreme Court found that a cable line installed on the outside of the owner's apartment building was a taking, even though the installation was for the benefit of the building occupants and the invasion was relatively minimal in size.

Eminent Domain

Eminent domain, or condemnation, refers to the power of the government to "take" (condemn) private land for a public purpose. The Fifth Amendment does not prohibit legitimate exercise of this power, so long as the landowner is justly compensated (usually determined by the fair market value of the property taken) and the proceedings are carried out with due process of law. Eminent domain is commonly used by local and state governments to acquire rights-of-way during highway and road construction, and for construction of other types of infrastructure and public facilities, such as schools. These are instances where the public purpose involved is well accepted and recognized as within the authority of local governments. Although individual instances of condemnation for road improvements, highway widening, or school construction may involve issues of unfairness, arbitrariness, or undue hardship, in general, eminent domain for these types of uses satisfies the public purpose requirement of the Fifth Amendment.

In other instances, what constitutes a public purpose may not be as clear. For example, in New London, Connecticut, the local government condemned private property for use as part of an economic development project and transferred the lots to a private development corporation. In June of 2005, the Supreme Court held that this was a legitimate public purpose, because the proceedings had been carried out under the auspices of the duly elected local governing council as part of a comprehensive redevelopment plan to revitalize New London's failing economy. Because of the strict separation of powers in our legal system, courts in general are reluctant to second guess the policy decisions made by local boards and other legislative bodies. In the New London case, the Supreme Court defined the concept of public purpose broadly, reflecting its long-standing policy of deference to legislative judgments as to what public needs justify the use of takings powers. In response, dozens of states and local governments have enacted legislation to prohibit the use of eminent domain for economic development purposes. Bills introduced in the U.S. Senate and House of Representatives have also proposed limits on the use of eminent domain for economic development when federal funds are involved.

5.6.4 Regulatory Takings

It is clear that physical occupations and eminent domain require the payment of just compensation under the Fifth Amendment Takings Clause. However, the takings rule also applies when the government "takes" an owner's land by severely restricting its use. As discussed earlier in the chapter, it is the duty of the landowner to obey all applicable laws and regulations in the jurisdiction where the property is located. But occasionally, those regulations may amount to a "taking."

In 1922 the U.S. Supreme Court decided that a particularly restrictive regulation may be considered an unconstitutional taking. In *Pennsylvania Coal Co. v. Mahon* the Court stated: "The general rule at least is, that while property may be regulated to a certain extent, if regulation goes too far, it will be recognized as a taking." The oft-cited rule from this case has prompted legal challenges by property owners against public land use regulations for many years. The state courts and the U.S. Supreme Court have developed a range of legal tests to determine when a regulation reaches the point found in the *Pennsylvania Coal* case and has gone too far. Many of these tests have multiple prongs or parts, dealing with a variety of issues, some of which are illustrated in the following list:

▲ The physical occupation of private land by the government is almost always a taking.

▲ All land use regulations must serve a valid public purpose.

▲ There must be a rational connection between the regulation and the purpose.

▲ Even a temporary loss of use that does not have a valid purpose and a rational connection is a taking.

▲ A regulation that deprives the owner of all economically beneficial use of the property is a taking.

Many cases involve a balancing of factors, including the character of the government action, the economic impact of the action, and whether the regulation interferes with the owner's expectations. The courts continue to apply the rule that economic loss figures into the balancing test, but have not developed a precise meaning. It is clear that the mere purchase of property with intent to develop it is not enough to create an investment-backed expectation that is protected under the taking clause.[19]

5.6.5 How Far Is Too Far? The Economically Beneficial Test

Most private property owners want to put their land to some sort of beneficial use, such as building a home to live in, developing the land for sale, or to profit from it in some other way. Often this beneficial use is economic in nature. But these desires may run up against government regulations that curtail the use, depending upon what the landowner expects and what the government is trying to achieve. In *Lucas v. South Carolina Coastal Council* (1992), the Supreme Court held that when a regulation denies an owner of all economically beneficial or productive use of the land, the regulation is a taking, even if the government's purpose is entirely legitimate, unless the use that is prohibited would also be prohibited by nuisance law or other state property law. The case study that appears in this chapter, "Takings Law and the South

Carolina Beachfront Management Act" tells the tale of the Lucas decision, including the somewhat bizarre turn of events that occurred at the conclusion of the trial proceedings.

Case Study: Takings Law and the South Carolina Beachfront Management Act

In *Lucas v. South Carolina Coastal Council* (1992), the U.S. Supreme Court issued the ruling that a regulation that deprives a landowner of all economically beneficial or productive use of land is a taking. David Lucas was the owner of two beachfront lots in the Wild Dunes subdivision on Isle of Palms, an extensively developed stretch of beach located on a barrier island in South Carolina. After Lucas acquired the lots, the South Carolina legislature enacted the Beachfront Management Act (the Act), which created a "dead zone" landward of the dune lines. This setback rule was intended to protect structures along the oceanfront from erosion, storm surge, and damage from coastal storms. Because of the size, shape, and boundary lines of the property, the Act prohibited construction on both of the Lucas lots except for wooden walkways and wooden decks as shown in Figure 5-2.

Figure 5-2

View of Lucas's two lots, on either side of large square house in the center. Note that Lucas's lots are the only vacant lots in sight along the beach. [20]

Mr. Lucas claimed that the Beachfront Management Act had unconstitutionally "taken" his property. He did not challenge the validity of the Beachfront Management Act itself, but claimed that when the Act was applied to his property, it destroyed all of its value. The South Carolina trial court awarded him $1.2 million dollars, stating that the regulation had made the Lucas property "valueless."

The South Carolina Coastal Council appealed the decision, and the South Carolina Supreme Court reversed the trial court decision, holding that the Act was intended to prevent a serious public harm and required no compensation, regardless of the effect on property value.

Mr. Lucas appealed that decision to the U.S. Supreme Court, which reversed the South Carolina Supreme Court. The U.S. Supreme Court decided that Mr. Lucas had suffered a "total taking" because the state had deprived him of all economically beneficial use of the land. The state owed him just compensation even though South Carolina had a legitimate interest in strict erosion control, because the owner could not build anything more substantial than a walkway or temporary structure on his lots (such as a tent). The U.S. Supreme Court did leave open a door for other regulations, however, saying that if a regulation is part of well-established legal doctrine, such as nuisance or property law, then no compensation would be required.

After making its decision in the *Lucas* case, the U.S. Supreme Court sent the case back to the South Carolina court to determine the ultimate outcome. When the South Carolina court applied the "economically beneficial use" rule to the case, it found that the Beachfront Management Act did not fall under the exceptions of nuisance or property law, and that Mr. Lucas should be compensated for the taking that had occurred.

Lucas Follow-up: After all the legal wrangling in the *Lucas* case, the ultimate disposition of the lots owned by Mr. Lucas took an interesting turn. Once the appeals process had taken its course and the final decision was made, the State of South Carolina compensated Mr. Lucas for the two lots that had been judged as "taken" by the setback regulation. In order to recoup its expenses, the State of South Carolina sold the Lucas lots to a developer. A large home has since been constructed on one of the lots, which in 1996 was threatened by renewed erosion as shown in Figure 5-3.

SELF-CHECK

- Define **takings** and **just compensation**.
- Explain how the Fifth Amendment relates to hazards management.

Figure 5-3

The cube-shaped house, as before, is between Lucas's original two lots. (Lucas did not own the cube-shaped house or its lot.) On the left is a new, 5000-square foot house built since 1994.

SUMMARY

To understand the process of hazards mitigation and preparedness we must first be familiar with the players involved and the legal framework within which they operate. This chapter introduces the federal, state, local, and regional levels of government that have jurisdiction over land use issues. Each level has its own means of dealing with the impacts of hazards, and the interactions among various levels of government determine how policy is made and affects the ways in which land uses are managed and how privately owned land is regulated. The chapter concludes with a discussion of the power of the government to restrict private land uses and the Constitutional limitations on government regulation to protect the public from the threat of hazards.

KEY TERMS

Dillon's Rule	Principle that a local government must have the proper delegation from the state in order to act.
Eminent domain	The right of the government to take (condemn) private property for public use; owner must be given just compensation for the taking.
Extraterritorial jurisdiction	Control towns have over development just outside the town limits and over areas that eventually could be annexed; usually extends one mile beyond the city limits.
Home Rule States	General police power is delegated by the state legislature to local governments to enact laws and to adopt and enforce regulations that are necessary for it to govern.
Just compensation	The payment of fair market value for whatever portion of the property is put to public use; used in takings cases.
Law of nuisance	An owner must refrain from undertaking any activity which interferes with the rights of adjoining property owners or which inflicts injury on the general public.
Police power	The inherent power of the government to make laws and regulations that promote the public health, safety, and general welfare.
States' rights	Powers that are reserved to the fifty states by the U.S. Constitution.
Takings	Law established by the Fifth Amendment to the U.S. Constitution that requires that the owner of private property must receive just compensation for property that is physically occupied by the government or regulated past a certain point.

ASSESS YOUR UNDERSTANDING

Go to www.wiley.com/college/schwab to evaluate your knowledge of the hazards management framework.
Measure your learning by comparing pre-test and post-test results.

Summary Questions

1. Keeping people and property out of hazardous areas is one of the main goals of mitigation. True or False?
2. Land use controls can be used to mitigate the impact of which of the following hazards?
   (a) wildfire
   (b) terrorism
   (c) hail
   (d) tornado
3. Land use controls have little effect on the hazard of flooding. True or False?
4. State governments regulate land uses
   (a) in diverse ways.
   (b) under federal mandates.
   (c) according to local action.
   (d) with undue process.
5. The Tenth Amendment relates to
   (a) separation of powers.
   (b) land ownership.
   (c) takings.
   (d) states' rights.
6. Towns have control over development outside of town limits through
   (a) acquisition.
   (b) extraterritorial jurisdiction.
   (c) zoning districts.
   (d) amortization.
7. Every state follows its own constitution as well as that of the U.S. Constitution. True or False?
8. Separation of powers is practiced at both the state and federal levels. True or False?
9. In addition to supplying disaster relief, the federal government is responsible for regulation of development in hazard zones. True or False?
10. Tools that states use for hazard areas include
    (a) flood insurance.
    (b) construction setbacks.

(c) Clean Water Act.

(d) tax deductions.

11. Most of the work in creating resilient communities takes place at the state level. True or False?

12. Geographic areas that share issues of public policy and resource management are

    (a) counties.

    (b) townships.

    (c) regions.

    (d) states.

13. Regional agencies typically set management policy and enact regulations. True or False?

14. A regulatory agency is one form of regional governance. True or False?

15. A property owner's right to disposition entitles him or her to

    (a) keep others off property.

    (b) hold land for investment purposes.

    (c) exploit the land's natural resources.

    (d) enforce police power.

16. Eminent domain gives the government the right to

    (a) enforce the law.

    (b) impose taxation.

    (c) change zoning.

    (d) condemn property.

17. Zoning is a legitimate form of police power. True or False?

18. Private property cannot be confiscated without just compensation. True False?

19. A regulation that deprives an owner of all economically beneficial use of the property is a

    (a) mitigation.

    (b) management act.

    (c) taking.

    (d) land trust.

20. The federal government delegates Home Rule power to local communities. True or False?

Review Questions

1. Why do we focus on the management of land use and development in hazard mitigation, and for which hazards is this approach appropriate?

2. List three land use controls that can reduce the risk of earthquakes.

3. Name two man-made hazards for which land use controls are not as effective.

4. What are some of the ways in which the government can manage development in hazardous areas?

5. Explain how the federal government uses ownership as a form of land management.

6. Name the three branches of the U.S. government.

7. When it comes to funding for emergency management what is the role of the federal government?

8. The federal government's involvement in managing hazard areas is not always beneficial. Discuss how the construction of dams and levees can have unintended negative results.

9. List four land use management tools of local governments.

10. What are some of the conflicting policy issues that face local governments who wish to use land use regulations to mitigate the impact of natural hazards?

11. What does the phrase "a patchwork of governance" mean in the context of hazards management?

12. Police power is granted to which level of government by the Tenth Amendment?

13. Explain what Home Rule means to a local government.

14. How does extraterritorial jurisdiction impact a community's resiliency?

15. Which type of governing body would be effective at managing a river basin that spans across three states?

16. Private property owners are a major stakeholder in the issue of land use control. List four privileges associated with ownership.

17. Property ownership carries with it more than rights. Define a landowner's duty under the law of nuisance and give an example.

18. How is zoning an exercise of the local government's police power?

19. What are two of the tests that the U.S. Supreme Court uses to judge whether a land use regulation is unconstitutional under the Fifth Amendment to the U.S. Constitution?

Applying This Chapter

1. Areas of the Northeast have suffered from some major ice storms in the past. Why is land use control not an effective way of preventing this and some other hazards? What other measures should emergency management officials factor into a mitigation plan for communities at risk of these types hazards?

2. Consider where you live and the different levels of government that have jurisdiction over the area. Outline the powers of the federal, state, local, and regional powers at play.

3. Think about any disaster events that occurred in your state in recent history. Even if that event did not affect you directly, it probably did have some impact on some part of your life. Explain.

4. The U.S. Army Corps of Engineers built a massive seawall to protect a stretch of coastline in New Jersey from storms and erosion. As a potential home buyer in the area, would you consider the seawall an advantage or disadvantage?

5. Assume you work for a small city that is experiencing an increase in pollution levels of streams, rivers, and lakes. Neighboring cities report similar increases. To share the burden of the research that must be done to identify and solve the problem, you think some sort of regional organization is necessary. Describe the mission of the organization and how it would fit into the local, state, and federal governments.

6. Assume you own 30 acres of rural property in Pennsylvania. You generally use the property for occasional camping trips, but there is no permanent structure on the land. You've put in a rough road and done selective logging throughout much of the property. You've also begun to fill in a portion of what you believe to be a wetland, in the hopes of building a cabin there one day. Of these activities, what falls within the rights of ownership, and what falls within the category of ownership duties?

7. As an emergency manager in a floodplain area of Pennsylvania, you've been charged with mitigating flood hazards through land use controls. Which controls might be effective? What would you need to keep in mind about private property rights under the U.S. Constitution?

Fireproofed Properties

Assume that you own a home in California, in an area that has experienced wildfires in the past. What types of preventive measures are you responsible for as the property owner? And what would be the concerns of local emergency management officials?

Flooded With Ideas

As the mayor of Davenport, Iowa, you're familiar with one particular hazard: flooding. Davenport often makes national headlines when the Mississippi River floods. It is the largest city bordering the Mississippi that has no permanent floodwall or levee. Aside from the floodwalls or levees, what federal, state, and local efforts could be made to protect your city and its citizens from future flooding?

Setting Back from Earthquakes

In your role as the Director of Emergency Management in your state, the Governor has asked you to prepare a draft setback rule to protect future development located along faultlines from earthquake hazards. What are some of the issues you might consider when drafting such a proposed rule? How would you ensure that the rule would not be challenged in court by private property owners?

6

THE ROLE OF THE FEDERAL GOVERNMENT
The Practice and Politics of Mitigation Policy

Starting Point

Go to www.wiley.com/college/schwab to assess your knowledge of the practices and politics of federal mitigation policy.
Determine where you need to concentrate your effort.

What You'll Learn in This Chapter

▲ How the federal role in emergency management has evolved
▲ Types of federal hazard mitigation programs
▲ The mission of the Federal Emergency Management Agency (FEMA)
▲ Which federal programs indirectly manage the impact of hazards
▲ Two ways the federal government gives incentives for development in hazard areas
▲ The role of federal disaster assistance in hazard mitigation

After Studying this Chapter, You'll be Able To

▲ Illustrate how federal programs encourage development in hazard areas
▲ Examine the role of the FEMA in formulating mitigation policy
▲ Appraise the strengths and weaknesses of various federal mitigation policies
▲ Examine how federal programs can actually be counterproductive to hazard mitigation
▲ Examine ways in which disaster assistance is counterproductive to mitigation

Goals and Outcomes

▲ Master the terminology and understand the perspective of federal hazard policies
▲ Evaluate the main issues regarding mitigation policy decisions
▲ Choose tools and techniques to analyze decisions made as part of mitigation policies
▲ Support or refute the proposition that the federal government subsidizes hazard risk
▲ Evaluate ways to limit the federal burden of disaster assistance
▲ Assess problems with federal programs
▲ Evaluate the effectiveness of federal mitigation programs for reducing vulnerability

INTRODUCTION

Most would agree that providing relief to people who have suffered the hardship and heartache of a catastrophic disaster is a worthwhile endeavor, even a moral obligation. This chapter discusses how the federal government's involvement in emergency management and its role in providing disaster assistance have evolved throughout its history. The chapter then outlines several federal programs that pertain directly to hazards management, as well as some other federal activities that are not focused on mitigation per se, but which nevertheless have some bearing on hazards management. The chapter also examines ways in which federal government programs offer incentives for development in hazard areas, with the result of increasing vulnerability in certain regions of the country. The chapter concludes by exploring the issue of federal disaster assistance as a "moral hazard" as well as some propositions for changing our current approach to hazards management at the federal level.

6.1 Evolution of Emergency Management at the Federal Level

The role of the federal government in emergency management has evolved over the years from distant observer to immediate responder, principal financier of disaster costs, and, more recently, champion of hazard mitigation.[1] As a way of introducing the federal role in hazard mitigation and preparedness, this section discusses some of the more dramatic changes in the federal approach to emergency management that have occurred from the 1800s up through the current War on Terrorism. This brief history might help explain some of the policies and programs that are in existence today, and provides a background for some of the impediments to and opportunities for mitigation that face emergency managers working in the field.

6.1.1 Federal Involvement: A Slow Trickle

As put forth in the United States Constitution, the function of protecting public health and safety rests primarily with the states. The role of the federal government is to step in and provide aid when state and local governments are overwhelmed or otherwise unable to provide the services that the citizenry needs. Over the years, however, this principle, while not eroding entirely, has come to mean that the federal government steps in on a regular basis, with more being expected of federal agencies and programs than ever before.

Between 1800 and 1950, there was a slow trickle of federal involvement in emergency management functions, but there was no national policy for responding to natural or man-made disasters.[2] Catastrophes ravaged portions of the nation periodically, including notable disasters such as the following:

▲ New Madrid, Missouri, Earthquakes of 1811-1812.
▲ Chicago Fire of 1873.
▲ Johnstown, Pennsylvania, Dam Break in 1889.
▲ Galveston Hurricane of 1900.
▲ San Francisco Earthquake and Fire of 1906.
▲ Miami Hurricane of 1926.
▲ Lower Mississippi Flood of 1927.
▲ New England Hurricane of 1938.

Deaths from such disasters numbered in the hundreds, sometimes in the thousands. Costs in present-day figures ran into the billions of dollars. Response to these disasters was ad hoc, organized by local groups and funded primarily by charities and some local and state monies. Any mitigation that took place was carried out by individual property owners or local governments in a piecemeal fashion,[3] but there was no concerted effort to push risk reduction at the community level.

The 1930s: The U.S. Army Corps of Engineers Becomes Active in Flood Control

The Flood Control Act of 1934 gave the U.S. Army Corps of Engineers increased authority to design and build flood control projects. This Act reflected a philosophy that man could control nature and eliminate the risk of floods, setting the tone for the basic approach to mitigating the impact of most natural hazards throughout the next several decades. The Corps' programs were very successful, in the sense that hundreds of dams, levees, floodwalls, diversions, and other structural flood control projects were built throughout the country. Although the Corps' programs promoted economic development and population growth along the nation's rivers and coastlines, history has proven that this attempt at emergency management was shortsighted and costly.

Emergency Management during the Cold War

The 1950s was a quiet time for large-scale natural hazards, although three significant hurricanes did occur: Hurricane Hazel, a Category 4 hurricane, inflicted significant damage in Virginia and North Carolina in 1954; Hurricane Diane hit several mid-Atlantic and northeastern states in 1955; and Hurricane Audrey, the most damaging of the three storms, struck Louisiana and North Texas in 1957.

The newly passed Disaster Assistance Act of 1950 picked up the tab for some of the costs from these disasters, introducing Americans to the concept of federal disaster assistance, but the amounts compared to later distributions of aid were paltry at best.[4] The focus of the nation at this time was not on hazards posed by nature but on the potential for nuclear war and nuclear fallout. The era of the Cold War in the 1950s meant that disaster management focused less on land use regulation to keep hazardous areas free of development and more on the threat of foreign invasion. The construction of bomb shelters in private homes and public buildings was fairly common, which coincidently provided protection from tornadoes and some other natural hazards, but only as a by-product of the more pressing need to combat the perceived threat of nuclear attack.

National Flood Insurance Act

In 1961, the Office of Emergency Preparedness was created to deal with natural disasters. As the 1960s progressed, the United States was struck by a series of major natural hazards: the Ash Wednesday Storm, a nor'easter that caused significant damage along the Atlantic Coast; the Prince William Sound earthquake, which set off a *tsunami* along the Pacific Coast; and Hurricanes Betsy and Camille, which killed and injured hundreds of people and caused millions of dollars in damage along the Atlantic and Gulf coasts.

The lack of insurance against such large-scale disasters prompted the passage of the National Flood Insurance Act of 1968, creating the National Flood Insurance Program (NFIP). The NFIP was unique in its day, as it called upon local governments to undertake community-based mitigation activities to lessen flood risk. We discuss the NFIP in greater detail later in this chapter.

Federal Disaster Activity in the 1970s: The Creation of FEMA

The federal Disaster Relief Acts of 1969 and 1970 further emphasized the role of the federal government as the primary source of disaster funding. By this time, more than 100 federal agencies bore some responsibility for risk and disasters. These agencies were scattered among the civil and defense departments—each operating on its own turf and with its own agenda—but none of these agencies focused primarily on mitigation as a viable way of reducing hazard risk.

In 1979, President Jimmy Carter created the Federal Emergency Management Agency (FEMA). Many of the responsibilities of other agencies were soon transferred to this agency. Integrating the diverse programs, operations, policies, and people into a cohesive operation was a mammoth task, fraught with political, philosophical, and logistical problems. At this point, mitigation was still not promoted or funded in any major way within FEMA itself. There were relatively few natural disasters during this period, so the disjointed nature of the agency, while inefficient and cumbersome, was not noticeable to any large degree.[5]

The 1980s and 1990s: An Explosion in Federal Aid

Abundant federal disaster assistance was made available through passage of the Robert T. Stafford Disaster Relief and Emergency Assistance Act in 1988. During the 1980s and 1990s, federal expenditures for disaster relief expanded by leaps and bounds. More disasters, larger dollar losses, and an inconsistent method of defining what qualifies as a "disaster" contributed to spending in the millions, and even billions, each year.

The purpose of the Stafford Act is to support state and local governments and their citizens when disasters overwhelm their capability to respond. A wide range of disaster assistance is available from FEMA under the Stafford Act. Such assistance generally falls into two categories. (1) *Individual and Family Assistance* grants provide funds to help meet the serious needs and necessary expenses of disaster victims that are not met through other means such as insurance, loans or charities. Eligible costs include housing, personal property, medical and dental expenses, funerals, and transportation. (2) The *Public Assistance Program* (PA) provides aid to help communities rebuild damaged facilities after a disaster. Grants cover eligible costs associated with the repair or replacement of facilities owned by state or local governments and some nonprofit organizations. Funds are used to restore water and wastewater services, establish emergency public transportation, remove debris, and other activities to return the community to pre-disaster conditions (see Figure 6-1). While mitigation can be a component of rebuilding public facilities using PA funds, restoration rather than mitigation is the primary goal of the Public Assistance Program.

The Stafford Act also created the **Hazard Mitigation Grant Program (HMGP).** The purpose of the HMGP is to reduce the loss of life and property due to natural hazards by providing money for mitigation as part of the disaster assistance package that state and local governments receive following a disaster declaration. Mitigation projects are meant to be implemented during the window of opportunity that opens when communities are rebuilding after a hazard event.

Other federal agencies also began to disburse greater disaster aid and loan packages during this time period. The Small Business Administration, for example, issues low-interest loans to help community businesses reestablish their enterprise activities following a hazard event. The Department of Housing and Urban Development administers disaster-related community development block grants (CDBG) to local governments impacted by disasters as well as other programs such as the Public Housing Modernization Reserve for Disasters and Emergencies, the HOME Investment Partnership Program, and the Section 108 Loan Guarantee Program. The Farm Service Agency of the U.S. Department of Agriculture provides numerous types of assistance to farmers following natural disasters, including loans, grants, and technical assistance, as well as catastrophic risk crop insurance.

Figure 6-1

Flooded sewer plants such as this one in eastern North Carolina are often repaired using federal Public Assistance funds following large scale disasters.

6.1.2 FEMA Incapable of Major Disaster Response

Although FEMA was up and running by this time, and although the Stafford Act provided a process to disburse disaster assistance to impacted communities fairly quickly, a series of major disasters between 1989 and 1993 highlighted some of the deficiencies in FEMA's capability to deal with catastrophic disasters. In 1989, Hurricane Hugo pummeled North and South Carolina and the U.S. Virgin Islands. It was the worst hurricane in a decade, with over $15 billion in damages and 85 deaths. FEMA was perceived as slow to respond. Soon after Hugo, the Loma Prieta Earthquake rocked California, with record damages but fewer deaths. In 1991, raging wildfires in Oakland, California, burned homes and businesses. In 1992, Hurricane Andrew struck with very costly consequences, devastating Florida and Louisiana. Hurricane Iniki soon followed, creating havoc in Hawaii.

In the eyes of many, FEMA, and the entire emergency management system failed. The public wanted, and by now expected, the government to be there to help in their time of need. FEMA seemed incapable of carrying out the essential government function of disaster assistance.[6] The extent of the damages incurred during these disasters emphasized the need for reducing the risk of future disasters—in other words, mitigation seemed an obvious choice.

The Midwest Floods of 1993: A Test for FEMA

President Bill Clinton nominated James Lee Witt to be Director of FEMA, who initiated sweeping reforms inside and outside the agency, including the creation of a Mitigation Directorate within FEMA. FEMA now placed emphasis on mitigation as a primary means of reducing vulnerability to future natural hazards. The need for a strong relationship between FEMA and state and local emergency managers was recognized as well, allowing for better coordination and communication before, during, and immediately following a hazard event.

Witt's reforms were quickly tested during the Midwest Floods of 1993. Devastating flooding occurred in an area covering 525 counties in 9 states, and much of it was caused by the failure of dams and levees that had been built by the Army Corps of Engineers. It was now evident that reliance on manmade structures was a dangerous approach to flood control, and the opportunity to change the focus of disaster recovery was realized. FEMA initiated a bold new approach to mitigation following the Midwest Floods, financing the largest buyout and relocation program that had ever been carried out in this country. For

FOR EXAMPLE

Pattonsburg Becomes More Sustainable with Federal Mitigation Funding

Before the Great Flood of 1993, Pattonsburg was a classic Midwest farm community of 400, occupying a couple of dozen square blocks in the middle of Missouri's countryside. But Pattonsburg was also an unsustainable community. Located at the confluence of Big Creek and the Grand River (a tributary of the Missouri River), the village had been flooded 33 times. The Great Flood swept through Pattonsburg on July 6, 1993, exactly 84 years after the community's first major flood disaster on July 6, 1909. In a well-rehearsed ritual, the villagers cleaned up their homes and shops, and moved back into the floodplain. Then the Great Flood came back a second time. On July 23, the Grand River sent another sickening surge of muck and debris back through the community. This latest flood was the last straw, bringing home the realization that Pattonsburg could not continue to survive in conflict with the river. In the fall of 1993, more than 90% of the residents voted in favor of relocating their town and rebuilding it on higher ground. In the spring of 1994, Pattonsburg got news that it would receive $12 million in federal disaster assistance. The new town located outside of the floodplain, and incorporated additional elements of sustainability into its rebuilding process, including codes for energy efficiency, solar access, and building orientation, plus guidelines for waste minimization and sustainable economic development.

the first time, removal of people and property from the floodplain was accepted as a long-lasting and cost-efficient method for avoiding future disasters. The Midwest buyouts were unique for a number of reasons, not the least of which was the massive scale of the projects; entire neighborhoods and even entire towns were moved—buildings, facilities, people, pets and all—and rebuilt on higher ground.

When President Clinton elevated the Directorship of FEMA to cabinet level status, the value and importance of emergency management and the federal role in that management were recognized. In 1995, FEMA published the first National Mitigation Strategy, which declared mitigation to be the "cornerstone" of emergency management, with two primary goals: increasing public awareness of hazards and reducing loss of life and injuries.

6.1.3 Project Impact

In the years following, FEMA steadfastly increased its emphasis on disaster mitigation—breaking the cycle of destruction and rebuilding that had been the norm. FEMA encouraged disaster-resistant communities, whereby the community would promote sustainable economic development, protect and enhance its natural resources, and ensure a better quality of life for its citizens. Project Impact, a program initiated by FEMA in 1997 that encouraged involvement of all sectors of the community in emergency management and mitigation activities, was an attempt to foster public-private partnerships for community-wide mitigation planning. Project Impact communities were designated in all 50 states, the Virgin Islands, and Puerto Rico.

While several worthwhile mitigation projects were undertaken with Project Impact funding, it has been criticized by some observers as having taken on a distinctly political quality with emphasis on launching a corporate-style marketing campaign complete with logos on baseball caps and tote bags. Other analysts noted that Project Impact lacked the inclusion of all the relevant stakeholders that should have been involved for a community-based mitigation plan.[7] Despite these criticisms, Project Impact was very successful in some communities by increasing awareness of mitigation, especially in the private sector among select businesses and industries. In any event, Project Impact funding was subsequently cut, and the initiative was replaced with passage of the Disaster Mitigation Act of 2000.

6.1.4 The Disaster Mitigation Act of 2000

On October 30, 2000, the President signed into law the **Disaster Mitigation Act (DMA)** of 2000 to amend the Robert T. Stafford Disaster Relief and Emergency Assistance Act of 1988. This legislation is aimed primarily at controlling and streamlining the administration of federal disaster relief and mitigation programs, and places emphasis on pre-disaster mitigation planning to reduce the nation's disaster losses. In fact, the DMA requires state and local mitigation plans as a prerequisite for certain disaster assistance, in effect, making states and local governments work for their mitigation dollars. We discuss the DMA in more detail later in this chapter.

6.1.5 The Threat of Terrorism Initiates Major Agency Reorganization

In the aftermath of the terrorist attacks against America on September 11, 2001, President George W. Bush decided 22 previously disparate domestic agencies needed to be coordinated into one department to protect the nation against threats of all kinds. The Department of Homeland Security (DHS) was created to serve this role. FEMA is now housed in this Department, where the agency carries out its long-standing role of disaster assistance and mitigation programming.

In the years following the creation of the DHS, the focus of emergency management shifted somewhat to terrorism and security threats and away from natural hazards. State and local emergency management agencies received grants and loans to beef up security and anti-terrorism capabilities, in some cases at the expense of natural hazard mitigation programs. However, the recurrence of major international disasters, including the Indian Ocean Tsunami of December 26, 2004, the Pakistan Earthquake of 2005, and the hyper-active hurricane seasons of 2004 and 2005, were harsh reminders to politicians and the public that natural hazards remain very real threats to communities throughout the nation and the world.

6.1.6 Hurricane Katrina: Enough Stink to Go Around

The devastation of communities along the Gulf Coast following the Hurricane Katrina disaster of 2005 once again portrayed FEMA in an unfavorable light. A lack of coordination, a failure in communication, and a dearth of strong leadership created a string of mistakes and misdirections, culminating in catastrophe on a scale never before seen in this country. Granted, the hurricane itself was a major natural hazard, with winds and waves reaching near-record heights as the storm made landfall along the Gulf Coast. However, it was the utter lack of timely response and the abysmal state of pre-disaster planning and preparedness that led to the wretched conditions that occurred in the aftermath of the storm.

Along with the hardship and heartache endured by thousands of Katrina victims whose lives were completely unraveled, another casualty of the disaster has been the reputation of federal, state, and local government emergency management agencies and their employees. Much of the disaster has been steeped in partisan political bickering, which, while providing a field day for the media, has stymied many of the genuine efforts of people dedicated to righting past wrongs and moving forward with recovery and reconstruction plans. At this point, we can only hope that mitigation is incorporated into those plans, as communities throughout the Gulf region are poised to establish themselves once more in the same location where Katrina wreaked such havoc.

SELF-CHECK

- Explain the effect of the Flood Control Act of 1934 on the U.S. Army Corps of Engineers.
- Define FEMA and give the year it was created.
- Name the program that preempted Project Impact.
- Discuss the reason for the creation of the Department of Homeland Security.

6.2 Federal Hazard Mitigation Programs

In the previous commentary about the evolution of federal involvement in emergency management, we briefly mentioned several programs that focus primarily on hazard mitigation. In this section we will discuss this type of program in more detail, including

- ▲ National Flood Insurance Program (NFIP).
- ▲ Community Rating System (CRS).
- ▲ Hazard Mitigation Grant Program (HMGP).
- ▲ Disaster Mitigation Act of 2000 (DMA).
- ▲ Pre-Disaster Mitigation Program (PDM).
- ▲ National Hurricane Program.
- ▲ National Earthquake Hazard Reduction Program.
- ▲ Flood Mitigation Assistance Program.
- ▲ Coastal Barrier Resources Act (CBRA).
- ▲ Structural Projects of the U.S. Army Corps of Engineers.

We might refer to these as obvious or explicit emergency management programs, because these programs are directly focused on emergency management and disaster mitigation. The majority of these programs are carried out by FEMA, with the exception of the CBRA and the activities of the U.S. Army Corps of Engineers.

6.2.1 The Role of FEMA

We begin this discussion of federal mitigation and preparedness functions with a brief review of FEMA. We noted earlier in this chapter that FEMA was created in the late 1970s to act as the lead agency for many aspects of disaster management, and that mitigation as a recognized discipline became a major focus of the agency in the 1990s. We also mentioned that FEMA is now housed within the larger DHS, where it is one of many different agencies responsible for protecting America from dangers of all kinds. Although FEMA has experienced trouble with management and other functions during which time the agency's essential role has come into doubt, it is still considered the preeminent force for supporting the creation of resilient communities.

FEMA's official mission is as follows: "to lead America to prepare for, prevent, respond to and recover from disasters with a vision of 'A Nation Prepared.'"[8] This involves fostering readiness for disaster at every level of the emergency management system. The Mitigation Division spearheads FEMA's efforts to reduce the loss of life and property and to protect our nation's institutions from all types of hazards through a comprehensive, risk-based emergency management program of preparedness and preventive techniques. The Mitigation Division administers the nationwide risk-reduction programs and Congressionally-authorized efforts that are discussed in this section.

6.2.2 The National Flood Insurance Program (NFIP)

Objective observers may quibble about whether insurance fully qualifies as a mitigation tool, because it merely transfers but does not reduce the financial risk of disaster from the property owner to the insurance company. However, in the case of the NFIP, the availability of flood insurance is often viewed as a mitigation technique, because the insurance does not become available merely through payment of premiums, but through community-wide efforts to reduce the risk of flooding.

Congress established the **National Flood Insurance Program (NFIP)** in 1968 through the National Flood Insurance Act to help control the growing cost of federal disaster relief. The program began as a voluntary program for local communities who wished to provide the opportunity for residents to purchase federally-backed flood insurance. In exchange, local governments had to enact ordinances to regulate development in floodplains. An **ordinance** is a local rule or law that the government can enact and that the government has the authority to enforce within its jurisdiction. The legislation was bolstered a few years later through the Flood Insurance Act of 1972, which required the purchase of flood insurance for all federally-backed home mortgages (Veterans Administration loans, for instance), as well as for all mortgages issued by lending institutions that are federally regulated or federally insured (the vast majority of lenders in the United States).

The NFIP is a self-supporting program that requires no taxpayer funds to pay claims or operating expenses for the average historical loss year. Expenses are covered through premiums collected for flood insurance policies. The program has borrowing authority from the U.S. Treasury for times when losses are heavy. These loans are paid back with interest.

The NFIP is the largest single-line writer of property insurance in the United States. In 2004, the NFIP had 4.4 million policies in force in nearly 20,000 communities. The NFIP estimates that mitigation efforts carried out under NFIP regulatory standards reduce America's flood losses by $1 billion each year. In an average year, NFIP policyholders receive approximately $800 million for flood insurance claims and related expenses.

Floodplain Management under the NFIP

Upon enrollment in the NFIP, communities are required to adopt floodplain ordinances that meet criteria established by FEMA. The ordinances must include construction standards for all development in the floodplain areas of the community. These construction standards must apply to both new development and to reconstruction of homes and other buildings that suffer "substantial damage"[9] during a flooding event, meaning the cost of repair or reconstruction after an event is more than 50% of the structure's value. Among the criteria for NFIP floodplain ordinances are requirements that the community issue permits for development in designated floodplains, that all new structures located in the 100-year flood zone be elevated above expected flood heights, that drainage ways and culverts be properly sized and maintained, and that all local water supply and sewage systems are protected to minimize infiltration of floodwaters.

Flood Insurance Rate Maps (FIRMs)

In order to enforce local floodplain ordinances, communities must have accurate information regarding the location of floodplains in the jurisdiction. As part of the NFIP, FEMA develops Flood Insurance Rate Maps (FIRMs) for each participating community. FIRMS are paper or digital maps that represent the full range of flood risk in the community. Each FIRM indicates certain areas using special designations that help the community prepare their development regulations and ascertain where these regulations will apply. See Chapter 2 for a description of FIRMs.

Keeping FIRMs Current

There is much riding on a community's FIRMs. Development permits, ordinance provisions, and structural requirements such as elevation are determined by the location of property as shown on the local FIRMs. The maps also determine the various insurance rates for covered properties. No map is perfect, and floodplains change due to a number of factors. From time to time, FEMA, communities, or individuals may find it necessary for a FIRM to be updated, corrected, or changed. Conditions that may warrant a change in a local FIRM include:

▲ The occurrence of significant construction within the already identified floodplains on the FIRM.

▲ Significant development of upstream communities since the FIRM was published.

▲ The occurrence of flooding for which inundation patterns indicate that the FIRM boundaries are no longer accurate.

▲ The completion of a major flood control project within the community or upstream of the community.

▲ Changes in topography in or adjacent to existing mapped floodplains.

In 1997, FEMA developed a Map Modernization Program to update and digitize the entire U.S. floodplain map inventory. The completed multiyear effort to update and digitize the flood map inventory will cost about $1 billion, but is projected to prevent $45 billion in flood losses over the next 50 years. Unfortunately, that time frame means that many communities will still be using out-of-date flood maps when determining standards for future development in their floodplains. In many of these communities, changes in development, topography, and inundation patterns have been so dramatic that homes and businesses may be unwittingly allowed in areas of flood risk, even in communities that faithfully enforce their floodplain regulations.

Some states have proceeded with their own flood map modernization programs. For example, the state of North Carolina has undertaken a massive flood mapping project. The decision to proceed was made following Hurricane Floyd in 1999, when flood hazard data and map limitations were dramatically revealed. At that time, approximately 75% of North Carolina FIRMs were at least 5 years old, and approximately 55% of North Carolina FIRMs were at least 10 years old. The flooding that occurred during and after Hurricane Floyd far exceeded the flood boundaries portrayed on the FIRMs. Many structures were flooded in locations that did not appear as flood hazard areas on the maps in existence at the time. Although FEMA had begun the process of updating FIRMs nationwide, the federal mapping budget was finite; on average, North Carolina would have received one updated flood study per county per year. In a state with 100 counties, the federal process was deemed inadequate to protect communities from future flood events.

Borrowing from the Treasury to Stay Afloat

The NFIP has been criticized over the years because of many significant flaws in its design and application. Foremost among these criticisms is the observation that the NFIP, by design, is not actuarially sound. The program does not

---

FOR EXAMPLE

New Maps after Katrina

Following Hurricane Katrina, FEMA began revising the federal flood maps for New Orleans, originally drawn in 1984, based on new flooding information and data. The new maps provide critical information for residents trying to decide whether—or how high—to rebuild their damaged homes. While the new maps were developed, the 1984 maps on the books were the law of the land. Citizens looking to renovate were allowed to do so without raising their floor levels as long as they fell into one of two categories: (1) their homes already meet the "base flood elevation" required in the 1984 maps, or (2) their homes did not receive "substantial" damage as defined by FEMA, meaning damage totaling more than 50% of the structure's pre-Katrina market value[10]. Those who follow those rules cannot be dropped from the flood program, and their flood insurance premiums can rise no more than 10% a year. However, some experts warn that, while rebuilding under the old maps may be the cheapest option—particularly for homes built on slabs—it's not necessarily the smartest, nor the most cost-effective over the long run. The higher that homeowners build, the less likely they are to flood, and the lower their flood insurance rates will be. Moreover, if owners of homes that were inundated during Katrina choose to rebuild and subsequently suffer another flood at a later date, FEMA may force them to raise their homes at that point by declaring them subject to repetitive flooding.

---

collect enough premium income to build reserves to meet long-term future expected flood losses, in part because Congress authorized subsidized insurance rates to be made available to some properties. FEMA has generally been successful in keeping the NFIP on a sound financial footing, but the catastrophic flooding events of 2004 (involving four separate hurricanes) required FEMA, as of August 2005, to borrow $300 million from the U.S. Treasury to help pay an estimated $1.8 billion on flood insurance claims. Following Hurricane Katrina in August 2005, legislation was enacted to increase FEMA's borrowing authority from $1.5 billion to $3.5 billion through fiscal year 2008. These figures indicate that the NFIP is heavily subsidizing properties in high-risk areas.

The Problem of Repetitive Losses

Even the most ardent supporters of the NFIP admit that the program is not run like a private insurance company—that is, with loss reduction as a primary goal. This problem is most evident with regard to the repetitive losses that occur on a regular basis, creating a significant drain on NFIP resources.

Repetitive loss properties (RLPs) are defined as properties with two or more NFIP claims over $1000 each within a ten year period. These properties represent 1% of the properties that are currently insured by the NFIP, but in an average loss year they account for 25-30% of the NFIP flood claim dollars. The NFIP pays out, on average, more than $200 million annually for repetitive loss properties.

Most RLPs are older, less safe homes that were grandfathered into the NFIP when the program first began. Most RLPs are residential structures, not vacation or investment properties, and many have been repaired multiple times. Most were built before NFIP construction standards were created and before the flood maps were issued. In other words, many RLPs were built before local flood hazard risks were fully known, and therefore were not constructed to resist water damage. The problem arises when RLPs suffer less than 50% damage, and are thus not required to be rebuilt to higher floodplain management standards designed to reduce future losses. Many RLPs never reach the 50% threshold because a majority of these buildings are in shallow flooding areas that flood only to the depth of a few feet. Consequently, such flooding does not result in the FEMA definition of "substantial damage[11]," allowing the owner to disregard the newer construction standards and merely patch up what damage does occur. The sheer number and cumulative amount of these losses create the repetitive loss payout problem.

Through its repetitive loss provisions, the NFIP has the unintended effect of helping people stay in areas which are repeatedly flooded when it would be in the property owners' and the communities' best long-term interests to mitigate the flood vulnerability of these properties or to move elsewhere. Furthermore, some policyholders of RLP structures are able to take advantage of and abuse the NFIP by making claim after claim on the same flood-prone properties, collecting much more than even the property is worth in some instances.

Attempts to Halt the Flood of Losses

Recent federal action to reduce NFIP losses from RLPs includes a strategy by FEMA to target severe RLPs for mitigation. The Flood Insurance Reform Act of 2004 established a pilot program requiring owners of RLPs to elevate, relocate, or demolish houses, with the NFIP bearing some of those costs. Funds from the Flood Mitigation Assistance program can be used to help with these activities. It is not clear yet whether the inventory of subsidized RLPs has been reduced. Implementation of the Act by FEMA has been slow, and guidelines for policyholders, insurance agents, and local communities have not been widely distributed to explain how the target program works. Congress has also made some proposals to phase out coverage or begin charging full and actuarially based rates for RLP owners who refuse to accept FEMA's offer to purchase or mitigate the effect of floods on these buildings. FEMA's strategy and the Congressional proposals appear to have the potential to reduce the number and vulnerability of RLPs, and thereby help reduce the number of flood insurance claims paid out.

6.2.3 The Community Rating System

The Community Rating System (CRS) is administered by FEMA as part of the NFIP. The CRS provides flood insurance premium discounts for residents in NFIP communities that undertake floodplain mitigation activities above and beyond the minimum NFIP requirements. By rewarding sound floodplain management with insurance savings for residents, the CRS program works towards the goals of reduced flood losses, accurate insurance ratings, and increased awareness of flood insurance. As of October, 2005, there were 1028 CRS communities spread throughout the United States. Over 67% of the NFIP's policy base was located in these communities. Communities receiving premium discounts through the CRS cover a full range of sizes from small to large, and a broad mixture of flood risks, including coastal and riverine.

CRS Classification

The reduction in insurance premiums is in the form of a CRS classification. There are 10 classes in the system, each providing an additional 5% premium rate reduction for properties in the community's mapped floodplain. A community's class is based on the number of credit points it receives for its floodplain management activities. Class 1 requires the most credit points and gives the greatest premium reduction. Class 10 receives no premium reduction. A community that does not apply for the CRS or does not obtain the minimum number of credit points is a Class 10 community.

CRS Floodplain Management Activities

The CRS schedule identifies 18 creditable activities, organized under four categories, or "series." The schedule assigns credit points based upon the extent to which an activity advances the goals of the CRS. The following list explains the four series of the CRS schedule:

1. **Public Information Activities:** This series credits programs that advise residents about the local flood hazard, flood insurance, and ways to reduce flood damage. These activities also provide data needed by insurance agents for accurate flood insurance rating. Activities in the Public Information Series include: elevation certificates, map information, outreach projects, hazard disclosure, flood protection information, and flood protection assistance.

2. **Mapping and Regulatory Activities:** This series credits programs that provide increased protection to new development, including: additional flood data, open space preservation, higher regulatory standards, flood data maintenance, and stormwater management.

3. **Flood Protection Activities:** This series credits programs that reduce the flood risk to existing development, including: floodplain management

plans, acquisition and relocation, flood protection (retrofitting), and drainage system maintenance.

4. **Flood Preparedness Activities:** This series credits: flood warning programs, levee safety, and dam safety.

The most possible credit points are awarded for acquisition and relocation projects to remove structures from the floodplain.

6.2.4 Hazard Mitigation Grant Program

The Hazard Mitigation Grant Program (HMGP) is the largest source of federal funding for state and local mitigation activities. HMGP funds are only available to communities after a disaster declaration has been made by the President, and the amount of mitigation funding is based on a percentage of the total disaster assistance package that is given, as calculated by damage loss estimates. As a result, the larger the disaster, the more mitigation funds are made available.

In recognition of the importance of planning, states that have an approved State Mitigation Plan in effect at the time of the declaration of a major disaster may receive additional HMGP funding. States, with local input, are responsible for identifying and selecting hazard mitigation projects.

Projects funded by the HMGP must be cost-effective; environmentally sound; conform to applicable environmental regulations; and substantially reduce the risk of future damage, hardship, loss, or suffering resulting from a major disaster. Types of projects for which HMGP funds can be used include, but are not limited to:

▲ Construction activities that will result in protection from hazards.
▲ Retrofit of facilities, structures, lifelines.
▲ Acquisition/relocation of structures from willing sellers.
▲ Elevation of flood-prone structures.
▲ Development of state or local mitigation standards.
▲ Development of comprehensive hazard mitigation programs.
▲ Preparedness/response equipment and services.
▲ Building code enforcement.
▲ Public awareness campaigns.

6.2.5 Disaster Mitigation Act of 2000

The Disaster Mitigation Act (DMA) of 2000 amends the Robert T. Stafford Disaster Relief and Emergency Assistance Act of 1988 and is intended to facilitate cooperation between state and local authorities, prompting them to work together. The DMA encourages and rewards local and state pre-disaster planning and promotes sustainability as a strategy for disaster resistance. The enhanced planning network is meant to enable local and state governments to better artic-ulate accurate needs for mitigation, resulting in faster allocation of funding and more effective risk reduction projects.

Significant changes brought about through enactment of the DMA include the requirement that local governments must create and adopt a mitigation plan in order to receive certain disaster assistance funds, including post-disaster pro-ject grants (bricks and mortar grants) under the HMGP and the Pre-Disaster Mitigation Program as well as assistance for rebuilding public infrastructure fol-lowing a major disaster, with some exceptions. See Chapter 7 for a discussion of the DMA as it pertains to state hazard mitigation planning and the conse-quences of not preparing a mitigation plan.

The rules that accompany the DMA lay out quite a rigorous planning process that states, local governments, and Native American Tribes must follow. FEMA is in charge of reviewing all the state and local plans that are submitted to it for approval, and certain criteria must be met before a plan will meet FEMA's guidelines. The plan must identify all the hazards that threaten a com-munity and must also include a thorough risk analysis for each of those hazards. The plan must contain mitigation goals and objectives and lay out strategies and actions that will reduce the community's vulnerability to the hazards iden-tified. These are not easy tasks to accomplish, and an effective mitigation plan requires many staff hours and much community networking to meet FEMA standards. However, the benefits of having a sound and well thought-out mit-igation plan in place before a disaster strikes are innumerable, and communi-ties that make the effort are rewarded by far more than their eligibility to receive future federal mitigation money.

6.2.6 Pre-Disaster Mitigation Program

Section 203 of the Disaster Mitigation Act of 2000 establishes the National Pre-Disaster Mitigation Program (PDM). The PDM Program provides techni-cal and financial assistance to state and local governments to assist in the implementation of pre-disaster hazard mitigation measures. PDM projects must be cost effective and designed to reduce injuries, loss of life, and dam-age and destruction of property, including damage to critical services and facilities.

Perhaps most notable about the PDM Program is the fact that it provides mitigation funding that is not dependent on a disaster declaration. Instead, funding through the PDM Program is provided in the form of a competitive grant system. PDM can provide funding for hazard mitigation activities (includ-ing planning) that complement a comprehensive mitigation program *before a disaster strikes*. PDM Program-funded multi-hazard mitigation projects must primarily focus on natural hazards, but may also address hazards caused by non-natural forces.

The following are eligible mitigation projects under the PDM:

▲ Acquisition or relocation of hazard-prone property for conversion to open space in perpetuity.

▲ Structural and non-structural retrofitting of existing buildings and facilities, such as elevation, floodproofing, storm shutters, hurricane clips, etc.

▲ Minor structural hazard control or protection projects, such as vegetation management, stormwater management (e.g., culverts, floodgates, retention basins, etc.) or shoreline/landslide stabilization.

▲ Localized flood control projects to protect critical facilities, such as ring levees, floodwall systems, etc.

▲ Development of hazard mitigation plans.

6.2.7 The National Hurricane Program

The goal of the National Hurricane Program is to significantly reduce the loss of life and property, economic disruption, and disaster assistance costs resulting from hurricanes. The program addresses population protection and evacuation, structural mitigation in hurricane-prone areas, and public education and awareness campaigns. The program has also funded hazard identification research as well as post-storm analyses to evaluate the effectiveness of mitigation measures and response activities. While the program's focus on hurricane mitigation and preparedness is well-defined, the program is woefully under funded, with FEMA receiving a paltry $3 million annually to combat hurricane risks along both the Atlantic and Gulf coasts.

6.2.8 National Earthquake Hazards Reduction Program

The National Earthquake Hazards Reduction Program (NEHRP) involves four agencies at the federal level: FEMA, the U.S. Geological Survey (USGS), the National Science Foundation (NSF), and the National Institute of Standards and Technology (NIST). The fundamental goal of the NEHRP is to reduce the impacts of earthquakes and subsequent loss of lives, property damage, and economic loss. To this end, the NEHRP provides financial and technical assistance to all levels of government and to the private sector to implement earthquake hazard mitigation measures. The NEHRP has fostered the development and implementation of seismic design and construction standards and techniques, as well as education and information dissemination of risk-reduction activities. Since the advent of the program, many building codes throughout the states where a seismic risk exists have been changed to include seismic resistance standards for new construction, although this is by no means uniform among all such states. The promotion of loss estimation studies is also a crucial component of the NEHRP.

6.2.9 The Flood Mitigation Assistance Program

The Flood Mitigation Assistance Program (FMA) is authorized by the National Flood Insurance Reform Act of 1994. The FMA Program expands FEMA's mitigation assistance to states, communities, and individuals by providing grants for cost-effective measures to reduce or eliminate the long-term risk of flood damage to the built environment and real property. The priority goal of the FMA is to reduce repetitive losses to the National Flood Insurance Program (NFIP).

Unlike the HMGP, which is available only after a presidentially-declared disaster, FMA funding is available to eligible communities every year. To be eligible for FMA grants, a community must be a participant in the NFIP and have jurisdiction over a particular area having special flood hazards.

The FMA Program provides three types of grants: planning, project, and technical assistance. Planning grants allow states and communities to determine flood risks and identify actions to reduce these risks. Creation and approval of a flood mitigation plan is a prerequisite to receiving FMA project grants. The regulations do not mandate that FMA plans be limited to flood hazards, although funds will only be provided for the flood portion of any mitigation plan.

Once a community has a flood mitigation plan approved by FEMA, it is eligible for flood mitigation project grants. Types of projects that are eligible for funding through the FMA include elevation, acquisition, and relocation projects; minor structural projects (flood retention ponds, floodproofing sewers, culvert modification, etc.); and beach nourishment activities.

6.2.10 Coastal Barrier Resources Act (CBRA)

Congress passed the Coastal Barrier Resources Act (CBRA) in 1982 in an attempt to reduce the costs to the federal government from development in the extremely fragile environment of coastal barrier islands. Besides bearing the brunt of impacts from storms and erosion, most coastal barriers are made of unconsolidated sediments such as sand, and gravel, etc. This geological composition alone makes them highly unstable areas on which to build (see Figure 6-2). CBRA prohibits the spending of federal money for growth-inducing infrastructure such as roads, bridges, wastewater systems, potable water supplies, and protective works including seawalls and groins in areas that are within the Coastal Barrier Resources System (CBRS). The CBRS consists of 585 "units" of land that were undeveloped at the time the legislation was passed and were mapped according to criteria developed by the U.S. Fish and

Figure 6-2

Undeveloped barrier island in North Carolina.

Wildlife Service. CRBA further stipulates that new development is ineligible for federal flood insurance in these areas.

A product of conservative political times, CBRA was intended to reduce threats to people and property as a cost-saving measure. It was widely recognized that federal programs such as flood insurance (through the NFIP) and infrastructure were encouraging building in areas that were prone to repeated natural hazards, including flooding, hurricanes, erosion, and coastal storms, and that the federal government would constantly be picking up the tab for damaged homes and businesses in a cycle of damage and reconstruction. CBRA is a free-market approach to conservation. These areas can be developed, but federal taxpayers do not underwrite the investments.

Effectiveness of CBRA

It is important to recognize that the purpose of CBRA is merely to prevent federal funds from being spent on islands that are included in the System. The Act applies only to these specific mapped areas and does not restrict activities of the private sector or state or local governments within the CBRS.

Many local coastal communities wish to increase job opportunities and expand their tax base by encouraging development. Many states are eager for the same economic benefits and are willing to invest in large infrastructure projects such as bridges and causeways to connect remote barrier islands to the mainland. Furthermore, some private developers are able to secure financial backing enabling them to construct their own infrastructure, such as roads, water, and sewer. In fact, some of the units have been developed with high-value projects such as multi-story condominiums in spite of the Act. However, studies have shown that, although local and state governments can step in to facilitate coastal development, areas that are not eligible for federal value-added programs are developed much more slowly than other areas, if developed at all.[12]

6.2.11 United States Army Corps of Engineers

The United States Army Corps of Engineers plays two very significant but different roles in managing development in hazardous areas. We discuss the role of the Corps in administrating the 404 wetlands program of the Clean Water Act later in this chapter. In this role, the Corps issues permits for dredge and fill activities in wetlands, providing at least some measure of protection for these important natural mitigation resources.

The second function of the Corps involves the design and construction of structural projects in the coastal zone and along the nation's rivers and streams. Corps flood control efforts range from small, local protection projects (small dikes and seawalls, for example) to major dams and levee systems. Today, most Corps-constructed flood protection projects are owned by sponsoring cities, towns, and agricultural districts, but the Corps continues to maintain and operate nearly 400 dams and reservoirs for flood control.

The original function of shoreline and riverbank protection projects was to protect development from the invading ocean and intruding rivers. This continues to be the major focus of Corps projects, but increasingly, new projects are designed to work more as a part of the natural system rather than as an effort to manage hydrological processes themselves. For example, beach nourishment projects that involve massive deposits of sand placed along eroding ocean beaches by the Corps is seen as a more environmentally responsible approach to erosion than hardened structures such as groins or bulkheads. Proponents argue that the projects do decrease vulnerability by deflecting wave energy, protecting against flooding, and by providing the extra protection of a wider beach (in the case of sand renourishment projects). Critics argue that if the projects do in fact reduce vulnerability it is only for the short term, and that these projects simply delay having to face the real problem of coastal erosion and riverine flooding. At worst they serve to exacerbate vulnerability by making the hazardous areas seem less vulnerable than they really are, thus encouraging development in areas prone to flooding and severe erosion. However, in internal evaluations of project performance, the Corps has found that federal protection projects have had no measurable effect on encouraging more development. The federal government plays no role in decisions regarding land use; state and local authorities make these decisions and are responsible for managing their shores and floodplains. Further discussion on structural engineering projects can be found in Chapter 12.

SELF-CHECK

- Explain the mission of FEMA.
- Discuss how the **National Flood Insurance Program** works to mitigate flood hazards.
- Identify the types of mitigation projects eligible under the Pre-Disaster Mitigation program.

6.3 Federal Programs That Indirectly Manage Hazard Impacts

In this section we will discuss a few federal programs that focus on protecting the quality of the natural environment, including the Clean Water Act (CWA), the National Environmental Policy Act (NEPA), and the Coastal Zone Management Act (CZMA). We refer to these as indirect emergency management programs, because they do not focus on reducing hazard vulnerability per se, but can result in risk reduction as a by-product of their main objective. We will also consider some other federal activities that may make these and the explicit hazard management programs less effective, including capital improvement programs and taxation policies that foster development in hazardous areas.

6.3.1 Clean Water Act

The primary purpose of the federal Clean Water Act (CWA), formally known as the Federal Water Pollution Control Act, is to increase quality of the waters of the United States by reducing pollutants discharged into them. The CWA consists of several pollution control programs, including point source (pollution that is discharged from a specific definable source, such as a pipe), local stormwater management, and non-point source (pollutants that do not discharge from a specific source, such as agricultural runoff). In so far as water quality and flood mitigation are interconnected objectives, these CWA programs can help mitigate the impacts of hazards in communities. In addition, Section 404 of the Clean Water Act contains provisions that restrict the discharge of dredge and fill materials into the nation's wetlands, the most significant of the CWA programs for flood mitigation purposes.

Section 404 of the Clean Water Act

Section 404 of the CWA requires a permit from the United States Army Corps of Engineers to discharge "dredge or fill materials" into the "waters of the United States." [13] Through a complicated series of regulations and guidelines, the term *waters of the United States* covers many types of wetlands. The term *discharge of dredge or fill* can cover many kinds of development, because it is very difficult to build in a wetland without creating dry areas suitable for construction. As a consequence, in the process of protecting water quality, Section 404 limits development activity in wetlands, including coastal and many freshwater wetlands. The Corps of Engineers may issue a permit only if it finds that there are no practicable alternative sites for the proposed activity. In addition to a permit, Section 404 requires that the impacts of the dredge and fill activity be mitigated through restoration or through the creation of new wetlands elsewhere.

The protection of the nation's wetlands is very significant for flood mitigation because in their natural state, wetlands can absorb floodwaters, acting much like a sponge (as shown in Figure 6-3). Wetlands also provide storage for floodwaters, releasing the excess water slowly during dry periods.

404 Flaws

Without the protections afforded by Section 404, a substantial portion of the nation's wetlands would undoubtedly have been lost to development. However,

Figure 6-3

Wetlands absorb floodwaters, helping to reduce flood risks to people and property.

FOR EXAMPLE

U.S. Supreme Court Decides Isolated Wetland Case

On January 9, 2001, the Supreme Court handed down *Solid Waste Agency of Northern Cook County (SWANCC) v. U.S. Army Corps of Engineers*. At issue in the SWANCC case was the scope of Clean Water Act Section 404, the charter for the federal wetlands permitting program.

SWANCC, a consortium of Chicago-area cities and villages, sought to develop a landfill for baled non-hazardous solid waste. The parcel of land selected for the landfill had been used for sand and gravel mining until about 1960. Since then, the excavation trenches from the mining had evolved into ponds ranging in size from a few feet across to several acres. SWANCC obtained the needed local and state permits, but the Corps, based on the presence of the ponds and their use by migratory birds, asserted jurisdiction under Section 404 and denied a permit. The Corps' "migratory bird rule" says that isolated waters include those "which are or would be used as habitat by . . . migratory birds that cross state lines . . ."[14] The Corps had found that the water areas on the SWANCC site were used as habitat by migratory birds that cross state lines. In the SWANCC decision, the U.S. Supreme Court explicitly held that the Corps of Engineers' use of the "migratory bird rule," adopted by the agency to interpret the reach of its Section 404 authority over "isolated waters" (including isolated wetlands), exceeded the authority granted by that section.

---

there are some inherent limitations to the program as a conservation tool. First, 404 permitting applies only to discharges of dredge and fill material. There is no prohibition against other methods of damaging or destroying wetlands, and many acres of wetlands have disappeared without any discharge taking place. Second, the definition of what qualifies as a wetland can be problematic. For instance, isolated wetlands (wetlands that are not adjacent to a navigable waterway) are not under the Corps of Engineers permitting authority, leaving many wetland areas unprotected because they do not have a visible connection with another larger body of water. In addition, some observers have commented that the Corps too readily issues permits, noting that very few permits are actually denied, and that those permits that are issued are not rigorously enforced, especially with regards to wetland mitigation and restoration requirements.

6.3.2 The Coastal Zone Management Act

When passing the Coastal Zone Management Act of 1972, Congress declared that the coastal zone of the United States is of tremendous importance to the entire nation, not just to the individual coastal states, and that the existing

NATIONAL OCEANIC AND ATMOSPHERIC ADMINISTRATION ACTIVITIES BEFORE, DURING, AND AFTER HURRICANE KATRINA

The National Oceanic and Atmospheric Administration (NOAA), an agency within the U.S. Department of Commerce plays a significant role in all stages of emergency management, including mitigation, preparedness, response, and recovery, as illustrated by ongoing activities carried out by several NOAA offices prior to and following the Hurricane Katrina disaster (see Figure 6-4). During preparedness operations before Hurricane Katrina, the National Weather Service (NWS), an agency within NOAA, was instrumental in providing real-time forecasts of Hurricane Katrina's condition. Operating out of the Hurricane Center in Miami, NWS predicted the track of Katrina with a high degree of accuracy as compared to average margins of error over the last 10 years. This accuracy (in part due to continuously improved modeling and tracking methodologies available through hurricane hunter aircraft missions, satellite imagery, and other state-of-the-art technologies) allowed for more precise estimations of landfall and increased warning time to initiate evacuation.[15] On August 27, 2005, the Director of the National Hurricane Center, Max Mayfield, made personal phone calls to the state governors and mayor of New Orleans describing the force of Katrina

Figure 6-4

NOAA Research Vessels such as the Research Vessel Nancy Foster are involved in monitoring activities after Katrina.

NOAA

and encouraging mandatory evacuations of the expected impact areas. The official warning from the Hurricane Center was equally urgent and strongly worded, and was proven later to be very accurate: "Hurricane Katrina…a most powerful hurricane with unprecedented strength…most of the area will be uninhabitable for weeks…water shortages will make human suffering incredible by modern standards."[16]

In terms of response and recovery after Katrina, NOAA has been actively involved in cleanup activities (removal of marine debris, mapping, financial assistance), restoring infrastructure related to fisheries, and recovering wetlands habitat.[17] NOAA research has included measurements of contamination in the Gulf of Mexico due to Katrina, as well as monitoring, sample evaluation, assessment of fish populations and fisheries, and satellite imagery of harmful algal bloom (HAB) outbreaks (HAB are rapid dense growths of algae that deplete the water of oxygen as they die and decompose). NOAA has also played a role in wetlands loss analysis and restoration activities. Included among NOAA's responsibilities were weekly reports on response and recovery efforts submitted to the White House Gulf Restoration Working Group.

NOAA also has the responsibility to participate in mitigation activities prior to the next disaster. The Administration has developed a Community Resiliency Index, an assessment tool intended to determine community resiliency and hazard impacts. Additionally, NOAA provides long term planning support through coordination with other federal agencies for storm surge mitigation investigations, including creation of evacuation decision support tools, topographic/bathymetric data, and storm surge/forecast systems. NOAA also prepares continuing support surveys to keep shipping lanes clear of debris, works with industry to clean up oil spills, and supplies water level measurements for the accurate determination of levee heights.

Several offices within NOAA engage in pre-disaster planning activities, such as the National Ocean Service's Office of Ocean and Coastal Resource Management (OCRM), which provides planning assistance under the Coastal Zone Management Act. Through the CZMA partnership, state governments work with this office to conduct a variety of pre-disaster activities, including: mapping and monitoring of erosion potentials, creation of permitting and setback systems to limit development in vulnerable areas, and establishing building codes.[18] This office also participates in post-Katrina planning efforts to mitigate disasters in the future.

management programs (largely state programs) were not adequately managing the coast. The Act establishes a national policy "to preserve, protect, develop, and where possible, to restore or enhance, the resources of the Nation's coastal zone for this and succeeding generations."[19] The CZMA is administered by the U.S. Department of Commerce, through the NOAA's

Office of Ocean and Coastal Resources Management (OCRM) and applies to states along the Atlantic and Pacific Oceans, the Gulf Coast, and the Great Lakes.

The CZMA: A Flexible Program

To participate in the Coastal Zone Management Program, states must respond to all of the requirements of the Act. Within the context of the Act, each state may determine the substantive content of its own coastal program. This flexible approach was established in recognition of the great differences in the nature of the coast from state to state. For example, Maine, which is characterized by rocky beaches with numerous coves and bays, has a very different type of coastline than Georgia, which consists of sandy beaches and a string of barrier islands. Both of these coasts are different from coastlines bordering the Great Lakes. In addition, this flexible approach recognizes the many social, economic, and political differences that exist in the coastal zone from state to state.

CZMA Incentives for State Participation

Although participation is voluntary, the CZMA provides two strong incentives for states to formulate coastal programs. The first incentive involves grants: grants under Section 305 assist states in preparing their Coastal Zone Management Programs, while Section 306 provides funding to administer approved programs. Grant allocations based on the extent and nature of the state's shoreline and population. The second incentive to encourage states to participate in the Coastal Zone Management Program is the "consistency doctrine,"[20] found in Section 307 of the CZMA.

Under the consistency doctrine, actions of any federal agency in a state's coastal zone must be consistent with that state's coastal management policies, giving the state a degree of control over activities of the federal government. The consistency provision covers activities and projects carried out directly by a federal agency (for instance, highway construction by the U.S. Department of Transportation), as well as activities and projects for which a federal permit or other form of approval is required (such as 404 permits issued by the US Army Corps of Engineers). Examples of other federal action that must be consistent with state coastal management programs include navigational and flood control projects, wastewater treatment facility funding, military activities, and federal fisheries management.

Hazard Mitigation through State Coastal Management Programs

In 1990 Congress amended the Coastal Zone Management Act and added several additional activities for which states may use CZMA grant funds. These activities include measures to prevent or significantly reduce threats to life and property destruction by eliminating development and redevelopment in high-hazard areas, managing development in other hazard areas, and anticipating and managing the effects of potential sea level rise and Great Lakes level rise. With this amendment, Congress made explicit the need to mitigate the impacts of natural hazards as a part of state coastal management programs.

Some states have been quite creative in establishing activities within their coastal management programs that are effective in mitigating the impacts of natural hazards. These activities include:

▲ Shoreline management and retreat (creating setback rules, regulating shoreline development, shoreline stabilization).

▲ Regulating shore-hardening structures (e.g., prohibiting or restricting seawalls, revetments, groins, and other shore-hardening structures).

▲ Managing post-hazard reconstruction (regulating the repair and reconstruction of buildings damaged by a coastal hazard).

▲ Managing unbuildable lots (regulating construction or lots that should not be developed because of their proximity to hazards).

▲ Promulgating building codes and construction standards (regulating construction through rules, inspections, and enforcement).

▲ Protecting coastal wetlands.

▲ Establishing policies to address sea level rise.

▲ Implementing land acquisition programs (purchasing private lots in hazardous areas).

▲ Promoting local land use planning (encouraging or requiring local governments to include hazard mitigation in their land use plans).

▲ Developing special area management plans (creating plans that deal with coastal hazards in designated areas of the coastal zone).

6.3.3 The National Environmental Policy Act

The primary purpose of the National Environmental Policy Act (NEPA) is to require federal agencies to take environmental issues into consideration when making significant decisions. The Act requires federal agencies to prepare a detailed explanation of the environmental impact of agency decisions and to inform other agencies and the public of that impact through various types of disclosure documents, including:

▲ Environmental Assessments (EA), prepared to assist the agency in deciding whether or not a more detailed study is required.

▲ Environmental Impact Studies (EIS) prepared when it is decided that an action is likely to cause a significant impact on the environment.

▲ Findings of No Significant Impact (FONSI), prepared if an EIS is not required.

NEPA as a Policy Act

NEPA is a policy act, merely requiring dissemination of information regarding potential environmental impacts, and lacks the regulatory muscle of other federal environmental statutes such as the Clean Air Act and the Clean Water Act. Because NEPA does not preclude an agency from implementing its decision, regardless of the action's impact, some observers have characterized NEPA as a toothless ogre. However, as a consciousness-raising device, NEPA does have the potential to require greater collaboration and transparency for activities that take place in environmentally sensitive areas, including the coastal zone, floodplains, and wetlands.[21] At a minimum, the requirements under NEPA slow down the progress of activities that could harm the environment, allowing citizens and affected local communities to respond[22].

SELF-CHECK

- List four programs that fall under the Clean Water Act.
- Explain the importance of wetlands for flood mitigation.
- Discuss the purpose of the CZMA.

6.4 Federal Incentives for Development in Hazard Areas: Driving With the Brakes On

The previous sections of this chapter sketch out the evolution of various federal mitigation approaches that have been in effect over the years, and discuss in more detail how some of these programs may reduce vulnerability to natural hazards. However, at the same time that these programs are being carried out to make development safer, there are dozens of other federal programs and policies that actively *encourage* development, even in some of the most hazardous areas of our country. These incentives are primarily in the form of federally funded infrastructure programs, and policies of the federal tax code. These counterproductive forces to national mitigation efforts have been characterized as "driving with the brakes on."[23]

6.4.1 The Internal Revenue Code as a *De Facto* Management Tool

The Internal Revenue Code (IRC) is administered by the Internal Revenue Service (IRS), a branch of the United States Treasury Department. The basic function of the IRC is to raise the revenue needed to operate the federal government. As a matter of tax policy, the Code includes provisions that allow taxpayers to make deductions, take credits, and otherwise lessen their tax burden. Pursuant to a major disaster declaration, homeowners and businesses may claim a casualty loss deduction for uninsured losses to real and personal property. Businesses in particular may write off many kinds of uninsured expenses involved in restoring property to pre-disaster condition. In essence, these deductions serve to reward, or at least subsidize, risky property decisions.[24]

Additional tax subsidies apply to investment properties, including property that is held for resale and for rental income, characteristics of much oceanfront and riverine real estate today. Some of the tax benefits for investment properties found in the IRC include:

▲ Mortgage interest and property taxes on second homes may be treated as deductions from taxable income.

▲ Damage to a property caused by a natural hazard may be treated as a casualty loss deduction.

▲ Expenses incurred in operating a second home as a rental property may be treated as business expenses (advertising, maintenance, management, etc.).

▲ Accelerated depreciation allowances on rental property may be permitted.

The cumulative effect of these various tax breaks has been described as "perhaps the most insidious federal stimulus to development along hazardous coasts."[25] The Internal Revenue Code removes much of the investment risk in hazard areas by softening the financial burden of property damage and offsetting the economic pain of unwise land use decisions.

6.4.2 Federal Infrastructure Programs

Capital improvement programs undertaken by federal agencies U.S. Army Corps of Engineers, provide significant stimulation for growth in hazard areas. All together, the federal government carries out approximately 40 different programs that foster development nationwide, including many programs that apply to high hazard areas such as the coastal zone.[26] Growth and rebuilding has been stimulated through several community development programs, and federal subsidies for water and sewer have eased the cost of development substantially in many hazard areas. One of the most aggressive growth stimulators is the federal Department of Transportation, which constructs highways, causeways, and bridges that connect barrier islands and other previously inaccessible areas with the mainland, greatly easing transportation to hazardous coastal lands. Many of these transportation projects are justified as supporting existing communities, but they also often serve to encourage new development as well.

These capital improvements are often made possible by the aggressive efforts of congressional representatives to secure funding for a variety of infrastructure and growth-inducing projects, from new highways to flood control to beach renourishment. Typically, these projects are supported by a specific member of

---

FOR EXAMPLE

Department of Transportation Provides Easy Access to Dauphin Island

Dauphin Island is located just off the coast of Alabama in the Gulf of Mexico. Because access to the island was only by ferry for many years, the island remained relatively undeveloped, until the U.S. Department of Transportation constructed a bridge linking the island to the mainland. Since that time, development on Dauphin Island has continued to grow, and with increased development came increased vulnerability to the impacts of hurricanes and other coastal storms. The bridge to Dauphin Island has been repeatedly damaged, and repeatedly rebuilt, at considerable federal expense. Following Hurricane Katrina, for example, the bridge was severely damaged, cutting the island off from the mainland. Since that time, construction on the bridge has begun anew, and homeowners have returned to rebuild on the island once again.

Congress and his or her local constituents as "earmarked" funds, but not necessarily by the federal agency in charge of implementing and administering the politically mandated "pork barrel project".[27] In general, the exposure of people and property to flooding and other hazards has been enhanced by federal financing of highway construction, sewers, and other infrastructure that serves to increase the development of hazard areas while reducing development costs.[28]

SELF-CHECK

- Name two ways that the federal government offers incentives to development.
- List four tax benefits for investment properties.
- Explain how federal infrastructure programs aid development of hazard areas.

6.5 Federal Disaster Assistance: Creating a Moral Hazard?

It is clear from our discussion in this chapter that some federal programs promote development in hazardous areas. The intent of these programs is to bring about public benefits such as a robust economy, growing communities, a healthy tax base, and the profitable use of private property. However, the net result of infrastructure programs and tax breaks that encourage unsafe development is increased vulnerability to natural hazards. Some observers argue that disaster assistance plays a similar role in stimulating development in hazard areas.

6.5.1 Federal Subsidies of Hazard Risks

The federal system of disaster assistance allows property owners and communities to recoup their losses whenever a disaster is declared. FEMA disburses public assistance funds to help communities reestablish facilities and services, and individual and family assistance grants to help residents get back on their feet. Numerous other agencies, such as the Farm Service Agency, the Small Business Administration, and the Department of Housing and Urban Development also provide grants and loan packages to victims to help them recover after a disaster and to rebuild in the same location. However, some observers have criticized the disaster assistance program as an enabler of unsafe and unsustainable development.

While federal assistance is technically available only as a supplement to state, local, and private resources, it has been characterized by some scholars as having become an "entitlement," at least in the eyes of the recipients. Americans want and expect the federal government to pay the expenses associated with a natural disaster. Politicians want and expect to be able to give it to them. Yet some believe the ready and willing provision of disaster assistance from the federal government negates all common sense or survival instinct when development decisions are made. This dilemma has been described as a **moral hazard**, as expressed by Professor Rutherford Platt in his book *Disasters and Democracy*:

> . . . to what extent does the likelihood of generous federal assistance serve to diminish the natural caution that individuals, communities, and businesses might otherwise exercise in adjusting to natural hazards in their investment and location decisions? At what point does compassion lead to "co-dependency" whereby potential disaster victims and their federal protectors become locked in a repetitive cycle of loss, compensation, reconstruction and new losses?[29]

According to the moral hazard paradox, the increasing amount of disaster funds and the ease with which many communities become eligible to receive assistance have lessened the incentives to take responsibility for hazard avoidance. Generous compensation for any losses that may occur makes spending money on mitigation seem pointless.[30] Federal insurance claim payments make investment in floodprone areas worthwhile, and beach nourishment programs make building on the coast a sure profit maker. The risk of building in a hazardous area has been reduced so significantly by federal programs that, in effect, the federal government is subsidizing the risk itself. The individual property owner shares in the risk only as one of millions of other taxpayers, spreading the cost to those who do not live in hazard areas equally with those who do.

Subsidizing Risk Through Mitigation Programs

For the past two decades, much of the post-disaster federal largess distributed to communities affected by natural hazards has included money for mitigation, not just for rebuilding in the same place in the same way. In theory, and more often than not in practice as well, mitigation funds—parceled out to the states as a percentage of the total disaster dollars that flow from the federal government following disaster declaration—do indeed make communities less vulnerable to future natural hazards. The finest example of mitigation successes can be found in communities that have chosen to engage in massive buyout projects, where residents are given the chance to sell their homes and businesses and relocate to drier, safer, higher ground and start again. But hazard mitigation itself involves the same dilemma as disaster assistance: what should the federal role be? In other words, how much should communities and individuals be expected to do for themselves as a condition of federal assistance?[31] We discuss this issue and other components of the moral hazard conundrum in the exploration of possible solutions in the next section.

6.5.2 Posing Solutions That Lead to More Questions

Many observers believe the federal government subsidizes the risks associated with development in hazard areas. The provision of affordable flood insurance, construction of shoreline protection and flood control works, tax deductions for hazard-damaged property losses, as well as payments of disaster assistance—all of these federal activities allow or even encourage people to build in hazard areas. Although the American public has come to view these payments and subsidies as their entitlement or right, hard choices about eliminating or reducing federal subsidies must be made by policy makers who hold the power of the purse.

Breaking the Cycle by Limiting Federal Disaster Dollars

Reduction in disaster payments, for example, could be phased in over time, with ample warning to state and local governments that they will soon be responsible for a larger share of relief following the next big disaster. Some commentators have proposed a type of deductible system, whereby state and local governments would have to pay on their own up to a certain amount before federal money is distributed.[32] This method should encourage state and local governments to take a more proactive and aggressive approach to regulating land uses in high hazard areas, such as the coastline or along known fault zones.

Charging Appropriate Premium Rates for the NFIP

The NFIP, notorious for providing low-cost flood insurance that does not reflect the actual level of risk involved, could be greatly strengthened if repetitive loss problems were addressed, perhaps by charging the owners of repetitive loss structures a higher premium for flood insurance. This would presumably encourage these owners to relocate their homes and businesses out of flood-prone areas or to strengthen their buildings against flood impacts, if only enough to reduce the premiums. Similarly, shoreline erosion would be excluded from insurance coverage, since it benefits wealthy, second-home oceanfront owners and investors much more than primary residential property owners.[33]

Making New Development Pay for Its Safety

Many critics of the current approach to hazards management believe the new development in hazardous areas should bear more of the burden of mitigation measures. This should encourage private developers and builders as well as homebuyers to avoid places prone to flooding, wildfire, erosion, or earthquake. Also, local and state governments should assess hazard districts with higher tax rates or impact fees, while reducing taxes and fees for properties built in safer locations.

Federal Dollars for Permanent Solutions

Most critics advocate that the federal government continue to play a major role in supporting particularly expensive mitigation strategies such as acquisition of hazardous areas and relocation of repetitive loss properties. By providing a significant portion of the initial outlay to purchase flood-prone, high-erosion, or seismic risk areas, the federal government can help local and state governments realize a long-term benefit, while also permanently eliminating the federal government's chances of having to pay for assistance for that area in the future. As for what the state and local governments should do in return, the hazard mitigation plans that are required by the Disaster Mitigation Act of 2000 are a fine start to sharing the responsibility.

Creating a Federal Vulnerability Impact Statement

In addition to reducing disaster assistance payments to state and local governments, we should also closely examine federal programs that increase hazard vulnerability and require exposure of how public infrastructure encourages unsafe development. The creation of a Federal Hazard Vulnerability Impact policy, modeled on the National Environmental Policy Act (NEPA), may be one approach. All federal agencies should prepare a vulnerability assessment that discloses how a proposed project may impact the vulnerability of the community where the action will take place. Such disclosure would force federal agencies to consider the hazard implications of their actions, as well as inform the public about possible increases in vulnerability. Analysis and disclosure may prompt alternative measures to accomplish the desired goal, without increasing the risk of hazard exposure.

Creating a Federal Hazard Mitigation Consistency Provision

The consistency provisions of the Coastal Zone Management Act (CZMA) encourage state governments to participate in the national coastal management program. The consistency doctrine assures states that activities of the federal government will be consistent with policies contained in the state's program. A

> ## FOR EXAMPLE
>
> ### The U.S. Virgin Islands Recommends a Vulnerability Impact Statement
>
> The U.S. Virgin Islands is a place of incredible beauty, with volcanic slopes covered in lush green foliage, white sandy beaches, coral reefs, mangrove swamps, and numerous sites of cultural and historical significance. Unfortunately, the U.S. Virgin Islands also faces serious issues of resource depletion, impaired water quality, and a high level of vulnerability to flooding. Many of these problems are due to poor land use decisions, both on the part of the government and the private sector—decisions that have resulted in development that disregards the suitability of the site in terms of natural resource protection or the risk of flooding.
>
> The U.S. Virgin Islands developed a Flood Hazard Mitigation Plan to address these multiple issues of concern. Although recognizing the territory has limited resources—financial, technical, and human—the plan sets forth several innovative strategies for reducing flood risks. The plan recommends that the governor of the U.S. Virgin Islands issue an executive order requiring all Virgin Islands agencies and departments to prepare a Flood Hazard Vulnerability Impact Statement that assesses and makes full disclosure of the impact that any proposed construction project or activity undertaken with public funds might have on flooding in territorial watersheds. Upon submission of the impact statement, the governor is to take the vulnerability impact statement under advisement and to consider termination of the project or activity if it is found to exacerbate the risk of flooding in or around the proposed site.

federal hazard mitigation consistency provision modeled on the successful CZMA may encourage states to develop and enforce strong mitigation policies in their own state mitigation plans. Through such a provision, the federal government would not undertake projects that could increase vulnerability if the activity is covered by an enforceable policy in the state's mitigation plan.

SELF-CHECK

- Define **moral hazard.**
- Explain how mitigation programs may provide a false sense of security to hazard-prone communities.
- Give examples of potential changes to federal disaster policies.

SUMMARY

The federal government steps in to provide relief after every major disaster that happens in our country. But do these disaster funds in fact contribute to the risk of future disasters? This chapter discusses how the federal government's involvement in emergency management has grown over the years. The Federal Emergency Management Agency and other federal programs each play a direct role in the country's hazard management activities. Other programs such as the Clean Water Act and Coastal Zone Management Act play a more indirect role. Still other federal programs actually work to encourage potentially counterproductive patterns of development in hazard areas. This, along with some increasingly questionable approaches to disaster relief, has spurred exploration of possible changes in the federal approach to disaster management.

KEY TERMS

Disaster Mitigation Act (DMA) of 2000	Amends the Robert T. Stafford Disaster Relief and Emergency Assistance Act of 1988; streamlines the administration of federal disaster relief and mitigation programs and places emphasis on pre-disaster mitigation planning to reduce the Nation's disaster losses.
Hazard Mitigation Grant Program (HMGP)	Funding program administered by FEMA. The purpose of the HMGP is to reduce the loss of life and property caused by natural hazards by providing funding for mitigation to state and local governments following a disaster declaration.
Moral hazard	Term used to describe how federal disaster relief may encourage citizens and communities to build in areas vulnerable to the impacts of natural hazards.
National Flood Insurance Program (NFIP)	Voluntary participatory program for local communities who wish to provide the opportunity for residents to purchase federally backed flood insurance. In exchange, local governments enact ordinances to regulate development in floodplains.
Ordinance	A local rule or law that the government can pass and that the government has the authority to enforce within its jurisdiction.
Repetitive loss properties (RLPs)	Property with 2 or more National Flood Insurance Program claims over $1000 each within a 10-year period.

ASSESS YOUR UNDERSTANDING

Go to www.wiley.com/college/schwab to evaluate your knowledge of practices and politics of mitigation policy.
Measure your learning by comparing pre-test and post-test results.

Summary Questions

1. Over the past several decades, federal involvement in emergency management has
   (a) increased.
   (b) decreased.
   (c) stayed the same.
   (d) been insignificant.

2. FEMA was created by President Carter to act as a lead agency for many aspects of emergency management. True or False?

3. The Small Business Administration's role in hazard management is to
   (a) provide technical assistance to farmers.
   (b) reduce the loss of life and property.
   (c) issue low-interest loans.
   (d) administer community grants.

4. FEMA took on a Mitigation Directorate during the Clinton Administration. True or False?

5. Which federal agency was created after the terrorist attacks of September 11, 2001?
   (a) FEMA
   (b) Office of Emergency Preparedness
   (c) Project Impact
   (d) Department of Homeland Security

6. The National Flood Insurance Program is supported by federal taxes. True or False?

7. National flood insurance is available to anyone who can afford the high premiums. True or False?

8. A 100-year flood floodplain
   (a) is an area that has flooded more than 10 times in a 100-year period.
   (b) has a 10% chance of flooding in any given year.
   (c) is the elevation of the water surface resulting from a major flood.
   (d) has a 1% chance of flooding in any given year.

9. A Flood Insurance Rate Map should be changed after a flood proves that the FIRM boundaries are no longer accurate. True or False?

10. The Community Rating System rewards
    (a) communities that have not experienced a flood in a given period.
    (b) companies that provide insurance in flood-prone areas.
    (c) communities that have undertaken extraordinary floodplain mitigation measures.
    (d) homeowners who relocate structures.

11. The Coastal Barrier Resources Act grants federal funds to aid the development of coastal areas. True or False?

12. The goal of Section 404 of the Clean Water Act is to protect wetlands from development. True or False?

13. The primary purpose of the National Environmental Policy Act is to
    (a) require federal agencies to acquire permits.
    (b) create Special Area Management Plans.
    (c) require federal agencies to consider environmental issues in the decision-making process.
    (d) deter land development.

14. The Internal Revenue Code includes provisions that increase a taxpayer's tax burden based on real estate investments. True or False?

15. The belief that federal disaster relief is an entitlement rather than assistance is growing in the United States. True or False?

Review Questions

1. Federal involvement in emergency management functions has increased in recent decades. Name five federal programs that directly relate to hazard mitigation or emergency management functions.

2. During the time of the Cold War, natural disasters were not a primary concern for U.S. citizens. Identify the act that introduced Americans to the concept of federal disaster assistance.

3. Explain what was unique about the National Flood Insurance Act of 1968.

4. Flood insurance is a major concern for many U.S. residents. Describe the purpose and major provisions of the National Flood Insurance Program (NFIP).

5. Those that make their living off the land can be particularly affected by natural disasters. In what way does the Farm Service Agency engage in disaster relief?

6. Hurricane Katrina opened a new chapter in the federal government's role in emergency management. Describe some of the reactions to FEMA's response.

7. Explain how a Flood Insurance Rate Map factors into flood mitigation.

8. Repeated losses cause a significant drain on the National Flood Insurance Program. Define repetitive loss properties.

9. The Pre-Disaster Mitigation Program provides mitigation funding that is not dependent on a disaster. Give three examples of qualified mitigation projects under PDM.

10. Explain what an "indirect mitigation program" is, and name three such programs at the federal level.

11. Explain why the Coastal Zone Management Act requires a level of flexibility.

12. How do states benefit from the Coastal Zone Management Act?

13. Explain ways in which the federal government encourages development in hazardous areas?

14. Explain how the risk of building in hazardous areas is transferred from an individual homeowner to taxpayers in general?

15. What would be the benefit of raising National Flood Insurance premiums to reflect the true risks of living in flood-prone areas?

Applying This Chapter

1. Your small horse riding and stable business was hit hard by a tornado. You lost 3 of your 15 horses, and one-third of your buildings were damaged beyond repair. In addition, 2 of your 3 employees have had to quit and relocate as a result of losing their homes in the storm. As the owner of this small business, which federal programs could you expect to get assistance from?

2. Nearly 20,000 communities participate in the National Flood Insurance Program. Your community, which hasn't had a major flood in more than three decades, is considering entering the program. Draft a proposal to your city council that describes the benefits of the program; be certain to include what, if any, steps your community will need to take to enter the program.

3. A developer has proposed to build a retail mall in a long-neglected area of your town. Most people in town support the move because it would bring business and interest to the area. A portion of the proposed site is believed to be wetlands, however. As the president of the local conservation group, how would you use the Clean Water Act to oppose the proposal? Alternatively, as the developer of the proposal, what would you do to satisfy requirements of the Clean Water Act and still get the job done?

4. Some critics have pointed to a major flaw in the Coastal Barrier Resources Act (CBRA) that manifests itself in the context of recovery from a natural hazards disaster. Based on the provisions in CBRA regarding the exemptions

discussed in this chapter, does the Act open the door to expanded development of barrier islands using federal funds, despite the clear intent of Congress when it passed the legislation? Consider the following hypothetical scenario to help you formulate your answer:

> *Suppose an 18-inch water line runs through a CBRA unit. The pipe connects development on one end of the unit to a water supply on the other end of the unit. Now suppose the pipe is damaged in a coastal storm. Does CBRA allow federal funds to be used to pay for the cost of replacing the 18-inch pipe? Can other funds, such as private financing or state and local government funds, be used to expand the pipe from 18 to 24 inches? What about the potential for more intense development that is made possible by the increased water capacity in the 24-inch pipe?*

5. Assume you live in a hurricane-prone area of the United States. Many say that the federal government is subsidizing the privilege of living in a coastal community, and other taxpayers are unfairly being asked to support the subsidy with their taxes. How do you respond?

YOU TRY IT

Mitigation Powers

Imagine you have just been appointed "Mitigation Czar" by the President of the United States. What would you do to enhance the role of the federal government in reducing the country's vulnerability to natural hazards?

Flood-Wise Ways

Although your 100-year-old home is in a Maryland floodplain, it has only been flooded twice since the early 1900s. Unfortunately, that's no guarantee it won't happen again. Using the National Flood Insurance Program's website at www.floodsmart.gov, estimate how much your flood insurance premium would be for both your home and its contents (note: you're in zone A).

Then, again using the site, come up with things you can do—in addition to buying insurance—to minimize potential loss.

Prevention Measures

It's clear from what's happened to other communities in the United States that it's not enough to recover from a natural disaster or event—a community must take steps to prevent future damage before a disaster strikes. The National Pre-Disaster Mitigation Program provides mitigation funding to communities that have not been declared disaster sites. Outline what mitigation programs your community might be eligible for under the PDM. Use the following website as a resource: www.fema.gov/government/grant/pdm/index.shtm.

7

MITIGATING HAZARDS AT THE STATE LEVEL
Divergent Views and Outcomes

Starting Point

Go to www.wiley.com/college/schwab to assess your knowledge of mitigating hazards at the state level.
Determine where you need to concentrate your effort.

What You'll Learn in This Chapter

▲ Responsibilities of state emergency management offices
▲ The role of the State Hazard Mitigation Officer
▲ The two levels of state plans under the Disaster Mitigation Act
▲ Four elements of a building code
▲ Types of problems associated with hazard insurance
▲ Common environmentally sensitive land areas
▲ Ideas on how to increase the mitigation capabilities of the states

After Studying This Chapter, You'll Be Able To

▲ Examine differences in state management of hazard areas
▲ Examine sources of funding for state mitigation programs
▲ Analyze the drawbacks of hazard insurance
▲ Analyze variations in effectiveness of state emergency management offices
▲ Examine the application of statewide building codes
▲ Distinguish weaknesses in hazard insurance programs
▲ Appraise the potential effectiveness of regulatory setbacks

Goals and Outcomes

▲ Compare and contrast divergent state approaches to hazardous land management
▲ Evaluate the procedures of hazard mitigation at the state level
▲ Compare and contrast agencies and levels of government involved in hazard mitigation
▲ Select appropriate tools and techniques to analyze emergency management operations
▲ Collaborate with others to compare the effectiveness of building codes
▲ Assess the role insurance plays in mitigation
▲ Evaluate land use planning in real hazard situations

INTRODUCTION

States have various ways of dealing with hazards and the impacts hazard events can have on communities under the states' jurisdictions. This chapter begins by discussing the functions and responsibilities of state emergency management offices and explores the significance of mitigation planning at the state level. Next, the chapter considers how state mandates for local government land use planning influence communities' approaches to hazards management. The chapter also takes a look at state building codes and state insurance laws. The chapter then examines some of the ways states directly intervene in land use decision making, particularly in environmentally sensitive areas such as the coastal zone and wetlands. The chapter concludes with a discussion of opportunities for states to increase the resiliency of their communities and the state as a whole.

7.1 Divergent State Approaches to Hazardous Land Management

Federal initiatives such as the National Flood Insurance Program (NFIP), the Coastal Zone Management Act (CZMA), the Clean Water Act (CWA), the Disaster Mitigation Act of 2000 (DMA), and other national programs provide incentive or directive for states to engage in a wide variety of regulatory and management activities that implicate hazard mitigation. See Chapter 6 for a discussion of these and other federal management programs. Apart from these federal initiatives, states have devised their own approaches to management of development in hazard areas. Some states intervene directly in private property development and land use decisions by imposing regulations on certain environmentally sensitive or hazardous areas such as wetlands, floodplains, or ocean erodible areas, sometimes surpassing federal standards. Other states have established planning mandates that force or encourage local governments to conform to state policy or provide guidance with regards to hazard measures. Still other states have recused themselves from involvement in development decisions in hazard areas, leaving local governments and market forces to regulate land uses.

Much of the divergence among states in their approach to hazards management and regulation of the built environment can be explained by differences in political climate and first-hand experience with natural hazards. Policy makers in states like Florida, where hurricanes occur frequently and cause widespread and very visible damage, have accepted that natural hazards are inevitable events in their states, and have been willing to expend state resources and political capital to mitigate hurricane impacts. Other states have been lulled into complacency and have not intervened in the private development market. This is perhaps an appropriate response where natural hazards are few and far between and public expenditure for hazards management is unwarranted. However, some of these

FOR EXAMPLE

Different States, Different Priorities

States set their own priorities for many federally regulated issues, and some states go beyond standards set by federal law. Both North Carolina and Florida recognize that being blessed with extensive stretches of coastline also brings the issue of beach erosion to the forefront that other states do not have to confront as a part of the NFIP. Thus, these two states impose stronger restrictions on development in coastal erosion zones than the NFIP. States like Illinois do not have to place as much emphasis on coastal erosion due to their geography. However, Illinois does exceed NFIP standards for development in the 100-year floodplain.

states may also be home to very strong building and development lobbies, which can often exert enough political pressure to counter state efforts to regulate development in hazard areas.

In this chapter, we will discuss various state approaches to emergency management and hazard mitigation, with a particular focus on land use issues and management of the built environment. Although generalities may be made about many state activities, it is important to remember that each state may act as a sovereign unit within the broad framework of the American federalist system of governance as dictated by the United States Constitution.

SELF-CHECK

- Discuss the different approaches states take to managing hazard areas.
- Describe factors that explain the divergence in state hazard management approaches.
- Explain how state and local governments interact.

7.2 State Emergency Management

States play an important role in carrying out the full range of emergency management functions, including mitigation and preparedness. State laws describe the responsibilities of the state government for emergencies and disasters, authorizing the Governor and state agencies to carry out plans and policies to respond to, recover from, and prepare for emergencies. In its pivotal position, the state serves as a key link between federal agencies and resources and local communities. One of the primary federal agencies that the states deal with is the Federal Emergency Management Agency (FEMA). Direct state interaction with FEMA is usually conducted through FEMA's ten regional offices, with FEMA's national office providing overall policy guidance and oversight.

7.2.1 State Offices of Emergency Management

Each of the 50 states, territories, and the District of Columbia maintain an office of emergency management. In some states, such as California, the Office of Emergency Services is housed in the Office of the Governor. In Tennessee, the Emergency Management Agency reports to the Adjutant General, while in Florida, the emergency management function is carried out in the Office of Community Affairs. In North Carolina, emergency management is in the Department of Crime Control and Public Safety. National Guard Adjutant Generals manage state emergency management offices in more than half of the 56 states and territories. The remaining state emergency management offices are lead by civilian employees.

7.2.2 Effectiveness of State Emergency Management Offices

The effectiveness of the emergency management office also varies widely from state to state. In general, policy-oriented offices (e.g., state planning) are more suited to carrying out mitigation and recovery programming, while tactical and operations-oriented offices (e.g., state police) are better at managing preparedness and response activities. However, while the orientation and prominence of the office may dictate to some degree the ability of emergency managers to promote mitigation policies, a more important factor in the overall effectiveness of emergency management is the relationship with the governor's office and the willingness of the chief executive officer of the state to support long-term reduction of vulnerability.

7.2.3 The State Hazard Mitigation Officer (SHMO)

Each state and U.S. territory has a State Hazard Mitigation Officer (SHMO) who serves as the primary contact between the federal government and the state. SHMOs are responsible for a multitude of tasks, not the least of which is to guide the state hazard mitigation planning process, as required under the Disaster Mitigation Act of 2000 (more on state hazard mitigation planning below). In addition to serving as a coordinator among different levels of government, SHMOs are also in charge of implementing statewide laws and programs for mitigation and for providing staff and resources to assist local governments in their own planning efforts and in implementing local hazard mitigation activities.

Despite the daunting tasks that face SHMOs, many SHMOs throughout the country lack full staff support or adequate resources to perform their duties.

FOR EXAMPLE

The North Carolina State Hazard Mitigation Advisory Group Supports the SHMO

In 2003, the State Hazard Mitigation Officer in North Carolina received support and guidance from the State Hazard Mitigation Advisory Group (SHMAG) throughout the process of developing the North Carolina Hazard Mitigation Plan. The SHMAG is a diverse committee made up of representatives from numerous state agencies; private industry groups, including the insurance, building, and housing industries; local government representatives; non-profit organizations; professional associations; the American Red Cross; academia; and several federal agencies, including FEMA and the National Weather Service. Not only was the SHMAG a useful vehicle for creating the state hazard mitigation plan, it also proved to be an effective forum for discussion of broader issues of concern to the state, including natural resource management, coordination and integration of agency activities, as well as data compatibility and technological consistency.

However, a good working relationship between the state and the FEMA regional office often bolsters the SHMO's commitment to mitigation. In addition, many SHMOs are supported in their coordinating efforts through interagency teams and committees at the state level, such as hazard mitigation advisory groups, task forces appointed by the governor of the state, and similar working groups that can provide advice and assistance for mitigation initiatives.

7.2.4 Funding for State Mitigation and Preparedness Activities

Most states are heavily dependent upon federal funding, especially funding from FEMA, to develop and implement mitigation programs. Significant support comes to the states in the form of grant programs such as the Hazard Mitigation Grant Program (HMGP), the mitigation portion of the Public Assistance Program (PAP), the Flood Mitigation Assistance Program (FMAP), and the Pre-Disaster Mitigation Program (PDMP). These federal mitigation assistance programs can vastly augment the capacity of state agencies to carry out major mitigation initiatives at the state level and to provide assistance to local governments for mitigation activities. States that experience repeated disasters—such as major flooding, damaging hurricanes, severe ice and winter storms, and destructive earthquakes—can receive massive amounts of financial assistance from the federal government for mitigation projects. However, much of this federal funding is only available after a disaster has been declared (with the exception of the FMAP and PDMP programs, which are available on an annual basis through a competitive grant process). Such dependence on federal disaster assistance is an unstable and unpredictable source of funding for ongoing mitigation activities.

Because most states depend on disaster-based funding for a majority of their mitigation programs, many state emergency management positions that focus on mitigation are time-limited. In some states, there is only enough money to fund a single position on a full-time basis, usually the SHMO, and perhaps a floodplain management coordinator to administer the NFIP. A few states have no full-time staff devoted to natural hazard mitigation at all. The remaining staff positions that are necessary to carry out mitigation programs and initiatives may fluctuate according to the level of disaster funding available at any given time. Although the occurrence of future hazards is inevitable, it is an unwise practice for state emergency management offices to remain dependent on disaster money in order to sustain long-term reductions in vulnerability. A few states are becoming more fluent in seeking additional ways to improve their mitigation capabilities, and are securing more permanent full-time positions in order to become less disaster-dependent and more proactive before the next hazard event occurs.

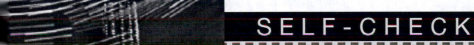

SELF-CHECK

- Explain the role of a state office of emergency management.
- Describe the duties of a state hazard mitigation officer (SHMO).
- List sources of funding for state emergency management offices.

MISSISSIPPI'S OFFICE OF RECOVERY AND RENEWAL: REBUILDING BIGGER AND BETTER AFTER HURRICANE KATRINA

In the wake of Hurricane Katrina, the State of Mississippi faces years of recovery and rebuilding. Under direction of the Governor, however, the spirit of Mississippi is strong, and the state intends to "rebuild bigger and better than ever."[1] To carry out this promise, Governor Haley Barbour created the Office of Recovery and Renewal in early 2006 to undertake the task of long-term recovery from Hurricane Katrina. Authorized by House Bill 22 and signed into law by Governor Barbour during the 2005 5th Extraordinary Session, the Office is the central agency charged with statewide mitigation. The Office is also responsible for coordinating Katrina relief efforts among federal and state agencies and other public and private entities within the State of Mississippi.

The primary focus of the Office of Recovery and Renewal is the implementation of long-term recovery plans and policies. The office has four primary objectives:

✔ Obtain maximum federal funds for recovery efforts and maximize use of credit in lieu of cash opportunities such as the concept of global match.

✔ Provide disaster recovery policy guidance and counsel to the Governor, his staff, state agencies, local government officials, and other organizations.

✔ Assist in the identification of appropriate organizations tasked with the implementation of the Governor's Commission on Recovery and Renewal Report: Building Back Better than Ever.

✔ Provide training, education, and outreach programs to government officials, organizations, and individuals in order to assist them in making more informed decisions regarding disaster recovery.

The Office of Recovery and Renewal is located within the Governor's Office in Jackson, Mississippi, and also has field staff working on the Coast. The Office focuses heavily on meeting local needs as defined by local residents. As a result, all staff, from the Director to those working in the field, rely on local knowledge of the disaster, including an understanding of the political, social, and economic conditions present as well as first-hand experiences of local officials, business leaders, and other individuals involved in recovery or directly impacted by Hurricane Katrina.[2]

7.3 Hazard Mitigation Planning at the State Level

Hazard mitigation planning is an important aspect of a successful state-wide mitigation program. States and communities use the hazard mitigation planning process to set short- and long-range mitigation goals and objectives. Hazard mitigation planning is a collaborative process whereby hazards affecting the state are identified, vulnerability to the hazards is assessed, and consensus is reached on how to minimize or eliminate the effects of those hazards on local communities and the state as a whole.

7.3.1 Mitigation Planning Under the Disaster Mitigation Act of 2000

The Disaster Mitigation Act of 2000 (DMA) reinforces the importance of pre-disaster mitigation planning to reduce the nation's disaster losses, and is aimed primarily at controlling and streamlining the administration of federal disaster relief and mitigation programs. States and communities must have an approved mitigation plan in place to be eligible for post-disaster funds from several non-emergency assistance programs administered by FEMA.

Section 322 of the DMA specifically addresses mitigation planning at the state and local levels. Tribal governments have the option of preparing mitigation plans as grantees of federal funds, in which case they prepare mitigation plans that follow the state planning regulations, or they may prepare plans as sub-grantees and follow the local planning regulations. Section 322(a) of the Act requires that state, local, and Tribal governments each develop and submit for approval a mitigation plan that follows criteria outlined in the Section 322 regulations and in guidance material published by FEMA.

7.3.2 DMA Planning Requirements

Rules accompanying the DMA lay out specific criteria that must be met and a planning process that must be followed by states seeking plan approval from FEMA. Many of the criteria that apply to state hazard mitigation plans parallel those required of local governments, including a risk assessment that consists of a hazard identification and profile, vulnerability assessment, and loss estimate; an evaluation of capabilities for mitigation; formulation of goal statements; and development of mitigation strategies and actions with identified sources of funding or potential funding. These specific criteria and the hazard mitigation planning process in general are described in detail in Chapter 13.

State Planning Requires Coordination and Cooperation

Many of the planning steps that states must follow under the DMA are identical to those that local governments follow when preparing their own mitigation plans. At the state level, however, a higher degree of coordination and integration is required because the state mitigation plan must cover the entire state, not just a single municipality or county.

States are also required to provide guidance and assistance to local communities in the development of local hazard mitigation plans that will meet DMA criteria. Services that some states provide to their local governments include training workshops and information sessions on risk assessment and hazard mitigation planning principles, planning assistance materials such as guidebooks and worksheets, and community outreach activities. Some states also may provide data sets for their local governments, including information on demographics, soils, wetlands, hazard histories, and updated floodplain maps.

Two Levels of State Plans: Standard and Enhanced

There are two levels of state plans under the DMA, standard and enhanced. Under an approved standard plan, states are eligible to receive 7.5% of the total disaster assistance amount granted from FEMA to be used solely for mitigation purposes. Under an approved enhanced plan, a state may qualify for a greater percentage of the total amount of disaster assistance to be used for mitigation projects. In addition to satisfying the requirements of the standard plan, the enhanced plan must demonstrate how the state will administer and implement its existing mitigation programs with a systematic and effective approach.

FOR EXAMPLE

Enhanced State Mitigation Plan, Washington's

The State of Washington's Enhanced Mitigation Plan was the first in the nation to be approved by FEMA as an enhanced plan on July 1, 2004. The enhanced portion of the plan can be found online at: emd.wa.gov/6-mrr/mit-rec/mit/mit-pubs-forms/hazmit-plan/comp-state-prgm.pdf.

7.3.3 Consequences of Not Preparing a State Hazard Mitigation Plan

The consequences that may arise when states do not prepare an acceptable mitigation plan are quite significant. The federal regulations state that

> States must have an approved Standard State Mitigation plan meeting the requirements of [the regulations] in order to receive [disaster] assistance. . . . In any case, emergency assistance provided under [several disaster act provisions] will not be affected.[3]

The distinction, then, is whether disaster assistance is "emergency" in nature. If a state does not have an approved plan in place, only emergency assistance will be provided. The Public Assistance (PA) categories that are considered emergency include only debris removal and protective measures. The remaining PA project categories are considered permanent restorative work and will not be funded. This means federal assistance will not be available to restore roads and bridges, water control facilities, public buildings, public utilities, and other facilities that are damaged in a hazard event. In addition, states will not be eligible for funding from the Individual and Family Grant (IFG), Hazard Mitigation Grant Program (HMGP), and Fire Suppression Assistance Program without an approved state hazard mitigation plan.

SELF-CHECK

- Explain the purpose of the Disaster Mitigation Act of 2000.
- Identify two levels of state mitigation plans.
- Describe the consequences of not having a state hazard mitigation plan in place if a disaster occurs.

7.4 State Mandates for Local Land Use Planning

For many years, planning advocates have touted the value of using a land use approach to hazard mitigation. The assumption is that by steering development away from hazard areas and towards more appropriate areas, we can decrease our vulnerability to the impacts of future hazards. Practically speaking, land use regulation is most effective when carried out through a process of careful planning that takes into account the numerous factors involved in managing growth and development. While this approach is most effective in areas where land remains undeveloped, there is still merit in using the land use planning approach for land that is already developed as well.

The responsibility to create land use plans and the regulations necessary to carry them out falls primarily to local governments. Because planning is so essential for the fair and comprehensive regulation of private property, some states have passed legislation requiring local governments to prepare comprehensive land use plans. Of these, a few states impose the planning mandate only on local governments in a certain region of the state, while the remaining communities are exempt from a planning mandate. In North Carolina, for example, the twenty counties that make up the coastal zone must prepare local land use plans, while the remaining 80 counties of the state are under no such mandate.

Some states that mandate local planning have made their policy objectives quite clear and have passed these on to the local governments with guidance as to how to achieve the state goals through the local land use planning process. Typically, states lay out criteria that the local communities must follow and specify the types of issues that the local land use plan must address. The states specify policy goals and objectives, but, to varying degrees, leave the specific details of the content and implementation of plans to local governments. A few states have included natural hazards and problems posed by development in hazardous areas as topics that local governments must consider in their plans. Florida, North Carolina, Washington,

FOR EXAMPLE

Oregon Planning Saves Millions

In 1996, FEMA estimated that Oregon had avoided about $10 million a year in flood losses because of strong land use planning that considered natural hazards. This was not accomplished by accident but through the foresight of Oregon administrations to call for local plans to include inventories, policies, and ordinances to guide development in hazard-prone areas for the previous 25 years. Using a comprehensive approach to planning has resulted in reduced losses from flooding, landslides, and earthquakes in communities throughout the state of Oregon.

Oregon, and a few other states have established planning mandates, with varying levels of incentives, to prod local governments into considering natural hazards as part of comprehensive planning.[4] However, even in these states, research tends to show that state planning mandates have had marginal effect in shifting land use and development policy making at the local level to include hazard reduction.

SELF-CHECK

- Describe the role of local land use planning in hazard mitigation.
- Explain how state governments influence local land use planning.

7.5 State Building Codes

A **building code** is a collection of laws, regulations, ordinances, or other statutory requirements adopted by a government that controls the physical structure of buildings. The purpose of a building code is to establish the minimum acceptable standards of construction necessary for preserving the public health, safety, and welfare, and to protect the built environment. These minimum requirements are based on principles of engineering, on properties of materials, and on the inherent hazards of climate, geology, and use of a structure.[5] Building codes primarily regulate new or proposed construction. They have little application to existing structures, except when buildings are undergoing reconstruction, rehabilitation, or alteration, or if the occupancy category of the building is being changed.

The term *building code* is frequently used to refer to a set of codebooks that are coordinated with each other to address specific technical applications. This set of codes usually consists of documents that deal with the structural, plumbing, mechanical, and electrical components of a building. The codes generally include provisions for structural modifications that deal with the impacts of various hazards. Natural hazards that can be addressed through building codes include earthquake, wildfire, snowstorms, high winds, storm surge, flooding, and wave action. Building codes usually contain maps indicating various wind and seismic zones, in which different levels of design standards apply depending upon the hazard risk.

Recent benefit/cost studies indicate that stronger minimum code provisions for natural hazards vulnerability reduction have positive benefit/cost ratios ranging from between 3 and 16. In other words, for every $1 increase in construction costs, there is a long-term savings of $3 to $16. This concept is similar to environmental and energy benefits when consumers invest in higher efficiency heating and cooling systems or add insulation, window and door sealants, and similar cost-effective measures that pay for themselves over the lifetime of the building or earlier.[6]

7.5.1 State Approaches to Building Codes

During the 1970s and earlier, very few states had statewide building codes. Where they existed at all, codes were enacted and enforced by local governments. Since then about half of the states have retracted this complete delegation of power to the local government and have enacted a building code that applies across the state. In many states, the statewide building code is administered through the state department of insurance, often through an engineering division or agency.

Many statewide codes are based on nationally-recognized model codes, including the International Building Code (IBC) and the International Residential Code (IRC) developed by the International Code Council (ICC). States vary widely in the version of the model codes that have been officially adopted. In addition, many states have enacted changes to the model codes, so that no two states in the nation have the identical statewide building code in effect. A few states have no building code regulations at all, while some states with statewide codes allow local governments to deviate from the state code. In some rural or semi-rural areas there are no building codes in place, or codes that exclude construction of single-family or two-family residential structures. When development is expanding into these areas, there is the possibility that a lack of codes or code enforcement may result in homes built and sold without safety standards for construction. In these instances, there is no control over how these buildings will perform in hazard events, possibly endangering the lives of occupants.

7.5.2 Building Code Enforcement

Even where a statewide code is in effect, the administration and enforcement of the building code rest with the local governments, with varying degrees of state

---

FOR EXAMPLE

Louisiana Adopts the International Building Code to Build Back Better and Stronger After Hurricanes Katrina and Rita

Louisiana Governor Kathleen Blanco signed a bill in December, 2005, that calls for the state to adopt the International Building Code (IBC), the International Residential Code (IRC), and other model codes developed by the International Code Council (ICC). The bill applies to buildings rebuilt in the wake of Hurricanes Katrina and Rita, and to all buildings built or rebuilt statewide starting in 2007. Under the legislation, the 11 parishes hit hardest by the hurricanes must put the new code into effect in 30 days if those parishes already have inspectors. If they do not, they have 90 days to begin enforcement. The bill also establishes a 19-member council to oversee enforcement of the codes by local governments.

oversight. The local government is responsible for creating the organizational structure for the code enforcement process, designating the person or persons responsible for enforcement and providing the necessary resources for code administration.[7]

Generally, the local government is responsible for building code enforcement at two separate stages of the construction process. First, municipal or county employees must review all plans and proposals submitted by landowners, builders, and developers who propose to build any type of structure in the local jurisdiction. The plans must be consistent with the current building code in order to receive a building permit. If the plans do not meet code as proposed, the local plan review office may require that modifications, additions, or corrections be made to the plans, or the office may reject the proposal. If the plans meet code standards, a permit is issued and the building process may begin. During construction, the local government has a second opportunity to enforce the building code by carrying out on-site inspections of the building as it is being constructed. Any deviation from the plans or other activity that is not consistent with either the permit as issued or the code itself is grounds for a halt-work order from the local building inspector. Corrections must be made to the building under construction before construction is allowed to resume. At the end of the building process, the local building inspector must review the finished product, and only if all conditions have been met will a certificate of occupancy be issued.

It is clear from this description of the building code enforcement process that a heavy burden is placed on the local government to ensure that the code is being followed and that any construction taking place in the jurisdiction will meet code standards. Knowledgeable, well-trained building officials and inspectors are essential to this process. Plan review and site inspections are time-consuming and complex. Adequate resources are essential in order for local enforcement agents to carry out their duties. In addition, inspectors must not be overburdened with so many daily inspections that they are not able to give each structure a thorough review. This is especially critical in the aftermath of a disaster, when local building inspection offices are inundated with permit requests from homeowners and businesses who wish to restore damaged structures quickly.

7.5.3 State Support for Local Code Enforcement

Because the quality of enforcement depends so heavily on the caliber of the local building code officials, some states require testing and licensing of all building officials. Many of these states also provide training and qualification certification for local building inspectors. Of these, however, only a few states require that licensed inspectors receive continuing education to keep their expertise up-to-date with building code changes. Some states also require that general contractors for projects over a certain dollar value (for example, projects over $30,000) be licensed by a state board or commission. Other state licenses that may be required include electrical, mechanical, and plumbing contracting.

South Florida has long had a reputation of having a strong coastal building code. But when Hurricane Andrew blew into the state in 1992, the storm and its aftermath highlighted some serious flaws in current assumptions about building codes and construction standards.[8] Problems that were discovered in the South Florida building code following Hurricane Andrew included unlicensed contractors, understaffed inspection offices, ineffective building inspection processes, poorly trained building inspectors, inadequate design wind standards, inadequate standards for manufactured and mobile homes, and egregious failure of building professionals to assume responsibility for safe construction. Ironically, many older structures fared better than newer buildings in the winds of Andrew.

SELF-CHECK

- Define **building code.**
- Cite the four elements of a building code.
- List the natural hazards that can be addressed through building codes.
- Name two model building codes used in the United States.
- Cite which level of government is responsible for enforcing building codes.

7.6 State Regulation of Hazard Insurance

Insurance can reduce the economic impact of a natural hazard event by distributing the cost of the loss among widespread rate payers. It can also serve as an inducement for property owners to follow structural hazard mitigation measures when premiums are reduced to reflect the additional protection provided to the property.

Insurance is generally available for some but not all natural disaster perils, varying from state to state and among carriers. Insurance coverage is nearly universally available for wildfires, winter storms, volcanoes, tornadoes, lightning, and hail. These perils are covered under most standard property insurance contracts. Generally speaking, these events are sufficiently random and widespread to permit the private insurance mechanism to operate effectively. Hurricane wind damage is included as part of the basic wind coverage in most property insurance policies. Flood damage from hurricanes is not included but can be purchased separately by homeowners under the National Flood Insurance Program (NFIP) in communities that participate in the program.[9]

7.6.1 Problems with Catastrophic Losses

The insurance industry is encountering serious problems in providing insurance for properties located in areas subject to catastrophic losses, particularly those exposed to hurricanes and earthquakes. The problems fundamentally arise from the fact that many insurers now realize they do not have the resources to pay for a so-called worst-case event in those high-risk areas.[10] For example, the massive amount of property damage caused by Hurricane Andrew in 1992 precipitated a major insurance crisis in South Florida, when more than $15 billion in insurance claims was paid. After Andrew, numerous smaller insurance companies went out of business, and many others stopped writing policies for South Florida. About 16,000 residents were left without homeowner's insurance following Andrew. Florida did have a state system in place, however, to cover insurance claims of failed companies, assuming, up to a certain amount, the liability of companies that failed.[11]

Insurers confronted by catastrophic loss situations have tried to deal with them in numerous ways, such as diversifying their book of business to avoid over-concentration in a given state or region, purchasing reinsurance to spread out the risk more broadly, and charging higher premiums in high-risk areas to cover catastrophic losses. In Florida and California, two of the highest-risk areas, emergency regulations and other laws have hampered insurers' pursuit of those solutions. Some companies have concluded that the resulting risk of insolvency is unacceptable and have attempted to withdraw entirely from those states. Others have stopped writing any new business there until their excessive risk exposure can be reduced.[12]

7.6.2 State Insurance Regulation

In the vast majority of state's nationwide, state insurance laws require that premiums not be excessive, inadequate, or unfairly discriminatory. Regulators are faced with a difficult challenge—that of assuring an adequate supply of affordable insurance coverage at a time when many insurers are seeking to decrease their disaster exposure and increase their prices for the catastrophic component of that risk. Resolution of this dilemma could have substantial implications for the economies of many disaster-prone areas and their residents.[13]

In general, state regulation influences the supply of disaster insurance by controlling various factors, such as capitalization, investments, diversification of risk, prices, and products. States also oversee the entry into and exit from insurance markets, as well as underwriting selection and trade practices. In theory, the job of state regulators is to protect the public from fraud and imprudent practices that threaten insurance companies' solvency and to ensure fair market practices. However, public policy is not forged in a political vacuum, and regulation increasingly has been influenced by voters' perceptions and preferences on how the cost of risk should be shared among different groups. In the process, insurers have largely lost the freedom to charge premiums based strictly on a structure's loss potential.[14]

FOR EXAMPLE

Insurance Coverage

Stopping the withdrawal of coverage by private insurance companies following Hurricane Andrew became a major public policy focus for the State of Florida. The state prohibited companies doing business in Florida from canceling more than 5% of their policies in a given time period, created a mechanism to insure homeowners who were unable to find insurance elsewhere, and created a state reinsurance fund to cover future hurricane-related claims.[16] The Florida Hurricane Catastrophe Fund was funded through surcharges on property insurance policies. Florida and Texas have also created "wind pools" to provide insurance coverage to property owners who otherwise would not be able to afford coverage.[17]

States have created a variety of political mechanisms to regulate insurance, including the state-mandated pool. A state-mandated pool serves as a market of last resort for property owners when coverage is not readily available from private insurers. Since the pools typically do not charge a premium high enough to cover the catastrophic loss potential of the properties involved, they subsidize people living in high-hazard areas and impose the excess cost on people residing elsewhere. Moreover, these state pools do not eliminate the problem of catastrophic losses. Private insurers in those states remain liable, on a market share basis, for the net losses generated by the state pools. Thus, any increase in voluntary business carries with it an increase in the insurer's share of the adverse results of the pool. This creates a disincentive for existing insurers to remain in those states or for new companies to establish operations there.[15]

SELF-CHECK

- Name the natural hazards for which insurance is generally available.
- Discuss three ways that insurers cope with catastrophic loss.
- Explain how the states regulate the supply of disaster insurance.

7.7 State Regulation in Environmentally Sensitive Areas

Most states leave the bulk of land use decision making to their local governments. Municipalities and counties usually have direct control over development and growth within their jurisdictions, with some states providing guidance and direction through statewide planning policies. Other states leave responsibility for land use regulation entirely in local hands. The one exception to this mostly hands-off approach is in areas of environmental concern, where many states play a direct role in controlling how these areas are used. The practice of direct state regulation overland uses most frequently occurs in coastal environments and in wetlands.

7.7.1 Combating Coastal Erosion and Storm Impacts

The coastal areas of the states that border the Atlantic Ocean, the Gulf of Mexico, the Pacific Ocean, and the Great Lakes are of immense value and importance to the states' economies and environmental integrity. These areas are also some of the most ecologically fragile as well as the most vulnerable to the impacts of natural hazards. Because their coastal areas represent resources that are of more than local value and are so susceptible to hazard impacts, most coastal states have enacted laws and policies that deal with the peculiar aspects of these regions.

Regulation is one method that states use to reduce the effects of natural hazards on people and property along the shore. State-imposed regulatory measures include setbacks, restrictions on post-storm reconstruction, and wetlands regulation. In addition, some states have designated certain areas as Areas of Particular Concern, where added protections for sensitive or hazardous resources are imposed. These types of state controls are discussed further in this section.

7.7.2 Regulatory Setbacks

Most coastal states impose some sort of regulatory setback requirements on development that takes place along the shore. Although the specifics vary among the coastal states, in general, **setbacks** work by prohibiting or limiting the erection of structures within a specified distance from the ocean. This method of strategic retreat can help reduce the risk to life and property from coastal hazards and prolong the life of the building. Setbacks also help protect public beaches, many of which are vital to state and local coastal tourism industries. Because hurricanes and other coastal storms can cause more damage when development is poorly located, setbacks also help reduce the amount of tax money that is spent responding to disasters.

Setbacks regulate construction in a zone that is a certain distance landward from the ocean. Methods of determining the setback line include the first line of stable, natural vegetation; the mean high water line; local erosion rates; or various other marks. In most states, construction must either take place landward of this line, or follow very strict guidelines for development. For example, in North Carolina, setbacks are determined by multiplying the average annual erosion rate by 30 for all single-family homes, regardless of size, with

Figure 7-1

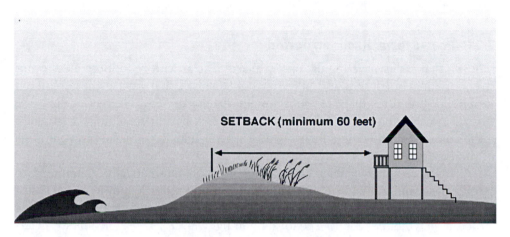

SETBACK (minimum 60 feet)

The minimum setback is 60 feet for all single-family homes in coastal North Carolina.

a minimum setback of 60 feet from the first stable line of natural vegetation. For buildings larger than 5000 square feet, the setback is determined by multiplying the erosion rate by 60, with a minimum setback being 120 feet as shown in Figure 7-1. In no case may development be seaward of the frontal dune system.

The problem with many of the methods of measurement used by coastal states to establish construction setbacks is that the distances can be relatively arbitrary, generally ranging from about 40 to 100 feet. As understanding of beach and dune processes has increased, and as coastal engineering has become more sophisticated, delineation of setback lines has also become more sophisticated

FOR EXAMPLE

Setting Back in Hawaii

The State of Hawaii uses a setback that prohibits development in a zone forty feet inland from the shoreline. The shoreline is defined as the debris or vegetation line that is visible on the shore. This line can fluctuate on a regular basis, which can lead to uncertainty on the part of property owners and state regulators. However, because Hawaii does not experience the same sort of erosion as beaches on the Atlantic coast, issues associated with fluctuating lines are minimal.

and highly technical. Setbacks based on seasonal fluctuations, vulnerability to storms and storm surges, and the rate of shoreline erosion are more scientifically valid, but they are also more difficult and costly for state regulators to implement and for landowners to understand.[18]

7.7.3 Post-Storm Reconstruction

Most coastal states have regulations in place to deal with rebuilding and reconstruction after hurricanes and other coastal storms. Usually a permit is required to rebuild structures that are "substantially damaged."[19] In North Carolina, the Coastal Area Management Act (CAMA) requires a permit to rebuild a structure if the cost of repairing the damage will be greater than 50% of the physical value of the building itself, as shown in Figure 7-2.

Owners of storm-damaged properties are not automatically guaranteed to receive a permit. All current regulations, including setback requirements, must be met in order to receive a permit to rebuild. If the setback cannot be met, the structure may not be rebuilt. The local building inspector is responsible for determining the extent of the damage. Usually, if a structure or septic system is damaged less than 50% of its value, an exemption is granted.

Figure 7-2

Structures damaged more than 50% may not rebuild in coastal North Carolina if current regulations cannot be met.

Following past hurricanes, the North Carolina Division of Coastal Management has refused permits to rebuild damaged properties along the coast. For example, erosion from Hurricane Fran in 1996 was so severe in a few areas that property owners lost entire lots. Some others lost such a large proportion of their lot that they could not meet setback requirements.

7.7.4 State Wetlands Protection

Many states provide some degree of regulatory protection for wetlands. Wetlands are well known for their water-quality protection function, and have been called nature's kidneys because of their ability to filter impurities from surface water as it makes its way through the hydrologic system. Wetlands also perform an important mitigative function in the coastal zone and in inland riverine floodplains. Among their many beneficial functions, wetlands serve to minimize the danger of damaging floods by storing and preventing rapid runoff of water. There are many different types of wetlands with different sorts of vegetation and wildlife, but in general each type provides a similar benefit for flood hazard mitigation, storing water after rains like a giant sponge and releasing it gradually into groundwater or through surface outflow. For instance, large pocosin wetlands can store enormous amounts of water and slow runoff of freshwater into brackish estuaries. Bottomland wetlands along streams provide holding basins for floodwater and slow the water to reduce flood damage. This function of wetlands helps maintain more constant water levels in streams, estuaries, and floodplains. Wetlands also protect against shoreline erosion. Wetland vegetation is often very dense, both above and below ground. This plant cover and root system can absorb energy from floods and wave action. By dissipating the energy, binding the soil, and encouraging sediment deposition, wetlands stabilize shorelines along coastal streams, lakes, and sounds.

As discussed in Chapter 6, Section 404 of the federal Clean Water Act imposes restrictions on activities carried out in wetlands and requires permits from the U.S. Army Corps of Engineers for any deposition of dredge or fill material into wetlands. A few states have undertaken the responsibility for administering the Section 404 program at the state level. In addition to the Section 404 regulations, some states have also imposed state-level restrictions on development in tidal or saltwater wetlands. A few states have extended restrictions to nontidal or freshwater wetlands. The wetlands programs of many states parallel the Section 404 guidelines and require that any permitted activity be a water-dependent use, refusing permits for any wetland activity where a practicable alternative is available. Often, state regulations cover more activities than provisions of the Section 404 program do.

Some states also require **wetland mitigation**, which involves the off-site preservation of another wetland located away from the development activity or the creation of a new wetland to take the place of one that is impaired or destroyed. States sometimes impose fairly rigorous mitigation ratios, ranging from 2:1 to 7:1 (that is, the amount of created, restored, or enhanced wetland acreage required for each acre of natural wetland destroyed or damaged).[20]

7.7.5 Areas of Particular Concern

In addition to the setback requirements for oceanfront development and the restrictions on wetland activities, many states designate certain areas of the state for added protection. These so-called **Areas of Particular Concern** are defined according to geographic boundaries, natural resources or habitats contained in the Area, or by the function performed by a particular natural feature.

In North Carolina, Areas of Environmental Concern (AEC) are the foundation of the Coastal Resources Commission's permitting program for coastal development, as dictated by the Coastal Area Management Act (CAMA). An AEC is an area of natural importance. It may be easily destroyed by erosion or flooding, or it may have environmental, social, economic, or aesthetic values that make it valuable to the state. The North Carolina Coastal Resources Commission designates areas as AECs to protect them from uncontrolled development, which may cause irreversible damage to property, public health, or the environment.

For example, the Estuarine and Ocean System AEC covers North Carolina's 2.2 million acres of estuarine waters, including public trust areas, estuarine waters, coastal shorelines, and coastal wetlands. Permits are required for development in any of these designated areas. AEC rules for estuarine and ocean system areas allow only projects that are "water dependent," such as navigation channels, docks, piers, and boat ramps.

The Ocean Hazard System AEC includes the band of narrow barrier islands that form the State's eastern border. The Ocean Hazard System is made up of oceanfront lands and the inlets that connect the ocean to the sounds, including ocean erodible areas, high hazard flood areas, and inlet hazard areas.[21] All development in the Ocean Hazard System AEC must be located and designed to protect human lives and property from storms and erosion, to prevent permanent structures from encroaching on public beaches, and to reduce the public costs (such as disaster relief aid) that can result from poorly located development. The development must incorporate all reasonable means and methods to avoid damage to the natural environment or public beach accessways. The Ocean Hazard System AEC rules further stipulate that no growth-inducing development paid for by public funds will be permitted if it is likely to require more public funds for maintenance and continued use—unless the benefits of the project will outweigh the required public expenditures.

SELF CHECK

- Define **setback, wetland mitigation,** and **Areas of Particular Concern.**
- Describe methods of determining regulatory setbacks.
- Discuss situations in which states play a direct role in land use regulation.
- Describe what happens when structures on the coast are damaged more than 50% during a hurricane or other coastal storm.

7.8 Increasing State Mitigation Capabilities

Many states are steadfastly increasing their capability for mitigation, and have progressed far beyond the days when the concept of mitigation was a foreign one to many state agencies, and hazard mitigation plans were few and far between. These states continue to implement programs, carry out policies, and formulate new strategies to increase resiliency throughout the state as awareness of hazards and the damage they can cause spreads. Outreach and education programs carried out at the state level have further educated the public about the threats of flooding, wildfires, hurricanes, earthquake, coastal erosion, and many other hazards, although residents in many states remain unaware of the specific risks their community or neighborhood faces.

Despite the many instances of successful collaboration for mitigation activity, many states need to bolster their efforts to increase interagency coordination. By finding areas of mutual expertise and interest, state agencies can often increase efficiency while supporting complementary goals and missions. For example, relatively little has been done to link water quality regulation with hazard mitigation strategies at the state level, despite the fact that all states with flooding hazards carry out these dual responsibilities. Taking a river basin approach to planning throughout the state could prove a highly effective means of dealing with both water quality and water quantity issues.

In addition to bolstering the level of collaboration and coordination, many states must also broaden their base of support for hazard mitigation planning and policy implementation. States should be sure that all relevant stakeholders are represented and contribute to the state's mitigation planning process. Although most state mitigation plans are developed by the state emergency management agency or its equivalent, many other state departments should have a place at the table during the planning process. For example, state departments of instruction (to ensure safe school construction and placement), departments of tourism (to add policies that protect visitors to hazardous areas such as beaches), state

FOR EXAMPLE

Partnership in Mississippi

Wetlands are invaluable in controlling floodwaters, recharging groundwater, and filtering pollutants. They serve as vital habitat for waterfowl and other wildlife, and on a global scale, wetlands are described as carbon dioxide sinks and climate stabilizers.[22] In 2001, The Nature Conservancy and the Mississippi Department of Transportation (MDOT) joined forces to protect wetlands in the state. MDOT purchased credits from The Nature Conservancy for over 5000 acres of wetland that were important habitat areas and also contributed to the state's DOT requirements for road development in less hazardous areas. "It's a win-win situation for all of us," said Southern District Transportation Commissioner Wayne Brown of the joint program. "Not only are we making a smart investment decision today, we are making an even more important investment for the future."[23]

departments of insurance or construction (where building code policy is often established), state infrastructure and transportation departments (to deal with issues of development in hazardous locations), and many other state departments and agencies can contribute to the overall resilience of the state.

The need to broaden participation in state mitigation policy formation spills over into the private sector and nonprofit communities as well, and many states should improve their efforts to engage in mutually beneficial partnerships with a wider range of stakeholders. Major employers, universities, corporations, and businesses all have a stake in increasing the resiliency of the state, and many can bring a new approach to mitigation if they are involved in the process. Nonprofit conservation organizations such as state-level Nature Conservancies and land trusts may readily support mitigation efforts that coincide with their goals of natural resource protection. Habitat for Humanity and other housing advocacy groups can contribute much to state efforts to provide housing that is both affordable and located out of dangerous areas such as floodplains. Charitable groups such as faith-based organizations, the Salvation Army, as well as the American Red Cross and its state-level chapters can also play a larger role in implementing mitigation policy during the critical post-disaster period if they are invited to the planning forum.

Although many states take a mostly single-hazard approach to their mitigation planning, focusing on the hazard with the greatest public attention, other states are placing greater emphasis on an all-hazards approach. Hazard identification and risk assessments in many states are now incorporating some of the less visible or pronounced hazards that may exist in their state, such as infectious disease, radon, arsenic contamination of groundwater, hoof and mouth disease, insect infestation, and bio-terrorism, to name a few.

The disaster assistance that has been provided to the states from the federal government has contributed significantly to their ability to respond to, prepare for, and recover from multiple disasters. But more importantly, many states are learning from their experiences, and are putting that knowledge to good use. Each disaster brings the states more knowledge about how to restore power quickly to utility customers, how to remove people and structures from hazardous areas, how to revive impacted businesses, how to gather perishable data quickly and efficiently, how to coordinate interagency efforts, how to engage the private and nonprofit sectors, and, most importantly, how to help people put their lives back together after a natural hazard. Despite these lessons learned, many states must capitalize more fully on that fleeting window of opportunity that occurs following a disaster. During the next hazard event, the states need to mobilize their mitigation forces faster and wider than ever before, implementing the many strategies and actions that have been put in place to further reduce their vulnerability to future hazard events.

Even better, the states should not wait that long, and should put greater effort into increasing the resiliency of the state in the calm before the storm, incorporating mitigation principles into the normal course of everyday state business. Mitigation criteria should be made a part of all state grants and loans, whether the administrating agency is an active participant in the state hazard mitigation plan or not. Local governments should be encouraged to consider hazard areas when making local infrastructure decisions and when regulating land uses in their jurisdictions. Mitigation principles should become routine measures in all investment, spending, and regulatory decisions made throughout the state.

> In practice, mitigation tends to be disaster-based, and opportunities are certainly optimized in the aftermath of a major disaster. But we need to move beyond this episodic approach to mitigation that relies on [federal funding] and other outside resources for program implementation which . . . after all . . . undercuts one of the principles of sustainability, and that is self-reliance. Ultimately, our goal is to incorporate mitigation into the day-to-day routines of government and business . . . this will take some time, but we're clearly making progress.[24]

SELF CHECK

- Discuss the role of interagency coordination.
- Explain the responsibilities of the private sector and nonprofit communities in increasing participation in mitigation efforts.
- Identify a main weakness associated with federal disaster assistance.

SUMMARY

How states approach disaster prevention varies greatly, depending on past hazard experience, resources that are available, and political commitment to reducing vulnerability. This chapter explores the responsibilities of state emergency management agencies and the role of mitigation planning at the state level. It also looks at the influence of state mandates on local government land use planning for addressing hazard issues at the community level. The chapter examines state building codes and state insurance laws, with an eye to understanding how different states approach regulation of construction in hazard areas and insuring against hazard losses. The chapter also discusses how some states directly intervene in land use decision making, particularly in environmentally sensitive areas such as the coastal zone and wetlands. The chapter concludes by outlining some opportunities for states to augment their capability to mitigate the impacts of hazards and increase the resiliency of their communities.

KEY TERMS

Areas of Particular Concern	Land designated for added state protection; defined by geographic boundaries, habitats, or natural resources.
Building code	A collection of laws, regulations, ordinances, or other statutory requirements adopted by a government that controls the physical structure of buildings.
Setback	Regulation that prohibits or limits the erection of structures within a specified distance from the ocean.
Wetland mitigation	The off-site preservation of another wetland located away from a development activity, or the creation of a new wetland to take the place of one that is impaired or destroyed.

ASSESS YOUR UNDERSTANDING

Go to www.wiley.com/college/schwab evaluate your knowledge of mitigating hazards at the state level.

Measure your learning by comparing pre-test and post-test results.

Summary Questions

1. States do not stray from federal regulations for land use planning and mitigation. True or False?
2. Few local governments are authorized to regulate land use and development. True or False?
3. What influence does a state have on local land use planning?
   (a) no influence
   (b) total control
   (c) varying influence
   (d) advisory capacity only
4. Each state maintains a regional FEMA office. True or False?
5. Funding for state emergency management offices is the sole responsibility of the states. True or False?
6. The Pre-Disaster Mitigation Program is one of the federally funded programs available to states to develop and implement mitigation efforts. True or False?
7. Hazard mitigation planning assesses vulnerability to hazards. True or False?
8. Section 322 of the Disaster Mitigation Act of 2000 requires that
   (a) state, local, and tribal governments submit a mitigation plan for natural hazards.
   (b) states submit proof of Clean Water Act compliance.
   (c) local governments apply for federal funding.
   (d) local and state governments comply with federal building codes.
9. A building code sets minimum acceptable standards of construction. True or False?
10. Which of the following is responsible for the enforcement of building codes?
    (a) local government
    (b) regional agencies
    (c) state management offices
    (d) federal programs

11. The federal government provides support to local code enforcement by requiring licenses for all building officials. True or False?

12. Insurance coverage is universally available for which of the following natural hazards?

    (a) tsunami

    (b) earthquake

    (c) flood

    (d) tornado

13. State regulation of hazard insurance controls both price and product. True or False?

14. A state-mandated insurance pool eliminates the problem of catastrophic losses from natural hazards. True or False?

15. The practice of direct state regulation occurs most frequently in

    (a) areas of repeat insurance claims.

    (b) environmentally sensitive areas.

    (c) earthquake zones.

    (d) urban areas.

16. A setback is used to shore up coastline to prevent erosion. True or False?

17. Which of the following are not used to establish setback distances for coastal construction?

    (a) mean low water mark

    (b) first line of natural vegetation

    (c) local erosion rate

    (d) mean high water mark

18. Owners of storm-damaged properties are not guaranteed the right to rebuild. True or False?

19. Areas of Particular Concern are determined by

    (a) local government.

    (b) regional agencies.

    (c) state government.

    (d) federal agencies.

Review Questions

1. Though states are responsible for some degree of regulation, local governments have the highest degree of control over land uses. Explain how.

2. Land use plans have been touted as a valuable mitigation tool. Explain why.

3. Give examples of states that have taken the initiative to establish responsible planning mandates that address the issue of development in hazard areas.

4. State governments serve as a key link between federal agencies and local communities. Describe the flow of interaction between the three levels.

5. Describe the role of a State Hazard Mitigation Officer and list some SHMO responsibilities.

6. Much of the funding for state emergency management offices comes from FEMA; list the types of grant programs that provide support to states.

7. Describe the role of hazard mitigation planning, an important aspect of a successful mitigation program.

8. The Disaster Mitigation Act of 2000 is an important element of state planning. Explain the goal of the DMA.

9. List the steps of the risk assessment portion of a state plan.

10. State hazard mitigation plans are serious business for the federal government. Describe the consequences of not preparing a plan.

11. A building code is used by a government to control the physical nature of buildings. List the four components of a building code.

12. Give examples of natural hazards that can be addressed through building codes.

13. Explain how strict building codes can be cost-effective in the long run.

14. The insurance industry faces great challenges in regard to areas subject to catastrophic losses. How are insurers coping?

15. What is the purpose of a state-mandated insurance pool?

16. Coastal areas are particularly vulnerable to the impacts of natural hazards. List three ways in which states regulate the coast.

17. Setbacks are a critical tool in protecting vulnerable coastal areas from development. Give ways in which setback lines are determined.

18. Many states provide some degree of protection for wetlands. Define wetland mitigation.

Applying This Chapter

1. As a developer looking to build a small housing development of homes in a former agricultural area, you are faced with the prospect of upgrading the infrastructure to accommodate the new homes. All that currently exists on the property is a narrow country road, well water, and public electric lines. Outline the infrastructure projects that would be required to go further with the plan.

2. What types of local land use planning would be required for a previously underdeveloped tract of lakeside property in Wisconsin? What support would be available from the state and federal governments?

3. As a public information officer in a small Texas town that experienced a minor wildfire last year, outline the various emergency management systems that support your community. Name your State Hazard Mitigation Officer and determine the location of his/her office.

4. The first step in risk assessment is to identify hazards; the second is to profile hazard events. Using these two steps, compare the risk assessment of New Orleans to San Francisco.

5. How would the building codes differ between a home along the Hudson River and a home in the plains of Kansas?

6. As an insurer in tornado-torn Indiana, a recent and dramatic increase in insurance claims has forced you to raise premiums. Draft a letter to your clients justifying your reasons.

7. Consider the different types of land areas in your state. Which could be classified as Areas of Particular Concern, and what protection should they be given?

8. If you were a state official in Colorado, how would you apply an all-hazards approach to your mitigation planning?

YOU TRY IT

Plan for the Worst

Define some area of your community (or state, if none exist locally) that you feel is prone to some type of natural hazard. Predict the worst-case scenario. What state-level mitigation efforts would better protect the area from a disaster?

Going Coastal

Imagine that your home was situated on the Outer Banks of North Carolina. What hazards would threaten your building? Assess how it would withstand those hazards. Using hurricane-preparedness information for homeowners from NOAA, (see www.nhc.noaa. gov/HAW2/pdf/avoid_hurricane_damage.pdf) determine what you could do to prevent or decrease damage from a hurricane.

Road Rules

Using information from your state's office of emergency management website, assess the types of hazards, both natural and manmade that your state informs its residents about. Were you aware of all the threats? Using the site, determine your evacuation route in the event of a natural hazard or disaster.

8

LOCAL GOVERNMENT POWERS
Building Resilience from the Ground Up

Starting Point

Go to www.wiley.com/college/schwab to assess your knowledge of local government powers.
Determine where you need to concentrate your effort.

What You'll Learn in This Chapter

▲ The principles of sustainable development
▲ The duty of local governments to protect public health and safety
▲ Forms of local authority
▲ Uses of powers delegated to local governments
▲ Types of local governments in the United States
▲ Ways of building resiliency at the local level

After Studying This Chapter, You'll be Able to

▲ Examine how the principles of resiliency contribute to a sustainable community
▲ Analyze ways that local governments utilize police power
▲ Describe mitigation tools that lie within local government authority
▲ Diagram the structure of your community's local government
▲ Evaluate ways local governments can collaborate with each other for mitigation purposes
▲ Examine how the characteristics of growth can determine local vulnerability to natural hazards

Goals and Outcomes

▲ Understand the policies and recognize the tools of local governments
▲ Compare and contrast forms of local government
▲ Assess the most effective way to promote hazard mitigation policies within the structure of a local government
▲ Select and apply chapter ideas to problems related to local control of community development
▲ Collaborate with others on ways to increase a community's involvement in the process of mitigation planning and goal formulation
▲ Evaluate the degree to which principles of resiliency and sustainability are expressed in a community

INTRODUCTION

This chapter offers a broad understanding of the types of powers that local governments can wield in managing the hazard areas within their jurisdiction. The chapter introduces the topic of local government policy with a short discussion of the sources of local government authority, as well as a brief mention of growth management. The chapter further develops the discussion of local policy with a description of the kinds of powers that states have delegated to their local governments, including regulation, acquisition, taxation, spending, education, and planning. It should be noted that these powers are generally quite broad. The authority to manage hazards is often limited only by local decision-makers' creativity and willingness to be proactive. The chapter then describes some of the basic forms of local government that are prevalent in the United States in order to provide an idea of the organizational structure where all local mitigation policy is developed and carried out. The chapter concludes with a discussion of ways in which local governments can collaborate to create communities that are more resilient to the impacts of hazards.

8.1 A Sustainable Community is a Resilient Community

Communities can be impacted by any number of calamities. The shutdown of a mill or factory can result in massive unemployment. The pollution of a river or lake can make water supplies unsanitary. Unchecked growth can bring about urban sprawl, leading to air pollution, traffic congestion, and inefficient use of land and public resources. Social injustice and racial and ethnic discrimination can lead to crippling poverty and violent crime. A lack of equal access to quality education, affordable housing, health care, and job opportunities can foster increased social unrest and discontent. Sustainable communities are those that face these issues head on and take proactive measures to combat the economic, environmental, and social problems that come their way.

In its most widely-used definition, sustainable development is development that "meets the needs of the present without compromising the ability of future generations to meet their own needs."[1] Sustainable development implies that those who are living on Earth now will not lessen the opportunities of future generations, but will strive to pass on a natural, economic, and social environment that ensures a high quality of life for all to come. Sustainability envisions a wise use of resources and a fair chance for all community members to live meaningful, productive lives both now and in the future. Sustainability also calls for seeing beyond our own borders and realizing that we are all interconnected in a complex system of natural processes.

But sustainable policies are meaningless if a community is exposed to natural and man-made hazards and does nothing to reduce its vulnerability. Earthquakes, hurricanes, ice storms, tornadoes, floods, wildfires, technological disasters, and other types of hazard events can be economically devastating, ecologically disruptive, and emotionally and psychologically draining. The occurrence of a natural or man-made hazard only serves to exacerbate problems a community may have been facing before the disaster. A truly sustainable community must also be a hazard-resilient community, and considers disaster prevention along with issues of environmental stewardship, quality of life, economic vitality, and a fair legacy for future generations.

8.1.1 Unsustainable Land Uses Lead to Vulnerability

How we develop our land and where we build our homes and businesses determines how vulnerable our communities are to all sorts of hazards. Patterns of growth that emphasize sprawling development place intense pressure on the natural environment, as wetlands, floodplains, wildlands, and seismic risk zones are built upon. This type of development is unsustainable and makes us more vulnerable to natural hazards than ever before. Nowhere is this more evident than in the coastal zone, an environment that is subject to devastating natural hazards on a regular basis. For example, in 1900, 11 million people lived in counties along the Gulf and Atlantic coasts. By 1950, these counties had increased in population by 136%, and by 2000, the population had doubled again (a 105% increase), with 53 million people living in these coastal counties.[2] The number of Americans at risk from earthquakes, landslides, and inland flooding has increased dramatically as well,[3] and the trends continue to rise.

8.1.2 Local Policy is Local

Each local community is unique, and there is no one-size-fits-all solution to every community's hazard problems. Even within a single state there is considerable variation among communities in terms of demographics, topography, climate, economics, natural resources, hazard exposure, and political and cultural character. There are large affluent metropolitan areas that are experiencing growing pains and unchecked sprawl. There are also isolated rural communities whose agricultural or manufacturing economic base is crumbling and whose populations are shrinking. There are mountain communities that must deal with the constraints of a steep terrain, and coastal communities that experience frequent violent storms. Some communities are progressive and promote a liberal agenda, while others are more conservative and espouse traditional values. Some local governments aggressively regulate land uses within their jurisdiction, and others vehemently oppose government interference with private property rights. While this diversity contributes to the richness of our nation's culture, it also means that every approach to increasing resiliency must reflect the community's individual mitigation and preparedness needs.

8.1.3 A Duty to Act

Fortunately, there are many ways to increase resilience available to local communities both large and small, ways that fall well within the power of local governments to pursue. Local policy to cultivate resilience indicates a community's commitment to reducing damage from high-risk hazards and provides the authority and guidance for mapping, regulation, planning, spending, and other local mitigation and preparedness activities.

Disaster prevention is more than a soapbox issue for politicians and community leaders—it is also an affirmative duty of local government. The responsibility of the government to protect the heath and safety of community residents is indisputable. Development decisions that do not take into account known risk factors such as flooding, earthquakes, sinkholes, high winds, storm surge, erosion, chemical spills, toxic wastes, and other natural or man-made hazards could place people and property in danger. It is in the best interests of the community at large to ensure that residents and property owners are fully aware of the inherent risks in building in hazard locations.

Issues of legal liability may also arise. When individuals experience damage from flooding or erosion, for example, they often file lawsuits against the government, claiming that the government has caused the damage, contributed to it, or (in some instances) failed to prevent or provide adequate warnings of the hazard. Such lawsuits are expensive for the public sector not only because damage awards are growing, but also because of attorney and expert witness fees.[4]

SELF-CHECK

- Define **sustainable development**.
- List five issues a sustainable community considers for its citizens.
- Explain how unsustainable land uses lead to vulnerability.

8.2 RATES: Local Government Powers to Manage Growth and Development

In this section we will examine some of the fundamental powers that local governments possess under their basic police power authority. These powers are popularly referred to by the acronym RATES: Regulation, Acquisition, Taxation, Education and Spending. We will also discuss planning as a tool to create a cohesive framework for all the other local powers in the context of mitigating the impacts of natural hazards (see Table 8-1).

> ## FOR EXAMPLE
>
> ### Nobody Told Us It Would Be Like This
>
> A family from Syracuse, New York, who purchased oceanfront property in North Topsail Beach, North Carolina, enjoyed a single weekend at their vacation home before Hurricane Ophelia washed away 60 feet of beach in front of the house in September, 2005. When the town condemned the building because of structural damage and because water, sewer, and power lines were no longer connected to the house, the new owners wondered why no one had told them of the dangers of oceanfront erosion. No law in North Carolina required the sellers to disclose the house's history, even though the home had been condemned before because of previous storms. In the meantime, the family is still responsible for paying the mortgage on the home, even though it is legally uninhabitable.[5]

8.2.1 Using Local Government Powers to Manage Growth

The powers available to local governments that fall under RATES can be used—either separately or in tandem—to manage the characteristics of growth in a community. Land use management tools and techniques influence one or more of the following characteristics of growth:

▲ **Quantity:** The total amount of development, such as the number of buildings, facilities, and structures; the amount of acreage developed; and the percentage of total land area that is developed.

▲ **Type:** The class of development. Major types include residential, commercial, government/religious/nonprofit, industrial, and open space. Subtypes can include single family/multifamily residential, light industrial/heavy industrial, or strip commercial/mall commercial.

▲ **Cost:** Expenses charged to the local government from development, such as *economic costs* (water/ sewer, schools, emergency/local services, or infrastructure), *distribution costs* (issues of who will pay, property taxation and assessments, efficiency of public services), *environmental costs* (water quality degradation/water resource depletion, increased impervious surfaces/stormwater flows, loss of open space/damage to habitats/decline in biodiversity, clear cutting/slope modification/changes in topography, waste management/landfill capacity, traffic congestion, or air/noise pollution), and *social costs* (stratification of incomes/class, deterioration of city centers, urban sprawl, overburdened/inadequate services, segregation by race, ethnicity, culture, etc.).

▲ **Timing & Rate:** When and how fast growth will be allowed for adequate facility construction or infrastructure capacity overload.

Table 8-1: Local Government Powers

Regulation	Local governments have the power to control land use through regulations such as zoning, subdivision ordinances, floodplain regulations, etc. Regulation also includes building codes and standards to make stuctures more hazard resilient.
Acquisition	Local governments are allowed to acquire and hold property for public benefit and use. Removing at-risk property from the private market can be a useful mitigation tool.
Taxation, Fees & Special Assessments	Taxes, impact fees, and special assessments can be an important source of revenue for governments to help pay for mitigation activities. In addition, the power of taxation can have a profound impact on the pattern of development in local communities. Special tax districts, for example, can be used to discourage intensive development in coastal hazard-prone areas.
Education	Public awareness and understanding of hazards that face the community are essential for effective hazard management activities. Education and information dissemination are important functions of local governments to protect the health and safety of the community.
Spending	Local governments can choose to pay for public facilities that are placed in non-hazardous areas and are built to withstand known hazard impacts. Local governments can also influence private development by withholding spending for public infrastructure and capital improvements in known hazard areas.
Planning	Local governments are authorized to make and carry out plans through the establishment of goals, policies, and procedures for a social or economic purpose. Planning provides a context for all other local government activities, ensuring that policies and actions are carried out according to a conscientious, organized, and rational process.

▲ **Quality:** Soundness of construction in terms of safety, energy efficiency, hazard resistance, aesthetics, etc.

▲ **Density:** Intensity of development in terms of distance between structures, lot size, building height, and number of people and structures per acre.

All these characteristics of growth determine the level of vulnerability in a community. When undertaken consciously and conscientiously, growth management can be used to control development in hazard-prone areas of the local jurisdiction.

As a general rule, local governments have used growth management techniques more frequently to control factors such as pollution, traffic congestion, aesthetics, and to make sure that adequate public services (schools, roads, water, and sewer, etc.) are available to serve new development, rather than for hazard mitigation purposes directly.

8.2.2 Using the Power of Regulation to Mitigate the Impacts of Hazards

Regulatory powers granted by the state to local governments are the most basic way that a local government can control growth and development within its jurisdiction. Local governments regulate private property to protect the natural environment, to encourage economic development, and to protect the public's health and safety. Regulatory powers discussed in this section include:

▲ Zoning ordinances
▲ Subdivision regulations
▲ Building codes
▲ Flood damage prevention ordinances

8.2.3 Zoning

Zoning is the traditional and nearly ubiquitous tool available to local governments to control land. **Zoning** regulates how property within the jurisdiction may be used by dividing the community into different districts (or zones). **Zoning maps** define the location of the various districts. An accompanying zoning ordinance defines the type and intensity of uses that are allowed within each district. Zoning districts are labeled according to the dominant use that will be permitted in that zone. Some communities have more elaborate systems of zonation than others, but the most basic zoning districts include Residential, Commercial, Industrial, Government, Open Space/Conservation, and Religious/Nonprofit.

The local zoning ordinance enumerates specific requirements that must be followed in each zone, such as lot size, building height, floor area or footprint, set backs (minimum/maximum distance of structures from property line and between structures), parking spaces, density of population, and so forth. For hazard mitigation purposes, local zoning maps may be accompanied by regulations that restrict inappropriate uses in designated hazard areas. This presupposes that the locality has mapped the locations of likely hazards and has incorporated this spatial information into the zoning map (see Figure 8-1).

Nonconforming Uses

Most zoning codes allow for prior uses to continue as nonconforming uses after changes in the code are made. As these buildings are replaced or destroyed, the former use becomes illegal. Over time, this process reduces the number of

Figure 8-1

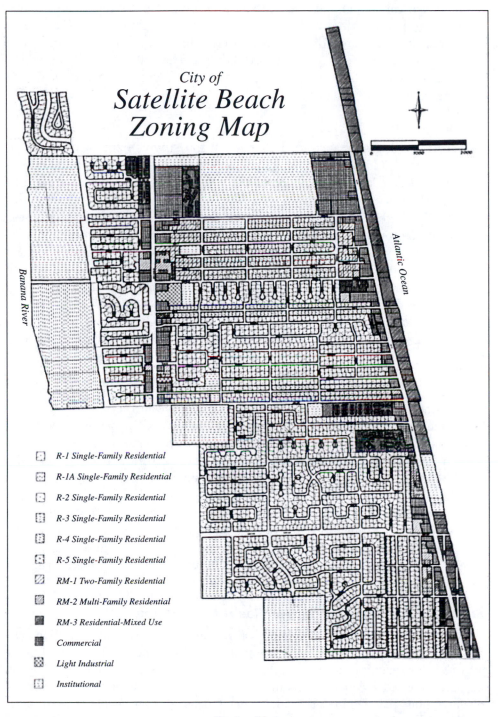

Zoning Map.

buildings that are out of compliance with a city's zoning code. Communities with less patience can require that nonconforming structures be replaced within a certain time period under a process known as **amortization**. For example, a community may require a homeowner to relocate his or her beachfront home outside the beach erosion zone by a specified date. The length of time over which amortization takes place must approximate the expected depreciation of the building or it could be challenged as unconstitutional.

Overlay Zones

Some local zoning ordinances include overlay zones, which apply conditions to development in addition to, or in place of, the standard zoning ordinance for a certain area. Overlay zones can be effective for use in high hazard areas. For example, floodplain overlay districts have been used to regulate development in mapped flood areas. Overlays have also been used in coastal high hazard areas such as beachfront, storm surge, and areas subject to rapid erosion.

Overlay zones can be triggered by a certain specified event or situation, such as a hurricane that causes substantial damage. Until the event occurs, the overlay zone remains transparent and has no effect on the property located in the overlay zone. Recovery overlay zones can include temporary regulations that restrict reconstruction in an area impacted by a disaster until a thorough damage assessment has been made or require any new development to include hazard mitigation techniques.

Bonus and Incentive Zoning

Bonus and incentive zoning is the practice of allowing developers to exceed the limits of current regulations, such as building height, floor area, or density, in return for certain concessions. This technique is generally used in metropolitan areas, where land is scarcer, and the market benefit to the developer is more easily realized. When used as a mitigation tool, communities offer bonuses to developers who avoid building in hazard-prone areas or who incorporate mitigation into their building designs. The developer may then build more intensely than is normally allowed on other portions of the property or elsewhere in the community. This method can be used to encourage developers to provide dune walkovers, open space, or on-site mitigation facilities such as retention ponds. Communities can also offer incentives for the developer to donate lands in the hazard-prone portions of the property or to cluster development away from the hazard areas.

Strengths of Using Zoning for Hazard Mitigation

There are notable strengths associated with zoning when used for mitigation purposes: Zoning can be used to keep inappropriate development out of hazard-prone areas by **down-zoning** (decreasing density) in hazardous areas. Down-zoning can be accomplished by increasing minimum lot size, or reducing the number of dwelling units permitted per acre. By reducing density, fewer people and structures are located in high hazard areas. This, in turn, helps protect the local tax base, matches the population with the capacity of local emergency shelters, lowers the amount of time needed to evacuate the population before a hazard strikes, and can prevent large, hard-to-relocate structures from being built in high-hazard zones like beach erosion areas. Safer areas can be zoned for higher-intensity uses including small-lot residential structures, apartments, and commercial businesses.

While zoning can be used to keep intensive uses out of hazardous areas, it can also designate hazardous areas for more appropriate low-intensity uses including parks, open space, greenways, resource conservation, wildlife habitat, agriculture, or beach access that benefit the entire community and add to local aesthetic and environmental quality. Zoning can also help preserve natural areas that mitigate against hazards such as wetlands, floodplains, and dunes. "As a rule of thumb . . . wetlands, floodplains, and slopes . . . take first priority for designation as open space, as they represent highly sensitive environmental resources that are generally considered to be unbuildable in a legal sense, in a practical sense, or for reasons of common sense."[6] Zoning can also prohibit the storage or handling of hazardous chemicals or other dangerous materials in floodplains and other at risk areas.

Weaknesses of Zoning for Hazard Mitigation

There are also some weakness and limitations to using zoning for hazard mitigation purposes. Zoning primarily affects new structures and vacant land rather than existing buildings and property that is already developed (except through nonconforming use provisions, which often take years to become effective). As a result, it is a poor way to make current development more hazard resilient. Also, zoning is a spatial control and is only suited to hazards that are spatially defined or clearly mapped (e.g., flooding, but not tornadoes). Furthermore, zoning can be subject to legal and political challenges: down-zoning may be viewed as exclusionary against low-income residents or discriminatory against minority residents, and zoning must allow the landowner to retain some economically viable use of the property to avoid Fifth Amendment takings claims. Down-zoning that decreases density may also increase the cost of providing public services, including mass transit, water and sewer lines, waste collection, and fire protection, all of which tend to become more expensive and less efficient when spread out over large land areas. Less dense areas may also mean lower tax revenues for the local government. Finally, zoning regulations are subject to a fluctuating political climate; as new leaders assume local elected and appointed positions, decision-making may change to suit the current administrative agenda. These factors usually preclude a blanket prohibition of development in hazard areas; however, they do not preclude the careful and precise application of the zoning ordinance to meet specific hazard problems.

8.2.4 Subdivision Ordinances

Subdivision ordinances govern the partition of land for development or sale. In addition to controlling the configuration of parcels and lot layout, subdivision ordinances set standards for developer-built infrastructure. The local government must approve the subdivision plat (map) prior to the division and sale of the land into individual lots. It is at the point of subdivision review that many communities impose conditions on the developer in exchange for plat approval. Local governments often charge exactions and fees to help pay for the demands that new construction will place on local facilities and services, such as schools, water and sewer, fire and police protection, and garbage pickup. Developers may also be required to pay for impacts on the community and the environment, such as traffic congestion, air and water pollution, excess noise, increased stormwater runoff, and similar burdens that result from increased development in a community. Many local governments also require dedication of land to build needed public facilities as a condition of subdivision approval.

Subdivisions regulations can be used for mitigation purposes in several ways, and are most commonly applied to prohibit the subdivision of land subject to flooding, wildfire, or erosion. When hazard zones can be identified on a map of the parcel, communities may require minimum distances between those zones and the site of construction. For instance, coastal communities may require the configuration of deep lots on the oceanfront. These lots allow homes to be relocated further inland on the same parcel if erosion or coastal storms threaten the structure.

If the subdivision layout does not keep entire lots out of the flood-prone area of a parcel, buffers can help minimize the amount of development exposed to flooding. A **buffer** is typically a setback of a specific distance, such as 25 or 100 feet, from a channel, floodway, wetland, or other water feature. In that area, no cutting, clearing of ground cover, or alteration of natural features is allowed, but the rest of the lot can be graded and built on. In the state of Maryland, for example, a 25-foot buffer is required next to all wetlands. Subdivision ordinances may also allow developers to cluster homes in greater densities away from hazard-prone sites, and require dedication of unbuildable lots to green space or parkland for use by all the residents (see Figure 8-2).

Figure 8-2

Subdivision with homes clustered together. Open spaces can be used for recreation, wildlife habitat, or flood control.

Subdivision regulations can also require that infrastructure meets standards that address known hazard risks. For example, the installation of adequate drainage and stormwater management facilities, as well as limits on impervious surfaces, can be required in flood-prone or landslide-prone areas. In order to reduce fire risk, for example, subdivision ordinances may require wide building spacing, installation of firebreaks, drought-resistant or indigenous vegetation and landscaping, on-site water storage, multiple access points, and streets built wide enough to accommodate fire trucks and emergency vehicles.

8.2.5 Building Codes

Building codes are laws, ordinances, or regulations that set forth standards and requirements for structural integrity, design, and construction materials used in commercial and residential structures. Building codes are generally permitted and enforced at the local level. The issuance of a building permit is a ministerial function of the local government, so that if building plans meet code requirements, a building permit must be issued. If the plans do not meet code, however, the local government can reject the proposal or require revisions before granting approval. Local building inspectors conduct site reviews during the construction process to ensure that construction complies with the approved plans.

Studies have found that regulations can be effective when supplemented with economic incentives. Local communities can help build public support for strict enforcement of building codes by initiating publicity campaigns with this objective in mind and alerting citizens about ways to strengthen structures beyond code requirements. See Chapters 7 and 12 for further discussion of building codes.

Post-Disaster Building Moratoria

Some communities have enacted moratoria to deal with construction in the post-storm environment. A **moratorium** is a short-term suspension of the right to develop, usually accomplished by a refusal of the local government to issue a building permit. Moratoria are only effective if they are ready to be activated by a pre-determined trigger, such as a disaster event. Moratoria give local officials time to assess the damage and set priorities for response, planning and mitigation efforts. They are often used to prevent property owners from rebuilding damaged structures before a complete damage assessment can be made or an acquisition program can go into effect. Moratoria can also allow officials to expand high-hazard designated areas to reflect the actual damages from a hazard event.

8.2.6 Flood Damage Prevention Ordinances

Structures built in the floodplain are subject to damage from rising water. In addition to increasing the number of properties at risk, development in the floodplain reduces the flood storage capacity of these areas, resulting in greater flood heights. Local floodplain regulations can keep people from locating in the most dangerous areas and require safe building designs for other flood-prone areas.

Local flood damage prevention codes prohibit or establish conditions for development in high risk areas. Conditions include setbacks, floodproofing, or elevation requirements for roads, bridges, pipelines, and buildings. These conditions are often imposed in addition to or in place of other zoning, subdivision, building codes, or other local regulations.

Many local flood prevention ordinances are enacted according to minimum standards issued by the National Flood Insurance Program (NFIP), a program administered by the Federal Emergency Management Agency (FEMA) that provides the opportunity for residents in participating communities to purchase federally-backed flood insurance. Development in the floodplain is regulated based on Flood Insurance Rate Maps (FIRMs) published by FEMA that show the boundaries of the 100-year flood zone (known as Special Flood Hazard Areas), as well as other types of flood areas in the jurisdiction.

There are many critical issues involved in local floodplain management. A significant problem in many communities involves inaccurate flood maps that do not reflect actual flood risks in the jurisdiction, often because new development has changed stormwater flows, which can increase flood levels dramatically.

Floodplain management programs can be foiled if development pressures in a community are heavy and there is insufficient leadership to honor mitigation goals. This is especially problematic in communities with a lack of suitable building sites located outside of the floodplain. Flood hazard risk reduction has often focused narrowly on the protection of structures in the floodplain rather than the preservation of the floodplain's natural functions. Restoration and conservation programs that protect wetlands and floodplains can help alleviate these limitations.

Since floodplains rarely fall within a single jurisdiction, floodplain management is often best addressed through regional governing bodies. A river basin-wide approach to flood management is often more effective than local regulatory programs enacted by individual communities. Collaborative agreements acknowledge that development in one community can affect neighboring communities both upstream and down. However, such multi-jurisdictional management agreements can be very difficult to achieve, especially if left solely to local initiative.

8.2.7 Using the Power of Acquisition to Mitigate the Impacts of Hazards

The types of land use regulations discussed above allow a local government to control land use and development within the jurisdiction without changing title or ownership patterns in the community. However, regulation of private property is not the only method available to local governments for controlling growth. Public land ownership and conscientious management of public lands provide a local government the most direct control over the use of property.

Willing Sellers, Willing Buyers

At times, the local government must use its power of eminent domain to condemn property for certain community needs, such as schools and roads. Eminent domain is rarely used, however, to acquire land for hazard mitigation purposes (and may never be used if federal funding is involved in the acquisition). More common is government purchase of land from a willing seller. Through the acquisition process, the local government offers to buy a home or business owner's property, and the owner must voluntarily agree to sell. Often, when property owners have experienced multiple hazards over the years, such as repetitive flooding that occurs on a regular basis, they are more than willing to participate in the local **buyout program,** as long as the program is explained fully, the purchase price reflects market value, and an affordable housing alternative is available. After the sale, the local government assumes title to the property, demolishes any structures on it, and the former owner may use the purchase price to move to another, safer location. Some acquisition programs include **relocation** rather than demolition, when the owner's house is moved to an alternative lot out of the hazard area.

Through a buyout program, the local government becomes the new owner of the formerly hazardous property. The local government must be able to maintain the property in perpetuity (forever) so that it will never again be used in a way that poses a risk to people or structures. For some impoverished communities or those located in rural areas, being responsible for maintaining the property can be burdensome. However, local governments can transfer the title to the acquired land to other government agencies (the state or county, for example), or the local government can deed the property to a non-profit agency, such as a conservation land trust or environmental protection organization. This option has allowed some communities to benefit from removal of people and buildings from hazard areas without the burden of continual property maintenance.

The Goals of Acquisition

Public acquisition serves to effectively hazard proof a particular piece of property. The property is removed from the private market, and the possibility of inappropriate development is reduced. Although acquisition is typically one of the most expensive mitigation tactics, in the long run it is often less expensive to acquire and demolish a building than to repeatedly provide for its reconstruction.

In addition to reducing the public cost of recovery and reconstruction, acquisition can be a tool for accomplishing other community goals, such as increasing floodplain storage capacity; preserving wetlands, maritime forests, estuaries and other natural habitats; protecting aquifer recharge zones and riparian buffers; and providing open space, beach access, and parks and recreation areas.

Acquisition is often paired with demolition or relocation of structures located on the property. This helps protect other structures from flying or floating debris that may be torn from damaged structures during high wind or severe flooding events. Removal of structures also allows the area to return to its natural function of absorbing hazard impacts, including storm surge, erosion, and floodwaters.

Types of Land Interests Acquired

Land ownership is often defined as a bundle of rights, or interests, of which the right to develop is only one. A local government may acquire the entire bundle of rights to a piece of hazard-prone property, or it may acquire a lesser interest such as an easement or right-of-use.

Fee Simple Acquisition of Land and Damaged Structures

When a single owner has all the rights associated with a parcel of land, that owner is said to hold the land in fee simple. Acquiring property in fee simple provides a local government with the greatest level of control over the use and disposition of a parcel.

Fee simple purchase is usually the most expensive method of land acquisition. In addition to the cost of buying the property, the local government must delete the property from its property tax rolls and assume its maintenance costs. Given its costs, this technique should be used only for property in the most hazardous areas, where structures and human lives are subject to repeated damage or extreme risk. Properties that match this description must not return to the marketplace. However, the cost of losing tax revenues from these properties is often lower than the cost of providing services to properties in hazard areas and the periodic costs of rescue and recovery from disasters. Acquiring land that is not yet developed may be significantly less expensive to purchase than developed parcels, and has the added advantage of preventing damage to structures before a hazard event occurs. Conversely, after a disaster, high-density, repetitive loss properties may drop in price and become a better long-term investment for mitigation purposes.

Acquisition of Easements

As an alternative to fee simple acquisition, a local government may acquire a lesser interest in hazardous property, such as an **easement**. The owner of an easement has one or more of the rights in a property, leaving the rest of the rights in the hands of the landowner. Easements either grant an affirmative right to use the property, such as a right of access, or can restrict the landowner's right to use the property in a particular way. Local governments can prevent development in hazard areas by purchasing a negative easement that prevents building on the land.

Easements that prevent development may be nearly as expensive to acquire as fee simple rights. Many governments also prefer to own land in fee simple because easements must be policed, and the terms of the easement must be enforced, often at considerable expense. Many governments offer to lower the tax burden for properties that cannot be developed due to an easement. As a result, the local government could see its property tax rolls decrease with each donated easement. For these reasons, easements have not frequently been used for hazard mitigation purposes.

Purchase of Development Rights (PDR)

Purchase of a property's development rights (PDR) is similar to acquiring a negative easement against development. Local governments can use this technique as an alternative to fee simple purchase or easements when the only purpose is to prevent building on the land. PDR may not be significantly less expensive than fee simple acquisition, but by owning development rights the government assumes a very high level of control over property without being responsible for its maintenance. PDR is particularly suited to land in forestry or farming, where the current use is compatible with hazard mitigation goals. In this case, PDR can prevent the land from changing into a higher-risk use, while allowing the landowner to benefit from harvesting crops or timber.

Transfer of Development Rights (TDR)

Like PDR, Transfer of Development Rights (TDR) programs treat development as a commodity separate from the land itself. The local government first awards the property owner in the "sending area" a set of development rights based on the value or acreage of land. The sending area contains land the local government seeks to protect. The government then establishes a "receiving area" for the development rights. The receiving area is located some distance from the sending area and is a more preferable site for development. Landowners in the sending area are typically prohibited from developing their land, but they can realize the value of their property by selling their development rights to developers in the receiving areas. Developers who acquire development rights can build to higher densities than would otherwise be permitted in the receiving zone.

TDR is a complex system, which often makes it difficult for local governments to implement and for landowners to understand and accept. However, by designating high hazard areas as "sending zones," and more appropriate, safer areas of the community as "receiving zones," the local government can effectively

---

FOR EXAMPLE

Transferring Development Away From Coastal Barrier Islands

Collier County, Florida, began a Transfer of Development Rights (TDR) program in the 1980s to protect 40,000 acres of coastal barrier islands, mangroves, salt marshes, and beaches. These areas were designated as sending zones. The receiving zones were already set for multi-family housing, but could be built to a higher density using the development rights. Parcels for which the development rights have been sold must be restricted from development or donated to the county or a conservation organization. The TDR program was halted when the transfer resulted in density concentration in only one receiving site, overwhelming it.[7]

shift the location of development without reducing the overall property value of the jurisdiction. Of course, to be successful, suitable receiving zones must be available outside of the hazard area, but because a large area of the community can be designated (not just specific individual parcels), TDR provides some flexibility to developers who put the purchased development rights to use.

Reusing Acquired Properties

Acquired properties become the responsibility of the local government, which must pay for its maintenance and management, except in the case of acquired easements. The local government is required to commit the purchased land to non-intensive uses in perpetuity, thereby avoiding future development that could put people and property in danger once again. Examples of permissible uses and public amenities include parks, open space, jogging and biking trails, ball fields, community gardens, dog parks, and wildlife refuges.

Hazard loss reduction is less pronounced and mitigation less effective when isolated parcels are purchased, creating a patchwork effect. Such a checkerboard pattern of purchases is also more costly and difficult for the local government to manage and maintain. Few large-scale acquisition projects undertaken with federal funds to date have been conducted in the context of a comprehensive management program to avoid a disorderly land use pattern; instead, local governments have largely acquired an inventory of scattered empty lots.

8.2.8 Using the Power of Taxation and Fees to Mitigate the Impacts of Hazards

Like other government powers, the local government's authority to raise revenue is dictated by state law. Taxes, especially property taxes, have traditionally been the largest single source of revenue for most local governments, sometimes providing more than half of all receipts. Local governments are also granted the power to charge user or administrative fees, make special assessments, issue bonds, and receive grants-in-aid. It is important to note that the power to levy taxes, assessments, and fees extends beyond merely the collection of revenue, and can have a profound impact on the pattern of development in the community.

By assessing certain areas of the community with differential tax rates or assessments, the local government can influence the affordability of development. The community can thereby steer development to desirable, safe areas, while providing disincentives for developers to build on lands identified as hazardous or environmentally sensitive. Tax abatements may also be used by local governments to encourage property owners and developers to integrate mitigation measures into new construction and to retrofit existing buildings. Incentives have been applied to promote storm proofing, flood proofing, wind strengthening, and seismic retrofitting. This is similar to programs that use taxation as an incentive for property owners to carry out energy conservation, historic preservation, and other activities of value to the community.

Real Property Taxes

Real property taxes are based on the assessed value of property, including the value of the land along with any improvements, such as structures. **Differential assessment** is a technique for reducing the tax burden on land facing development pressure by recognizing that undeveloped properties require fewer public services. This technique can moderate the pressure to develop land at its highest and best use by reducing the tax rate applied to land so that payments are equal to its essential services. Tax assessments may also reduce the assessed value of land to a percentage of urban land, or assess the land based on its income-producing capacity, as opposed to its market value.

Preferential taxation has been used to preserve land that is valuable to the community in ways other than monetary, such as farmland, forestland, historical properties, open space, and wildlife habitat. Although preferential taxation has not been used extensively for mitigation purposes per se, local governments can apply differential assessments to reduce the development pressure on hazard-prone lands including floodplains and open space. This is especially effective where hazard areas overlap other sensitive lands such as wildlife habitat or aquifer recharge areas, effectively linking multiple community goals.

Special Assessments

Many local governments levy special assessments against property owners who receive a direct benefit from a public improvement. This technique shifts the financial burden from the general public to those who gain the most. Local governments typically levy special assessments for public improvements such as streets and sidewalks that serve a particular neighborhood or section of the community.

There are a number of ways to apply this technique for mitigation purposes, from one-time assessments that raise revenue for a specific improvement to long-term assessments that fund ongoing projects. Special assessments for hazard mitigation include:

▲ Construction of structural projects, such as seawalls, retention basins, dikes, berms, etc.
▲ Establishing a regional floodplain management organization.
▲ Creation of a special storm services district, where funds go toward mitigation, disaster recovery, and response activities in that district, including replacement of damaged infrastructure.
▲ Maintaining stormwater management systems.
▲ Implementing beach erosion programs.
▲ Floodproofing water, sewer, or other public service systems.

These charges may or may not have the effect of discouraging development in the assessment district. However, they do transfer some of the cost of living or doing business in environmentally sensitive or hazard-prone areas to those who choose to do so.

Impact Fees

Impact fees require new developments to share in the financial burden that their arrival imposes on a community. **Impact fees** are typically one-time up-front charges (although some jurisdictions allow payments over time) against new development to pay for off-site improvements, including schools, sewer and water treatment plants, fire stations, community centers, and other local facilities. The fees can also be set up to allow new development to buy into existing services with excess capacity.

Impact fees are typically based on ratios that show what services the average new resident will require. While there are several methods for analyzing impacts, most consider only a single project in isolation. An alternative method is to carry out a **cumulative impact assessment,** which looks at the total effect of all development in a particular environment. For example, this approach can be used to estimate the combined effects of several potential developments on the flood storage capacity of the watershed. The fee in this case would go toward mitigating increased flood heights, perhaps by creating flood storage elsewhere in the floodplain.

Despite the theoretical advantages, local governments have made little use of hazard-related impact fees, even when public facilities are damaged by natural hazards. Communities have typically preferred to insure against losses than to pass the cost of service along to developers.[8]

8.2.9 Using the Power of Spending to Mitigate the Impacts of Hazards

In order to provide the services that their residents need, local governments have the authority to spend public funds for public purposes. The power to spend also includes the power to withhold spending when that is in the best interest of the public at large. Most local government spending involves a considerable amount of discretionary decision making and policy formation, and is key to accomplishing broader growth management goals. This authority to make expenditures in the public interest can be a powerful tool for communities to mitigate the impacts of some types of hazards.

There are basically two types of expenditures that local governments make on a regular basis. The first includes payment for ongoing services, such as waste collection, fire and police protection, drainage maintenance, and the like. These types of expenditures are usually covered in the annual operating budget of the municipality. The second type of expenditure involves major one-time capital improvement projects.

Spending for Capital Improvements

The definition of a **capital improvement** differs from community to community. The common definition of a capital improvement includes new or expanded physical facilities that are relatively large in size, expensive, and permanent. Some common examples include streets and bridges, schools, public libraries, water and sewer lines and treatment plants, parks and recreation facilities, and government offices. In smaller communities certain expenditures, such as the purchase of a fire engine, may also be considered a capital expenditure.

Capital Improvement Programs and Budgets

Most communities make plans in advance to help guide decisions about how, when, and where public spending for major projects will take place. A capital improvements program is a multiyear schedule of public physical improvements. The scheduling is based on studies of fiscal resources available and the choice of specific improvements to be constructed for a period of five to six years into the future. The capital improvements budget refers to those facilities that are programmed for the next fiscal year.

An important distinction between the capital improvements budget and the capital improvements program is that the one-year budget may become a part of the legally adopted annual operating budget. In contrast, the longer-term program does not necessarily have legal significance, nor does it necessarily commit a local government to a particular expenditure in a particular year. It merely serves as a planning tool to guide future decisions about upcoming expenditures.

Spending for Government Buildings and Facilities

When local governments build new structures and facilities or renovate old ones, they have the opportunity to build them according to hazard-resistant standards. These standards can be incorporated directly into local capital improvement policies. At a minimum, public buildings should conform to the standards set for private development. Ideally, government structures should be built to even higher standards if the risk of loss is significant.

The decision of where to locate public facilities is also critical. By locating public facilities outside of hazardous areas, local governments can reduce the costs of repair and replacement following a disaster. Locating **lifeline services** such as fire, police, hospitals, emergency operations centers, and rescue stations outside of hazard areas is especially important to ensure that the response capability of the local government is not impaired during a disaster. Building public facilities to high standards and in non-hazard areas also makes the local government a good leader in mitigation practice, setting the example for private property owners.

Influencing Private Development through Public Spending Decisions

In addition to being directly involved in the siting and construction standards of public buildings, capital improvement programs can also be used to influence private development decisions.

Spending policies have long been considered a growth management tool, since growth and development tend to follow the availability of public services.

In particular, highways and water and sewer utilities have been called growth shapers. The conscientious withholding of public spending can also impact patterns of development in the community. By establishing certain areas where the local government will *not* extend essential services, such as water and sewer systems, growth may be limited in those areas. Local governments can use policies about where (and where not) to provide public infrastructure to discourage development in identified hazard areas.

Withholding public spending to discourage private development is less effective in areas that have already reached build-out, or where private developers are able to provide the expensive infrastructure necessary to support new construction. In localities where soils and other topographical conditions can support on-site sewer (septic tanks) and water services (wells), the refusal to extend public infrastructure is also limited in its effectiveness as a hazard management tool. Public health laws may restrict the use of septic systems or private wells in some areas, but these laws are rarely tied to natural hazard considerations.

Effectiveness of Capital Improvement Programs for Mitigation

A key component of a resilient community is the location of public infrastructure. This is particularly true following a disaster. The placement of roads, water, sewer, schools, libraries, and other public facilities is crucial during the rebuilding phase to guide overall community development patterns. After a hazard event, where and how capital improvements are built and rebuilt can dramatically shape future vulnerability of the community. Some communities have made use of the window of opportunity following a disaster to revamp their public investment policies. For example, Nags Head, North Carolina, has implemented a policy not to expend public funds to repair any private road that is damaged or destroyed as a result of a severe storm, except in conjunction with the repair of the town's water system.

Despite the theoretical potential, research has shown that in practice, capital improvement programs are not widely used for hazard mitigation in either pre- or post-disaster environments. Such policies tend not to alter the basic spatial pattern of private development in hazardous areas.[9] Moreover, restricting public services is not usually very popular with property owners who require the infrastructure in order to develop their land. Local governments may feel obligated to limit the geographic scope of the program to make it more acceptable politically. Local governments may also count on receiving federal support to rebuild public facilities in the event of a disaster and therefore have little incentive to spend their own funds on protecting them. Most researchers would agree that these policies are much more effective when linked with complementary land use regulations and tax policies.

Not All Spending Decisions Are Made Locally

Although local governments are responsible for providing much of the infrastructure and many of the facilities that support community development, a significant number of spending decisions are not within the control of local governments. Federal and state agencies, as well as many regional entities often enact legislation or carry out programs and policies that trump local government authority. For example, most major highway projects are funded with federal and/or state funds, with little local influence on road capacity, location, or even maintenance and repair. Numerous examples demonstrate the impact of highway construction on hazardous area growth, such as Interstate 40 linking central North Carolina with Wilmington and the beach communities.[10] Capital improvement programs, such as beach nourishment undertaken by the U.S. Army Corps of Engineers, provide additional stimulation for growth in coastal areas.

Water resource development in many parts of the country is also controlled by state and regional agencies, with relatively little local input. State law can also dictate that local governments provide necessary infrastructure to developed land within their jurisdiction. These adequate facilities laws can make it difficult for local governments to control growth by withholding spending.

8.2.10 Using the Power of Education to Mitigate the Impacts of Hazards

Among the powers held by local governments is the authority, and even the duty, to educate the community. An informed and educated citizenry is an integral part of managing hazards at the local level. Many residents assume that current building codes, zoning regulations, subdivision review processes, and permitting will adequately protect them and their property from the impacts of hazards, but this is not always the case. Making the public aware of the hazards it faces is the first step towards making the community safer, and overcoming a lack of awareness should be an integral part of any local mitigation program.[11]

Many local governments have carried out programs to alert residents to natural hazards—both the dangers as well as the opportunities to lessen hazard risks. Other communities have focused on educating visitors about fragile ecosystems, sensitive natural areas, endangered wildlife and plant species, or other natural wonders that need to be protected and conserved. In addition to residents and tourists, local target audiences for education and awareness include a wide range of community members, such as lenders and insurance agents; builders, architects, and realtors; and local elected and appointed officials and public staff, including the governing board, building inspectors and zoning officials, and emergency first responders.

It is not uncommon that the prevailing perception of risk in a community is skewed, even in areas where natural hazards have occurred in the past. Information regarding hazard frequency is often misunderstood. For example, the common understanding of the 100-year floodplain is that this area will only be flooded once in a century. Residents also often fail to grasp the extent of past hazard events, such as flood heights. Such misperceptions highlight the need for publicizing accurate information.

There are several different methods that local communities can use to promote community awareness, including real estate disclosure, community awareness campaigns, hazard maps, and disaster warnings.

8.2.11 Local Government Planning

Local government planning provides a cohesive framework for managing all aspects of growth and development in the community. Most large and mid-sized municipalities and county governments in the United States carry out some sort of planning function. There is a wide variety of plan types, some of which are narrow in scope and deal with only one particular topic, while other local plans are broader and combine multiple objectives. Some local plans are freestanding documents, others are included as part of a wider community management program. Some communities have officially adopted all their plans and view them as regulatory devices, while other communities merely use plans as policy guidance without the force of law. The degree to which plans are actually implemented and the level of their effectiveness for influencing land uses also varies widely.

Among the types of plans that local governments use are hazard mitigation plans, post-disaster recovery plans, land use plans, comprehensive plans, floodplain management plans, capital improvement plans, emergency operations plans, transportation plans, economic development plans, park and recreation plans, and open space management plans, to name but a few. Many communities have come to realize the value of incorporating principles of hazard resiliency in their current planning efforts. Other communities continue to compartmentalize the various planning functions and have yet to consider a sustainable development approach to planning and growth management.

Land Use/Comprehensive Plans

In many jurisdictions, a land use plan serves as the basis for much of the regulation of property use. A comprehensive plan also addresses economic development, environmental, transportation, and social concerns. City and county planners study the physical characteristics of the land. Where are the steep slopes? What areas are subject to flooding? They map existing streets, rail lines, water lines, sewers, schools, parks, fire stations, and other facilities that can support development. They also note current uses of the land. Where are the factories, the warehouses, the stores and offices, the residential neighborhoods?

On the basis of their studies, planners prepare maps showing how various areas might be developed to make use of existing public facilities and to avoid mixing incompatible land uses. The maps may also indicate where new water lines and sewers might be built. These maps are then presented to the public for comment. After the public has reviewed the maps, the planners prepare a detailed set of maps showing current and possible future uses of the land. The local governing board might review and vote on this final set of maps itself or delegate authority to an appointed planning board. The approved maps and supporting narrative become the official land use plan for the community, called a Comprehensive Plan.[12]

Local officials can use land use plans to guide their decisions about where to locate new public facilities. Some governments use them only for these non-regulatory purposes. A land use plan also establishes a basis for regulation of property uses. However, the plan itself does not set up a system of regulation. Zoning and subdivision ordinances are systems of regulation based on a land use plan.

The main advantage of land use or comprehensive plans as a hazard mitigation tool is that they guide other local measures, such as capital improvement programs, zoning ordinances, and subdivision ordinances. Comprehensive planning requires local governments to collect and analyze information about land's suitability for development. This process helps policy makers and local residents understand the limitations to development in hazard-prone areas. In turn, land uses can be tailored to the hazard risk, typically by reserving dangerous areas for less intensive, hazard-compatible uses such as parks, golf courses, backyards, wildlife refuges, or natural features.

Hazard Mitigation Planning

Planning is the key to transforming mitigation from a reactive process to a proactive one. Hazard mitigation planning is the comprehensive and orderly process of determining how to reduce or eliminate the loss of life and property damage resulting from natural and man-made causes. However, in the past, many communities have undertaken mitigation actions with good intentions but with little advance planning. In some cases, decisions have been made on the fly in the wake of a disaster. In other cases, decisions may have been made in advance but without careful consideration of all options, effects, or contributing factors. Chapter 13 discusses the process of hazard mitigation planning in detail.

The primary purpose of hazard mitigation planning is to identify community policies, actions, and tools for implementation over the long term that will result in a reduction of risk and potential for future losses community wide. Under the Disaster Mitigation Act of 2000 (DMA), local and state governments are required to prepare hazard mitigation plans in order to receive federal mitigation funds in the future. As a result, many more communities are now preparing mitigation plans than ever before, and it is an exciting time for those in the planning and emergency management fields as they find ways to work together to bring these plans to life (the Disaster Mitigation Act is discussed in more detail in Chapter 6). Effective planning forges partnerships that will bring together the skills, expertise, and experience of a broad range of groups to achieve a common vision for the community, and can also ensure that the most appropriate and equitable mitigation projects will be undertaken. Hazard mitigation planning is most successful when it increases public and political support for mitigation programs, results in actions that also support other important community goals and objectives, and influences the community's decision-making to include hazard reduction considerations.[13]

Emergency Operations Plans

All counties and many municipalities develop and adopt an emergency operations plan (EOP), which predetermines actions to be taken by government agencies and private organizations in response to an emergency or disaster event. EOPs typically describe the local government's capability to respond to emergencies and establish the responsibilities and procedures for responding effectively to the actual occurrence of a disaster. To keep plans up to date, local governments must conduct real-life exercises based on actual risk scenarios. Issues that emerge from post-disaster scenarios often draw attention to pre-disaster activities that can be undertaken now to prevent future losses. FEMA makes available post-disaster mitigation and recovery exercises for flood, earthquake, and hurricane disaster scenarios, as do many state emergency management agencies.

Most local EOPs do not specifically address hazard mitigation, but do identify operations to be undertaken by counties to protect lives and property immediately before, during, and immediately following an emergency. There are usually few foreseeable conflicts between a county's hazard mitigation plan and its EOP, primarily because they are each focused on separate phases of emergency management (mitigation versus preparedness and response). Local EOPs do identify which officials or positions within the county are to play the lead role in the long-term reconstruction phase following a disaster, which can present a window of opportunity for implementing hazard mitigation strategies. Typically, however, these actions are not specified within the EOP.

SELF-CHECK

- Define **building codes, zoning maps, cumulative impact assessment, capital improvement,** and **lifeline services.**
- Name five basic local government powers (RATES).
- List four regulatory powers of local governments.
- Discuss two weaknesses of **zoning** for hazard mitigation.
- Explain the benefit of public acquisition as a way to hazard proof a piece of property.

8.3 Local Government Structure

So far in this chapter we have reviewed the authority of local governments under the police power to make communities more resilient to the impacts of natural hazards. To understand how these powers are executed during the day-to-day business of the community, we must be aware of how local governments are organized and the political machinery that is necessary to implement mitigation strategies.

For purposes of federal disaster assistance and mitigation planning under DMA, FEMA defines a *local government* as

> *any county, municipality, city, town, township, public authority, school district, special district, intrastate district, council of governments . . . regional or interstate government entity, or agency or instrumentality of a local government; any Indian tribe or authorized tribal organization, or Alaska Native village or organization; and any rural community, unincorporated town or village, or other public entity.*[14]

In the following sections of this chapter, we will describe how some of these units of governance are typically established, the processes by which decisions are made, and how policy is formulated and adopted at the local level.

8.3.1 Types of Local Governments

There are five basic types of local government in the United States, which can be grouped into general-purpose and single-purpose governments.

▲ **General-purpose local governments** perform a wide range of government functions, and include: counties, municipalities, towns and townships.

▲ **Single-purpose local governments** such as school districts and special districts are created a specific purpose and perform one function.

8.3.2 Counties

All states, except Connecticut and Rhode Island, are divided into counties (in Alaska these subunits of government are called boroughs and in Louisiana they are called parishes). Counties can be urban or rural. They can combine municipalities within them or can have no incorporated communities within their borders.

Counties were originally created to act as an administrative unit of the state and to perform activities of statewide concern at the local level. Today counties often have more policy- and decision-making responsibility. Basic county functions include property assessment, revenue collection (taxation), law enforcement, jails, elections, land records, road maintenance, and emergency services. Counties may also provide additional services, including health care, social services, pollution control, mass transit, and industrial and economic development.

Organization of County Governments

There are three main types of county government in the United States:

1. A *County Board* is made up of "Supervisors" or "Commissioners." This is the most common type of county government in the United States, where the board is elected by voters in the county. The board serves as the central policy maker, approves the county budget, and appoints other officials. In some counties, the board shares power with other elected officials, including the sheriff, public safety officer, county prosecutor or district attorney, county tax assessor, coroner, and the county clerk or clerk of court.

2. In the *County Council-Elected Executive* form of local government, the board and all executive officers are elected by the county voters. In these counties, the board performs legislative (rule-making) functions, adopts the budget, sets policy, and performs financial audits. The executive officer performs executive functions such as preparing the budget, implementing policy, and appointing department heads.

3. In the *County Council-Administrator* form of local government, the board is more hands off in the day-to-day running of the government. In these counties, the board performs legislative functions such as setting policy and adopting the budget, while a professional administrator hired by the Board manages government affairs.

8.3.3 Municipalities

Municipalities are incorporated units of government, formed by the state through charter or other means. Throughout the United States, municipalities are variously referred to as cities, towns, hamlets, villages, or boroughs. These are the most frequently used terms to describe urban areas, which, in general, are more densely populated than unincorporated areas (areas outside municipal boundaries). In some states, the various terms have no special legal meaning, while in others different status is afforded to each type. In all states, municipalities are authorized to make decisions for the community and to implement policies and programs that fall within their delegated powers and responsibilities. Like counties, municipalities are general-purpose units of government. Unlike counties, they generally have greater decision-making authority and discretion, especially in home-rule states.

Organization of Municipalities

There are three main types of municipal government: (1) Mayor-Council, (2) City Commission, and (3) Council-Manager.

1. *Mayor-council* is the oldest and most common type of local government in both the smallest and largest of cities. There are two varieties, depending upon the strength of the mayor:

▲ In the *Strong Mayor-Council,* the mayor is elected by the voters and is the source of executive leadership. The mayor prepares the budget, hires and fires top-level city officials, performs daily administrative duties, and has veto power over the council.

▲ In the *Weak Mayor-Council,* power and authority are fragmented. The council is the source of executive power, while the mayor is considered an executive figurehead ("ribbon cutter"). The council appoints city officials, develops the budget, and elects the mayor.

In some municipalities, a weak mayor may be elected by constituents in lieu of being appointed. The mayor has the power to veto with the possibility of being overridden by the council. The mayor may also be in a position to break a tie vote.

2. In the *City Commission* plan, the legislative and executive functions are merged. Each commissioner, who is a politician, tends to be an advocate for his or her own department (usually by asking for a larger share of the city budget). The commissioners generally make policy and lead major departments. One commissioner serves as mayor, presiding over commission meetings.

3. The *Council-City Manager* form of municipal government predominates in cities of 10,000 to 50,000, especially in suburban communities and cities of the Sunbelt. In theory, the politics and policy-making functions of government are separated from the administration and execution of policies. The City Manager serves at the pleasure of the council, appoints and removes department heads, oversees delivery of services, prepares the budget, and makes policy recommendations to the council. In many communities, the manager is quite powerful, and can play an activist role in local affairs. Because of the heightened level of professionalism and degree of coordination between departments that this organizational structure involves, local governments conducted under the council-manager

FOR EXAMPLE

Hurricane Response Galvanizes a New Galveston Administration

The city commission plan of municipal government was largely created as a reaction to the mayor-council form of government. In Galveston, Texas, in 1900 the then mayor-council government was viewed as ineffective in its response to a hurricane disaster that had killed 6000 people and demolished the city. The Texas legislature authorized the creation of the commission, and by 1904 the new city government had entirely rebuilt Galveston, running the city as a business.

plan are more likely to infuse mitigation into all local government operations, from keeping new school buildings away from the dangers of landslides, to designating stream banks as recreational greenways, to constructing safe rooms in all government buildings.

8.3.4 Towns and Townships

Towns and townships are general-purpose units of local government, distinct from counties and municipalities. In some states, towns and townships have broad powers, acting like other general-purpose units of government. Examples of this type of township can be found in New England, New Jersey, Pennsylvania, Michigan, New York, and Wisconsin.

In other states, towns and townships have more limited authority. These tend to be more rural in nature, offering limited services such as roads and law enforcement. These townships are found in Illinois, Indiana, Kansas, Minnesota, Missouri, Nebraska, North Dakota, Ohio, and South Dakota.

Some communities may regionalize certain areas of government to expand their response capacity and overall effectiveness. Such regionalization must be well planned so as not to interfere with other community functions. Laws, ordinances, and employee contracts must be adjusted accordingly.

8.3.5 Special Districts

Special districts are single-purpose local governments that are authorized to perform one function or to meet the service needs of one particular area. Special districts are created to address specific issues in the community such as fire protection, sewage and water management, mosquito control, drainage and flood control, soil and water conservation, school administration, redevelopment and disaster recovery, and mass transit, among others.

Special districts tend to overlap the general-purpose local governments, and concern themselves solely with one service. Special district officials may be elected or appointed by another government, such as the county. Budgets and staff of special districts range from very large to minimal. Examples of powerful special districts include the Port Authority of New Jersey, the Chicago Transit Authority, and the Los Angeles County Sanitation District.

Service districts can extend services beyond the borders of a general-purpose local government and can tackle regional problems that transcend political jurisdictions. For example, a flood control district can deal with flooding of a river that runs through several counties. Service districts are often used to provide services that are inefficient to provide on an individual basis, based on economies of scale. For example, electric power can often be provided more efficiently to several counties than to one single county's population. Regional utilities may also be better equipped to handle power outages and other emergencies.

Some special districts can charge user or service fees and may not be bound by the same taxation and debt limitations that often fall on municipalities. Because of this flexibility in revenue collection, some special districts have been criticized for a lack of accountability; often the public is not aware of their existence or function.

8.3.6 Local Government Departments

Most local governments carry out the day-to-day business of running a municipality or county through local government employees located in individual government departments. The number, size, and organizational complexity of the various departments depend on the size, relative wealth, and geographical location of the community itself, but there are a few basic types of departmental functions that are typical nationwide. For instance, most local governments have an administrator or manager's office, as well as a budget and financial office. Local governments may have their own building code enforcement and inspections departments, or may share such functions among several smaller municipalities in a single county. These offices are often combined with planning and zoning, as well as floodplain management. Local governments must have an attorney on staff or on retainer office, and counties are required to have an emergency management or preparedness department or agency, as well as fire protection, public safety, medical emergency office, and hazardous materials manager. Most counties and municipalities also have departments that deal with day-to-day services, such as mass transit, housing, sanitation, and public works. Increasingly, municipalities have offices that deal with historic preservation, tree preservation, parks, recreation and open space, floodplain management, economic development, and tourism, as well as a tribal liaison office.

Often, citizen advisory boards work with department staff and report to the governing board with advice and recommendations about departmental policy. Many of these departments are either directly related or can or should play some role in the hazard mitigation efforts of the community. Other departments may be carrying out practices and policies that are detrimental to a community's efforts at becoming more disaster resilient.

8.3.7 Relationships among Local Governments

In many respects local governments act as freestanding, autonomous units, each with its own power base, its own basic governmental structure, and its own decision-making and policy-formation processes. Yet while a strong identity and unique character are essential to a community's sense of place, many of the challenges that face communities are broader in scope and are best addressed with a regional approach. Natural hazards clearly fall into this category of issues that communities must deal with, because many types of hazards do not strike solely within clearly defined political boundaries and their impacts can be experienced over a wide geographic area. This is particularly true of flooding, which can be exacerbated by communities living in the same watershed or river basin. A parochial view is not uncommon among local governments, and cooperative, joint-venture activities are not entered into lightly. Nevertheless, finding solutions to some of these problems in a collaborative way can often be more effective than individual local governments working alone.

Multi-Jurisdictional Planning

In its administration of the DMA, FEMA encourages communities to cooperate with one another when preparing their mandatory local hazard mitigation plans.[15] Planning on a broader scale can bring additional resources, such as staff, funding, technical ability, and experience to the effort, and can help mitigate hazards that originate outside of a community's jurisdictional boundaries. For example, a multi-jurisdictional planning area may include several towns located along the same fault line whose main hazard is earthquake, or communities that lie within the same watershed. Multi-jurisdictional plans may also be created by communities that are contiguous to one another (for example, a tri-county plan), or by a county government and the municipalities and townships within it.

Councils of Government (COGs)

In some regions of the country, local governments band together loosely to form Councils of Government, or COGs. These voluntary organizations of county and municipal governments provide services that are more effectively handled on a regional basis rather than by individual local governments. Some COGs are fairly small, consisting of a pair of local governments working together, while other COG-like structures are much larger. In Washington, DC, for example, the local COG in essence covers three states, while a quad-state partnership exists in the eastern panhandle of West Virginia.

Typical services provided by COGs include programs for senior citizens, land use planning, economic development, environmental protection, and other types of collaborative efforts. Member governments pay dues to support the work of the regional council and appoint representatives to discuss problems they share and to work out ways to deal with issues of mutual concern. Frequently, areas of a state that are least advantaged and that have fewer resources (often rural counties) rely on COGs to help administer federal and state programs, write grants, and provide assistance with plan writing and other local functions. Despite the potential, not many COGs have dealt with natural hazards on a larger than local scale, although some have provided assistance to local communities to carry out federal disaster recovery programs and develop local hazard mitigation plans.

Mutual Aid Agreements

Legislation in some states allows municipalities and counties to enter into inter-local agreements to cooperatively perform any function that can be carried out as an individual local government. Many of these mutual aid agreements enable local governments to work together to provide emergency services. The agreements

CREATIVE REBUILDING PLANS FOR COASTAL MISSISSIPPI

For six days in October 2005, a group of 200 architects, engineers, urban planners, and code writers met to discuss ideas on how to rebuild the coast of Mississippi after Hurricane Katrina (see Figure 8-3) The experts of the Mississippi Renewal Forum were concerned with using lessons learned from both Hurricane Katrina and Hurricane Camille, which struck the area in 1969, as an opportunity to guide the redevelopment of more sustainable, resilient communities along the Gulf Coast. The creation of the Governor's Commission Policy Plan, "After Katrina: Building Back Better than Ever," was the highlight of an intense four-month Commission on Recovery, Rebuilding and Renewal spon-sored by the Governor of Mississippi, Haley Barbour. The plan contains a "roadmap of accountability" that describes mitigation practices that were not implemented following Hurricane Camille, "so that the people of the Gulf Coast will not forever be seen as victims of tragedy, but as a generation of those fortunate enough to have been there for the Mississippi renaissance."[16]

The members of the Forum and participating local community members overwhelmingly agreed that they wanted to provide coastal towns the ability to rebuild in a way that allowed for higher quality, better form, more green space, and restoration of small town character rather than allowing the urban sprawl that characterized rebuilding in the years after Hurricane Camille. They decided to accomplish these goals through transect planning and the use of a SmartCode.

The SmartCode for Mississippi is a unified land development ordinance adopted by the state of Mississippi that provides guidelines to local govern-ments to follow during the rebuilding process. The ordinance is not a building code, but as a form-based code it offers local governments a variety of plan-ning tools to improve their resilience to natural hazards while incorporating local character, housing diversity, open space, transportation options, and mixed-use neighborhoods that traditional zoning would disallow. The SmartCode incorporates transect methodology, adapted from ecology field studies, which uses a continuous cross section to classify human habitat environments ranging from rural to urban areas. The SmartCode is applied to each transect classifica-tion according to the section's particular set of characteristics. Mississippi selected six transect zones: T-1 Natural, T-2 Rural, T-3 Sub-Urban, T-4 General Urban, T-5 Urban Center, and T-6 Urban Core. Although SmartCode has not been described or used as a tool to address hazard resilience, it certainly could be (i.e., by decreasing density adjacent to natural areas or by including those same areas that are high hazard, such as ocean front, barrier islands, wetlands, etc., in their transects). Use of the SmartCode and transects template empowers communities devastated by Katrina to rebuild without repeating the unsustainable mistakes of the past.[17]

Figure 8-3

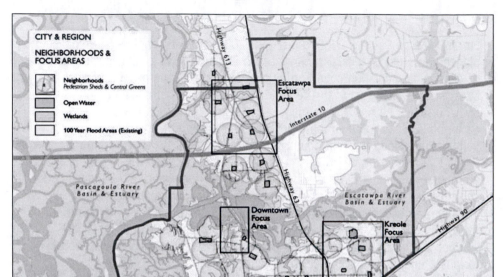

Three focal areas — Escatawpa Village, Kreole and Moss Point's downtown — have been identified as places to concentrate retail and commercial centers.

Image showing an example of rebuilding plans generated from the Mississippi Renewal Forum, extracted from the summary report.

establish a means through which signatories can offer and receive assistance in times of disaster. Mutual aid agreements address logistics, deployment, compensation, and liability issues, and can also assist in faster reimbursement of disaster aid from FEMA. The pre-established policies and procedures of a mutual aid agreement make intra-government cooperation more expansive and efficient, serving to protect property, minimize costs, and save lives.

SELF-CHECK

- Define **general-purpose local governments** and **single-purpose local governments**.
- Discuss the role of the city or county manager.
- List the issues addressed in a mutual aid agreement.
- Describe two types of local collaborative activities.

SUMMARY

Local communities have a number of ways within the powers delegated to them by the state to increase hazard resilience. Local governments represent only one of the many layers of management in hazardous areas, but they are arguably the most critical for creating resilient communities. It is at the local level that land use patterns are determined, infrastructure is designed, and many other developmental issues are decided. It is also at the local level where hazards are experienced and losses are suffered most directly. This chapter provides a broad understanding of the types of powers that local governments can use to manage the hazard areas within their jurisdiction in the effort to become more resilient.

KEY TERMS

Amortization	Process that requires nonconforming structures to come into compliance with local zoning regulations or be removed from the property within a certain time period.
Buffer	A setback of a specific distance, such as 25 or 100 feet, from a channel, floodway, wetland, or other water feature. In that area, no cutting, clearing of ground cover, or alteration of natural features is allowed.
Buyout program	Public acquisition of privately held property located in hazardous areas.
Capital improvement	New or expanded physical facilities that are relatively large in size, expensive, and permanent.
Cumulative impact assessment	An evaluation that looks at the total effect of all development in a particular environment.
Differential assessment	A technique for reducing the tax burden on land facing development pressure by recognizing that undeveloped properties require fewer public services.
Down-zoning	Used to keep inappropriate development out of hazard-prone areas; can be accomplished by increasing minimum lot size, or reducing the number of dwelling units permitted per acre.
Easement	Used to grant an affirmative right to use a property, such as a right of access; may also restrict the landowner's right to use the property in a particular way.

General-purpose local government	Type of local government that performs a wide-range of functions; examples: counties, municipalities, and towns and townships.
Impact fees	Typically one-time, up-front charges against new development to pay for off-site improvements, including schools, fire stations, community centers, and other local facilities.
Lifeline services	Services such as fire, police, hospitals, and rescue stations.
Moratorium	A short-term suspension of the right to develop, usually accomplished by a refusal of the local government to issue building permits.
Relocation	Removing privately owned structures from hazardous areas and relocating them on non-hazardous sites; most often used in combination with acquisition.
Single-purpose local government	Type of local government that has a specific purpose and performs one function; example: school district.
Subdivision ordinance	Local regulations that govern the partition of land for development or sale. In addition to controlling the configuration of parcels, subdivision ordinances set standards for developer-built infrastructure.
Zoning	The traditional tool available to local governments to control land use; zoning maps divide the jurisdiction into zones where various regulations apply as described in the zoning ordinance.
Zoning maps	Divide the area under local government control into zones where various zoning regulations apply.

ASSESS YOUR UNDERSTANDING

Go to www.wiley.com/college/schwab to evaluate your knowledge of the local government powers.

Measure your learning by comparing pre-test and post-test results.

Summary Questions

1. Sustainable communities are those that reduce opportunities of future generations to meet their own needs. True or False?

2. A sustainable community should also be a
   (a) federally subsidized community.
   (b) local government.
   (c) resilient community.
   (d) hazardous area.

3. Development of environmentally fragile areas decreases a community's resiliency. True or False?

4. A building code is an example of a local government's taxation powers. True or False?

5. Which of the following is an example of a local government's regulatory powers?
   (a) impact fees
   (b) planning
   (c) floodplain ordinances
   (d) special assessments

6. A zoning ordinance defines the types and intensity of uses that are allowed within a zone. True or False?

7. Moratoria are used by communities to
   (a) prevent rebuilding of damaged structures.
   (b) update hazard maps.
   (c) re-assess zoning districts.
   (d) all of the above.

8. Local governments require developers to provide infrastructure in subdivisions according to the highest profit margin. True or False?

9. New developments share in the financial burden that they impose on a community through
   (a) property taxes.
   (b) user fees.

(c) capital improvements.

(d) impact fees.

10. A special district is an example of a single-purpose government. True or False?

11. Jails and law enforcement are the responsibility of county governments. True or False?

12. Which of the following is the most common type of local city government?

(a) Strong mayor-council

(b) Mayor-council

(c) City commission

(d) Council-manager

13. Special districts can tackle regional problems that transcend political jurisdictions. True or False?

14. Keeping hazard information from local residents helps bolster property values. True or False?

Review Questions

1. Consider a community that has been affected by a natural hazard. In what ways are hazard mitigation and preparedness linked to the sustainability of a local community?

2. A sustainable community must be hazard resilient. What are four other issues that a sustainable community must consider?

3. How does suburban sprawl affect a community's sustainability and vulnerability to hazards?

4. When is the pressure to rebuild after a disaster most intense, and why?

5. How can local government powers be used to manage a community's growth and mitigate the impacts of natural hazards?

6. How is acquisition a long-term solution to repeatedly paying for rebuilding?

7. Give reasons why easements are not used for hazard mitigation purposes.

8. Explain the relationship between eminent domain and acquisition of private property for hazard mitigation purpose.

9. A disaster warning system is a critical part of a community's hazard planning process. What are the inherent weaknesses in disaster warning systems?

10. What are the five types of local government structure in the United States? Which are general-purpose and which are single purpose?

11. Counties were originally created as an administrative unit of the state. Name the two states that are not divided into counties.

12. Special districts are single-purpose governments created to meet service needs in a particular area. List five types of special districts.

13. A community that seeks hazard resilience must be willing to invest in the capability for developing and carrying out mitigation programs and policies. List five government activities that demonstrate this principle.

Applying This Chapter

1. Keeping in mind the considerations of a sustainable community, assess the sustainability of where you live. Is there a particular unsustainable land use that has increased the vulnerability of your community to hazards?

2. In what ways could a local government use zoning to try to control rampant growth associated with the arrival of a large communications company that plans to build an industrial park in the area? In particular, consider ways to address traffic concerns, pollution, and housing issues.

3. How might special assessments discourage development in areas vulnerable to hazards? Identify a type of special assessment at work in your area.

4. If you were the emergency manager in a mid-sized municipality, what would be some of the advantages to having a council-manager type of local government for pushing a hazard mitigation agenda through the local policy-making process?

5. Explain any ways that local governments would manage the risk of human-induced hazards versus natural hazards.

Hazard Maps and You

To determine how best to protect a community from disaster, it is necessary to first identify any local hazard risks. Hazard maps can dramatically illustrate where areas of development overlap with areas of hazards such as floods, landslides, earthquakes, and hurricanes. Using the Internet or other resources, find hazard maps of your area, determine the distance between your home and the hazard(s), and assess your risk of experiencing a disaster event.

Power to the People

States empower local governments to control the use of land. How are the four local regulatory powers of zoning ordinances, subdivision regulations, building codes, and flood damage prevention ordinances at work in your community?

Community Resiliency

What are some of the principles of resilience and sustainability that you would need to employ when crafting a hazard mitigation program for your local community? Which activities are in place in the community's capability for developing mitigation policies?

9

COMMUNITY RESILIENCE AND THE PRIVATE SECTOR
Maintaining a Strong Economy through Wise Land Use and Business Protection Planning

Starting Point

Go to www.wiley.com/college/schwab to assess your knowledge of community resilience and the private sector.
Determine where you need to concentrate your effort.

What You'll Learn in This Chapter

▲ The importance of economic resilience for a sustainable community
▲ Role of private land ownership in creating resilient communities
▲ Economic impacts of disasters on a community
▲ The planning process a business can use to become more resilient
▲ Mitigation actions a business can use to protect assets, inventories, and human resources
▲ Ways the private sector can participate in community mitigation efforts

After Studying This Chapter, You'll Be Able To

▲ Describe the foundations of a resilient economy
▲ Examine the role of developers and investors in creating resilient communities
▲ Highlight the important aspects of small business continuity planning
▲ Outline the process a business can follow to formulate a mitigation plan
▲ Appraise mitigation measures a business might use to reduce its vulnerability to hazards
▲ Explain how businesses and communities can work together to mitigate the impact of hazards

Goals and Outcomes

▲ Assess the connection between private sector development decisions and local vulnerability
▲ Support and apply the process of business continuity planning to mitigate hazard impacts
▲ Apply the principles of a risk assessment to make informed investment decisions
▲ Distinguish among types of insurance that are available to businesses for hazard perils
▲ Collaborate with others to protect a company's assets, employees, and business viability in the face of hazards
▲ Evaluate incentives for businesses to participate in community resiliency

INTRODUCTION

At the heart of a resilient community is a resilient economy. Economic resilience calls for wise use of privately owned real estate, as well as for a strong business sector that can withstand the impacts of natural hazards. Communities that have built resilience into the local economy before a disaster strikes are more likely to experience fewer disruptions in productivity, and are better able to maintain a stable tax base, a vibrant marketplace, and a higher quality of life for community members. This chapter discusses the decision-making process of private land owners and real estate investors, and how choices they make regarding the location of property can impact community vulnerability. The chapter also describes how public sector actions can influence locational decisions made by the private sector. The chapter then explores ways that local businesses, particularly small businesses, can protect their assets, their employees, and their businesses' viability in the face of natural hazards. The chapter concludes with a discussion of private sector participation in community mitigation programs.

9.1 Resilient Economies, Resilient Communities

At the heart of any hazard resilient community is a resilient economy. Residents need a reliable source of decent jobs and affordable housing options. Businesses need an accommodating venue for commerce and trade and a steady workforce. The local government needs a stable source of revenue in order to build and maintain infrastructure and provide services to community members. All these elements of a vibrant economy depend upon a steady flow of capital investment from both the public and private sectors. At no time are these issues more critical than during the period of recovery and reconstruction following a disaster. After a hazard event, it is essential for the recovery of the community at large that the economy remains stable or quickly returns to stability after a short period of readjustment. Communities that have built resiliency into the local economy *before* a disaster strikes will be in a much better position to make this happen. Sustainable communities are able to maintain economic vitality even in the face of disaster.

9.1.1 The Foundations of a Resilient Economy

A local community's overall resiliency depends upon the ability of its economy to withstand the impacts of a wide range of hazards and the speed with which the economy can bounce back when a disaster occurs. This is accomplished by placing people and property in hazard-safe locations and by integrating mitigation building techniques into the construction process, such as installing wind-resistant roofing or elevating flood-prone structures. The local government plays a major role in determining what types of structures are permitted within its jurisdiction and where they are allowed to be built; however, the private sector is the main driving force behind a community's patterns of land use. Choices that property owners make about how to use their land and protect their property have a profound effect on community vulnerability.

Private Land Ownership

A major controlling factor in a community's economic staying power lies in the patterns of land use that predominate in the area. Because the built environment is such a critical determinant of vulnerability, the first section of this chapter deals with the issue of land ownership, particularly private land ownership in hazardous areas. Chapter 5 discusses what it means to be a private landowner in our legal system, including the various rights and duties that are inherent in ownership. That discussion should serve as a backdrop to this chapter, where we discuss the extent to which private developers and investors can exert their own will in the real estate market and some of the reasoning behind their development and investment decisions.

9.1.2 Community Resiliency Depends on Business Resiliency

Creating disaster-resilient community depends not only locational and structural decisions made by private property owners, but also decisions regarding the types of economic activity that are most appropriate for the area in terms of hazard exposure. A truly sustainable local economy is diversified and less easily disrupted by internal or external events, including natural disasters. For instance, a coastal town that depends solely on tourism as its economic mainstay is more likely to suffer dire long-term consequences after a major hurricane than a community with a more diversified economy. Economies that include a mix of industries are much more stable. Making the private sector more resistant to disasters through mitigation and diversification provides fiscal insurance to the local government by making the local tax base more secure, residents safer, and businesses more competitive.[1]

Although many factors play into whether or not the local economy will survive following a disaster, much of the economic resiliency of a community depends on the individual businesses and industries located there, how well they are able to prevent large-scale damages, and how quickly they are able to resume operations. A resilient economy is one where productivity is only minimally disrupted by a hazard event. Disasters can have the effect of accelerating economic trends that were present in the community before the disaster hit. For example, if a downtown is experiencing a slow decline, a disaster might fast-forward the negative trend, compounding the difficulties of sanitation, public safety, transportation, and general deterioration.[2] On the other hand, a disaster can also provide an opportunity for a community to make positive changes and to focus new energy on revitalizing areas of blight or neglect.

FOR EXAMPLE

Positive Changes

After many repetitive losses due to flooding in their community, citizens of Soldiers Grove, Wisconsin, relocated the entire downtown (including the main business district) to higher ground in the early 1980s. The town seized the opportunity following the last flooding event to prevent future repetitive losses and build a disaster-resistant economy. Upon making the move, community members went a step further, adapting the building code to incorporate principles of sustainable development. In the relocated town, all new structures were required to receive at least half of their energy from renewable sources. This protected these businesses from future disasters and associated economic shocks, as well as contributed to new job creation and reduced energy costs.[3]

Business Protection through Mitigation and Preparedness

In addition to an exploration of the role played by private landowners in hazardous land management, this chapter also gives a broad overview of how hazards can impact individual businesses, as well as a brief introduction to some of the steps that business and industry can take to protect their inventory, income stream, employees, and other assets to become more resilient. This is important not only for the individual businesses that choose to take the mitigation and preparedness steps necessary to protect their livelihood, but also for the local economy as a whole. A healthy, viable economy is highly dependent upon healthy, viable businesses that are resilient to the impacts of hazards and that work to lessen, rather than contribute to, a community's overall level of vulnerability.

SELF-CHECK

- Describe the foundations of a resilient economy.
- Explain why a resilient economy is important to a community and integral to a resilient community.
- Describe how recovering from a disaster can strengthen the sustainability of a local economy.

9.2 Private Land Ownership in the United States

Private land owners have rights and privileges with regard to their property, such as the right to cut the timber; divert the surface water; graze livestock; mine ore, coal, and mineral deposits; and otherwise extract the land's natural resources. The rights and privileges of property ownership also include the right to develop and build upon the land as well as to sell it and profit from the sale. These rights of ownership are not absolute. Owners of private property also have duties and responsibilities. Owners must conform to all applicable public laws, regulations, and ordinances, even when such regulations interfere with the landowner's wishes as to use of the property. Nevertheless, within the boundaries established by federal, state, and local laws, there is wide latitude for putting one's property to uses that meet investment-backed expectations. Sometimes, however, these uses are not in the best interest of the community at large.

9.2.1 Location, Location, Location

It is often quipped that the three most important factors in determining the value of real estate are "location, location, location." This is equally true for determining a property's vulnerability to many kinds of natural hazards. The experience of past hazard events in this country has made it clear that patterns of land use are one of the primary determinants of a community's level of vulnerability to natural hazards. When growth and development take place in the floodplain, along the coastline, in areas of seismic risk, and other hazardous areas, there is a greater likelihood that property will be damaged and that death or injury may occur as the result of a flood, hurricane, or major earthquake. When we consider this probability, it is important to realize that the majority of land in the United States is held by private landholders and investors. This includes land owned by individual homeowners, small businesses, and large corporations. In addition to the raw and developed land in private ownership, nearly 85% of the nation's infrastructure is also controlled by the private sector.[4]

9.2.2 The Role of Developers and Investors

One of the most important rights of land ownership is the right to put the land to economically beneficial use, which often includes development. While many owners use their property to locate a business, build their primary residence, or construct a vacation home for their own families, a great deal of real estate is purchased, held, built upon, leased, and sold as a money-making venture. This is particularly true in the coastal zone, which is an especially hazardous area, subject to high rates of erosion, frequent hurricanes and storms, inlet migration, and other coastal hazards. As such, we will use the coastal zone as an example during the following discussion about the ways that many property investment decisions are made. However, the same considerations apply in the development decisions of other types of hazardous lands as well, such as floodplains, wildfire areas, and seismic risk zones.

To understand how coastal lands are developed, and the degree to which natural hazards may or may not be considered during the development process, we must understand the interests of developers and investors. Generally speaking, the private sector operates with regard to expected profits. Development occurs where and when the investor will likely receive an acceptable return on the investment. Some development projects are relatively small in scale—a single building, for instance—while other developments involve hundreds of individual units complete with supporting facilities and infrastructure. Whatever the scale of the particular project, developers analyze markets and trends and build where there is sufficient demand for their products with a minimum of risk.

Factors in Coastal Development Decisions

There are a few common factors that all investors take into consideration before making a major investment decision:[5]

- ▲ **Demand:** In economics, demand is the desire for a commodity together with the ability to pay for it. Scarcity increases the desire for a particular product, such as beachfront property in highly-developed coastal areas. When demand is high, the private sector will try to meet that demand.

- ▲ **Risk:** As a general rule, investors are risk averse. The degree of risk that is acceptable depends upon the likelihood and magnitude of the potential profit. Developers consider many aspects of the region, community, and site, as well as the general market and economy, when deciding what and where to build. Natural hazards are sometimes, but not always, one of the factors considered along with other characteristics of a site when deciding upon the feasibility of a particular project.

- ▲ **Regulation:** The regulatory requirements that apply in a particular location play a major role in investment decision making. Some of the land use regulations imposed by state and local governments dictate the height, square footage, setback distances, and occupational capacity of buildings constructed in the coastal zone. Zoning and subdivision ordinances, building codes, fire regulations, environmental protection laws, and other types of regulatory mandates can increase the cost of construction many times over. These constraints are factored into the profitability of an investment project.

- ▲ **Infrastructure:** The availability of infrastructure also plays a major role in development decisions, including where to build and at what density. Development cannot take place without adequate water, sewer, roads, and public services to support it. All but the very largest development companies are dependent to some degree upon public infrastructure in order to build. Much infrastructure is provided by local governments, often subsidized by state and federal monies. The extension of infrastructure into hazardous areas can encourage inappropriate development. Likewise, the refusal to extend municipal services and infrastructure to hazardous lands may help prevent or delay intense development.

▲ **Time value of money:** Investors also consider the time value of money when deciding on the viability of a proposed project. Returns on investment that can be realized quickly maximize the profitability of a development project. If a structure is in imminent danger of damage or collapse from storms, rapid erosion, or other coastal hazards before rents or sales can recoup the cost of construction, developers may determine that potential gains are not worth the risk. Part of this calculation depends on what types of mitigation techniques are available to safeguard the property from the impacts of future hazards. The relative ease or difficulty in obtaining government permits to build can also influence investment decisions. Delays in the permitting process add substantially to development costs.

Hazards Awareness in Investment Decision-making

As these development decision factors indicate, investors always consider the level of risk involved in a proposed project or venture. In order to incorporate natural hazards into this calculation of risk, investors must first be aware of the hazards that could potentially impact their properties. Furthermore, the risk must be articulated in ways the investors can understand and appreciate—how will it affect the bottom line? A thorough hazards identification and risk assessment that includes the probability of various hazard events, their expected magnitude and intensity, as well as the severity of potential impacts should be carried out for all projects proposed in vulnerable locations. In the case of projects with heavy up-front capital expenditures (such as a multi-story high-rise structure located directly on the beachfront), studies of hazard risk factors are essential.

Despite the obvious need for a complete understanding of risk, investors and developers do not always perform a thorough assessment of potential hazards. Some investors, especially those from out of state who are not familiar with the geography and climate of the local environment, may be unaware of the degree of risk posed by natural hazards. Other investors may rely too heavily on state and local government hazard assessments, which may or may not speak directly to the building site in question. Developers may also rely on the agency in charge of issuing building permits to gauge whether a site is safe for property investment. If a permit is issued, the reasoning goes, the area must be free of hazards. Unfortunately, this assumption is not always correct. There remains a high degree of personal and corporate responsibility for thoroughly investigating all of the risks associated with the use of private property.

FOR EXAMPLE

Responding to Coastal Change: Going with the Flow[6]

The fundamental problem with living (and investing) in the coastal zone, is that all of our static, immobile construction (buildings, roads, bridges, and utility supply lines) is placed in a dynamic zone. The shoreline, inlets, dune fields, overwash terraces, marshes, and maritime forests shift landward as well as laterally in response to ongoing changes in the coastal environment. Changes in the levels of the sea and the land, changes in storm frequency and wave regime, change in the patterns of currents, change in the offshore topography, change in sand supply, changes in growth, and changes we are only just beginning to realize (e.g., climatic change and changes in water quality due to pollution)—change is the rule, especially for barrier islands. Awareness of these dynamic factors is essential to living within this ever-changing environment.[7] The price for not paying attention to the natural processes along the coast is property damage, costly rebuilding, loss of investment, and risk to human life.

Incorporating Mitigation into Investment Decisions

The understanding of hazard risk must be further translated into terms of trade-offs—how should capital resources be allocated to protect the investment? The more hazards can be linked to the financial viability of a project, the more weight they will be given in the developer's decision process. Many site-specific conditions can be mitigated, if adequate funds are expended.[8] For example, structures located along the oceanfront can be elevated above the expected flood height to reduce the risk of flooding and damage from storm surge. However, modifying a structure or a site to correct hazardous conditions often adds considerably to the engineering and construction costs of the project. A developer will avoid costs considered unnecessary in order to increase the financial attractiveness of a project.

9.2.3 Public Sector Actions to Influence Private Sector Decisions

Although private property owners have many choices and opportunities to realize profit and make financial gains from investment property in the coastal zone and other hazardous locations, the private sector is not granted free reign in exercising their property rights. While developers may avoid unnecessary costs when making financial projections for a development project, regulations and policies set by all levels of government can partially determine the importance that hazard exposure plays in those development decisions. For example, many coastal states have setback regulations that determine how far back from the shoreline a structure must be built. Larger structures are usually required to be built further back from the oceanfront than smaller, one-family units. A developer/investor must have enough space on the lot to build the size structure that will realize a profit. Some states also prohibit shoreline hardening structures like groins and bulkheads that damage fragile coastal ecosystems and transfer erosion risks to other locations along the shore. Building codes and construction regulations also play into the determination of profitability. Stringent building standards typically increase the cost of construction, but provide added security to the building against hazard impacts. These types of trade-offs can result in wiser investment decisions where a developer may still realize a profit, but projects that are unsustainable or considered inappropriate will not receive the regulatory green light. While the imposition of regulatory requirements does not supersede the requirement of personal responsibility in land use decision making, actions by the public sector can help prevent some of the more foolish property investment choices.

Local communities benefit immensely from the value that is added to the tax base when private property is put to its best use. At the same time, it is in the best interest of both the public and the private sectors that coastal lands, as well as other lands of intense natural beauty, environmental significance, and cultural and societal value, are used in a way that is sustainable over the long term. The case study included in this chapter ("Shell Island: A Case Study in Hazardous Coastal Development") illustrates some of the complex issues associated with private development in hazardous locations.

SELF-CHECK

- Describe five factors considered during development investment decisions.
- List six public sector actions that can influence private sector building and investment decisions.
- Explain how hazard awareness can help make sound investment decisions.

9.3 Economic Resiliency: Protecting Businesses From Hazards

So far in this chapter we have been discussing the private sector in terms of land ownership and investment in privately held real estate. But the vulnerability of a community depends upon more than the decisions that landowners make regarding use of their property. We know when a disaster strikes that individual

SHELL ISLAND: A CASE STUDY IN HAZARDOUS COASTAL DEVELOPMENT[9]

One of the biggest challenges for coastal resource managers is balancing personal property rights with the public's right to access and enjoy our nation's shoreline.[10] This challenge is compounded by the need to avoid costly public expenditures for erosion control and other hazard mitigation measures solely for the protection of private investment property.

In the late 1970s, the North Carolina Coastal Resources Commission (CRC), the policy-making and rule-adopting authority for the state's coastal zone management program, began prohibiting the use of hard erosion control structures such as seawalls, bulkheads, jetties, and similar devices to protect new buildings. In 1985, the commission revised the rules to prohibit the construction of hard erosion structures to protect any building, unless it is historic and cannot be relocated, or there is an overriding public need for the erosion structure to protect a waterway used for navigation purposes. Temporary sandbag protection is allowed under the rule if a building is considered "threatened," meaning the erosion escarpment must be within 20 feet of the foundation or the rate of erosion is so great that the building is in imminent danger of collapse.

The North Carolina state ban on erosion control construction projects was imposed in response to research and information demonstrating that hardened structures on beachfronts most often lead to the demise of sandy beaches. The complex cycles of sand accretion and erosion, long-shore drift of sand deposits, inlet formation and closure, and other processes of a dynamic coastal ecosystem are interrupted when manmade structures interfere with the natural progression of barrier island evolution. The goal of the regulatory prohibition is to protect the state's long-term economic and environmental interests, which means protecting sandy beaches to attract tourists and tourist dollars throughout the coastal zone, as well as providing some measure of protection against hurricanes and other coastal storms that a wide, sandy beach and healthy dune system offers.

In 1985, developers built the Shell Island Resort on the northern end of Wrightsville Beach in New Hanover County, prompting a sequence of events that led to multiple attempts to stave off the ravages of rapid erosion, triggered a lawsuit, and ultimately resulted in the physical relocation of Mason Inlet. To obtain permission from the State of North Carolina to construct the nine-story building on that site, the developers signed an agreement that stated: "In signing this permit, the permittee acknowledges the risks of erosion associated with developing on this site and recognizes that current state regulations do not allow shoreline erosion control structures such as seawalls to be erected for developments initiated after June 1, 1979."[11] The statement acknowledged that the condominium was being built in a designated **inlet-hazard area** under the North Carolina Coastal Area Management Act (CAMA). The signed statement further indicates that the developers were aware of state rules prohibiting erosion control structures to protect the condos if they were ever threatened by erosion in the future.

The northern end of Wrightsville Beach and the southern end of Figure Eight Island, which flank Mason Inlet, are naturally prone to erosion because of wave action, tides, sea-level rise, and a migrating inlet with a tendency to move in a southerly direction. Barrier islands and tidal inlets are constantly fluctuating and are key components of the coastal ecosystem, providing unique habitats, nursery areas, and buffers for the estuaries and mainland. They are also important to the movement of water, sand, and larval fish and shellfish along the coast and are owned by the public, which has the right to enjoy and benefit from them.

In 1985, as construction on the Shell Island Resort began, Mason Inlet, located just north of the construction site, exhibited accelerated movement to the south (see Figure 9-1). From 1993 to 1995, the inlet moved 650 feet to the south, which represents an average annual rate of 325 feet a year. When Mason Inlet began to get dangerously close to the Shell Island Resort, owners made repeated requests to the state to construct a protective barrier. The Coastal Resources Commission approved a large temporary sandbag seawall in January 1997—the first substantial exception to official state policy.

Realizing that the sandbag wall was not a permanent solution, the Shell Island property owners sued the state to build a permanent wall. The lawsuit was one of the first major challenges to the state's seawall ban. The property owners at Shell Island claimed that they were the victims of a mapping error. During court proceedings regarding the matter, representatives of the Resort owners alleged that the official state and county maps delineating inlet hazard

Figure 9-1

Mason Inlet migrating towards Shell Island Resort.

areas in the mid-1980s indicated that the site for the Resort was safe from Mason Inlet. It is not possible to ascertain whether more accurate maps would have resulted in denial of building permits for Shell Island Resort. However, it is clear that the Resort was built in a known inlet hazard area, and the developers and buyers had acknowledged the inherent risks involved. Later, the North Carolina Court of Appeals upheld the state's ban on seawalls and dismissed the lawsuit.

Faced with a deadline for removing the sandbags, the property owners requested that the sandbag barrier be allowed to remain until December 2001. The property owners then decided to join the privately funded Mason Inlet Preservation Group, and throw their efforts behind the dredging and moving of Mason Inlet.

Despite repeated warnings and advice from environmental groups, members of the Mason Inlet Preservation Group partnered with New Hanover County to proceed with the inlet movement project (see Figure 9-2). The Mason Inlet plan called for borrowing money from a public beach nourishment fund to cover the initial expenses of the project, which would later be repaid through a special assessment to the private property owners who comprised the membership of the Mason Inlet Preservation Group.

However, legal challenges to the assessment have purented the county from recouping the full cost of the project. Today, Shell Island is located several hundred yards from the inlet, but the area remains vulnerable to erosion and coastal storms.

Figure 9-2

Mason Inlet relocation after project completion.

families are affected, property is damaged, roads are blocked, power outages occur, and local government services such as drinking water and sewer treatment are disrupted. But one of the longest-lasting and most pervasive effects of a hazard event often involves the local economy. The roots of a community's economic troubles can be traced to the way hazards impact local businesses.

9.3.1 Economic Impacts of Natural Hazards

Staggering economic losses can be suffered following natural hazards. For example, Hurricane Andrew, which devastated much of southern Florida in 1993, seriously affected 8000 businesses and more than 100,000 jobs in Dade County alone. The area's $500 million-per-year tourist industry was disrupted for several years; agriculture experienced $1 billion in damages with permanent income loss of $250 million; and storm-affected areas suffered daily lost outputs of $22 million.[12] Flooding from Hurricanes Dennis and Floyd in eastern North Carolina in 1999 affected about 60,000 businesses, resulting in more than $955 million in business losses. The average repair cost for physical damage was about $40,000 per business, with an average revenue loss of nearly $80,000[13]. As a result of Hurricane Katrina in 2005, the majority of businesses in the affected Gulf Coast region have suffered significant declines in net income while others have simply ceased to exist. Property damage, destroyed assets, lost revenues, and other financial losses are estimated in the billions of dollars. The economic repercussions of Hurricanes Katrina, Wilma, and Rita will be felt in the Gulf region and throughout the country for years to come.

A Temporary Boost

Ironically, in some cases a major disaster can actually boost a local economy, at least in the short term. As disaster assistance funding and insurance payments pour into the community for reconstruction and recovery, a building boom often results. Construction jobs, and the services needed to support the construction activity, can often bring in more income to a community than previously existed. However, these jobs are temporary and are often filled by workers from outside the affected area.

Businesses associated with preparedness and recovery activities, such as building material suppliers, roofers, and appliance and furniture stores, are also likely to have increased levels of business in the recovery period following a disaster. Some of these industries may experience a significant rise in profits. Large building supply outlets, such as The Home Depot, routinely warehouse plywood, generators, and other materials needed for disaster response and recovery. They can send supplies quickly to a targeted region, extend store hours, and otherwise respond to the increased demand, often experiencing record sales in both retail and wholesale markets.[14]

As the physical reconstruction phase winds down, economic activity can flatten out to a more normal pace, and the structure of the local economy begins to regain its pre-disaster balance. It is at this juncture that local communities have an opportunity to rebuild an economic structure that is less vulnerable to future disruptions from natural disasters.[15] Much of this work involves strengthening the businesses that make up the community's economic sector.

9.3.2 Community Resiliency Depends on Business Resiliency

Communities depend upon their business and industries for their very existence. The local business sector provides jobs and tax revenue, and stimulates commerce, trade and other economic activity. Aside from the temporary boost that occurs from selected business operations during the recovery phase of a disaster, the ripple effect of a disaster can permeate all other sectors of community life. Destroyed businesses have multiplier effects on community difficulties, as residents lose jobs, property values decline, and tax receipts diminish.[16] When a business protects itself from natural disasters, it also is protecting one of its community's most valuable assets.

A community's business sector consists of thousands of individual businesses, including manufacturers, corporate offices, retailers, utilities, service providers, and other types of organizations where any number of people work or gather. Some businesses operate from a high-rise building, others in an industrial complex, and still others from a single office. Some businesses work from buildings they own, others rent or lease their property. Some companies are large, with hundreds or even thousands of employees, while others are small with only a handful of workers. Each of these businesses has its own characteristics and its own degree of resiliency to natural and man-made hazards. Every year hazards take their toll on all sorts of businesses and industries—in lives and dollars. However, business and industry can take action to limit injuries and damages and return more quickly to normal operations if they plan ahead.[17] In the following sections of this chapter, we will discuss business protection planning—a process that begins with a thorough risk assessment and hazard impact analysis—as a way to support the resilience of the business community.

Small Businesses is Big Business

Of all employers in the United States, 99.7% are small businesses.[18] All businesses and industries are subject to hazards, but small ones (generally defined as those employing less than 50 people) are especially susceptible, with some 30% not surviving when stricken by a natural disaster.[19] The percentage of small business failures can be even higher in some disasters. For instance, it is estimated that about 50% of the smaller or newer businesses in North Carolina did

> ## FOR EXAMPLE
>
> ### The Big Guys Get Back First
>
> The first businesses to reopen in southern Florida following Hurricane Andrew in 1993 were almost exclusively national fast-food franchises and retail chain outlets. In contrast to small owner-operated businesses, these centrally-administered businesses could access multinational and national capital resources to quickly resume operations.[22]

not recover following Hurricane Floyd, a storm that caused massive flooding throughout the eastern third of the state. Of the larger, more well-established businesses in the state, approximately four out of six have recovered. In general, many small local businesses are lost after a major event.

In addition to direct impacts that can damage property and destroy company assets and inventories, small businesses typically suffer a host of burdens associated with their relative size and place in the local economy when a disaster strikes. For example, small businesses typically rely on a local customer base[20], much of which can be eroded when residents and surrounding businesses can no longer patronize the company. Small businesses also suffer disproportionately from a shortage of employees when community residents are displaced, in addition to experiencing cash flow problems, lack of capital, and a loss of suppliers.

Many small companies fail primarily because of a lack of knowledge and resources to develop property and business protection plans. Many small business owners do not fully understand how the local economy is structured, nor do they comprehend the ways in which the economy may change because of a hazard event. Small companies may exhaust personal and business sources of capital in an attempt to revive and may fail to adjust their business plans to meet the changing post-disaster economy (see Figure 9-3).[21] All these factors point to the need for all businesses, but especially small businesses, to prepare a business protection plan well in advance of a hazard event.

SELF-CHECK

- List several economic impacts of disasters on businesses.
- Describe how some communities experience a temporary economic boost following a disaster.
- Explain why small businesses take a harder hit from disasters than large corporations.

Figure 9-3

Festus, Missouri, July 9, 1993: Businesses big
and small were hit hard during the Midwest
floods of 1993.

9.4 Business Risk Assessment and Impact Analysis

Businesses that are aware of the hazards that face them and take action before
a disaster strikes can often prevent many of the losses and damages associated
with natural and man-made hazards. There are many different approaches to
business protection planning, but all preventive measures begin with an assessment of risk and an analysis of the potential impacts of hazards on business
viability.

9.4.1 Types of Business Protection Plans

Various terms are used to describe the types of planning activities that many companies carry out in order to protect the business. **Contingency planning**, for example, is the process of developing advance arrangements and procedures that enable an organization to respond to a disaster so that critical business functions resume within a defined time frame, the amount of loss is minimized, and the stricken facilities are repaired or replaced as soon as possible. **Business Continuity Planning** is another commonly used term to describe this process, as is **Continuity of Operations Planning** (COOP). These plans are usually directed toward maintaining the business's viability when one or more functions are impaired or disrupted. Since the advent of computerized business operations, many of these plans focus on data protection, retrieval, and restoration.

Some businesses have very specific plans for dealing with situations peculiar to that industry or activity, such as a **Spill Prevention Control and Countermeasures (SPCC)** plan, or similar procedure for handling hazardous waste or dangerous substances. Many businesses also maintain a **safety and health plan** designed for workplace safety and employee health. Many of these planning activities are undertaken in response to regulations issued by state and federal agencies, including the Occupational Health and Safety Administration (OSHA) and the Environmental Protection Agency (EPA).

Fewer businesses, however, have a comprehensive emergency plan that covers all the types of hazards, including natural hazards and man-made hazards, and that covers all the components of the business, including physical assets as well as operations. Many of the various stand-alone plans that businesses may have in place can be consolidated into a comprehensive emergency management program or process, but it is essential that mitigation and preparedness be a part of that system. If the business already has an emergency plan, mitigation for natural and man-made hazards can often be incorporated into the existing plan.

A comprehensive disaster preparedness and mitigation plan for a business involves three main elements:

1. **Property Protection:** safeguarding physical facilities and their contents—equipment, furniture, inventories, raw materials, etc. from known hazards.

2. **Contingency Planning:** anticipating all the emergencies that could occur and creating plans accordingly to minimize disruptions.

3. **Insurance:** determining adequate coverage and purchasing the right kinds of insurance to help defray immediate and long-term costs if a disaster does occur.

To become more disaster resilient, a business must first identify and understand what hazards it faces and what is at risk from those hazards. A business risk assessment helps answer these questions.

9.4.2 Business Risk Assessment

Thousands of communities throughout the nation experience social and economic disruption from natural and man-made hazards every year. For instance, the string of hurricanes that made landfall in 2004—including Hurricanes Charley, Frances, Ivan, and Jeanne—struck hundreds of thousands of homes and businesses from Florida and the Gulf Coast to the Appalachian Mountains. Buildings were damaged, power was out for weeks in some places, roads were washed away, sewer service was disrupted, schools were closed, and scores of people died.

Every year thousands of businesses also experience emergencies internal to their operations, such as a frozen pipe that bursts over a long holiday weekend and floods the facility. Hazardous materials and dangerous chemicals can be unintentionally released, causing plant closure and downtime while containment and decontamination measures are carried out. In 1991, 25 people died and another 49 were injured as the result of a tragic fire in a chicken processing plant in Hamlet, North Carolina, where workers were trapped inside a locked facility as flames raged through the building. These scenarios clearly demonstrate the vulnerability of businesses located in every region to all sorts of hazards. For these reasons, a business mitigation and preparedness program begins with a thorough risk assessment that factors in the types of hazards that might occur, the vulnerability of the business to those hazards, and the losses that might result if the hazard event does happen.

Elements of a Business Risk Assessment

Central to preparing a business for the potential consequences of natural and technological hazards is an understanding of risk. Chapter 10 covers the steps involved in a risk assessment in greater detail, but the process is outlined here as it pertains to businesses. There are three basic levels of hazard assessment that businesses should carry out for a complete understanding of their risks:

1. **Hazard identification**, the first level, defines the magnitudes (intensities) and associated probabilities (likelihood) of hazards that may pose threats to the business and community.
2. **Vulnerability assessment**, the second level, characterizes the exposed populations and property, and the extent of injury and damage that may result from a hazard event of a given intensity in a given area.

3. **Risk assessment** is the third and most sophisticated level of analysis. It considers issues associated with an entire range of hazard intensities and probabilities, from the fairly common, low-intensity event (e.g., minor flooding from groundwater seepage) to the relatively rare, catastrophic event (e.g., a magnitude 6.5 earthquake). Risk analysis captures the full range of potential casualty and damage experiences, and provides the basis for a business impact analysis and strategy to minimize losses.[23]

9.4.3 Hazard Identification

The first step in a business risk assessment is to identify and list the full range of potential hazards that can impact the company. For business planning purposes, a hazard is any unplanned event that can cause death or significant injuries to employees, customers, or the public; or that can shut down a business, disrupt operations, cause physical or environmental damage; or can threaten the company's financial standing or public image.[24] These include emergencies that can occur within a facility, emergencies that can occur in the community, and emergencies that occur to businesses with links to other businesses. Hazards include the full range of natural hazards that face the community where the business is located, including tornadoes, earthquakes, flooding, hurricanes, landslides, sinkholes, and other natural events. In addition to the natural hazards that can potentially affect a business are numerous types of technological events, including nuclear facility accidents, terrorism, hazardous material incidents, cyber-risks, and energy emergencies. Each of these types of events must be addressed within the context of the impact it has on the company and the community. What might constitute a nuisance to a large industrial facility could be a disaster to a small business.[25]

Gathering Hazard Information

There are numerous ways a business can gather information about the hazards that are present in the community and that may affect its facility. Some factors to consider include:

▲ **Historical:** What types of emergencies have occurred in the community, at this facility, and at other facilities in the area?
▲ **Geographic:** What can happen as a result of the facility's location? Factors to consider include proximity to floodplains, coastal areas, seismic faults, forested areas, dams, and so forth. Proximity to potential man-made hazards, such as facilities that produce, store, use, or transport hazardous materials, or proximity to major transportation routes and airports is also pertinent.
▲ **Technological:** What could result from a process or system failure? Possibilities include fire, explosion, hazardous materials incidents, safety

system failures, telecommunications failures, power failures, or heating/cooling system failures.

▲ **Human Error:** What emergencies can be caused by employee error? Are employees trained to work safely? Do they know what to do in an emergency? Human error is the single largest cause of workplace emergencies and can result from poor training, poor maintenance, carelessness, or fatigue.

There is a wide variety of sources businesses can rely on information about hazards including local and state emergency offices; federal, state, and local regulatory agencies; local planning/zoning/building/public works departments; fire/police/emergency medical services; electric and telecommunications utilities; local emergency planning committee (LEPC); the American Red Cross; National Weather Service; and neighboring businesses. If the community where the business is located has a current local hazard mitigation plan in place, the company can also refer to that plan during its hazard identification, as well as to the state hazard mitigation plan.

9.4.4 Vulnerability Assessment

Armed with information about the natural and technological hazards that could conceivably impact the business, a company is in a position to assess its vulnerability to these hazards. During the vulnerability assessment, a business determines the probability and potential impact of each hazard. In other words, a prediction is made about what will happen to the business if any one of the hazards identified were to actually occur. The location of the business relative to probable natural hazard events is one of the primary determinants of vulnerability (e.g., businesses located on the coast are more vulnerable to hurricanes and storm surge). Business vulnerability is also a function of the community's overall vulnerability, including the infrastructure and local services that the business depends upon for daily operations.

FOR EXAMPLE

Expecting the Unexpected

While researching potential emergencies, a company in Beaver County, Pennslyvania discovered that a nearby dam had been classified as a High Hazard. The State Division Dam Safety was able to provide information about the possibility of a dam break, the amount of warning time that people downstream could expect, and likely velocities and depth of flooding that could occur because of a dam failure. The company was able to plan accordingly.

While the hazard remains constant over time, vulnerability will change as the business grows (or decreases), and new buildings are constructed, more inventory and customers are acquired, and greater value is accumulated. For this reason, it is important to assess future vulnerability to hazards based on probable trends and changes, as well as present vulnerability based on current conditions.

A business can gauge its vulnerability using a ranking system such as low, moderate, or high for each hazard based on frequency, as determined by historical records and trends, the relative strength of typical hazard events, and the direct and indirect impacts that can be expected from each type of hazard.

▲ **Direct impacts** include physical damage to structures, such as buildings and other facilities. Direct impacts also include losses to inventories, equipment, and other physical assets.

▲ **Indirect impacts** result from the closure of roads and disassembly of transportation networks; loss of utilities, such as water, sewage, electric power; and disruptions to telecommunications.

Offsite damages and losses can have a significant impact on the operation of a business. Following Hurricane Floyd, for example, road closures temporarily prevented thousands of customers, suppliers, and employees from accessing businesses in the most flooded areas.[26]

9.4.5 Business Impact Analysis

Once a business has a general idea of its vulnerability to certain identified hazards based on location, probabilities, and intensities, the analysis must turn toward the specific impacts these hazards will have on that particular business. This is done by conducting a **business impact analysis**, which involves calculating the types of damages and losses that can be expected during any one of the identified hazard events and relating them to the characteristics of the business itself. This in turn will determine the types of actions that must be taken to reduce vulnerability.

The conditions that make a business operate smoothly and profitably vary from company to company. For example, the protection of inventory and business records may be most critical to a retailer or a business in the service sector (e.g., finance, insurance, real estate, restaurant, hotel). A small manufacturing plant may have equipment or machinery that is essential for the success of the business. For farmers, it may be the protection of crops that have been harvested and stored, livestock and poultry, or critical farm equipment. The purpose of a business impact analysis is to identify the parts of the business that need to be up and running as soon as possible in the aftermath of a disaster as well as those that the business must keep intact to remain viable.

Factors that determine the impact a hazard will have on a business include:

▲ **Services or products provided:** Whether the product or service can be deferred is an important consideration in assessing the financial impact of a disaster on a business. For example, if a burger stand cannot sell hamburgers for one week because the kitchen is closed for repairs due to damage from an earthquake, the owner cannot make up for the lost income from the missed sales. The same applies to a bed and breakfast, where every day without a patron represents lost revenue. However, in the case of a store that sells appliances, the customer can defer his purchase if the store is closed, which does not necessarily result in lost income for the business (assuming the inventory has been adequately safeguarded).

▲ **Site Dependence:** Whether a business is at a fixed site or whether business functions can be temporarily moved to a safer location has an important bearing on preparedness and risk reduction strategies. If the business is unable to relocate in the event of an emergency, it is more important to consider mitigation actions to protect or strengthen the building and its contents. A manufacturing plant or a restaurant, for example, cannot easily transfer operations to another locale, while an investment firm or travel agency may be more flexible and can work temporarily out of alternative office space.

▲ **Dependence on Information Technology:** In the case of customer service and similar industries, business continuity is very dependent on the functionality of information technology and the protection of critical data and files. These businesses will focus on securing continual access to their vital records in order to minimize disruption from hazards.[27]

Operational problems due to disasters are not always connected to property damage or impacts on the business itself. External impacts include disruptions to the flow of supplies and in the ability to ship goods or deliver services to customers and clients.[28] Therefore, the business impact assessment will also consider losses that can occur upstream from the business as well as those downstream.

Upstream and Downstream Losses

Even if a business escapes a disaster unharmed and its employees are unhurt, there is still a risk that the business will suffer significant losses. When some local businesses fail, there is a chain reaction because of the negative impact on the local economy and the interrelationships among various members of the economic sector. These can be broken down into two types of losses: upstream and downstream. Upstream losses are those the business will suffer when one or more of its suppliers are affected by the disaster and cannot deliver the goods or services the business needs. Many businesses depend on

daily deliveries, such as produce to a restaurant or machine parts to a manu-
facturer. If the supplier's building is damaged by the disaster and it cannot
keep up its pre-disaster schedule, this upstream loss will affect other firms,
even those that are undamaged. Downstream losses occur when a key customer
and/or the lives of residents in the community are affected by a disaster. For
example, if residents in the area are cleaning up debris and repairing their
homes after a major flood, a local theater or restaurant may experience a dramatic loss of customers. If supplying a component to a large assembly plant
is a major source of a firm's cash flow and that plant is closed because of tornado damage, the business will suffer a downstream loss even if it escaped
unscathed from the disaster itself.[29]

SELF-CHECK

- What is a business protection plan?
- What are four factors to consider when gathering hazard informa-
  tion for a business?
- What are the elements of a business risk assessment?

9.5 Preparing a Plan to Minimize Losses

Upon completion of a thorough hazard risk assessment and business impact
analysis, a business will be able to create a mitigation and preparedness plan to
bolster resiliency. The plan will list mitigation strategies and actions that the
business intends to carry out when timing and resources make implementation
feasible within the company's larger business plan. There are three major components to an effective business protection plan: property protection, business
continuity, and insurance.

9.5.1 Reviewing the Business Impact Analysis

When a business reaches the point of devising mitigation strategies to protect
the company, it should review the particular impacts that various hazards can
have. In this way, the business can target its mitigation actions to the precise
problems that it faces. Table 9-1 summarizes the impacts that certain natural
hazards can have on a business.

  With this information in hand, a business is in a better position to: (1) assess
whether the company should take steps to protect its building and contents from

Table 9-1: Selected Hazards Confronting Businesses and Their Expected Impacts

Expected Impacts	Flood	Hurricane	Tornado	Earthquake	Wildfire	Winter Storm	
Wind Damage		X	X			X	
Water Damage	X	X				X	
Damaging Hail/ Ice			X				
Earth Movement				X			
Electric Power Outage	X	X	X	X	X	X	
Roadway Blockage	X	X	X	X	X	X	
Water System Outage	X	X	X	X		X	
Sewer System Outage	X	X	X	X		X	
Telecommunications System Outage	X	X	X	X	X	X	
Employee Endangerment		X	X	X	X	X	X
Business Disruption	X	X	X	X	X	X	

Source: Adapted from FEMA.

the effects of flooding, ice, ground shaking, high winds, and fires; (2) prepare a continuity plan that will ensure the business can remain operational during and after a hazard event; and (3) re-evaluate the company's insurance coverage.

9.5.2 Property Protection

A business strategy to protect company property from hazard losses covers the building(s) and other structures, the building interior, as well as exterior components and surroundings. The building's physical condition and how well it can survive a natural disaster can determine whether the company is able to keep the business open following an incident.[30] Though building owners typically have more control over their property than renters, business tenants have many of the same concerns, as the issues remain the same whether the occupants own the building or rent space in it.

An ideal time for structural improvements that make company property more hazard resistant is during a major addition or renovation. Replacement windows and doors, materials for a new roof, and other items can improve structural integrity and overall building safety, and might also have other positive benefits, such as increased energy efficiency or ease of maintenance. Whether the company is planning to remodel or build an entirely new facility, the plans must conform to state and local building code requirements. These codes reflect the lessons experts have learned from past disasters and incorporate engineering and structural specifications to strengthen buildings against known hazard impacts. Older buildings may need to be inspected by a professional engineer to check whether they are up to code.[31] If a business is located in a particularly hazardous area (along the oceanfront, for example), constructing or retrofitting a structure to exceed minimum code requirements can often provide additional protection. Although these added improvements may increase the cost of construction, it is often a wise investment that enables the company to reopen its doors to customers or clients quickly after a hazard event.

Examples of physical retrofitting measures that businesses may consider include:

▲ Upgrading facilities to withstand the shaking of an earthquake or high winds.
▲ Elevating buildings above expected flood heights.
▲ Constructing tornado safe rooms.
▲ Installing fire-resistant roofing materials.
▲ Installing storm shutters for all exterior windows and doors.

Businesses located in special flood hazard areas may wish to consider floodproofing, a term that covers a variety of techniques that provide some protection to certain types of buildings. Although the National Flood Insurance Program (NFIP) does not allow new residential buildings to be floodproofed, nonresidential buildings, such as commercial space or manufacturing facilities, can be retrofitted or floodproofed. There are two approaches to floodproofing:

▲ **Dry floodproofing** involves strengthening walls to withstand hydrostatic and dynamic forces, including debris impacts. Openings, including doors, windows, and vents, are sealed or filled with special closures to block entry of floodwater. In some instances, walls can be coated with waterproofing compounds or plastic sheeting.
▲ **Wet floodproofing** intentionally allows floodwater to enter certain enclosed areas to reduce the damaging pressures that can collapse walls and foundations. Flooring and wall materials must be resistant to flood damage, and the contents of floodable areas should be removed when flood warnings are issued. The NFIP regulations allow wet floodproofing measures, called "enclosures below base flood,"[32] only under very limited

circumstances in new buildings. However, such measures can be used to reduce damage to existing buildings.

There are also nonstructural mitigation measures for protecting business property from hazards, such as:

▲ Moving valuables—including equipment—from basement if prone to flooding.
▲ Elevating or relocating main breaker, fuse box, HVAC, etc. above anticipated flood levels.
▲ Installing sewer backflow valves.
▲ Anchoring fuel tanks and gas-fired hot water heaters.
▲ Securing light fixtures and other items that could fall or shake loose in an earthquake.
▲ Moving heavy or breakable objects to low shelves.
▲ Attaching cabinets and files to low walls or bolting them together.
▲ Installing automatic sprinkler systems.
▲ Installing fire-resistant landscaping around the exterior of the business.
▲ Insulating water piping to prevent frozen or burst pipes.

These and similar strategies can help ensure that the business will not fail because of physical damage to the structure during an anticipated hazard event. Many property protection measures can serve double duty, enhancing safety for one or more hazards. Securing roof shingles, for example, helps protect a building from high winds due to hurricanes, as well as from tornadoes and thunderstorms.

9.5.3 Business Contingency Planning

Even the best-designed and well-maintained buildings can be damaged, forcing a business closure. Even if a building sustains no damage, a major hurricane, earthquake, or other catastrophic event can close roads, cause power outages, or create other problems that force a business to shut down. This is why every business needs a continuity plan to get up and running as quickly as possible in case disaster strikes.[33] Based on the business impact assessment performed earlier, each company will need to create a plan that specifically speaks to its particular risk and minimizes downtime by bolstering its most critical elements to withstand hazard impacts.

Minimizing Upstream Business Disruptions

The ability of many businesses to resume operations following a disaster relies on the ability of suppliers to deliver what the business needs and to make the delivery on time. To ensure that critical suppliers of services and materials will be available when needed and to encourage the continuity of the supply chain, there are several things a business can do, such as:

▲ Diversify the pool of principal suppliers, making sure they are not all located in the same geographical area.

▲ Request or require that all critical suppliers have a business continuity plan of their own.

▲ Encourage a mutual aid agreement between the main supplier and similar companies.

▲ Maintain a list of backup vendors that can provide the business with materials, supplies, and services in case the primary ones are disabled.

These and other measures can keep the business going, even when a widespread hazard cripples much of the community. By planning in advance, a business won't be left scrambling in the aftermath of a disaster in an attempt to resume operations with contacts that are unfamiliar.

Protecting Data and Vital Records

Certain records are essential to perform critical business functions. Without access to data and information, business operations can come to a standstill. Some business records are required for legal or contractual reasons, others are required by regulatory or oversight agencies. Certain vital records may also be necessary to support recovery efforts following a disaster and to make insurance claims. A company's vital records might include:

▲ Employee data/payroll/financial records.

▲ Strategic plans/research data.

▲ Product lists and specifications.

▲ Formulas/trade secrets.

▲ Supplier contacts/inventory lists.

▲ Customer/client/patient/student records.

▲ Building plans/blueprints/engineering drawings.

▲ Property lease/insurance records.

Any number of hazards can cause data to become lost, corrupted, or damaged, and a crucial element of a business contingency plan must include provisions to protect data and vital records. The majority of businesses today are dependent on computers and computer networking systems. Many businesses communicate and conduct business transactions with vendors, customers, clients, and partners via the internet. Online security is a critical consideration for these businesses, and maintaining connections during power failures and other disruptions caused by natural hazards must be addressed in the pre-disaster phase.

The most important records should be backed up on one or more forms of media (printed copies, electronic, removable storage devices, etc.). Vital information should be stored securely onsite and in a secure offsite location at least 50 miles away. Some companies and universities contract for a "hot site" or "mirror site" at a host institution or facility in a different state where important backup information is stored. Contracting with a mobile information technology service is another option, but this assumes the downed business will have transportation access as well as a source of power. Procedures for protecting and accessing vital records may include:

- ▲ Labeling vital records.
- ▲ Backing up computer systems.
- ▲ Making copies of records.
- ▲ Storing tapes and disks in insulated containers.
- ▲ Increasing security of computer facilities.
- ▲ Arranging for evacuation of records to backup facilities.
- ▲ Backing up systems handled by service bureaus.
- ▲ Arranging for backup power.

The services of a data center and disaster recovery facility can be helpful in securing vital records, as data is backed up on a regular basis and can be made available if normal business operations are interrupted.

9.5.4 Preparing a Business Relocation Plan

In areas of the country that experience repetitive floods and other disasters on a fairly regular basis, it is important to identify alternate sites for business relocation following a disaster. Moving to a safer location can save money, prevent lost revenues, and break the cycle of destruction and rebuilding that occurs when businesses are located in hazardous areas. The three main elements of a business relocation plan include (1) Land use planning and site selection: the location and siting of businesses to promote business continuity; (2) Building standards: design and construction features that promote building resistance to hazards; and (3) Temporary business relocation (recovery location): the identification of viable business locations that can temporarily accommodate displaced businesses.[34]

Land Use Planning and Site Selection

In the long term, the most direct and cost-effective strategy to minimize or prevent damages and losses from natural hazards is to guide development away from hazard-prone areas when other development locations are available. Local governments, working with private businesses and organizations such as the local chamber of commerce can use a combination of planning and regulatory tools, ordinances, and interagency cooperative agreements to reduce the number of people and value of property at risk from hazards. This involves planning for the construction of new businesses that might enter the community in the future, as well as selecting sites where current businesses may move after a hazard has caused severe damage.

In selecting a location for new businesses or business relocations, there are several factors to consider, including (1) access to customers, (2) access to suppliers, (3) access to employees, (4) cost to lease or purchase office/retail/manufacturing space, (5) access to key services—electrical, water, telecommunications, and (6) the vulnerability of the property and building to natural and technological hazards, including flooding, landslides, earthquakes, fires, hazardous materials spills, etc.[35]

Temporary Business Locations/Sites

When business owners are displaced from their buildings as the result of a disaster, income is disrupted and the solvency of the business becomes a critical issue. A valuable piece of a business relocation plan is the identification of viable alternative business locations that can accommodate—at least temporarily—the displaced business. Before a disaster strikes, a business should select an alternative site, perhaps even from the owner's home, to recover. Some businesses have established mutual aid agreements with similar businesses, or made pre-arrangements to rent available space at another location if base operations are unusable or inaccessible. Some businesses may have other facilities or branch offices that can be used to resume some or all of their operations.

Considerations to be made during the business recovery location plan include:

▲ Selecting a site that is not on the same electric power grid.
▲ Factoring in the ability of vendors/suppliers or rental companies to quickly transport critical items such as computers, inventory, and equipment to the recovery location.
▲ Pre-arranging for an industrial cleanup or emergency repair service and/or a security service to protect damaged facilities.
▲ Reviewing the lease of the primary location space to determine who is responsible for what in case of damage from a natural disaster.
▲ Exploring rental options to replace damaged equipment, machinery, vehicles, and other assets during the time they are being repaired or replaced.

9.5.5 Protecting Employees and Their Families

The traditional approach to business protection focuses on planning for continuity of operations, strengthening buildings and facilities against hazard impacts, and carrying out nonstructural mitigation measures. Unfortunately, businesses often have overlooked the impact of disasters on their employees, yet employees are a company's most important asset. "A business can be as secure as Fort Knox, but if employees cannot make it to work, the bottom line will be affected."[36] Businesses should always consider ways to help employees prepare themselves and their families for emergencies. This will increase their personal safety and help the facility get back up and running. Those who are prepared at home will be better able to carry out their responsibilities at work.[37]

There are many tactics for making employees safer on the job as well as enhancing their ability to withstand a disaster in their own homes so they can return to work as soon as the facility is open for business. Types of activities in an employee assistance plan may include:

▲ Disseminating hazard information to all employees.

▲ Allowing employees time off to implement home protection measures.

▲ Pre-arranging alternate forms of transportation for employees, such as a carpool or pick-up service, including four-wheel drive if necessary.

▲ Providing or assisting with emergency housing for displaced employees.

▲ Addressing immediate needs of employees, including short-term financial aid.

▲ Pre-arranging for childcare at the primary or alternate site.

▲ Offering flexible work schedules/reduced hours.

▲ Arranging for crisis counseling.

▲ Providing information on property insurance for employee homes and belongings.

Another important consideration involves employee compensation. Payroll continuity following a disaster is key to continued loyalty of employees. Examples of companywide policies that can help employees handle disaster-related problems at home and meet their personal financial obligations include direct deposit of paychecks for all employees, cash advances, overtime pay during disaster, and payment of one week's salary (or other amount) even if the business is not operational.

Businesses should also make it a priority to ensure the safety of all employees during a hazard event at company facilities. Many companies establish policies to convene all employees at least once a year to review emergency plans, practice evacuation drills, and provide CPR, first aid, and other emergency training. It is also essential that employees have direct access to emergency phone numbers, such as fire department, police department, ambulance service, and the local emergency management agency. Installing weather radios to listen for tornado, hurricane, ice, thunderstorm, and other severe weather warnings issued by the media and the National Weather Service can alert employees to impending events. Onsite sheltering measures to protect employees, including space for their families, during a hazard event can also create a safer and more secure workplace.

FOR EXAMPLE

Taking Care of Employees

One of the hardest hit communities during Hurricane Floyd was the town of Greenville, North Carolina, where the Grady-White Boat Company is located. When the company was cut off from the rest of the community after the Tar River crested at over 20 feet, the company president turned his full attention to his employees, many of whom lost their homes and vehicles during the storm. Acknowledging that production would not resume at full throttle until the needs of employees were addressed, priority was given to a company-wide self-help initiative that focused on three objectives: providing transportation to employees, arranging for housing of the displaced, and addressing the immediate needs of workers (including short-term financial needs). As a result of the spontaneous company-driven relief effort, the Grady-White Boat Company was able to resume business operations quickly. Equally important, the disaster served as the impetus in a new effort to launch a county-wide business vulnerability assessment project. The premise is that with advances in risk assessment tools, it is possible to anticipate the consequences of natural disasters and take necessary measures to protect employees and customers alike.[38]

9.5.6 Business Protection through Insurance

Most companies discover that they are not properly insured only after they have suffered a loss. Lack of appropriate insurance can be financially devastating. On the other hand, the proper amount and kind of insurance can allow a business to resume operations, make up for lost revenues, repair damaged property, replace equipment and materials, and otherwise recover from a disaster. There are three main types of insurance protection for businesses: (1) property insurance for all structures, equipment, and vehicles; (2) business interruption insurance to cover lost income during downtime; and (3) extra expenses insurance, which compensates the business for additional expenses that are incurred due to a disaster. Despite the availability and wisdom of purchasing insurance to cover base assets and operations of a business, a surprising number of small businesses fail to take this basic step to protect their investment. For example, a survey of businesses following Hurricane Floyd determined that while most businesses carried liability, property, casualty, and fire insurance, almost one of every six small businesses reported having none. As a result, many businesses were under-insured, and in some instances were forced to close.[39]

Checking the Policy

Of the small businesses that do carry insurance, many are not fully aware of the details of their insurance policies. Businesses should always include a discussion with insurance advisors as part of a thorough hazard mitigation and preparedness effort. For instance, most policies do not cover flood or earthquake damage; these hazards may require separate policies for coverage. The insurance should be tailored to the individual business and take into consideration not only property damage, but also the loss of revenues and extra expenses that occur when business is halted by a disaster.

Like many aspects of a viable business plan, the devil is in the details when it comes to insurance. Issues that should be addressed in the pre-disaster stage include a wide range of topics addressing property valuation and extent of coverage. Sample questions a business may wish to pose include:

- ▲ How will property be valued?
- ▲ What perils or causes of loss does the policy cover?
- ▲ What does the policy require the business to do in the event of a loss?
- ▲ To what extent is the business covered for loss due to interruption of power?
- ▲ Is coverage provided for both on- and off-premises power interruption?
- ▲ Is the business covered for lost income in the event of business interruption because of a loss?
- ▲ Is there enough coverage?
- ▲ For how long is coverage provided?
- ▲ How long is the coverage for lost income if the business is closed by order of a civil authority (for example, a mandatory evacuation order)?
- ▲ To what extent is the business covered for reduced income if customers do not come back once the business reopens?
- ▲ Does the policy cover the cost of required upgrades to meet current building codes if a structure is in need of repair following a disaster?
- ▲ Will mitigation and preparedness measures result in a decrease in premium rates?[40]

These and other questions can help a business specify the type of coverage it chooses to carry, as well as other options that may be available through additional insurance products.

Property Insurance

Typically, property insurance policies exclude coverage for flood or earthquake damage. These hazards are usually covered through additional policies to supplement the fire insurance that many businesses routinely carry. If a business is located in the flood zone of a community that participates in the National Flood Insurance Program (NFIP), the company may be able to purchase a federally-backed flood insurance policy. Under NFIP rules, buildings located in the flood zone that are damaged in excess of 50% of the market value of the structure must be torn down. Some businesses purchase ordinance or law-compliance coverage to help pay for the extra costs of tearing down a structure and rebuilding it to meet code standards.

Business Interruption Insurance

Business interruption insurance can help even when businesses sustain significant losses during a hazard event. Just a short duration without customers, suppliers, and other critical operations can create a huge gap in revenue and net income. Furthermore, businesses typically experience a lag in revenues even after reopening following a disaster. Customers may seek alternative sources to fill their needs and may not readily resume relations with previous service providers. Business interruption insurance can help fill some of these gaps until the company is up and running again.

Business interruption insurance compensates for income lost if the company must vacate the premises due to disaster-related damage (see Figure 9-4). Business interruption insurance also covers the profits that would have been earned,

Figure 9-4

Falls City, Texas, July 8, 2002: Local businesses were hit hard by flooding in Texas.

based on financial records, had the disaster not occurred. The policy covers recurring operating expenses—such as utilities—even though business activities have come to a temporary halt. The price of the policy is generally related to the risk of a fire or other disaster damaging the premises.[41]

Extra Expense Insurance

As income shrinks following a disaster, expenses—both previous ongoing business expenses and new expenses due to the disaster—will rise. Extra expense insurance reimburses a company for expenditures made over and above normal operating expenses to avoid a shutdown during recovery and reconstruction following a qualifying disaster. Extra expense insurance is generally calculated by estimating projected revenues and expenses, calculating anticipated income, and then determining the potential losses from a temporary closure.[42] Extra expense insurance will usually only be paid if the extra expenses help to decrease business interruption costs. In some instances, extra expense insurance alone may provide sufficient coverage, without the purchase of business interruption insurance.[43]

SELF-CHECK

- Describe upstream and downstream losses.
- List four business mitigation strategies to lessen the impact of natural hazards.
- Explain the purpose of property insurance, business interruption insurance, and extra expense insurance.

9.6 Private Sector Participation in Community Mitigation

Business continuity planning, property protection, and insurance can help a company safeguard its assets against hazard impacts, but these measures alone cannot guarantee the post-disaster viability of the business. Any pre-disaster planning must be carried out within the context of the larger community, or a business will find it very difficult to survive a temporary closure. It is in the best interests of businesses to engage in mitigation practices that not only provide a direct benefit to an individual company by minimizing potential downtime, but that also make the community as a whole more resilient to hazards. By looking beyond its own plant, factory, retail, or office space and broadening its mitigation efforts, private sector business owners can also secure a work force that is able to return to their jobs; facilitate the reactivation of utilities, roadways, and government services; and help commerce resume quickly following a disaster.

Specific information on how private sector involvement has reduced (or can be a factor in reducing) community vulnerability is scarce.[44] However, it is clear that public-private partnerships are needed to address disaster preparedness and mitigation. In response, an increasing number of public-private partnership models are emerging around the country, and are being used to channel business sector involvement into the adoption of local hazard mitigation as well as sustainable development practices.[45] Partnerships are likely to lead to more viable solutions than would be developed by any one group working independently.[46]

Mitigation partnerships bring together the leadership and expertise of business, state and local governments, utilities, research and academia, nonprofit groups, and other community organizations to develop integrated strategies to reduce exposure to hazards and make post-disaster recovery easier. Partnership activities can include awareness and education activities, integration of business and community vulnerability assessment programs for identifying community-wide hazards and risks, a team approach to disaster response and recovery, and sponsorship of community-based programs that address hazard mitigation and sustainability.

One of the most important actions the business sector can take to bolster community resiliency is to support the building code—a strong and well-enforced building code actually costs businesses less in the long run. Even though initial outlays for new construction may be higher to incorporate the latest disaster-resistant materials and construction techniques, these standards are generally designed to ensure safety at certain specified impact levels, such as wind speed or seismic ground shaking.

9.6.1 Using Incentives to Promote Community Resiliency

Sometimes being a good corporate citizen is not sufficient motivation for private businesses to become involved in hazard mitigation initiatives at the community level. There are a variety of incentives that communities can use to encourage the private sector to become engaged. Some incentives are offered by the local government, such as lowered tax rates or tax discounts for property that is built or retrofitted to withstand hazard impacts (e.g., hurricane shutters to prevent wind damage to homes and businesses, elevation to protect against flooding, seismic retrofit to strengthen a building against earthquake shaking). Other types of incentives can be offered by the building supply and home improvement industry, such as rebates or discounts on purchases of mitigation-related materials and supplies. In return, the retailer, wholesaler, or distributor receives increased sales, good public relations, and recognition in the community as a partner in mitigation efforts. The lending and insurance industries can also play a part in stimulating mitigation actions by home and business owners through premium discounts and lowered loan rates. In return, both the lender and the insurance provider benefit from the increased safety of the secured property.

When properly applied, incentives can be a powerful lever to engage individual businesses and homeowners in a community-based risk reduction initiative. Combinations of incentives can also be used to reward risk reduction efforts. Sample incentives are displayed in Table 9-2.[47]

There are impediments to adoption of incentives as an integral feature of a local mitigation strategy. Incentives can be complex, cumbersome to administer, and in the short-term can have negligible impacts on reducing risk. In the long-term, however, it can be argued that incentives, when applied as a package and in combination with accurate hazard assessment and risk analysis information, can motivate homeowners, business, and communities to take action to protect their property from the effects of natural hazards.[48]

Table 9-2: Incentives for Community-Based Risk Reduction Initiatives

Incentive	Provisions
Tax	Reduction in local government taxes for property protection measures undertaken by homeowners and business owners. Waiver of sales taxes on building materials to retrofit structures.
Insurance	Differentiated premiums in hazard areas based on mitigation measures. Waiver of deductible on natural hazard losses for strengthened buildings. Reduced premiums/waived deductibles for strengthened public facilities. Building code enforcement grading system to allow property owner premium discounts on new construction built at or above code.
Retailer, manufacturer, or wholesaler pricing	Manufacturer's rebates on products used for mitigation. Discounts or rebates at point-of-sale (e.g., The Home Depot). Project-specific discounts or rebates.
Financial	Building fee waivers/reductions for structures built with mitigation features. Discounted construction loans/lower rates for retrofitted structures.

FOR EXAMPLE

Property Protection Rebates

The village of South Holland, Illinois, has a rebate program to help property owners fund retrofitting projects to protect against surface and subsurface flooding. If a project is approved, installed, and inspected, the village will reimburse the owner 25% of the cost up to $2500. About 650 floodproofing and sewer backup protection projects have been completed under this program. Perhaps not surprisingly, contractors have become some of the best agents to publicize this program.[49]

Project Impact

One of the best publicized public-private partnerships for hazard mitigation was Project Impact: Building Disaster Resistant Communities. Project Impact was an initiative developed by the Federal Emergency Management Agency (FEMA) in the late 1990s for identifying risk, prioritizing needs, and implementing long-term plans to protect communities with a strong emphasis on private sector participation. Under the program, FEMA and state offices of emergency management designated local communities as Project Impact sites. Many Project Impact communities specifically targeted business, encouraging their support and providing ways for them to become directly involved. Membership targets included insurance agencies, real estate firms, homebuilders, and financial institutions. For further discussion of Project Impact, see Chapter 6.

SELF-CHECK

- Why is it important for a business to be engaged in community-wide mitigation planning and programs?
- List four incentives for community-based risk reduction and describe their provisions.
- Describe Project Impact and how businesses were involved.

SUMMARY

Economic resilience is a vital part of creating a disaster-resilient community. This chapter describes the planning process a business can follow to become more resilient to disaster and identifies a number of mitigation actions a business might take to reduce its vulnerability to natural hazards. This chapter provides a list of factors considered during private land investment and development decision-making, and describes how these decisions are related to a community's economic resiliency. This chapter also outlines several types of business protection plans and describes business impact analysis. It is important for a community and its businesses to work together to mitigate the impact of hazards. This chapter explores that connection, as well as the processes by which a business can mitigate the impact of hazards on its own facilities and operations.

KEY TERMS

Business Continuity Planning or Continuity of Operations Planning (COOP)	Plans directed toward maintaining a business's viability when one or more functions are impaired or disrupted. Since the advent of computerized business operations, many of these plans focus on data protection, retrieval, and restoration.
Business impact analysis	A calculation of the types of damages and losses that can be expected during an identified hazard event; the damages are related to the characteristics of the business. The business impact analysis assists in determining the types of actions that must be taken to reduce vulnerability.
Contingency planning	The process of developing advance arrangements and procedures that enable an organization to respond to a disaster so that critical business functions resume within a defined time frame, the amount of loss is minimized, and the stricken facilities are repaired or replaced as soon as possible.
Demand	The desire for a commodity together with the ability to pay for it. Scarcity increases the desire for a particular product—for example, beachfront property in highly developed coastal areas.
Direct impact	Includes physical damage to structures, such as buildings and other facilities.

	Direct impacts also include losses to inventories, equipment, and other physical assets.
Dry floodproofing	A structural mitigation technique that strengthens walls to withstand hydrostatic and dynamic forces, including debris impacts. Openings, including doors, windows, and vents, are sealed or filled with special closures to block entry of floodwater. In some instances, walls can be coated with waterproofing compounds or plastic sheeting.
Hazard identification	A step of the business risk assessment that defines the magnitudes (intensities) and associated probabilities (likelihood) of hazards that may pose threats to the business and community.
Indirect impacts	Result from the closure of roads and disassembly of transportation networks; loss of utilities, such as water, sewerage, electric power; and disruptions to telecommunications.
Infrastructure	Facilities and systems that support development, such as water, sewer, roads, etc.
Regulation	Legislation that controls property uses, including zoning and subdivision ordinances, building codes, fire codes, environmental protection laws, and other types of mandates that dictate where and how development and building take place.
Risk	The potential losses associated with a hazard, defined in terms of expected probability and frequency, exposure, and consequences.
Risk assessment	A process or method for evaluating risk associated with a specific hazard and defined in terms of probability and frequency of occurrence, magnitude and severity, exposure and consequences.

Safety and health plan	Plan for ensuring workplace safety and protecting employee health.
Spill Prevention Control and Countermeasures (SPCC) Plan	Plans and procedures for dealing with hazardous waste or dangerous substances.
Time value of money	One of the basic concepts of finance, the time value of money is based on the premise that faster returns on investment maximize the profitability of a development project.
Vulnerability assessment	A step of the business risk assessment that characterizes exposed populations and property and the extent of injury and damage that may result from a hazard event of a given intensity in a given area.
Wet floodproofing	Structural mitigation measure that intentionally allows floodwater to enter certain enclosed areas to reduce the damaging pressures that can collapse walls and foundations.

ASSESS YOUR UNDERSTANDING

Go to www.wiley.com/college/schwab to evaluate your knowledge of community resilience and the private sector.
Measure your learning by comparing pre-test and post-test results.

Summary Questions

1. A resilient community needs a resilient economy in order to contribute to geo-global stability. True or False?

2. Land ownership in the United States means that an owner can do anything she wants on her land. True or False?

3. A diverse economy is advantageous for a community because it offers jobs to people of diverse ethnic backgrounds. True or False?

4. Community infrastructure planning can be used to steer development away from hazardous areas. True or False?

5. Investors are required to take natural hazards into consideration when deciding when and where to build. True or False?

6. Established businesses are usually not affected by natural hazards because they are insured. True of False?

7. Small businesses typically open sooner than larger stores or chains simply because they are smaller and easier to clean up. True or False?

8. A COOP is a
   (a) residence for poultry.
   (b) a term of endearment for a person named Cooper.
   (c) a continuity of operations plan.
   (d) a community optional operations plan.

9. As part of a business risk assessment a business should
   (a) identify the hazards that can impact the business.
   (b) withdraw all of its funds from the neighborhood bank.
   (c) fire the CFO.
   (d) none of the above.

10. A risk assessment should inform the business about
    (a) the extent to which the business is vulnerable to a particular hazard.
    (b) the time and date of the next natural hazard.
    (c) alternative methods of preventing natural hazards.
    (d) all of the above.

11. Upstream losses refer to the damage that is caused by development in the river basin that results in increased flowage in the community. True or False?

12. Building codes
    (a) regulate the methods and materials used in construction.
    (b) prevent unauthorized entrance to a building during a natural hazard.
    (c) are rarely used because they are difficult to administer.
    (d) decrease the cost of construction.

13. Local mitigation plans may play an important part in mitigating the impact of natural hazards on business operations
    (a) by discouraging development from locating in hazardous areas.
    (b) by encouraging business to relocate to the community following a disaster.
    (c) by extending infrastructure only to areas that are hazardous for development.
    (d) all of the above.

14. Insurance should be tailored to the particular business and should take into consideration (indicate all applicable)
    (a) property damage.
    (b) loss of revenues.
    (c) extra expenses resulting from the disaster.
    (d) vacation plans.

Review Questions

1. What is a resilient economy?
2. What two things does land ownership consist of?
3. Can a community completely control the viability of a local economy?
4. What is a factor following a disaster that may have long term impacts on resilience?
5. What does community resiliency have to do with economics?
6. Describe why business protection plans are important.
7. Name three elements that a comprehensive disaster preparedness and mitigation plan should contain.
8. Why is hazard awareness important for businesses?
9. Describe the positive and negative aspects of hazards insurance as a mitigation action for businesses.
10. How can a local jurisdiction's mitigation plan contribute to economic resilience?

Applying This Chapter

1. Imagine that you have just inherited a business from a somewhat foggy relative in a community you are not familiar with. What steps would you take to make your newly acquired business resilient to natural hazards?

2. Still focusing on the inherited business: what are some of the mitigation actions that you might consider?

3. In this same situation, what factors would you consider in choosing an insurance policy?

4. After moving to this community, how would you rely on the community to make you less vulnerable to the next natural hazard event? How would you contribute to the community's hazard mitigation efforts as a member of the business sector?

5. Imagine that you are a local economic development director and have been invited to give a speech to the local chamber of commerce on "Building a Resilient Community." Outline such a speech.

6. Imagine that you are a city manager. What sort of policies, programs, and projects would you promulgate to insure that the business community in your jurisdiction was moving toward resilience?

YOU TRY IT

READY . . . Set . . . Go!

Natural hazards are a part of the natural environment and will be with us forever. There are indications that disasters resulting from the impact of natural hazards on the built environment are increasing in frequency and magnitude. This means, of course, that businesses may be impacted more heavily than in the past. Think of possible careers that this generates. Explore the Internet to find possibilities in business administration, management, continuity planning, insurance, and so forth.

Mock Interview

Contact a local business owner and discuss with them their business contingency plans for natural hazards in your community. What are they doing to be prepared? Are they taking any mitigation measures? Are they concerned about disaster striking their business? What types of insurance do they have? What help from the community do they desire?

Turning Lemons into Lemonade!

As a kid, did you ever run your own lemonade stand? If you were to start your own business today (whether it be selling lemonade or otherwise), what from this chapter would you incorporate into your business location, design, and policies?

10

RISK ASSESSMENT
Identifying Hazards and Assessing Vulnerability

Starting Point

Go to www.wiley.com/college/schwab to assess your knowledge of identifying hazards and assessing vulnerability.
Determine where you need to concentrate your effort.

What You'll Learn in This Chapter

▲ The purpose of a risk assessment
▲ The steps of the risk assessment process
▲ Sources of data to carry out a risk assessment
▲ Types of mapping and data collection
▲ The purpose of a hazard profile
▲ The three tasks involved in inventorying assets and populations
▲ Ways of estimating hazard loss
▲ The role of future development and land use trends
▲ Ways in which communities make use of risk assessment information

After Studying This Chapter, You'll Be Able To

▲ Analyze the role of risk assessment in hazard mitigation and preparedness
▲ Appraise the probability of a hazard
▲ Compare the differences between inventories for natural hazards and manmade hazards
▲ Estimate hazard losses using risk assessment programs
▲ Identify where undeveloped areas intersect with hazard areas
▲ Examine the advantages of a mitigation plan that is based on a risk assessment

Goals and Outcomes

▲ Select tools to use during hazard risk assessment
▲ Choose tools to inventory community assets and estimate losses
▲ Assess vulnerability using hazard maps
▲ Collaborate with others to identify community practices that may increase future vulnerability
▲ Support the need for mitigation actions to reduce community vulnerability
▲ Evaluate hazard risk assessment strategies used by communities

INTRODUCTION

Communities that are resilient to the impacts of natural hazards are not built by chance. The decisions we make about how and where to build determine how successful we are at avoiding disasters. This chapter explains how a risk assessment informs us about the hazards we face, so that we can choose the most appropriate mitigation and preparedness strategies in the effort to become more resilient. A risk assessment consists of several different elements, or steps. To conduct a thorough risk assessment, the community must first identify the hazards that could affect that particular jurisdiction. There must then be a determination of how likely these hazards are, as well as their potential intensity and severity. The community must also assess its level of vulnerability to the hazards identified. Assessing vulnerability includes identifying the people and property that could suffer harm, estimating losses in dollar figures, and predicting who or what could be affected in the future. The final step involves assembling and analyzing the relevant data and information in order to form conclusions as to whether the level of risk the community faces is considered acceptable or unacceptable. Each step in the risk assessment process provides additional information to use in creating local mitigation and preparedness strategies. When completed, a careful risk assessment allows the community to direct mitigation efforts to where they are most needed, as proposed in the local hazard mitigation plan.

10.1 The Purpose of a Risk Assessment

Risk assessment is the process of defining which hazards could impact a community and describing how these hazards could affect people and property. A risk assessment is most often performed as part of a comprehensive hazard mitigation planning process, which uses data obtained during the risk assessment to formulate policies and strategies based on community capabilities and resources (we discuss mitigation strategies in Chapter 12). States, local governments, and Native American tribes are required under the Disaster Mitigation Act of 2000 to prepare an all-hazards mitigation plan to be eligible for certain federal disaster assistance and mitigation funding. The risk assessment is one of the required steps in preparing such a plan. See Chapter 13 for a discussion of the mitigation planning process.

This chapter describes how a typical risk assessment is carried out and how the information may be put to most effective use for reducing community vulnerability to hazards. We focus on mitigation plans prepared at the local level here; while there a few different steps for state-level plans, in general the process is similar for all risk assessments. Many of the steps described in this chapter are based on risk assessment procedure as outlined by the Federal Emergency Management Agency (FEMA) in guidance materials designed to help communities and states prepare hazard mitigation plans under the Disaster Mitigation Act of 2000. Therefore, this chapter closely follows the FEMA publication *State and Local Mitigation Planning How-to Guide: Understanding Your Risks: Identifying Hazards and Estimating Losses*,[1] which is available free of charge online at www.fema.gov/plan/mitplanning/howto2.shtm. This chapter also relies heavily on material produced by the North Carolina Division of Emergency Management (DEM) to assist local governments prepare hazard mitigation plans, including *Keeping Hazards From Becoming Disasters: A Mitigation Planning Guidebook for Local Governments*, available online at the North Carolina DEM website[2].

Throughout this chapter, we use a fictitious community named Hazard City to illustrate the risk assessment process. As you go over the material in this chapter,

HAZARD CITY

Hazard City, nestled in the Mountain-Coastal Territory of Atlantic State, is home to 10,000 residents. It's an area of incredible beauty, with mountains, forests, a lovely river, and fine white sand beaches. Hazard City is undergoing tremendous population growth. The investment in public and private infrastructure has been in the millions of dollars for the past five straight years. New schools and shopping centers are being built, and roads and water and sewer lines are being planned for areas not yet developed, including the marsh near the river, which is slated to be drained and filled in soon. New subdivisions are springing up to accommodate families moving into the area. Investors are considering building a large hotel on the beach to attract more tourists. Developers, the mayor, and the town's tax assessor are ecstatic.

Over the years, however, natural hazards such as Hurricane Zelda in 2000, devastating tornadoes in 1991, 1997, and 2001, as well as annual, intense forest fires have impacted local residents, businesses, and the tourism industry. Flooding threatens Hazard City every year, as the river swells its banks with melted snow from the mountains. In 1999, back-to-back snowstorms shut the city down for nearly a week. Power was out for two weeks in some neighborhoods, and roads were impassable for days. Occasionally, mild earthquakes can be felt in the area, although no damage from quakes has been recorded since 1910, when a grain elevator just outside of town was toppled. Periodic landslides have closed some of the mountain roads with rock and debris.

The scars of Zelda, a powerful Category 3 hurricane, can still be seen throughout the city. In some neighborhoods, many of the damaged homes have not been fully repaired, where roofs and siding were ripped off by high winds and entire buildings were uprooted. A majority of the town's small businesses have never re-opened. The coastal areas took the brunt of the storm, and numerous oceanfront lots have yet to be redeveloped.

FOR EXAMPLE

Statewide Risk Assessment Methodology for the North Carolina Natural Hazard Mitigation Plan

North Carolina residents do not have to go back very far in history to remember the devastating effects that natural disasters can have on their livelihoods, their homes, and their families. Hurricanes Isabel (2003), Floyd (1999), and Fran (1996) brought flooding, severe wind damage, and the loss of life and property. Risk assessment—the identification of vulnerabilities to natural hazards in a community—cannot prevent these hazards from occurring, but it can help minimize future damage.

In 2004, FEMA approved the State of North Carolina's hazard mitigation plan, which includes strategies to reduce the state's vulnerability to multiple natural hazards. The foundation for the state's plan was based on the background data compiled during the risk assessment, a process that involved the review of historical records, examination of damage reports from past hazard events, and extensive discussions with meteorological and geological experts to identify, describe, and assess the various natural hazards that affect North Carolina. Once the background data was assembled, the state applied HAZUS-MH, FEMA's loss estimation database, to incorporate the scope, frequency, intensity and destructive potential of all the natural hazards. This process was essential to allow the state to focus on those hazards that posed the most severe threats to special populations, economic activity, infrastructure, critical facilities, and environmental resources.

you may wish to imagine yourself the emergency manager of this community, so you can visualize going through the steps as both a concerned citizen and as a professional tasked to improve your community's resiliency to hazards. Please read the Hazard City Case Study before you begin this chapter.

SELF-CHECK

- Define **risk assessment**.
- Discuss the purpose of a hazard risk assessment.
- List the hazards that confront Hazard City.

10.2 Steps in the Risk Assessment Process

In this chapter, we describe the risk assessment process followed by our fictitious community, Hazard City, to determine its level of risk to both natural and man-made hazards. Each local community is unique, and no two towns or counties would carry out an identical risk assessment. However, there are certain steps common to all hazard risk assessments, and we will cover those main points in this chapter. Figure 10-1 shows the steps we will describe in the following sections.

The steps of the risk assessment process are applicable to all sorts of hazards. There are some unique aspects of the hazard profiling, asset inventory, and loss estimation steps for man-made hazards, but in general, a similar process to assess risk is used whether the community is dealing with natural hazards, threats of terrorism, or hazardous material accidents.

Figure 10-1

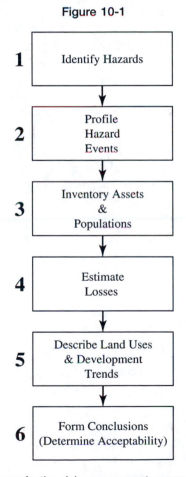

Steps in the risk assessment process.

10.2.1 Mapping and Data Collection

Much of the information gathered during the risk assessment process is best displayed on maps, which illustrate the geographic area that could be affected by various hazards. There are many methods of creating hazard assessment maps, ranging from simple traced maps to elaborate geographic information systems (GIS) products. Both types of maps will illustrate local hazard-prone areas and locate important community features. **HAZUS** (Hazards U.S.) is a computer modeling system that can also be helpful in creating maps and gathering and analyzing data for many of the steps in the risk assessment process. HAZUS was developed by FEMA to estimate losses from earthquake hazards, high winds, and flooding, but it also contains useful information for preparing inventories and mapping community features vulnerable to other hazards as well.

Geographic information system (GIS) is software that can be used on a desktop computer by users with varying degrees of skill and training and at varying levels of sophistication, from basic applications to sophisticated analysis. In essence, GIS capitalizes on the fact that everything on earth has a unique location (a specific address) in space, allowing the user to create layers of spatial data and superimpose them on one another. For example, maps that show where residential structures are located in a community can be overlaid with flood maps, thus illustrating the relationship between the two layers. The GIS software captures this spatial information, helping us to visualize correlations, analyze relationships, and identify patterns over time and space. This information can then be leveraged to formulate conclusions and make decisions about the conditions present.

It is important to remember during the data gathering stage that the quality of the information source directly affects the quality of the assessment and its results. Raw data that is not entirely accurate or complete should not prevent a community from carrying out a useful risk assessment. FEMA requires that local and state governments use "best available data," a phrase which reflects the fact that very rarely does a community have access to perfect information. However, communities should always make note of the source of the data used, its date, and any other metadata (data about data) that could indicate potential errors,

FOR EXAMPLE

Problems with Out-of-Date Maps

Following Hurricane Floyd in 1999, it was very apparent in portions of eastern North Carolina that the existing flood maps were out-of-date. Entire communities were flooded, even though many of these areas did not show up as flood-risk areas on the official maps. The state of North Carolina has since begun the long and expensive process of updating and digitizing (computerizing) the state's flood maps in order to more accurately indicate the location of flood risk areas.

gaps, inaccuracies, or other imperfections. The end results of any data analysis, including (or especially) an assessment of hazard risk should always be viewed with a critical eye that acknowledges possible flaws.

10.2.2 Creating a Base Map

Hazard mapping begins with a base map, upon which hazard-specific information can be superimposed. A **base map** shows the basic topography, physical elements, and infrastructure of the community. A good base map for hazard assessment purposes will include political boundaries, such as city limits, extraterritorial jurisdiction, and ownership patterns; streets and roads; water features, including rivers, streams, and watersheds; and other natural features such as wetlands, beaches, and steep slopes. The base map should also indicate where development is currently located, as well as the location of infrastructure, such as water and sewer lines, that is scheduled to be laid in the future. The majority of these features can be found on local and state highway maps, local land use and zoning maps, in capital improvement plans, and from aerial photography.

Much of the area inside the town limits of Hazard City is already developed. But there are also areas that are not developed, and water and sewer lines will be located in some of these places soon (scheduled infrastructure). The map in Figure 10-2 displays the river running through the town limits, the beach area, and the main roads. We refer back to the main features of Hazard City as we conduct a risk assessment for the community throughout the remainder of this chapter.

Figure 10-2

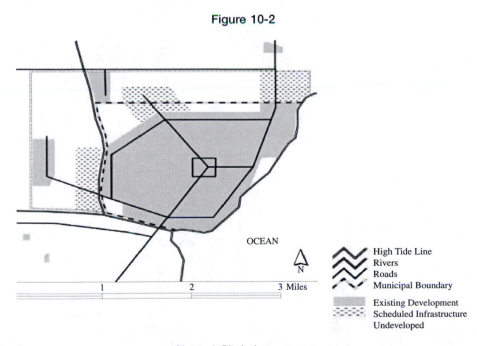

Hazard City's base map.

SELF-CHECK

- List the steps in the risk assessment process.
- Define **HAZUS** and **GIS**.
- List several of the basic layers that would help create a good base map.

10.3 Risk Assessment Step One: Identifying Hazards

The first step in the risk assessment process asks the question: "What kinds of natural hazards can affect the community?" **Hazard identification** involves listing all the hazards that might occur in the local region and providing a description of each one. Some hazards occur quite infrequently, while others are regularly recurring events in a community. Even very large hazard events may occur in rapid succession. For example, during the 2004 hurricane season, Florida experienced four major hurricanes within the span of a few weeks. The hurricane season of 2005 saw a similar rapid sequence of huge coastal storms, including Hurricanes Katrina, Rita, and Wilma. Hazard identification involves researching all potential hazards and including them all in a list of possible events.

Some hazards may be chronic (regularly occurring but not causing extensive damage each time). These repetitive occurrences can lead to a cumulative impact over time, such as flooding or landslides that can result from numerous rainfalls of average amount. Other hazards may be less regular, but can have more catastrophic impacts when they do occur, such as large hurricanes and earthquakes.

10.3.1 Finding the Information

There is a wide variety of information sources useful for hazard identification. Research into the community's past can indicate the types of hazards that typically occur in the local area. Newspapers, weather reports, past disaster declarations and other historical records from community archives can contain a treasure trove of information. Interviews of long-time residents can also be a good source of information about the types of hazards that have struck the community in the past.

Collecting old accounts of hazard events will provide an overview of the major hazards in the area, but contacts should be widened in order to obtain information about all the possible hazards, not just the "big ones" that community members easily recall or that made major headlines at the time. Local plans and documents that are publicly available often contain information about hazards, even though hazards might not be the focus of these documents. For example, transportation, environmental, or public works reports could have references to local hazard possibilities. Local comprehensive plans, land use plans, and building codes and regulations often contain information about hazards as well. Personnel in local departments may also be able to provide information about hazards that are likely in the area. Police, fire, rescue, and emergency management workers who deal with emergencies on a regular basis are also familiar with hazard possibilities.

The search for information about potential hazards should be expanded beyond local sources. Some hazards are more common in large regions of the country or throughout the state, and these regional hazard possibilities should be included in the hazard identification as well. For example, communities located in "tornado alley" in the Midwest will likely experience more tornadoes in any given year than other parts of the United States. The assumption is simply based on the fact that tornadoes have often impacted that area in the past. State and federal agencies have databanks and other records of hazards on a county or regional level. Many government agencies maintain hazard-specific websites, including state emergency management offices, the National Oceanic and Atmospheric Administration (NOAA), FEMA, the U.S. Geological Survey (USGS), the National Hurricane Center, the National Weather Service, and others.

10.3.2 Finding Information on Man-Made Hazards

Terrorist attacks and technological disasters occur infrequently enough in the United States that there may be few relevant records that can help determine what man-made hazards could affect a local community. The Department of Homeland Security (DHS), the Federal Bureau of Investigation (FBI) and the U.S. Department of State issue annual reports on terrorism activity domestically and around the world. State emergency agencies and environmental resource departments, as well as the U.S. Environmental Protection Agency (EPA) are sources for data on hazardous material incidents. Also, in many communities, plans are in place to respond to numerous types of technological hazards, and these plans—and the people who develop them—may be valuable sources of information about human-induced risks. Such plans include emergency operations plans, chemical stockpile contingency plans, toxic release inventory reports, community right-to-know reports, local emergency planning committee files (LEPC, as described in Chapter 11), and other types of emergency and notification documents.

SELF-CHECK

- Define **hazard identification.**
- List sources of information for identifying potential natural hazard events.
- List sources of information for identifying potential man-made hazard events.

FOR EXAMPLE

Describing the Hazards in Hazard City

Review the description of Hazard City at the beginning of this chapter. The types of hazards that would be listed in the hazard identification step of the community's risk assessment include hurricane, flood, tornado, forest fire, severe winter storm, and earthquake. Of course, in reality, additional sources of information to complete the hazard identification step for Hazard City would be available, including government websites for the region, interviews with residents, a review of local documents and plans, reports of municipal employees, old weather reports and archives, and so forth. In fact, information overload is often experienced when planners and emergency managers begin gathering information about local hazards. It can be difficult to determine when to stop the data gathering stage and move on to the next step in the planning process.

10.4 Risk Assessment Step Two: Profiling Hazards

A hazard profile asks the question: "What is the potential impact of identified hazards on the community?" The **hazard profile** helps determine how each hazard will affect the community, how often each hazard may occur, and where the hazards might take place. It is important to ascertain whether the hazards the community has identified are cyclical, seasonal, or otherwise predictable. It is also important to know the location and geographic extent of each hazard type. Certain portions of the community will be affected on a regular basis in identifiable areas, such as floodplains surrounding streams and rivers. Other types of hazards, such as earthquakes or snowstorms, will affect the entire community. Hazards of various intensities will also affect the community in different ways. For example, a tornado that ranks 4 or 5 on the Fujita scale would probably cause more damage than a class 1 or 2 tornado (see Chapter 2 for a description of the Fujita tornado rating scale). This is important information for the hazard profile.

10.4.1 Creating a Hazard History

A good way to begin the hazard profile is to provide information on past occurrences of each hazard. These hazard histories can provide a snapshot of specific events from which we can make some general assumptions about future hazard events based on patterns and trends. A community that has experienced a tornado in the past might assume that another could occur in that locality. On the other hand, the fact that a community has experienced an average of three

> ## FOR EXAMPLE
>
> ### Hazard City's Hazard History
>
> Instead of merely mentioning that Hurricane Zelda occurred in 2000, the hazard history for Hazard City should indicate the critical features of Zelda, including wind speeds, depth of flooding, height of storm surge, as well as a description of property damages and the number of deaths and injuries. A complete hazard history would also indicate longer-lasting impacts of a past hazard event, such as whether businesses closed, either permanently or temporarily, whether people were displaced and moved away, and other pertinent facts about how the event affected the local economy, social networks, and the built environment.

tornadoes each year for the last thirty years does not mean that a tornado will hit any particular point in the locality in the following year. It is clear that there are limitations to using historical data to estimate events that are likely to occur in the future. Nevertheless, a hazard history can provide a good sense of what lies within the range of possibilities. Sources of information of past occurrences are often the same as the sources used to create the hazard identification list in the previous step, such as archived news accounts, weather records, and interviews with local residents and community officials. The hazard history developed during the profile step provides more extensive information with details about how each historical event actually affected the community.

The local hazard history should contain a description of all the elements of a past hazard event, as well as how long the hazard lasted, how severe the event was, and what damage resulted. Some hazards are single-force events, such as tornadoes that bring high winds. Other types of hazards are made up of multiple elements, such as a hurricane, which can involve the combined threats of high winds, storm surge, and flooding. Each of these hazard characteristics should be described in detail for each event mentioned in the hazard history.

10.4.2 Identifying the Extent of Each Hazard

The hazard profile must assess the extent of each potential hazard listed during the identification step, which involves identifying the magnitude and intensity.

▲ **Magnitude:** A measure of the strength of an event.
▲ **Intensity:** A measure of the effects of a hazard at a particular place.

The estimates of hazard extent should be based on local historical evidence and regional data. The potential extent of a hazard may be described using relative terms or the profile may refer to standardized intensity scales (see Table 10-1). Reliable hazard rating scales include the Saffir-Simpson Scale that categorizes hurricanes, the Fujita rating scale for tornadoes, and the Modified Mercalli Scale that ranks earthquakes (see descriptions of these rating scales in Chapters 2 and 3). Flood severity is often measured in terms of water depth and velocity. For wildfires, severity can be expressed as fire line intensity (a measure of the rate at which a fire releases heat, or the unit length of the fire line), the rate of fire spread (feet per second), and flame length. For other types of hazards with no formal rating scale (ice storms, for instance), severity may be indicated through general terms, such as mild, moderate, or severe.

The extent of a hazard event also includes a measure of its potential impact, which is a combination of the magnitude of the event, how large an area within the community is affected, and the amount of human activity. Table 10-1 can help determine various levels of impact that a hazard could have on a community.

Table 10-1: Hazard Impact Levels and Effects on Communities

Level	% Area Affected	Impact
Catastrophic	More than 50%	Multiple deaths. Complete shutdown of facilities for 30 days or more. More than 50% of property severely damaged.
Critical	25%–50%	Multiple severe injuries. Complete shutdown of critical facilities for at least 2 weeks. More than 25% of property severely damaged.
Limited	10%–25%	Some injuries. Complete shutdown of critical facilities for more than 1 week. More than 10% of property severely damaged.
Negligible	Less than 10%	Minor injuries. Minimal quality-of-life impact. Shutdown of critical facilities and services for 24 hours or less. Less than 10% of property severely damaged.

Table 10-2: Likelihood of a Hazard Based on Frequency of Occurrence

Likelihood	Frequency of Occurrence
Highly likely	Near 100% probability in the next year.
Likely	Between 10% and 100% probability in the next 10 years, or at least one chance in the next 10 years.
Possible	Between 1% and 10% probability in the next year, or at least one chance in the next 100 years.
Unlikely	Less than 1% probability in the next year, or less than one chance in the next 100 years.

10.4.3 Determining the Probability of Each Hazard

Some hazards are more likely to occur in a particular community than others. An estimate of **probability**, or likelihood of occurrence, is not an actual prediction, but based on regional data and local historical evidence the hazard profile can indicate whether each hazard is likely or unlikely. Table 10-2 is used to determine likelihood, based on frequency of occurrence.

Standardized information is available to help determine the probability of some types of hazards within a range of frequencies or **recurrence intervals**. For instance, the probability of a flood is based on a statistical chance of a particular size flood (expressed in cubic feet per second of water flow) occurring in any given year. The annual flood is usually considered the single greatest event expected to occur on an annual basis. The flood that has a 1% probability (1 in 100) of being equaled or exceeded in any year is referred to as the 100-year flood. This term is simply a convenient way to express probability. It should not be interpreted to mean a flood that happens exactly once every 100 years, nor does it imply that once a 100-year flood occurs there is little risk of another 100-year flood occurring in the near future. To the contrary, changes in climate conditions, such as those caused by El Niño often result in clusters of floods that occur over relatively short times in the same location.

10.4.4 Identifying the Location of Each Hazard

The hazard profile must identify the location—the geographic area—that will be affected by each potential hazard. Some types of hazards occur in fairly predictable areas. For instance, floodplains and steep slopes (where landslides can occur) can be identified and described geographically. Other types of hazards are not site-specific and cannot be geographically defined so readily, such as tornadoes, ice storms, and severe winds. For these types of hazards, the entire community is considered exposed.

The most effective means of identifying the location of potential hazards (for those hazards that can be geographically defined) is to create or obtain a map that shows the hazard boundaries. Many types of hazards are mapped by state and federal agencies and made available to local communities. For instance, Flood Insurance Rate Maps (FIRMs) are provided by FEMA to communities participating in the National Flood Insurance Program (NFIP). Other commonly mapped hazards include earthquakes, coastal erosion, storm surge inundation areas, wind speed zones, tsunamis, landslides, and wildfires. The U.S. Nuclear Regulatory Commission (NRC), which regulates all nuclear power facilities in the country, can provide information about Nuclear Planning Zones (NPZ), which are safety and evacuation zones delineated around all nuclear power plants.

Mapping Hazard City's Hazards

The emergency manager of Hazard City has obtained many hazard maps from state and federal agencies, including the town's FIRM, storm surge inundation maps, erosion rate maps, topographical maps (for steep slope and landslide areas), seismic zone maps, and wildfire maps. The community has also chosen to show the historic dates of major flood events that occurred outside the official floodplain. By layering all these maps onto the base map, the Hazard City emergency manager has created a map as shown in Figure 10-3 that shows the boundaries of all the city's potential hazards.

Figure 10-3

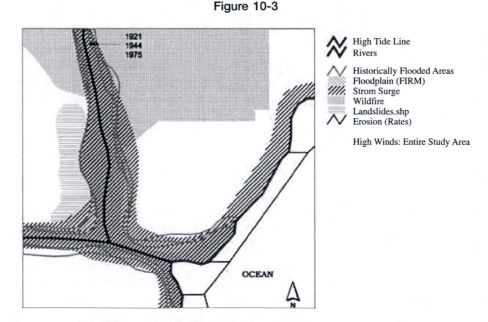

Map of boundaries of all of Hazard City's potential hazards.

HAZARD RISK ASSESSMENT IN THE STATE OF LOUISIANA

Before Katrina struck Louisiana on August 29, 2005, the risk of hurricanes in the area was well known and thoroughly documented (see Figure 10-4). The Hurricane Center at Louisiana State University (LSU) ran computer-generated SLOSH models (an acronym for Sea, Lake, and Overland Surges from Hurricanes) in 2003 that showed a significant risk of flooding for all of New Orleans with the occurrence of a Category 3 hurricane. In addition to the models run by LSU, many other models also forecasted the flooding of New Orleans and surrounding parishes. Numerous news and informational articles had been published in popular periodicals over the years, including an article published in *National Geographic* that predicted with eerie accuracy the effects of a hurricane such as Katrina on New Orleans.[3] *Scientific American* magazine

Figure 10-4

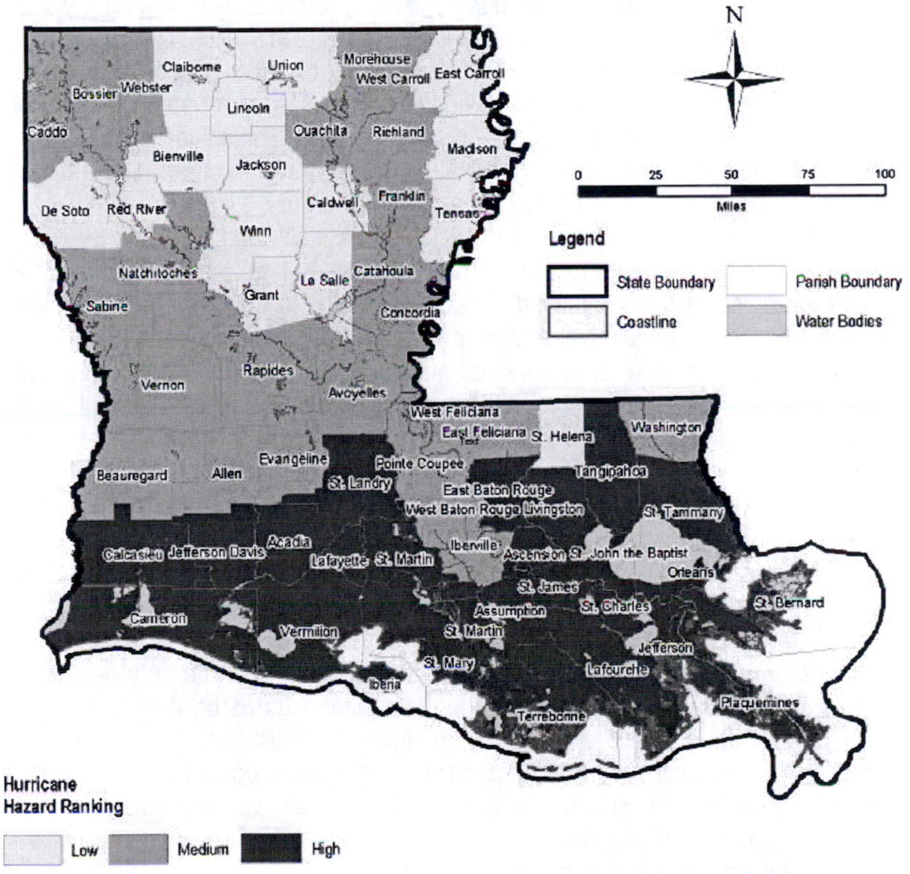

Maps from the State of Louisiana hazard mitigation plan risk assessment, April 2005.

had published a report on a similar theme in October 2001. But one of most telling indicators of what might happen during a large hurricane in the Gulf Coast region came from actual historic events.

Flooding of catastrophic proportions had occurred in New Orleans during Hurricane Betsy in 1965, the descriptions of which sound much like the aftermath of Katrina. It was reported after Betsy that 5000 square miles of Louisiana were inundated with flood waters, including extensive flooding due to levee breaches in Orleans, Plaquemines, and St. Bernard Parishes; thousands were left homeless; entire buildings were swept away; and over 80 people died and 17,000 people were injured. Hurricane Audrey in 1957 landed as a Category 4 storm with winds of 150 miles per hour and 12-foot storm surge, killing between 390 and 550 people. Several other well known hurricanes have hit Louisiana over the years as well, including Andrew, Camille, and the August Hurricane of 1940.

In addition to the forecasting models, published articles, and past history, it was also well known that the loss of wetlands in southern Louisiana had accelerated to a point that the area's natural buffers against storm surge and flooding were disappearing at an unprecedented rate.[4] Ecologists and coastal managers warned that the disappearance of the region's extensive system of marsh and wetlands increased the vulnerability of development in the area many fold. It was also common knowledge that levees surrounding the city of New Orleans were built by the U.S. Army Corps of Engineers to "Standard Project Hurricane" levels, a building standard that is not intended to withhold storm surges above those caused by a strong Category 3 hurricane.[5]

These existing indicators all served to identify risks and warn the public about the destructive potential of future hurricanes in Louisiana. In addition, the State of Louisiana had conducted a risk assessment to guide the policy making process of the state as required by the Disaster Mitigation Act of 2000.[6] The Louisiana risk assessment is based on statewide data for several different natural hazards. As shown on state hazard maps, risk was classified as high (red), medium (orange), or low (yellow) for each natural hazard throughout the state. The hurricane hazard risk map shows the majority of the southern half of the state as falling into the high risk category, while the risk of storm surge hazard is much more confined (directly surrounding New Orleans in Jefferson and Orleans Parishes). The subsidence and levee failure hazard maps focus on the very southern portion of the state. All state hazard maps display hazards related to flooding, and several of these hazards are specifically focused on the areas surrounding New Orleans. This spatial information can be very helpful in the long term for implementation of the state plan in terms of identifying high risk areas, setting mitigation goals and priorities, and discovering gaps in knowledge about certain hazard potentials. As Louisiana continues to recover from the impacts of Hurricane Katrina, updated risk assessment data will help inform future mitigation policies and action strategies to lower vulnerability of the coastal region to future tropical storm events.[7]

10.4.5 Profiling Man-Made Hazards

There are significant differences between natural and man-made hazards when carrying out the profile step, particularly with regard to terrorism. The most poignant difference lies in the fact that terrorists have the ability to choose among targets and tactics, designing their attack to maximize the chances of achieving their objective. Similarly, accidents, systems failures, and other mishaps are also largely unforeseeable. This increases the difficulty in identifying how and where these hazards may occur. We do know from comprehensive reviews of terrorist activities in the United States that man-made hazards impact not only large cities, but can also strike small to mid-sized communities as well. Where within a particular community a man-made hazard could occur depends upon the types of potential targets or accident sites that exist. Terrorist incidents generally occur at a specific location such as a building rather than encompassing a wider area such as a floodplain, although the intentional or accidental release of chemical and biological agents could be distributed widely throughout a community in a relatively short amount of time.

Despite the difficulty in predicting and locating the occurrence of man-made disasters, a profile for various man-made hazards can be useful for analysis and decision-making purposes. A variety of resources, including charts and tables available from FEMA and other agencies, provide information about event profiles for terrorism and technological hazards. These profiles include information about the characteristics of man-made hazards, such as:

▲ **Application Mode:** describes the human act or unintended event that causes the hazard (for example, detonation of an explosive device, rupture of a chemical storage container).

▲ **Duration:** the length of time the hazard is present on the target (for example, the duration of a tornado may be just minutes, but a chemical warfare agent such as mustard gas can persist for days or weeks under the right conditions).

▲ **Dynamic/Static Characteristic:** describes the tendency of the hazard's effects to either expand, contract, or remain confined (for example, the physical destruction caused by an earthquake is generally confined to the place in which it occurs and does not usually get worse unless there are aftershocks or secondary impacts; in contrast, a cloud of chlorine gas leaking from a storage tank can change location by drifting with the wind and can diminish in danger by dissipating over time).

▲ **Mitigating Conditions:** characteristics of the target and its physical environment that can reduce the effects of a hazard (for example, earthen berms can provide protection from bombs, exposure to sunlight can reduce the effectiveness of some biological agents).

▲ **Exacerbating Conditions:** characteristics that can enhance or magnify the effects of the hazard (for example, depressions or low areas can trap heavy vapors; obstacles in the street such as parked cars, mail boxes, etc. can provide concealment opportunities for explosive devices).

These hazard profiles can provide useful information for assessing the various risks associated with man-made hazards. However, more important for the purposes of hazard mitigation than details about the various agents' characteristics are the ways in which they can impact the built environment and human populations, and what actions can be taken to reduce or eliminate the resulting damage. The various consequences of these events are generally familiar to emergency management professionals who already specialize in them: injuries and deaths, damage to buildings, contamination of the environment, breakdowns in services and systems, and other impacts.

10.4.6 Completing Steps One and Two

At the conclusion of the hazard identification and profile steps, the community will have created a map indicating the areas impacted by each hazard type or a report containing information regarding the characteristics of hazard events affecting the community. In some cases, such as those involving flooding, both types of information will be available. The importance of hazard mapping becomes clear during the next step of the risk assessment process, inventorying assets and populations.

SELF-CHECK

- What are the three major questions associated with the hazard profile step in the risk assessment process?
- Review ways of determining the probability of a hazard.
- List several characteristics of man-made hazards that are important to include in a hazard profile.

10.5 Risk Assessment Step Three: Inventorying Vulnerable Assets and Populations

Steps one and two of the risk assessment process determine whether a community might experience various types and intensities of hazards, what the level of impact those hazards might have, and where within the community those hazards are likely to occur. Step three helps answer the question: "What will be affected by the hazard event?"

During this step the community will assess the number of people and amount of existing assets that are at risk from the identified hazards. **Assets** are all those features of a community that have value, including buildings, facilities (such as wastewater treatment plants), infrastructure (roads, bridges, etc.), historic and cultural landmarks, and other important local resources. Combined with Steps four and five, the community will also be able to estimate losses to assets and determine whether the locality is encouraging or allowing additional development to take place in locations that have been identified as unsafe. In other words, by building on the information gathered during the previous steps, and by following the subsequent steps, the community can gauge its level of **vulnerability** to hazards, both now and in the future. As always during the risk assessment process, it is important to remain focused on the ultimate goal—creating and implementing mitigation and preparedness measures that will reduce vulnerability.

10.5.1 Tasks in Step Three

To create a complete inventory of assets and populations, we gather and analyze information in three stages or tasks, and compile the information into a spreadsheet, chart, GIS, or other type of report.

- ▲ **Task One:** Identify assets throughout the community. This community-wide perspective is useful because some types of hazards can affect the entire area, such as earthquakes, ice storms, and tornadoes. It is also useful for indicating the types of land uses that are prevalent in non-hazardous areas of the community, so that if possible, the community can steer future growth and development to these safer areas.
- ▲ **Task Two:** Review assets and populations that are located in mapped hazard areas.
- ▲ **Task Three:** Determine what proportion of total community assets are located in known hazard areas. This task indicates the percentage of community assets that is vulnerable to hazards as compared to the rest of the community.

10.5.2 Sources of Information

Sources of information to carry out the asset inventory vary from community to community. Some communities have elaborate data management and GIS capabilities. These communities may also wish to use HAZUS to assist in inventorying assets and populations. Other communities may rely more on local property tax records, land use plans, or aerial photography (for information on buildings) and U.S. Census data (for information on populations). Some communities' emergency 911 systems, especially those that are contained in a GIS format, can also provide valuable information about the location of populations and assets.

10.5.3 Task One: Inventorying Assets and Populations in the Community

The first task in the inventory step involves creating a list and description of assets located throughout the community, identifying each one on a map, and tallying up the total amount of assets. Local assets include properties such as residential and commercial buildings, religious and nonprofit centers, and industrial or manufacturing plants. Particularly important to identify are the community's **critical facilities** that are necessary for the health and safety of the population, especially following a hazard event. These include hospitals and clinics, police, fire and emergency operations stations, and evacuation centers. **Lifeline utilities** and other infrastructure should also be listed, including water and sewer systems, communications lines, energy services, as well as major transportation routes. **Essential facilities** that aid in recovery following a disaster should also be included, such as government and civic buildings, major employers, banks, schools, daycare centers, and certain commercial establishments such as grocery stores, hardware stores, and gas stations. Hazardous materials facilities that manufacture, store, or process industrial/hazardous materials, such as corrosives, explosives, flammable materials, radioactive materials, toxins, and so forth should also be identified. Data from HAZUS, tax records, aerial photography, or local planning documents are useful for gathering this information and displaying it on a map.

Estimate the Value of Each Asset in the Community

The estimated value of the buildings and facilities in the entire community must be determined, and the information must be recorded on a chart or spreadsheet. Property tax records provide information about the privately-owned buildings in the jurisdiction, while government records provide estimates of the insurance or replacement value of public buildings and facilities.

Count the Number of People in the Community

The community-wide inventory will also include an estimate of the number of people that live and work in the area. Current census data is a reliable source of information for these figures, as are state and local population records. The inventory should note whether the local population tends to fluctuate seasonally, so that the community is adequately protected year round. For instance, tourist destinations can attract visitors during certain months of the year, significantly swelling the population that could be affected by a hazard event, such as beach towns that experience huge influxes of visitors during the summer, which coincides with the height of the hurricane season.

10.5.4 Task Two: Inventorying Assets and Populations in Each Hazard Area

The hazard areas that were identified and mapped in step one—such as floodplains and landslide areas—provide the basis for this task, which involves a more detailed inventory of the number and value of buildings and the populations that could be affected in each one of the hazard areas. For those types of hazards that cannot be geographically defined (such as tornadoes and ice storms), asset information gathered during task one regarding the entire community is sufficient.

Total the Number of Assets in Each Hazard Area

The total number of each type of building and facility inside each hazard area must be totaled. A tax assessment map, aerial photography, HAZUS, or GIS can be used to establish the number and location of buildings in the hazard area. Record the information in a spreadsheet, GIS map layer, or other report.

Estimate the Value Assets in Each Hazard Area

GIS, HAZUS, public documents, or tax records can be used to estimate the total value of the buildings and facilities inside each hazard area. The approximate replacement value for each type of building, accessible through local tax assessment records (for privately-owned buildings) and government records (for public buildings and facilities), indicates the cost of rebuilding these structures if they are damaged severely or destroyed by a hazard event. Insurance replacement value is also a good indication of asset value for risk assessment inventory purposes, although these figures may be more difficult to obtain for privately-owned structures. Record the information in a spreadsheet or other report.

Estimate Current Population Numbers in Each Hazard Area

This task estimates current population numbers for people living and working in the hazard area, using HAZUS, census data, or state and local records. Particularly vulnerable populations such as non-English speakers, the elderly, special needs, or impoverished citizens may require special response assistance or medical care after a disaster, and their location should be noted. Record this information on a spreadsheet or other report.

10.5.5 Task Three: Calculating the Proportion of Assets Located in Hazard Areas

Task three requires calculation of the proportion of assets and their values that are located in hazard areas as compared to the community total. This task is carried out by dividing the number or value in each hazard area by the total number or value in the community as a whole. For example, if 20 residential structures are located in the community and 10 of those are located in the 100-year floodplain, then 50% (10 divided by 20) of local residential structures are located in the flood hazard area. This information should be recorded on a spreadsheet or other report.

By presenting information about the percentage of the building stock (and the community tax base) that is susceptible to hazard damages, we can see by the numbers how vulnerable the community is to hazards. These figures can serve as a real eye-opener to local officials and citizens, encouraging them to financially and politically support mitigation and preparedness efforts. If the proportion of community assets that are exposed to hazards is significant, the community may be propelled to be proactive in its mitigation strategies.

Inventorying Hazard City's Assets

Table 10-3 indicates the proportion of Hazard City assets that are located in the town's flood hazard area (Table 10-3). We can see from the last row in the chart that 40% of Hazard City's structures and 42% of the town's property

Table 10-3: Hazard City Asset Inventory: Flood Hazard Area

Type of Structure	Number of Structures			Value of Structures			Number of People		
	Total # in city	# in hazard area	% in hazard area	Total $ in city	$ in hazard area	% in hazard area	Total # in city	# in hazard area	% in hazard area
Residential	2500	100	40%	250,000,000	100,000,000	40%	10,000	4000	40%
Commercial	10	8	80%	10,000,000	7,000,000	70%	570	345	61%
Industrial	0	0	0	0	0	0	0	0	0
Government	7	5	71%	7,055,000	2,555,000	36%	570	170	30%
Education	4	2	50%	6,000,000	3,000,000	50%	3000	1500	50%
Utilities	4	4	100%	4,750,000	4,750,000	100%	30	30	100%
Religious/ Non-Profit	3	1	33%	3,450,000	1,500,000	43%	351	10	0.03%
Total	2528	1020	40%	281,255,000	118,805,000	42%	14,521	6055	42%

(Note that counting the number of people that live in the residential structures and adding them to the number of people who work and go to school in the other types of buildings results in some double counting of the people who live, work, and go to school in the same area. However, it is better to overestimate rather than underestimate population numbers for purposes of a risk assessment.)

value are located in flood areas. We can also see that 42% of the town's population lives and works in the flood hazard area. This chart tells us that a very significant percentage of the town's total property value and many of its people are in danger from flooding.

10.5.6 Inventorying Assets for Man-made Hazards

Defining borders for man-made hazard areas is much more difficult than for natural hazards. Therefore, an inventory of assets in hazard-prone areas is less useful than for natural hazards. Instead, the community must use an asset-specific approach, identifying potentially at-risk critical facilities and systems in the area, and then assessing each one individually for its particular vulnerabilities. Critical infrastructure and systems that should be inventoried during this step include those whose incapacity or destruction would have a debilitating effect on the defense or economic security of the community, state, region, or nation. These critical infrastructure categories include:

▲ Food supplies, storage, and distribution systems.
▲ Water and wastewater.
▲ Public health (hospitals, medical clinics, etc.).
▲ Emergency services.
▲ Defense industries.
▲ Telecommunications.
▲ Energy (oil, gas, electric power lines, nuclear reactors).
▲ Transportation (airports, roads, railroads, etc.).
▲ Banking and finance.
▲ Chemicals and hazardous materials.
▲ Postal and shipping.

The vulnerabilities of these assets can be identified through two basic approaches: inherent vulnerability and tactical vulnerability.

▲ **Inherent vulnerability:** The way a building or facility is used, how visible it is, how accessible it is, how many people are located there, and other factors determine that asset's level of inherent vulnerability. For example, a football stadium is a setting where thousands of people gather and is relatively easy to gain entry. A terrorist may find such a target attractive because many people could be hurt during an attack. An assessment of such inherent vulnerabilities must be conducted for each asset to determine its weaknesses.

▲ **Tactical vulnerability:** The way a building is designed, built, landscaped, and engineered determines its tactical vulnerability. For example, if an

FOR EXAMPLE

Mapping Hazard City's Critical Facilities

The map in Figure 10-5 indicates where hazards intersect with critical facilities in Hazard City.

Hazard City has layered its all-hazards map over a map that shows the location of its critical facilities and we can now identify which critical facilities, roads, and development are exposed to which hazards. Note that on this map, a significant area of the town that is scheduled for infrastructure is exposed to flooding, storm surge, and landslide. Areas where development is already located are also exposed to numerous hazards, as you can see where flooding, storm surge, wildfire and landslide areas intersect with development. Note also that the entire community is subject to high winds.

HVAC system is designed so that it is not easily accessible and has security cameras aimed at it, a terrorist may be less likely to attempt to use the system as a weapon to release poisonous gas. A tactical vulnerability assessment should be completed for each asset to determine how well it is protected from attack.

10.5.7 Mapping Assets and Populations

The next step in the vulnerability assessment involves creating map overlays. Hazard maps created during step two of the risk assessment process can be overlaid on the community's base map to visualize the number and value of buildings and the populations that could be impacted in these areas. Overlay maps that show community features and the ways that hazards can affect these features can be produced by hand using a light table and transparencies, or through the use of GIS.

SELF-CHECK

- What are the three tasks associated with step three in the risk assessment process?
- Define **assets, vulnerability, inherent vulnerability,** and **tactical vulnerability.**
- Describe several types of information that you might want to gather during an inventory of hazard areas.

10.6 Risk Assessment Step Four: Estimating Potential Losses

The fourth step in the risk assessment process answers the question: "What could the community lose in a hazard event?" So far, the risk assessment has determined that one or more hazards may affect the community (step one), profiled hazard events (step two), and inventoried the assets and populations that could be damaged by a hazard event (step three). In this step, the community estimates losses using dollar amounts that indicate how the community could be impacted economically by the various hazards that threaten it. HAZUS and HAZUS-MH (Hazards United States-Multi-Hazard), the loss estimation software produced by FEMA, has been useful to many communities when carrying out this step.

A **loss estimate** assesses the level of damage that could happen to each individual asset in the inventory from each type of hazard. This involves calculating the losses that could occur to each structure, based on the building's replacement value. The loss to the contents of each structure is also added to the calculation. A very detailed loss estimate adds to this the costs that would occur when the use and function of each structure is disrupted (this occurs when the service provided in that structure would have to be carried out from an alternative location). When added together, these various figures provide an estimated total loss for assets in the community if a natural hazard event occurs.

Loss Estimate Calculation

Structural loss + Content loss + Use and Function loss = Total loss

The loss estimation step of the risk assessment provides one more piece of information illustrating the community's level of vulnerability. The ultimate goal is to reduce that vulnerability; knowing exactly what is at stake can help develop the most appropriate mitigation strategies for achieving that goal.

10.6.1 Calculating Human Losses

The costs from a flood, earthquake, or other type of hazard that are captured during the loss estimate are only financial in nature. The human losses are much more difficult to calculate. There are credible estimates available from various state and federal sources that project the number of people that may be hurt or killed in different types of buildings under different hazard conditions. For the risk assessment it is important to note that the likelihood of people being injured or killed depends upon such factors as warning time, the quality and age of the structures, and the characteristics of the hazard itself. For some hazards, such as flooding, deaths or injuries are relatively rare in our country, and most often occur when people fail to heed evacuation warnings or when they drive through floodwaters in their vehicles. In any event, it is extremely problematic to place a dollar value on human lives; rather, the planning process should incorporate every opportunity to reduce the risk of human injuries and casualties to the greatest extent possible for all sorts of hazards.

10.6.2 Using HAZUS Software to Estimate Hazard Losses

HAZUS-MH is a powerful risk assessment software program for analyzing potential losses from floods, hurricane winds, and earthquakes. The software is made available from FEMA to help communities estimate losses from various hazards as the first step in creating mitigation and preparedness strategies.

In HAZUS-MH, current scientific and engineering knowledge is coupled with the latest GIS technology to produce estimates of hazard-related damage before, or after, a disaster occurs. One of FEMA's principal objectives in promoting HAZUS is to encourage users to analyze, in advance, potential estimates of deaths, injuries, building damage, economic loss, the need for shelters and medical aid, and disruption to lifelines, infrastructure, and critical facilities due to hazards, and then to design and implement measures to reduce expected losses.

It is important to note that HAZUS-MH and other loss estimation methodologies are intended to be used only for planning purposes. The figures derived from loss analyses are not meant to provide an absolute prediction about dollar losses to any particular building or a precise number of deaths. Instead, these tools can help us gauge what might happen during various hazard scenarios.

FOR EXAMPLE

Using HAZUS to Estimate Earthquake Losses

FEMA first developed its HAZUS software to estimate potential losses from earthquake. The HAZUS earthquake loss estimation methodology uses mathematical formulas and data about building stock, local geology, the location and size of potential earthquakes, economic and population figures, and other information. Once the size and location (epicenter) of a hypothetical earthquake is selected, the HAZUS software, using a series of mathematical formulas, calculates the violence of ground shaking, the amount of damage, the number of casualties, the number of people displaced by damaged structures, and the disruption and economic losses caused by the earthquake. These formulas describe the relationship between earthquake magnitude, violence of ground shaking, building and utility system damage, cost of repair, and indirect economic impact. HAZUS allows the user to change the size and location of the hypothetical earthquake to see the range of damages that may occur to the community.

10.6.3 Estimating Losses from Man-made Hazards

As with the natural hazard risk assessment process, the potential losses from man-made hazards are generally grouped into three categories: people (death and injury), assets (structures and their contents), and functions (provision of services and generation of revenue). However, terrorism and technological disasters present some unique implications for loss estimation. Because it is so difficult to predict the frequency of occurrence, the location, and the consequences of man-made hazards, it is more difficult to estimate losses with any precision.

For some hazards, worst-case scenarios can be generated and losses estimated if the hazard can be characterized with some accuracy. For example, using the location of rail lines and the kinds and quantities of hazardous materials that are transported over them, computer models can be used to estimate the consequences of various types of train accidents where chemicals and other hazardous materials are released.

For other man-made hazards such as bombs, however, our ability to analyze damage to buildings is still evolving. Software can be used to model blast effects on structures, but methodologies that can easily translate this information into dollar loss figures are not yet widley available. When dealing with these difficult-to-quantify risks, planners and emergency managers often assume worst-case scenarios (such as total building destruction) and estimate the losses by applying the same techniques that are used for estimating losses from natural hazards.

SELF-CHECK

- Describe the **loss estimate** equation.
- Describe HAZUS-MH.
- Discuss the difficulties in estimating losses from man-made hazards.

10.7 Risk Assessment Step Five: Describing Future Land Use and Development Trends

So far during the risk assessment process, we have been focusing on the impact a hazard event could have on a community as it exists right now. But communities are constantly changing. As towns and cities grow and develop their level of vulnerability changes. We might assume that, in general, more assets and more people mean greater vulnerability, and in many cases this is true. Yet we do not have to accept this assumption. Communities can choose to grow and develop in such a way that their vulnerability to hazards does *not* increase. This does not mean that the hazards will disappear, but it does mean that a community will be conscious of its direction of growth, and will make decisions so that new development is not located in places of danger. Step five in the risk assessment process evaluates the community's future vulnerability by asking the question: "What people and property will be at risk from hazards in the future if we continue to grow and develop as we are right now?"

Although there is no sure way to foretell a community's future, trends in population and land uses can be used to indicate future directions in growth. The community's attitude towards new growth is also indicative of future growth trends. These attitudes are articulated through the local ordinances and regulations that control land use in the jurisdiction. We predict where future development might occur during the risk assessment so that if development is being allowed in hazard risk areas, mitigation strategies can be formed to change the regulatory systems currently in place.

10.7.1 Describing Undeveloped Areas

A good place to start when assessing a community's potential future vulnerability is to describe all the areas within the county or town limits that are currently undeveloped. Local land use maps, tax data, aerial photography, or a tour of the community can determine the major features of land that has few if any structures located on it. For each undeveloped area, the risk assessment includes a description of the dominant form of land cover, such as forest, desert, wetland, farmland, parkland, and so forth.

In addition to describing the current state of undeveloped areas, the risk assessment also describes potential future conditions by considering the types of development that are likely over the course of the next few years in these undeveloped areas. Most local governments have policies, plans, and regulations that deal with future land uses that dictate what types of new development are allowed. For example, a local comprehensive plan often spells out how and where a community wants to grow over the next 10 to 20 years. Local zoning ordinances and subdivision regulations are usually more specific and describe how many and what types of buildings are allowed in certain areas of the community. These rules and policies provide information about what could be built where if the rules remain unchanged and if developers and landowners take full advantage of those rules. See Chapter 8 for a more detailed discussion of local regulations and land use policies.

10.7.2 Describing Scheduled Infrastructure Areas

In addition to looking at the community's plans and regulations to determine the type of development that is permissible, the risk assessment should also include a review of local capital improvement programs and local infrastructure plans. These plans indicate where and when public services will be extended into undeveloped areas, including roads, water lines, sewer lines, schools, and other community facilities. These types of decisions are usually contained in a capital improvement plan, a plan that schedules where and when a local government will build all its public assets during the next 5 to 10 years, or a master or comprehensive plan, which describes the overall land use pattern for the community over the next decade.

Scheduled infrastructure is a good predictor of future development because once these services are provided, development will usually soon follow. These items are necessary to support new neighborhoods, shopping centers, factories, office complexes, and other sorts of construction, and they are typically very expensive to build and maintain. Most large-scale development projects rely on hookups to public water and sewer, as well as other public facilities to be viable investments for the developer and builder.

If the community has not enacted land use regulations or a formal capital improvement plan, planners and emergency managers can rely on their own sense of judgment about how and where the community is growing and whether there is potential for development to take place in areas that are currently undeveloped. Insight derived from local residents, business owners, elected officials, and local staff can help inform these conjectures about future land use trends. Is the locality considered a bedroom community for a growing city nearby? Are large employers likely to be attracted to the area? Is a major interstate or connector road going to be constructed to which the community will have access? Has the state or local government created tax incentives or other economic development programs to lure business and industry to the area? These and other questions help predict, at least in a general way, the future development potential, and therefore future vulnerability, of the community.

10.7.3 Determining Where Undeveloped Areas Intersect with Hazardous Areas

Knowing which areas of the community are undeveloped and which of these areas may be developed in the future provides a basis for determining whether developable portions of the community are located in known hazard areas. This step involves comparing the hazard area descriptions created during step two of the risk assessment process with the descriptions of undeveloped land and scheduled-infrastructure areas created during this step. An overlay of hazard maps onto the community base map is helpful for visualizing this step.

If the overlays indicate that undeveloped lands intersect with hazardous areas, then more specific information about this potential for future vulnerability is necessary. An overlay of the hazard map with the community's zoning map, for instance, can indicate the types of development that are allowed in hazard areas. If it appears that development will be allowed that could put more people and property in danger in the future, the community will want to change the rules before a disaster happens.

FOR EXAMPLE

Ignoring the Obvious: A Recipe for Disaster

A few years ago, public officials in a small town in the southeast decided that they were going to solve the town's repetitive flood problems. The officials took a field trip to visit an area of town that had recently flooded. They stood near the edge of the river, viewing the area to the south, debating about various ways to protect the existing homes in the neighborhood from future flooding. What the officials failed to realize, however, was that the vacant land just up the river to the north was zoned for residential development, and was subject to the same flood hazards as the existing flooded neighborhood! When this oversight was pointed out to them, the officials (all of whom were elected by the local citizenry) declared that rezoning the area was out of the question because it would be politically contentious. Unfortunately, this stance could result in more people and property at risk from future flooding.

SELF-CHECK

- Discuss the role of undeveloped areas in assessing a community's future vulnerability.
- Explain why scheduled infrastructure is a good predictor of future development.
- Describe how to determine where undeveloped areas intersect with hazardous areas.

10.8 Risk Assessment Step Six: Forming Conclusions (Determining Acceptability)

The risk assessment process can provide a wealth of information about the community's level of vulnerability to a wide range of potential hazards. Much of this information will be in the form of charts, spreadsheets, tables, and reports full of figures and projections, as well as maps that illustrate the locations of community assets in relation to known hazard areas. But the value of this information lies in the conclusions that are formulated, conclusions that are based on the data collected and the analysis conducted.

10.8.1 Each Community Must Decide for Itself

Each community must look at its risk assessment in its entirety, and decide whether the sum of all the various bits of information put together equal a risk scenario that is either acceptable or unacceptable. In other words, are the problems presented during the risk assessment so great that the community would agree to do something about it? If so, then the level of risk will be considered unacceptable, and the community should then take the necessary steps through mitigation and preparedness to reduce those risks. On the other hand, it might be discovered that only an insignificant portion of the community is actually vulnerable to known hazards, and the community might decide to forgo spending the necessary money, time, and energy in trying to solve its relatively minor hazard problems. Either way, it is important that the conclusions that are formed at the end of the risk assessment process be based on the information gathered and analyzed.

There is no magic formula for developing conclusions and determining acceptability of risk. Each community must determine on its own where it draws the line in terms of the level of vulnerability it is willing to live with. Usually, the greater percentage of a community's assets and tax base that are located in known hazard areas indicates a more compelling need to reduce vulnerability. And certainly, the greater number of people that are shown to be located in hazard areas should prompt action to reduce the vulnerability of local populations. However, each community will need to weigh its other community goals and needs with the need to reduce its hazards risks, and no two communities will come to the same conclusion.

10.8.2 Creating a Mitigation Plan Based on the Risk Assessment

If a community decides that its level of risk is unacceptable, the risk assessment can provide a factual basis for creating and targeting mitigation strategies. This is often most effectively done by developing a mitigation plan, a policy document that lays out goals, objectives, and actions intended to reduce the vulnerabilities highlighted during the risk assessment process. The risk assessment and loss estimations are just one element of a complete hazard mitigation plan, but it is the plan itself that will put measures in action to reduce vulnerability. Through a mitigation plan, we can use the information obtained during the risk assessment to protect existing buildings and to retrofit older buildings against hazard impacts. Where land is not yet developed, we can guide future development and keep people and property out of areas we know are hazardous. In this way, we can choose to make our communities more resilient by using the information gathered during the risk assessment process to create a sound and targeted mitigation plan that reduces both present and future vulnerability.

FOR EXAMPLE

Opening the Eyes of the Community

Over twenty years ago (before the use of GIS was widespread), the forward-thinking town planner for the Town of Nags Head, North Carolina, made large, oversized maps showing all of the community's taxable property. The town is located on the Outer Banks of North Carolina, an area that is frequently hit by very large hurricanes. The planner taped the maps to the wall, and during a town council meeting he took a red pencil and drew a line that marked an area 300 feet landward from the ocean. This line, although only an approximation, represented the area that typically suffers the majority of damage from hurricane winds and storm surge. It also represented the area where the majority of the town's tax base was located! Despite the fact that few hurricanes had visited the area in the previous decade, the town council, on being graphically informed of the risk they were taking, decided to create one of the first hazard mitigation plans in the region.

SELF-CHECK

- List ways to incorporate the results of the risk assessment into actions that will reduce vulnerability.
- Discuss factors that influence a community's decision to act on a risk assessment.
- Explain how a risk assessment can be used to steer development away from hazardous areas.

SUMMARY

This chapter explains how a risk assessment informs us about the hazards we face, so that we can choose the most appropriate mitigation and preparedness strategies in the effort to become more resilient. To begin, a community must identify all the hazards that might occur, information that is largely based on events of the past, as well as other local and regional data. In the second step of the risk assessment process the community creates a profile of the hazards that includes what areas may be affected, the possible impacts, and the probability of recurrence. The third step involves an inventory of those assets and populations that are vulnerable to hazards. In the fourth step, the community estimates what could be lost in a hazard event, using dollar figures, as well as projected numbers of deaths and injuries. The community uses the fifth step of the process to anticipate future vulnerability by describing growth and development trends. The chapter concludes with a discussion of the sixth step, outlining ways that communities can arrive at conclusions about the acceptable level of risk based on risk assessment findings.

KEY TERMS

Asset	Any man-made or natural feature that has value, including, but not limited to, people; buildings; infrastructure like bridges, roads, and sewer and water systems; lifelines like electricity and communication resources; or environmental, cultural, or recreational features like parks, dunes, wetlands, or landmarks.
Base Map	Graphic that shows the basic topography, physical elements, critical facilities, and infrastructure of a community; can be used to superimpose hazard-specific information for an illustration of vulnerability.
Critical facilities	Facilities critical to the health and welfare of the population, especially following hazard events. Critical facilities include, but are not limited to, shelters, police and fire stations, hospitals, life line infrastructure such as water and sewer treatment facilities, power generation stations, and communication and transportation networks.
Essential facilities	Facilities important for a full recovery of a community following a hazard event. These include: government functions, major employers, banks, schools, and certain commercial establishments such as grocery stores, hardware stores, and gas stations.
Geographic Information Systems (GIS)	A computer software application that relates physical features on the earth to a database to be used for mapping and analysis.
Hazard identification	The process of identifying hazards that threaten an area.
Hazard profile	A description of the physical characteristics of hazards and a determination of various descriptors

including magnitude, duration, frequency, probability, and extent. In most cases, a community can most easily use these descriptors when they are recorded and displayed as maps.

Hazus (Hazards U.S.)
A risk assessment tool used to estimate earthquake and other hazard losses. HAZUS contains a database of economic, census, building stock, transportation facilities, local geology, and other information.

Inherent vulnerability
Factors such as the way a building or facility is used, how visible it is, how accessible it is, how many people are located there, and other factors that determine the asset's level of susceptibility, often in reference to man-made hazards.

Intensity
A measure of the effects of a hazard at a particular place.

Lifeline utilities
Services that are essential to a community's health and well-being, such as potable water, wastewater treatment, oil, natural gas, electric power, and communication systems

Loss estimate
A calculation in dollar amounts of the potential damage to structures and contents, interruption of services, and displacement of residents and businesses caused by a hazard.

Magnitude
A measure of the strength of a hazard event, or how much energy is released. The magnitude (also referred to as severity) of a given hazard event is usually determined using technical measures.

Probability
A statistical measure of the likelihood that a hazard event will occur.

Recurrence interval
The time between hazard events of a similar size in a given location. It is based on the probability that the given event will be equaled or exceeded in any given year.

Risk assessment
The process or methodology used to evaluate risk. Risk assessment typically includes five preliminary steps: (1) identify hazards; (2) profile hazard events; (3) inventory assets and populations; (4) estimate losses; (5) determine future development and population trends. A sixth step, (6) determine acceptable level of risk, is often

included in a risk assessment to decide whether further action is warranted.

Tactical vulnerability   Factors such as the way a building is designed, built, landscaped, and engineered that determine the asset's susceptibility to hazard impacts, often in reference to man-made hazards.

Vulnerability   The extent to which people will experience harm and property will be damaged from a hazard. Present vulnerability involves who and what is at risk now; future vulnerability indicates who and what may be at risk in the future under projected development and population trends.

ASSESS YOUR UNDERSTANDING

Go to www.wiley.com/college/schwab to evaluate your knowledge of identifying hazards and assessing vulnerability.

Measure your learning by comparing pre-test and post-test results.

Summary Questions

1. The purpose of a risk assessment is to determine what would happen if a hazard event occurred in a community. True or False?

2. Repetitive occurrences of chronic hazards do not lead to a cumulative impact over time. True or False?

3. The risk assessment process for a hurricane greatly differs from that used for hazardous material accidents. True or False?

4. A base map is used
   (a) to periodically update HAZUS maps.
   (b) to view hazard-specific information against basic topography.
   (c) to illustrate zoning districts in a community.
   (d) to depict floodplains.

5. Hazard identification involves creating a hazard history. True or False?

6. For which of the following hazards was HAZUS-MH *not* designed to analyze potential losses?
   (a) wildfire
   (b) floods
   (c) hurricane winds
   (d) earthquakes

7. Research into a community's past hazard events should include major events as well as those that are less significant. True or False?

8. A hazard profile identifies the severity of a potential hazard, in some cases using terms such as mild, moderate, or severe. True or False?

9. A hazard's potential impact is
   (a) equal to its probability.
   (b) greater than its severity.
   (c) a combination of frequency of occurrence and magnitude of event.
   (d) a combination of magnitude of event, area affected, and amount of human activity.

10. The 100-year flood is one that has:
    (a) near 100% probability in the next year.
    (b) a 1% chance of occurring in a given year.

(c) at least one chance in the next 10 years.

(d) less than one chance in the next 100 years.

11. An evacuation center is one example of a community asset. True or False?

12. Tactical vulnerability is partly determined by how a facility or building is used. True or False?

13. Potential losses from a man-made hazards area are typically divided into three groups: people, assets, and functions. True or False?

14. Methods to estimate losses from natural hazards work equally well with hazards of a terrorist or technological nature. True or False?

15. Over the years, a community's vulnerability

(a) remains the same.

(b) decreases.

(c) increases.

(d) varies.

16. An evaluation of a community's undeveloped areas and their potential for growth helps determine a community's potential future vulnerability. True or False?

17. A geographic information system is

(a) a type of computer software product.

(b) a tool for creating digital overlays of geographic features.

(c) a tool for creating printed maps.

(d) all of the above.

Review Questions

1. How does a risk assessment factor into mitigation efforts?

2. What are the six steps of the risk assessment process?

3. Which steps in the risk assessment process help you determine the community's level of vulnerability?

4. List several components of a good base map.

5. Describe three example of where to find information about past hazard events.

6. What three sources can be used to find information about man-made hazards?

7. Which types of hazards are commonly mapped?

8. What are the limitations of using historical information to estimate what will happen in the future?

9. List three examples of community assets.

10. The extent of a hazard is identified in the second step of the risk assessment process. Which scale could be used to describe the potential severity of a tornado?

11. Step three of a risk assessment, inventorying vulnerable assets and populations, involves three tasks. Describe each of the three tasks.

12. As part of the inventory process, you must estimate the value of each community asset. Explain how.

13. Two approaches can be used to identify the vulnerability of an asset. Define tactical vulnerability and give an example.

14. What is the name of the risk assessment program used for analyzing potential losses from floods, earthquakes, and hurricane winds?

15. Explain why it is more difficult to determine potential losses from terrorism or technological hazard than for a natural hazard?

16. What is scheduled infrastructure, and what does it indicate for the future?

17. A community with unacceptable risks may decide to do something about it. Define mitigation plan.

18. Explain hazard probability for flooding and what a 100 year floodplain means.

Applying This Chapter

1. What elements of your community's risk assessment process would you choose to display on maps? Why? What are some of the sources you would use to create your maps?

2. As a planner in Biloxi, Mississippi, you have been charged with carrying out the city's risk assessment. What role does the risk assessment play in creating the city's mitigation strategies? Identify the natural hazards that affect your community; determine if any are chronic hazards.

3. In the past eight years, two trains have derailed on the rail line that runs through your community. One was significant, involving a hazardous material and two deaths. Create a hazard profile for this hazard. How does this profile differ from one for a natural hazard?

4. How would you go about determining the level of vulnerability to natural hazards for Lewes, Delaware? What resources, internet or otherwise, would you go to for the information you needed for the three tasks required for this step?

5. Using the formula provided in the text for calculating estimated total losses, determine the total loss that would result from a hazard event impacting your home or residence. Would that loss vary depending on the hazard? If so, indicate why?

6. As a conservationist, what would you do if you discovered an undeveloped area of your community was vulnerable to landslides? You've already read about plans to build a bigger road and bring water and power to this potentially hazardous area.

7. Imagine you live a rural farming community in Ohio. Why is a future project to install water and sewer lines in an area an indicator of future development? What does this tell you about the future vulnerability of this area?

YOU TRY IT

Describing the Future

Part of assessing a community's vulnerability is determining what's at stake for loss in the future. Describe areas of your town or county that are undeveloped; include their current state as well as their potential future condition. Use resources such as the Internet, aerial maps, tax maps, and local land maps. Whenever possible, indicate who owns the property.

Hazard History 101

Choose what you think is the most significant natural hazard that threatens your community. Complete a hazard profile, determining the hazard's extent, probability, and location.

Risk Assessment

Consider the hazard-prone areas of your community where people live or work. Predict the feasibility of a mitigation plan based on your community and local government's attitudes toward growth and mitigtion.

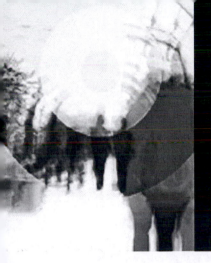

11

PREPAREDNESS ACTIVITIES
Short-term Planning in the Emergency Management Cycle

Starting Point

Go to www.wiley.com/college/schwab to assess your knowledge of the basics of short-term planning in the emergency management cycle.
Determine where you need to concentrate your effort.

What You'll Learn in This Chapter

▲ The role of preparedness as part of the emergency management cycle
▲ Responsibilities of government authorities in preparedness
▲ Responsibilities of businesses in preparedness
▲ Responsibilities of families and individuals in preparedness
▲ Hazard-specific examples of preparedness exercises

After Studying This Chapter, You'll Be Able To

▲ Distinguish between hazard mitigation and preparedness actions
▲ Illustrate how coordination between all preparedness programs is essential
▲ Describe the vital responsibility of all citizens to cooperate in the continual updating of preparedness activity
▲ Describe several types of exercises that are hazard-specific examples of preparedness
▲ Describe several opportunities for further education and training of emergency managers and individuals

Goals and Outcomes

▲ Evaluate the effectiveness of all levels of preparedness
▲ Select the necessary preparedness players and help coordinate their actions
▲ Create informed disaster plans, whether contributing to a local emergency operations plan or a family disaster plan
▲ Analyze the importance of preparedness in the creation of hazard-resilient communities
▲ Compare and contrast preparedness actions on an individual level and community level

INTRODUCTION

This chapter outlines the differences and similarities between hazard mitigation and preparedness and discusses the role of preparedness in the disaster management cycle. This chapter also gives a brief overview of how preparedness helps ensure an efficient response to a disaster, including an introduction to the National Response Plan. The chapter then goes on to describe various preparedness activities undertaken by governments, businesses, families, and volunteer organizations such as the American Red Cross. The chapter illustrates the responsibilities of government and individuals for preparedness by focusing on an evacuation scenario. The chapter concludes with a discussion of various preparedness programs that help make communities and individuals ready for many types of hazard situations.

11.1 Drawing the Lines between Mitigation, Response, and Preparedness

When a community receives word that a hurricane is approaching, a frenzy of activity takes place to ensure that citizens and businesses are warned and the best possible attempt is made to move the targeted populous out of harm's way. In the midst of these activities, it is to the advantage of the community to have planned out a course of action ahead of time. Determining the most efficient methods for communicating warnings, evacuating large numbers of people, and setting up shelters is not something community officials should do on the fly, especially when it is possible to make these preparations ahead of time in thoughtful detail.

The core of preparedness is planning for the activities that will take place immediately before, during, and immediately after a disaster occurs. It is a vital portion of the hazard mitigation cycle discussed in Chapter 1, and one that is not to be confused with mitigation per se. There can be significant overlaps between mitigation and preparedness, but also some key distinctions. These distinctions are important in building resilient communities, so we will restate the definitions of each phase, as well as their respective roles in the disaster management cycle.

11.1.1 The Role of Preparedness in the Disaster Management Cycle

Resilient communities are towns, cities, counties, Native American tribes, states, and other forms of communities that take action prior to a hazard event so that a disaster does not result. Resilient communities do this in two stages: (1) preparedness and (2) mitigation.

Mitigation and Preparedness in the Emergency Management System

Hazard mitigation and preparedness are often referred to as integral parts of the comprehensive emergency management system. **Comprehensive emergency management** is a widely used approach at the local, state, and federal levels to

---

Table 11-1: Phases of Comprehensive Emergency Management

Preparedness	• Activities to improve the ability to respond quickly in the immediate aftermath of an incident. • Includes development of response procedures, design and installation of warning systems, evacuation planning; exercises to test emergency operations, and training of emergency personnel.
Response	• Activities during or immediately following a disaster to meet the urgent needs of disaster victims. • Includes time-sensitive operations such as search and rescue, evacuation, emergency medical care, and food and shelter programs.
Recovery	• Actions that begin after the disaster, when urgent needs have been met. Recovery actions are designed to put the community back together. • Include repairs to roads, bridges, and other public facilities, restoration of power, water and other municipal services, and other activities to help restore normal operations to a community.
Mitigation	• Activities that prevent a disaster, reduce the chance of a disaster happening, or lessen the damaging effects of unavoidable disasters and emergencies. • Includes engineering solutions such as dams and levees; land use planning to prevent development in hazardous areas; protecting structures through sound building practices and retrofitting; preserving the natural environment to serve as a natural buffer against hazard impacts; and educating the public about hazards and ways to reduce risk.

---

deal with the inevitability of natural hazards and the possibility of man-made hazards and their potential to cause disasters in a community. The four phases of a comprehensive emergency management system are **Preparedness, Response, Recovery,** and **Mitigation** as described in Table 11-1.

The Disaster Management Cycle

These four phases are often illustrated in a circular relationship as in Figure 11-1, signifying the cyclical nature of disaster and emergency management. We prepare for disasters before they occur. When a disaster happens, a community must first respond to that particular event, and soon thereafter begin recovery. But

Figure 11-1

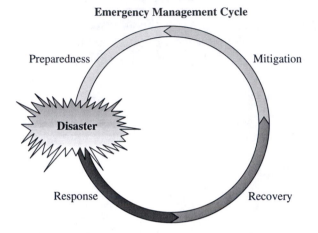

Emergency Management Cycle.

even while the community is still recovering from one disaster, we begin the process of mitigating the impacts of the next disaster.

Preparedness can be characterized as a state of readiness to respond to any emergency or disaster. It involves anticipating what might happen during different sorts of hazard events, making sure that plans are in place to deal with those possibilities and training and educating everyone involved about what their various roles will be as the situation evolves. Along with mitigation, preparedness focuses on the future, and is one of the building blocks of a resilient community.

The Difference between Preparedness and Mitigation

Preparedness involves the functional and operational elements of emergency management. Although preparedness activities are carried out in advance of a hazard event, they are generally directed to the response and recovery phases. During preparedness, we gather our supplies and make our plans for what to do prior to impact of a disaster and immediately thereafter to recover from the effects of a disaster. Mitigation, in contrast, is the ongoing effort to lessen the impacts of disasters on people and property through predisaster activities. Mitigation can take place months, years, and even decades before a hazard event, and continues after a disaster occurs with an eye to the future. In sum, the difference between these two predisaster phases is mainly temporal. Mitigation involves a long-term commitment that ensures fewer people are victims of disasters in the future, while preparedness is planning for emergency services that must be delivered prior to and following a specific event.

Preparedness and Response

Preparedness is directly related to response—the phase of the emergency management cycle that occurs immediately after a disaster. In order to experience a successful response to a disaster, the plans for the response must be in place prior to the response effort. Preparedness takes care of much of the preplanning for response. There are many activities to coordinate in a response effort. The more planning that can be done ahead of a disaster makes the response to that particular disaster more efficient. Without preparedness, a timely, coordinated response would not be possible.

During a response effort, many activities must be coordinated. The **National Response Plan (NRP)** serves to coordinate response responsibilities and logistics at the federal level. The current NRP was developed by FEMA in 2004 to supersede the Federal Response Plan of 1992, and represents a binding agreement among 27 government agencies and the American Red Cross. The intention of the NRP is to coordinate the delivery of federal assistance in concert with local governments during a presidentially-declared disaster response effort. The plan provides monetary support to local and state governments overwhelmed by a disaster for initial response resources such as food, water, emergency generators, shelters, and debris clearing of vital access roads. The NRP establishes 15 emergency support functions that must be coordinated during the immediate disaster recovery, which inherently are important preparedness functions as well.

The 15 emergency support functions established in the NRP are:

▲ Transportation.
▲ Communications.
▲ Public works and engineering.
▲ Firefighting.
▲ Emergency management.
▲ Mass care, housing, and human services.
▲ Resource support.
▲ Public heath and medical services.
▲ Urban search and rescue.
▲ Oil and hazardous materials response.
▲ Agriculture and natural resources.
▲ Energy.
▲ Public safety and security.
▲ Long-term community recovery and mitigation.
▲ External affairs.

Each of these response-oriented functions is highly dependant upon the others. For example, the agencies in charge of urban search and rescue must coordinate with the health and medical services professionals, understand the modes of transportation available, and have communications capabilities to contact each other and the other organizations involved. The individual functions carried out under the NRP are not stand-alone activities during a response effort. Agencies must coordinate their efforts while also executing their own individual training exercises to ensure readiness for these situations.

11.1.2 Preparedness in a Nutshell

The definition of preparedness issued by FEMA encompasses many of the issues discussed above. As described by FEMA, preparedness is:

> . . . *the leadership, training, readiness and exercise support, and technical and financial assistance to strengthen citizens, communities, State, local and Tribal governments, and professional emergency workers as they prepare for disasters, mitigate the effects of disasters, respond to community needs after a disaster, and launch effective recovery efforts.*[1]

Preparedness plays a vital role in the emergency management cycle. Preparedness involves predisaster readiness and planning for the immediate emergency response, but also involves restoration of government services, utilities, and businesses to predisaster status as quickly as possible. Preparedness is a concept that overarches most aspects of emergency management. It entails coordination between many government officials, emergency workers, volunteers, and citizens. Emergency management agencies, businesses, and residents alike need to have preparedness capabilities. These capabilities can only come about through planning, training, and performing emergency exercises ahead of a disaster. Knowing what to do in a disaster can reduce the confusion, anxiety, fear, and even panic that often occur as a disaster unfolds. Most significantly, pre-disaster preparedness planning can save lives and minimize injuries.

FOR EXAMPLE

Girl Scouts Can "Be Prepared" Too

The shared Boy Scout and Girl Scout motto "Be Prepared" can be applied to many situations, but Junior Girl Scouts wearing the Safety Award decided to use their abilities to help each other, their families, and their communities "Be Prepared," too. In order to obtain the award, the Girl Scouts must complete eight safety preparedness activities. Among the qualifying activities include developing a family fire safety plan, learning about local 911 services, conducting an emergency evacuation drill as described by the FEMA Family Disaster Plan or American Red Cross Disaster Services, learning first aid, becoming a FEMA Disaster Action Kid, and learning severe weather signs as described by the National Weather Service.[2]

HURRICANE PAM: A PRE-KATRINA PLANNING AND PREPAREDNESS EXERCISE

Hurricane Pam was a planning and preparedness exercise that took place in July 2004 at the Louisiana State Emergency Operations Center in Baton Rouge (see Figure 11-2). The five-day exercise was based on a hypothetical scenario named Hurricane Pam, a storm conceptualized as a slow-moving, strong Category 3 hurricane that would hit the city of New Orleans at some undetermined time in the future. FEMA provided funding for the exercise because out of 25 disaster scenarios nationwide, a hurricane hitting New Orleans was selected as one of the most disastrous scenarios possible. The exercise was designed and facilitated by the private contracting firm Innovative Emergency Management Inc., and involved emergency management officials from over 50 parish, state, federal, and volunteer organizations located throughout southeastern Louisiana. The purpose of Pam was to facilitate the development of joint disaster response plans between all of the participants and to determine what should be done to prepare and respond to this type of disaster.

The essentials of the hypothetical scenario were amazingly similar to the actual conditions wrought by Hurricane Katrina a little over a year later in

Figure 11-2

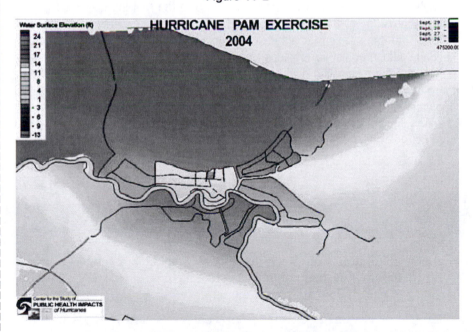

Computer model from the Hurricane Pam exercise in June 2004.
SOURCE: www.pbs.org/wgbh/nova/orleans/vanh-02.html

August 2005. Models run during Hurricane Pam visualized sustained winds of 120 miles an hour, up to 20 inches of rain in some areas of Louisiana, and storm surges that topped the levee system in New Orleans. Additionally, the scenario specified that 300,000 people would not evacuate, over 500,000 buildings would be destroyed, sewer services and communications would be knocked out, about 1000 shelters would be needed, boats and helicopters would be required to rescue stranded residents, and flood waters would create large uninhabitable areas across the southeast.[3] The predicted consequences also included over 175,000 injured, over 200,000 ill, and over 60,000 dead. In this respect, the resemblance of Hurricane Pam to Hurricane Katrina is close—but, fortunately, not too close.[4]

During the Hurricane Pam exercise, the 300 workshop participants were split into groups and asked to devise responses to each part of the scenario as it unfolded, focusing on search and rescue, sheltering, debris removal, and medical care. Post-landfall and recovery issues were emphasized.[5] The outcome of the exercise was formulated into a to-do list consisting of 15 guiding principles that each level of government should use to revise their plans. The list includes diagrams for distribution of supplies to storm victims; action plans for debris removal, sheltering, and search and rescue; and ideas for evacuation plan revisions. The detailed workshop summary also identifies the appropriate lead and support agencies for each of the tasks mentioned.[6]

After Katrina, a number of Hurricane Pam participants reported that the workshop had increased their ability to respond to the real-life disaster by anticipating some of the most critical problems in advance. However, the aftermath of the Katrina disaster also exposed many more lessons that were not heeded.[7] Although history provides the benefit of 20/20 hindsight, it is indeed unfortunate for those who died and whose lives were disrupted so brutally that more of the lessons learned during the Hurricane Pam exercises were not fully implemented before the 2005 hurricane season arrived. The funding for the second planned phase of the Pam exercise was cut by Congress before it could take place.[8]

SELF-CHECK

- Define **mitigation** and **preparedness** as distinct but related phases of the emergency management cycle.
- List examples of response activities that involve preparedness.
- Explain why a basic knowledge of weather-related hazards is necessary in hazard mitigation and preparedness.

11.2 Preparedness Is Everyone's Responsibility

Although there are a number of different organizations involved in potential preparedness activities, it is important to realize that every individual, whether as family member or business owner, must accept responsibility for his or her own readiness for disaster. Although government agencies and volunteer organizations have a significant role to play, responsibility lies with each citizen to take these preventative actions as well. Working together to achieve preparedness at each level is the key to any successful response effort.

11.2.1 Government Agencies

Each level of government in the United States—federal, state, local, and tribal—has a role in preparedness activities.

Federal Level

There are many federal organizations with responsibility for preparedness. The following are the federal partners in the NRP authorized to provide some form of response during a disaster:

- ▲ American Red Cross.
- ▲ Corporation for National and Community Service.
- ▲ Department of Agriculture.
- ▲ Department of Commerce.
- ▲ Department of Defense.
- ▲ Department of Education.
- ▲ Department of Energy.
- ▲ Department of Health and Human Services.
- ▲ Department of Homeland Security.
- ▲ Department of Housing and Urban Development.
- ▲ Department of the Interior.
- ▲ Department of Justice.
- ▲ Department of Labor.
- ▲ Department of State.
- ▲ Department of Transportation.
- ▲ Department of the Treasury.
- ▲ Department of Veteran Affairs..
- ▲ Environmental Protection Agency.
- ▲ Federal Bureau of Investigation.
- ▲ Federal Communications Commission.
- ▲ General Services Administration.

▲ National Aeronautics and Space Administration.

▲ National Transportation Safety Board.

▲ National Communications System.

▲ Nuclear Regulatory Commission.

▲ National Voluntary Organizations Active in Disaster.

▲ Office of Personnel Management.

▲ Small Business Administration.

▲ Social Security Administration.

▲ Tennessee Valley Authority.

▲ U.S. Agency for International Development.

▲ U.S. Postal Service.

These agencies must prepare ahead of a disaster in order to effectively carry out their designated response effort. By signing the NRP, these organizations have agreed to "develop, exercise, and refine headquarters and regional capabilities to ensure sustained operational readiness"[9]. This involves the development of hazard-specific contingency plans; providing coordination of federal interagency planning, training, and exercising; and facilitating federal coordination with state, local, and tribal entities and the private sector, as specified in the plan.

Through the Department of Homeland Security (DHS), NRP member agencies are responsible for contributing to a **National Preparedness Assessment and Reporting System**, which provides a report of the nation's level of preparedness to the President. As a part of the assessment system, the agencies adopt quantifiable performance measurements of preparedness in the areas of training, planning, exercises, and equipment. The assessment system additionally calls for the maintenance of a federal response capability inventory, which includes performance parameters of capabilities, timeframes necessary for the capability to be applied to an incident, and the readiness of the capability to make a difference in domestic incidents.

The NRP is built upon the **National Incident Management System (NIMS)** established in 2003. NIMS also provides guidance to federal agencies in disaster preparedness. NIMS is directed under the Department of Homeland Security and can be described as follows:

> This system will provide a consistent nationwide approach for Federal, State, and local governments to work effectively and efficiently together to prepare for, respond to, and recover from domestic incidents, regardless of cause, size, or complexity. To provide for interoperability and compatibility among Federal, State, and local capabilities, the NIMS will include a core set of concepts, principles, terminology, and technologies covering the incident command system; multiagency coordination systems; unified command; training; identification and management of

resources (including systems for classifying types of resources); qualifications and certification; and the collection, tracking, and reporting of incident information and incident resources."[10]

Standardized guidance for federal agencies in terms of preparedness is established through NIMS and includes instructional components of planning, training, exercises, personnel qualifications and training, equipment acquisition and certification, mutual aid, and publications management. NIMS encourages integrating all preparedness components and conducting activities regularly at the federal level to ensure preparedness for an **incident of national significance**. Incidents of national significance are declared as such after meeting any of the following four criteria:

▲ A federal agency has requested the help of the Secretary of Homeland Security.

▲ A state or local government has requested the help of the federal government because its capabilities to respond to a disaster are overwhelmed.

▲ Multiple federal agencies have become involved in a response effort.

▲ The President requests the involvement of the Department of Homeland Security.

To prepare for an incident of national significance, all signatories of the NRP work together—and independently—to provide overall preparedness at the national level. Each is responsible for meeting the requirements of the NRP during a disaster and the requirements of the more steady-state NIMS. Yet, in general, the federal government's contribution to preparedness is to make available adequate resources to augment state and local efforts. These resources include public outreach materials on hazards preparedness; grants for training, personnel, programs, equipment, and exercises; grants for response and recovery efforts during a disaster that is beyond the capability of local and state governments; and technical assistance to help build stronger programs.

One of the most significant federal resources that is made available to the public for hazard preparedness efforts is provided by the National Oceanic and Atmospheric Administration (NOAA). NOAA's National Weather Service is responsible for the **NOAA Weather Radio (NWR) All Hazards Network.** This network of radio stations across the country broadcasts continuous weather and hazards information. Warnings, watches, and forecasts are transmitted directly from the closest National Weather Service office in a local area. The network is called "All Hazards" for a reason—it includes warnings and post-event information for all hazards, even non-meteorological hazards under the purview of the Weather Service (such as earthquakes or oil spills).[11] Information on purchasing a NOAA weather radio receiver that is configured specifically to the NWR can be found at www.nws.noaa.gov/nwr/nwrrcvr.htm.

State Level

State governments are responsible for assisting their local governments when support and resources are needed beyond what the local level can provide. These resources include money, personnel, and equipment to supplement the capabilities of local-level response. State-level responsibilities also include the coordination of planning and preparedness efforts among local jurisdictions such that they do not conflict with each other and the coordination of training and exercising programs among multiple jurisdictions. The states must also coordinate activities of state agencies outside of emergency management that are involved in response efforts, similar to the coordination of federal-level agencies by the Department of Homeland Security.

Each state maintains an emergency management office. The following are examples of the emergency management offices for various states:

▲ North Carolina Division of Emergency Management within the Department of Crime Control and Public Safety.

▲ Louisiana Governor's Office of Homeland Security and Emergency Preparedness.

▲ Colorado Division of Emergency Management within the Department of Local Affairs.

▲ Mississippi Emergency Management Agency (MEMA).

▲ Washington Military Department's Emergency Management Division.

Regardless of which department each state emergency management office is housed in or the name of the division, they all perform similar functions. All emergency management agencies must have well-maintained emergency plans for facilities and equipment, oversee the development of local hazard plans, and provide funding for training and assistance to local governments. To carry out these functions, state emergency management offices receive funding for preparedness activities primarily from FEMA and state budgets.

While the state governments play an important role in preparedness, the responsibilities of emergency managers are better suited for mitigation and recovery functions in certain cases. Preparedness in terms of response efforts are oftentimes put in the hands of different state divisions with more tactical and operational capabilities, such as state troopers and emergency responders. It is important that all of these organizations work together at the state level; the coordinating function is most often found within the emergency management office.

The governor of each state also has responsibilities to coordinate with the state emergency management office (see Figure 11-3). As the chief executive of the state, the governor has final word on ordering mandatory evacuations, calling in the National Guard, and communicating with the federal government about state and local capabilities.

Figure 11-3

The Governor of Indiana, Mitch Daniels, meets with members of the National Guard.

A governor's prime resource is the **National Guard.** When called upon, the National Guard provides the capability to greatly assist in disaster response in terms of providing communications systems; construction equipment; emergency supplies such as medical supplies, beds, food, water, and blankets; as well as personnel to assist with distribution. Upon calling in the National Guard, the governor becomes commander in chief of state military forces. The governor also has police powers to amend, rescind orders, or create regulations during a declared state of emergency. He or she must also be involved in evacuation coordination between intrastate agencies, local level governments, and interstate agencies. Although these are largely response-related activities, the governor's office must participate in preparedness activities to ensure the state's readiness to respond to disasters.

Local Level

Just as a governor has chief executive responsibilities for the state, the city or town manager or mayor has responsibility as leader of the jurisdiction to provide for the welfare and safety of the municipality. The mayor must coordinate the local resources available to ensure preparedness and communicate with the governor when those resources are exhausted during an emergency. Local law determines the powers of the mayor to establish curfews, order quarantines, direct evacuations, or suspend local laws. In addition, the mayor is also responsible for communicating warnings to citizens, working with the local emergency managers, and facilitating resource sharing with other jurisdictions.

Each local jurisdiction also has some form of emergency plan that assigns the responsibilities of **first responders** such as police, fire, and paramedics for a variety of emergency scenarios, including natural hazard events and technological emergencies. These first responders each have their own protocols and preparedness activities. Similar to other levels of government, these procedures can be detailed and coordinated in the local **emergency operations plan,** which is usually developed and maintained by local emergency managers, often at the county level.

At the local level, there are many activities to coordinate and prepare logistically in addition to the deployment of first responders. Communications, notifications and warnings, search and rescue, shelter and mass care, traffic detours, evacuations, law enforcement, and power failure are a few of the issues emergency managers face. The numerous details for which local governments are responsible highlight the critical need for preparedness and emergency operations plans that are developed in advance of a disaster.

FEMA has developed the following list of some of the emergency management responsibilities of local governments:[12]

▲ Identifying hazards and assessing potential risk to the community.
▲ Enforcing building codes, zoning ordinances, and land use management programs.
▲ Coordinating emergency plans to ensure a quick and effective response.
▲ Fighting fires and responding to hazardous materials incidents.
▲ Establishing warning systems.
▲ Stocking emergency supplies and equipment.
▲ Assessing damage and identifying needs.
▲ Evacuating the community to safer locations.
▲ Taking care of the injured.
▲ Sheltering those who cannot remain in their homes.
▲ Aiding recovery efforts.

The local emergency manager is in the unique position of being able to coordinate all these aspects of preparedness, and can establish and maintain personal contacts with partners outside the emergency management office. Maintaining and implementing the local emergency operations plan is greatly facilitated by an understanding of the various agencies, organizations, and individuals involved.

A very important, but often overlooked, responsibility of local emergency management officials involves educating the public about preparedness activities and providing information to citizens about the safest course of action to take during different disaster scenarios. Heightened awareness within the community plays a critical role in implementing a local emergency plan for effective response. The best possible preparation for any community is to have a populace that is prepared to act in its own best interest. Public announcements about weather conditions, emergency care kits, safe water and food handling practices, and other emergency-related information can be very effective for educating the community. Local governments have used a variety of methods to get the word out, including public access websites, newspaper and radio announcements, brochures, flyers, and school children's educational materials.

11.2.2 Families and Individuals

In addition to the emergency management functions carried out by local, state, and federal governments, each of us plays an important role in preparedness at an individual level as well. Those who are well prepared can be proactive, rather than reactive, during a disaster. It is our individual responsibility to know what hazards could potentially affect us and our families and to take action in preparation.

In 2004, FEMA published an informative handbook targeted to citizens entitled *Are You Ready? An In-depth Guide to Citizen Preparedness*. This handbook can be found online at www.fema.gov/areyouready/index.shtm. An accompanying DVD, entitled *Getting Ready for Disaster – One Family's Experience*, is downloadable from the same website and also provides steps citizens can take toward preparedness. These resources provide details for how to:

▲ Get informed about hazards and emergencies that may affect you and your family.
▲ Develop an emergency plan.
▲ Collect and assemble a disaster supplies kit.
▲ Learn where to seek shelter from all types of hazards.
▲ Identify the community warning systems and evacuation routes.
▲ Include in your plan required information from community and school plans.
▲ Learn what to do for specific hazards.
▲ Practice and maintain your plan.[13]

Additionally, the handbook lists suggestions for actions to take during each stage of preparation. Before the disaster, the guide suggests that individuals know their risks and learn to recognize signs of danger, purchase insurance, including additional insurance not covered by traditional homeowner's insurance policies (such as flood insurance), develop disaster plans, assemble a kit of supplies, and volunteer to help others. During the disaster, plans can then be put into action, citizens can help others, and should look to the advice of emergency officials. Families should prepare escape routes, and make advance plans for communicating among family members during emergencies, for shutting off utilities, protecting vital records, and caring for pets. Knowing the emergency plans for local schools can also assist in making preparations for families with children in terms of communication, safety, and evacuation measures.

All of these are important responsibilities for individuals to take seriously. Using this handbook can be extremely helpful in understanding the best ways to be prepared. Those who are well prepared will be more available to help others, becoming part of the solution rather than part of the problem.

The FEMA handbook *Are You Ready? An In-depth Guide to Citizen Preparedness* lists the following items that should be included in any family's basic disaster supplies kit:

▲ Three-day supply of non-perishable food.

▲ Three-day supply of water—1 gallon of water per person, per day.

▲ Portable, battery-powered radio or television and extra batteries.

▲ Flashlight and extra batteries.

▲ First aid kid and manual.

▲ Sanitation and hygiene items (moist towelettes and toilet paper).

▲ Matches and waterproof container.

▲ Whistle.

▲ Extra clothing.

▲ Kitchen accessories and cooking utensils, including a can opener.

▲ Photocopies of credit and identification cards.

▲ Cash and coins.

▲ Special needs items, such as prescription medications, eye glasses, contact lens solutions, and hearing aid batteries.

▲ Items for infants, such as formula, diaper, bottles, and pacifiers.

▲ Blankets, sleeping bags, and warm clothing such as jackets, pants, hats, gloves, scarves, and sturdy shoes if in a cold climate.[14]

11.2.3 Business and Commercial Preparedness

As members of the community, local businesses and commercial operations are also responsible for preparedness. Chapter 9 covers in detail the risks businesses face and the mitigation and preparedness measures they can use to reduce the risks from hazards. This chapter discusses strategies to meet the responsibilities of property protection, business contingency planning, business relocation planning, protecting employees and their families, and purchasing adequate insurance coverage.

In addition to protecting their own assets and investments, businesses can also contribute to preparedness efforts of the wider community. Providing adequate supplies for families in the community takes preparation and coordination on the part of local businesses. For example, families interested in securing their properties from damage, such as boarding up their houses for a hurricane, need to be able to purchase plywood, nails, and hammers. Citizens evacuating the area prior to a wildfire need to fill up their gas tanks. Prior to an oncoming winter storm, individuals flock to grocery stores to buy milk, bread, and canned goods. Businesses are not usually accustomed to accommodating large influxes of customers and in these special instances need to be prepared for bringing in additional supplies if possible.

11.2.4 Highlight on Evacuation: Roles and Responsibilities

Evacuation is a prime example of an emergency-related action that involves preparedness at all levels of responsibility. Evacuation can be planned for ahead of time at the individual, business, local, state, and federal levels, although its execution takes place just before an event. Thus far, this chapter has identified roles and responsibilities of these different levels separately, but in this section we will tie all of them together in a specific evacuation situation in order to highlight the degree of coordination necessary.

Imagine you are a resident of a town on a barrier island. While making dinner in the early evening of a lazy summer day, you are keeping an eye on your children playing outside and you have the television on in the background. Suddenly, you hear on the newscast that there is a tropical storm gaining strength

---

FOR EXAMPLE

Pop Tart Preparedness

The retail company Wal-Mart implemented many disaster preparedness strategies to safeguard the business from the impacts of hazards, particularly in stores located in hurricane-prone Florida. In addition, the corporation has also focused its preparedness efforts towards shipping targeted items that will be of assistance to local stores and customers. Prior to a hurricane, the company has historically sent trucks full of dry ice and backup generators to protect frozen food from power outages. After studying customer buying patterns in hurricane hazard areas, Wal-Mart was able to determine that before a hurricane, customers typically raid the shelves for certain items. Based on these consumer studies, Wal-Mart has contingency plans in place to deliver additional shipments of items shown to be in high demand, including bottled water, flashlights, generators, tarps...and strawberry pop tarts.[15]

in the Atlantic Ocean. NOAA NWS forecasters are predicting that it will turn into a hurricane and your barrier island is within the projected path. Of course, there is only a certain amount of reliability to their predictions, but over the next two days, it is still heading in your direction and has become a Category 3 hurricane. What do you do?

Now imagine you are the local emergency manager for the same town and are receiving frequent hurricane condition updates from the National Weather Service. You have the community's emergency plans at hand. You also know that you will need to recommend a mandatory evacuation to the mayor and governor with adequate notice to ensure there is enough time for citizens and visitors to evacuate. Your plans show that in order for a town of your size to evacuate during the peak of the tourist season, it will take at least two days notice prior to landfall to successfully move the entire population off the island. Yet, you feel the pressure from local businesses, many of whom cater to tourists, to wait until the hurricane is predicted to make landfall in the area with greater certainty before asking the mayor and governor to call for a State of Emergency and mandatory evacuation. The two-day evacuation window is quickly approaching. What do you do?

As an owner of a local hardware store, what do you do? As governor, what do you do? As resident or visitor, what do you do? Luckily, you are prepared.

As a local hardware store owner, you called for extra shipments of plywood and other supplies at the first notification of a hurricane. You ensure that your employees are aware of the situation and are preparing for the safety of their families. You have a business contingency plan in place and have purchased flood insurance.

As the emergency manager, you alert citizens and tourists about impending hurricane conditions, encouraging them to evacuate voluntarily several days ahead of expected landfall. When NWS predictions indicate the hurricane will make landfall in two days time, you advise a mandatory evacuation. You contact the mayor, who calls the governor, who enlists the National Guard to assist with the reverse traffic flow and set up shelters according to the state's evacuation plan. The governor commands the local police, state police, and the National Guard, including those requested from other states, to enforce the evacuation order. The governor also is working in coordination with federal officials to guide evacuation activities. The NRP is invoked because of the large number of people evacuating from along the coastline of the surrounding areas and states. Your local emergency officials are ready and start assisting with door to door notifications of mandatory evacuation and helping those that have special needs. The local chapter of the American Red Cross is gearing up its volunteers and supplies and moving them out of harm's way. The hospitals and nursing homes are preparing to evacuate all of the patients they can according to their emergency plans. And the local utility companies are preparing for power outages.

As a resident, you are boarding up your windows, have ensured that gasoline is in your car and have identified several locations you can go before the mandatory evacuation is called. You have detailed maps of the area ready in case the traditional roads are overwhelmed and a NOAA Weather Radio to receive updates on the path of the hurricane and local evacuation instructions. You have your children's medicines, a suitcase of extra clothing, copies of important documents such as identification and insurance papers, as well as food and water for the car trip ready to go. When the evacuation is called, you are ready to leave immediately to avoid being trapped by any severe weather and know your children's school emergency plan so picking them up does not slow things down. The single bridge leaving the island is crowded, but traffic is moving, and you and your neighbors are able to successfully evacuate.

Without preparation and coordination in advance of the evacuation, however, it is evident that the evacuation process could easily become a nightmare. If the citizens, local emergency officials, business owners, governor's office, and federal weather forecasters did not all work together and know their individual responsibilities through education, exercises, and training, many parts of the evacuation would fail to be executed successfully.

Without warning systems alerting citizens and officials of an approaching hurricane, no one would know to be concerned or begin the evacuation process. Without the local residents having the knowledge of what to do upon hearing that a hurricane is approaching, they would not make early preparations for a mandatory evacuation or initiate their family disaster plans. The hardware store would be overwhelmed with residents waiting until the last minute to purchase supplies to secure their homes, and inventories would be depleted quickly. If the emergency manager waited too long to recommend a mandatory evacuation, the governor could not activate the National Guard with enough time to provide quality pre-hurricane assistance. The highways would turn into a parking lot with cars attempting to cross the lone bridge off the island. Hospitals and nursing homes would not have time to evacuate and they would have no choice but to keep patients in place. Traffic conditions would discourage other residents from evacuating and they would stay in their homes to ride out the storm, placing themselves and rescue workers in danger. All this commotion would happen while the hurricane continues to barrel down upon the community with ever-increasing speed and force.

Each of the participants described in this scenario plays an important role in the evacuation process. The better prepared each is, the more efficient and effective the evacuation can be. Yet, if only one of these participants is not prepared, a domino effect can result. Other community members, no matter how well prepared as individuals, will not be able to perform their functions because of a broken link elsewhere in the chain of interdependence. Personal responsibility to take preparedness seriously is essential in an evacuation situation, for ourselves and for the safety and welfare of others around us.

SELF-CHECK

- List the levels of preparedness players.
- Describe the **National Response Plan** and the **National Incident Management System.**
- Give a summary of what can be found in the FEMA handbook: *Are You Ready? An In-depth Guide to Citizen Preparedness.*

11.3 Preparedness Programs

There are a number of programs, training activities, and exercises available, each of which plays an important role in preparedness. These ensure that the best possible instructions are in place when a disaster occurs and a response effort is necessary. Activities include, but are certainly not limited to, planning for warning systems and evacuations, providing training for emergency response officials, evaluating the efficiency of response exercises, anticipating population trends and special needs, and detailing the coordination between numerous organizations involved. This section highlights several volunteer programs, education programs, and hazard-specific exercises to demonstrate the many preparedness resources available to citizens, families, businesses, and government officials.

11.3.1 Volunteer Programs

There are a large number of volunteer programs throughout the United States that make lasting contributions to preparedness. These include nationally known organizations such as the American Red Cross, Salvation Army, Second Harvest, Catholic Charities, Mennonite Disaster Service, and others that are a part of the National Voluntary Organizations Active in Disaster (NVOAD), as well as numerous locally-driven groups.

The American Red Cross

The American Red Cross was created by Clara Barton in 1881 to aid the victims of disaster. Ninety-seven percent of the Red Cross is composed of volunteers. These volunteers provide humanitarian aid to people all over the United States. As described on the American Red Cross website, activities carried out by the ARC include:

▲ Every year, the Red Cross is there for hurricane, earthquake, and other disaster victims—including 150 families forced from their homes by fire *every day.*

- ▲ 175,000 volunteers worked to prevent, prepare for, and respond to nearly 64,000 disaster incidents in 2005.
- ▲ Over 15 million Americans turn to the Red Cross to learn first aid, CPR, swimming, and other health and safety skills. Last year, more than 230,000 people volunteered to teach those courses.
- ▲ Half the nation's blood supply—six million pints annually—is collected by more than 190,000 Red Cross volunteers.
- ▲ Among emergency services for the men and women of the armed forces is the delivery of urgent family messages—one every 22 seconds.
- ▲ Over 24,000 volunteers serve as chairs, members of boards of directors, or on advisory boards for local Red Cross units—chapters, Blood Services regions, and military stations.
- ▲ As part of the International Red Cross Movement, the ARC works to ease human suffering on a global scale.[16]

The American Red Cross provides shelter and supplies, helps people contact their loved ones, and has local chapters ready to mobilize quickly and efficiently in the event of a disaster. In addition, the Red Cross contributes to community preparedness through education and outreach materials and training courses for its volunteers. The Red Cross partnership with FEMA in the Community and Family Preparedness Program is only one example (www.redcross.org/services/disaster/0,1082,0_601_,00.html) of preparedness activity. Other publications can be found online as well (www.redcross.org/ pubs/dspubs/cde.html), including *Preparing for Disaster for People with Disabilities and other Special Needs* and *Preparing Your Business for the Unthinkable.*

FOR EXAMPLE

Katrina Quilting Project

When Hurricane Katrina hit, groups across the country sprang into action to find ways to support the storm's victims. Many of the country's quilters were no exception, going to work immediately to give storm victims something to hold onto as they started their recovery. The "Quilters Comfort America" project broadcasted a message to quilters across the country to make a quilt for hurricane evacuees and to make a financial donation to the Red Cross. Within days the group raised $1 million for the Disaster Relief Fund, and quilter's guilds started their sewing machines and got to work. Upon delivery to American Red Cross National Headquarters, the quilts were distributed to Katrina evacuees living in the greater Washington, D.C. area. Since then, quilting veterans and Red Cross employees have coordinated the distribution of quilts to some of the thousands of Katrina evacuees.

CERT

The Community Emergency Response Team (CERT) was formed to support local response capabilities. Through the CERT, local volunteers receive training to learn how to provide immediate assistance to victims and to assist responders' efforts when they arrive on the scene. This way, following a disaster, individuals that are trapped in an area without communications can be educated ahead of time on how to help themselves and others until help can reach them. Local emergency management offices sponsor most CERT training courses, which include 20 hours of instruction in disaster preparedness, fire safety, disaster medical operations, light search and rescue, team organization, and disaster psychology.[17] For more information on CERT training courses, visit training.fema.gov/EMIWeb/CERT.

11.3.2 Education and Training Programs

The following are examples of the many education and training programs that focus on disaster preparedness, including the Emergency Management Institute (EMI) and FEMA's Ready Kids Program.

EMI

The Emergency Management Institute (EMI) was created in 1979 by FEMA to provide emergency management courses for students and working professionals. The Institute has assisted in the establishment of numerous degree programs across the United States in emergency management and also provides distance learning programs. Its mission is to enhance U.S. emergency practices through a national training program. EMI is described by FEMA as

> the national focal point for the development and delivery of emergency management training to enhance the capabilities of federal, state, local, and tribal government officials, volunteer organizations, and the public and private sectors to minimize the impact of disasters on the American public. EMI curricula are structured to meet the needs of this diverse audience with an emphasis on how the various elements work together in emergencies to save lives and protect property.[18]

Thousands of participants attend courses at the EMI campus located in Emmitsburg, Maryland, every year, while many more participate in EMI supported exercises, non-resident programs run cooperatively by EMI, FEMA, and state emergency management agencies, and the EMI Independent Study program. The Independent Study program, EMI's free distance learning program, provides training to professionals and volunteers to promote disaster preparedness. For a listing of the courses and how to enroll, see the EMI IS Program website at training.fema.gov/EMIWeb//IS/crslist.asp.

Ready Kids!

The U.S. Department of Homeland Security launched a program called *Ready Kids!* in the spring of 2006 to educate children about emergencies. Parents and teachers can point their children to a website (www.ready.gov/kids) that is understandable and appropriate for several age groups. The site features games, puzzles, and in-school lessons developed by Scholastic, Inc. that focus on steps children can take with their families to prepare for emergencies while learning important language arts, geography, and social studies skills. The *Ready Kids!* mascot, Rex the mountain lion, is designed to engage children in active learning for their role in preparedness activities. The American Psychological Association, American Red Cross, National Association of Elementary School Principals, National Association of School Psychologists, National Parent Teacher Association, National Center for Child Traumatic Stress, U.S. Department of Education, and U.S. Department of Health and Human Services all contributed to the design of the *Ready Kids!* program. *Ready Kids!* is part of the larger public service *Ready* campaign, designed to educate all citizens, young and old, about how to prepare for emergencies.[19]

11.3.3 Exercise Programs

Adequate preparedness depends on solid training and exercises that mimic real-life emergency scenarios in a controlled setting, such as the Homeland Security Exercise and Evaluation Program (HSEEP) carried out by the Department of Homeland Security.[20] Many other government agencies also carry out routine exercises to prepare officials, volunteers, and responders for various types of hazards and emergency incidents. The following sections describe some examples of hazard-specific exercise programs.

Flash Floods/Dam Failure Exercises

Every year, in conjunction with Colorado's statewide Flood Awareness Day on April 18, the city and county of Boulder jointly conduct an annual flood exercise. Due to Boulder's location at the foot of the Rocky Mountains, a flash flood is possible during any heavy, slow moving rainstorm event; the risk of such an event is especially high during the flash flood season of April through September. A flash flood in 1976 called the "Big Thompson Flood" took place to the north near Loveland, Colorado, but could have easily caused flash flooding of the same magnitude in Boulder had the rain event occurred within the Boulder Creek watershed. If such an event were to happen in Boulder, the downtown would be under two to four feet of raging water while other areas of Boulder and Boulder County within the Boulder Creek floodplain could be inundated up to eight feet deep with very little warning (see Figure 11-4).

The annual Boulder flood exercise involves the entire community and encourages preparedness improvements at all levels. The exercise is designed to raise public awareness, practice using public notification systems (including warning sirens, NOAA all-hazard radio warnings, emergency warning evacuation

Figure 11-4

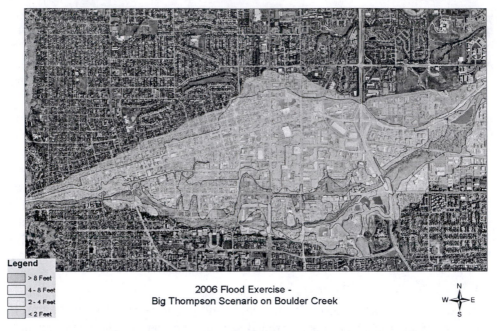

Legend

- [ ] > 8 Feet
- [ ] 4 - 8 Feet
- [ ] 2 - 4 Feet
- [ ] < 2 Feet

2006 Flood Exercise -
Big Thompson Scenario on Boulder Creek

Estimated Boulder Creek flood path map in a Big Thompson flash flood scenario.
(Disclaimer: this is an approximated flood map, and variable factors such as debris
may result in a different flood path during a real event.)
www.co.boulder.co.us/emergency/BldrCreekFlood_map.htm

systems, television warnings, and other communication systems), assess and
practice evacuation and response plans, and assess and practice communication
and coordination of emergency response personnel. In addition to the annual
exercise, on the first Monday of each month from May through August, the warning system sirens are tested throughout the city and county at 10 A.M.[21]

Earthquake Exercises

NASA's Disaster Assistance and Response Team (DART), FEMA's Urban Search
and Rescue Team, California's Urban Search and Rescue Team (Task Force-3) and
many other local emergency response agencies came together in 2004 to conduct an earthquake preparation exercise. The scenario called for "the big one," a
7.2 magnitude earthquake along the San Andreas Fault that would demolish
many parts of the San Francisco Bay area.

The exercise took place at the NASA Ames Research Center and was
employed to test and strengthen the coordination capabilities of attending organizations. The exercise simulated the response needed for a major earthquake
through specialized training in disaster management support, participation in
FEMA incident support team functional drills, and participation in a simulation

of the three days following the disaster itself. In full, the workshop tested the abilities of the various levels of responders in their ability to work together to mobilize and respond to such a large-scale disaster.[22]

Tornado Exercises

Every year during the month of March, in partnership with the National Weather Service, the state of Missouri conducts a statewide tornado drill.[23] All citizens, businesses, and schools are invited to participate. Members of the Missouri General Assembly also participate in the drill, where all taking part in the exercise are encouraged to respond to the storm sirens by seeking a safe place and tuning to their NOAA weather radios to wait for further instruction.

The American Red Cross also conducts tornado exercises to test their response capabilities to tornado events. In one example, volunteers belonging to the Jefferson County, Florida, chapter of the Red Cross coordinated tornado efforts with the Jefferson County Emergency Operations Center and state emergency management officials by setting up mock shelters in schools, providing hot meals to mock disaster victims, and identifying areas needing mass care.[24]

Terrorism Exercises

The city of Nashville, Tennessee, and the Greater Nashville Homeland Security District (District 5) conducted an Emergency Preparedness Challenge in April 2006. This exercise was intended to test local first responders' abilities to respond to a full-scale terrorist attack on the city. It involved responders at every level of government in Nashville and its four surrounding counties. The challenge is one of the nation's largest local disaster response exercises. Through the recruitment of over three thousand volunteers that played the role of the sick, injured, or dead, or the role of volunteer coordinators of food and beverages, local emergency teams, law enforcement agencies, and 14 area hospitals were able to evaluate their capability to respond to this type of terrorist event. The exercise examined District 5's strategies for "responding to mass casualties, search and rescue for victims, triage and transportation preparation of survivors, hospital processing and treatment, processing of deceased victims and other disaster management efforts".[25] The exercise is also intended to educate the volunteers involved as to their role in participating in preparedness.

SELF-CHECK

- Describe the role of The American Red Cross.
- Describe the Emergency Management Institute (EMI) Program.
- Select a natural hazard and give an example preparedness exercise for that hazard.

SUMMARY

Preparedness is a continuous process that requires constant updating and revision to remain current. Updates to preparedness activities can be implemented after a disaster, when emergency managers can incorporate lessons learned from the event, as well as after organizational or administrative changes in preparedness functions. Preferably, our preparedness actions are proactive rather than reactive, but in understanding the role of preparedness within the emergency management cycle, we realize that emergency managers must be flexible in order to adapt established plans and protocol to meet emergency situations as they arise. This chapter describes the framework within which preparedness functions are carried out at all levels of government, within the business sector, and by private citizens. All citizens are responsible for continuing preparedness education and for contributing to improvements in governmental, community, and individual readiness.

KEY TERMS

Comprehensive emergency management	A widely used approach at the local, state, and federal levels to deal with the inevitability of natural hazards and their potential to cause disasters in a community.
Emergency operations plan	Contains procedures that can be detailed and coordinated for emergency responders; developed and maintained by local emergency managers.
First responders	Groups that are the first to arrive at the scene of the emergency, such as police, fire, and paramedics.
Incident of national significance	Declared after a federal agency has requested help from the Department of Homeland Security, a state or local government has requested help from the federal government, multiple federal agencies have become involved, or the President requests the involvement of the Department of Homeland Security.
Mitigation	Any sustained action to reduce or eliminate long-term risk to people and property from hazards and their effects.
National Guard	Provides the capability to greatly assist in disaster response in terms of providing communications systems; construction equipment; emergency

such as medical supplies, beds, food, water, and blankets; as well as personnel to assist with distribution.

National Preparedness Assessment And Reporting System

Provides a report of the nation's level of preparedness to the President and gives guidance to participating agencies on adopting quantifiable performance measures of preparedness in the areas of training, planning, exercises, and equipment.

National Incident Management System (NIMS)

Provides guidance to the federal agencies participating in the National Response Plan in disaster preparedness.

National Response Plan (NRP)

Serves to coordinate response responsibilities and logistics at the federal level. Represents a binding agreement among 27 government agencies and the American Red Cross.

NOAA Weather Radio All Hazards Network (NWR)

A network of radio stations across the country that broadcasts continuous weather and hazards information.

Preparedness

Activities to improve the ability to respond quickly in the immediate aftermath of an incident. Includes development of response procedures, design and installation of warning systems, evacuation planning, exercises to test emergency operations, training of emergency personnel.

Recovery

Phase in the emergency management cycle that involves actions that begin after a disaster, after emergency needs have been met; examples include road and bridge repairs and restoration of power.

Resilient communities

Towns, cities, counties, Native American tribes, states, and other forms of communities that take action prior to a hazard event so that a disaster does not result.

Response

Phase in the emergency management cycle that involves activities to meet the urgent needs of victims during or immediately following a disaster; examples include evacuation as well as search and rescue.

ASSESS YOUR UNDERSTANDING

Go to www.wiley.com/college/schwab to evaluate your knowledge of the basics of short-term planning in the emergency management cycle.
Measure your learning by comparing pre-test and post-test results.

Summary Questions

1. Preparedness overlaps with all phases of the emergency management cycle. True or False?

2. Which of the following is not a true preparedness activity?
   (a) training
   (b) exercises
   (c) emergency response planning
   (d) land use planning

3. Preparedness is
   (a) first response by paramedics.
   (b) a long-term activity.
   (c) pre-planning for response.
   (d) building levees or retrofitting houses.

4. The National Response Plan has 10 emergency response functions. True or False?

5. Emergency response functions are independent of each other. True or False?

6. The All Hazards Network is broadcast over the
   (a) NOAA Weather Radio.
   (b) USGS hazards radio.
   (c) The Weather Channel.
   (d) FEMA Weather Radio.

7. State level emergency management offices have different office or agency names, but perform similar functions. True or False?

8. During an incident of emergency, a governor's prime resource is
   (a) the local police station.
   (b) the President.
   (c) the hardware store owner.
   (d) the National Guard.

9. Local governments do not share in which of the following preparedness responsibilities?
   (a) calling for the help of the Department of Homeland Security.

(b) providing warning systems.

(c) stocking emergency supplies and equipment.

(d) evacuating the community.

10. Business owners hold preparedness responsibilities within your community. True or False?

11. The *Are You Ready? An In-depth Guide to Citizen Preparedness* describes where to seek shelter from all types of hazards. True or False?

12. Evacuation involves which of the following:

(a) the local police station.

(b) the governor.

(c) the National Guard.

(d) all of the above.

13. Which of the following is not a volunteer agency involved in preparedness and response:

(a) The American Red Cross.

(b) Catholic Charities.

(c) The Emergency Management Institute.

(d) all of the above are involved in preparedness and response.

14. The Department of Homeland Security does not want to involve children in preparedness because it is too scary. True or False?

15. There are preparedness exercises that can be done for every hazard. True or False?

Review Questions

1. Name ten federal departments or agencies that participate in the National Response Plan.

2. Describe an example of mitigation.

3. Describe an example of preparedness.

4. Describe an example of response.

5. Explain why preparedness is everyone's responsibility.

6. What are some of the ways citizens can participate in preparedness activities?

7. What other volunteer organizations are out there other than The American Red Cross?

8. What is an example of a preparedness exercise using a warning system?

Applying This Chapter

1. Imagine that you are the mayor of a town that is prone to wildfires. What are the different preparedness activities that you can participate in to improve your town's state of readiness? What are other examples from other local warning systems that you could use to apply to your town? What exercises would you want to employ and who would be involved?

2. Set aside time to create a preparedness plan with your family or roommate. What would you include? Where would you start to look for good examples? Would you encourage others to use your plan as a template?

3. What are ways that you, as a citizen, can get others in your community involved in preparedness activities taking place in the area?

The American Red Cross

The American Red Cross relies on volunteers to carry out most of its programs. Following every disaster in the United States, ARC chapters spring into action to provide emergency aid, care, and comfort. To contact a local Red Cross chapter near you, follow the instructions on the Red Cross Web site: www.redcross.org/where/chapts.asp. Write a paper or how The American Red Cross can help your community after a disaster.

READY? . . . Set . . . Go!

There are so many responsibilities for emergency managers that vary from place to place—you'll just have to see for yourself. Take a look at the list of responsibilities for emergency management coordinators in Baltimore County, MD: www.co.ba.md.us/Agencies/fire/emergencyplan/index.html, and the 13 functions of emergency management in Allegheny County, PA: www.county.allegheny.pa.us/emerserv/emerman. Then, look for the emergency plan in your locality. Check to see if disaster response responsibilities are clearly described, delineated, and coordinated for the officials that are there to protect you and your community—and see what you can do to get involved.

12

HAZARD MITIGATION TOOLS AND TECHNIQUES
Creating Strategies to Reduce Vulnerability

Starting Point

Go to www.wiley.com/college/schwab to assess your knowledge of hazard mitigation tools and techniques.
Determine where you need to concentrate your effort.

What You'll Learn in This Chapter

▲ The major categories of mitigation strategies
▲ Common types of structural engineering projects
▲ Ways of protecting shorelines using structural engineering
▲ Community-level methods of structural engineering
▲ Three ways of preventing disasters
▲ The four strategies used to strengthen buildings and facilities
▲ The mitigation benefits of wetland preservation
▲ Ways of mitigating through public information
▲ Examples of funding sources for mitigation
▲ Mitigation techniques for man-made hazards

After Studying This Chapter, You'll Be Able To

▲ Examine the important factors in choosing a mitigation strategy
▲ Discuss the disadvantages of structural engineering projects
▲ Compare the benefits of disaster-prevention techniques
▲ Appraise the role of building codes in hazards mitigation
▲ Examine the role of real estate disclosure in hazard mitigation
▲ Compare the differences between mitigation for natural and man-made disasters

Goals and Outcomes

▲ Master the terminology, understand the procedures, and recognize the strategies to reduce vulnerability to hazards
▲ Evaluate the pros and cons of various mitigation tools
▲ Assess the relationship between risk assessment and strategy selection
▲ Select mitigation strategies in the context of a comprehensive mitigation plan
▲ Collaborate with others to select the most appropriate mitigation strategies for a community
▲ Evaluate mitigation techniques used to reduce hazard vulnerabilities of real communities

INTRODUCTION

Though we cannot prevent hazards from occurring, we can reduce our vulnerability to many natural and man-made hazards that face our communities. This chapter introduces action strategies that can increase the resiliency of a community, beginning with an outline of five broad approaches to mitigation. The chapter then details some of the advantages and disadvantages of structural engineered projects, with attention given to projects used to protect shorelines. The chapter next discusses preventative mitigation strategies, using examples such as acquisition of properties located in hazard areas and land use regulatory techniques such as zoning. The chapter describes property protection next, followed by a discussion of various tools for natural resource protection and ways of informing community members about potential hazards through public education and awareness programs. In addition, this chapter reviews some of the sources of funding that are available to communities to implement mitigation efforts at the local level. The chapter also contains a short description of some of the methods that can be used to deal with various man-made hazards. The chapter concludes by describing how a community can incorporate its mitigation strategies and actions into a local hazard mitigation plan to provide a cohesive and coordinated approach to reducing vulnerability.

12.1 Types of Mitigation Tools and Techniques

Mitigation tools and techniques can be as varied as the communities that use them, and no two communities use the same set of strategies. In general, there are five broad approaches to mitigation, as shown in the following table. Within each of these categories, different mitigation actions target specific types of problems. Some communities may choose to focus on one type of mitigation strategy, while other communities may use a mix and match approach. Whatever strategy (or combination of strategies) is used depends on various factors, such as the cost of each type of action, the technical ability of the community to put the strategy into place, and the benefit that the community will receive once the strategy is implemented. Some mitigation techniques are best suited to prevent future disasters by keeping people and property out of harm's way before development occurs (these are strategies in the prevention category). Other categories of mitigation are more effective for protecting existing structures (such as strategies in the property protection group) and are appropriate for areas where development has already occurred. Table 12-1 summarizes the types of mitigation strategies that communities can use as part of a comprehensive mitigation program and provides a few examples of each.

Table 12-1: Types of Mitigation Strategies

Type of Strategy	Purpose and Critique	Examples
Structural Engineered Project	Lessen the impact of a hazard by modifying the environment or progression of the hazard event. Can have the potential to increase vulnerability over the long-term and/or cause environmental degradation.	• Dams and reservoirs • Dikes/levees/floodwalls/berms • Diversions • Seawalls/groins/jetties • Revetments • Beach nourishment • Storm sewers/drainage system • Vegetative buffers
Prevention	Avoid hazard problems or keep hazard problems from getting worse. Most effective in reducing future vulnerability, especially in locations where development has not yet occurred.	• Land use planning • Zoning/subdivision • Floodplain regulation • Acquisition and relocation • Shoreline/faultzone setbacks • Capital improvement programs • Taxation and fees
Property Protection	Protect structures by modifying/strengthening the building to withstand hazard impacts. Effective in protecting existing structures in hazard areas.	• Building codes and construction standards • Elevation • Floodproofing/windproofing • Seismic retrofit • Safe rooms
Natural Resource Protection	Reduce the impacts of natural hazards by preserving or restoring natural areas and their mitigation functions. Can also serve other community interests of providing open space/recreation areas/greenways.	• Floodplain protection • Beach/dune preservation • Riparian buffers • Fire resistant landscaping • Erosion/sediment control • Wetland preservation and restoration • Habitat protection • Slope stabilization
Public Information	Advise residents, business owners, potential property buyers, and visitors about hazards, hazardous areas, and mitigation techniques to protect themselves and their property.	• Outreach projects • Hazard map information • Real estate disclosure • Warning systems • Libraries • Education programs for school children

FOR EXAMPLE

No Critical Facilities in High-Hazard Areas

Dade County, Florida's 1988 Comprehensive Development Master Plan prohibited the construction of critical facilities (such as hospitals, emergency services, and emergency command centers) in coastal high hazard areas. The county was intent on being able to rescue citizens and provide emergency response even during a hurricane or other coastal storm.

SELF-CHECK

- Cite the five types of mitigation strategies.
- Discuss the factors involved in choosing a mitigation strategy.

12.2 Mitigation through Engineering Projects

For many years in our country, the favored technique for preventing disasters was to try and control the hazard itself. It was assumed that engineering and technology could be used to armor against the forces of nature. Agencies such as the U.S. Army Corps of Engineers have built dams, levees, seawalls, and other large projects throughout the country designed to make communities resistant to natural hazards. In many cases, these hard structures do indeed protect people and property from rising floodwaters, erosion, wave action, and other natural hazards. When communities are located in an area that depends on a particular natural resource, such as a river, it may make sense to protect residents in this way. In some places, structural projects have been in place so long that they must be maintained in order to keep the community intact. However, although some communities have benefited from structural mitigation measures, others have experienced some of the serious disadvantages associated with these projects.

12.2.1 Disadvantages of Structural Engineered Mitigation Projects

While structural engineered projects are appropriate in some locations, in general, this approach to mitigation is based on a flawed assumption. By armoring communities to resist hazards, it is assumed that these communities can defeat the forces of nature. This is a never-ending proposition, one with few guarantees of success and can lead to a false sense of security.

Providing a False Sense of Security

The major drawback of many structural mitigation projects is that in the process of reducing short-term risk they can actually make future disasters worse, particularly by encouraging development in hazard-prone areas when residents feel a false sense of security. Civil engineers, planners, and others interested in flood-control management have observed that damage from floods in this country has actually gone up despite our huge investment in flood-control infrastructure.

Reducing the Mitigation Function of Natural Resources

Structural engineered projects can also reduce nature's ability to mitigate the impacts of storms and floods. Often these negative effects are experienced at some distance from the site of the project itself. For example, levees may worsen upstream or downstream flooding by changing the natural flow and volume of a river. Groins, which are meant to protect the shore from erosion by trapping sand, can worsen erosion on neighboring beaches. Channel diversions that are built for flood control purposes can rob surrounding wetlands and marshes of silt deposits and starve them of nutrients, reducing the floodplain's natural capacity to absorb floodwaters. It is important to consider the wider region when thinking about structural mitigation projects to avoid simply shifting problems from one neighborhood to another.

The Expense of Structural Mitigation Projects

Armoring against nature is very expensive. Many structural projects are technically difficult and costly to build and their benefits are often short-lived. When budgets are tight, routine maintenance and repairs to levees, seawalls, and other large projects may be postponed, increasing the likelihood of failure. Few local governments can afford to build and maintain big mitigation projects, and most large-scale engineering works are funded by the federal and state governments. Federal funds are most often used for mitigation projects in areas that are of national interest, such as large ports or shipping channels, or where significant tax revenues and jobs are created, such as along the oceanfront where property values are high. Unfortunately, some of these projects are funded through "pork barrel" appropriations of federal tax dollars—when a member of Congress is able to direct large amounts of money to his or her own district, even though there may only be a direct benefit to relatively few people.

These disadvantages apply mostly to very large-scale structural projects that require complicated engineering plans and millions of dollars to construct. A description of large structural projects follows, along with potential advantages and disadvantages of each project. Not all structural projects are carried out on this scale, however. Some of the smaller projects that are carried out at the local level will also be discussed, such as storm sewers and drainage systems, where many of these disadvantages do not apply.

12.2.2 Dams and Reservoirs

A dam is an artificial barrier designed to impound water, wastewater, or any liquid-borne material for the purpose of storage or flood control. Dams can be effective flood-control devices by retaining water and releasing it at a controlled rate that does not overwhelm the capacity of downstream channels. Dams are also used to maintain water depths for navigation, irrigation, water supply, hydropower, and other purposes. Reservoirs are water storage facilities that are located behind dams and are used to hold water during peak runoff periods, to serve as a source of drinking water and to provide recreational and fishing opportunities.

Dam Ownership in the United States

Although very large dams are owned and operated by state or federal agencies, the majority of dams in the United States are privately owned, as is demonstrated by Figure 12-1. Dam owners are responsible for the safety and the liability of the dam and for financing its upkeep, upgrade, and repair. Most states have a dam safety program that helps monitor dams and carries out inspections on a regular basis, yet the large number of dams that are owned and controlled by private landowners makes it difficult for state and local officials to ensure their safety. In many states, the dam safety office is understaffed and underfunded, and dam officials cannot inspect all privately-owned dams in the state. Dam repair and maintenance can be costly, and many state dam safety

Figure 12-1

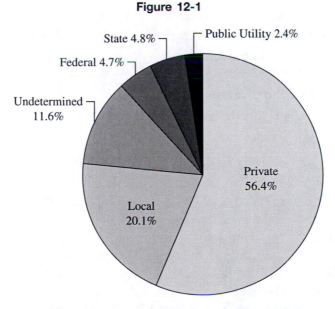

Ownership and operation of dams in the United States.
National Inventory of Dams, February 2005

programs do not have enforcement authority to require private dam owners to make repairs.

Environmental Costs Associated with Dams

As with other structural projects, dams and reservoirs are expensive and land consumptive, require regular maintenance, and only prevent damage from floods for the capacity that they are designed to handle. Dams and reservoirs can have many environmental costs, such as the flooding of natural habitat or farming areas when the reservoir is filled. Dams can eliminate the natural and beneficial function of the floodplain, including its ability to absorb floodwater. Dams can also change the hydrology of an entire watershed, causing negative impacts in areas far removed from the dam itself.

Dam Break Hazards

The potential for dam failure is an extremely serious hazard in many states. Leaks and cracks that form in ill-maintained dams can cause dam failure, resulting in very rapid flooding downstream, often with little warning, putting property and human life in grave danger. Dams can fail for one or a combination of the following reasons:[1]

▲ Overtopping caused by floods that exceed the capacity of the dam.
▲ Deliberate acts of sabotage.
▲ Structural failure of materials used in dam construction.
▲ Movement and/or failure of the foundation supporting the dam.
▲ Settlement and cracking of concrete or embankment dams.
▲ Piping and internal erosion of soil in embankment dams.
▲ Inadequate maintenance and upkeep.

Dam Failures in the United States

A series of dam failures in the 1970s caused the nation to focus on inspecting and regulating dams.

▲ On February 26, 1972, a tailings dam owned by the Buffalo Mining Company in Buffalo Creek, West Virginia, failed. In a matter of minutes, 125 people were killed, 1100 people were injured, and over 3000 were left homeless.
▲ On June 5, 1976, Teton Dam, a 123-meter high dam on the Teton River in Idaho, failed, causing $1 billion in damage and leaving 11 dead. Over 4000 homes and over 4000 farm buildings were destroyed as a result of the Teton Dam failure.
▲ In November 1977, Kelly Barnes Dam in Georgia failed, killing 39 people, most of them college students.

FOR EXAMPLE

The Johnstown Flood

At 4:07 P.M. on the afternoon of May 31, 1889, the residents of Johnstown, Pennsylvania, heard a low rumble that grew to a "roar like thunder."[2] After a night of heavy rains, the South Fork Dam had failed, sending tons of water crashing down the narrow valley. Boiling with huge chunks of debris, the wall of flood water grew at times to 60 feet high, tearing downhill at 40 miles per hour and leveling everything in its path. Thousands desperately tried to escape the wave. Those caught by the wave found themselves swept up in a torrent of oily, muddy water, surrounded by tons of grinding debris, which crushed some, provided rafts for others. Many became helplessly entangled in miles of barbed wire from a destroyed wire works. Although the event was over in 10 minutes, for some the worst was yet to come. As darkness fell, thousands were huddled in attics, others were floating on the debris, and many more had been swept downstream to the old Stone Bridge at the junction of two rivers. Piled up against the arches, much of the debris caught fire, entrapping and killing 80 people who had survived the initial flood wave.

12.2.3 Dikes, Levees, Floodwalls, and Berms

The terms dike and levee are often used synonymously. Dikes are usually earthen or rock structures built partially across a river for the purpose of maintaining the depth and location of a navigation channel. Levees are earthen embankments used to protect low-lying lands from flooding. A floodwall is a reinforced concrete wall that acts as a barrier against floodwaters. Berms are barriers created by grading or filling areas with soil and are meant to keep floodwaters from reaching buildings.

Environmental Damage Caused by Flood Control Structures

Dikes, levees, floodwalls, and berms can cause environmental damage similar to that of dams and reservoirs. These structures interfere with the environment's ability to naturally mitigate floods, which it can do under normal circumstances by absorbing excess water into wetlands and low-lying areas. Levees and other floodwalls prevent floodwaters from flowing into the natural floodplain. As a result, they frequently concentrate flooding in locations upstream and downstream from their location. These flood control structures can also deprive wildlife and fish habitats, such as marshes and estuaries, of the water and nutrients they need to function properly.

The Dangers of Breached Flood Control Structures

To be effective, levees and similar flood control structures must be located outside of the floodway and must make up for the flood storage they take up. Levees, dikes, and floodwalls should not be used to reclaim land in the floodplain

THE FAILURE OF NEW ORLEANS LEVEES FOLLOWING HURRICANE KATRINA

For many successive generations, the tools and techniques used in New Orleans, Louisiana, for flood hazard prevention have focused on structural means through the construction of levees. Historically, the levees surrounding New Orleans and those built along the banks of the Mississippi River have repeatedly failed to keep flood waters out.

After each successive flooding event, the levees of New Orleans have simply been built higher as a preventive measure against the next flood. The levees also work to increase the volume of water by channeling river flow into a concentrated area. These factors combine with the routine subsidence that occurs in the area due to natural soil conditions, effectively creating a never-ending challenge for the protection of New Orleans. The fact that the levees of New Orleans were breached by the forces exerted by Hurricane Katrina in 2005 is a dramatic demonstration of how levees in general are not foolproof flood protection measures. What happened in New Orleans after the levees breached is an even more telling example of the worst-case scenario, with excessive inundation of most of the city and devastation of the neighborhoods in the vicinity of the levee breaches.

As Katrina passed through the area in and surrounding New Orleans, bringing high storm surges and large amounts of rainfall, the level of Lake Pontchartrain rose rapidly, straining the entire levee system in the New Orleans area, especially in the 17th Street Canal and London Avenue Canal. It is not known exactly when the levees were breached or overtopped, but several of the levees were breached on the day of landfall. On August 29, the surging water overtopped the eastern levees around New Orleans, spilling into Orleans Parish and St. Bernard Parish and pushing water up the Industrial Canal and Intracoastal Waterway.[4] There were breaches along the 17th Street Canal and the London Avenue Canal that day as well, resulting in flooding of 80% of New Orleans with flood waters reaching up to 20 feet in parts of the city. It was difficult and time consuming to repair the breaches, especially with the arrival of Hurricane Rita a short time later. The U.S. Army Corps of Engineers was not able to drain all of the flood waters out of the city until October 11, 43 days after Katrina's landfall.

There is considerable speculation as to exactly why and how the levees of New Orleans failed so completely. What is known for certain is that the Army Corps of Engineers had purposely built the levees to a specified level known as the "Standard Project Hurricane."[5] This standard is designed to withstand up to and including a Category 3 hurricane in terms of storm surge levels and a Category 2 hurricane in terms of wind speed. As a consequence, the levees of New Orleans were not designed or constructed to withstand a strong Category 3 hurricane like Katrina. Further complications arose due to the numerous agencies that were responsible for managing the levee system after it was built, resulting in variable maintenance and repair policies and practices, and weaknesses in transition areas between jurisdictional responsibilities. These issues are in addition to the basic problems encountered by building levees on deltaic soils that are prone to subsidence, which causes levees to sink and become unstable over time. Leaks in the 17th Street Canal levee that were reported before Hurricane Katrina may have been due to weakened structural components caused by this subsidence.

Continuation of a system of levees is not the only mitigation technique that is available to the City of New Orleans. The following adaptation strategies were recommended for New Orleans in an article in the 2002 Natural Hazards Observer, a publication of the Natural Hazards Research and Applications Information Center at the University of Colorado. At that time, the article recommended a variety of tools and techniques for mitigating future flood hazards, including:

- ✔ Protect and restore natural coastal defenses.
- ✔ Upgrade levees and drainage systems to withstand Category 4 and 5 hurricanes.
- ✔ Develop maps of potential flood areas that integrate local elevations, subsidence rates, and drainage capabilities (for use in the design of ordinances, greenbelts, and other flood damage reduction measures).
- ✔ Design and maintain flood protection based on historical and projected rates of local subsidence, rainfall, and sea-level rise.
- ✔ Minimize drain and fill activities, shallow subsurface fluid withdrawals, and other human developments that increase subsidence.
- ✔ Improve evacuation routes to increase the ability of residents to escape an approaching hurricane.
- ✔ Encourage floodproofing of buildings and infrastructure.
- ✔ Foster the purchase of more National Flood Insurance Program policies by homeowners and businesses.[6]

for development. The Midwest Floods of 1993 clearly demonstrated that each of these structures is subject to being overtopped or breached by floods that exceed their design. One flood control official has summed up the danger by observing, "There are two kinds of levees: those that have broken and those that are going to break. After all, they're just packed dirt."[3]

12.2.4 Reducing Coastal Hazard Impacts through Structural Engineered Projects

A traditional approach to hurricane and coastal storm mitigation is to strengthen, reinforce, or replenish the natural environment so that it is less susceptible to the damaging forces of storms. Most hurricane-related deaths and property damage are a result of storm surges. Shoreline protection works are designed to combat storm surge and storm-induced waves. Some shoreline protection works are also designed to protect existing development from ongoing coastal erosion. However, these measures often have high costs, both in monetary and environmental terms, and should primarily be used as the last defense before abandoning existing major buildings. Some coastal states, mindful of the environmental damage and high cost of these projects, have passed legislation that prohibits most shore-hardening devices.

Sediment-Trapping Structures

Beaches and dunes are the coast's first line of defense against storm winds and waves. The sand that provides this defense is constantly moving from offshore bars to channels, to beaches and dunes, and back again in response to the natural forces of wind, waves, currents, and tides. Sand-trapping structures are designed to protect, maintain, or enhance beaches and dunes by interrupting this cycle as sand is deposited on the beaches or dunes. Some structures, such as groins or jetties, are designed to capture sand as it flows parallel to the shore, a natural process known as littoral drift. Planting and fencing are designed to capture sand as it is blown through the air. However, by interrupting the natural cycle, these techniques can create unintended negative consequences. They may starve downstream beaches or create currents that swish sand away from the shore.

Groins

Groins are wall-like structures, built of timber, concrete, metal sheet piling, or rock, placed perpendicular to the beach to capture sand traveling in littoral drift (see Figure 12-2). Usually constructed in groups called groin fields, their primary purpose is to trap and hold onto the sand, filling the beach compartments between them.

Figure 12-2

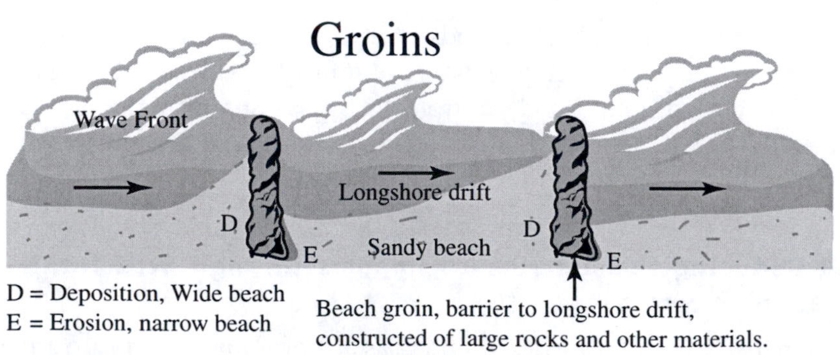

Groins

D = Deposition, Wide beach
E = Erosion, narrow beach

Beach groin, barrier to longshore drift, constructed of large rocks and other materials.

Groins

Groins are mainly designed to create a wider beach for recreational purposes and to reduce the need for sand replacement on beaches. A wider beach can help slow erosion by making storm waves break further out to sea, but it is not an effective means of protecting shorefront buildings from coastal surge or high winds. By interrupting the normal patterns of drift, groins starve downstream beaches of their diet of sand and may worsen a shoreline's overall erosion problem.

Jetties

Jetties are wall-like structures built perpendicular to the coast, often in pairs, to keep sediment from building up in inlets. Inlets are natural waterways that run between barrier islands and connect the ocean to the sound, and are very important to navigation. The main function of jetties is to allow safe passage for boats.

While the primary function of jetties is to protect navigation channels, they can restrict the movement of sediment traveling parallel to the shore, even more so than groins. Jetties can also create currents that transfer sand offshore, leading to net sand loss from the beach. The effects of jetty systems are sometimes difficult to predict and frequently are not evident until years or decades later.

Seawalls and Bulkheads

Seawalls are vertical coastal walls designed to protect buildings from shoreline erosion. They may or may not also protect against storm wave attacks. Bulkheads are vertical walls set back from the shoreline, often constructed of wood or steel. Unlike seawalls, bulkheads are designed to *retain* loose fill and sediment behind them. Despite their differences, the terms seawall and bulkhead are often used interchangeably.

Seawalls are costly to build and can block public access to the shoreline. They reflect waves and make currents more intense, which can make the profile (slope) of the beach steeper and actually makes erosion in front of the wall and on property at both ends of the wall worse. Seawalls require continual maintenance and investment since loosened materials can become a hazard during storms. Temporary seawalls constructed from sandbags are unlikely to withstand the force of a storm and should be used only to repel normal erosion until the structure they are protecting can be relocated.

Construction and Stabilization of Sand Dunes

Dunes are naturally very useful to protect buildings from damage during severe storms and long-term erosion. They also prevent overwash flooding (when ocean-side waves are driven onto an island, usually through gaps in the dune field) during storms and minimize the scouring that occurs when the overwash water flows back to the sea. Dunes also shelter buildings from high winds. Dunes can be constructed artificially by trapping sand with fences or by piling sand into dunes with bulldozers. Dune stabilization is a technique for anchoring sand in dune form using plants.

Dune fields can be difficult to place in between existing beachfront homes. To provide any storm protection, dune fields must be wide, about 100 feet, and the dunes must be as high as 10 feet. There also must be no gaps between the dunes, which limits oceanfront views and public access to the beach. Dunes migrate as part of their natural life cycle. Attempts to anchor dunes in place generally result in "seawall" dunes that narrow beaches and can cause erosion at their ends. Areas with low sand supplies will have trouble building dunes artificially.

Beach Nourishment

A beach that is relatively stable or growing provides natural protection to structures behind it. Beaches that are losing sand through erosion or starvation cannot provide this natural protection. **Beach nourishment** is the artificial replacement or addition of sand to beaches to widen the backshore and move the high-water line further toward the sea.

Large-scale nourishment programs can be very expensive, on the order of $1-$5 million per mile per application. The frequency of nourishment required to maintain a beach is difficult to predict. Most nourishment projects along the Atlantic Ocean have a lifespan of two to ten years depending on how often storms occur. Artificially renourished beaches tend to erode more quickly than natural beaches.

While nourishment programs create wider beaches for recreational use, they can also unintentionally worsen the hazard risk. The sand used to nourish beaches is often taken from nearby offshore banks because these banks offer a less expensive source of matching sand. But robbing these banks is shortsighted, since they act as an offshore speed bump. The result is that larger waves reach the shore, causing more severe erosion. Nourishment programs may also spur oceanfront development, putting even more structures at risk.

SELF-CHECK

- List six ways dams can fail.
- Explain how structural engineering projects can encourage development of hazard-prone areas.
- Discuss the environmental costs of large-scale engineering projects such as dams.

12.3 Storm Sewers and Drainage Systems

Not all structural mitigation projects are huge and expensive. On a smaller scale—at the community level—structural projects are usually designed by engineers and managed by public works staff and include such necessary actions as

> ## FOR EXAMPLE
>
> ### Using GIS to Project Flooding from Future Development
>
> Planners and engineers of the Charlotte-Mecklenburg Storm Water Service in North Carolina use geographic information system (GIS) technology to create computer models of the impact of future flood events and to assess the impact of various land use, development patterns, and growth scenarios. The department uses the GIS data to choose the most appropriate stormwater flood control measures in the floodplains of the metropolitan area.

the construction and maintenance of stormwater systems, sanitary sewer systems, and drainage systems.

12.3.1 Building Drainage Systems with Adequate Capacity

A number of floods occur in urban areas for the simple reason that drainage systems are not built with the capacity to handle stormwater runoff. **Runoff** is rainwater that does not soak into the soil, evaporate, or become trapped by plant roots, and thus flows over the surface of the ground into the first depression, stream, lake, or other low-lying area. Stormwater systems are designed to catch runoff and channel it into a series of drains and pipes to a catch basin or other containment device. When drainage systems are installed, a community should make sure that culverts, ditches, channels, pipes, and all other components are built with enough capacity to meet the volume of stormwater that is expected during normal and above-average rainfalls.

When designing a new or updated stormwater system, a community would do well to anticipate any changes that could occur to flood levels due to future development and growth. Increased development usually brings an increase in **impervious surfaces**—paved areas that rainwater cannot soak through, such as parking lots, roofs, streets, and other nonporous surfaces—resulting in a greater volume of water entering the stormwater system. Rapid urbanization that is not well planned can quickly overwhelm a community's ability to manage increased levels of stormwater runoff.

12.3.2 Drain System Maintenance

Drainage systems will not continue to function properly without a well-planned, on-going preventive maintenance program of inspection, de-silting, and repair. Maintenance work can be expensive, but not nearly as expensive as fixing flooding problems. Problematic road gullies, stormwater intakes, drains, and watercourses should be inspected on a regular basis, especially before and during the rainy season. Some municipalities use closed-circuit television surveys to inspect existing drains where human-entry inspections are not possible.

12.3.3 Nontraditional Stormwater Management

Traditional municipal stormwater management and flood-control projects involve hard, invasive techniques that disturb natural urban stream channels. Some communities are choosing alternative methods such as soil bioengineering, the use of vegetation along streambeds to slow runoff, and other nontraditional ways to stabilize stream banks and control floodwaters. Some communities are also restricting the amount of impervious surfaces that developers can create and encourage such innovative solutions as garden roofs, where small trees, shrubs, and other plantings are grown on rooftops to filter and soak up rainwater before it meets the drainage system. These and other types of approaches can improve water quality at the same time they reduce flood hazards, and can also add to the beauty of a community.

12.3.4 Moving Away from Structural Engineered Mitigation Projects

Mitigation practice is moving away from the engineered approach as a way of reducing hazard impacts. Experience has shown that while the actions described above might work in the short term, their long-term effectiveness is often questionable. Many structural projects are expensive to build and maintain. They can be vulnerable to sudden failure, and they encourage development to take place in their shadow. They can cause unintended damage to the environment or to people downstream. Strategies with long-term costs that outweigh their benefits are unsustainable, and over the long run such actions can decrease rather than increase community resiliency. Mitigation experts are tending toward activities that are more sustainable, such as the prevention, natural resource protection, and property protection strategies that we will discuss next.

SELF-CHECK

- Define **runoff** and **impervious surface**.
- Explain the relationship between urban flooding and maintenance of drainage systems.
- Discuss the long-term effectiveness of structural engineering projects.

12.4 Mitigation through Prevention

Over the long term, the most sustainable approach to minimize damages and losses from natural hazards is to guide development away from hazard-prone areas. This means not building on floodplains, avoiding steep-slope and landslide areas, and setting development back from high-erosion coastal areas. In other words, we try to avoid disasters altogether by removing people and property from the location where the built environment intersects with the hazard event. This section describes three ways of preventing disasters:

1. The most direct way to prevent future disasters is through public acquisition of hazardous land: paying the owners to leave and then demolishing or relocating any buildings located on the site.
2. A second method to prevent disasters involves local land use regulations, such as zoning, subdivision ordinances, and setback regulations.
3. A third method involves the community's power to spend public money for capital improvements in order to discourage development in hazardous areas.

The prevention approach is most useful when other, safer development locations are available in the community to which growth can be steered. Communities that have reached build-out already have more limited options for using prevention strategies, although there are ways that the local government can encourage new structures to be built on existing lots (a practice called infill) in safe locations. Prevention techniques apply only to hazards that can be geographically delineated and located on a map (flooding, for example). Preventive mitigation measures are less effective for hazards that are not locally geographically specific, such as tornadoes and ice storms.

12.4.1 Acquisition and Relocation

By acquiring property in hazardous areas, a community can ensure that the land will be used only for purposes that are compatible with the hazard. Picnic shelters and dog parks, for example, are a better choice for the floodplain than homes and shops. Although acquisition is typically one of the most expensive mitigation tactics, in the long run acquisition can be very cost effective. Through acquisition, the local government takes ownership of privately-held residential or business property that has been subjected to repeated hazards, most often flooding. Acquisition is often accompanied by relocation, when the owner's home is moved to a safer location.

Saving Money through Acquisition

Although buyout programs require an initial outlay of thousands, sometimes millions, of dollars (depending upon the price and number of homes involved), over the long term these funds are paid back in full through cost savings realized by avoiding future disasters. Initially, since title to the acquired property is transferred to the public domain, acquisition can remove properties from the tax rolls, so that the local government can no longer collect real estate taxes on that property, a major source of revenue for most communities. However, the cost of losing tax revenue from these properties is usually much lower compared to the cost of repairing and rebuilding homes repeatedly after they are damaged during hazard events. The local government also avoids the expense of rescue and recovery operations, emergency sheltering, and financial assistance that arises when residents are displaced due to a disaster. Cost savings are also realized since the local government no longer is responsible for providing municipal services (such as garbage pickup and road maintenance) to these properties once they are acquired. Over the long term, acquisition allows communities to save a great deal by preventing repetitive losses.

Communities have put their acquired properties to any number of uses, such as parks, greenways, open space, tennis courts, and community gardens. These new uses can serve the community in numerous ways, including protecting habitat, enhancing water quality, conserving open space, and contributing to the beauty and recreational attributes of the area.

12.4.2 Land Use Regulation

Another very effective method of preventing disasters is to keep people and property from locating in known hazard areas *before* these areas become developed. Communities carry this out by writing a land use plan or comprehensive plan that creates a vision of how the community wants to grow, and then passing ordinances that follow the plan to control where and how property can be developed. This section discusses some of the more commonly used types of regulation that local governments can use to control growth in hazardous locations, including zoning ordinances, subdivision ordinances, and setbacks.

Zoning Ordinances

The majority of local governments in the United States use zoning as a tool to control the use of land within their jurisdiction. The local government is authorized to divide its jurisdiction into districts, and to regulate and restrict the construction and use of buildings within each of those districts. Land uses controlled by zoning include the type of use (residential, commercial, industrial, etc.), as well as minimum specifications for use such as lot size, building height, and street setbacks, density of population (how many people can be accommodated in one area), and other elements of development.

A local zoning ordinance consists of maps and written text. Some communities have made good use of their zoning ordinances by showing hazard areas on the map. The corresponding text of the ordinance may require that these areas be used for low-intensity uses such as recreation, open or green space, or

> ## FOR EXAMPLE
>
> ### Subdividing in Colorado, California, and Oregon
>
> In Colorado, local governments require subdivision applicants to prepare drainage plans to prevent flooding and erosion. In California, municipalities require subdividers to incorporate wildfire suppression facilities in the development plans. In Portland, Oregon, developers must locate public facilities and utilities, such as sewer and water systems, in a way that minimizes flood damage.

agriculture. Zoning can also be used to prohibit environmentally hazardous uses, such as junkyards and chemical storage facilities in areas exposed to natural hazards. At the same time, a zoning ordinance can be used to encourage development in safe areas, by allowing greater density in parts of the community that are not subject to hazards.

Subdivision Ordinances

Subdivision regulations control land that is being divided into smaller parcels for sale or development. Subdivision ordinances typically set construction and location standards for lot layout and for infrastructure such as roads, drainage systems, sidewalks, lighting, and the like. Subdivision ordinances are not as broad as zoning and only indirectly affect land use. Nonetheless, subdivision regulation has been used to limit development on hazardous land, especially flood-prone property and wildfire hazard areas. Subdivision ordinances can require increased distances between structures and hazard areas, and can set limits for the amount of impervious surfaces to control stormwater flow. Subdivisions ordinances are also useful for clustering development, so that homes are more densely located in safer areas, while floodplains, high erosion areas, and firebreak zones are left clear of development.

12.4.3 Setback Regulations

Setback regulations establish a minimum distance between a hazard area and the portion of the lot that may be built upon. Ocean shoreline setbacks are designed to prevent damage to structures from coastal storms and regular erosion. Fault-zone setbacks work in similar fashion, establishing the distance that construction can take place from a known fault line to prevent damage to structures from earthquakes.

A major problem with setbacks is that some communities grant too many **variances** (exceptions that allow development to go ahead, even though the rules prohibit it), which weakens the regulations' effectiveness. Some variances are granted to homeowners who want to rebuild their oceanfront homes after a major storm has reduced the amount of beachfront on the lot. Constitutional issues can arise when state and local officials deny a permit to build or rebuild based on the setback. Some of the constitutional issues associated with setback regulations are illustrated in Chapter 5.

12.4.4 Capital Improvement Programming

Local governments are empowered to spend public money for public purposes—including capital improvements—which include physical assets such as bridges, police stations, schools, recreation centers, and similar community facilities. Most local governments plan for these big-ticket items with a capital improvement program (CIP). The CIP lays out the government's intentions to provide public facilities over the next five to ten years, and specifies where they will be located and when and how they will be built.

Using Capital Improvement Plans to Protect Public Facilities from Hazards

Communities can protect public facilities by requiring that capital improvements not be built in known hazard areas. Such careful siting can protect lifelines and critical facilities and can also reduce public expense for repair and reconstruction of public structures that might be damaged during hazard events. Local governments can also use capital improvement and maintenance programs to require that public facilities be built using durable materials and constructed in ways that make them strong enough to withstand the impacts of hazards.

Using Capital Improvement Plans to Prevent Private Development in Hazard Areas

In addition to using the capital improvement plan to limit damage to public structures, local governments can also use the spending power to discourage growth and private development in hazardous areas. By limiting the availability of public services such as roads, schools, water and sewer lines, and other infrastructure that is necessary to support development, the community can make it much more expensive and difficult for a developer to build in hazardous areas. Many communities enact prohibitions on extensions of services to outlying areas in an attempt to curb urban sprawl. Local governments can also use capital improvement planning to encourage growth and development to take place in desirable sections of the community, such as areas where hazards are not present. However, capital improvement programs have not been used extensively for hazard mitigation purposes, even in highly hazardous, fast-growing areas. In the rare instances that capital improvement spending has been used as a mitigation tool, it is only effective when used in combination with other land use regulations and planning.[7]

SELF-CHECK

- Define **variance**.
- Cite three ways to use mitigation as a disaster-prevention tool.
- Explain the costs and benefits associated with land acquisition as a mitigation strategy.

12.5 Mitigation through Property Protection

In a perfect world, communities would be built in locations that are never exposed to the impacts of hazards. But when hazards cannot be avoided, it is imperative to reduce potential disaster losses by strengthening buildings and facilities so they can better withstand hazard impacts. Local governments can encourage or in some instances require property owners to take steps that will improve the hazard resilience of homes and businesses. Local governments can also make sure that public facilities, such as sewage treatment plants, fire and police stations, schools, libraries, government buildings, water and power distribution lines, roads, bridges, and other infrastructure are built to high standards that make them less vulnerable to the elements.

From studying structures that were damaged during past disasters, we now understand many of the factors that can contribute to property damage, including:

▲ Ground-level construction (makes structures more susceptible to flooding).
▲ Poor framing (causes structures to be vulnerable to high winds, snow loads, and earthquakes).
▲ Inadequate anchoring (contributes to instability during earthquakes and susceptibility to high winds).
▲ Pilings and supports that are not buried deep enough (making structures vulnerable to erosion and the scouring action of storm surge).
▲ Low-quality building materials (increasing vulnerability to multiple hazards).
▲ Shoddy workmanship (significantly weakens structures against all types of hazards).

Some of the ways that communities can combat these deficiencies and make sure that buildings are able to withstand hazard conditions include strengthening buildings and facilities, enforcing building codes, and municipal improvements. The following sections explore these methods of property protection.

12.5.1 Strengthening Buildings and Facilities

Among the mitigation strategies that are used to strengthen buildings and facilities are: (1) elevation, (2) floodproofing, (3) windproofing, and (4) seismic retrofitting.

Elevating Buildings above Flood Level

Many communities have successfully used elevation to reduce future flood losses while allowing property owners to remain in the same location. Elevation-in-place also works for some public facilities such as wastewater treatment plants, lift stations, water storage facilities, and other public buildings. Elevation raises the lowest habitable floor above the 100-year flood level, so that rising water flows under the building without harming the structure. Along the oceanfront, elevation may also mean raising the building above storm surge and storm wave heights.

While elevating a building protects it from flooding, it may also increase vulnerability to high winds and earthquakes. Elevating buildings in areas that are subject to erosion must be done carefully to make sure that the foundation is not swept away in a storm or over time. This problem can be addressed by building an open foundation, with parking spaces or other open storage below the house, and sinking the piles deep into the ground, below the anticipated depth of erosion. Many buildings, including masonry buildings and multi-story buildings are heavy to raise and may be damaged in the process.

One less expensive way to reduce flood damage is to elevate only the heating, ventilating, and cooling (HVAC) equipment, such as furnaces and hot water heaters. This equipment can often be moved to an upper floor or attic. However, relocating HVAC systems is likely to involve plumbing and electrical changes. Electrical system components, such as service panels (fuse boxes and circuit breakers), switches, meters, and outlets should also be elevated at least one foot above the 100-year flood. These components suffer water damage easily and could short and cause fires. By elevating electrical and mechanical equipment, buildings should be able to recover more quickly and less expensively after a flooding event.

Floodproofing

There are two major types of floodproofing. Dry floodproofing means that all areas below flood level are made watertight. With wet floodproofing, floodwaters are intentionally allowed to enter a building to reduce the pressure exerted by deep water. The property owner floodproofs the interior by removing water-sensitive items from parts of the building that are expected to flood. Backflow valves (also referred to as "check valves") can help homeowners prevent the reverse flow of sewage into the house by temporarily blocking drainpipes.

Although floodproofing makes construction more expensive, it can be an effective mitigation tool and provides a high level of protection from water damage. Dry floodproofing is typically done by coating walls with waterproof compounds or plastic sheeting and protecting building openings with removable shields or sandbags. Dry floodproofing cannot extend more than two or three feet above the foundation of the building because the pressure exerted by deeper water would collapse most walls and floors.

Windproofing

Windproofing involves changing the design and construction of a building to enable it to withstand wind damage. Windproofing typically involves improvements to the aerodynamics of a structure, the materials used in its construction, or adding features such as storm shutters and shatter-resistant window panes. Windproofing can also help protect a building's occupants and their possessions from broken glass and flying objects.

Residential structures are never completely windproof, but can be made wind-resistant. Construction techniques that can increase resistance without raising the cost of construction by more than a few percent include fairly simple techniques such as using larger than usual timbers, using bolts instead of nails, and reinforcing roof braces. These techniques can help prevent roofs or even entire buildings from coming loose during high wind events and becoming flying projectiles that cause further damage to neighboring structures and endanger human life.

Seismic Construction and Retrofitting

Seismic construction involves designing and building new structures to withstand the shaking force of an earthquake. It also includes nonstructural improvements to the inside of buildings to reduce earthquake damage. The cost of including seismic techniques during the building process can be relatively minor, such as adding reinforcing rods to concrete or using wood frame with brick veneer rather than all brick when building new homes.

In contrast, **retrofitting** existing buildings is often a more challenging process. Rebuilding is vastly more expensive than incorporating design improvements during initial construction. Seismic retrofitting may be a low priority for the public in areas that are rarely affected by serious earthquakes. But even in these areas, fairly inexpensive tactics can go a long way to reducing earthquake risk.

Structural improvements to buildings typically include adding braces and removing overhangs. Bridges, water towers, and other non-occupied structures should also be retrofitted with earthquake-resistant materials. Sources of secondary damage, such as sprinkler pipes, water connections, and gas service lines that can rupture during a quake should be secured or fitted with shutoff valves. Fuel tanks and their supply lines should be securely anchored so that they do not become dislodged by earthquakes.

Nonstructural mitigation techniques include securing bookcases, computer monitors, and light fixtures to the wall; covering glass windows with shatter-resistant film; and locating hazardous materials where they are less likely to be spilled during an earthquake.

FOR EXAMPLE

Shoddy Workmanship Makes for Huge Losses

In August 1992, more than 75,000 homes and 8,000 businesses in South Florida were destroyed or severely damaged by Hurricane Andrew, a storm with sustained winds of over 120 miles per hour. Damage reports following the storm showed that Andrew caused *more* damage to *recently built* structures than to those built before 1980. Much of the damage was attributed to the widespread practice of shoddy workmanship, poor design, and lax enforcement of the building codes.

12.5.2 Building Codes: Requiring and Enforcing Safe Construction

An effective way of protecting buildings from hazard impacts is through strict enforcement of a stringent building code. Building codes are laws, ordinances, or regulations that set forth standards and requirements for the construction, maintenance, operation, occupancy, use, or appearance of buildings. Building codes usually require a certain level of fire resistance and also regulate for earthquake, flooding, and high wind impacts in order to save lives and reduce building collapse.

Strict compliance with the letter as well as the spirit of the building code is essential so that structures are built as safe as possible. Strict enforcement is especially critical in the aftermath of a disaster. It is understandable that residents and property owners want to rebuild their homes and businesses as quickly as possible following a hurricane or other large-scale event. Political pressure may be put on building officials in the post-disaster period to expedite the permitting process. However, this urge to get back to normalcy should not be indulged at the sacrifice of public health and safety.

12.5.3 Other Municipal Improvements

In addition to strengthening buildings and facilities, there are other techniques local communities can use to protect public facilities, such as burial of utilities and routine pruning. These steps are described below.

Burying Utility Lines

Burying utility lines underground can help keep power and telecommunications running during a hazard event, particularly during high winds and winter storms. During normal weather conditions, underground systems can also be more reliable than overhead systems, with fewer interruptions. However, the gain in reliability is offset by an increase in repair time, because specialized crews must identify and locate the problem, dig up the area, and repair the cable. During severe weather events, such as hurricanes and ice storms, customers with underground facilities are less likely to be interrupted, but will be among the last to have power restored when there is an underground failure.

Burying existing overhead lines is often prohibitively expensive, and can take years to complete. Customers might see their utility bills go up as much as 125% to cover the cost of burial and to cover the higher operation and maintenance costs. However, the costs of burying utility lines in newly developed areas can be a cost-effective alternative.[8]

Pruning and Planting

Pruning is the thinning of trees and tall bushes that interfere with utility lines. Pruning not only removes branches that pose an immediate threat to power lines, it also strengthens trees and makes them less likely to topple over completely or drop heavy branches on power lines, cars, and buildings during high winds or ice storms. Pruning requires near constant effort to keep up with the rate of new growth. Where the public right-of-way is not wide enough to allow for sufficient pruning, communities should consider the purchase or lease of additional rights-of-way. Communities can choose to plant wind-resistant species of trees and plants and to plant larger stands of trees, which are less vulnerable to windfall than widely separated trees.

SELF-CHECK

- Define **retrofitting**.
- List three ways of protecting property from hazards.
- Cite four strategies used to strengthen buildings.
- Discuss ways of protecting utilities and public facilities.

12.6 Mitigation through Natural Resource Protection

A community's wetlands, hillsides, shorelines, floodplains, riparian areas, forests, and habitats can provide important and cost-effective natural services and benefits, not the least of which is hazard mitigation. Often, the best way to reduce vulnerability of people and property is to preserve a healthy, well-functioning ecosystem.

12.6.1 Preserving Wetlands

Wetlands are areas that naturally flood with water at least a portion of the year, and are some of the most dynamic, valuable, and diverse ecosystems on earth. Wetlands serve as natural flood controls by storing tremendous amounts of floodwaters and slowing and reducing downstream flows. The federal government, along with state and local governments, have protected wetlands through

> **FOR EXAMPLE**
>
> **Returning the Land to the Mark Twain Wildlife Refuge**
>
> The Wapello Levee District in Louisa County, Iowa, chose to buy out farmers after the 1993 Midwest Floods damaged the local levee system. The land has been annexed by the neighboring Mark Twain National Wildlife Refuge and is being returned to natural uses. In addition to providing permanent flood mitigation, the program is restoring natural habitats and allowing the river to return to its natural meandering course.[9]

regulations and permitting requirements for dredge and fill activities, as well as through acquisition and purchase of easements in wetland areas. For further discussion of wetland regulation, see Chapter 7.

The Demise of the Nation's Wetlands

Over the past century, coastal and inland watersheds of the United States have changed dramatically. Up to 80% of wetlands in some locations have been converted to agriculture and urbanization. In other areas, the construction of massive flood control structures designed to keep rivers from switching channels in their natural meandering patterns has resulted in a restriction of sediment flow and freshwater supplies to many floodplains and deltas.

Among the human actions that physically alter, degrade, or destroy wetlands are conversion to agriculture; clearing for development; draining for irrigation; dredging for navigation, energy exploration and extraction; and the construction of levees, dikes, and dams. Wetlands are also commonly degraded through water and air pollution, introduction of invasive (non-native) species, sedimentation, and changes in temperature and salinity. In the future, sea level rise may be the most serious long-term threat to wetlands in the coastal zone. A sizable portion of coastal wetlands may be inundated if even the mildest of sea level predictions comes true.

12.6.2 Soil Conservation and Steep Slope Preservation

Most slopes greater than 15 degrees have enough soil and loose rock to cause a landslide. Avalanche risk greatly increases when steep slopes and loose soils are drenched with water, either from torrential rainfall, broken water pipes, or misdirected runoff.

Soil conservation and steep slope preservation are measures that place restrictions on the grading of hillsides and put limits on development of landslide-risk areas. Some methods of slope stabilization involve changes to the structure of the slope, such as reducing the steepness of the grade. Other techniques involve planting vegetation to help anchor loose rubble and soil. Because water greatly increases the risk of landslides, wise water management can help reduce the hazards associated with steep slopes. One method is to cover the surface with impermeable material to prevent water from reaching the loose material beneath it. However, this technique will increase stormwater runoff and may create flood hazards downhill. A better approach is to redirect stormwater or install a subsurface drainage system.

SELF-CHECK

- Name two ways of mitigating through natural resource protection.
- Explain the mitigation benefit of wetland preservation.

12.7 Mitigation through Public Information

Often, the key to building a resilient community is educating the public about the nature and consequences of hazards. As citizens, elected officials, planners, builders, emergency managers, school children, and others in the community learn about the hazards around them, they can also learn about the steps that can be taken to minimize injuries and death, damage to property, and economic losses. There are many methods for informing the public about hazards and mitigation, including hazard mapping, disclosure requirements during real estate sales, disaster warning systems, and community awareness campaigns.

12.7.1 Hazard Mapping

Some communities choose to relay information about local hazards by publishing maps. Mapping of hazards includes inventories of at-risk populations, hazardous areas, hazardous structures, and environmentally-sensitive areas. Hazard maps can range in sophistication from simple paper maps that show the outlines of hazardous areas (storm surge inundation zones, for example) to multi-layered computerized maps created through a geographic information system (GIS). GIS supports the inventory and analysis of spatial data related to the location and characteristics of hazardous areas, demographic data, characteristics of the built environment, and other factors that are necessary to mitigation and preparedness efforts.

Hazard maps are often made available to the public for viewing in local government offices. Other communities make their maps accessible over the internet through links from a municipal or county website so that new and current residents have access to the maps at any time at relatively little cost. Using web-based maps also facilitates dissemination of up-to-date and interactive mapping information. Maps that clearly portray the extent of hazard exposure a community faces can create an awareness and understanding among local officials, as well as the general public, that often is more vivid than other methods of information dissemination. These graphic depictions of community vulnerability can be worth a thousand words, and can serve to notify residents of where the dangers lie in relation to both public and private property. A map of the town's property tax base overlaid with hazard maps of storm surge or flood zones, for example, can be a real eye-opener. When the intersection of the built environment with the potential hazard area is illustrated on a map, it can highlight the need for management practices that will reduce the community's level of vulnerability.

12.7.2 Real Estate Disclosure Laws

Hazard maps can be used to define the boundaries within which hazards must be disclosed during real estate transactions. Real estate disclosure laws require that the buyer and lender be notified if property is located in a hazard-prone area. Supporters of disclosure laws claim that a better-informed marketplace should result in better decision making—lenders will be hesitant to extend credit in hazard areas, and well-informed purchasers will choose to avoid purchasing in hazard areas, demand a lower price, or require mitigation as a bargaining chip. Only a handful of states have mandated real estate disclosure about natural hazards. Currently, federally-regulated lending institutions (which include the vast majority of banks and mortgage issuers in the United States) are required to advise applicants for a mortgage or other loan if the building is in the floodplain as shown on an official Flood Insurance Rate Map.

Studies have shown that notification may not have much of an impact on home-buyers. Notification of a hazard risk usually occurs too late in the real estate process, and most warning messages have been found to be weak or confusing. For instance, federal lending laws require that flood hazard notification must be made five days before closing, by which time the applicant has usually signed a contract or has otherwise committed to purchasing the property.

Local real estate boards can help make notification practices more effective by requiring that newcomers be advised about hazard risks thoroughly and early in the home-buying process. Real estate boards may also require homeowners to disclose past disaster events, whether or not the property is in a mapped high-risk zone. However, sellers in many communities retain the option to make no representation about the hazard risks or about past hazard events, including flooding, erosion, or coastal storms that have affected the property.

12.7.3 Disaster Warning

Disaster warnings are critical for protecting residents from flash floods, dam breaks, thunderstorms, winter weather, tornadoes, and other rapid-onset hazards. Many disaster warnings are issued through the National Weather Service and are disseminated to the public in numerous ways, including sirens, radio, television, cable television, mobile public-address systems, telephone trees, reverse 911 systems, or door-to-door contact. Posted signs can be used to identify risks at a particular site. Informational signs have been installed in riptide areas along the coast, in falling rock and landslide risk zones, areas of localized flooding, and other hazard areas.

Many people fail to respond to emergency warnings of imminent disaster, and even fewer residents heed warnings that are projected further into the future. Individuals ignore warnings for a variety of psychological or social reasons, including:

▲ Misperception of disaster probability.
▲ Underestimation of the effectiveness of mitigation measures.
▲ Fatalistic belief that it is impossible to control one's destiny.
▲ Refusal to believe hazards are present.
▲ Assumption that after a hazard occurs once, it will never recur.
▲ Warnings in the past might have proven unwarranted (i.e., the hazard they were warned about never actually happened).[10]

On the other hand, people might rely too heavily on warnings, leading them to unnecessary exposure to risk. The practice of hazard prediction and warning is not an exact science. This is particularly obvious in the case of hurricanes. Most hurricane experts admit that we have reached a plateau in the ability to predict the future direction of a hurricane and to warn coastal communities of an oncoming storm.

12.7.4 Community Awareness Campaigns

Even though communities cannot single-handedly change the fatalistic outlook or combat all of the psychological factors that lead people to ignore warnings and cautionary words, community awareness programs can be used to directly educate the general public about hazard risks and mitigation strategies. Information can be presented in a number of ways, including outreach projects, hazard information centers and kiosks, school-age education programs, booths at county and state fairs, brochures, media releases, or workshops.

General awareness campaigns can include a wide variety of topics, such as practical information specific to the community and individual households. Residents should be informed about ways they can limit exposure, how they can retrofit their property to reduce damage, items to pack for any type of emergency, and local evacuation routes and procedures. Awareness campaigns can also cover information that the public should know about how their community fits into a larger environment, such as how uncontrolled floodplain use impacts downstream neighbors, the ways in which wetlands naturally absorb and filter flood waters, barrier island and inlet migration, and how dunes protect inland areas from wave action and storm surge.

General awareness programs have a mixed record for building public support for hazard mitigation and preparedness activities. More successful are self-help programs with a narrow scope, such as residential floodproofing workshops or property insurance informational sessions.

> ### FOR EXAMPLE
>
> #### Fun with Maps
>
> During the 1999 hurricane season, New Hanover County in coastal North Carolina distributed hurricane tracking maps that allowed users to trace the paths of hurricanes as they crossed the Atlantic Ocean. The user-friendly maps, which had information about household preparedness and evacuation routes, proved very popular and helped increase awareness of the number of hurricanes that make landfall or come close to the state's coast each year.

SELF-CHECK

- Explain how public information is an effective hazard mitigation technique.
- Discuss obstacles to disaster warning systems.
- Give examples of community awareness campaigns.

12.8 Mitigation Funding

There is no doubt that communities can incur significant costs in implementing many of the mitigation tactics mentioned in this chapter. Local government officials must balance many competing interests when deciding how to distribute limited resources. Hot-button issues such as crime control, education, affordable housing, public transit, homelessness, and health services often grab the immediate attention of voters. Many local government budgets are stretched thin in meeting the urgent needs of citizens, and mitigation may receive low priority, particularly if the community has not experienced a hazard event in the recent past. However, it is a well-accepted principle in planning and emergency management circles that current dollars invested in mitigation greatly reduce the demand for future dollars by reducing the amount needed for emergency response, recovery, and reconstruction following a disaster. Keeping businesses open, residents in their homes, and basic services operating following an emergency results in economic security and social stability for local communities. Financial resources that are directed toward lowering risk represent money well spent.

There are many sources of funding available to local communities to carry out mitigation activities. The possibilities for grants and loans are endless, limited only by the energy, time, and persistence of those seeking funds. Potential sources of funds include federal and state agencies, nonprofit organizations, charitable giving, public-private partnerships, and more.

12.8.1 State and Federal Funding Sources

State and federal aid is a large part of many local government revenue streams. The vast majority of buyouts, elevation projects, and other expensive mitigation activities are paid for with federal funds, through programs such as the Hazard Mitigation Grant Program (HMGP), the Pre-Disaster Mitigation Program (PDM), and the Pubic Assistance (PA) Program administered by FEMA. Other funding sources include the Small Business Administration Disaster Assistance Program and Community Development Block Grants issued by the Department of Housing and Urban Development. Most of these programs are available to communities after the President of the United States has issued a disaster declaration for the area. You can find descriptions of these and other federal programs in Chapter 6. Some programs, such as the PDM program administered by FEMA are not tied to a disaster declaration, and local governments may apply for this funding annually.

12.8.2 Combining Mitigation with Other Goals

In addition to disaster assistance programs, other federal and state programs may fund mitigation activities, even though the programs are not directly related to hazards. Mitigation goals can often be coupled with other objectives, such as affordable housing, pollution prevention, water quality protection, natural resource preservation, wildlife conservation and other mutual interests. For instance, wetland restoration funding may be available from the federal Environmental Protection Agency (EPA), soil and water loans may be granted by the U.S. Farm Service Agency, and watershed protection grants may come from the Natural Resources Conservation Service. Although these programs may not have mitigation as a primary objective, they can provide an opportunity to fund hazard mitigation as a side benefit.

12.8.3 Finding Matching Funds

Many federal grant programs require the local government to contribute what is known as a **nonfederal match**—usually a percentage of the total grant amount awarded—that must come from another source. This is true of many federal hazard mitigation grants. Local or state funds can be used to meet the match, although federal funds from another source cannot.

When the state does not provide the needed match, local governments applying for grants can often meet the nonfederal match with **in-kind contributions** instead of cash outlays. In-kind resources can consist of labor or salaries paid to local staff to carry out the mitigation activities (such as project managers, engineers, planners, public works crews, etc.). In-kind contributions can also include donated services, supplies, equipment, and office space. Partnerships and coalitions formed with other organizations can also be a source of in-kind resources.

> ### FOR EXAMPLE
>
> #### Pay As You Flow
>
> Tulsa, Oklahoma, has established a stable financing source to pay for its stormwater management program. Each home and business in the watershed is assessed a monthly stormwater fee as part of its utility bill. Businesses are assessed based on the amount of impervious surface. The fee raises over $8 million a year, which the city uses to pay for enforcement of regulations on new development, a master drainage plan for the city, and acquiring lands along creek beds to be used as biking and hiking trails.

12.8.4 Finding Mitigation Funds at Home

Although outside sources of funding pay for the bulk of large mitigation projects, many creative local governments are becoming more self-reliant when it comes to paying for mitigation activities. Local governments have used a variety of sources, including capital budgets, taxation and special assessments, municipal bonds, utility and permitting fees, and partnerships with nonprofit organizations to fund mitigation activities.

Local governments can also study their annual operating budgets carefully to see where mitigation can fit into ongoing community programs. Often a change in spending priorities is all that is needed to finance some mitigation ideas. And sometimes, the most effective mitigation activities require no new money at all, just a shift in thinking so that the community includes mitigation principles in day-to-day operations and decision making.

SELF-CHECK

- Define **non-federal match** and **in-kind contribution**.
- List five local sources of mitigation funding.
- Cite five sources of federal and state funding for mitigation.

12.9 Mitigation Strategies for Man-Made Hazards

Instead of preventing man-made disasters by avoiding hazardous locations, it is necessary to create a built environment that is protected from attack or is better able to withstand an attack or hazardous materials accident. This can

FOR EXAMPLE

Embassy Prototype Design

Working on behalf of the U.S. Department of State, a contracted team of architects, engineers, and planners developed a prototype design for embassy office buildings and associated support facilities. It features a flexibility of design and engineering systems so it can be adapted to diverse climates and different topographical and geologic conditions. The prototype incorporates the latest in antiterrorist design principles to help protect these buildings against potential attacks on U.S. targets overseas. These include a blast-resistant hardened shell, safe havens, and emergency alert systems. For security reasons, most antiterrorism-related design features are classified.

be achieved through target hardening and other strategies. It is also possible to carry out public awareness campaigns so that members of the community are better informed about ways to protect themselves, their families, and their businesses.

Target-hardening strategies can be fairly simple—for example, installing security fencing around an HVAC system's air intake to avoid the insertion of poisonous gas. Target hardening can also be more elaborate, such as blocking off large areas as buffer zones around particularly sensitive buildings. Some of the strategies that are appropriate for mitigating natural hazard impacts can also be used to increase protection against man-made hazards. For example, earthquake mitigation techniques can also strengthen a building against the effects of a bomb blast. Mitigation against wildfire may help protect structures from incendiary devices. And property protection measures that strengthen buildings against high winds can help mitigate the impact of an explosion. Table 12-2 gives a few examples of the types of strategies that can be used to mitigate the impacts of man-made hazards.[11]

SELF-CHECK

- Define **target-hardening strategies**.
- List seven mitigation techniques for terrorism and technological hazard mitigation.
- Explain a key difference between man-made and natural disasters.

Table 12-2: Terrorism and Technological Hazard Mitigation Strategies

Type of Mitigation Technique	Sample Action
Site planning and landscape design	• Minimize concealment opportunities such as hedges, bus shelters, trash cans, mailboxes, etc. • Limit entrances/exits. • Provide adequate lighting.
Architectural and interior	• Do not locate toilets and service spaces in non secured areas. • Locate delivery/mail service facilities at remote locations; prevent vehicles from driving into or under building. • Restrict roof access.
Structural engineering	• Create blast-resistant exterior envelope. • Ensure structural elements can withstand blast loads. • Enclose critical building components within hardened floors, walls, ceilings.
Security	• Develop backup control center capabilities. • Implement intrusion detection systems. • Install screening systems (metal detectors, x-ray machines, etc.).
Mechanical engineering	• Protect utility lifelines (water, power, communications) by concealing, burying, encasing. • Locate air intakes on roof. • Provide filtration of intake air.
Electrical engineering	• Secure primary and backup fuel supply areas. • Implement separate emergency and normal power systems. • Locate utility systems away from entrances, loading areas, etc.

12.10 Putting It All Together: Local Mitigation Planning

All of the mitigation strategies described in this chapter are put to their best advantage as part of a comprehensive mitigation plan. Hazard mitigation planning is the most effective way of establishing a community's commitment to mitigation goals, objectives, policies, and programs. By expressing what a community hopes to achieve, the plan can be an important connection between the public interest

---

FOR EXAMPLE

Planning for Drainage in Orland Hills

The village of Orland Hills, Illinois, had a varied and widespread flooding and drainage problem that affected buildings, yards, and streets throughout town. Heavy rains caused water problems several times each year. In 1995, the village developed a flood protection plan that explained the problem to the public and helped launch more public information and mitigation activities, including tougher enforcement of existing flood rules; initiation of a formal drainage maintenance program; development of small scale projects to correct local problems, including televising storm sewers and rehabilitating broken ones; implementation of site visits to determine the causes of local flooding problems and to advise property owners about what they can do; and creation of a public information program that includes articles in the village newsletter, annual letters to residents in problem areas, cable TV "crawlers," and an annual public information campaign theme, such as "Don't forget your drainage."[13]

---

that is being served and the mitigation strategy to be put in action. A plan can help a local community avoid the uncoordinated and often inconsistent results of an ad hoc, project-by-project attempt at mitigation by identifying what it wants to do before a hazard event occurs. That way, as soon as money is available and the opportunity arises, the community can implement mitigation strategies as quickly as possible.

Not only does a local mitigation plan make sense, it is also required by law that local governments have an approved mitigation plan in place before they can receive federal disaster assistance. This includes funds from the Hazard Mitigation Grant Program and the Pre-Disaster Mitigation Program, two significant FEMA funding sources. (Chapter 6 discusses the Disaster Mitigation Act of 2000).

According to the Disaster Mitigation Act, the primary purpose of hazard mitigation planning is to identify community policies, strategies, and tools for action over the long term that will reduce risk and the potential for future losses throughout the community. This is accomplished by using a systematic process of learning about the hazards that can affect the community, setting clear goals, identifying appropriate strategies, following through with effective implementation, and keeping the plan up-to-date. Hazard mitigation planning is most successful when it increases public and political support for mitigation programs, results in actions that also support other important community goals and objectives, and influences the community's decision making to include reducing vulnerability at every opportunity.[12]

SELF-CHECK

- Explain the role of a comprehensive mitigation plan.
- Discuss the importance of a mitigation plan in regards to federal disaster funding.

SUMMARY

This chapter describes some of the many tools and techniques that local communities can use to reduce vulnerability to natural and man-made hazards. These tools include a variety of structural engineering projects, ways of strengthening buildings and facilities to withstand hazard impacts, land use regulations and building codes, natural resource and wetland preservation strategies, techniques for informing the public and increasing community awareness of hazards, as well as mitigation strategies aimed at reducing the impacts of man-made hazards. Additionally, the chapter provides examples of funding sources for mitigation, including federal and state resources, and ways that local governments can fund mitigation activities using internal revenue sources. The chapter concludes with a discussion of hazard mitigation planning as a way to coordinate and integrate resilience into all community programs and policies.

KEY TERMS

Beach nourishment	The artificial replacement or addition of sand to beaches to widen the backshore and move the high-water line further toward the sea.
Impervious surfaces	Paved areas that rainwater cannot soak through, such as parking lots, roofs, streets, and other non-porous surfaces.
In-kind contributions	Non-cash contributions of goods and/or services. Can include items such as equipment, technical or consulting services, furniture, office supplies, etc. May also include donated staff or volunteer time.
Nonfederal match	The amount of funds, usually a percentage of the total grant amount awarded, required by many federal grant programs that must come from a source other than the federal grant program.

Retrofitting	Rebuilding existing buildings to withstand the shaking and ground movement associated with an earthquake.
Runoff	Rainwater that does not soak into the soil, evaporate, or become trapped by plant roots, and thus flows over the surface of the ground.
Target-hardening strategies	Methods of protecting structures from man-made hazard impacts.
Variances	Exceptions that allow development to proceed, even though the rules prohibit it.

ASSESS YOUR UNDERSTANDING

Go to www.wiley.com/college/schwab to evaluate your knowledge of hazard mitigation tools and techniques.

Measure your learning by comparing pre-test and post-test results.

Summary Questions

1. Mitigation is based on short-term preventative measures. True or False?
2. Which of the following is an example of a property protection mitigation strategy?
   (a) safe room
   (b) capital improvement
   (c) revetment
   (d) vegetative buffer
3. Levees are an example of which type of mitigation strategy?
   (a) natural resource protection
   (b) property protection
   (c) prevention
   (d) structural engineered project
4. A hazard mitigation plan is the first step of a risk assessment. True or False?
5. Which of the following is an example of a public information strategy?
   (a) taxes and fees
   (b) building codes
   (c) warning system
   (d) diversions
6. A revetment is an example of a structural engineered project. True or False?
7. Dams increase the natural function of a floodplain. True or False?
8. Which of the following is used to reduce coastal hazard impacts?
   (a) riparian buffer
   (b) groin
   (c) levee
   (d) slope stabilization
9. Groins are hardened materials on the shore to protect against erosion. True or False?
10. Stormwater systems should have the capacity to meet the volume of stormwater expected in a lower than normal rain season. True or False?
11. Keeping development out of hazard-prone areas is the most sustainable approach to hazard mitigation. True or False?

12. A buyout program is one method of
    (a) public information.
    (b) property protection.
    (c) prevention.
    (d) natural resource protection.
13. Acquisition is only used in cases where property owners are willing to sell. True or False?
14. A land use plan and the resulting zones and ordinances can be used to keep people and property from locating in hazard areas. True or False?
15. Setback regulations can be used to
    (a) build capital improvements.
    (b) reuse acquired properties.
    (c) establish the distance between building zones.
    (d) establish the distance between construction and a fault line.
16. In situations where communities cannot avoid hazards they must then protect property from as much damage as possible. True or False?
17. Wet floodproofing uses special paints and compounds to protect walls from water damage. True or False?
18. Seismic construction includes structural and nonstructural improvements to reduce earthquake damage. True or False?
19. Wetlands reduce pollution by
    (a) increasing floodwaters.
    (b) filtering pollutants.
    (c) reducing floodwaters.
    (d) diluting pollutants.
20. Wetland mitigation requires communities to restrict certain types of development in a wetland area. True or False?
21. A wetland mitigation bank is used to fund mitigation efforts in wetland areas. True or False?
22. A non-federal match requires that
    (a) a community apply for alternative grant sources.
    (b) a state government match a grant.
    (c) local governments contribute a percentage of a grant.
    (d) a state government provide funding to the local level.
23. Which of the following is an example of a mechanical engineering mitigation technique?
    (a) filtration of intake air
    (b) intrusion detection systems
    (c) metal detectors
    (d) blast-resistant exterior

Review Questions

1. Mitigation is a long-term approach to reducing hazard risk. List the five different mitigation strategies that communities can use to control hazards and disasters.

2. Dams, seawalls, and vegetative buffers are all examples of structural engineered projects. Describe the purpose of this type of strategy.

3. A risk assessment can help a community choose a mitigation strategy. How?

4. By building dams, levees, and seawalls, humans assume that they can defeat the powers of Mother Nature. What are three disadvantages to such projects?

5. What are the drawbacks of seawalls and bulkheads?

6. What are some relatively inexpensive ways a community can control its stormwater flow?

7. List five ways that communities can reuse acquired properties.

8. Discuss the role of setback regulations in preventative mitigation.

9. What is a buyout program, and why does it work best when it involves blocks of homes or a neighborhood?

10. Wetlands are a valuable part of the environment. How do they act as a natural flood control?

11. What are five of the activities humans have done to damage our wetlands?

12. Whose responsibility is it to determine a property's vulnerability to hazards—potential buyers, sellers, or mortgage companies?

13. List seven different funding sources available to communities that wish to carry out mitigation strategies.

14. Which of the state and federal aid programs does not require a disaster situation?

15. There is no such thing as a terrorism zone. Explain what this means for mitigation strategies for man-made hazards.

16. To prevent man-made disasters, local governments need to focus more on building a community that can withstand a man-made event. Define target hardening.

17. Law requires that local governments have an approved mitigation plan before they can receive federal disaster money. Explain why.

Applying This Chapter

1. Explain how a mitigation plan can help a community in an earthquake-prone area carry out mitigation strategies.

2. What rationale would you give to support a proposal to remove a dam on a river in Minnesota? Opponents of the proposal claim that the loss of hydropower and flood control will negatively affect this rural area.

3. A small coastal town in Georgia is exploring the idea of using a seawall to protect a stretch of shoreline where a dozen homes and several small businesses are located. What factors determine the effectiveness of such a seawall? What are other options available to this community?

4. As a mitigation planner in a tornado-prone area of Kansas, what property protection mitigation measures could be used to protect the homes in the community? What resources would you use to research the potential strategies?

5. Look around your community and think about the wetlands that have been impaired or destroyed because of development or other means. What impact, if any, has that had on flooding in the area? Are there wetlands that are still vulnerable?

6. What disaster warning systems are in place for your community? How do they compare to another community, one with different hazard issues?

7. As the owner of a warehouse in an industrial area, you've decided to build an adjacent building to house part of your business. A chemical explosion at the other end of the industrial park has caused you to think about protecting your new building and your investment. What types of mitigation strategies could you put to use in the design, construction, and security of the building?

8. Assume you are the emergency manager in a town that has experienced major flooding for the fourth time. Homes in several neighborhoods located in the floodplain were damaged severely, and many people are living in trailers and other types of temporary housing. The mayor of your town asks you to seek funding from FEMA to carry out some mitigation projects. What would you advise the mayor and the town council to do? What factors would you consider as you propose your ideas?

Savings Plan

Think about any areas or neighborhoods in your community or county that should not be developed or that cannot be protected well enough from hazards. Come up with an acquisition plan that would protect this area from development and protect residents and property from injury or damage. How would you defend the high cost of such a strategy?

Public Support

Think about some mitigation action that has been proposed for your community (or one that you believe would be beneficial). What is the general sentiment of the community about the action? What could be done to gain more support for the mitigation?

Going for the Green

Choose a particular mitigation action for your community and consider the funding options available to pay for it. What resources would you investigate?

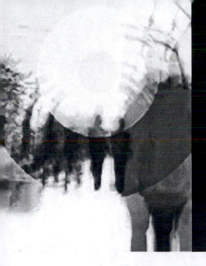

13

HAZARD MITIGATION PLANNING

Assessing Risk, Developing Goals, and Creating Strategies for Resilient Communities

Starting Point

Go to www.wiley.com/college/schwab to assess your knowledge of hazard mitigation planning.
Determine where you need to concentrate your efforts.

What You'll Learn in This Chapter

- ▲ Types of mitigation plans
- ▲ Steps common to successful planning
- ▲ Ways to organize before preparing a plan
- ▲ Components of a risk assessment
- ▲ Types of local government capabilities
- ▲ The difference between mitigation goals and objectives
- ▲ Types of mitigation actions
- ▲ Elements of plan implementation
- ▲ Procedures for monitoring and updating a mitigation plan

After Studying This Chapter, You'll Be Able To

- ▲ Examine an all-hazards approach to mitigation planning
- ▲ Analyze the importance of public participation in the planning process
- ▲ Practice the steps of a risk assessment
- ▲ Compare a mitigation plan's goals and objectives
- ▲ Appraise what it takes to create implementation procedures
- ▲ Distinguish criteria for a periodic assessment of a plan

Goals and Outcomes

- ▲ Master the terminology, understand the procedures, and recognize the tools of hazard mitigation planning
- ▲ Distinguish among types of mitigation plans and their strategies
- ▲ Collaborate with others to organize information for plan development
- ▲ Apply chapter ideas to develop goals for a community mitigation plan
- ▲ Evaluate hazard mitigation plans for real-world communities

INTRODUCTION

Through hazard mitigation planning, communities learn about the hazards they face, develop goals to reduce their hazard risks, and devise actions to meet those goals. This chapter outlines the steps involved in the hazard mitigation planning process. The chapter describes the elements of a risk assessment, as well as how communities can assess their capabilities for mitigation action. The chapter also outlines ways that local communities can develop goals, objectives, and policies for mitigation. The chapter then discusses how implementation procedures help put mitigation recommendations into action. The chapter concludes with a description of the writing process, followed by guidelines for how to submit, adopt, and put a plan into motion at the local level.

13.1 Hazard Mitigation Planning Overview

Hazard mitigation planning is the process of determining how to reduce or eliminate the loss of life and property damage that can occur as a result of hazards. An **all-hazards approach** to mitigation planning involves consideration of all the hazards with the potential for causing harm, including natural hazards as well as man-made hazards such as technological accidents and terrorism. The end product of the process is a hazard mitigation plan—a document that presents policies and strategies that aim to reduce vulnerability to hazards when those policies and strategies are put into action. These policies and action strategies should be based on a sound and thorough assessment of the hazards present in the community and an analysis of what is at risk from those hazards. The planning process helps pull together these important analyses and uses them as background support for changes that will contribute to the resiliency and overall sustainability of the community.

The planning process as we describe it in this chapter is largely based on the requirements of the Disaster Mitigation Act of 2000 (DMA), as administered by the Federal Emergency Management Agency (FEMA). Regulations implementing the DMA establish standards and criteria that states, local governments, and tribal governments must meet in order to be eligible for certain federal disaster funds. FEMA has produced guidance material for governments to use during their planning process that is freely available on the FEMA website and through its documents warehouse.[1] Many states have also developed guidance material for mitigation planning that is available free of charge.[2] This chapter focuses primarily on hazard mitigation planning at the local level, and while additional factors must be considered when preparing a statewide plan, the essential concepts and many of the actual planning steps are identical whether the plan is prepared at the state, tribal, or local level.

13.1.1 Why Prepare a Mitigation Plan?

Mitigation plans, especially those that are prepared well in advance of a hazard event, can help a state or local government avoid the ad hoc approach to mitigation that occurs when individual projects are carried out in isolation from each other or from other state and local activities. By providing an overall context for mitigation, a mitigation plan can help articulate a vision of what the state or local community wants to look like in the future. The plan can establish goals, objectives, policies, and strategies for attaining that vision in a thoughtful and methodical way. Through this process, the mitigation plan can serve to educate the public and to guide policy makers so that decisions regarding development, growth, and infrastructure are made with an eye towards reducing vulnerability to hazards. Such informed decision making is more likely to increase the resiliency of the state or community as a whole.

Another pragmatic reason for preparing a mitigation plan appears in the DMA itself: state and local governments must have a mitigation plan that meets FEMA's approval in order to be eligible for certain federal disaster recovery program funds. Mitigation plans are required for or facilitate access to many other government programs as well, including the Small Business Administration Disaster Assistance Program, the Community Development Block Grant Program, and the Community Rating System, among others.

13.1.2 Types of Mitigation Plans

This chapter focuses primarily on hazard mitigation plans that are prepared as distinct, freestanding plans. Many local communities prepare such stand-alone plans because of the advantage of high visibility within the community. However, communities that choose to prepare a single-purpose hazard mitigation plan are cautioned to link the mitigation plan with other planning and policy documents that may exist in the community. The mitigation plan should support and be supported by the local land use plan, comprehensive plan, zoning ordinance, floodplain management plan, and any other policies that govern land use and development.

Aside from creating a stand-alone mitigation plan, there are many other ways to develop local mitigation plans. Some communities incorporate a hazard mitigation element or chapter into their local land use or comprehensive plan. This is appropriate in localities that use their comprehensive and land use plans as part of an integrated development process. This approach has the advantage of highlighting mitigation as a necessary component of all other government operations, and calls for integration of mitigation into the day-to-day decision-making processes of the jurisdiction. On the other hand, inserting the hazard mitigation plan into other local plans may not be the best option in communities that use their land use or comprehensive plans only as general guides for local policy making. In these localities, the mitigation plan may become lost and not given the credibility it needs to be fully implemented. Other communities tie the mitigation plan to the local emergency operations plan. Some jurisdictions can attach other hazard elements to the local floodplain management plan (if multiple types of hazards are present in that locality). There is no one right way to prepare a mitigation plan—its importance lies in the way the plan guides development decisions so that vulnerability to hazards is reduced.

Local governments can prepare plans singly or in conjunction with neighboring communities in a **multi-jurisdictional** planning process. Local governments are allowed to combine forces with other local governments of their choice, or the county can cooperate with one or more municipalities to create a single plan that covers the entire county area. Multi-jurisdictional plans are acceptable under the FEMA rules as long as each jurisdiction participates in the process and officially adopts the plan.

13.1.3 Four Phases of the Planning Process

The mitigation planning process is as individual as the jurisdiction that engages in it. Each community or state approaches growth and change in a unique way, and each planning process should fit that community's particular personality. As a result, the step-by-step sequence that is described here is not the only way to pursue mitigation planning.[3] At the same time, the process illustrated in this chapter is based on certain steps common to successful planning, paralleling materials issued by FEMA to guide the creation of a DMA-compliant plan. In general, a well-accepted planning process comprises four basic phases, each of which is made up of several steps:

1. Organize for the effort and involve affected parties, especially the public.
2. Assess the hazard and the community's exposure to damage from the hazard.
3. Set goals and review and select appropriate measures to reach those goals.
4. Adopt, implement, evaluate, and revise the plan periodically.

SELF-CHECK

- Define **hazard mitigation planning, all-hazards approach,** and **multi-jurisdictional.**
- Explain reasons for preparing a mitigation plan.
- Explain why one approach to planning isn't feasible for all types of communities.

FOR EXAMPLE

Cherokee Planning Process

The Eastern Band of the Cherokee Indians in North Carolina has completed a hazard mitigation plan that is compliant with the DMA. Specifically, the plan is a comprehensive look at identifying hazards that can be anticipated by the tribe and is organized into seven primary areas of concern. The seven sections include: an introduction, familiarizing the reader with the environmental setting of the Cherokee Reservation holdings; providing a profile of the community; detailing the process followed in preparing the plan; a description of the hazards affecting the reservation and an analysis of the vulnerability of the existing infrastructure, housing, and other development; an overview of current and anticipated land use and development trends; an analysis and recommendation of hazard-specific mitigation strategies with a timeline for completion; and an outline of how the plan was initially adopted and how it will be reviewed and updated.

13.2 Organizing to Prepare the Plan

Before embarking on the planning process itself, the community must establish the commitment and political will to see the plan through to the end. Planning can be a protracted procedure, and sustaining support is critical to its success. An important component of garnering the necessary support depends on the knowledge base of the community at large. A certain level of understanding about hazard mitigation planning and risk reduction is necessary for a successful outcome. There must also be a general awareness of the hazards the community faces and of the need to do something about them. Of course, the planning process itself will serve an educational role as participants in the process become more knowledgeable about their community's vulnerability and ways to decrease it, but an assessment of how much citizens and elected and/or appointed officials actually know about hazards from the outset can help direct later steps in the most efficient and effective manner. The planning team that will develop the hazard mitigation plan should be made up of local staff that have the authority to carry out the detailed studies as well as the analysis and policy recommendations that are part of the planning process. Many communities establish an advisory committee or task force to meet regularly and oversee the mitigation planning process. It is also important to coordinate with other agencies within the local government and with other jurisdictions. This is particularly important if the plan is to be a multi-jurisdictional plan, that is, one that covers all the local governments in a county or region.

FOR EXAMPLE

Using the Web

When creating a mitigation plan in response to the Cerro Grande Fire, the town of Los Alamos, New Mexico, created a web page to announce public meetings, gain public input into the process and development of the plan, and to inform the public about the potential mitigation measures and the progress of the mitigation plan.

13.2.1 Public Participation

It is good practice to involve the public when planning to mitigate the impacts of hazards so that the plan reflects the community's specific needs. Regulations of the DMA require that the public be invited to participate in at least two phases of the process: when the plan is in draft stages, and prior to plan approval.[4] Public meetings, workshops, informational presentations, websites, resident mailings, and other forms of communication are often effective ways to solicit citizen participation.

13.2.2 Document the Planning Process

In order to meet FEMA planning criteria, the planning process must be fully documented, including efforts to engage the public. The plan must include a narrative description of the process followed to prepare the plan, justifications for any assumptions made during the planning process, the outcomes of meetings, sources of data, and other pertinent information. In addition, the plan must indicate who was involved in the planning process. For example, FEMA wants to know who led the development at the staff level, whether any external contributors were involved such as contractors or consultants, and who participated on plan committees. The plan should also indicate who provided information for the plan and who reviewed any drafts.

SELF-CHECK

- Discuss the importance of a qualified planning team.
- Explain the role of public participation.
- Review FEMA criteria for planning documentation.

13.3 Risk Assessment

The risk assessment step is the backbone of the hazard mitigation plan. The regulations of the DMA state that the hazard plan "shall include a risk assessment that provides the factual basis for activities proposed in the strategy section of the plan to reduce losses from identified hazards."[5] The regulations go on to require that the local risk assessment "provide sufficient information to enable the jurisdiction to identify and prioritize appropriate mitigation actions to reduce losses from identified hazards."[6] Essentially, the risk assessment provides the justification and rationalization for policies written in the plan. This section of the chapter gives a brief overview of the risk assessment process. More detailed information is provided in Chapter 10.

13.3.1 Hazard Identification

First and foremost, the community must become aware of what hazards it faces. An initial decision must be made whether the plan will cover all possible hazards—both natural and man-made—or whether the plan will start out by identifying its natural hazards, with additional hazards to be added at a later date as resources and time permit. The regulations of the DMA require that all natural hazards that can affect the jurisdiction be described.[7] If the hazard identification omits without explanation any hazards commonly recognized as threats to the jurisdiction, this part of the plan cannot receive a satisfactory score from FEMA.

At this stage, the planning team will compile a list of what hazards affect the locality. This list is created by researching past hazard events in the region, talking to residents and experts, and reviewing hazards data available from the state and federal governments and other sources.

13.3.2 Hazard Profile

During the hazard profile, the planning team analyzes the hazards identified earlier in terms of likelihood, magnitude, and potential impact. This also involves locating what geographic areas of the community could be subject to the various hazards and depicting them on a map, if possible. Some areas will be affected repeatedly by a particular hazard, such as a floodplain adjacent to a stream or river. Other hazards may affect the entire jurisdiction, such as a hurricane or earthquake. Some hazards come in varying strengths and will have different effects depending upon the severity of the particular event.

The DMA regulations require that the plan provide information on previous occurrences of each type of hazard addressed in the plan.[8] The hazard history should present a clear picture of the hazards' impact through descriptions of the events, including the location, magnitude, and severity of each event chronicled. The hazard profile must also include the probability of future events (i.e., the chance of occurrence) for each hazard identified in the plan.[9]

13.3.3 Vulnerability Assessment

During this step, the planning team discovers what is located in each of the hazard areas identified during the first two steps. Inventorying assets and populations provides a sense of how vulnerable property and people are to hazards. Infrastructure, properties, critical facilities, and other community features will all be displayed on maps, which can be overlaid with the hazard maps to show where the built environment intersects with hazard areas. Maps are an important and striking way to visualize what is at risk within the community.

Identifying Structures and Populations

The planning team must first prepare an inventory of populations and structures located in hazard areas. An inventory of critical and lifeline facilities and infrastructure is an important part of this analysis. Using census data, property tax maps, aerial photography, and other data sources, the planning team will identify structures and residents that are vulnerable to each hazard addressed in the plan and display them on a map.

Estimating Potential Losses

The DMA regulations state that the mitigation plan should describe vulnerability in terms of "an estimate of the potential dollar losses to vulnerable structures" identified earlier.[10] This step helps the community discover the extent to which assets could be damaged by each hazard, and how much it might cost to replace and/or repair them if they are destroyed or damaged. The loss estimate also calculates figures if the contents of businesses and homes are affected as well as the accumulated cost of various types of indirect effects that could occur.

Analyze Development Trends

DMA regulations suggest that local plans describe vulnerability in terms of a general description of land uses and development trends within the community so that mitigation options can be considered in future land use decisions.[11] The plan should discuss development trends over the past 20 to25 years and consider how areas of growth will increase or decrease the jurisdiction's future vulnerability to the hazards identified above. In this step, the planning team will be making some educated guesses about future population growth and how that may affect the built landscape. This is a very critical component of assessing vulnerability, because the mitigation plan should deal not only with the here and now (although existing development is also critical for mitigation purposes), but should also look ahead to avoid costly development mistakes that could be made if there is no attention paid to where and how future growth will occur.

FOR EXAMPLE

Coastal Vulnerability Assessment Tool

The NOAA Coastal Services Center in Charleston, South Carolina, has created a tool to assist communities in carrying out a vulnerability assessment. The CD-ROM provides a step-by-step guide for conducting community-wide risk and vulnerability assessments for emergency managers, planners, building officials, and others. It also provides an illustrative case study demonstrating the process for analyzing physical, social, economic, and environmental vulnerability to hazards at the local level. Details on this tool can be found on the Coastal Services Center Web site at www.csc.noaa.gov/products/nchaz/startup.htm.

SELF-CHECK

- Describe a hazard profile.
- List three elements of a vulnerability assessment.
- Discuss the role of a risk assessment in a hazard mitigation plan.

13.4 Capability Assessment

The capability assessment describes the legal authority vested in local governments to pursue mitigation measures. The assessment also evaluates the community's institutional framework, technical know-how, and ability to pay for mitigation. The capability of all levels of government (local, state, tribal, federal, and regional), as well as the contributions made by nongovernmental organizations (churches, charities, community relief groups, the Red Cross, hospitals, for-profit and nonprofit businesses) should be included, with a description of their utility to the community in terms of hazard mitigation. Preparing a capability assessment assures that local mitigation strategies will be based on existing authorities, policies, programs, and resources, and that the community's ability to expand on and improve its existing tools is duly noted.[12]

The political willpower necessary to carry out mitigation strategies should not be underestimated. In some communities the most difficult hurdle to overcome may be reluctance on the part of citizens or local officials to engage in something new. Some property owners may view hazard mitigation as a restriction on their rights. Other community members may mistakenly think hazard mitigation will pose an impediment to growth and economic development. In times of fiscal restraint, expenditure of limited resources may be a challenge. On the other hand, some residents and elected officials may have experienced personally the devastation of a past disaster and will support local hazard mitigation efforts wholeheartedly. The planning team should consider the local political climate carefully when assessing the community's capability.

13.4.1 Capability of Local Departments and Agencies

The capability assessment should include a list of all the local government departments, agencies, and organizations that have a direct impact through specifically delegated responsibility to carry out mitigation activities or hazard control tasks, and describe briefly what those responsibilities are (for example, the public works department is responsible for drainage system maintenance, which helps prevent flooding when carried out on a regular basis). At a minimum, the planning team should list local government agencies, departments, and offices with responsibility for planning, building code enforcement, mapping, building, and/or managing physical assets, as well as for emergency management functions.

13.4.2 Review Existing Policies, Programs, and Ordinances that May Affect Vulnerability

The capability assessment should include a description of mitigation initiatives that the community may have in place, and the policies, programs, ordinances, regulations, and other activities that guide these efforts. The capability assessment should also include policies and practices that are not directed at mitigation or natural hazards per se, but which may have an effect on mitigation-related efforts (for instance, a greenway program that could be targeted for acquiring open space in the floodplain). Some of these directives will be found in formal, adopted documents, such as the local land use plan, zoning ordinance, or stormwater management plan. Other practices and policies may be unwritten or

FOR EXAMPLE

Eastern Band of Cherokees Assess Mitigation Capabilities

When the Eastern Band of Cherokee Indians developed a hazard mitigation plan, the planning team carried out a thorough capability assessment. The team evaluated the existing authorities, policies, programs, and fiscal resources within the tribal community. The tribe went further and also prepared an assessment of the Federal Bureau of Indian Affairs' legal, fiscal, and regulatory roles within the community. By including an assessment of the federal role, the capability assessment gave a clear picture of the Tribe's full complement of resources to engage in mitigation actions.

less official, but nevertheless have implications for mitigation (for instance, a practice of allowing public access to the beach over the dunes, causing deterioration of the dune system's protective features). The planning team might want to talk to department heads and local government employees to find out what unwritten practices and policies they follow that affect mitigation.

SELF-CHECK

- Describe political will for mitigation action.
- Identify policies, programs, and ordinances that affect vulnerability.
- List the agencies and departments that carry out mitigation activities.

13.5 Develop Mitigation Goals and Objectives

The steps that have been taken so far have identified the populations and assets that are vulnerable to specific identified hazards and the capabilities of the community to address its hazard threats. The planning team must now develop appropriate mitigation actions to reduce vulnerability. Goals and objectives are useful for guiding mitigation decisions and are developed to address the hazard and risk assessment findings made earlier.

▲ **Goals** are general guidelines that describe what the community hopes to achieve.

▲ **Objectives** provide a more specific way to achieve the goals. In general, each goal statement will have 3 or 4 objectives that spell out steps to reach that goal.

▲ **Mitigation actions** are developed later, and are the most specific proposals for reaching goals.

Together, goals, objectives, and actions make up a mitigation strategy that is designed to increase community resiliency. (See box on p 456.) The regulations that accompany the DMA state that the plan "shall include a mitigation strategy that provides the jurisdiction's blueprint for reducing the potential losses identified in the risk assessment . . . . [The hazard mitigation strategy shall include a] description of mitigation goals to reduce or avoid long-term vulnerabilities to the identified hazards."[13]

13.5.1 Developing Goal Statements

Goals establish a vision of how the community wants to protect itself from hazards and how the community wants to grow and develop in the future. Goals are phrased in fairly general terms, focus on the long-term, and establish broad

GOALS, OBJECTIVES, AND ACTIONS

Goals are general guidelines that explain what is to be achieved. They are usually broad, policy-type statements, long-term, and represent a global vision. Example goal statements are:

- ✔ Reduce the vulnerability of flooding in the community.
- ✔ Minimize wildfire losses.
- ✔ Protect the local economy from the impacts of future hazard events.

Objectives lay out intermediary steps to reach the stated goals. Objectives are more specific than goals, and their attainment can be measured. Example objectives are:

- ✔ Protect structures in the downtown area from flooding.
- ✔ Educate homeowners about wildfire risks.
- ✔ Create incentives for local businesses to take mitigation actions.

Mitigation Actions are the most specific statements of all, and articulate how goals and objectives will be attained. Example actions are:

- ✔ Elevate three structures located in the downtown district.
- ✔ Create and distribute an educational brochure about wildfire hazards.
- ✔ Provide tax credits for local businesses that add hurricane storm shutters to their structures.

policy approaches to mitigation. Goal statements should acknowledge the findings of the risk assessment and be formulated to address the most serious problems that were raised. Combining other community priorities with hazard mitigation can make mitigation goals more effective. For example, community concerns such as improving water quality, preserving open space, conserving historic and cultural resources, protecting watersheds, and maintaining a stable economy are all compatible with hazard mitigation. Many of these goal statements may exist in previously-adopted local documents, and can be referred to in the hazard mitigation plan.

13.5.2 Creating Objectives

Objectives are statements that lay out steps to reach the goals. Objectives are more specific and narrower in scope than goals and are usually phrased so that it is easy to see when (or if) they have been reached. Objectives are the interim step between goals (very broad statements) and mitigation actions (the most specific, targeted statement of how mitigation is to be carried out). Objectives expand on

> ## FOR EXAMPLE
>
> ### Mitigation Goals for the Village of Gurnee, Illinois
>
> In November, 2001, the village of Gurnee adopted a series of mitigation goals and objectives to address its frequent flooding problems. The first goal is to "Protect existing properties," the second is to "Protect health and safety," the third goal statement is to "Improve the quality of life in Gurnee," and the fourth goal is to "Ensure that public funds are used in the most efficient manner." While these are fairly broad and generalized statements, the village further clarified each statement with a series of objectives designed to accomplish each goal.

the goals and provide more detail on the ways to accomplish them. Objectives often include time frames and specific targets within the time frame to reach identified outcomes. Performance-based objectives can be phrased so that a percentage of mitigation actions are taken or a certain number of outcomes are achieved.

SELF-CHECK

- Define **goals, objectives,** and **mitigation actions.**
- Give examples of mitigation goals and objectives.
- Discuss the characteristics of a good objective.

13.6 Develop Mitigation Actions

Once the community has concluded that it faces an unacceptable risk to certain identified hazards and has made the commitment to reducing its level of vulnerability by establishing meaningful goals and objectives, it is time to formulate a plan that meets those goals. This is the action part of the planning process, where the planning team will establish what will be done, and where, to reduce vulnerability. This section of the plan will identify, evaluate, and prioritize a comprehensive range of specific mitigation actions and projects to reduce the effects of each hazard identified earlier. The policies created will help guide both the day-to-day and long-range decision making of the community. Since the focus of this step is to recommend solutions to the problems the community faces, it is important to refer to the hazard studies conducted earlier in the planning process in order to target the areas identified as most vulnerable.

The mitigation actions considered should cover a wide range of options to reach the objectives laid out previously. Every single action may not necessarily be acted upon, but the planning team should think of multiple alternatives, each with its own set of relative merits. Some of the actions that are identified may be "brick and mortar" projects, such as constructing tornado-safe rooms or retrofitting existing school buildings to withstand earthquake shaking. Other mitigation actions may be non-construction projects, such as acquisition of flood-prone properties or changes to the zoning ordinance or building code. In general, mitigation actions should cover each of the six broad categories of mitigation activities, including prevention, property protection, natural resource protection, structural projects, and public education and awareness strategies as well as emergency operations. It is important that the identified actions and projects address both reducing the effects of hazards on new buildings and infrastructure, as well as existing buildings and infrastructure. In addition, the actions should include some that are appropriate to carry out after a disaster has occurred, while others can be instituted at any time, including in the pre-disaster period.

13.6.1 Sources for Mitigation Action Ideas

A series of brainstorming sessions can be an effective way to develop mitigation alternatives. Many communities use this opportunity to solicit ideas and suggestions from local public officials, residents, business owners, community and civic organizations, and representatives from state, federal, and regional agencies. Scientists and hazard experts (e.g., geologists, seismologists, hydrologists, etc.) as well as floodplain managers, emergency managers, fire marshals, public works engineers, transportation engineers, and civil engineers who are expert in applying mitigation and emergency management principles all have valuable experience in mitigating hazards. These experts can help the planning team evaluate whether the mitigation alternative will fulfill the stated objectives, if the action provides a long-term solution to the problem, and possibly what some of the social, administrative, environmental, and economic implications are for the planning area. Some potential alternative actions involve complex engineering and may require additional study before a solution or alternative mitigation action can be identified.

In addition to talking with the experts, the planning team can review many of the resources made available by FEMA and state emergency offices that describe mitigation actions, some of which include specific design features and approximate cost ranges for various actions. Many of these are available at state and federal websites.[14] Another good source for mitigation ideas is the Community Rating System Coordinator's Manual, which lays out specific mitigation tasks for each major category of mitigation strategies.[15] Learning about what has worked for other communities is another way to scope out possibilities for mitigation in jurisdictions with similar conditions. These so-called mitigation success stories can also go a long way towards convincing reluctant community members to support mitigation actions.[16]

13.6.2 Select and Prioritize Mitigation Actions

Brainstorming sessions and talking with the experts will result in a long list of possible mitigation actions. The list needs to be narrowed down to include only those that are the most reasonable and have a chance of becoming reality. The process of selecting and prioritizing the mitigation action alternatives will help the planning team create a realistic list of mitigation recommendations. But those ideas that don't make the final list should not be discarded completely. The planning team may wish to prepare a secondary file of possible alternatives that may become feasible at a later time.

Form Selection Criteria

The mitigation actions that have been developed so far include any and all possibilities for reducing vulnerability. Before selecting those actions that will be pursued further, the community should evaluate each alternative. One way to do this is to develop selection criteria through which all the ideas are passed, much like a filter. When devising selection criteria, first and foremost, every mitigation action proposed must be technically capable of solving the problem it is intended to solve. Later, when the plan is actually ready to be implemented, a thorough cost-benefit analysis will have to be performed to decide which projects are put in line for full funding. A cost-benefit analysis will also help in prioritizing mitigation actions. Beyond that, each community will have its own emphasis when selecting and prioritizing mitigation alternatives. What follows is a list of possible criteria that communities may consider when deciding which mitigation actions to pursue. These are based on the STAPLE/E method of evaluative criteria (see box on page 460). STAPLE/E is an acronym for a general set of criteria common to public administration officials and planners. It stands for social, technical, administrative, Political, legal, economic, and environmental criteria for making planning decisions. The STAPLE/E approach provides a series of questions to help make planning decisions and determine benefits and costs of various mitigation activities.

Select the Mitigation Actions

As the planning team reviews the various mitigation actions that have been proposed, it should look for ways to eliminate from consideration those actions that, from a technical standpoint, will not meet the objective, even though may have been indicated as generally applicable to the situation. For example, if an alternative mitigation action is to relocate a building out of the floodplain, the building may be structurally unsound and might not survive a move. Such an action could then be eliminated from the list, and there is no need to undertake a detailed evaluation of the remaining criteria, thereby saving time and effort. The planning team must document the process used to evaluate all the actions, as well as the reasons for eliminating any of the proposed measures.

STAPLE/E CRITERIA

Social, Technical, Administrative, Political, Legal, Economic, and Environmental

Social:

- ✔ Is the proposed action socially acceptable to the community?
- ✔ Are there equity issues involved that would mean that one segment of the community is treated unfairly?
- ✔ Will the action cause social disruption?

Community development staff, local non-profit organizations, or a local planning board can help answer these questions.

Technical:

- ✔ Will the proposed action work?
- ✔ Will it create more problems than it solves?
- ✔ Does it solve a problem or only a symptom?
- ✔ Is it the most useful action in light of other community goals?

The community public works staff and building department staff can help answer these questions.

Administrative:

- ✔ Can the community implement the action?
- ✔ Is there someone to coordinate and lead the effort?
- ✔ Is there sufficient funding, staff, and technical support available?
- ✔ Are there ongoing administrative requirements that need to be met?

Elected officials or the city or town administrator can help answer these questions.

Political:

- ✔ Is the action politically acceptable?
- ✔ Is there public support both to implement and to maintain the project?

Consult the mayor, city council, or board of aldermen, city or town administrator, and regional planning agencies to help answer these questions.

Legal:

- ✔ Is the community authorized to implement the proposed action?
- ✔ Is there a clear legal basis or precedent for this activity?
- ✔ Are there legal side effects?
- ✔ Will the activity be challenged? Could the activity be construed as a taking?
- ✔ Will the community be liable for action or lack of action?

Include legal counsel, land use planners, risk managers, and city council or town planning commission members, among others, in this discussion.

Economic:

- ✔ What are the costs and benefits of this action? Do the benefits exceed the costs?
- ✔ Are initial, maintenance, and administrative costs taken into account?
- ✔ Has funding been secured for the proposed action? If not, what are the potential funding sources (public, non-profit, and private)?
- ✔ How will this action affect the fiscal capability of the community?
- ✔ What burden will this action place on the tax base or local economy?
- ✔ What are the budget and revenue effects of this activity?
- ✔ Does the action contribute to other community goals, such as capital improvements or economic development?
- ✔ What benefits will the action provide? (This can include dollar amount of damages prevented, number of homes protected, credit under the CRS, potential for funding under the HMGP or the FMA program, etc.)

Community economic development staff, civil engineers, building department staff, and the assessor's office can help answer these questions

Environmental:

- ✔ How will the action impact the environment?
- ✔ Will the action need environmental regulatory approvals?
- ✔ Will it meet local and state regulatory requirements?
- ✔ Are endangered or threatened species likely to be affected?
- ✔ Do the actions comply with the state's Environmental Justice Policy?

Watershed councils, watershed basin teams, environmental groups, land use planners, and natural resource managers can help answer these questions.

Prioritize the Mitigation Actions

It is a very rare local government that has at its immediate disposal all the resources it needs to meet all its mitigation goals and solve all its hazard problems at once. Most communities will need to set priorities to determine which problems are most critical to the health and safety of the community and focus on those problems first. For example, if a certain hazard area contains a significant number of people, properties, or critical facilities and is also exposed to a highly probable, high-magnitude event, this area would receive top priority, and mitigation actions that target this area would receive top billing. Referring to the vulnerability maps performed during the risk assessment will help review the

---

FOR EXAMPLE

City of Quincy Provides Mitigation Choices

Recovery after disaster declarations for nor'easters in 1991 and 1992 gave Quincy, Massachusetts, the opportunity to address its quality of life goal of increasing the availability of financing for affordable housing within the city. The city provided a range of options for homeowners whose property was located in flood-prone areas. The goal was to reduce vulnerability through retrofit, relocation, and structural improvements. The three strategies demonstrate the city's commitment to incorporating multiple objectives into its mitigation strategies.

---

areas that are highly vulnerable to multiple hazards. Some communities may choose to implement easy actions first, to show quick results, while others may wish to place priority on those that fulfill multiple community objectives, like protection of habitat areas along with floodplain protection. Still other communities will want to focus on preserving historic structures. Whatever the particular ranking criteria that are used, the mitigation strategy selection process should reflect the community's overall priorities.

Benefit-Cost Analysis

The regulations that accompany the DMA require that the prioritization process for selecting mitigation actions include an emphasis on the use of a cost-benefit review to maximize benefits. All projects using federal funds must be justified as being cost-effective. This can be determined through the use of various benefit-cost analysis methodologies.

▲ A **Benefit-Cost Analysis (BCA)** is a quantitative procedure that assesses the desirability of a hazard mitigation project by taking a long-term view of avoided future damages to insurable structures as compared to the cost of the project.

▲ A **Benefit-Cost Ratio (BCR)** is the outcome of the analysis, which demonstrates whether the net present value of benefits exceeds the net present value of costs.

FEMA's BCAs are governed by guidance from the Office of Management and Budget (OMB).[17] A BCA is required for all mitigation projects submitted to FEMA for funding, and mitigation projects with a BCR less than 1.0 will not be considered for funding under most programs. Mitigation projects with higher BCRs will be more competitive.

The benefits of mitigation projects are counted broadly, not narrowly. In simple terms, it is proper to count all of the direct benefits of mitigation projects. The direct benefits are simply the avoided damages, losses, and casualties that may occur in natural disasters. As a general rule of thumb, if a natural hazard results in direct damages, losses, or casualties and a mitigation project avoids or reduces them, then it is acceptable to count these benefits for a FEMA BCA. Office of Management and Budget guidance on BCAs excludes some benefits from consideration when conducting a BCA. The most important of these are indirect, or "multiplier," effects. For example, long-term changes in regional economic activity, future employment, or tourism cannot be considered benefits of mitigation projects because they are not directly linked to the project.

13.6.3 Recommendations for Mitigation Action

The end result of the evaluation, selection, and prioritization process will be a set of recommendations for mitigation action. These will be included in the strategy portion of the plan. The decision-making process can lead to a variety of different types of recommendations—from clear-cut actions that target a specific hazard location to seeking more information about a particular action item's feasibility to combinations of different mitigation strategies that cover a wide range of hazard areas.[18] Whatever the method used for selecting and prioritizing mitigation actions, it is important that the plan include a discussion of the process and criteria used. Documentation that explains the rationale for selecting particular actions can ease implementation and is required by the DMA regulations.

When communities create a multi-jurisdictional plan, the DMA rules require that the plan include at least one identifiable action item for each jurisdiction.[19] The mitigation action item can be any type of strategy, so long as it targets the particular hazard problem of that jurisdiction.

SELF-CHECK

- Define **benefit-cost analysis** and **benefit-cost ratio.**
- List six types of mitigation actions.
- Discuss ways of finding action ideas.
- Explain STAPLE/E.

13.7 Create Implementation Procedures

The real challenge of hazard mitigation planning involves converting the plan into action. A hazard mitigation plan that sits on the shelf does nothing to reduce a community's vulnerability to hazards. It is only through implementation, or putting the plan into action, that a community can hope to increase its resiliency and make the area safer for all its residents. One way to ensure that the mitigation plan is implemented in a timely fashion is to include procedures within the plan itself for how the plan will be put into action and administered by the local community. Even the best mitigation action ideas are meaningless unless a responsible party is assigned to carry them out, funding is made available, and a realistic time frame for accomplishing tasks is established. This step will take care of these details to make sure the plan is implemented as fully as possible. The more specific and precise the implementation procedure is, the more likely that it will actually be followed. The DMA regulations require that the mitigation strategy section of the plan describe how the actions identified earlier will be implemented and administered by the local jurisdiction.[20]

13.7.1 Assign Responsibility

A particular person or department within the local government will need to put each specific mitigation action into place and follow it through to completion. The capability assessment performed earlier can be quite helpful for identifying the right person or agency for the job. The planning team should refer to the list of organizations and agencies prepared as part of the capability assessment to identify who has the authority and will be most effective in carrying out the action. The city or county manager can also be very helpful in deciding who might be the most appropriate contact to take responsibility for each type of mitigation action, and can facilitate making that assignment for many of the departments in the community.

13.7.2 Identify Potential Funding Sources

Most (but not all) mitigation actions will require money. The planning team should list a funding source, or a potential funding source, for each of the mitigation actions proposed. The capability assessment can be helpful for identifying what types of financing are available in the community. Often funding sources can be combined, so that some actions may have more than one source listed. If no funding source can be identified for a particular mitigation action immediately, it should not necessarily be eliminated. Instead, the action plan should indicate that funding is not available at this time. Funding sources often become apparent at a later date.

For some mitigation actions, additional resources aside from money will be necessary. For example, vehicles, equipment, supplies, and other tools may

> **FOR EXAMPLE**
>
> **Multiple Funding Sources for Multiple Objectives**
>
> Boone, North Carolina, a small town in the mountainous northwestern corner of the state, is vulnerable to flooding and also subject to development pressure because of its scenic location. The town achieved multiple objectives in a broad flood mitigation program through partnerships that tackled such community needs as affordable housing, open space and recreation, and removing repetitive damaged properties from the floodplain. The town of Boone was able to attract and administer multiple sources of funding to carry out mutually compatible objectives. A total of $4.5 million was raised from several sources, including the town, federal Hazard Mitigation Grant Program and Housing and Urban Development funds, and state water quality and acquisition funds.

be required, especially for the "brick and mortar" type projects when they come online. Some of these resources may already be available in the various departments assigned to the task, such as the Public Works Department that may have the excavating, grading, and construction equipment needed to upgrade stormwater drainage facilities. But other projects may require additional resources, and the implementation strategy will need to make note of those requirements and factor securing them into the budget projection for that action.

13.7.3 Establish a Time Frame

A definite time line for accomplishing mitigation actions is necessary to make sure that implementation is not delayed unnecessarily or that the action ideas get forgotten or buried under other priority activities. The time line for each mitigation action should include a start date, an ending date, as well as interim dates to check on progress while the action is being implemented. Determining the time frame with staff members from the departments or agencies that are responsible for the mitigation action will greatly enhance the chance of the mitigation plan succeeding.

The planning team should establish the starting and ending dates by first identifying any special scheduling parameters, such as seasonal weather conditions, funding cycles, agency work plans, and other responsibilities, budgets, and staff constraints. The time frame for implementing each action should be as realistic as possible, without causing undue delay or pressure to complete an action too quickly to ensure a quality end result.

13.8 Establish a Plan Maintenance Process

Mitigation is an ongoing process. Effective plans are dynamic and evolving, and must be continually tested. Therefore, an essential element of the written mitigation plan is a section that spells out in detail the procedures to monitor and evaluate the plan's progress on a regular basis. The plan should designate a specific person or position within the local government to perform these functions.

The primary question to be addressed in monitoring and evaluating a hazard mitigation plan is, "Has the area's vulnerability increased or decreased as a result of planning and mitigation efforts?" Where vulnerability has decreased, the planning team should determine if other methods could be used to achieve even greater improvement in reducing the area's vulnerability. Where vulnerability has increased, or has not decreased as projected, mitigation efforts must be evaluated to determine if other mitigation strategies might provide greater effectiveness than those currently in use.

13.8.1 Procedures for Monitoring Implementation

The planning team should set a regular schedule for monitoring implementation of the plan. This schedule can be quarterly, semi-annually, or annually—whatever best suits the needs and ability of the local government to stay on top of things. The person or committee charged with routine monitoring should check whether the policies in the plan are being implemented within the timeframe assigned during the implementation procedure. If implementation is not occurring as scheduled, the person in charge of monitoring should note any explanations. A brief progress report from or conversation with those responsible for implementation of each action may aid this task.

13.8.2 Procedures for Evaluating Plan Progress

Beyond checking whether the policies and actions of the plan are being implemented on time, the community should undertake an evaluation of the plan's effectiveness regularly. Some communities find it useful to establish firm indicators or benchmarks against which progress can be measured. The indicators should be linked specifically to individual actions, so each one can be evaluated

> **FOR EXAMPLE**
>
> ### Louisa County, Iowa, Takes Stock
>
> In 1993, a severe flood occurred in Louisa County, located along the Mississippi River, resulting in damage to more than 275 homes and the evacuation of nearly 200 families. Following this flood event, the county used both acquisition and relocation to mitigate future flooding problems. In May 2001, the flood pattern of 1993 repeated itself, and the Mississippi River and its tributaries flooded Louisa County yet again. By comparing calculated damages from the 1993 flood to the 2001 flood, the effectiveness of the acquisition program could be measured. Significant reductions in emergency shelter, family assistance, and public assistance expenditures were realized in 2001 as a result of the acquisitions and housing relocations that occurred in the aftermath of the 1993 flooding.[21]

on its own merits. Indicators and benchmarks can be quantifiable measures of progress, or more quality-oriented and subjective. For example, the community may wish to track the number of housing units permitted each year in hazard areas or the number of businesses that purchase flood insurance. More general criteria could involve assessing whether the nature or magnitude of the risk has changed or whether current resources are adequate for continued implementation of the plan.

13.8.3 Procedures for Revising and Updating the Plan

Revisions to the hazard mitigation plan are necessary to correct flaws that are discovered as the plan is set in motion. There are always some contingencies that cannot be foreseen or events which cannot be predicted. Revisions incorporate those changes necessary to better fit the plan to real-life situations. Periodic revision of mitigation plans will also help to ensure that local mitigation efforts include the latest and most effective mitigation techniques. Technology is rapidly advancing, and the community will want to take advantage of any improvements in hazards analysis, geographic data collection, and mitigation techniques that become available.

Updates address changes that have taken place in the local area. At a minimum, under the DMA the plan must be updated within a 5-year cycle.[22] The plan should include a statement that declares the community will review and update the plan every five years, and that it will re-submit the plan to the State Hazard Mitigation Officer and to FEMA for review and approval.

Changes that should be reflected in the regular plan update may result from additional development, implementation of mitigation efforts, development of new mitigation processes, and changes to state or federal statutes and regulations. Additional development in the area may result in an increase, little change, or a decrease in the community's vulnerability to hazards depending on the location, type, density, and design of the development. The occurrence of a disaster or emergency can also cause the need for an update to the mitigation plan. A hazard event can drastically change vulnerability, capability, and the local political and physical landscape. A hazard event can also provide a good indicator of whether mitigation actions implemented so far have produced the desired result.

Another important change in a local community that may warrant revision or an update to the local mitigation plan occurs with each local election, when a potentially new political scene occurs. Turnover among the decision makers of the community may impact the policies of the mitigation plan, as the political climate becomes more accepting or more adverse to controlling growth and development in hazardous areas.

13.8.4 Incorporation into Existing Planning Mechanisms

The maintenance section of the plan must also include provisions for incorporating the mitigation policies into other existing local planning activities.[23] The mitigation plan should identify other local planning mechanisms available, such as land use plans, subdivision regulations, zoning ordinance, capital improvements plan, transportation plan, floodplain management plan, emergency management plan, and other types of local plans where mitigation would be appropriate for inclusion. For example, the mitigation plan could describe a process whereby the hazard mitigation plan will be presented to advisory committees or local employees whenever other local plans are being created or updated and that recommendation for inclusion of mitigation principles will be made. The mitigation plan should also indicate that the goals and strategies of new and updated local planning documents will be consistent with the hazard mitigation plan and will not contribute to increased vulnerability in the jurisdiction.

13.8.5 Continued Public Involvement

Keeping the plan alive and actionable is a very important part of the mitigation planning process. Maintaining plan action will involve continued participation by the public if the plan is to remain on the front burner of the community's priorities. The plan must contain a section that explains how continued public participation will be obtained and how the public will have the opportunity to comment on plan progress. The DMA regulations are quite flexible about the actual method that the community chooses to keep the public involved, so long as it effectively communicates opportunities for participation to members of the community, and the commitment to carry out the method is clearly documented in the plan itself.[24] For example, communities may send notices to residents periodically, place a copy of the plan on reserve in the public library or town hall, or post draft changes of the plan on the community website.

SELF-CHECK

- List ways of determining how an area's vulnerability has changed as a result of mitigation efforts.
- Review various schedules for monitoring.
- Discuss the importance of continued public involvement in a plan's success.

13.9 Putting It All Together: Writing and Adopting the Hazard Mitigation Plan

After following all the steps of the planning process, the community will have a wealth of information in the form of worksheets, lists, maps, and narrative summaries. This material needs to be presented in a written document in a way that the reader can easily identify what the major hazard problems are, the goals for the community to reduce risk to those hazards, and the solutions recommended for solving the problems and reaching the goals. There are numerous ways to put the mitigation plan together, and each community will need to decide for itself what the final product should look like, so long as the basic elements of the written plan are in conformance with FEMA regulatory requirements as laid out in the DMA.

The written document should emphasize the action part of the plan—the strategies and implementation measures that will serve to reduce vulnerability in the community. While the analyses performed during the first steps of the planning process were essential to creating the goals and policies, they are not the plan itself. Therefore, many communities choose to include the hazard identification, risk analysis and capability assessment as appendices to the plan itself.

13.9.1 Putting Pen to Paper: Writing Style and Format

There is no set format or style that a local mitigation plan must follow. The language used and organization of the plan should reflect the needs and the personality of the community that the plan serves. Some mitigation plans are quite short and get to the point quickly, without a lot of background verbiage or extra commentary. Other communities might choose to wax lyrical, and use the mitigation plan as a forum to articulate what's best about the community, describing its character and why it is home to community residents, emphasizing the need to protect its sense of identity from the impacts of hazards. The planning team might wish to review other local documents, to make the mitigation plan consistent in style and format with similar policy statements. The planning team should also check with the state to see if a common format and style have been mandated or requested for local governments to follow.

Whether the mitigation plan is lengthy or concise, simplified or involved, the mitigation plan must be clear, current, and as complete as practicable. Language should not be overly technical, or if technical terms must be used, they should be clearly defined, either in the text or in a glossary or appendix. The reader should be able to find where the plan discusses a particular topic quickly and easily. A table of contents or other type of indexing system can be helpful for this purpose. A "Crosswalk", which is a table-like compendium that indicates where certain topics are covered in the plan (page number and/or section or chapter) can also be a good way to lead the reader quickly to the right spot, especially for official reviewers of the final plan.[25] Above all, the mitigation plan should leave no doubt in the reader's mind about what the plan is to achieve, how it will be done, and who will be in charge of carrying it out. Every attempt should be made to make the mitigation plan as comprehensive as possible; however, some gaps in information are inevitable. The plan should make note of any items that are lacking and prepare a statement that describes how the community will address any existing gaps in the future.

13.9.2 Adopting the Plan

The governing body of the local government must officially adopt the hazard mitigation plan in order to make the plan enforceable. A series of recommendations made by planning or emergency management staff does not have nearly the impact as an official document that clearly lays out the government's policies for dealing with hazards and reducing vulnerability. In fact, adoption of the plan is a prerequisite for plan approval by FEMA under the DMA regulations.[26]

Hold Public Meetings

Prior to official adoption, the planning team should arrange to hold a public meeting to offer citizens an opportunity to comment on the plan. Many local communities have a standard legal process for adoption of regulations and policy that often includes specific requirements for how, when, and where public hearings are to be held, and certain rules about how the public is to receive notice in advance of the meeting. State laws may also require certain procedures for public notice and hearings before adoption of important local policy. It is important that the planning team follow these rules and documents these efforts to involve the public. Documentation should include copies of the actual public notices used to advertise the meeting (newspaper clippings, flyers, memos, etc.), copies of meeting invitations, a list of invited individuals, sign-in sheets, recorded minutes, and other records from the meeting. After holding the public meeting, the planning team may need to incorporate public comments and revise the plan accordingly. Once the revisions have been made, the final plan will be ready for submission to the local governing body for official adoption.

Formal Plan Adoption

The final version of the plan will be presented to the lead governing body of the community, usually at a regularly scheduled meeting that is open to the public. Depending upon the structure of the local government, this may be a meeting of the city council, board of supervisors, county commissioners, board of aldermen, or other official policy-making group (see Chapter 8 for a discussion of the various forms of local government in the United States). The mitigation plan must be adopted through the government's normal legal process. Generally, most local governing bodies adopt a hazard mitigation plan by resolution. A **resolution** is an expression of a governing body's opinion, will, or intention that is usually legally binding, but not always. A legally binding resolution must be supported by an official vote of the majority of members of the governing board. If this is the proper procedure for the local community, supporting documentation, such as a copy of the resolution, must accompany the plan when it is submitted to FEMA for approval. Depending upon the laws of the state and the local jurisdiction, adoption of the plan gives the local government legal authority to enact ordinances, policies, or programs to reduce hazard losses and to implement the recommended mitigation actions contained in the plan.

13.9.3 Submit the Plan for Approval

Once the local governing body has adopted the plan, it must be submitted to the State Hazard Mitigation Officer (SHMO). Some states impose requirements upon local governments for hazard mitigation plans that go beyond the requirements

---

FOR EXAMPLE

Passing Public Muster

In 1981, Nags Head, North Carolina, began addressing its severe exposure to coastal storms and erosion by developing a hazard mitigation plan that identified specific pre- and postdisaster responsibilities, including building moratoria, reconstruction priorities and guidelines, and restrictions on public capital improvements following major storms. The controversial nature of the effort is demonstrated by its 1989 adoption date, *eight years* after discussions were initiated.

of the DMA, and the SHMO will review the plan to make sure these additional requirements are met. Local plans must also be consistent with the state hazard mitigation plan, and the SHMO will review the local plan carefully to check that it does. After reviewing the local plan, the SHMO then forwards the plan to the appropriate FEMA Regional Office for review. If a tribal government has developed a state-level mitigation plan, the tribal plan should be submitted directly to the FEMA Regional Office. The FEMA Regional Office will review each local plan, and may approve the local plan immediately, or may require modifications or changes to be made to make the plan compliant with DMA regulations. Once the FEMA Regional Office and the state give final approval to the local mitigation plan, the local jurisdiction is then officially eligible to apply for federal mitigation project funds under several different pre-and post-disaster assistance programs.

13.9.4 Putting the Plan in Motion: Mitigation in Action

One of the most important reasons for having a hazard mitigation plan is to help the community make decisions that will reduce its vulnerability to hazards. Activities that local governments do every day, such as issuing building permits, approving development plans, and repairing roads and bridges, should reflect the community's vision and goals, whether it's using the most up to date building code, restricting growth in hazard-prone areas, or making infrastructure decisions based on the latest risk assessment findings. The hazard mitigation plan is a guide to keep the community on track and serves as documentation of the thoughts and considerations that were the foundation of the planning process. As community leadership changes, and during intense decision-making situations, such as the postdisaster setting and when undertaking major land development decisions—the plan will serve as the representation of the community's principles for hazard loss reduction.[27]

SELF-CHECK

- Define **resolution**.
- Discuss the necessity of adopting the plan.
- Explain how and where to submit a plan for approval.
- Review the steps that must be taken before putting a mitigation plan into action.
- Discuss the day-to-day activities that a community will do to meet its mitigation goals.

SUMMARY

A hazard mitigation plan makes the community eligible for certain federal mitigation funding, but more importantly, a hazard mitigation plan can help guide decision making to make the community more disaster resilient, both now and in the future. This chapter reinforces the importance of mitigation planning, reviewing the types of plans and the steps involved. The roles of both risk assessments and capability assessments are covered. The chapter offers guidance on developing mitigation goals, objectives, and actions. Implementation procedures, or ways of converting a plan into action, are outlined. The chapter concludes with guidelines for the actual writing process, as well as how to go about submitting, adopting, and putting a plan into action.

KEY TERMS

All-hazards approach	Mitigation planning that involves consideration of all the hazards with the potential for causing harm, including natural and man-made hazards.
Benefit-cost analysis	A quantitative procedure that assesses the desirability of a hazard mitigation project by taking a long-term view of avoided future damages to insurable structures as compared to the cost of the project.
Benefit-cost ratio	The outcome of a benefit-cost analysis, which demonstrates whether the net present value of benefits exceeds the net present value of costs.
Goals	What a community hopes to achieve with a mitigation plan.
Hazard mitigation planning	Process of determining how to reduce or eliminate the loss of life and property damage that can occur as a result of hazards.
Mitigation actions	Specific proposals for reaching mitigation goals.
Multi-jurisdictional	Two or more local governments that prepare a joint hazard mitigation plan.
Objectives	Provide specific ways to achieve mitigation goals.
Resolution	An expression of a governing body's opinion, will, or intention that is usually legally binding.

ASSESS YOUR UNDERSTANDING

Go to www.wiley.com/college/schwab to evaluate your knowledge of hazard mitigation planning.

Measure your learning by comparing pre-test and post-test results.

Summary Questions

1. An all-hazards approach to mitigation planning addresses both natural and man-made hazards alike. True or False?
2. Which level of government is primarily responsible for preparing mitigation plans?
   (a) local
   (b) regional
   (c) state
   (d) federal
3. A multi-jurisdictional plan is prepared in conjunction with neighboring states. True or False?
4. A standardized planning process must be used for all communities in order to be accepted by the federal government. True or False?
5. Which of the following steps follows the capability assessment?
   (a) create implementation procedures
   (b) risk assessment
   (c) develop mitigation goals and objectives
   (d) write the plan
6. Proper documentation of a planning process is required both by FEMA and the DMA. True or False?
7. The role of a risk assessment in a hazard mitigation plan is to define a community's hazard problem. True or False?
8. In which stage of the risk assessment process does a planning team inventory assets and population?
   (a) hazard profile
   (b) vulnerability assessment
   (c) hazard identification
   (d) development analysis
9. The DMA requires that a risk assessment identify all man-made hazards in a community. True or False?
10. Secondary hazards cause less damage than the initial hazard event. True or False?

11. Local governments are required by the DMA to complete a capability assessment. True or False?

12. A capability assessment should review a community's funding as part of its
    (a) environmental capability.
    (b) legal capability.
    (c) political capability.
    (d) fiscal capability.

13. Which of the following is an example of a mitigation objective?
    (a) minimize landslide losses
    (b) retrofit city hall to prevent additional earthquake damage
    (c) improve disaster warning system
    (d) reduce coastal erosion

14. "Reduce Hazard City's vulnerability to terrorism" is an example of a mitigation goal. True or False?

15. In general how many objective statements should be required to reach a goal?
    (a) 1
    (b) 3 to 4
    (c) 5 to 7
    (d) 10

16. Which of the following actions is an example of the property protection type of mitigation?
    (a) fault zone setback
    (b) slope stabilization
    (c) retention ponds
    (d) seismic retrofit

17. Preventive mitigation actions are particularly effective in reducing future vulnerability in undeveloped areas. True or False?

18. Floodplain protection is an example of which type of mitigation?
    (a) emergency services
    (b) structural projects
    (c) acquisition
    (d) natural resource protection

19. Mitigation actions address only new buildings and infrastructure. True or False?

20. What is STAPLE/E?
    (a) criteria for evaluating mitigation activities
    (b) criteria for vulnerability assessments

(c) criteria for prioritizing mitigation activities

(d) criteria for implementation

21. Civil engineers and community development staff can answer questions about which part of STAPLE/E?

(a) environmental

(b) economic

(c) legal

(d) political

22. As part of implementation procedures, responsibility must be assigned for each mitigation action, from putting it into place to its completion. True or False?

23. How often are updates required by the DMA of plan maintenance and progress?

(a) annually

(b) bi-annually

(c) every five years

(d) every ten years

24. Public meetings should take place before a plan is submitted for official adoption. True or False?

25. Once a local government adopts a plan, it must be submitted to

(a) FEMA national office.

(b) Office of the Governor.

(c) State Hazard Mitigation Officer.

(d) County Commissioners.

Review Questions

1. List three examples of government aid and programs that require a local government to have a hazard mitigation plan in place.

2. Many communities choose to prepare a distinct, free-standing hazard mitigation plan. For those that do not, what options are available to them?

3. Which federal law is the standard hazard mitigation planning process based on?

4. List the four phases of the mitigation planning process.

5. A planning process takes time, but organization done in the beginning can help. What three elements of organization should a community take care of?

6. The DMA requires public participation in a plan at which two stages?

7. A risk assessment is a critical part of a mitigation plan. Review the steps of a hazard risk assessment.

8. A risk assessment must provide information on previous occurrences of any hazards addressed in a plan. What is the name of this process?

9. Inventorying assets and populations provides a sense of how vulnerable property and people are to hazards. How do maps facilitate this process?

10. Define capability assessment.

11. A capability assessment should include a list of all the departments, agencies, and organizations that carry out mitigation activities. Give five examples.

12. Explain the difference between the goals and objectives of a mitigation plan.

13. Write an objective to follow a community's goal of reducing coastal erosion.

14. Give some characteristics of workable objectives.

15. Review the six broad categories of mitigation actions.

16. Once a community identifies its hazards it must still come up with mitigation ideas. Give an example of a resource for such ideas.

17. What does the acronym STAPLE/E stand for?

18. What types of people can answer questions as part of the environmental element of STAPLE/E?

19. How does a benefit-cost analysis differ from a benefit-cost ratio?

20. In addition to responsibility and funding, what other element needs to be determined in the implementation step of the planning process?

21. What happens after the planning process is just as important as the planning itself. Which step of the process addresses the future of a plan?

22. What type of writing style is most effective for mitigation plans?

23. Before a plan can be put into action, what must first happen?

Applying This Chapter

1. Consider the hazards faced by your community and those that surround it. Determine any benefit of preparing your community's hazard mitigation plan in a multi-jurisdiction process. How would it differ from a process that focused singly on your community?

2. As a planner in Seaside, a small town in coastal Oregon, what steps would you take to organize before embarking on a hazard mitigation planning process? Take into consideration the 12 homes that have been repeatedly flooded in a particularly flood-prone area of the bay.

3. As a planner in Seaside, part of your town's mitigation planning is a risk assessment. What would be the direct and indirect losses from the three most significant hazards faced by your community?

4. As part of the capability assessment for Seaside's mitigation plan, it appears that your community is fiscally and legally capable to undertake its mitigation efforts. Politically, however, the town is very divided. What can be done to convince plan opponents to change their minds?

5. Given the three most significant hazards faced by Seaside, determine one goal and objective for each.

6. Once you've established goals and objectives for hazards, it is time to formulate a plan that meets those goals. Develop mitigation actions based on the three goals of your community, including specific projects.

7. Using the four different considerations used to prioritize mitigation activities, put Seaside's mitigation actions in order of highest to lowest priority; give an explanation for each.

8. Putting Seaside's mitigation plan into action requires the creation of implementation procedures. What needs to be done to implement Seaside's plan? Identify any areas that may prove difficult to determine.

9. The Disaster Mitigation Act of 2000 requires that a plan be evaluated every five years; Seaside has voted to increase the frequency of the monitoring to every three years. What benchmarks will you use to judge the success of your town's plan?

Hazards Hit Home

Consider where you live and what hazards threaten your community. Determine if a hazard mitigation plan exists at the local level. Which, if any, of the mitigation actions directly affect you and your property?

Capabiltiy Assessment

Assess the capability of your government to address the hazards that impact your community. Look at a variety of factors, including resources, policies, legal capacity, political capacity, and fiscal capacity. Determine which aspect might prove least capable.

Making Progress

Evaluate your community's hazards and prioritze them according to ease of implementation. Determine a goal, objective, and mitigation action for the hazard with the greatest ease; predict how long it would take to see results.

14

BUILDING A CULTURE OF PREVENTION
Resilient Communities for a Safer Tomorrow

Starting Point

Go to www.wiley.com/college/schwab to assess your knowledge of building a culture of prevention.
Determine where you need to concentrate your effort.

What You'll Learn in This Chapter

▲ Three spheres of sustainable development
▲ Ways hazard mitigation contributes to community sustainability
▲ The role of the private and nonprofit sectors in creating resilient communities
▲ Several structural and nonstructural mitigation strategies
▲ How economic vitality supports community sustainability
▲ Features of the natural environment that serve a mitigation function
▲ The importance of hazards awareness and risk terminology

After Studying This Chapter, You'll Be Able To

▲ Illustrate how resiliency supports and complements community sustainability
▲ Examine the aspects of sustainable development that can change current thinking about hazard mitigation
▲ Examine the features of a resilient community
▲ Examine the linkages between the three spheres of community sustainability
▲ Analyze how unsustainable patterns of development increase community vulnerability to hazards
▲ Analyze how poverty exacerbates community vulnerability to hazards
▲ Appraise several pre- and postdisaster sustainable development opportunities

Goals and Outcomes

▲ Evaluate the effectiveness of sustainable development
▲ Assess the opportunities available for mitigation with a sustainable development mindset
▲ Create opportunities for communities to incorporate sustainable development principles into local policy and practices in the pre- and postdisaster settings
▲ Synthesize the art and technical skills of emergency management to reduce local vulnerability to hazards
▲ Collaborate with others to determine an acceptable level of risk to natural hazards
▲ Appraise the role of personal responsibility in preventing disaster
▲ Assess the cost-benefits of various mitigation measures

INTRODUCTION

While hazards are a function of the natural world, vulnerability to disasters is a function of human action and behaviors. The ways in which we create our communities and choose to live determine how resilient we are to the impacts of hazards. Infusing an ethic of mitigation—a culture of prevention—can help us achieve a more sustainable future. This chapter discusses the unsustainable patterns of land use that have led to more and greater disasters in the United States, and how a sustainable development approach to resilience can help us break the cycle of disaster and rebuilding that has plagued our communities for decades. The chapter also discusses the economic vitality, environmental integrity, and social equity that are essential characteristics of a sustainable community, and how hazard resiliency can contribute to these efforts. The chapter concludes with a discussion about the role of personal responsibility in building a culture of prevention, and how the art of emergency management can help bring the vision of sustainability to fruition for a safer tomorrow.

14.1 Vulnerability as a Function of Human Behavior

The United States has witnessed an exponential increase in material losses due to natural disasters over the past several decades. While the number of deaths has not equaled those experienced in other nations that have suffered natural disasters of similar or greater proportions[1], the extent of property damage has been astronomical in our country and has outstripped that of other developed countries.[2] A partial explanation for this rise in disaster losses may be attributed to increasing risk from weather and sea-level-related hazards caused by global climate change.[3] We may also attribute some of the increase in recent disaster figures to increases in capabilities for reporting and documenting disaster losses (the "CNN syndrome").[4] Primarily, however, vulnerability to disasters is a function of human action and behaviors.

Vulnerability describes the degree to which socioeconomic systems or physical assets are either susceptible or resilient to the impact of natural hazards. It is determined by a combination of several factors, including awareness of hazards, the condition of human settlements and infrastructure, public policy and administration, and the relative wealth and resourcefulness of a given community. Vulnerability is also determined by the capacities of workers in all fields of disaster and risk management to prepare for and respond quickly to emergency situations.

14.1.1 A Change in Thinking

What is needed is a change in thinking about where and how we want to live. We must consider the natural world and the threats it presents when we build or rebuild our neighborhoods and city centers. The objective of preventing disaster must permeate all our actions and behaviors to promote safer living conditions. Yet, as Secretary-General of the United Nations, Kofi Annan, has noted:

> *Building a culture of prevention is not easy. While the costs of prevention have to be paid in the present, its benefits lie in a distant future. Moreover, the benefits are not tangible; they are the disasters that did **not** happen.*[5]

While there are currently methods for measuring the benefits of prevention in terms of losses avoided, this is still a field in progress, and calculating the benefits in numerical or financial terms is fairly subjective. However, despite the difficulties in measuring what does *not* happen, it is clear that our rising disaster costs require a change to a more sustainable pattern of living.

Unsustainable Patterns of Land Use Are Disaster Prone

Traditional development patterns and urban growth in the United States have created communities that fail in some very fundamental social, economic, and environmental ways.[6] Development patterns are brittle when they do not take hazards into account. Sprawling suburban tracts and homes constructed with little or no protection against high winds, flooding, wildfire, earthquakes, landslides, or other natural hazards are the norm in many communities. Building is often permitted on environmentally-sensitive lands because it satisfies an economic need or a locational preference.[7] The traditional approach to preventing disasters was for many years to contain or control the hazard itself, often through the construction of large-scale engineering works, such as dams, dikes, levees, seawalls, and similar projects. "It was humans against the elements, and no one doubted that humans could out-engineer the forces of nature."[8]

In many instances, these structural mitigation projects have provided a false sense of security, leading to massive displacement and property damage when they ultimately fail. "In trying to reduce vulnerability by taming nature, the situation is often made worse, not better."[9] Large-scale protection works can also impair nature's ability to mitigate against extreme events. "Many mitigation efforts themselves degrade the environment and thus contribute to the next disaster."[10] Numerous studies provide examples of engineering works that have been counterproductive at best, or have even exacerbated vulnerability by interfering with natural process. An ecological view of sustainable place recognizes that events such as hurricanes, earthquakes, and floods are natural (although they may be exacerbated by human activities), and that only when we choose to build structures and place settlements in their paths do they become disasters. [11]

Sustainable Human Settlement Patterns

Efforts to reduce the impacts of natural hazards are ultimately and fundamentally about promoting a more sustainable human settlement pattern and living more "lightly and sensibly" on the earth.[12] Over the past couple of decades, sustainable development has emerged as a paradigm with the potential to give human beings the perspective and the power they need to live more lightly and sensibly.

In its classic sense, sustainable development "meets the needs of the present without compromising the ability of future generations to meet their own needs."[13] This definition has become universally accepted as the standard, and was established by the World Commission on Environment and Development (the Brundtland Commission) in 1987. Other words that encompass the basic concepts of sustainable development include "excellence in development," "smart growth," "sustainable ecosystems," "livability," and similar phrases that convey the principle of living within our means, treating land and other natural resources as finite, and reducing the human footprint on the earth.

14.1.2 The Three Spheres of Sustainable Development

Sustainable development is often conceptualized as three interlocking spheres of community existence: the economic, social, and environmental.[14]

▲ The **social sphere** consists of human interactions—families, neighborhoods, workplaces, houses of worship, community centers, schools—all the factors that forge a sense of community and contribute to a feeling of belonging.

▲ The **environmental sphere** is the physical setting in which the community exists—the natural landscape that is determined by geography, topography, hydrology, and climate, as well as the as the manmade environment—buildings, infrastructure, utilities, and facilities.

▲ The **economic sphere** consists of all the activities, transactions, and decisions that are based on producing and exchanging goods and services. This sphere encompasses jobs, markets, investment, capital, and other aspects of our economic existence in the modern world.

Sustainable communities work to maximize the overlap among environmental, economic, and social values as shown in Figure 14-1; communities that successfully integrate each of its spheres of existence approach a quality of life for all their residents.[15]

All of these community "spheres" have an aspect of futurity associated with them – the capacity to sustain desired levels of development at given resource use rates over time.[16] Also known as intergenerational equity, this concept speaks to allowing future generations to enjoy equal or better conditions and opportunities than we experience today. A sustainable community thrives from generation to generation because its social foundation supports and is supported by a healthy and vibrant ecological system and a diverse and inclusive economy that provides opportunities for self-sufficiency and long-term security while recognizing the limits of available resources.

Figure 14-1

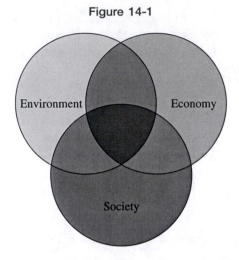

The three spheres of sustainable development.

The Principles of Sustainability Include Hazard Resilience

To sustainability's economic, environmental, and social criteria is added a fourth dimension—to be sustainable, development must be resilient to the natural variability of the earth.[17] "An essential characteristic of a sustainable community is its resilience to disasters."[18] Sustainable development implies efforts to create and maintain communities that avoid or mitigate natural hazards.[19] Resilient communities are self-reliant and depend on predisaster action rather than postdisaster handouts to minimize risk.[20]

How does resiliency fit into the three spheres of sustainability? By bolstering each one of these components.

> *Resilient communities may bend before the extreme stresses of natural hazards, but they do not break. They are consciously constructed to be strong and flexible rather than brittle and fragile. This means that their lifeline systems of roads, utilities, and other support facilities are designed to continue functioning in the face of rising water, high winds and shaking ground. It means that their neighborhoods and businesses, their hospitals and public safety centers are located in safe areas rather than in known high-hazard areas. It means that their buildings are constructed or retrofitted to meet building code standards based on the threats of natural hazards faced. It means that their natural environmental protective systems, such as dunes and wetlands, are conserved to protect their hazard mitigation functions as well as their more traditional purposes.[21]*

"Sustainability means that a locality can tolerate—and overcome—damage, diminished productivity, and reduced quality of life from an extreme event without significant outside assistance."[22] A community has a better chance of retaining its special character over time, and of being a livable place for current and future residents if it is resilient in the face of multiple hazards.

14.1.3 Reaching Resiliency

Many terms have been used to describe the actions that communities can take to reach a state of resilience, including disaster prevention, risk minimization, loss reduction, hazard avoidance, hazard resistance, strategic retreat, as well as mitigation and preparedness. These phrases embody a similar objective—we want to make our community more resilient against the effects of natural hazards by mitigating their impacts, preparing for the effects, reducing the losses, and minimizing the risk that losses will occur. The one thing that is not a part of resilience building is hazard prevention—we cannot stop the hazard from occurring (with some exceptions, such as elevated flood levels caused by development in floodplains, drought caused by depletion of groundwater resources, landslides caused by slope alteration, and wildfires that are started by arson or accidental burning).

14.1.4 What is Mitigation?

Because it is one of the more action-oriented terms for building resilience, we will focus on mitigation as a necessary step for community sustainability. Natural hazard mitigation is generally described as advance action taken to reduce or eliminate long-term risks to people and property from hazards and their effects. Typically carried out as part of a coordinated mitigation strategy or plan, such actions, usually termed either structural or nonstructural depending on whether they affect buildings or land use, include the following:[23]

▲ Strengthening buildings and infrastructure exposed to hazards by means of building codes, engineering design, and construction practices to increase the resilience and damage resistance of the structures, as well as building protective structures such as dams, levees, and seawalls (structural mitigation).

▲ Avoiding hazard areas by directing new development away from known hazard locations through land use plans and regulations and by relocating damaged existing development to safe areas following a disaster (nonstructural mitigation).

▲ Maintaining protective features of the natural environment by protecting sand dunes, wetlands, forests and vegetated areas, and other ecological elements that absorb and reduce hazard impacts, helping to protect exposed buildings and people (nonstructural mitigation).

FOR EXAMPLE

Napa, California, Widens the River

The city of Napa experienced 27 floods between 1862 and 1997. In 1996, residents, businesses, local government, and numerous resource agencies became part of a community coalition to create a flood protection project—widening the river. The project restored over 650 acres of tidal wetlands, protecting 2700 homes, 350 businesses and over 50 public properties from flood levels at a projected savings of $26 million annually in flood damage costs. In 1998, Napa culminated 2 years of community planning and partnering with the development of a 20-year Napa Flood Management Plan, and voters approved a ½-cent sales tax increase to provide the local funding match for federal, state, and private sector funds to implement the plan. Up and down the river, the plan has resulted in new energy and investment, including renovation of a historical structure on the banks of the Napa River as a major tourist center, a non-profit arts and design school for promising arts students, and three planned hotels in the city of Napa. Before the flood management plan, the city could not attract lodging due to investor fear of damages from frequent flooding.[24]

▲ Informing the public about hazard risks and increasing awareness of mitigation strategies and building techniques to educate residents, business owners, community leaders, and decision makers about hazards and what they can do about them (nonstructural mitigation).

By putting these types of mitigation strategies into action, communities can effectively break the cycle of damage, reconstruction, and repeated damage that often occurs in places that experience disasters on a repetitive basis.

Using Mitigation to Build Sustainable Communities

Mitigation helps build community resilience, which in turn contributes to community sustainability. By viewing mitigation as a step toward the larger goal of sustainability, we can recognize this phase of the emergency management system as an art rather than a science, and emergency managers as artists rather than mere technicians.

The next section of the chapter will review how resiliency, and specifically how hazard mitigation, contributes to each of the three spheres of community sustainability. As we discuss the issues of economic vitality, environmental integrity, and social equity, keep in mind the *art* of emergency management, and the role that emergency managers play in bringing the vision of sustainable communities to reality.

SELF-CHECK

- List the three spheres of sustainable development and explain how they are interrelated and interdependent.
- Discuss what sustainable human settlement patterns should look like.
- Explain how resiliency contributes to all three spheres of sustainable development.

14.2 Economic Vitality

Economic prosperity is one of the foundations of sustainability. A healthy economy that grows sufficiently to create meaningful jobs, reduce poverty, nurture agriculture, and promote small businesses can provide a high quality of life for all. Sustainable development communicates a concern with what *kind* of development, rather than how much, while hazard mitigation encourages development that is built to hazard-resistant standards and is located in areas that minimize hazard impacts. Neither principle necessarily proposes a no growth policy for communities. Rather, these concepts advocate for the safe accommodation of future population rise through conscientiously controlled growth and development, fostering a stable tax base, secure housing opportunities, and a robust business sector.

14.2.1 Economic Losses Following a Disaster

A resilient community can better withstand the negative economic effects of a disaster, including:

▲ Imbalances in local government budgets as resources are reallocated to meet the urgent and unexpected emergency needs associated with a disaster, such as emergency road repair, reconnecting utilities and water and sewer connections, and debris removal.

▲ Deferment or cancellation of other important projects that rely on public funding.

▲ Market disorders, both immediate and long-term, as supply lines and deliveries are disrupted.

▲ Loss of the local employment base, and changed or reduced work forces as residents are displaced.

▲ Loss of major employers, including large-scale industries as well as smaller companies.

▲ Increases in welfare rolls, food stamp receipts, unemployment compensation, and demand for public housing.

The closure of small businesses can be especially devastating to a local community following a disaster. Small businesses are often impacted more severely than major industries as they have fewer resources for recovery and rebuilding, and many do not carry adequate insurance to cover losses from hazards. The loss of "mom and pop" businesses can dramatically impact a locality's economy as well as its sense of community and character. In a resilient community, business downtime following a disaster is reduced. Stores, factories, and offices can reopen more quickly if they are located, designed, and built to withstand the impacts of hazards.

14.2.2 Local Mitigation Strategies to Protect the Economy

Communities can undertake a wide variety of hazard mitigation activities to protect the local tax base and ensure job security. Among these techniques is the strict enforcement of tough building codes, and vigilant inspection of construction during the site selection, design and building stages of new development. Zoning and subdivision ordinances and other land use planning activities that take hazards into account, and that disallow building in the most hazardous areas can also help protect the local economic base from disasters. Capital improvement planning and long-range strategic planning for infrastructure can help discourage development in hazard areas by restricting public facilities such as water and sewer in the most fragile areas. And partnerships with the business sector, encouraging and facilitating business continuity planning and structural mitigation practices can greatly increase the local government's economic resiliency to natural hazards.

Fiscal Accountability: Loss Avoidance or Loss Compensation?

Not only must we encourage economic vitality through protection of the business sector and the local tax base, but we must also make sure that our disaster policies are fiscally sound. There is a decided moral or ethical component to this discussion, and we will discuss the issue of personal responsibility later in the chapter, but there is also an aspect of financial accountability that must be considered. The issue can be summed up by asking: does it make fiscal sense to continue to pay for the losses experienced by property owners over and over again? "Are people more likely to invest in property in hazardous locations in the belief that, if worse comes to worst, the federal government will hold them relatively harmless? Are communities, concerned about property values and tax revenue, more likely to allow, or even tacitly encourage, building or rebuilding in unsafe locations in the expectation of a federal bail-out if disaster strikes?"[25]

Taxpayers spend billions of dollars each year to help others recover from disaster, but recovery costs are not borne equally. We allow some people to build in environmentally-sensitive areas susceptible to natural hazards, and then we pay to help them recover when disaster strikes. This is not sound environmental or fiscal policy. In many cases, decisions about where to locate development are made because they appear to save money in the short term. Ultimately, these decisions cost more because the vulnerability of these sites has never been fully examined.[26]

Weighing the Benefits and Costs of Mitigation

A more fiscally responsible approach to disasters is to invest heavily in strategies that are proven to produce benefits that outweigh their costs. Mitigation has been shown in research studies to be exceedingly cost effective when money is invested wisely to meet a community's specific disaster prevention needs. Recent research conducted by the Multi-hazard Mitigation Council (MMC) of the National Institute of Building Sciences focused specifically on mitigation funded by the Federal Emergency Management Agency (FEMA) as part of a three-year, congressionally-mandated independent study.[27] The study provides independent evidence to support what nearly every member of the hazards community knows anecdotally—generally, mitigation grants issued by FEMA are highly cost-effective. On average, each dollar spent on mitigation saves society an average of four dollars in avoided future losses. These research findings are important, because FEMA continues to provide the bulk of mitigation funding used by state and local governments throughout the country.

As described in the MMC research study, there are basically two classes of mitigation activities undertaken by communities, both of which are funded by FEMA:[28]

▲ **Project mitigation activities** are akin to investments in physical capital and are frequently referred to as brick-and-mortar projects because they result in tangible physical change to the built or natural environment. Quantitative benefit-cost assessments are more easily conducted for grants funding these types of activity. Typical project mitigation activities funded by FEMA include drainage enhancement, acquisition and relocation of at-risk structures, structural and nonstructural improvements, lifeline improvements, and land improvement projects.

▲ **Process mitigation activities** lead to policies, practices, and plans to reduce risk and are much like investments in human, social, or institutional capital. Outcomes of these activities are less tangible than project activities and tend to be difficult to predict and quantify, particularly over the short term. Examples of process mitigation activities include vulnerability assessments, community priorities and action plans, education and awareness campaigns for decision makers and constituents, and development of codes and regulations. These activities stimulate the commitments needed to instigate and sustain mitigation over the long term and play a

FOR EXAMPLE

Shelby County, Tennessee, Counts Projected Savings

Shelby County is located within the new madrid seismic zone. The water supply system that provides water to the area is owned by Memphis Light, Gas, and Water. The company has initiated a seismic retrofit project to protect its pumping station and enhance the survivability of the connections between the water distribution lines. Retrofit plans include reinforcement and anchorage of masonry walls; strengthening of steel frames; improved connections of concrete wall and roof, secured anchorage of pipes and valves, and bracing of pipelines; bracing of treatment and control equipment; and protection of an overhead crane. The estimated cost to replace the pumping station in the event of a large earthquake exceeds $17 million. Each day the station is not in service costs an additional $1.4 million. Total projected savings are expected to be $112 million with a total project cost of $968,800.[29]

large role in building community resilience. This added-commitment feature of hazard mitigation grant funding is important, because until mitigation and resilience are institutionalized and embodied in everything a community does, mitigation will continue to be a piecemeal, haphazard occurrence.

14.2.3 Revamping the NFIP to Make Flood Insurance Actuarially Sound

Measuring the benefits of mitigation projects and translating them into economic resiliency for communities is relatively straightforward compared to assessing the fiscal integrity of the National Flood Insurance Program (NFIP). Numerous studies have indicated weaknesses in the program, and while this is a policy dilemma that must be addressed at the federal level, it impacts the economic resiliency of local communities directly.

In recognition of growing flood losses, the NFIP was established in 1968 as a mechanism to provide federal flood insurance for individuals that reside in a community that adopts and abides by certain floodplain management criteria. Since then, the NFIP has done a notable job of bringing floodplain management to most of the nation's communities. Furthermore, the staff of FEMA, which administers the NFIP, has significantly influenced the role and acceptance of nonstructural measures among other federal agencies. However, because the NFIP is viewed primarily as an insurance program, FEMA has been reluctant to promulgate regulations that account for *future* damage resulting from floodplain encroachment or development-induced runoff. Granted, local and state governments could and should be doing more, but due to lack of information or due to a presumption that a minimum standard set by the federal government is adequate, most communities are not effectively dealing with increasing flood damage.[30]

Economic analysis would show that this does not make economic sense. The reality is, that when floods hit, people are forced from their homes and businesses, and many never recover financially from the impact. Local, state, and federal officials must undertake rescue operations at great personal risk and financial cost; there are housing needs for displaced people and immediate expense for the repair of infrastructure. Dollars are diverted from necessary public efforts to pay for the emergency. In the end we reposition to wait for the next flood.[31] One commentator has summed up problems of the NFIP thusly: "Our National Flood Insurance Program is an actuarial joke. It is as if we had a federal auto insurance company that only insured teenage boys with alcohol problems. By definition the properties covered by the program are doomed to be flooded, damaged and even destroyed, not just once, but time and time again."[32]

Are these increased and repetitive flood losses simply the price the nation pays for growth? From a purely cost-benefit standpoint, many argue that the nation as a whole is better off as a result of these investments in flood-prone development—flood losses are part and parcel of growth and development. Economic arguments such as this have become a key factor in establishing federal government interest in flood control. Others have compared flood losses to the gross national product and found no adverse trend. Unfortunately, an alternatives analysis has never been performed to determine if the same level of expenditure and investment *outside* the floodplain would have led to a better return.[33]

SELF-CHECK

- List several possible economic losses following a disaster.
- Describe **project mitigation activities**.
- Explain some of the critiques of the current National Flood Insurance Program.

14.3 Social Equity

Sustainable development at its highest and best embodies issues of equity. Equity is perhaps one of the slipperiest as well as the most critical of the three circles of sustainability, but a thorough and complete discussion of sustainable resilient communities must involve issues of race, ethnicity, gender, income disparities, and socio-economic class stratification. In true social and intergenerational equity, each person has an inherent right to exist, survive threats, have access to resources, and pursue a decent life, despite his or her social or economic status. By the same token, unborn generations must inherit opportunities for a good life that have not been diminished by those who came before them. Social equity and acceptance of responsibility to future generations are essential parts of a holistic approach to sustainability and resiliency. This means avoiding disproportionate treatment of or impacts to vulnerable populations from known hazard risks and not displacing costs and risks to others.[34]

14.3.1 Poverty Exacerbates Vulnerability

Poverty, in particular, along with its associated racial and ethnic undertones, increases an individual's vulnerability, as well as that of the community as a whole. The reasons that racial, ethnic, and low income populations are more vulnerable to natural disasters are many, but include such factors as language, housing patterns, building construction, community isolation, and cultural insensitivities. In the best of times, poverty is a drain on the economy, on communities, on an individual's sense of worth. Following a disaster, these problems are magnified, as communities struggle to regain economic stability and social equanimity. Research in this area indicates that disasters may actually serve as a catalyst for the reproduction or exacerbation of inequality throughout the community.[35] The

---

FOR EXAMPLE

Poor, Black, and Wet in New Orleans; High and Dry in White Neighborhoods

Much of the discussion about the racially differential impact of Katrina has emphasized the Lower Ninth Ward, a neighborhood in New Orleans where many homes were entirely demolished by the breach in the levee on the Industrial Canal. Most neighborhoods in this planning district were more than 85% black, and most residences were damaged. A majority of residents were homeowners, although relatively few carried flood insurance. More than a third of Lower Ninth Ward residents were below the poverty line, and nearly 14% were unemployed. At the other extreme, poststorm data shows that few residents in the French Quarter, a predominantly white neighborhood with a poverty rate of about 11% and unemployment below 5%, lived in tracts that were flooded. Among other neighborhoods with a national reputation for affluence, the Garden District neighborhood was not flooded and only 40% of the Audubon/University neighborhood (home of Tulane University and Loyola University) was damaged.[36]

poor are much more likely to live in areas of high hazard risk and to have little if any insurance to cover losses when the risk is realized. (The exception to this generalization can be found in parts of the coastal zone, where high-end residential structures are placed in exceptionally risky ocean-front areas.) The poor are also often located in neighborhoods that are less resilient because of dilapidated infrastructure and substandard housing, where routine maintenance and repair of even life-protection facilities are inadequate, making the impacts of a hazard event much more severe than in more affluent neighborhoods that are well serviced.

14.3.2 Disparities in Risk Perception

In addition to disparities in the physical vulnerability of low income populations as compared to upper income groups, there may also be differences in the psychological impact of hazards, both during and after a disaster event. Studies by sociologists, anthropologists, economists, and others show that there exist variations among racial and ethnic groups in the ways they perceive natural hazard risks and respond to warnings, as well as in the ways they are affected psychologically by disasters. "Disaster effects vary by race and ethnicity during the periods of emergency response, recovery and reconstruction."[37] We could add to this observation the period of predisaster mitigation and preparedness, where disparities among racial and income groups result in different levels of prevention and protection within a community. "Calls to stockpile water and food for four days seem ludicrous to those who barely have enough money to eat everyday."[38] Calls for evacuation, whether mandatory or voluntary, are equally ineffectual when residents have no form of transportation and no public transit is made available to remove them from the scene of impending danger.

Research conducted immediately following Hurricane Katrina highlights the significance of race and class issues in postdisaster situations, with implications for predisaster insufficiencies in planning and preparedness for these population groups. For many Hurricane Katrina survivors, issues of race and class were central to their evacuation experiences. Specifically, of the residents that evacuated in a timely fashion from the city of New Orleans and its environs as Hurricane Katrina approached, it was found that predominately working-class African Americans did not evacuate because they did not have the financial resources to do so. Although race and class were significant issues for many evacuees, issues of age, gender, religion, physical and mental disability, previous disaster experience, and care for dependents were also formative influences on evacuees' catastrophe experiences.[39]

14.3.3 Social Equity Makes Economic Sense

Aside from the moral or ethical concerns involved with racial and income disparities in hazard vulnerability, a purely economical approach to the issue would indicate the need to eradicate inequalities in vulnerability in order to reduce the fiscal drain on a community from a disaster. Disasters are expensive, even when residents and business owners have adequate resources and insurance payments to pay for their individual rebuilding and recovery needs. But when a majority, or even a significant portion of the community, is unable to take care of its own daily needs, let alone the increased costs of disaster recovery, the local, state, and federal governments must cover those costs. While charities, faith-based organizations, and volunteer groups provide generous aid to disaster victims, these sources are a drop in the bucket compared to the unmet needs that linger after a hazard event has passed. Prevention and mitigation strategies that encompass risk reduction for low-income groups saves money for everyone in the long term. "Taking action to help the poor lower their everyday risk [to hazards] is the best form of self-interest becoming common interest."[40]

14.3.4 Determining an Acceptable Level of Risk[41]

One of the ethical issues that emergency managers must deal with when managing hazard impacts is how to define acceptable risk. We cannot eliminate 100% of all risk from natural or man-made hazards, even with the latest technologies, building techniques, or state-of-the art land use planning practices. There will always be a degree of risk inherent in living anywhere on earth. Of course, in some locations this risk is more prevalent than others. New Orleans is one such place, where the entire city has been described as a "bowl," lying 8 meters below sea level. In many respects, the possibility of a hurricane hitting New Orleans and causing massive damage has been called a disaster waiting to happen. When Hurricane Katrina arrived in 2005, the hypothetical became reality.

Over 169 miles of levees and flood walls were damaged in New Orleans during and immediately after Hurricane Katrina, causing massive flooding, property damage, displacement of thousands of residents, and the loss of hundreds of human lives. What went wrong? A lethal combination of physical factors, engineering factors, and human and organizational factors led to the overtopping and breaching of the protective features surrounding the city. Many of these factors are rooted in happenstance, bad luck, bad timing, or a seemingly random set of coincidences. However, many other of the factors leading up to the devastation of New Orleans were the result of deliberate, well-considered decisions that were based on known facts and established protocol. One such decision involved the level of risk that was considered appropriate for flooding in the city.

What Are Our Aims for Flood Prevention?

Before we can discuss the ramifications of setting a particular level of acceptable risk, we must first establish the means that will be used to achieve that level of protection. The fundamental question involves whether to use a structural approach to flood prevention in New Orleans and elsewhere, including flood walls, levees, dams, dikes, and other types of engineered structures, or whether we will rely on land use planning, acquisition, urban development patterns, education, and other nonstructural methods of mitigation, or a combination of both. Once the commitment has been made to build a system of levees and flood control structures, the discussion can then turn to how to make the best use of that approach. Defining an acceptable level of risk will revolve around the policy decisions—including funding decisions—that are related to such a project, which in turn must be translated into technical engineering standards and construction practices for building a structural hazard mitigation project.

Setting the Limit of Acceptable Risk: A Visit to the Netherlands

To understand some of the considerations that are made in setting an acceptable level of risk for a given population in a given area, we can look for a moment at an international corollary of New Orleans—the country of The Netherlands. The Netherlands have, for hundreds of years, designed and built structures allowing the country to maintain an entire nation below sea level. The Netherlands is one of the lowest geographical countries in the world; its name literally means "low countries," and the first dikes were built as early as the twelfth century. The similarities between The Netherlands and the city of New Orleans are striking in many ways. The Netherlands lie 80% below sea level; New Orleans is 80% below sea level. The Netherlands uses an elaborate system of sea walls and levees to protect the population from the sea; New Orleans relies on a system of levees and dikes to protect its population from the Gulf of Mexico. Dutch engineers look to soil samples, engineering techniques, and building materials to construct massive walls and barriers to limit flooding. Engineers and contractors working in New Orleans conduct similar studies and engage in similar tactics to reduce flooding. The differences lie in part in how each community implements the details of construction, some of which may be accounted for by differences in topography, soil types, expertise, and other technicalities. But more importantly, the difference between the way in which The Netherlands approaches its task and the situation in New Orleans is rooted in the divergence between the two communities in the definition of risk and the level of protection that is desired.

In simple terms, The Netherlands provides a higher level of protection from flooding for its population than that which is provided in New Orleans. The Dutch commitment to flood mitigation is based on a probability of flood occurrence in urban areas of 1 in 10,000. This means that the Dutch have protected the country against an event that could occur once in 10,000 years with regard to the size of event and the pressure that can be expected to be exerted on the floodwalls. The United States, as a matter of national policy, does not consider such a level of protection feasible at this time. Instead, we focus on a 1 in 100 chance of flooding as the basis of our flood prevention strategies. Much of the blame for this policy is targeted towards the U.S. Army Corps of Engineers, the agency responsible for the construction and maintenance of levees in New Orleans and elsewhere throughout the country. However, the Corps is merely an instrument of larger forces—policy makers and decision makers at several different levels of government, including the holders of the purse strings that determine the level of funding that is appropriated towards Corps projects.

What Does it Take to Have Such a Higher Threshold?

A simple answer to the question of why The Netherlands provides a higher level of protection than that which is found in New Orleans is a matter of national will. The Dutch citizens and their elected leaders long ago put the country on its current track of maintaining and even augmenting the dry land—much of it reclaimed over the course of many years from the North Sea. The political will of the people is behind the system of dikes and levees that keep The Netherlands safe from the onslaught of waves, winds, and storm surge. The Dutch have deliberately chosen this course and are willing to continue to pursue the way of life they have known for generations.

The political will of the Dutch is surpassed only by their ongoing diligence. The Dutch not only maintain their dikes and seawalls, but every year they seek to improve the system of flood prevention. Dutch engineers are constantly seeking new ways to heighten the structures' integrity and soundness in the face of ongoing hazard risks. Money is certainly a part of this issue. Due diligence is matched by the willingness of the Dutch to expend public monies, and significant funding is allocated towards the dike system and levees that keep the country safe and dry. The level of risk that is acceptable in The Netherlands drives the decisions surrounding the dike system—engineering decisions, political decisions, and financial decisions. The choice of material and technique fit the risk that the residents are trying to reduce. They recognize every year that they are at war with the North Sea.

In the United States there is not such a long history of prevention mentality as exists in The Netherlands. Since adoption of a structural protection approach to flooding nearly 200 years ago, the United States generally takes a hurry up and wait approach to maintenance and repair, whereby levees are allowed to decay, sag, collapse, settle, and develop cracks over the course of a decade or more. When a catastrophic event such as Katrina occurs, emergency appropriations from state, federal, and local coffers are required to fund expensive short-term fixes to the problem. Several more years of neglect and decline are allowed, until another hazard event recurs. The Netherlands do not maintain such a 30-year cycle. Their national will, funding, and diligence mean that their levees are never considered finished.

14.3.5 Describing Risk in Terms that People Can Understand

Once the threshold for what is considered acceptable has been established and the standard of protection has been decided, the ethical implications of risk determination are not yet completely resolved. Risk must be communicated in ways that are useful to the decision maker, whether the decision is being made by an individual homeowner who is contemplating building in a floodplain, the local official who implements the floodplain ordinance, or the elected representative who establishes the hazard mitigation policy and associated financial commitments.

Hazards Awareness: Getting the Message Across

A major obstacle to implementing hazard reduction measures involves the public's misunderstanding of risk and the fact that most people do not want to believe that their community will ever experience disaster, much less experience another if they've already been through one.[42] All people, no matter where they live, deserve to know the level of risk they are undertaking by living in a particular place. The need for hazards awareness and an understanding of risk goes beyond issues of race and class. Even the affluent and highly educated can be placed in vulnerable locations if the hazard potential is not clearly articulated and their understanding of risk is incomplete.

Although it is true of most natural hazards (and man-made hazards as well), flood risk is couched in the most frequently misunderstood terms. Our standard method of describing flood risk is through the delineation of the 1% chance flood as shown on a local map illustrating the 100-year floodplain. The all-or-nothing quality conveyed by the delineation of a 1% chance floodplain is a continuing and insidious problem. The public, local officials, and insurance agents usually interpret the flood map to mean that there is *no* flood risk whatsoever just outside the line showing the 1% zone. The terms "1% annual chance flood" and "100-year flood" have been sources of continual misunderstanding for the public and decision makers.[43]

Deeper understanding is needed of how to better communicate to the public the meaning of probability of flooding, the flood risk, damage that can be expected, frequency intervals, and related flood risk issues. Descriptions of flood hazard must be fully understood so that decision makers can convert the information into sound policy for construction and development. Citizens and community leaders must seek and obtain accurate information on flood risk before building, and property owners must acquire flood insurance because of the risk, not because it is required by regulations that are randomly applied.[44]

14.3.6 Incorporating Future Build-Out into Flood Risk Determinations

Stepping aside for a moment from problems associated with the terminology used in setting the 100-year flood risk, the concept itself is inherently flawed, because it does not change as rapidly as flood levels change due to increased development. Changing conditions in the floodplain and elsewhere in the watershed have profound impacts on flood levels. As watersheds are developed, the increase in impervious surfaces, such as pavement and rooftops, causes more water from a storm to run off the land's surface into the drainage system and streams, and usually at a faster pace, than was the case before development. The flood depths and flood boundaries that were calculated and mapped before such urbanization took place become inaccurate within a short period of time.

What this means is that today's 1% (100-year) standard, which allows encroachments into the floodplain, in actuality may be tomorrow's 50-year standard, and may only be a 10-year standard once the watershed is fully developed. These trends do not bode well for controlling the escalation of flood damage, and left unchecked could become significantly worse than anticipated by the founders of the flood insurance program.[45]

As an alternative to the current method of flood risk determination, changes in development patterns—which result in increases in flood damage even though the area is being managed—can be accounted for by using a future-conditions scenario when determining the expected runoff. As new levels of development are factored into the determination of flood elevations, regulations for lowest-level floor elevations can anticipate where flood heights might be within the lifetime of the structure, greatly increasing the level of protection afforded to a particular residence.

A few communities have made use of development projections when setting flood regulations, such as Charlotte-Mecklenburg in North Carolina. The City-County floodplain management authority stresses identification of the flood hazard area based on future developed conditions. Maps incorporate increased runoff rates from development that has not yet taken place within the watershed, and corresponding regulations reflect these levels.

14.3.7 No Adverse Impact: A Do No Harm Policy[46]

In addition to incorporating the effects of future development into the determination of acceptable flood risks, another approach involves the concept known as **no adverse impact.** The no adverse impact approach to floodplain management strives to ensure that the actions of one property owner do not increase the flood risk of other property owners.

The no adverse impact approach focuses on planning for and lessening flood impacts resulting from land use changes. It is essentially a do no harm policy that can significantly decrease the creation of new flood damages. No-impact floodplains become the default management criteria, and can be extended to entire watersheds. Development is permitted in a way that creates no negative changes in hydrology, stream depths, velocities, or sediment transport functions; impacts are only allowed to the extent they are offset by mitigation. Examples of "wise use" or the "most beneficial use" include using the floodplain as dedicated open space for flood storage and low-impact uses such as recreation. Site-specific mitigation techniques range from the installation of detention and retention basins to adequate drainage channels to improved stormwater management features.

The no adverse impact approach promotes fairness, responsibility, community involvement, pre-flood planning, sustainable development, and local land use management. It places responsibility for managing floodplain risks squarely on local governments, since the specific details for land use are decided at the community level. It also supports private property rights because property owners can have input on management strategies that impact their own property. This approach can especially benefit those property owners that are not currently in regulated flood areas, but who could be in the future.

SELF-CHECK

- Compare how The Netherlands and the United States approach the determination of what is an acceptable level of risk to flood hazards.
- List some of the problems associated with our current description of flood risks.
- Give an example of a **no adverse impact** mitigation strategy.

14.4 Environmental Integrity

Traditional sustainable development theory embodies an ethic of preservation and conservation of the natural environment in order to promote healthy ecosystems, support biodiversity, and encourage habitat protection. The need for resilience in the face of disasters lends support to arguments for restoring and enhancing the natural environment as a form of protection against hazard impacts on human communities. Hazard mitigation calls for conservation of natural and ecologically sensitive lands, such as wetlands, floodplains, barrier islands, and dunes, features which enable the environment to efficiently and cost-effectively absorb some of the impact of hazardous events. These ecosystems also serve as important pollution filters that enhance water and air quality, as well as provide habitat for fish and wildlife. In this way, preservation and protection for mitigation follow one of the fundamental premises of sustainable development: that we respect our natural heritage and allow its systems to operate as designed, without alteration or interference.

14.4.1 Using Land Wisely

In sustainable communities, land is viewed as a limited resource, land is consumed sparingly, and environmentally-sensitive lands (wetlands, shorelines, hillsides, fault zones) are placed off-limits to intensive development. Development patterns promote compact urban areas, curtailing scattered development and sprawl. Sustainable communities also take advantage of underutilized urban areas and encourage infill and brownfield development. Energy and resource conservation are high priorities and a greater emphasis is placed on public transit and creating mixed-use environments that are less dependent upon the automobile.[47] A sustainable community acknowledges the presence of natural features and processes—such as riverine flooding, wildfires, and barrier island migration—and arranges its land use and settlement patterns so as to sustain rather than interfere with or disrupt them.[48]

RESPECTING THE NATURAL DYNAMISM OF THE COAST: BARRIER ISLAND MIGRATION

Barrier islands, such as those dotted along the coastline of the Gulf of Mexico, are dynamic places. What is here today may be gone tomorrow.[49] Natural forces build and erode shorelines in a subtle, never-ending process combining the effects of winds, waves, currents, and tides. Under normal circumstances, barrier islands shift landward in a process called island migration. This form of "strategic natural retreat" is carried out slowly through the action of inlet currents and wind, and more dramatically during storms, when forceful waves wash sand over the island as overwash. The island literally rolls over, as sand moves from the seaward side to the back of the island in a cycle of perpetual motion.

Perhaps more powerful than forces of nature, human impacts can threaten the existence of barrier islands. Island roads leading to the shoreline that go through dunes (as opposed to winding over dunes) are especially damaging. Roads that cut straight to the beach and through, not over, dunes act as overwash passes during storms. Notches cut or worn through the dune to allow public access to the beach may also allow storm flooding.[50]

Sand dunes along the front of a barrier island can act as a buffer against storm activity, and the existence of a healthy dune system provides some protection to island structures. Dunes are also necessary for evolution and survival of the beach during a storm. In general, wide dunes mean less damage. Vegetation on sand dunes also provides a degree of protection to property. Unvegetated sand dunes are usually moving sand dunes.[51] Unfortunately, many builders remove natural sand dunes in order to maximize ocean views and ease access to the recreational beach. These alterations to the natural functioning of a barrier island can severely impair its protective features.

Dramatic changes that can take place on a barrier island during a hurricane or other coastal storm event. Dauphin Island is located directly south of Mobile, Alabama, more than 110 kilometers east of the region where the eye of

Katrina came ashore in Plaquemines Parish, Louisiana. The island suffered extensive overwash, and a major breach was formed toward the western end of the island. Changes occurred in the recent hurricane seasons to a developed section of Dauphin Island. There was a significant increase in overwash penetration across the island through these successive hurricanes. Unfortunately, the homes located there are not intended to rebound so reflexively as the land underneath them. As a result, the first line of structures on the seaward side of the island come dangerously close to the ocean as the beach in front of them erodes. And while the backside of the island is relatively better protected from rapid erosion, houses on the last row are by no means safe from future storms or the slow barrier island migration process.

Sustainable communities also recognize that natural systems do not necessarily correspond to political boundaries and approach planning and resource management on a broader scale to account for impacts that cross jurisdictional lines. **River basin management** is a planning mechanism that is an effective, although underutilized system for addressing issues of water quality, habitat protection, rural land conservation, and flood hazard mitigation on a regional scale. Since a river basin consists of all the land draining to a major river system, the streams, tributaries, and watersheds of a river basin exist as a continuum through many communities, land cover types, and various land usages. Several states use

FOR EXAMPLE

A River Runs Through It

Despite the fact that the topography and climate of North Carolina are extremely diverse from east to west—including mountains, the coastal plain, and the piedmont in between—one common tie among the various regions is river basins. There are 17 major river basins in the state, ranging in size from over 9000 square miles in the Cape Fear River Basin to barely 150 square miles in the Savannah. The North Carolina Department of Environment and Natural Resources takes a river basin approach to planning for water quality purposes. Planning for flood mitigation on the river basin scale has been recommended by the North Carolina Division of Emergency Management. Given the massive scale of flooding in the eastern third of the state during Hurricane Floyd, taking a broad view of flood hazards would seem to be a logical step. However, to date, no action has been taken to pursue such an approach.[52]

a basin-wide approach to planning for water quality purposes. However, fewer states use the river basin as a unit for planning for flood control purposes, despite the obvious utility of such an approach.

14.4.2 Green Infrastructure

Infrastructure is a term that usually encompasses the public works and utilities that serve development, such as roads, sewer lines, and drainageways. The **green infrastructure** concept views natural areas as another form of infrastructure needed for both the ecological health of an area and for the quality of life that people have come to expect. Green infrastructure is a strategic approach to conservation that addresses many of the negative impacts of sprawl and the accelerated consumption and fragmentation of open land. Green infrastructure can include parks, buffers along waterways, greenways, farms, backyards, residential landscaping, and urban gardens, each of which can serve multiple purposes in the community. Not only can green infrastructure protect natural resources and habitat, but these spaces also act as floodwater storage facilities, water conveyance areas, and runoff filters to reduce the impacts of excess water in the community.[53] Green infrastructure also lessens the amount of impervious surface area in a community, effectively reducing the volume and velocity of stormwater flows.

14.4.3 The Role of Nonprofit Conservation and Environmental Protection Organizations

Whether through floodplain preservation, river basin planning, or green infrastructure initiatives, hazard reduction and environmental protection are mutually reinforcing activities that often promote more sustainable communities.[54] In many communities, the job of preservation and conservation of natural areas is undertaken by nongovernment organizations (NGOs). The growing nonprofit sector encompasses environmental activist groups, land trusts, conservancies, recreational clubs, watershed protectionists, hunting and fishing associations, watchdog groups, and other organizations focused on environmental quality and natural resource protection. They range in size from large-scale, nationally-recognized organizations such as the Sierra Club, Nature Conservancy, and the Natural Resources Defense Council, to local grass-roots volunteer groups with shoestring budgets and tiny resource pools, to radical fringe elements that practice eco-terrorism. These NGOs, also known as the third sector, are a growing and powerful force in our society and often are quite visible and vocal in presenting their agenda.[55]

Each type of nonprofit environmental organization pursues its own priorities, but many of their objectives may overlap with local or state management goals for hazard mitigation in environmentally sensitive or ecologically fragile lands. Even though environmental organizations may not target their efforts to natural hazards per se, many of their resultant outcomes can have the effect of reducing hazard impacts. For instance, purchasing acreage for conservation and environmental protection purposes may also result in increasing the hazard mitigating function of these natural areas. Wetlands, for example, can reduce flood losses while also providing important habitat and breeding grounds for fish and wildlife. Placing land under conservation easements or in permanent holding will also keep these areas out of the development stream, thereby preventing structures from being built in hazard areas. The complementary relationships between hazard mitigation efforts, environmental protection, and, ultimately, sustainability become clear when consideration is given to how healthy natural systems often serve to protect communities from hazards and how land use strategies in turn often serve to keep those natural systems healthy.[56]

SELF-CHECK

- Define **green infrastructure.**
- Discuss the value of using a river basin scale to manage flooding.
- Describe how nonprofit environmental organizations can contribute to community resiliency.

14.5 Pre- and Postdisaster Opportunities for Sustainable Development

In the best of all worlds, communities strive to become more resilient as part of their daily activities. "Mitigation is most effective when carried out on a comprehensive, communitywide, and long-term basis. Single grants or activities can help, but carrying out a slate of coordinated mitigation activities over time is the best way to ensure that communities will be physically, socially, and economically resilient to future hazard impacts."[57] Any and all selected mitigation measures must be joined with the political will and the institutionalized systems with the power to enforce them. How well a community integrates mitigation objectives with community growth and development, and balances competing priorities, will determine the extent to which the community has a sustainable future.[58]

14.5.1 Recognizing the Opportunities for Postdisaster Sustainable Redevelopment

Sometimes the best opportunity for encouraging a resilient and sustainable approach to community life arises after a major disaster. One of the impediments to local implementation of the principles of sustainability is the fact that much of the land within a local jurisdiction has already been developed according to practices and traditions that are far from sustainable.

Ironically, the time immediately following a natural disaster may provide a community with a unique **window of opportunity** for inserting an ethic of sustainability in guiding development and redevelopment in high-risk areas. With forethought and planning, communities that are rebuilt in the aftermath of a natural hazard can be built back so that they are more resilient to future hazards, breaking the cycle of hazard-destruction-rebuilding. At the same time, the community is given the opportunity to incorporate other attributes of sustainability into its second chance development, such as energy efficiency, affordable housing, walkable neighborhoods, use of recycled building materials, reduction of water use, and environmental protection.

If a community has not yet formally considered broader issues like environmental quality, economic parity, social equity, or livability, the period of recovery after a disaster can be a good time to start, primarily because disasters "jiggle the status quo, scrambling a community's normal reality and presenting chances to do things differently."[59] Some of the changes that occur in the routine business of a community after a disaster include:[60]

▲ **Hazard awareness increases:** immediately following a disaster event, people become personally aware of the hazards that can beset the community and the extent of the impact. In other words, it suddenly becomes real.

▲ **Destruction occurs:** In some cases, the disasters will have done some of the work already. For example, a tornado, earthquake, or fire may have damaged or destroyed aging, dilapidated, or unsafe buildings or infrastructure.

▲ **Community involvement increases:** A disaster forces a community to make decisions, both hard and easy. Community involvement and citizen participation in policy formation often increase after a disaster.

▲ **Help arrives:** Technical assistance and expert advice become available to a disaster-impacted community from a variety of state, federal, regional, academic, and nonprofit sources.

▲ **Money flows in:** Financial assistance becomes available from state and federal government agencies, both for private citizens and the local government for disaster recovery and mitigation projects; insurance claim payments can also provide a source of funds for recovery and mitigation work.

▲ **Hazard identification changes:** Sometimes a hazard may change a community's assessment of where hazard areas are located. A disaster may provide opportunities to update flood maps, relocate inlet zones, re-establish erosion rates, modify oceanfront or seismic setback regulations, and change other indicators of vulnerability to reflect actual hazard risks based on new conditions.

The best way to ensure that a community has a sustainable recovery from a future disaster is to prepare a comprehensive, holistic plan. But even if a community has not prepared such a plan, there are many common-sense things that can be done during the recovery process that will make a community more sustainable than it was before.[61] Integrating sustainable development into disaster recovery requires some shifts in current thinking, land use, and policy. Some broad guidelines for developing recovery strategies that promote sustainable hazards mitigation include:[62]

▲ **Adopt a longer time frame:** Sustainable hazards mitigation calls for the adoption of a much longer time frame in recovery decision making. Particularly foolhardy are short-term actions that destroy or undermine natural ecosystems and that encourage or facilitate long-term growth and development patterns that expose more people and property to hazards.

▲ **Consider future losses:** Substantial attention must be paid during rebuilding to future potential losses from hazards.

▲ **Remember hazards are recurrent events:** Postdisaster reconstruction and land use policies must recognize that natural disasters are recurrent events in natural ecological cycles and thus impose limits on redevelopment.

▲ **Protect natural resources:** Features of the natural environment that serve important mitigation functions, such as wetlands, firebreak zones, and sand dunes, should be taken into account and protected during rebuilding.

▲ **Use the best available data:** Scientific uncertainty about frequency intervals, prediction, or vulnerability should not postpone structural strengthening or hazard avoidance during rebuilding.

▲ **Invest in redevelopment wisely:** Postdisaster reconstruction that does not account for future natural disasters is an inefficient investment of recovery resources.

It must be remembered, however, that the postdisaster recovery period is one of high stress and anxiety for the victims of a recent disaster. There may be community resistance to any redevelopment effort that appears to slow the process down. In addition, people whose lives have been disrupted by disaster often want to put their lives back together just the way they were before the hazard event occurred. Such an attitude, while understandable, may prove to be an impediment to changing the community during the redevelopment phase. The "need for speed, [however] is a myth. Agencies believe that emergencies always require speedy response from the outside. More important than speed is timeliness. To be timely is to be there when needed. Timeliness requires that agencies look before they leap."[63] For a successful recovery, timelines need to be adjusted for long-term sustainable recovery and vulnerability reduction.[64]

FOR EXAMPLE

Oakland Firestorms Lead to New Action Plans

In October 1991, a major fire ravaged the hills of Oakland, California. Over the span of 4 days, more than 18,000 acres of land and 3000 residential units were destroyed. The fire burned through residential neighborhoods, wooded and grassland hillsides. After immediate danger from the fire had passed, concerns arose about the potential for erosion and mudslides on the denuded slopes. Oakland developed a short-term action plan for erosion and drainage control, implementing measures such as aerial seeding by helicopter, hydro mulching, construction of silt fences and debris dams, and protection of storm drain inlets. As a result of the firestorm, the city also implemented new, future-oriented development regulations that seek to deter future firestorms. A 1999 development ordinance addresses density issues in fire hazard areas. Before additional structures can be built on property located in fire hazard areas, the city must evaluate their plans, thereby preventing development conditions that can lead to increased fire risk. Oakland's 1991 experiences have significantly reduced risk of damage caused by flooding, debris and sediment flows, slides, blowing ash, and erosion, illustrating the commitment of city officials and residents not only to understanding the threat wildfires pose, but also to preventing them in the future.[65]

14.5.2 Paradigms of Sustainable Redevelopment

Examples of communities that have taken a sustainable redevelopment approach following a natural disaster are many and widespread. Among such communities that have taken advantage of the post-disaster window of opportunity to become more sustainable are:

▲ Located on the Arkansas River, **Tulsa, Oklahoma,** has a history of vulnerability to flooding. After years of repeated flooding, in the 1980s Tulsa initiated a multi-prong approach to mitigation. Projects to reduce flood risks include moving homes out of the floodplain, adopting watershed-wide regulations on new development, developing a master drainage plan for the city, establishing a funding source for stormwater management, and creating open space and recreational areas in the floodplain.

▲ After the 1993 Midwest Floods, **Soldier's Grove, Wisconsin,** rebuilt the community while following many sustainable development guidelines. Among other activities to promote resilience and sustainability, the town relocated its business district entirely out of the floodplain, required new businesses to obtain at least half their energy from solar, conducted life-cycle analysis of building materials, sited buildings and landscaping based on a detailed site analysis, and mixed housing into downtown development.

▲ *Pattonsburg, Missouri,* relocated completely out of the floodplain after the 1993 Midwest Floods. The community adopted a Charter of Sustainability, adopted sustainable design features such as energy efficient and resource conservation standards, created a pedestrian-friendly and solar-oriented street layout, created a Sustainable Economic Development Council, and adopted a waste minimization policy for the town.

▲ *Valmeyer, Illinois,* moved completely out of the Mississippi River floodplain after the 1993 Midwest Floods. The relocated town was designed and built to encourage energy conservation and promote the use of solar and geothermal energy.

▲ During rebuilding following Hurricane Andrew, Habitat for Humanity constructed an affordable housing complex called **Jordan Commons,** near Homestead, Florida. The project was designed as a community rather than built as individual housing units. The project incorporated design standards and building practices to withstand future hurricanes while providing affordable housing to low- and middle-income residents who participated in the rebuilding process.

▲ Following a devastating tornado in the spring of 1997, the city of **Arkadelphia, Arkansas,** used funding from the U.S. Department of Housing and Urban Development (HUD) to develop a comprehensive downtown recovery program as part of a larger community redevelopment initiative. Key projects that were developed in reaction to local commitment to keeping downtown as the heart of the community included the construction of a new city hall and town square complex, implementing streetscape improvements, construction of a new riverfront park, attracting middle-market housing to affected neighborhoods and the creation of a housing rehabilitation program. In addition, changes to the zoning code encouraged a greater diversity of housing types throughout the city, compact neighborhood design, and energy-efficient home building practices. The city took advantage of the HUD funding after the tornado to develop a sustainable recovery plan that benefited the entire community.

Calhoun Street: A Center for Sustainable Living

113 Calhoun Street in Charleston, South Carolina, is used as a learning center to demonstrate various sustainable building techniques, including flood mitigation. The 113 Calhoun Street Foundation's Center for Sustainable Living is dedicated to the premise that living within the "earth's means" is the key to a sustainable society. The 125-year old building, located in the historic downtown district, was already abandoned when it was further damaged by Hurricane Hugo in 1989. The 113 Calhoun Street Foundation, a private, nonprofit organization established

Figure 14-2

113 Calhoun Street, Charleston, South Carolina.

by the South Carolina Sea Grant Consortium, Clemson University Extension Service, and the city of Charleston, decided to transform the building into a real-life example of sensible building practices and use it as a demonstration project. The house as shown in Figure 14-2 serves as a focal point for hazard-related education and research in South Carolina, and is open to the public for tours and other educational programs.[66]

SELF-CHECK

- List the six guidelines for sustainable recovery strategies.
- Describe the postdisaster **window of opportunity** and what that entails for mitigation.
- Select a sustainably-redeveloped community and describe its mitigation actions.

14.6 The Art of Emergency Management: Resilient Communities for a Sustainable Future

We have discussed in this chapter how mitigation can lower risk and reduce vulnerability to natural hazards, thereby contributing to a community's overall resilience and sustainability. The nuances and subtle features of infusing an ethic of prevention into community policy and practices highlight the function of emergency management as an art form, and illustrate how emergency managers serve as local artists rather than mere technicians.

Many of the mitigation functions carried out by emergency managers are indeed technical. We need meteorologists and geologists to inform us of the likely hazard events in our area and how they can affect people and property. We rely on civil engineers and architects to develop building codes and to design structurally sound buildings and infrastructure that can resist hazard impacts. We need GIS technicians to gather data and display it in a geospatial format that captures the intersections between the built environment and potential impacts. We need hydrologists and hydraulic engineers to create flood maps that indicate where structures are at risk of flooding and to establish flood heights on which to base regulatory requirements for building in the floodplain. We need planners and resource managers to direct growth and development out of hazard areas and to encourage more sustainable patterns of land use. The science of emergency management relies on good data, accurate mapping, and the expertise to interpret them. But emergency management also involves critical thinking, application of that knowledge to practice, and the giving of sound advice based on the data to decision and policy makers. Ultimately, it is not until the data is interpreted and translated into policy that mitigation will make a difference. It is here—at the juncture of science and policy, that mitigation builds resiliency and sustainability. Emergency management can contribute to each of the three community spheres—social, economic, and environmental—through policy and practice based on science and technology.

A discussion of the sustainable development features of hazards management would not be complete without reference to the issue of personal responsibility. Assuming that individuals and their families, businesses, and local government officials have accurate, reliable information regarding hazards in the community, a certain level of responsibility comes into play for addressing those hazards in the way we live.

At the individual and family level, we must assume that one cannot completely rely on others, even the government, the Red Cross, one's neighbors, or church to always be there to help in times of disaster—ultimately we all are responsible for our own safety. Having said that, we live in a society that, while it values personal responsibility, independence, and self reliance, we recognize that some do not have the capacity to help themselves (the young, the old, the poor, the dispossessed and disenfranchised, the mentally ill, those who are sick and infirm, and others less fortunate in their life circumstances). Therefore, responsibility also lies with the community as a whole, both because this is the more socially acceptable approach, as well as the more efficient and cost-effective means of addressing issues of hazard vulnerability.

It is not always law and governments that encourage adoption of risk reduction practices. A certain level of engagement by the citizenry that are able and willing to take action is needed. The vision of sustainability in part embodies a spirit of responsibility and self-sufficiency, and heavy reliance on outside resources (i.e., federal and state funding) for disaster assistance is inconsistent with this. Communities must be better prepared to cope with the financial implication of disaster events and should be expected to utilize more of their own resources, at least in all but the most catastrophic of disaster events. Partly this means accepting more responsibility for allowing, or even actively promoting, development in vulnerable places, and striving to reduce this over time.[67]

By sharing the responsibility for a community's all-hazards preparedness and disaster prevention efforts, community involvement is the key to successful emergency management programs. Government will never have enough resources or money to mitigate alone, and a sustainability model based on personal and community responsibility requires that government not be the sole source for mitigation action. Businesses, nonprofit organizations, professional associations, neighborhood activists, and other members of a community can become more involved and make a difference. Every level and individual in a community is ultimately responsible for their community's resilience, first by taking care of themselves and their family, and then by participating in taking their community to the next level of resilience.[68] In terms of building a sustainable legacy, the future lies in the hands of those living today.

FOR EXAMPLE

Multi-Objective Planning in Del Rio, Texas

A flash flood in August, 1998, totally destroyed a historic neighborhood along San Felipe Creek. The town's recovery efforts are an excellent example of multi-objective planning: acquiring flood-damaged homes, providing increased recreational opportunities along the creek, restoration of a natural floodplain habitat, and protection of a federally threatened species—the Devils River Minnow. The lack of affordable housing opportunities for displaced residents was addressed by a publicly funded subdivision that incorporates many sustainability concepts, including mixed-use development, a range of housing types, open space, and an emphasis on the use of adobe, an environmentally friendly or "green" construction technique for the Southwest.[69]

SELF-CHECK

- Describe the ways in which emergency management may be viewed as an art form rather than merely as an application of technical skills.

- List some of the other fields that can contribute to emergency management functions.

- Discuss the role of the government in creating safe communities. What is the role of business and industry? What are the responsibilities of individuals and families?

SUMMARY

Our current patterns of land use are unsustainable because they increasingly put people and property in harm's way. A more sustainable approach to community growth involves incorporating principles of social equity, environmental integrity, and economic vitality, along with an ethic of resiliency, into pre- and postdisaster development in order to reduce community vulnerability to the impact of hazards. This approach will require a change in thinking, so that a culture of prevention is nurtured and integrated into all community decision making. Mitigation is a fiscally responsible means of increasing community resiliency when benefits and costs are carefully considered. However, the value of hazard mitigation projects that prevent or avoid disaster can be difficult to quantify. Preserving and protecting the natural environment, including wetlands, dunes, floodplains, and shorelines is an effective means of protecting the built environment, while also adding aesthetic, cultural, and recreational value to community open space. We must take into account disparities in risk perception when we establish an acceptable level of risk for communities in hazardous locations, and make every effort to describe risk in terms that people can understand. In the end, we are all responsible for making our communities more resilient to the impacts of hazards, to ensure a safer tomorrow.

KEY TERMS

Economic sphere	Consists of all the activities, transactions, and decisions that are based on producing and exchanging goods and services and encompasses jobs, markets, investment, capital, and other aspects of our economic existence in the modern world.

Environmental sphere
The natural and physical setting in which the community exists—the visible landscape as well as resources such as water, air, and soil, on which communities rely.

Green infrastructure
Views natural areas as a form of infrastructure (public works and utilities such as sewer lines and roads) that supports not only quality of life but the ecological health of an area.

No Adverse Impact
An approach to floodplain management that attempts to ensure that the actions of one property owner do not increase the flood risk of other property owners through land use planning and mitigation strategies.

Process mitigation activities
Mitigation projects that are difficult to quantify from a cost-benefit perspective, but lead to policies, practices, and plans to reduce risk, including vulnerability assessments, community priorities and action plans, education and awareness campaigns for decision makers and constituents, and development of codes and regulations.

Project mitigation activities
Brick and mortar mitigation projects that result in tangible physical change to the built or natural environment, such as drainage enhancement, acquisition and relocation of at-risk structures, structural and non-structural improvements, lifeline improvements, and land improvement projects.

River basin management
A technique for addressing issues of water quality, habitat protection, rural land conservation, and flood hazard mitigation on a regional scale in recognition of the fact that natural systems do not necessarily correspond to political boundaries.

Social sphere
Consists of all of the interactions among people—cooperating in their neighborhood activities, practicing their religion, enjoying their families, sharing cultural identities, solving problems together, uniting as a community.

Window of opportunity
The time immediately following a disaster during which a community can insert an ethic of sustainability in guiding development and redevelopment in high-risk areas.

ASSESS YOUR UNDERSTANDING

Go to www.wiley.com/college/schwab to evaluate your knowledge of prevention culture building.
Measure your learning by comparing pre-test and post-test results.

Summary Questions

1. Development patterns are brittle when they do not take hazards into account. True or False?

2. Which of the following is not one of the three traditional spheres of sustainable development?

    (a) social

    (b) economic

    (c) environmental

    (d) hazard resilience

3. Hazard resilience works as a fourth dimension to the three basic spheres of sustainable development. True or False?

4. Which of the following is a structural mitigation action?

    (a) avoiding hazard areas through land use plans

    (b) protecting sand dunes

    (c) strengthening buildings to withstand hazard impacts

    (d) increasing awareness of building reinforcement techniques

5. Which of the following is a nonstructural mitigation action?

    (a) building levees

    (b) installing hurricane shutters on a home

    (c) constructing sounder infrastructure

    (d) maintaining floodplains as open space

6. Hazard mitigation is not the only phase of emergency management that is especially dedicated to breaking the cycle of damage, reconstruction, and repeated damage. True or False?

7. Resilient communities can better withstand which negative economic effects of a disaster?

    (a) displacement of residents and loss of local employment base

    (b) deferment of other publicly funded projects

    (c) loss of major employers

    (d) all of the above

8. Which is an example of a process mitigation activity?

    (a) land improvement projects

    (b) vulnerability assessment

(c) relocation of at-risk structures

(d) lifeline improvements

9. Which of the following is not part of the social equity sphere of sustainable development?

    (a) budgetary financial impacts

    (b) gender

    (c) race

    (d) income disparities

10. The simple answer to the question of why The Netherlands provides a higher level of protection than that which is found in New Orleans is a matter of global economics. True or False?

11. Most people believe that their community will experience disaster. True or False?

12. Which of the following is not an ethic of preservation and conservation that can be translated to sustainable development practices?

    (a) promotion of healthy ecosystems

    (b) protection of biodiversity

    (c) building in the floodplain

    (d) habitat protection

13. Which of the following is an example of green infrastructure?

    (a) roads

    (b) farms

    (c) sewer lines

    (d) utility lines

14. Infusing a mitigation ethic into all land use planning and development activities is the best way to increase local vulnerability. True or False?

15. We can rely on others, such as the Red Cross or the government to be responsible for our safety. True or False?

Review Questions

1. Define sustainable development.

2. Define the economic sphere of sustainable development.

3. Define the social sphere of sustainable development.

4. Define the environmental sphere of sustainable development.

5. List six economic protection mitigation strategies available at the local level.

6. What is the difference between a project mitigation activity and a process mitigation activity?

7. Why is the standard method of describing flood risk as a 1 percent chance flood illustrated as the 100 year floodplain a misconception?

8. What are the benefits of a natural floodplain?

9. What are some of the changes that occur in a community after a disaster?

10. List six guidelines communities can use to promote sustainable redevelopment following a disaster.

11. Describe some of the complementary goals of local governments and nonprofit environmental organizations in reducing hazard vulnerability.

12. Describe why emergency management can be seen as an art form.

Applying This Chapter

1. What river basin are you located in? Are you upstream near the headwaters, downstream near the outflow point, or somewhere in between? How do the actions of your community affect the entire river basin as a whole?

2. Think of a disaster that could affect your community. After that disaster, if you were an emergency manager, what would you do to insert a sustainable development ethic into guiding development and redevelopment in high risk areas? Would you take advantage of that window of opportunity? And if so, how? What recovery strategies would you use to promote sustainable hazards mitigation?

3. Identify some of the natural features of your community. If you live near a river, can you identify the extent of the floodplain? Are there wetlands present or nearby? If so, are they allowed to function in their natural capacity as catchments for excess rainfall? If not, what measures should be in place to protect their mitigation function?

4. Consider the sustainability of your community. What factors might you look at to determine the economic vitality of the business sector? What social equity features might you want to investigate? How would you rate the environmental quality of the area you live in? How do these features impact the resiliency of your community to natural hazards?

5. Describe how structural engineers in New Orleans might approach levee repair and reconstruction following a major hurricane if they were trained in The Netherlands. What obstacles to their approach might they encounter? Consider the budget they might be allocated. Consider too the traditions of land use planning and development.

6. Outline the strategy you might take to developing floodplain regulations if your community were to take a no adverse impact approach to flood mitigation. How would you assess the boundaries of the floodplain? Would you take into account future development? Why or why not?

7. You are the emergency manager of a small town that has experienced repeated flooding. The town manager has asked you for a report detailing the costs and benefits of a proposed structural mitigation project. What factors will you consider when compiling your report? What basis for your information will you use?

Greening Your Infrastructure

The Maryland Department of Natural Resources is working to identify those undeveloped lands that are most critical to the state's long-term ecological health. These lands, referred to as Maryland's green infrastructure, provide the natural foundation needed to support diverse plant and animal populations, and enable valuable natural processes like filtering water and cleaning the air to take place. Identifying and setting priorities for protection of the green infrastructure is an ongoing process. A description of Maryland's green infrastructure, including county-by-county maps, can be found at hwww.dnr.state.md.use/greenways/gi.gi.html. Using Maryland's approach as a guide, find out how your community treats its open spaces. If you live in an urban area, does your city protect urban forests or other natural areas? If your community is suburban or rural in nature, is agricultural or habitat protected in any way? What water quality protections are in place at the local level? State level?

Environmental Justice at Home

Seeking information from your local planning department, community affairs, or housing agency, identify where low-income or minority populations live in your community. Now identify the hazards that may be present there. Look at the local flood maps. Are toxic waste sites or local landfills nearby? Are disadvantaged people living in areas that are more vulnerable to hazards than other sectors of society? If so, what might you do as an emergency manager to safeguard all members of your community?

Risky Business

The terms we use to describe risk are often confusing and misleading to the general population. Take an informal poll of friends, colleagues, and family members. Ask them what comes to mind when you mention the "100-year flood risk." How many people respond that it must mean a flood that occurs once every 100 years? Does the phrase "1% chance of flooding in any given year" help clarify the concept of risk for them? Confuse them more? How would you describe flood risk in terms that people who are not in the emergency management field could understand?

ENDNOTES

Chapter 1

1. Coch, Nicholas K. 1995. *Geohazards: Natural and Human*. Englewood Cliffs, NJ: Prentice-Hall, p.12.
2. Coch, Nicholas K. 1995. *Geohazards: Natural and Human*. Englewood Cliffs, NJ: Prentice-Hall.
3. North Carolina Hazard Mitigation (409) Plan. Undated.
4. Brower, David J., and Charles C. Bohl. 1998. *Principles and Practice of Hazard Mitigation Instructor Guide*. FEMA National Emergency Management Institute.
5. Platt, Rutherford H. 1999. *Disasters and Democracy: The Politics of Extreme Natural Events*. Washington, DC: Island Press.
6. Platt, Rutherford H. 1999. *Disasters and Democracy: The Politics of Extreme Natural Events*. Washington, DC: Island Press.
7. Knabb, R. D., J. R. Rhome, and D. P. Brown. 2005. "Tropical Cyclone Report, Hurricane Katrina, 23–30 August 2005." National Hurricane Center. www.nhc.noaa.gov/2005atlan.shtml.
8. Knabb, R. D., J. R. Rhome, and D. P. Brown. 2005. "Tropical Cyclone Report, Hurricane Katrina, 23–30 August 2005." National Hurricane Center. www.nhc.noaa.gov/2005atlan.shtml.
9. Dyson, Michael Eric. 2006. *Come Hell or High Water*. NY: Basic Civitas.
10. The H. John Heinz III Center for Science, Economics and the Environment. 2000. *The Hidden Costs of Coastal Hazards: Implications for Risk Assessment and Mitigation*. Washington, DC: Island Press.
11. FEMA. *The Disaster Life Cycle*. last modified: April 5, 2006. www.fema.gov/about/what.shtm. (May 17, 2006).
12. This is the official definition of mitigation as it appears in the Stafford Act (*Robert T. Stafford Disaster Relief and Emergency Assistance Act*. 1988. *Code of Federal Regulations*. Title 44, Part 206.40.) and the definition most often used by the Federal Emergency Management Agency in its published works and guidance materials.
13. Blanchard, Wayne. 1997. Emergency Management USA: Student Manual. FEMA Emergency Management Institute.
14. FEMA. 2003. Planning for a Sustainable Future: The Link Between Hazard Mitigation and Livability. Publication 364. FEMA.
15. The H. John Heinz III Center for Science, Economics and the Environment. 2000. *The Hidden Costs of Coastal Hazards: Implications for Risk Assessment and Mitigation*. Washington, DC: Island Press.

16. FEMA News Release. March 21, 2005. Release Number: R4-05-085.

17. FEMA. 2001. State and Local Hazard Mitigation Planning How-to Guide. Publications 386-1-386-7. FEMA.

18. This is the definition of "sustainable development" developed by the Brundtland Commission in 1987, World Commission on Environment and Development, Our Common Future 43 (1987).

19. FEMA. 2003. Planning for a Sustainable Future: The Link Between Hazard Mitigation and Livability. Publication 364. FEMA.

20. NC Department of Crime Control and Public Safety. August 2001. Disaster Debris Management/Deconstruction Initiative. Environmental Sustainability Report Update.

Chapter 2

1. The information about Hurricane Katrina is derived from (1): Knabb, R. D., J. R. Rhome, and D. P. Brown. 2005. "Tropical Cyclone Report: Hurricane Katrina, 23–30 August 2005." National Hurricane Center. www.nhc.gov/2005atlan.shtml. (2) personal communication with Gavin Smith, Ph.D., Director of the Mississippi Office of the Governor's Office of Recovery and Renewal, May 2006.

2. NC Department of Environment and Natural Resources. Undated. Discover North Carolina's River Basins. NCDENR, Office of Environmental Education.

3. www.noaanews.noaa.gov/stories/s688.htm.

4. This section contains excerpts from: FEMA. June 2005. Reducing Damage from Localized Flooding: A Guide for Communities. Publication 511. FEMA.

5. www.spc.noaa.gov/efscale.

6. Kocin, P. J., and L. W. Uccellini. 2004. A Snowfall Impact Scale Derived From Northeast Storm Snowfall Distributions. *Bulletin of the American Meteorological Society* 85:177–194.

7. www.ncdc.noaa.gov/oa/climate/research/snow-nesis.

8. www.news14charlotte.com/content/top_stories/?ArID=31523.

9. www.srs.fs.usda.gov/sustain/report/pdf/chapter_25e.pdf.

10. www.tncfire.org/resource/keetch.htm.

Chapter 3

1. Coch, Nicholos K. 1995. *Geohazards: Natural and Human*. Englewood Cliffs, NJ: Prentice Hall.

2. Coch, Nicholos K. 1995. *Geohazards: Natural and Human*. Englewood Cliffs, NJ: Prentice Hall.

3. FEMA. August 2001. State and Local Hazard Mitigation Planning How to Guide: Understanding Your Risks. Publication 386-2. FEMA.

4. FEMA. August 2001. State and Local Hazard Mitigation Planning How to Guide: Understanding Your Risks. Publication 386-2. FEMA.

5. Coch, Nicholos K. 1995. *Geohazards: Natural and Human*. Englewood Cliffs, NJ: Prentice Hall.

6. Coch, Nicholos K. 1995. *Geohazards: Natural and Human*. Englewood Cliffs, NJ: Prentice Hall.

7. Bradley, Bob. 2006. Louisiana Coastal Erosion: The Effects of Storms: An Interactive Lesson and Activity. (April 19, 2006) www.leeric.lsu.edu/educat/lessons/erosion (April 19, 2006.)

8. Brown, M. February 15, 2006. Coastal losses greater than thought. *The Times Picayune*. Quotation by Carlton Dufrechou, Lake Pontchartrain Basin Foundation. Available at www.nola.com/news/t-p/index.ssf?/ base/news-3/113998708880320.xml.

9. U.S. House of Representatives. 2004. The Water Resources and Environment Subcommittee background memorandum on the July 15, 2004, U.S. Army Corps of Engineers' proposed Louisiana Coastal Area Ecosystem Restoration Project testimony. Available at www.house.gov/ transportation/water/07-15-04/07-15-04memo.html.

10. USGS. 2006. Press Release: USGS Reports Latest Land-Water Changes for Southeastern Louisiana. Available at www.nwrc.usgs.gov/hurricane/Land%20Water%20Changes%20for%20SE%20LA.pdf.

11. USGS. Land and People: Finding a Balance: Los Angeles Student Guide, Glossary. January 29, 2002. interactive2.usgs.gov/learningweb/students/landpeople_s_la_glossary.htm (January 9, 2006).

Chapter 4

1. Waugh, William L. Winter 2004. The all-hazards approach must be continued. *Journal of Emergency Management* 2(1): 1112.

2. *Code of Federal Regulations*. Title 28, Part 0.85.

3. More information on EMAC can be found at www.emacweb.org/ index.cfm.

4. U.S. Environmental Protection Agency.

5. A list of the hazardous substances is published in *Code of Federal Regulations*. Title 40, Part 302: Table 302.4.

6. The list of extremely hazardous substances is identified in Title III of *Superfund Amendments and Reauthorization Act (SARA). 1986. Code of Federal Regulations*. Title 40, Part 355.

7. The list of toxic chemicals is identified in Title III of *Superfund Amendments and Reauthorization Act (SARA). 1986. Code of Federal Regulations*. Title 40, Part 355.

8. *Code of Federal Regulations*. Title 40, Part 261.33.

9. *Code of Federal Regulations*. Title 49, Parts 170–179.

10. *Code of Federal Regulations*. Title 29, Part 1910.120, which resulted from Title I of SARA.

11. Occupational Health and Safety Administration. Recommended Format for Material Safety Data Sheets. Publication 174. OSHA.

12. Occupational Health and Safety Administration. Recommended Format for Material Safety Data Sheets. Publication 174. OSHA.

13. North Carolina Department of Environment and Natural Resources, Division of Water Quality. Stormwater Control.

14. U.S. Nuclear Regulatory Commission. *U.S. Nuclear Regulatory Commission: Who We Are.* August 17, 2004. www.nrc.gov/who-we-are.html (November 18, 2005).

15. Nuclear Regulatory Commission. Fact Sheet on the Accident at Three Mile Island.

16. U.S. House of Representatives. 2006. A Failure of Initiative: Final Report of the Select Bipartisan Committee to Investigate the Preparation for and Response to Hurricane Katrina. Available at katrina.house.gov.

17. Minerals Management Service News Release. September 16, 2005. Release Number: 3349. Available at www.mms.gov/ooc/press/2005/ press0916a.htm.

18. Knabb, R. D., J. R. Rhome, and D. P. Brown. 2005. "Tropical Cyclone Report, Hurricane Katrina, 23–30 August 2005." National Hurricane Center. Available at www.nhc.noaa.gov/2005atlan.shtml.

19. NOAA Office of Response and Restoration. Incident News. (November 18, 2005). www. incidentnews.gov/6001 (November 18, 2005).

20. NOAA CCMA. *National Status and Trends*. (November 18, 2005). www.ccma.nos.noaa.gov/cit/katrina/welcome.html (date of last access).

21. Waugh, William L., Jr. November 2005. The Disaster that Was Katrina. *Natural Hazards Observer* 30 (2).

22. Waugh, William L., Jr. November 2005. The Disaster that Was Katrina. *Natural Hazards Observer*. 30 (2).

23. FEMA. 2003. State and Local Hazard Mitigation Planning How-To Guide: Integrating Manmade Hazards into Mitigation Planning. Publication 386–7. FEMA.

24. FEMA. 2003. State and Local Hazard Mitigation Planning How-To Guide: Integrating Manmade Hazards into Mitigation Planning. Publication 386–7. FEMA.

Chapter 5

1. McDowell, Bruce D. 1986. The Evolution of American Planning. In *The Practice of State and Regional Planning*, edited by Frank So. Chicago: American Planning Association.

2. May, Peter J., and Robert E. Deyle. 1998. Governing land use in hazardous areas with a patchwork system. In *Cooperating with Nature: Confronting Natural Hazards with Land-Use Planning for Sustainable Communities*, edited by Raymond J. Burby. Washington, DC: Joseph Henry Press.

3. May, Peter J., and Robert E. Deyle. 1998. Governing land use in hazardous areas with a patchwork system. In *Cooperating with Nature: Confronting Natural Hazards with Land-Use Planning for Sustainable Communities*, edited by Raymond J. Burby. Washington, DC: Joseph Henry Press.

4. Singer, Paul. A port in the storm. *National Journal*. May 27, 2006.

5. Singer, Paul. A port in the storm. *National Journal*. May 27, 2006- p. 34. Quoting Rep. Earl Blumenauer, D-Ore.

6. Singer, Paul. A port in the storm. *National Journal*. May 27, 2006.

7. These and other statistics regarding federal real property ownership and control may be found in the General Services Administration Office of Government-wide Policy Report Overview of U.S. Government's Owned and Leased Real Property: Federal Real Property Profile as of September 30, 2004, available at http://www.gsa.gov/realpropertyprofile.

8. Singer, Paul. A port in the storm. *National Journal*. May 27, 2006.

9. Singer, Paul. A port in the storm. *National Journal*. May 27, 2006.

10. Singer, Paul. A port in the storm. *National Journal*. May 27, 2006.

11. Beatley, Timothy, David J. Brower, and Anna K. Schwab. 2002. *An Introduction to Coastal Zone Management*. Washington, DC: Island Press.

12. May, Peter J., and Robert E. Deyle. 1998. Governing land use in hazardous areas with a patchwork system. In *Cooperating with Nature: Confronting Natural Hazards with Land-Use Planning for Sustainable Communities*, edited by Raymond J. Burby. Washington, DC: Joseph Henry Press.

13. U.S. House of Representatives. 2006. A Failure of Initiative: Final Report of the Select Bipartisan Committee to Investigate the Preparation for and Response to Hurricane Katrina. Available at katrina.house.gov.

14. State of Louisiana Emergency Operations Plan. April 2005. Supplement 1A: Emergency Operations Plan: Southeast Louisiana Hurricane Evacuation and Sheltering Plan.

15. City of New Orleans. 2004. Comprehensive Emergency Management Plan, p. 104.

16. City of New Orleans. 2004. Comprehensive Emergency Management Plan, p. 113.

17. City of New Orleans. 2004. Comprehensive Emergency Management Plan, p. 113.

18. Madelker, Daniel R. 1993. *Land Use Law*. Charlottesville, VA: The Michie Company.

19. Madelker, Daniel R. 1993. *Land Use Law*. Charlottesville, VA: The Michie Company.

20. William A. Fischel. 1995. Lucas v. South Carolina Coastal Council: A Photographic Essay. Hanover, New Hampshire: Dartmouth College Dept. of Economics.

Chapter 6

1. Platt, Rutherford H. 1999. *Disasters and Democracy: The Politics of Extreme Natural Events*. Washington, D.C.: Island Press.

2. Haddow, George D., and Jane A. Bullock. 2003. *Introduction to Emergency Management*. Burlington, MA: Butterworth-Heinemann.

3. Platt, Rutherford H. 1999. *Disasters and Democracy: The Politics of Extreme Natural Events*. Washington, D.C.: Island Press.

4. Platt, Rutherford H. 1999. *Disasters and Democracy: The Politics of Extreme Natural Events*. Washington, D.C.: Island Press.

5. Haddow, George D., and Jane A. Bullock. 2003. *Introduction to Emergency Management*. Burlington, MA: Butterworth-Heinemann.

6. Haddow, George D., and Jane A. Bullock. 2003. *Introduction to Emergency Management*. Burlington, MA: Butterworth-Heinemann.

7. The H. John Heinz III Center for Science, Economics and the Environment. 2002. *Human Links to Coastal Disasters*. Washington, D.C.: The Heinz Center.

8. FEMA. FEMA History. March 21, 2006. /www.fema.gov/about/history.shtm (March 21, 2006).

9. Federal Regulation 44CFR59.1

10. Federal Regulation 44CFR59.1

11. Federal Regulation 44CFR59.1

12. Godschalk, David, and David Salveson. Undated. "Development on coastal barriers: Does the Coastal Barrier Resources Act make a difference?" Report to the Coastal Alliance, Washington, DC.

13. 33 U.S.C. 1344

14. 51 Federal Regulation 41217

15. Knabb, R. D., J. R. Rhome, and D. P. Brown. 2005. "Tropical Cyclone Report, Hurricane Katrina, 23–30 August 2005." National Hurricane Center. Available at www.nhc.noaa.gov/2005atlan.shtml.

16. U.S. House of Representatives. 2006. A Failure of Initiative: Final Report of the Select Bipartisan Committee to Investigate the Preparation for and Response to Hurricane Katrina. Available at katrina.house.gov.

17. Murawski, Steven, and Kristin Koch. Hurricanes Katrina and Rita: NOAA's next steps in response and rebuilding. Presentation to the NOAA Science Advisory Board, March 9, 2006, Washington, D.C. Available at www.sab.noaa.gov/Meetings/2006/march/05_Hurricane_Murawski.pdf.

18. Ocean and Coastal Resource Management. *Coastal Hazards*. July 19, 2005. coastalmanagement.noaa.gov/pcd/coastal_hazards.html (date of last access).

19. 16 C.F.R. 1452

20. 16 C.F.R. 1456

21. Beatley, T., et al. 2000. *An Introduction to Coastal Zone Management*. Washington D.C.: Island Press.

22. Kalo, Joseph. J. 1990. *Coastal and Ocean Law*. Houston, TX: The John Marshall Publishing Co.

23. Platt, Rutherford H. 1999. *Disasters and Democracy: The Politics of Extreme Natural Events*. Washington, D.C.: Island Press, p. 291.

24. The H. John Heinz III Center for Science, Economics and the Environment. 2002. *Human Links to Coastal Disasters*. Washington, D.C.: The Heinz Center.

25. Platt, Rutherford H. 1999. *Disasters and Democracy: The Politics of Extreme Natural Events*. Washington, D.C.: Island Press, p. 292.

26. The H. John Heinz III Center for Science, Economics and the Environment. 2002. *Human Links to Coastal Disasters*. Washington, D.C.: The Heinz Center.

27. The H. John Heinz III Center for Science, Economics and the Environment. 2002. *Human Links to Coastal Disasters*. Washington, D.C.: The Heinz Center.

28. Miletti, Dennis. 1999. Disasters By Design: *A Reassessment of Natural Hazards in the United States*. Washington, D.C.: Joseph Henry Press.

29. Platt, Rutherford H. 1999. *Disasters and Democracy: The Politics of Extreme Natural Events*. Washington, D.C.: Island Press.

30. Godschalk, David, et al. 1999. *Natural Hazard Mitigation: Recasting Disaster Policy and Planning*. Washington, D.C.: Island Press.

31. Platt, Rutherford H. 1999. *Disasters and Democracy: The Politics of Extreme Natural Events*. Washington, D.C.: Island Press.

32. Burby, 1998. Burby, Ragmonds, ed. 1998. *Cooperating with Nature: Confronting Natural Hazards with Land-Use Planning for Sustainable Communities*. Washington, D.C.: Joseph Henry Press.

33. Burby, 1998.

Chapter 7

1. Governor's Office of Recovery and Renewal News Release. May 15, 2006. Available at www.governorbarbour.com/Recovery. Quoting Governor Haley Barbour.

2. Gavin Smith, Ph.D., Director of the Mississippi Office of the Governor's Office of Recovery and Renewal, personal communication with author. May 14, 2006.

3. *Code of Federal Regulations*. Title 44, Part 201.1.

4. Burby, Raymond J., and Linda C. Dalton. 1994. Plans can matter! The role of land use plans and state planning mandates in limiting development of hazardous areas. *Public Administration Review* 54(3): 229–238.

5. Mileti, Dennis S. 1999. *Disasters By Design: A Reassessment of Natural Hazards in the United States*. Washington, D.C.: Joseph Henry Press.

6. Institute for Building and Home Safety. *The Benefits of Statewide Building Codes*. 2005. www.ibhs.org/building_codes/view.asp?id=173 (date of last access).

7. Mileti, Dennis S. 1999. *Disasters By Design: A Reassessment of Natural Hazards in the United States*. Washington, D.C.: Joseph Henry Press.

8. Godschalk, David R., Timothy Beatley, Philip Berke, David J. Brower, and Edward J. Kaiser. 1999. *Natural Hazard Mitigation: Recasting Disaster Policy and Planning*. Washington, D.C.: Island Press.

9. Mileti, Dennis S. 1999. *Disasters By Design: A Reassessment of Natural Hazards in the United States*. Washington, D.C.: Joseph Henry Press.

10. Mileti, Dennis S. 1999. *Disasters By Design: A Reassessment of Natural Hazards in the United States*. Washington, D.C.: Joseph Henry Press.

11. Godschalk, David R., Timothy Beatley, Philip Berke, David J. Brower, and Edward J. Kaiser. 1999. *Natural Hazard Mitigation: Recasting Disaster Policy and Planning*. Washington, D.C.: Island Press.

12. Mileti, Dennis S. 1999. *Disasters By Design: A Reassessment of Natural Hazards in the United States*. Washington, D.C.: Joseph Henry Press.

13. Mileti, Dennis S. 1999. *Disasters By Design: A Reassessment of Natural Hazards in the United States*. Washington, D.C.: Joseph Henry Press.

14. Godschalk, David R., Timothy Beatley, Philip Berke, David J. Brower, and Edward J. Kaiser. 1999. *Natural Hazard Mitigation: Recasting Disaster Policy and Planning*. Washington, D.C.: Island Press.

15. Mileti, Dennis S. 1999. Disasters By Design: *A Reassessment of Natural Hazards in the United States*. Washington, D.C.: Joseph Henry Press.

16. Godschalk, David R., Timothy Beatley, Philip Berke, David J. Brower, and Edward J. Kaiser. 1999. *Natural Hazard Mitigation: Recasting Disaster Policy and Planning*. Washington, D.C.: Island Press.

17. Burby, Raymond J. 1998. Natural Hazards and Land Use: An Introduction. *In Cooperating with Nature: Confronting Natural Hazards with Land-Use Planning for Sustainable Communities*, edited by Raymond J. Burby. Washington, D.C.: Joseph Henry Press.

18. Christie, Donna R., and Richard G. Hildreth. 1999. *Coastal and Ocean Management* Law. 2d ed. St. Paul, MN: West Group.

19. 44CRF59.1

20. Beatley, Timothy, David J. Brower, and Anna K. Schwab. 2000. An *Introduction to Coastal Zone Management*. Washington, DC: Island Press.

21. North Carolina Administrative Code. Title 15A, Part 7H, Section 0306.

22. The Nature Conservancy. *Investing in Wetlands*. 2006. www.nature.org/wherewework/northamerica/states/ohio/science/art5437.html (March 3, 2006.)

23. The Nature Conservancy News Release. January 11, 2001. Available at www.nature.org/pressroom/press/press150.html.

24. North Carolina Division of Emergency Management. 1999. Hazard Mitigation Successes in the State of North Carolina. North Carolina Department of Crime Control and Public Safety. Quoting Dr. Gavin Smith.

Chapter 8

1. United Nations World Commission on Environment and Development. 1987. Our Common Future, p. 43.

2. The H. John Heinz III Center for Science, Economics and the Environment. 2002. *Human Links to Coastal Disasters*. Washington, D.C.: The Heinz Center.

3. FEMA. 2003. Planning for a Sustainable Future: The Link Between Hazard Mitigation and Livability. Publication 364. FEMA.

4. Kusler, Jon A. 2004. *No adverse impact: floodplain management and the courts*. Madison, WI: Association of State Floodplain Managers.

5. Barrett, Barbara. November 7, 2005. Topsail homes in no man's land: Condemned houses leave owners few options. *Raleigh, NC News & Observer*.

6. Arendt, Randall G. 1996. *Conservation Designs for Subdivisions*. Washington, D.C.: Island Press, p. 42.

7. North Carolina Division of Emergency Management. 1998. Tools and Techniques: Putting a Hazard Mitigation Plan to Work. North Carolina Department of Crime Control and Public Safety. Available at www.ncem.org/mitigation/Library/Full_Tools_and_Tech.pdf.

8. Burby, Raymond J., ed. 1998. *Cooperating With Nature: Confronting Natural Hazards with Land Use Planning for Sustainable Communities*. Washington, D.C.: Joseph Henry Press.

9. Olshansky, Robert B., and Jack D. Kartez. 1998. Managing Land Use to Build Resilience. In. *Cooperating With Nature: Confronting Natural Hazards with Land Use Planning for Sustainable Communities*, edited by Raymond. J. Burby. Washington, D.C.: Joseph Henry Press.

10. The H. John Heinz III Center for Science, Economics and the Environment. 2002. *Human Links to Coastal Disasters*. Washington, D.C.: The Heinz Center.

11. FEMA. 2002. Getting Started: Building Support for Mitigation Planning. Publication 386-1. FEMA.

12. Institute of Government, the University of North Carolina at Chapel Hill. Undated. Local Government in North Carolina.

13. FEMA. 2002. Developing the Mitigation Plan: Identifying Mitigation Actions and Implementation Strategies. Publication 386-3. FEMA.

14. *Code of Federal Regulations.* Title 44, Part 201.2.

15. FEMA. 2002. Getting Started: Building Support for Mitigation Planning. Publication 386-1. FEMA.

16. Mississippi Renewal Forum Summary Report: Recommendations for Rebuilding the Gulf Coast. 2005. Quoting Andres Duany, a leader of the Congress for New Urbanism (CNU), which was hired to help communities develop plans focused on design and city form following Hurricane Katrina.

17. Examples of rebuilding ideas for the various coastal communities in Mississippi can be found in the complete report by the Commission on Recovery, Rebuilding and Renewal at www.governorscommission.com/ final or within the summary report of the Mississippi Renewal Forum at www.mississippirenewal.com/documents/ Rep_SummaryReport.pdf.

Chapter 9

1. Schwab, Jim., et al. 1998. *Planning for Post-Disaster Recovery and Reconstruction.* Chicago: American Planning Association Planning Advisory Service. Report No. 483/484.

2. Eadie, Charles. 2001. *Building Economic Vitality into Disaster Recovery in Holistic Disaster Recovery: Ideas for Building Local Sustainability After a Natural Disaster.* Boulder: Natural Hazards Research and Applications Information Center, University of Colorado.

3. Schwab, Jim., et al. 1998. *Planning for Post-Disaster Recovery and Reconstruction.* Chicago: American Planning Association Planning Advisory Service. Report No. 483/484.

4. Johnson, Laurie, Laura Dwelley Samant, and Suzanne Frew. 2005. *Planning for the Unexpected: Land-Use Development and Risk.* Chicago: American Planner Association.

5. Much of this discussion on private investment decision making is based on French, Steven P. May 2002. Incorporating Resilience in Private Sector Project Planning and Review. In. *Building Disaster Resilient Communities Instructor Guide,* edited by Raymond J. Burby. Federal Emergency Management Agency Emergency Management Institute.

6. Lennon, Gered, William J. Neal, David M. Bush, Orrin H. Pilkey, Matthew Stutz, and Jane Bullock. 1996. *Living with the South Carolina Coast.* Durham, NC: Duke University Press, p. 41.

7. Lennon, Gered, William J. Neal, David M. Bush, Orrin H. Pilkey, Matthew Stutz, and Jane Bullock. 1996. *Living with the South Carolina Coast.* Durham, NC: Duke University Press, p. 41.

8. French, Steven P. May 2002. Incorporating Resilience in Private Sector Project Planning and Review. In. *Building Disaster Resilient Communities Instructor Guide,* edited by Raymond J. Burby. Federal Emergency Management Agency Emergency Management Institute.

9. Sources for this case study include: NOAA Coastal Services Center. 2000. *Coastal Services,* March/April; Surfrider Foundation. State of the Coast 2005; Carolina Coastal Science. The Shell Island Dilemma: Educators' Guide. NC State University; The North Carolina Coastal Federation; and the North Carolina Division of Coastal Management, Department of Environment, Health and Natural Resources.

10. NOAA Coastal Services Center. 2000. *Coastal Services,* March/April.

11. As quoted in the publication: NOAA Coastal Services Center. Coastal Seawall Magazine, "NC Seawall Ban Stands Up to Legal Challenge." March/April 2000.

12. Schwab, Jim., et al. 1998. *Planning for Post-Disaster Recovery and Reconstruction.* Chicago: American Planning Association Planning Advisory Service. Report No. 483/484.

13. Delia, A. A. 2001. Population and economic changes in eastern North Carolina before and after Hurricane Floyd. In *Facing Our Future: Hurricane Floyd and Recovery in the Coastal Plain,* edited by J. R. Maiolo, et al. Wilmington, NC: Coastal Carolina Press.

14. The H. John Heinz III Center for Science, Economics and the Environment. 2002. *Human Links to Coastal Disasters*. Washington, D.C.: The Heinz Center.

15. Schwab, Jim., et al. 1998. *Planning for Post-Disaster Recovery and Reconstruction.* Chicago: American Planning Association Planning Advisory Service. Report No. 483/484.

16. The H. John Heinz III Center for Science, Economics and the Environment. 2002. *Human Links to Coastal Disasters*. Washington, D.C.: The Heinz Center.

17. Much of the discussion on business preparedness and mitigation planning in this chapter is based on guidance material produced by the Federal Emergency Management Agency, including the Business and Industry Guide for Emergency Management available from the online resource library accessible through the FEMA website. Additional resources for this section include material produced by the North Carolina Emergency Management Division. 2001. Managing Your Business to Minimize Disruption: A Guide for Small Businesses in North Carolina, available from the NCEM website www.ncem.org; and Open For Business: A Disaster Planning Toolkit for the Small to Mid-Sized Business Owner produced by the Institute for Business and Home Safety. 2005.

18. Small Business Administration. (Date not available) www.sba.gov. (April 3, 2006).

19. Schwab, Jim., et al. 1998. *Planning for Post-Disaster Recovery and Reconstruction.* Chicago: American Planning Association Planning Advisory Service. Report No. 483/484.

20. Small Business Administration. (Date not available.) www.sba.gov/disaster. April 3, 2006.

21. Eadie, Charles. 2001. *Building Economic Vitality into Disaster Recovery in Holistic Disaster Recovery: Ideas for Building Local Sustainability After a Natural Disaster.* Boulder: Natural Hazards Research and Applications Information Center, University of Colorado.

22. The H. John Heinz III Center for Science, Economics and the Environment. 2002. *Human Links to Coastal Disasters*. Washington, D.C.: The Heinz Center.

23. NC Division of Emergency Management, 2001. Managing Your Business to Minimize Disruption: A Guide for Small Businesses in North Carolina. NCEM.

24. Federal Emergency Management Agency. October 1993. Emergency Management Guide for Business and Industry: A Step-by-Step Approach to Emergency Planning, Response and Recovery for Companies of All Sizes. Publication 141. FEMA.

25. Federal Emergency Management Agency. October 1993. Emergency Management Guide for Business and Industry: A Step-by-Step Approach to Emergency Planning, Response and Recovery for Companies of All Sizes. Publication 141. FEMA.

26. North Carolina Division of Emergency Management, 2001. Managing Your Business to Minimize Disruption: A Guide for Small Businesses in North Carolina. NCEM.

27. North Carolina Division of Emergency Management, 2001. Managing Your Business to Minimize Disruption: A Guide for Small Businesses in North Carolina. NCEM.

28. Institute for Business and Home Safety. 2005. Open For Business: A Disaster Planning Toolkit for the Small to Mid-Sized Business Owner.

29. Institute for Business and Home Safety. 2005. Open For Business: A Disaster Planning Toolkit for the Small to Mid-Sized Business Owner.

30. Institute for Business and Home Safety. 2005. Open For Business: A Disaster Planning Toolkit for the Small to Mid-Sized Business Owner.

31. Institute for Business and Home Safety. 2005. Open For Business: A Disaster Planning Toolkit for the Small to Mid-Sized Business Owner.

32. FEMA Mitigation Directorate. "Wet Floodproofing Requirements for Structures Located in Special Flood Hazard Areas in Accordance with the National Flood Insurance Program." Technical Bulletin 7–93.

33. Institute for Business and Home Safety. 2005. Open For Business: A Disaster Planning Toolkit for the Small to Mid-Sized Business Owner.

34. North Carolina Division of Emergency Management, 2001. Managing Your Business to Minimize Disruption: A Guide for Small Businesses in North Carolina. NCEM.

35. North Carolina Division of Emergency Management, 2001. Managing Your Business to Minimize Disruption: A Guide for small Businesses in North Carolina. NCEM.

36. The H. John Heinz III Center for Science, Economics and the Environment. 2002. *Human Links to Coastal Disasters*. Washington, D.C.: The Heinz Center. p. 92.

37. Federal Emergency Management Agency. October 1993. Emergency Management Guide for Business and Industry: A Step-by-Step Approach to Emergency Planning, Response and Recovery for Companies of All Sizes. Publication 141. FEMA.

38. North Carolina Division of Emergency Management, 2001. Managing Your Business to Minimize Disruption: A Guide for Small Businesses in North Carolina. NCEM.

39. North Carolina Division of Emergency Management, 2001. Managing Your Business to Minimize Disruption: A Guide for Small Businesses in North Carolina. NCEM.

40. Institute for Business and Home Safety. 2005. Open For Business: A Disaster Planning Toolkit for the Small to Mid-Sized Business Owner.

41. North Carolina Division of Emergency Management, 2001. Managing Your Business to Minimize Disruption: A Guide for Small Businesses in North Carolina. NCEM.

42. Institute for Business and Home Safety. 2005. Open For Business: A Disaster Planning Toolkit for the Small to Mid-Sized Business Owner.

43. North Carolina Division of Emergency Management, 2001. Managing Your Business to Minimize Disruption: A Guide for Small Businesses in North Carolina. NCEM.

44. The H. John Heinz III Center for Science, Economics and the Environment. 2002. *Human Links to Coastal Disasters*. Washington, D.C.: The Heinz Center.

45. North Carolina Division of Emergency Management, 2001. Managing Your Business to Minimize Disruption: A Guide for Small Businesses in North Carolina. NCEM.

46. The H. John Heinz III Center for Science, Economics and the Environment. 2002. *Human Links to Coastal Disasters*. Washington, D.C.: The Heinz Center.

47. Adapted from North Carolina Division of Emergency Management, May 2003. Keeping Natural Hazards from Becoming Disasters: A Mitigation Planning Guidebook for Local Governments. North Carolina Department of Crime Control and Public Safety.

48. North Carolina Division of Emergency Management, May 2003. Keeping Natural Hazards from Becoming Disasters: A Mitigation Planning Guidebook for Local Governments. North Carolina Department of Crime Control and Public Safety.

49. FEMA. 2005. Reducing Damage from Localized Flooding: A Guide for Communities. Publication 511. FEMA.

Chapter 10

1. FEMA. 2001. State and Local Mitigation Planning How-to Guide, Understanding Your Risks: Identifying Hazards and Estimating Losses. Publication 386–2. FEMA.

2. North Carolina Division of Emergency Management, 2003. Keeping Natural Hazards from Becoming Disasters: A Mitigation Planning Guidebook for Local Governments. North Carolina Department of Crime Control and Public Safety.

3. Bourne, JK. 2004. Gone with the water. *National Geographic Magazine,* October. Available at magma.nationalgeographic.com/ngm/0410/feature5/?fs=www3.nationalgeographic.com.

4. Brown, M. 2006. Coastal losses greater than thought. *The Times Picayune,* 15 February. Quote by Carlton Dufrechou, Lake Pontchartrain Basin Foundation. Available at www.nola.com/news/t-p/index.ssf?/ base/news-3/113998708880320.xml.

5. U.S. House of Representatives. 2006. A Failure of Initiative: Final Report of the Select Bipartisan Committee to Investigate the Preparation for and Response to Hurricane Katrina. Available at katrina.house.gov.

6. Statewide Risk Assessment, Section 5. State of Louisiana Hazard Mitigation Plan. April 2005. Available at www.ohsep.louisiana.gov/hlsmitigation/hazmitplan/Section05StatewideRiskAsses.pdf.

7. For more information on the risk assessment and the entire Louisiana plan, visit: www.ohsep.louisiana.gov/hlsmitigation/hazmitigatpln.htm.

Chapter 11

1. Federal Emergency Management Agency. About FEMA: Preparedness. April 5, 2006. www.fena.gov/about/prepare.shtm. (May 15, 2006.)

2. Girl Scouts of the USA. *Safety Award for Junior Girl Scouts.* (date not available). www.girlscouts.org/program/gs_central/insignia/online/ safety/junior_safety_award.asp (March 13, 2006.)

3. U.S. House of Representatives. 2006. A Failure of Initiative: Final Report of the Select Bipartisan Committee to Investigate the Preparation for and Response to Hurricane Katrina. Available at katrina.house.gov.

4. Beriwal, Madhu. 2005. Hurricanes Pam and Katrina: A Lesson in Disaster Planning. *Natural Hazards Observer* 30 (November), no. 2.

5. U.S. House of Representatives. 2006. A Failure of Initiative: Final Report of the Select Bipartisan Committee to Investigate the Preparation for and Response to Hurricane Katrina. Available at katrina.house.gov.

6. U.S. House of Representatives. 2006. A Failure of Initiative: Final Report of the Select Bipartisan Committee to Investigate the Preparation for and Response to Hurricane Katrina. Available at katrina.house.gov.

7. U.S. House of Representatives. 2006. A Failure of Initiative: Final Report of the Select Bipartisan Committee to Investigate the Preparation for and Response to Hurricane Katrina. Available at katrina.house.gov.

8. Gavin Smith, Ph.D., Director of the Mississippi Office of the Governor's Office of Recovery and Renewal. Personal communication. May, 2006.

9. U.S. Department of Homeland Security. 2004. *National Response Plan.* Quick Reference Guide page 4. Available at www.dhs.gov/interweb/assetlibrary/NRP_quick_reference_guide_5-22-06.pdf.

10. U.S. Department of Homeland Security. 2004. *National Information Management System.* Available at NIMS online: www.nimsonline.com/nims_3_04/introduction_and_overview.htm.

11. NOAA. *National Weather Service: NOAA Weather Radio All Hazards.* (Date not available). www.nws.noaa.gov/nwr (May 9, 2006).

12. Federal Emergency Management Agency 2004. Are You Ready? An In depth Guide to Citizen Preparedness. IS-22. FEMA.

13. Federal Emergency Management Agency 2004. Are You Ready? An In depth Guide to Citizen Preparedness. IS-22. FEMA.

14. Federal Emergency Management Agency 2004. Are You Ready? An In depth Guide to Citizen Preparedness. IS-22. FEMA.

15. Leonard, Devin. 2005. The Only Lifeline Was the Wal-Mart. *Fortune,* 3 October. Available at money.cnn.com/magazines/fortune/fortune_archive/2005/10/03/8356743/index.htm.

16. Extracted from American Red Cross. *Volunter Services.* (Date not available). www.redcross.org/services/volunteer/0,1082,0_325_,00.html (May 10, 2006).

17. Federal Emergency Management Agency 2004. Are You Ready? An In depth Guide to Citizen Preparedness. IS-22. FEMA

18. Emergency Management Institute. *Welcome to the Emergency Management Institute (EMI)*. (May 10, 2006.) www.training.fema.gov/ EMIweb (May 10, 2006).

19. 2006. DHS Wants Kids to Get Ready!. *Natural Hazards Observer* Vol. 30 (March), no. 4.

20. Homeland Security Exercise and Evaluation Program. *Welcome to the HSEEP Website*. (Date not available). hseep.dhs.gov (May 11, 2006).

21. Boulder County Colorado Government Online. Emergency Information and Preparedness: April 18: Citywide Flood Exercise. (Date not available). www.co.boulder.co.us/emergency/flood_exercise.htm (May 11, 2006).

22. NASA Ames Research Center Disaster Assistance and Rescue Team. Mobex 2000. (Date not available). dart2.arc.nasa.gov/Exercises/ MOBEX2000/MOBEX-2000.html (May 11, 2006).

23. State of Missouri Emergency Management Agency. 2004. *Informational Notes for First Responders and Officials*. Bulletin #45 (20 February). Available at sema.dps.mo.gov/Bulletin45.pdf.

24. American Red Cross Capital Area Chapter. *Jefferson County Tornado Exercise*. (Date not available). www.tallytown.com/redcross/jcte.html (May 11, 2006).

25. Metropolitan Nashville and Davidson County, TN, Mayor's Office of Emergency Management. *Office of Emergency Management Home*. (Date not available). www.nashville.gov/oem (May 11, 2006).

Chapter 12

1. FEMA. *Dam Ownership in the United States*. (Date not available). www.fema.gov/hazard/damfailure/ownership.shtm. (November 9, 2005). Visit National Dam Safety Program Partners for more information.

2. National Park Service Guide to the Johnstown Flood National Memorial. Undated. Quoting named newspaper source of June, 1889.

3. Pottinger, Lori. 1997. California Flood Control System Springs Leaks. *World Rivers Review* 12 (February), No. 1, p. 1.

4. Knabb, R. D., J. R. Rhome, and D. P. Brown. 2005. "Tropical Cyclone Report," Hurricane Katrina, 23–30 August 2005." National Hurricane Center. www.nhc.noaa.gov/2005atlan.shtml.

5. U.S. House of Representatives. 2006. A Failure of Initiative: Final Report of the Select Bipartisan Committee to Investigate the Preparation for and Response to Hurricane Katrina. Available at katrina.house.gov.

6. Leatherman, S. P. and V. R. Burkett. 2002. Sea-Level Rise and Coastal Disasters: Lessons from the East Coast and New Orleans. *Natural Hazards Observer* 26 (March), no. 4. Available at www.colorado.edu/ hazards/o/maro02/maro02e.htm.

7. Burby, Raymond J., ed. 1999. *Cooperating with Nature: Confronting Natural Hazards with Land-Use Planning for Sustainable Communities*. Washington, D.C.: Joseph Henry Press.

8. State of North Carolina Hazard Mitigation Plan, Capability Assessment. 2005.

9. North Carolina Division of Emergency Management. 1998. Tools and Techniques: Putting a Hazard Mitigation Plan to Work. North Carolina Department of Crime Control and Public Safety. Available at www.ncem. org/mitigation/Library/Full_Tools_and_Tech.pdf.

10. Burby, Raymond J., ed. 1999. *Cooperating with Nature: Confronting Natural Hazards with Land-Use Planning for Sustainable Communities*. Washington, D.C.: Joseph Henry Press.

11. FEMA. 2003. State and Local Hazard Mitigation Planning How-To Guide: Integrating Manmade Hazards into Mitigation Planning. Publication 386–7. FEMA.

12. FEMA. 2003. State and Local Hazard Mitigation Planning How-To Guide: Integrating Manmade Hazards into Mitigation Planning. Publication 386–7. FEMA.

13. FEMA. 2005. Reducing Damage from Localized Flooding: A Guide for Communities. Publication 511. FEMA.

Chapter 13

1. The FEMA publications warehouse can be contacted at 1-800-480-2520, or visit the FEMA website at fema.gov/fima.

2. See, for example, the North Carolina Division of Emergency Management, Mitigation Section website for planning guidance documents that may be downloaded free of charge: www.ncem.org.

3. FEMA. 2002. Getting Started: Building Support for Mitigation Planning. Publication 386–1. FEMA.

4. *Code of Federal Regulations.* Title 44, Part 201.6(b)(1).

5. *Code of Federal Regulations.* Title 44, Part 201.6(c)(2).

6. *Code of Federal Regulations.* Title 44, Part 201.6(c)(2).

7. *Code of Federal Regulations.* Title 44, Part 201.6(c)(2)(i).

8. *Code of Federal Regulations.* Title 44, Part 201.6(c)(2)(i).

9. *Code of Federal Regulations.* Title 44, Part 201.6(c)(2)(i).

10. *Code of Federal Regulations.* Title 44, Part 201.6(c)(2)(ii)(B).

11. *Code of Federal Regulations.* Title 44, Part 201.6(c)(2)(ii)(C).

12. *Code of Federal Regulations.* Title 44, Part 201.6(c)(3).

13. *Code of Federal Regulations.* Title 44, Part 201.6(c)(3)(i).

14. See, for example, the FEMA Mitigation Publications Library at www/fema.gov/library/prepandprev/shtm. For examples of state publications, see the North Carolina Division of Emergency Management, *Tools and Techniques for Mitigating the Effects of Natural Hazards,* at www/dem.dcc.state.nc.us/mitigation/Library/Full_Tools_and_Tech.pdf, and the Oregon Department of Land Conservation and Development, *Planning for Natural Hazards: Oregon Technical Resource Guide* at www/lcd.state.or.us/hazhtml/Guidehome.htm.

15. Visit the CRS website at www.fema.gov/nfip/crs/htm for more information.

16. See FEMA's Mitigation Success Stories at www.fema.gov/fima/success.shtm. See also the North Carolina Division of Emergency Management publication, *Hazard Mitigation in North Carolina: Measuring Success* Volume 2 (February 2000), available at www.dem.dcc/state.nc.us/mitigation/planning_publications.htm.

17. OMB Circular A-94 describes the economic principles and methods by which most Federal programs must determine the cost-effectiveness (i.e., BCR) of funded projects.

18. FEMA. April 2003. Federal Emergency Management Agency. April 2003. Developing The Mitigation Plan: Identifying Mitigation Actions and Implementation Strategies. Publication 386-3. FEMA.

19. *Code of Federal Regulations.* Title 44, Part 201.6(c)(3)(iv).

20. *Code of Federal Regulations.* Title 44, Part 201.6(c)(3)(iii).

21. FEMA. 2003. Bringing the Plan to Life. Publication 386–4. FEMA.

22. *Code of Federal Regulations.* Title 44, Part 201.6(c)(4)(i).

23. *Code of Federal Regulations.* Title 44, Part 201.6(c)(4)(ii).

24. *Code of Federal Regulations.* Title 44, Part 201.6(c)(4)(iii).

25. See, for example, the sample crosswalk that is used by FEMA Region IV to review local hazard mitigation plans that are submitted for approval under the Disaster Mitigation Act of 2000.

26. *Code of Federal Regulations.* Title 44, Part 201.6(c)(5).

27. FEMA. April 2003. Federal Emergency Management Agency. April 2003. Developing The Mitigation Plan: Identifying Mitigation Actions and Implementation Strategies. Publication 386-3. FEMA.

Chapter 14

1. The number of fatalities in recent years from international natural disasters has far outpaced those of the United States. For example, the United Nations Office of the Special Envoy for Tsunami Recovery estimates that 229,866 people are missing or confirmed dead after the Indian Ocean Tsunami of 2004; in contrast, the highest number of fatalities from a natural disaster in the United States in recent history is 1336 during Hurricane Katrina in 2005.

2. Between 1993 and 2003, FEMA spent more than $20 billion in over 5000 counties on disaster recovery. These figures do not include the damage costs from the hurricanes of 2004 or 2005.

3. However, while there are ongoing debates on the increase of the frequency and intensity of extreme hydrometeorological events due to climate change, there is no evidence of more frequent or intense geological hazards and yet disaster costs for earthquakes are also very high. Many experts theorize that California is due for an exceptionally large earthquake some time in the current generation's lifetime. When and where exactly the epicenter may occur is highly speculative, but predictions are that damage costs will be immense.

4. Platt, Rutherford. 1999. *Disasters and Democracy: the Politics of Extreme Natural Events.* Washington, D.C.: Island Press.

5. Annan, Kofi. 1999. "Introduction to Secretary-General's Annual Report on the Work of the Organization of United Nations," emphasis in the original.

6. Beatley and Manning. 1997. *The Ecology of Place: Planning for Environment, Economy, and Community.* Washington, DC: Island Press.

7. FEMA. 2003. Planning for a Sustainable Future: The Link Between Hazard Mitigation and Livability. Publication 364. FEMA.

8. Bush, David M., Orrin H. Pilkey, Jr., and William J. Neal. 1996. *Living by the Rules of the Sea.* Durham, NC: Duke University Press, 66.

9. Burby, Raymond J., ed. 1998. *Cooperating with Nature: Confronting Natural Hazards with Land Use Planning for Sustainable Communities.* Washington, D.C.: Joseph Henry Press, 1. "structures have been found to actually induce development in hazardous areas and to increase, not decrease the likelihood that when a large flood or hurricane does occur, losses truly will be catastrophic." Burby, p. 8.

10. Mileti, Dennis. 1999. *Disasters By Design: A Reassessment of Natural Hazards in the United States.* Washington, D.C.: Joseph Henry Press, 3.

11. Beatley and Manning. 1997. *The Ecology of Place: Planning for Environment, Economy, and Community.* Washington, D.C.: Island Press.

12. FEMA. 2003. Planning for a Sustainable Future: The Link Between Hazard Mitigation and Livability. Publication 364. FEMA, quoting Timothy Beatley.

13. This is the definition of "sustainable development" developed by the Brundtland Commission in 1987, World Commission on Environment and Development, Our Common Future 43 (1987).

14. These three spheres are described in a report produced by the Natural Hazards Research and Applications Information Center. 2001. *Holistic Disaster Recovery: Ideas for Building Local Sustainability After a Natural Disaster.* Boulder. CO: University of Colorado.

15. FEMA. 2003. Planning for a Sustainable Future: The Link Between Hazard Mitigation and Livability. Publication 364. FEMA.

16. Curwell, A., M. Deakin, M. Symes, eds. 2005. *The framework and protocols for environmental assessment*, Vol. 1 of *Sustainable urban development*. London: Routledge.

17. Godschalk, David, et al. 1999. *Natural Hazard Mitigation: Recasting Disaster Policy and Planning.* Washington, D.C.: Island Press.

18. FEMA. 2003. Planning for a Sustainable Future: The Link Between Hazard Mitigation and Livability. Publication 364. FEMA. p. 9.

19. Beatley, Timothy. 1998. "The Vision of Sustainable Communities." In *Cooperating with Nature: Confronting Natural Hazards with Land Use Planning for Sustainable Communities*, edited by Raymond J. Burby. Washington, D.C.: Joseph Henry Press, 237.

20. Natural Hazards Research and Applications Information Center. 2001. *Holistic Disaster Recovery: Ideas for Building Local Sustainability After a Natural Disaster.* Boulder. CO: University of Colorado.

21. Godschalk, David, et al. 1999. *Natural Hazard Mitigation: Recasting Disaster Policy and Planning.* Washington, D.C.: Island Press, 526.

22. Mileti, Dennis. 1999. *Disasters By Design: A Reassessment of Natural Hazards in the United States.* Washington, D.C.: Joseph Henry Press, 4.

23. Godschalk, David, et al. 1999. *Natural Hazard Mitigation: Recasting Disaster Policy and Planning.* Washington, D.C.: Island Press, 5.

24. FEMA. 2003. Planning for a Sustainable Future: The Link Between Hazard Mitigation and Livability. Publication 364. FEMA.

25. Platt, Rutherford. 1999. *Disasters and Democracy: the Politics of Extreme Natural Events.* Washington, D.C.: Island Press, xvii.

26. FEMA. 2003. Planning for a Sustainable Future: The Link Between Hazard Mitigation and Livability. Publication 364. FEMA.

27. The two-volume study report, Natural Hazard Mitigation Saves: An Independent Study to Assess the Future Savings from Mitigation Activities was released in December, 2005. The study report is available for free download at www.nibs.org/MMC/mmchome.html.

28. The description of research findings in this chapter includes excerpts from an invited comment by Philip T. Ganderton, et al. 2006. MMC releases study on savings from mitigation March 2006. *Natural Hazards Observer* 30 (March), no. 4.

29. FEMA. 2003. Planning for a Sustainable Future: The Link Between Hazard Mitigation and Livability. Publication 364. FEMA.

30. Larson, Larry, and Doug Plasencia. 2001. No Adverse Impact: A New Direction in Floodplain Management Policy. *Journal of Natural Hazards* Review (Fall).

31. Larson, Larry, and Doug Plasencia. 2001. No Adverse Impact: A New Direction in Floodplain Management Policy. *Journal of Natural Hazards Review* (Fall).

32. Merriam, Dwight H. n.d. *A Response in Losing Ground: A Nation on Edge.* Environmental Law Institute, forthcoming. (Page not available)

33. Larson, Larry, and Doug Plasencia. 2001. No Adverse Impact: A New Direction in Floodplain Management Policy. *Journal of Natural Hazards Review* (Fall).

34. Natural Hazards Research and Applications Information Center. 2001. *Holistic Disaster Recovery: Ideas for Building Local Sustainability After a Natural Disaster.* Boulder. CO: University of Colorado.

35. Barnshaw, John. 2005. The Continuing Significance of Race and Class among Houston Hurricane Katrina Evacuees." *Natural Hazards Observer* 30 (November), no. 2.

36. Logan, John R. 2005. *The Impact of Katrina: Race and Class in Storm-Damaged Neighborhoods.* Providence, RI: Brown University Press.

37. Fothergill, Alice, Enrique Maestas, and JoAnne DeRouen Darlington. 1999. Race, Ethnicity and Disasters in the United States: A Review of the Literature. *Disasters* 23, no. 2, 156–173.

38. Waugh, William J. 2005. The Disaster that Was Katrina. *Natural Hazards Observer* 30 (November), no. 2.

39. Barnshaw, John. 2005. The Continuing Significance of Race and Class among Houston Hurricane Katrina Evacuees." *Natural Hazards Observer* 30 (November), no. 2.

40. Siembieda, William. 2006. Urban risk reduction's role in sustainable development. *Natural Hazards* Observer 30 (March), no. 4. p. 9.

41. Much of the discussion in this section is based on a transcript of the *Diane Rheam Show* broadcast by WAMU 88.5 FM American University Radio on March 16, 2006. Guests on the show include Col. Lewis Setliff, US ACOE Task Force for Levee Reconstruction in New Orleans; Edward Link, Senior Fellow, Civil and Environmental Engineering at University of Maryland, Director of ACOE Task Force for Levee Failure in New Orleans; and Raymond Seed, Professor of Engineering at University of California at Berkley, head of an independent investigative Katrina Task Force funded by the National Science Foundation.

42. FEMA. 2003. Planning for a Sustainable Future: The Link Between Hazard Mitigation and Livability. Publication 364. FEMA.

43. Association of State Floodplain Managers. 2005. "Is the 1% Chance Flood Standard Sufficient?" Actions Needed to Reduce Flood Losses in the United States: A Summary of Issues from the Gilbert F. White Flood Policy Forum.

44. Association of State Floodplain Managers. 2005. "Is the 1% Chance Flood Standard Sufficient?" Actions Needed to Reduce Flood Losses in the United States: A Summary of Issues from the Gilbert F. White Flood Policy Forum.

45. Larson, Larry, and Doug Plasencia. 2001. No Adverse Impact: A New Direction in Floodplain Management Policy. *Journal of Natural Hazards Review* (Fall).

46. Association of State Floodplain Managers. June 2001. No Adverse Impact: A Common Sense Strategy to Protect Your Property.

47. FEMA. 2003. Planning for a Sustainable Future: The Link Between Hazard Mitigation and Livability. Publication 364. FEMA.

48. Beatley, Timothy. 1998. "The Vision of Sustainable Communities." In *Cooperating with Nature: Confronting Natural Hazards with Land Use Planning for Sustainable Communities*, edited by Raymond J. Burby. Washington, D.C.: Joseph Henry Press.

49. National Park Service. 2003. Islands. Gulf Islands National Seashore- Mississippi District.

50. Pilkey, Orrin H., Sr., et al. 1983. *Coastal Design: A Guide for Builders, Planners, and Home-owners.* NY: Van Nostrand Reinhold Co., Inc.

51. Pilkey, Orrin H., Sr., et al. 1983. *Coastal Design: A Guide for Builders, Planners, and Home-owners.* NY: Van Nostrand Reinhold Co., Inc.

52. NC Division of Emergency Management 2004. North Carolina State Hazard Mitigation Plan. NC Department of Crime Control and Public Safety.

53. FEMA. June 2005. Reducing Damage from Localized Flooding: A Guide for Communities. Publication 511. FEMA.

54. Paterson, Robert G. 1998. "The Third Sector: Evolving Partnerships in Hazard Mitigation." In *Cooperating with Nature: Confronting Natural Hazards with Land-Use Planning for Sustainable Communities,* edited by Raymond J. Burby. Washington, D.C.: Joseph Henry Press.

55. Beatley, Timothy, et al. 2002. *An Introduction to Coastal Zone Management.* Washington, D.C.: Island Press.

56. Paterson, Robert G. 1998. "The Third Sector: Evolving Partnerships in Hazard Mitigation." In *Cooperating with Nature: Confronting Natural Hazards with Land-Use Planning for Sustainable Communities*, edited by Raymond J. Burby. Washington, D.C.: Joseph Henry Press.

57. Ganderton, Philip T., et al. 2006. MMC releases study on savings from mitigation March 2006. *Natural Hazards Observer* 30 (March), no. 4, p. 3.

58. FEMA. 2003. Planning for a Sustainable Future: The Link Between Hazard Mitigation and Livability. Publication 364. FEMA.

59. Natural Hazards Research and Applications Information Center. 2001. *Holistic Disaster Recovery: Ideas for Building Local Sustainability After a Natural Disaster.* Boulder. CO: University of Colorado. p. 35.

60. Natural Hazards Research and Applications Information Center. 2001. *Holistic Disaster Recovery: Ideas for Building Local Sustainability After a Natural Disaster.* Boulder. CO: University of Colorado.

61. Natural Hazards Research and Applications Information Center. 2001. *Holistic Disaster Recovery: Ideas for Building Local Sustainability After a Natural Disaster.* Boulder. CO: University of Colorado.

62. Mileti, Dennis. 1999. *Disasters By Design: A Reassessment of Natural Hazards in the United States.* Washington, D.C.: Joseph Henry Press, 238.

63. Anderson, Mary, and Peter Woodrow. 1989. *Rising from the Ashes: Development Strategies in Times of Disaster.* Boulder, CO: Westview Press. (Page not available).

64. Peterson, Kristina J. 2005. Recovery by Design: The Ongoing Challenges Presented by Katrina and Rita. *Natural Hazards Observer* 30 (November), no. 2.

65. FEMA. 2003. Planning for a Sustainable Future: The Link Between Hazard Mitigation and Livability. Publication 364. FEMA.

66. More information about 113 Calhoun Street and the Center for Sustainable Living, as well as a virtual tour, can be found at 113calhoun.org.

67. Beatley, Timothy. 1998. "The Vision of Sustainable Communities." In *Cooperating with Nature: Confronting Natural Hazards with Land Use Planning for Sustainable Communities,* edited by Raymond J. Burby. Washington, D.C.: Joseph Henry Press.

68. Pearce, Ines. 2005. Building Community Partnerships. *Natural Hazards Observer* 30 (November), no.2.

69. FEMA. 2003. Planning for a Sustainable Future: The Link Between Hazard Mitigation and Livability. Publication 364. FEMA.

GLOSSARY

100-year flood floodplain   The area that has a 1% chance, on average, of flooding in any given year as shown on a community's FIRM.

500-year flood floodplain   An area with a 0.2% chance of flooding in any given year.

Acceleration   The rate at which speed of ground movement is increasing.

All Hazards Network   A network of radio stations across the country that broadcasts continuous weather and hazards information.

All-hazards approach   Consideration of all the hazards with the potential for causing harm in a community, including natural hazards and man-made hazards, such as technological accidents and terrorism.

Amortization   Process that requires nonconforming structures to come into compliance with local zoning regulations or be removed from the property within a certain time period.

Antiterrorism   Defensive measures used to reduce the vulnerability of people and property to terrorist acts.

Areas of Particular Concern   Land designated for added state protection; defined by geographic boundaries, habitats, or natural resources.

Asset   Any man-made or natural feature that has value, including, but not limited to, people; buildings; infrastructure like bridges, roads, and sewer and water systems; lifelines like electricity and communication resources; or environmental, cultural, or recreational features like parks, dunes, wetlands, or landmarks.

Base Flood   The 100-year flood floodplain as shown on a community's FIRM.

Base flood elevation (BFE)   The elevation of the water surface resulting from a flood that has a 1% chance of occurring in any given year as shown on a community's FIRM.

Base Map   Graphic that shows the basic topography, physical elements, critical facilities, and infrastructure of a community; can be used to superimpose hazard-specific information for an illustration of vulnerability.

Beach nourishment   The artificial replacement or addition of sand to beaches to widen the backshore and move the high-water line further toward the sea.

Benefit-cost analysis   A quantitative procedure that assesses the desirability of a hazard mitigation project by taking a long-term view of avoided future damages to insurable structures as compared to the cost of the project.

Benefit-cost ratio   The outcome of a benefit-cost analysis, which demonstrates whether the net present value of benefits exceeds the net present value of costs.

Biological agent   Infectious organisms or toxins that are used to produce illness or death in people.

Blizzard   Snowstorm characterized by low temperatures and accompanied by winds that are at least 35 miles per hour.

Buffer   A setback of a specific distance, such as 25 or 100 feet, from a channel, floodway, wetland, or other water feature. In that area, no cutting, clearing of ground cover, or alteration of natural features is allowed.

Building code   A collection of laws, regulations, ordinances, or other statutory requirements adopted by a government that controls the physical structure of buildings.

Business Continuity Planning or Continuity of Operations Planning (COOP)   Plans directed toward maintaining a business's viability when one or more functions are impaired or disrupted. Since the advent of computerized business operations, many of these plans focus on data protection, retrieval, and restoration.

Business impact analysis   A calculation of the types of damages and losses that can be expected during an identified hazard event; the damages are related to the characteristics of the business. The business impact analysis assists in determining the types of actions that must be taken to reduce vulnerability.

Buyout program   Public acquisition of privately held property located in hazardous areas.

Capital improvement   New or expanded physical facilities that are relatively large in size, expensive, and permanent.

Catchment   A river basin, or the area surrounding a river that collects water from higher surrounding elevations.

Chemical agent   Poisonous gases, liquids, or solids that have toxic effects on people, plants, or animals.

Cinder cones   The simplest type of volcano; they have a single vent and are built of cinders.

Cinders   Lava that erupts into the air and breaks into small fragments that solidify.

Civil unrest   Unexpected or planned events that can cause disorder and disruption to a community.

Coastal erosion   The wearing away of the land surface by detachment and movement of soil and rock fragments.

Coastal erosion   The wearing away of the shoreline along the ocean.

Coastal flooding   Flood event that is the result of storm surge, wind-driven waves, and heavy rainfall.

Coastal high hazard area   Areas that are subject to a velocity hazard (wave action).

Cold air damming (CAD)   A surface-based layer of cold air entrenched against the eastern slopes of the Appalachian Mountains; results in freezing rain or sleet.

Cold wave   An unusual fall in temperature, to or below the freezing point, exceeding 16 degrees in twenty-four hours or 20 degrees in thirty-six hours.

Collapse   When the land surface opens up and surface materials fall into cavities below.

Collapse pit   Hole created when too much supporting material is removed during mining; the surface will collapse into the mine below.

Composite volcanoes   Large volcanoes that are also mountains; also called stratovolcanoes.

Comprehensive emergency management   Approach used to deal with natural hazards and human-caused hazards and their potential to cause disasters in a community.

Contingency planning   The process of developing advance arrangements and procedures that enable an organization to respond to a disaster so that critical business functions resume within a defined time frame, the amount of loss is minimized, and the stricken facilities are repaired or replaced as soon as possible.

Continuity of Operations Planning (COOP)   Plans directed toward maintaining a business's viability when one or more functions are impaired or disrupted. Since the advent of computerized business operations, many of these plans focus on data protection, retrieval, and restoration.

Core   The innermost region of the Earth.

Coulees   Short, steep-sided lava flows.

Countermeasures (SPCC) Plan   Plans and procedures for dealing with hazardous waste or dangerous substances.

Counterterrorism   Offensive measures taken to prevent, deter, and respond to terrorism.

Crater   Bowl-shaped hole at the summit of a volcano.

Critical facilities   Facilities critical to the health and welfare of the population, especially following hazard events. Critical facilities include, but are not limited to, shelters, police and fire stations, hospitals, life line infrastructure such as water and sewer treatment facilities, power generation stations, and communication and transportation networks.

Crust   The thin layer on the surface of the Earth.

Cumulative impact assessment   An evaluation that looks at the total effect of all development in a particular environment.

Debris flow   Fast-moving landslides that generally occur during intense rainfall on water-saturated soil.

Demand   The desire for a commodity together with the ability to pay for it. Scarcity increases the desire for a particular product—for example, beachfront property in highly developed coastal areas.

Differential assessment   A technique for reducing the tax burden on land facing development pressure by recognizing that undeveloped properties require fewer public services.

Dillon's Rule   Principle that a local government must have the proper delegation from the state in order to act.

Direct impact   Includes physical damage to structures, such as buildings and other facilities. Direct impacts also include losses to inventories, equipment, and other physical assets.

Disaster   The result when a natural hazard takes place where humans have situated themselves.

Disaster life cycle   The cycle of the four phases of the comprehensive emergency management system as it interacts with a disaster event.

Disaster Mitigation Act (DMA) of 2000   Amends the Robert T. Stafford Disaster Relief and Emergency Assistance Act of 1988; streamlines the administration of federal disaster relief and mitigation programs and places emphasis on pre-disaster mitigation planning to reduce the Nation's disaster losses.

Disaster resilient community   A community or region developed or redeveloped to minimize the human, environmental, and property losses and the social and economic disruption caused by disasters. A resilient community understands natural systems and realizes that appropriate siting, design, and construction of the built environment are essential to advances in disaster prevention.

Domestic terrorism   Groups or individuals whose activities are directed at elements of U.S. government or without foreign direction.

Down-zoning   Used to keep inappropriate development out of hazard-prone areas; can be accomplished by increasing minimum lot size, or reducing the number of dwelling units permitted per acre.

Dry floodproofing   A structural mitigation technique that strengthens walls to withstand hydrostatic and dynamic forces, including debris impacts. Openings, including doors, windows, and vents, are sealed or filled with special closures to block entry of floodwater. In some instances, walls can be coated with waterproofing compounds or plastic sheeting.

Dynamic equilibrium   The Earth's natural systems maintain a balanced state over long periods of time through a series of adjustments.

Earthquake   Geologic hazard caused by the release of stresses accumulated as a result of the rupture of lithosphere rocks along opposing boundaries in the Earth's crust.

Easement   Used to grant an affirmative right to use a property, such as a right of access; may also restrict the landowner's right to use the property in a particular way.

Economic sphere   Consists of all the activities, transactions, and decisions that are based on producing and exchanging goods and services and encompasses jobs, markets, investment, capital, and other aspects of our economic existence in the modern world.

Emergency Management Assistance Compact (EMAC)   A congressionally ratified organization that provides form and structure to interstate mutual aid.

Emergency operations plan   Contains procedures that can be detailed and coordinated for emergency responders; developed and maintained by local emergency managers.

Eminent domain   The right of the government to take (condemn) private property for public use; owner must be given just compensation for the taking.

Enhanced Fujita Scale   An updated tornado index based on the Fujita scale that incorporates 28 damage indicators and degrees of damage estimates to more clearly classify tornado intensity during a tornado event.

Environmental sphere   The natural and physical setting in which the community exists—the visible landscape as well as resources such as water, air, and soil, on which communities rely.

Epicenter   Causative fault of an earthquake; damage is generally most severe at or near the epicenter.

Episodic erosion   Erosion induced by a single storm event.

Essential facilities   Facilities important for a full recovery of a community following a hazard event. These include: government functions, major employers, banks, schools, and certain commercial establishments such as grocery stores, hardware stores, and gas stations.

Estuary   A semi-enclosed area where fresh water from a river meets salty water from the sea.

Extraterritorial jurisdiction   Control towns have over development just outside the town limits and over areas that eventually could be annexed; usually extends one mile beyond the city limits.

Extra-tropical cyclones   Storms that form outside the tropics; severe winter storms.

Eye   Calm center of a hurricane.

Fault planes   Ruptures in the Earth's crust that are typically found along borders of the tectonic plates.

First responders   Groups that are the first to arrive at the scene of the emergency, such as police, fire, and paramedics.

Flash flood   A flood event occurring with little or no warning where water levels rise at an extremely fast rate.

Flood fringe   The area on both sides of the floodway with lower depths and velocities. The flood fringe stores water during a flood.

Flood Insurance Rate Map (FIRM)   Map of a community that shows both the SFHAs and the risk premium zones applicable to the community. FIRMs are prepared by FEMA.

Floodplain   Low-lying flat areas that typically lie to either side of a river or stream.

Floodway   The central portion of the floodplain with the greatest water velocities and highest depths.

Freezing rain   Moisture falling in liquid form but freezing upon impact when surface temperatures are below freezing.

Frostbite   A severe reaction to cold exposure that can permanently damage its victims.

General flood   Flood event caused by precipitation over an extended period and over a given river basin.

General-purpose local government   Type of local government that performs a wide-range of functions; examples: counties, municipalities, and towns and townships.

Geographic Information Systems (GIS) A computer software application that relates physical features on the earth to a database to be used for mapping and analysis.

Goals What a community hopes to achieve with a mitigation plan.

Green infrastructure Views natural areas as a form of infrastructure (public works and utilities such as sewer lines and roads) that supports not only quality of life but the ecological health of an area.

Ground motion The vibration or shaking of the ground during an earthquake.

Groundwater Subsurface water.

Hazard identification A step of the business risk assessment that defines the magnitudes (intensities) and associated probabilities (likelihood) of hazards that may pose threats to the business and community.

Hazard Mitigation Grant Program (HMGP) Funding program administered by FEMA. The purpose of the HMGP is to reduce the loss of life and property caused by natural hazards by providing funding for mitigation to state and local governments following a disaster declaration.

Hazard Mitigation Plan A document that presents policies and strategies to reduce vulnerability to hazards when those policies and strategies are put into action. These policies and action strategies are based on a sound and thorough risk and vulnerability assessment.

Hazard mitigation planning Process of determining how to reduce or eliminate the loss of life and property damage that can occur as a result of hazards.

Hazard profile A description of the physical characteristics of hazards and a determination of various descriptors including magnitude, duration, frequency, probability, and extent. In most cases, a community can most easily use these descriptors when they are recorded and displayed as maps.

Hazardous material Chemical or toxic substances that pose a potential threat or risk to life or health.

Hazards U.S (HAZUS) A risk assessment tool used to estimate earthquake and other hazard losses. HAZUS contains a database of economic, census, building stock, transportation facilities, local geology, and other information.

Home Rule States General police power is delegated by the state legislature to local governments to enact laws and to adopt and enforce regulations that are necessary for it to govern.

Hot spot Area prone to volcanic activity.

Hurricane An intense tropic cyclone, formed in the atmosphere over warm ocean waters, in which wind speeds reach 74 miles per hour or more and blow in a large spiral around a relatively calm center or "eye."

Hydrological hazard Weather event that occurs as part of the Earth's water systems.

Hypothermia A condition brought on when the body temperature drops below 95°F.

Impact fees Typically one-time, up-front charges against new development to pay for off-site improvements, including schools, fire stations, community centers, and other local facilities.

Impervious surfaces   Paved areas that rainwater cannot soak through, such as parking lots, roofs, streets, and other nonporous surfaces.

Incident of national significance   Declared after a federal agency has requested help from the Department of Homeland Security, a state or local government has requested help from the federal government, multiple federal agencies have become involved, or the President requests the involvement of the Department of Homeland Security.

Indirect impacts   Result from the closure of roads and disassembly of transportation networks; loss of utilities, such as water, sewerage, electric power; and disruptions to telecommunications.

Infrastructure   Facilities and systems that support development, such as water, sewer, roads, and so forth.

Inherent vulnerability   Factors such as the way a building or facility is used, how visible it is, how accessible it is, how many people are located there, and other factors that determine the asset's level of susceptibility, often in reference to man-made hazards.

In-kind contributions   Non-cash contributions of goods and/or services. Can include items such as equipment, technical or consulting services, furniture, office supplies, etc. May also include donated staff or volunteer time.

Inland flooding   Rivers and streams overflow as a hurricane moves across land.

Intensity   How the damage potential of an earthquake is measured.

International terrorism   Groups or individuals whose activities are foreign-based and/or directed by countries or groups outside the United States, or whose activities cross international boundaries.

Just compensation   The payment of fair market value for whatever portion of the property is put to public use; used in takings cases.

Keetch-Byram Drought Index (KBDI)   The current scale of fire conditions that estimates the potential risk for wildfire based on daily temperatures, daily precipitation, and annual precipitation levels on an index of 0 (no drought) to 800 (extreme drought).

Land subsidence   A gradual settling of the Earth's surface.

Landfall   The point where a hurricane crosses the coastline from the ocean.

Landslide   When masses of rock, earth, or debris move down a slope.

Lateral spread   Type of ground failure in an earthquake that develops on gentle slopes and entails the sidelong movement of large masses of soil as an underlying layer liquefies.

Lava   Magma that reaches the Earth's surface.

Lava dome   Type of volcano that grows by layering lava upward and outward, largely by expansion from within.

Lava flows   Moving lava; because of its excessive heat, lava quickly burns any consumable material it covers.

Law of nuisance   An owner must refrain from undertaking any activity which interferes with the rights of adjoining property owners or which inflicts injury on the general public.

Laze   Lava haze produced when lava enters the sea and chemical reactions produces hydrochloric acid fumes.

Lifeline services   Services such as fire, police, hospitals, and rescue stations.

Lifeline utilities   Services that are essential to a community's health and well-being, such as potable water, wastewater treatment, oil, natural gas, electric power, and communication systems.

Liquefaction   When ground shaking causes loose soils to lose strength and act like viscous fluid.

Lithosphere   The Earth's crust and upper mantle.

Looting   Plundering or stealing of valuables or other goods triggered by a change in authority or the absence of authority.

Loss Estimate   A calculation in dollar amounts of the potential damage to structures and contents, interruption of services, and displacement of residents and businesses caused by a hazard.

Loss of bearing strength   Type of ground failure in an earthquake that results when the soil-supporting structures liquefies.

Magma   Molten rock.

Magnitude   A measure of the strength of a hazard event, or how much energy is released. The magnitude (also referred to as severity) of a given hazard event is usually determined using technical measures.

Major hurricane   Category 3, 4, and 5 hurricanes; most potentially dangerous.

Man-made hazards   Intentional or accidental occurrences caused by human activity; examples include oil spills and acts of terrorism such as bombings.

Mantle   Middle layer of the Earth.

Material Safety Data Sheet (MSDS)   Provides useful information regarding acceptable levels of toxin exposure, including data regarding the properties of a particular substance, the chemical's risks, safety, and impact on the environment; OSHA requires that MSDS be available to employees for potentially harmful substances handled in the workplace.

Meteorological hazard   Weather event that occurs because of processes in the Earth's atmosphere.

Microearthquake   An earthquake with a magnitude of less than 2.0.

Mitigation actions   Specific proposals for reaching mitigation goals.

Mitigation   Any sustained action to reduce or eliminate long-term risk to people and property from hazards and their effects.

Moral hazard   Term used to describe how federal disaster relief may encourage citizens and communities to build in areas vulnerable to the impacts of natural hazards.

Moratorium   A short-term suspension of the right to develop, usually accomplished by a refusal of the local government to issue building permits.

Multi-jurisdictional   Two or more local governments that prepare a joint hazard mitigation plan.

National Flood Insurance Program (NFIP)   Voluntary participatory program for local communities who wish to provide the opportunity for residents to purchase federally backed flood insurance. In exchange, local governments enact ordinances to regulate development in floodplains.

National Guard   Provides the capability to greatly assist in disaster response in terms of providing communications systems; construction equipment; emergency supplies such as medical supplies, beds, food, water, and blankets; as well as personnel to assist with distribution.

National Incident Management System (NIMS)   Provides guidance to the federal agencies participating in the National Response Plan in disaster preparedness.

National Preparedness Assessment And Reporting System   Provides a report of the nation's level of preparedness to the President and gives guidance to participating agencies on adopting quantifiable performance measures of preparedness in the areas of training, planning, exercises, and equipment.

National Response Plan (NRP)   Serves to coordinate response responsibilities and logistics at the federal level. Represents a binding agreement among 27 government agencies and the American Red Cross.

Natural hazards   Inevitable and uncontrollable occurrences such as floods, hurricanes, winter storms, and earthquakes.

No Adverse Impact   An approach to floodplain management that attempts to ensure that the actions of one property owner do not increase the flood risk of other property owners through land use planning and mitigation strategies.

NOAA Weather Radio All Hazards Network (NWR) A network of radio stations across the country that broadcasts continuous weather and hazards information.

Nonfederal match   The amount of funds, usually a percentage of the total grant amount awarded, required by many federal grant programs that must come from a source other than the federal grant program.

Northeast Snowfall Impact Scale (NESIS)   A scale that has recently been developed to characterize and rank high-impact snowstorms in the Northeast United States.

Nuee ardente   French for "glowing cloud"; an incinerating mixture of gas and volcanic debris; also called pyroclastic flow.

Objectives   Provide specific ways to achieve mitigation goals.

Ordinance   A local rule or law that the government can pass and that the government has the authority to enforce within its jurisdiction.

Pancaking   When high-rise buildings collapse in on themselves.

Police power   The inherent power of the government to make laws and regulations that promote the public health, safety, and general welfare.

Preparedness   A state of readiness to respond to any emergency or disaster.

Probability   A statistical measure of the likelihood that a hazard event will occur.

Process mitigation activities   Mitigation projects that are difficult to quantify from a cost-benefit perspective, but lead to policies, practices, and plans to reduce risk, including vulnerability assessments, community priorities and action plans, education and awareness campaigns for decision makers and constituents, and development of codes and regulations.

Project mitigation activities   Brick and mortar mitigation projects that result in tangible physical change to the built or natural environment, such as drainage enhancement, acquisition and relocation of at-risk structures, structural and non-structural improvements, lifeline improvements, and land improvement projects.

Pyroclastic flow   An incinerating mixture of gas and volcanic debris; also called nuee ardente.

Race riot   Outbreak of violent civil unrest in which race issues are a key factor.

Rain band   A spiraling arm of rain radiating out from the eye of a hurricane.

Recovery   Phase in the emergency management cycle that involves actions that begin after a disaster, after emergency needs have been met; examples include road and bridge repairs and restoration of power.

Recurrence interval   The time between hazard events of a similar size in a given location. It is based on the probability that the given event will be equaled or exceeded in any given year.

Regulation   Legislation that controls property uses, including zoning and subdivision ordinances, building codes, fire codes, environmental protection laws, and other types of mandates that dictate where and how development and building take place.

Relocation   Removing privately owned structures from hazardous areas and relocating them on non-hazardous sites; most often used in combination with acquisition.

Repetitive loss properties   Property with 2 or more National Flood Insurance Program claims over $1000 each within a 10-year period.

Resilient communities   Towns, cities, counties, Native American tribes, states, and other forms of communities that take action prior to a hazard event so that a disaster does not result.

Resolution   An expression of a governing body's opinion, will, or intention that is usually legally binding.

Response   Phase in the emergency management cycle that involves activities to meet the urgent needs of victims during or immediately following a disaster; examples include evacuation as well as search and rescue.

Retrofitting   Rebuilding existing buildings to withstand the shaking and ground movement associated with an earthquake.

Richter Scale   An open-ended logarithmic scale that describes the energy release of an earthquake through a measure of shock wave amplitude.

Risk   The potential losses associated with a hazard, defined in terms of expected probability and frequency, exposure, and consequences.

Risk assessment   A process or method for evaluating risk associated with a specific hazard and defined in terms of probability and frequency of occurrence, magnitude and severity, exposure and consequences.

River basin management   A technique for addressing issues of water quality, habitat protection, rural land conservation, and flood hazard mitigation on a regional scale in recognition of the fact that natural systems do not necessarily correspond to political boundaries.

River basin   The area surrounding a river that collects water from higher surrounding elevations; the drainage area of a river.

Riverine flooding   Flood event that is a function of precipitation levels and runoff volumes within the watershed of a stream or river.

Runoff   Water that is unable to soak through impervious surfaces such as rooftops or pavement.

Safety and health plan Plan for ensuring workplace safety and protecting employee health.

Secondary hazard A technological hazard that occurs during, often as a result of, a primary natural event.

Seismic waves When the rock on both sides of a fault snaps, it releases this stored energy; waves are what cause the ground to shake in an earthquake.

Seismograph The instrument that records the amplitude of the seismic waves.

Seismology The study of earthquakes.

Setback rules Regulations based on the erosion rate along the shoreline. The setback is a line behind which construction must take place.

Setback Regulation that prohibits or limits the erection of structures within a specified distance from the ocean.

Severe blizzard Snowstorm with temperatures near or below 10°F, winds exceeding 45 miles per hour, and visibility reduced by snow to near zero.

Shield volcanoes Type of volcano that can have many eruptions from the fractures, or rift zones, along the flanks of their cones.

Single-purpose local government Type of local government that has a specific purpose and performs one function; example: school district.

Sinkholes Spaces and caverns that develop underground as the rock below the land surface is dissolved by groundwater circulating through them.

Sleet Ice pellets.

Snowstorm Any storm with heavy snow.

Social sphere Consists of all of the interactions among people—cooperating in their neighborhood activities, practicing their religion, enjoying their families, sharing cultural identities, solving problems together, uniting as a community.

Soil slumps Loose, partly to completely saturated sand or silt, or poorly compacted man-made fill composed of sand, silt, or clay.

Special Flood Hazard Area (SFHA) An area within a floodplain having a 1% or greater chance of flood occurrence in any given year (100-year floodplain); represented on Flood Insurance Rate Maps by darkly shaded areas with zone designations that include the letter A or V.

Spill Prevention Control and Countermeasures (SPCC) Plan Plans and procedures for dealing with hazardous waste or dangerous substances.

States' rights Powers that are reserved to the fifty states by the U.S. Constitution.

Storm surge Rise in the water surface above normal water level on the open coast due to the action of wind stress and atmospheric pressure on the water surface.

Storm tide The combination of a hurricane's surge and the normal tide.

Stratovolcanoes Large volcanoes that are also mountains; also called composite volcanoes.

Subdivision ordinance Local regulations that govern the partition of land for development or sale. In addition to controlling the configuration of parcels, subdivision ordinances set standards for developer-built infrastructure.

Surface faulting The differential movement of two sides of a fracture; the location where the ground breaks apart.

Sustainable development   Development that meets the needs of the present without compromising the ability of future generations to meet their own needs.

Tactical vulnerability   Factors such as the way a building is designed, built, landscaped, and engineered that determine the asset's susceptibility to hazard impacts, often in reference to man-made hazards.

Takings   Law established by the Fifth Amendment to the U.S. Constitution that requires that the owner of private property must receive just compensation for property that is physically occupied by the government or regulated past a certain point.

Target-hardening strategies   Methods of protecting structures from man-made hazard impacts.

Technological hazard   Incidents that occur when hazardous materials are used, transported, or disposed of improperly and the materials are released into a community.

Tectonic plates   Moving layers of the Earth's surface that contain the continents and oceans.

Terrorism   The unlawful use of force and violence against persons or property to intimidate or coerce a government, the civilian population, or any segment thereof, in furtherance of political or social objectives.

Time value of money   One of the basic concepts of finance, the time value of money is based on the premise that faster returns on investment maximize the profitability of a development project.

Tornado   A violently rotating column of air extending from the base of a thunderstorm.

Tropical cyclones   Storms that form in the tropics; hurricanes.

Urban flooding   Flood event that occurs where there has been development within stream floodplains.

Variances   Exceptions that allow development to proceed, even though the rules prohibit it.

Vog   Volcanic fog; occurs a short distance downwind from volcanic eruption site.

Volcanic ash   Produced by volcanic eruption; can form thick deposits on the ground, causing extensive environmental damage.

Volcanic mudflows   A mixture of water and volcanic debris.

Volcano   A vent in the surface of the Earth through which magma and associated gases and ash erupt.

Vulnerability   The extent to which people will experience harm and property will be damaged from a hazard. Present vulnerability involves who and what is at risk now; future vulnerability indicates who and what may be at risk in the future under projected development and population trends.

Vulnerability assessment   A step of the business risk assessment that characterizes exposed populations and property and the extent of injury and damage that may result from a hazard event of a given intensity in a given area.

Water force   The wave action of water during a hurricane that makes flooding particularly destructive.

Watershed   All the land drained by a river, stream, or lake; many watersheds make up a river basin.

Waterspout   Weak tornadoes that form over warm ocean waters.

Wet floodproofing   Structural mitigation measure that intentionally allows floodwater to enter certain enclosed areas to reduce the damaging pressures that can collapse walls and foundations.

Wetland mitigation   The off-site preservation of another wetland located away from a development activity, or the creation of a new wetland to take the place of one that is impaired or destroyed.

Wildfire   An uncontrolled burning of grasslands, brush, or woodlands.

Wind velocity   The speed of wind.

Windchill factor   As wind increases, heat is carried away from the body at a faster rate.

Windchill temperature   Unit of measurement to describe windchill factor.

Window of opportunity   The time immediately following a disaster during which a community can insert an ethic of sustainability in guiding development and redevelopment in high-risk areas.

Zoning   The traditional tool available to local governments to control land use; zoning maps divide the jurisdiction into zones where various regulations apply as described in the zoning ordinance.

Zoning maps   Divide the area under local government control into zones where various zoning regulations apply.

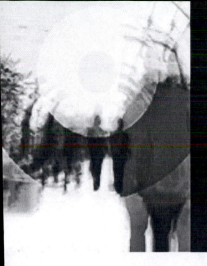

CREDITS

Figure 7-2:   Photo by Cynthia Hunter/FEMA, FEMA Web site, Image Number 8868

Figure 8-3:   www.mississippirenewal.com/documents/Rep_SummaryReport.pdf

Figure 9-1:   www.surfrider.org

Figure 9-2:   www.surfrider.org

Figure 9-3:   Photo by Andrea Booher/FEMA, FEMA Web site, Image Number 13708

Figure 9-4:   Photo by Bob McMillan/FEMA, FEMA Web site, Image Number 7359

Figure 11-2: www.pbs.org

Figure 11-3: www.in.gov/gov/photo/militarybriefing.html

Figure 11-4: www.co.boulder.co.us/

Figure 14-2: www.113calhoun.org

INDEX